AN INTRODUCTION TO THE NEW TESTAMENT

AN INTRODUCTION TO THE NEW TESTAMENT

D. A. Carson, Douglas J. Moo, and Leon Morris

ZondervanPublishingHouse
Grand Rapids, Michigan

A Division of HarperCollinsPublishers

An Introduction to the New Testament
Copyright © 1992 by D. A. Carson, Douglas J. Moo, and Leon Morris

Requests for information should be addressed to:
Zondervan Publishing House
Academic and Professional Books
Grand Rapids, Michigan 49530

Library of Congress Cataloging-in-Publication Data

Carson, D. A.
    An introduction to the New Testament / D.A. Carson, Douglas J.
Moo, Leon Morris.
    p. cm.
    Includes bibliographical references and indexes.
    ISBN 0-310-51940-3
    1. Bible. N.T.–Introduction. I. Moo, Douglas J. II. Morris,
Leon, 1914- . III. Title.
    BS2330.2.C34 1992
    225.6'1–dc20
                                        91-26371
                                          CIP

Edited by Craig Noll and Leonard G. Goss
Interior designed by Leonard G. Goss
Cover designed by Terry Dugan
Cover illustration: The Last Supper, *11th Century, State Museum for Russian Art, Kiev*

Printed in the United States of America

96 97 / DH / 10 9

This edition is printed on acid-free paper and meets the American National Standards Institute Z39.48 standard.

*This book is gratefully dedicated to
Joy, Jenny, and Mildred*

contents

pReface

The primary focus of this book is on what used to be called "special introduction"—that is, on historical questions dealing with authorship, date, sources, purpose, destination, and the like. Not a few recent books devote more space than we do to literary form, rhetorical criticism, and historical parallels. We do not minimize the importance of such topics and have introduced them where they directly bear on the subject at hand. In our experience, however, they are better given extended treatment in courses on exegesis, especially the exegesis of particular books, and we fear that too much focus on these topics at the expense of traditional questions of introduction tends to divorce the New Testament books from their historical settings, and students from some important debates in the first centuries of the Christian church. This also means that we have often referred to primary sources. In debates over such questions as what Papias means by "John the elder," we have tended to cite the passage and work through it, so that students may see for themselves what the turning points in the debate are (or should be!).

Although the emphasis of this book is on "special introduction," we have included a brief outline or résumé of each New Testament document, sometimes providing a rationale for the choices we have made. In each case we have provided a brief account of current studies on the book and have indicated something of the theological contribution that each New Testament document makes to the canon. Our ultimate concern is that new generations of theological students will gain a better grasp of the Word of God.

We have tried to write with the first- and second-year student of seminaries and theological colleges in mind. Doubtless in most instances the material will be supplemented by lectures. Some teachers will want to use the material in some order other than that presented here (e.g., by assigning chapters on Matthew, Mark, and Luke before assigning the chapter on the Synoptic Gospels). Bibliographies are primarily in English, but small numbers of works in German, French, and other modern languages appear. These bibliographies are meant to be brief enough not to be daunting, and comprehensive enough not to be reductionistic. Lecturers may provide guidance as to what in these lists is especially useful in particular contexts.

Not least important, we have restricted the length of this *Introduction* so that it can be used as a textbook. One or two well-known introductions are so long that only relatively short parts of them are assigned to students. This means it is possible to graduate from a seminary without ever having read a single New Testament introduction right through. Although the brevity of this volume precludes detailed discussion of many topics we would have liked to pursue, we hope the constraints we have chosen will enhance its value.

Confessionally, the three authors are Evangelicals. Doubtless that heritage biases our readings somewhat but (we hope) not too greatly our awareness of our biases, and no more, we suggest, than other New Testament students are influenced by their heritage. If we have tried to eschew obscurantism, we have nevertheless sometimes raised possibilities and questions that are too quickly turned aside in some introductions. We have tried to engage a representative sampling of the vast amount of current literature, sometimes following traditional paths, and at other times suggesting a fresh way of looking at an issue. Where the evidence seems entirely inconclusive to us, we have left questions open.

Each of us has written about a third of this volume and offered written critiques of the work of the other two. One of us has tried to reduce stylistic and other differences to a minimum. In two or three instances, references in the text betray the individual author. Elsewhere, readers are warmly invited to identify the redactor and the individual sources.

Soli Deo gloria.

D. A. Carson
Douglas J. Moo
Leon Morris

abbreviations

AB	Anchor Bible
AGJU	Arbeiten zur Geschichte des antiken Judentums und des Urchristentums
AGSU	Arbeiten zur Geschichte des Spätjudentums und Urchristentums
AJT	*American Journal of Theology*
ALGHJ	Arbeiten zur Literatur und Geschichte des hellenistischen Judentums
AnBib	Analecta Biblica
ANRW	*Aufstieg und Niedergang der römischen Welt*
ASNU	Acta Seminarii Neotestamentici Upsaliensis
ATR	*Anglican Theological Review*
AusBibRev	*Australian Biblical Review*
AUSS	*Andrews University Seminary Studies*
b.	Babylonian Talmud
BAGD	Walter Bauer, William F. Arndt, F. Wilbur Gingrich, and Frederick W. Danker, *A Greek-English Lexicon of the New Testament and Other Early Christian Literature*, 2d ed. (Chicago: University of Chicago Press, 1979)
Barker/Lane/ Michaels	Glenn W. Barker, William L. Lane, and J. Ramsey Michaels, *The New Testament Speaks* (San Francisco: Harper & Row, 1969)
BETL	Bibliotheca Ephemeridum Theologicarum Lovaniensium
BFCT	Beiträge zur Förderung christlicher Theologie
BGBE	Beiträge zur Geschichte der biblischen Exegese
BIP	Biblical Institute Press
BJRL	*Bulletin of the John Rylands Library*
BL	Bampton Lectures
BNTC	Black's New Testament Commentaries (= HNTC)
Bornkamm	Günther Bornkamm, *The New Testament: A Guide to Its Writings* (London: SPCK, 1974)
BR	*Biblical Research*
BS	*Bibliotheca Sacra*
BSNTS	*Bulletin* of the *Studiorum Novi Testamenti Societas*
BU	Biblische Untersuchungen
BZ	*Biblische Zeitschrift*

BZNW	Beihefte zur Zeitschrift für die neutestamentliche Wissenschaft
c.	circa
CAH	*Cambridge Ancient History*
Cartledge	Samuel A. Cartledge, *A Conservative Introduction to the New Testament* (Grand Rapids: Zondervan, 1957)
CBQ	*Catholic Biblical Quarterly*
CBQMS	Catholic Biblical Quarterly Monograph Series
CGSTJ	*China Graduate School of Theology Journal*
CGTC	Cambridge Greek Testament Commentary
Childs	Brevard S. Childs, *The New Testament as Canon: An Introduction* (Philadelphia: Fortress, 1984)
CIL	*Corpus Inscriptionum Latinarum*
CJT	*Canadian Journal of Theology*
Clogg	Frank Bertram Clogg, *An Introduction to the New Testament* (London: University Press and Hodder & Stoughton, 1940)
CNT	Commentaire du Nouveau Testament
Collins	Raymond F. Collins, *Introduction to the New Testament* (Garden City, N.Y.: Doubleday, 1983)
CTJ	*Calvin Theological Journal*
d.	died
Davidson	Samuel Davidson, *An Introduction to the Study of the New Testament*, 2 vols. (London: Longmans, Green, 1868)
Davies	W. D. Davies, *Invitation to the New Testament* (London: DLT, 1957)
DBI	*A Dictionary of Biblical Interpretation*
Dibelius	Martin Dibelius, *A Fresh Approach to the New Testament and Early Christian Literature* (London: Ivor Nicholson & Watson, 1936)
DLT	Darton, Longman and Todd
EBC	*The Expositor's Bible Commentary*
EBib	Etudes bibliques
EGT	*The Expositor's Greek Testament*
EKKNT	Evangelisch-katholischer Kommentar zum Neuen Testament
Enslin	Morton Scott Enslin, *Christian Beginnings* (New York: Harper, 1936)
EphThLov	*Ephemerides Theologicae Lovanienses*
EQ	*Evangelical Quarterly*
EstBib	Estudios bíblicos
ET	English translation
Exp	*The Expositor*
ExpTim	*Expository Times*
FRLANT	Forschungen zur Religion und Literatur des Alten und Neuen Testaments
Fs.	*Festschrift*

Fuller	Reginald H. Fuller, *A Critical Introduction to the New Testament* (London: Duckworth, 1955)
GNC	Good News Commentaries
Goodspeed	Edgar J. Goodspeed, *An Introduction to the New Testament* (Chicago: University of Chicago Press, 1937)
GP	*Gospel Perspectives: Studies of History and Tradition in the Four Gospels*, 6 vols., ed. R. T. France, David Wenham, and Craig Blomberg (Sheffield: JSOT, 1980–86)
Grant	Robert M. Grant, *A Historical Introduction to the New Testament* (London: Collins, 1963)
Guthrie	Donald Guthrie, *New Testament Introduction*, 4th ed. (Downers Grove, Ill.: IVP, 1990)
Harrington	Wilfrid J. Harrington, *Record of the Fulfillment of the New Testament* (London: Chapman, 1958)
Harrison	Everett F. Harrison, *Introduction to the New Testament*, rev. ed. (Grand Rapids: Eerdmans, 1971)
Hennecke	E. Hennecke, ed., *New Testament Apocrypha*, 2 vols. (ET London: Lutterworth, 1963–65)
Herklots	H. G. G. Herklots, *A Fresh Approach to the New Testament* (London: SCM, 1950)
HNT	Handbuch zum Neuen Testament
HNTC	Harper's New Testament Commentaries (= BNTC)
HTKNT	Herders theologischer Kommentar zum Neuen Testament
HTR	*Harvard Theological Review*
HTS	Harvard Theological Studies
Hunter	A. M. Hunter, *Introducing the New Testament* (London: SCM, 1945)
IB	*Interpreter's Bible*
IBS	*Irish Biblical Studies*
ICC	International Critical Commentary
ICE	Institute for Christian Economics
IDB	*Interpreter's Dictionary of the Bible*
IDBSup	*Interpreter's Dictionary of the Bible Supplement*
Int	*Interpretation*
ISBE	*International Standard Bible Encyclopedia*
IVP	InterVarsity Press
JASA	*Journal of the American Scientific Affiliation*
JB	Jerusalem Bible
JBL	*Journal of Biblical Literature*
JBR	*Journal of Bible and Religion*
JCE	*Journal of Christian Education*
JETS	*Journal of the Evangelical Theological Society*

Johnson	Luke T. Johnson, *The Writings of the New Testament* (Philadelphia: Fortress, 1986)
Jones	Maurice Jones, *The New Testament in the Twentieth Century* (London: Macmillan, 1934)
JSNT	*Journal for the Study of the New Testament*
JSNTSupp	Journal for the Study of the New Testament Supplements
JSOT	*Journal for the Study of the Old Testament*
JTC	*Journal for Theology and the Church*
JTS	*Journal of Theological Studies*
Jülicher	Adolf Jülicher, *An Introduction to the New Testament* (London: Smith, Elder, 1904)
KBW	Katholisches Bibelwerk
KEK	Meyer's Kritish-exegetischer Kommentar über das Neue Testament
KJV	King James Version
Klijn	A. F. J. Klijn, *An Introduction to the New Testament* (Leiden: Brill, 1967)
Köster	Helmut Köster, *Einführung in das Neue Testament* (New York: de Gruyter, 1980)
Kümmel	Werner Georg Kümmel, *Introduction to the New Testament*, rev. ed. (Nashville: Abingdon, 1975)
Lake	Kirsopp Lake and Silva Lake, *An Introduction to the New Testament* (London: Christophus, 1938)
LCL	Loeb's Classical Library
LouvStud	*Louvain Studies*
LSJ	Henry George Liddell, Robert Scott, and Henry Stuart Jones, *A Greek-English Lexicon*, 9th ed. (Oxford: Clarendon, 1940)
LW	*Luther's Works*
LXX	Septuagint
m.	*Mishnah*
McNeile	A. H. McNeile, *An Introduction to the Study of the New Testament*, 2d ed., revised by C. S. C. Williams (Oxford: Clarendon, 1953)
Martin	Ralph P. Martin, *New Testament Foundations: A Guide for Christian Students*, 2 vols. (Grand Rapids: Eerdmans, 1975–78)
Marxsen	Willi Marxsen, *Introduction to the New Testament* (Philadelphia: Fortress, 1968)
Metzger	Bruce M. Metzger, *A Textual Commentary on the Greek New Testament* (London: UBS, 1971)
MNTC	Moffatt New Testament Commentary
Moffatt	James Moffatt, *An Introduction to the Literature of the New Testament*, rev. ed. (Edinburgh: T. & T. Clark, 1918)
Moule	C. F. D. Moule, *The Birth of the New Testament*, 3d ed. (San Francisco: Harper & Row, 1981)
MS(S)	manuscript(s)
NA[26]	Nestle-Aland Greek New Testament, 26th ed.

NAG	*Nachrichten der Akademie der Wissenschaften in Göttingen, philologisch-historische Klasse*
NBC	New Bible Commentary
NCB	New Century Bible
NClarB	New Clarendon Bible
NEB	New English Bible
Neot	*Neotestamentica*
NewDocs	*New Documents Illustrating Early Christianity*
NICNT	New International Commentary on the New Testament
NIGTC	New International Greek Testament Commentary
NIV	New International Version
NovT	*Novum Testamentum*
NPNF2	*The Nicene and Post-Nicene Fathers*, ed. Philip Schaff and Henry Wace, 2d ser., 14 vols. (reprint, Grand Rapids: Eerdmans, 1975)
NTAbh	Neutestamentliche Abhandlungen
NTC	New Testament Commentary
NTD	Das Neue Testament Deutsch
NTS	*New Testament Studies*
ÖstK	*Östkirchliche Studien*
Perrin/Duling	Norman Perrin and Dennis C. Duling, *The New Testament: An Introduction*, 2d ed., ed. Robert Ferm (San Diego: Harcourt Brace Jovanovich, 1982)
PL	*Patrologia Latina* (Migne)
PNTC	Penguin New Testament Commentaries
Pullan	Leighton Pullan, *The Books of the New Testament* (London: Rivingtons, 1926)
RefThRev	*Reformed Theological Review*
RevBib	*Revue biblique*
RevQ	*Revue de Qumran*
RHPR	*Revue d'histoire et de philosophie religieuses*
RNT	Regensburger Neues Testament
Robert/ Feuillet	A. Robert and A. Feuillet, eds., *Introduction to the New Testament* (New York: Desclée, 1965)
Rowland	Christopher Rowland, *Christian Origins: From Messianic Movement to Christian Religion* (Minneapolis: Augsburg, 1985)
RSV	Revised Standard Version
RVV	Religionsgeschichtliche Versuche und Vorarbeiten
SAB	*Sitzungsberichte der königlichen preussischen Akademie der Wissenschaften zu Berlin*
SBG	Studies in Biblical Greek
SBLDS	Society of Biblical Literature Dissertation Series
SBLMS	Society of Biblical Literature Monograph Series

SBS	Stuttgarter Bibelstudien
SBT	Studies in Biblical Theology
Schürer	E. Schürer, *The History of the Jewish People in the Age of Jesus Christ*, 3 vols., new ed. (Edinburgh: T. & T. Clark, 1973–87)
SE	*Studia Evangelica*
SJLA	Studies in Judaism in Late Antiquity
SN	Studia Neotestamentica
SNT	Studien zum Neuen Testament
SNTSMS	Society of New Testament Studies Monograph Series
SNTU	*Studien zum Neuen Testament und seiner Umwelt*
SP	Scholars Press
SPB	Studia Postbiblica
SR	*Studies in Religion = Sciences religieuses*
ST	*Studia Theologica*
SUNT	Studien zur Umwelt des Neuen Testaments
SuppNovT	Supplements to *Novum Testamentum*
TDNT	*Theological Dictionary of the New Testament*
Tenney	Merrill C. Tenney, *New Testament Survey* (London: IVP, 1951)
Theol	*Theology*
THNT	Theologischer Handkommentar zum Neuen Testament
ThR	*Theologische Rundschau*
TLZ	*Theologische Literaturzeitung*
TNTC	Tyndale New Testament Commentary
TOTC	Tyndale Old Testament Commentary
TrinJ	*Trinity Journal*
TSK	*Theologische Studien und Kritiken*
TU	Texte und Untersuchungen
TynB	*Tyndale Bulletin*
UBS	United Bible Societies
UBS3	United Bible Societies Greek New Testament, 3d ed.
UPA	University Press of America
van Unnik	W. C. van Unnik, *The New Testament* (London: Collins, 1964)
WBC	Word Biblical Commentary
WC	Westminster Commentaries
WEC	Wycliffe Exegetical Commentary
Weiss	Bernhard Weiss, *A Manual of Introduction to the New Testament*, 2 vols. (New York: Funk & Wagnalls, n.d.)
WH	B. F. Westcott and F. J. A. Hort, *The New Testament in the Original Greek* (London: Macmillan, 1881)
Wikenhauser	Alfred Wikenhauser and Josef Schmid, *Einleitung in das Neue Testament*, 6th ed. (Freiburg: Herder, 1973)
WMANT	Wissenschaftliche Monographien zum Alten und Neuen Testament

WTJ	*Westminster Theological Journal*
WUNT	Wissenschaftliche Untersuchungen zum Neuen Testament
Zahn	Theodore B. Zahn, *Introduction to the New Testament*, 3 vols. (Edinburgh: T. & T. Clark, 1909)
ZNW	*Zeitschrift für die neutestamentliche Wissenschaft*
ZTK	*Zeitschrift für Theologie und Kirche*

1

the synoptic gospels

INTRODUCTION

The first three gospels were first labeled the Synoptic Gospels by J. J. Griesbach, a German biblical scholar, at the end of the eighteenth century. The English adjective "synoptic" comes from the Greek συνόψις (*synopsis*), which means "seeing together," and Griesbach chose the word because of the high degree of similarity found among Matthew, Mark, and Luke in their presentations of the ministry of Jesus. These similarites, which involve structure, content, and tone, are evident even to the casual reader. They serve not only to bind the first three gospels together but to separate them from the gospel of John.

Matthew, Mark, and Luke structure the ministry of Jesus according to a general geographic sequence: ministry in Galilee, withdrawal to the North (with Peter's confession as a climax and point of transition), ministry in Judea and Perea while Jesus is on his way to Jerusalem (less clear in Luke), and final ministry in Jerusalem. Very little of this sequence can be found in John, where the focus is on Jesus' ministry in Jerusalem during his periodic visits to the city. In content, the first three evangelists narrate many of the same events, focusing on Jesus' healings, exorcisms, and teaching in parables. John, while narrating several significant healings, has no exorcisms and no parables (at least of the type found in Matthew, Mark, and Luke). Also, many of the events we think of as characteristic of the first three gospels are absent from John: the sending out of the Twelve, the transfiguration, the Olivet discourse, the last-supper narrative. By having Jesus constantly on the move and by juxtaposing actions—miracles, especially—with (usually) brief teachings, the first three evangelists convey a tone of intense, rapid-fire action. This is quite in contrast to the more meditative tone of John, who narrates far fewer events than do the synoptic evangelists and prefers to present Jesus as speaking in long discourses rather than in brief parables or pithy sayings.

Over the last two centuries, scholars have scrutinized the Synoptic Gospels from many angles and with many different results. This is an inevitable result of the vital importance of these books for Christian belief and life. Here we have narrated the life of the One in whom God has chosen especially to make himself known to human beings. These books depict the events on which the significance of history and the destiny of every single individual depend: the death and resurrection of Jesus the Messiah. Issues pertaining to these books individually will be treated in the section devoted to each; here we address significant issues that embrace all three accounts. Specifically, we examine three questions: How did the Synoptic Gospels come into being? How should we understand the Gospels as works of literature? And what do the Gospels tell us about Jesus?

THE EVOLUTION OF THE SYNOPTIC GOSPELS

How did the Synoptic Gospels come to be written? A simple and in some ways adequate answer would be to identify the people who, under inspiration of God's Spirit, wrote these books and to note the circumstances in which they were written. These issues are addressed in the introductions devoted to each of the four gospels. But simply identifying the authors of the Synoptic Gospels leaves some questions unanswered. How did the authors get the material about Jesus that they have used? Why are the three accounts so similar at so many places and so different at others? What was the role of the evangelists themselves—recorders of tradition? Authors with a viewpoint of their own? And, to raise the larger question that lurks behind all of these, why *four* gospels? These and similar questions have occupied thoughtful Christians since the beginning of the church. A second-century Christian, Tatian, combined all four gospels together in his *Diatessaron*. Augustine wrote a treatise entitled *The Harmony of the Gospels*.[1] But scholars have pursued these questions especially vigorously since the rise of modern biblical criticism at the end of the eighteenth century.

While we may dismiss as inconsequential some of the questions raised during this time, and even more of the answers as simply wrong, the issue of synoptic origins and relations is one that cannot be avoided. The number and nature of the Gospels raise such literary and historical questions. Moreover, one of the evangelists refers to the process by which the gospel material has come to him.

> Many have undertaken to draw up an account of the things that have been fulfilled among us, just as they were handed down to us by those who from the first were eyewitnesses and servants of the word. Therefore, since I myself have carefully investigated everything from the beginning, it seemed good also to me to write an orderly account for you, most excellent Theophilus, so that you may know the certainty of the things you have been taught. (Luke 1:1–4)

In this introduction to his two-volume "history of Christian origins," Luke acknowledges three stages in the genesis of his work: the "eyewitnesses and servants of the word" who "handed down" the truth of Jesus; those "many" who have already written *drawn up* accounts of Jesus and the early church; and Luke himself, who, having "carefully investigated" these sources, now composes his own "orderly" account. Investigation of the process to which Luke refers appears to be quite in order. We look first, then, at the earliest stage of transmission, during which eyewitnesses and others handed down the tradition about Jesus, much of it orally; then at the stage when written sources began to grow and become more important; and last, at the stage of final authorship.[2]

---

[1]It can be found in *NPNF* 6:77–236.
[2]Martin uses Luke 1:1–4 in a similar way in his introduction (1:119–21).

The Stage of Oral Traditions: Form Criticism

In the course of the investigation into the origins of the Gospels, several distinct approaches have emerged over the last two centuries, each of them emphasizing different aspects or stages of the problem. Three approaches in particular have made distinct and significant contributions to the problem of gospel origins and development: form criticism (*Formgeschichte*), which focuses on the period of oral transmission; source criticism, which focuses on the way different literary units were put together to make up the Gospels; and redaction criticism (*Redaktionsgeschichte*), which focuses on the literary and theological contributions of the authors of the Gospels. These methods correspond generally to the three stages mentioned by Luke in his introduction. Yet they are not mutually exclusive; most contemporary gospel critics employ all three simultaneously in what is called traditions analysis or tradition criticism (*Traditionsgeschichte*). Nevertheless, these three approaches are both historically and methodologically distinct, and we examine each in turn.

We begin with form criticism because, though arising only after the heyday of source criticism, it concentrates on the earliest stage in the process by which the Gospels came into being: the oral stage. This was the period of time before any substantial written accounts of the life and teaching of Jesus existed, during which the material that has become our Gospels was transmitted by word of mouth. If we date Mark at the earliest in the mid-50s, with other possible written gospel sources not much earlier, this stage of mainly oral transmission must have lasted at least twenty years.

Description Form criticism was first applied to the Old Testament by scholars such as Hermann Gunkel and was then brought into New Testament studies in the second and third decades of this century by a trio of men who had come to recognize that the source-critical approach, pursued rigorously for several decades, had exhausted its potential. These men were Karl Ludwig Schmidt, Martin Dibelius, and Rudolf Bultmann.[3] Though differing at several important points, these pioneers of form criticism had in common at least six assumptions and beliefs that came to be the basis for form criticism.

1. The stories and sayings of Jesus circulated in small independent units. The early form critics saw an exception in the passion narrative, which they thought was a self-contained literary unit from a very early period.[4] Even this exception is not admitted by many contemporary form critics.

2. The transmission of the gospel material can be compared to the transmission of other folk and religious traditions. Responsibility for this transmission rests not with individuals but with the community, within which the material takes shape and is handed down. Certain laws of transmission, generally observable in such instances of oral transmission, can be applied to the transmission of the Gospels.

---

[3]Schmidt's *Der Rahmen der Geschichte Jesu: Literarkritische Untersuchungen zur ältesten Jesus-überlieferung* was published in 1919 (by Trowitzsch & Son in Berlin) and has never been translated. Also appearing in 1919 in its original German edition was Martin Dibelius's *From Tradition to Gospel* (ET New York: Charles Scribner's Sons, n.d.); *The History of the Synoptic Tradition* by Rudolf Bultmann was published in 1921 (ET New York: Harper & Row, 1963).

[4]E.g., Dibelius, *From Tradition to Gospel*, pp. 178–79.

Table 1
Terminology of Form Criticism

Form	Dibelius	Bultmann	Taylor[5]
Brief sayings of Jesus set in a context (e.g., Mark 12:13–17, which climaxes in Jesus' saying "Give to Caesar what is Caesar's and to God what is God's")	Paradigms	Apophthegms	Pronouncement Stories
Stories about Jesus' miraculous deeds (e.g., the feeding of the 5000)	Tales	Miracle Stories	Miracle Stories
Stories that magnify Jesus as a "hero" (e.g., Luke's story about Jesus in the temple at twelve years of age [2:41–52])	Legends	Historical Stories & Legends	Stories about Jesus
Teaching of Jesus which does not climax in a single saying (e.g., the Lord's Prayer)	Paranesis	Dominical Sayings	Sayings and Parables

3. The stories and sayings of Jesus took on certain standard forms (hence "form" criticism, or "the history of forms"), for the most part still readily visible in the Gospels. Form critics have not agreed on the number and exact nature of these forms. Table 1 presents three influential schemes. [5]

4. The form of a specific story or saying makes it possible to determine its *Sitz im Leben* ("setting in life"), or setting in the life of the early church. According to Bultmann, "The proper understanding of form-criticism rests upon the judgement that the literature in which the life of a given community, even the primitive Christian community, has taken shape, springs out of quite definite conditions and wants of life from which grows up a quite definite style and quite specific forms and categories. Thus, every literary category has its 'life situation.'"[6]

5. As it passed down the sayings and stories of Jesus, the early Christian community not only put the material into certain forms, it modified it under the impetus of its own needs and situations. With this point we move from what may be called form criticism proper (a literary enterprise) into a broader conception of the discipline in which historical judgments that by and large do not grow out of the discipline as such are being rendered.

Form critics differ widely over the degree to which the early church modified and created gospel material. Bultmann, for instance, thinks the influence was huge, attributing most of the gospel material to the early church and finding relatively little that can be reliably considered to have come from the earthly ministry of Jesus. He can attribute so much of the material to the early church

---

[5]In addition to the Dibelius and Bultmann works mentioned, see Vincent Taylor, *The Formation of the Gospel Tradition*, 2d ed. (London: Macmillan, 1935). Taylor uses form criticism with less historical skepticism than does either Dibelius or Bultmann.

[6]Bultmann, *Synoptic Tradition*, p. 4.

because he, with many other form critics, believes that the early church was not concerned to distinguish between things Jesus said while on earth and things that he was continuing to say through prophets in the life of the church. As Norman Perrin puts it, "The modern distinction between historical Jesus and risen Lord is quite foreign to the early church."[7]

Radical historical judgments such as these are not intrinsic to form criticism, and many form critics are much more conservative in their historical assessments. Vincent Taylor is one, and there are others still more conservative who confine the influence of the early church mainly to the arrangement of material (e.g., the series of controversy stories in Mark 2:1–3:6 and parallels). But these are exceptions to the rule, and it must be said that the great majority of form critics have viewed their enterprise as including a good measure of historical skepticism.

6. Classic form critics have typically utilized various criteria to enable them to determine the age and historical trustworthiness of particular pericopes. These criteria are based on certain laws of transmission that are thought to hold good for any orally transmitted material. According to these so-called laws, people tend to (1) lengthen their stories, (2) add details to them, (3) conform them more and more to their own language, and (4) generally preserve and create only what fits their own needs and beliefs. On the basis of these laws, many form critics have declared that gospel material that is shorter, lacks details, contains Semitisms, and does not fit with the interests of the early church or first-century Judaism is earlier and thus more likely to be historical. The last criterion, which we might call the criterion of dissimilarity, is especially important for the more radical form critics. By eliminating *anything* that was likely to have been introduced by the early church or that could have been picked up from the Jewish milieu, it is able to secure a "critically assured" minimum number of sayings and activities on which a supposedly historical understanding of Jesus can be based. This criterion, for instance, suggests that Mark 13:32—"No one knows about that day or hour, not even the angels in heaven, nor the Son, but only the Father"—may well be original with Jesus, since it uses language not typical of Judaism ("the Son") and contains a premise (Jesus' ignorance) that runs counter to a view in the early church. A fifth criterion is a by-product of this one, holding material to be authentic that agrees with material isolated by a "criterion of dissimilarity," while a sixth criterion, "multiple attestation," gives preference to material found in more than one stream of tradition (e.g., Mark and "Q").

Evaluation The historical skepticism that characterizes many of the most prominent form critics has given form criticism itself the reputation of attacking the historicity of the Gospels. But as we have suggested above, this need not be the case. As a literary discipline, form criticism entails no a priori judgment about the historicity of the material that it analyzes. Moreover, many of the assumptions on which form criticism is based appear to be valid: there was indeed a period of mainly oral transmission of the gospel material; much of it was probably in small units; there probably was a tendency for this material to take on certain standard forms; and the early church has undoubtedly influenced the way in which this

---

[7]Normann Perrin, *Rediscovering the Teaching of Jesus* (London: SCM, 1967), p. 27; cf. Bultmann, *Synoptic Tradition*, pp. 127–28.

material was handed down. Defined narrowly in this way, there is undoubtedly a place for form criticism in the study of the Gospels.

Nevertheless, we must register certain cautions even about this narrow application of the discipline. First, it is probable that more of the gospel material than many form critics allow existed from very early periods in written form and that much of the rest of it may already have been connected together into larger literary units.[8] Second, we must be careful not to impose a straitjacket of specified, clearly delineated forms on the material. The existence of so-called mixed forms suggests that any classification must be viewed as provisional and general at best. Third, the claims of form critics to be able to identify the setting in the life of the church from specific forms must be treated with healthy skepticism. Often— perhaps usually—we lack sufficient data for any such identification. Finally, and perhaps most damaging, the assumptions of many of the form critics about the nature of the transmission process are suspect. Several authors have argued that most form critics have not sufficiently appreciated the dynamics and nature of oral transmission and that far too little attention has been given to the role of individuals in shaping and handing down the material.[9]

More serious criticisms must be directed against the antihistorical application of form criticism typified by Bultmann, Dibelius, and many of their heirs. First, the claim that the early church did not distinguish the earthly Jesus from the risen Lord, and thus felt free to place on the lips of the earthly Jesus sayings uttered by early Christian prophets, is unjustified. Bultmann claimed that verses such as 2 Corinthians 5:16b—"if, indeed, we have known Christ according to the flesh, we now no longer will know him in this way" (authors' translation)—demonstrated that Paul and others in the early church had no interest in the earthly Jesus as such. But Paul is saying in this text not that he would no longer have any interest in a "fleshly" (i.e. earthly) Jesus but that he was determined no longer to regard Jesus "from a fleshly point of view." In fact, nothing in the New Testament substantiates the notion that early Christians did not distinguish the earthly Jesus and the risen Lord, and the radical form critics have never come near to explaining how the utterance of a Christian prophet in, say, Antioch in A.D. 42 would have been put on the lips of Jesus as he taught in a specific locale in Galilee thirteen or so years earlier. That Christian prophecy actually functioned in this way is being questioned more and more.[10]

Second, we must question whether the transmission of the gospel material over a period of twenty or so years can appropriately be compared with some of the other material that form critics use to draw conclusions about the Gospels. The rabbinic literature, for instance, with which both Bultmann and Dibelius compare the Gospels, was a very undefined body of material, being gathered over the

---

[8]C. H. Dodd, for instance, proposes that from the beginning, the pattern of early Christian preaching had imposed a certain pattern in the gospel material ("The Framework of the Gospel Narrative," *ExpTim* 43 [1932]: 396–400).

[9]See esp. Erhardt Güttgemanns, *Candid Questions Concerning Gospel Form Criticism: A Methodological Sketch of the Fundamental Problematics of Form and Redaction Criticism* (ET Pittsburgh: Pickwick, 1979), and Werner H. Kelber, *The Oral and the Written Gospel* (Philadelphia: Fortress, 1983).

[10]E.g., David Hill, *New Testament Prophecy* (Richmond: John Knox, 1979), pp. 160–85; J. D. G. Dunn, "Prophetic T-Sayings and the Jesus Tradition: The Importance of Testing Prophetic Utterances Within Early Christianity," *NTS* 24 (1978): 175–98; David Aune, *Prophecy in Early Christianity and the Ancient Mediterranean World* (Grand Rapids: Eerdmans, 1983), p. 245.

course of centuries. And the rabbis never produced anything remotely resembling a gospel.

Third, and related to this last point, are doubts about the validity of the so-called laws of transmission. E. P. Sanders and others have shown that oral transmission by no means always tends to lengthen material.[11] The use of such laws, then, to attribute stories and sayings to the church rather than to Jesus is not valid. Particularly to be criticized is the criterion of authenticity. To be sure, the application of this criterion is often misunderstood: most who utilize it do not claim that *only* those sayings that it can isolate are authentic, but rather that these are the only ones we can be sure about. Nevertheless, its use has the tendency to focus attention on what was peculiar to Jesus over against both his Jewish environment and the early church. Its use thus tends to skew our view of Jesus.[12] More conservative form critics insist that the criterion must not be used in isolation and only with the positive purpose of providing evidence of historicity rather than with the negative purpose of disproving historicity.[13] Even so, the use of the criterion assumes a discontinuity in the process of transmission that needs to be questioned.

A fourth problem with radical form criticism is its failure to come to grips with the presence of eyewitnesses, some of them hostile, who were in a position to contest any wholesale creation of gospel incidents and sayings. As McNeile puts it, "Form-critics write as though the original eye-witnesses were all caught up to heaven at the Ascension and the Christian Church was put to live on a desert island."[14] Fifth, many form critics are guilty of underestimating the degree to which first-century Jews would have been able to remember and transmit accurately by word of mouth what Jesus had said and done. The so-called Scandinavian School, represented particularly in the work of Birger Gerhardsson,[15] looked to key authoritative figures in the early church as the transmitters of the gospel tradition and argued that the process would have been akin to the transmission of the rabbinic traditions, in which both written materials and careful memorization would have played key roles. Criticism that this particular approach assumes a similarity between the scholastic setting of the rabbis and the more popular setting of early Christianity is warranted. But the importance of memorization in first-century Jewish society is undeniable, and we are justified in thinking that this provides a sufficient basis for the careful and accurate oral transmission of gospel material.[16] We have every reason to think, then, that the early Christians were both able and willing to hand down accurately the deeds and words of Jesus.

---

[11]E. P. Sanders, *The Tendencies of the Synoptic Tradition*, SNTSMS 11 (Cambridge: Cambridge University Press, 1969).

[12]See, e.g., M. D. Hooker, "On Using the Wrong Tool," *Theol* 75 (1972): 570–81.

[13]See esp. Robert Stein, "The 'Criteria' of Authenticity," in *GP* 1:225–63; Ben F. Meyer, *The Aims of Jesus* (Philadelphia: Fortress, 1979), pp. 85–87.

[14]McNeile, p. 53.

[15]Birger Gerhardsson, *Memory and Manuscript: Oral Tradition and Written Transmission in Rabbinic Judaism and Early Christianity*, ASNU 22 (Lund: Gleerup, 1964). For a review of this proposal, see Peter Davids, "The Gospels and Jewish Tradition: Twenty Years After Gerhardsson," in *GP* 1:75–99.

[16]Rainer Riesner, *Jesus als Lehrer*, WUNT 2.7 (Tübingen: Mohr, 1981); idem, "Jüdische Elementarbildung und Evangelienüberlieferung," in *GP* 1:209–23.

Table 2
Synoptic Parallels: The Healing of a Paralytic

Matthew 9:6	Mark 2:10–11	Luke 5:24
"But so that you may know that the Son of Man has authority on earth to forgive sins. . . ." Then he said to the paralytic, "Get up, take your mat and go home."	"But that you may know that the Son of Man has authority on earth to forgive sins. . . ." He said to the paralytic, "I tell you, get up, take your mat and go home."	"But that you may know that the Son of Man has authority on earth to forgive sins. . . ." He said to the paralyzed man, "I tell you, get up, take your mat and go home."

The Stage of Written Sources: Source Criticism (the Synoptic Problem)

Introduction The oral stage of the development of the Synoptic Gospels, which we examined in the last section, probably also included some written traditions about Jesus' life and teachings. Some of the apostles may have taken notes on Jesus' teachings and activities during the ministry itself, and they and other eyewitnesses probably accelerated that process after the resurrection. But it is probable that a predominantly oral period of transmission only eventually gave way to a period during which more substantial bodies of written tradition began to be produced, in a procedure that led eventually to the canonical Gospels. Source criticism is devoted to the investigation of this written stage in the production of the Gospels. It asks, and seeks to answer, this question: What written sources, if any, did the evangelists use in compiling their gospels?

The question is of particular interest to the historian of the early Christian movement, and one that any student of the Synoptic Gospels is bound to ask. For there are startling similarities, both in general outline and in particular wording, among the Synoptic Gospels. Consider the example in table 2, from the account of the healing of a paralytic.

Not only is the wording almost exact (as is true in the Greek original), but each of the three evangelists inserts an abrupt break in Jesus' words at the same point. Such duplication of unusual or awkward constructions occurs at other places, along with passages in which two or three of the evangelists use precisely the same words, in the same order, over several lines of text. In table 3 note, for instance, how Matthew and Luke use almost exactly the same words to record Jesus' lament over Jerusalem.[17] The student of the Gospels naturally wants to know how we can account for so exact a similarity in wording.

But what makes the synoptic problem particularly knotty is the fact that, alongside such exact agreements, there are so many puzzling differences. In the incident cited in table 2, for instance, we note that Matthew omits the "I tell you" found in both Mark and Luke. And in the story from which the extract in table 3

---

[17]The agreement in the Greek text is almost as close, with variations only in the tense of an infinitive, the inclusion of a nonessential verb in Luke, and the choice of a particle at the beginning of the last sentence. Notice the "for" in Matthew, with nothing comparable in Luke (the Greek text has δέ [*de*], "and," "but"). Why the NIV has an exclamation point at the end of the first sentence in Luke and a period at the same place in Matthew is a mystery.

Table 3
Synoptic Parallels: Jesus' Lament over Jerusalem

Matthew 23:37–39	Luke 13:34–35
O Jerusalem, Jerusalem, you who kill the prophets and stone those sent to you, how often I have longed to gather your children together, as a hen gathers her chicks under her wings, but you were not willing. Look, your house is left to you desolate. For I tell you, you will not see me again until you say, "Blessed is he who comes in the name of the Lord."	O Jerusalem, Jerusalem, you who kill the prophets and stone those sent to you, how often I have longed to gather your children together, as a hen gathers her chicks under her wings, but you were not willing! Look, your house is left to you desolate. I tell you, you will not see me again until you say, "Blessed is he who comes in the name of the Lord."

is taken, Matthew omits the part about the paralyzed man's friends opening a hole in the roof in order to let his mat down in front of Jesus.

This combination of agreement and disagreement extends to the larger structure of the Gospels as well. Consider the list of events in table 4, which follows Mark's order. (Any place where one Gospel has deviated from the other two in order of events is indicated with bold type). We find here, though not perhaps in the same proportion, the kinds of agreements and disagreements that recur throughout the Synoptic Gospels. All three roughly follow the same order of events, even when there is no clear chronological or historical reason to do so. Each evangelist, however, omits material found in the other two, each contains unique incidents, and some of the events that are found in one or both of the others are put in a different order.

The question behind the synoptic problem, then, may be reformulated in light of these data: What hypothesis best accounts for the combination of exact agreement and wide divergence that characterizes the first three gospels?

The Main Solutions While the number of solutions to the synoptic problem is proportionate to the amazing amount of research and imaginative thinking that has been devoted to the matter,[18] we may single out four main options.

Common dependence on one original Gospel. In 1771, the German writer and literary critic G. E. Lessing argued that the relationships among the Synoptic Gospels could be explained if they had independently used one original gospel written in Hebrew or Aramaic.[19] This proposal was adopted by others and received modification at the hands of Eichhorn, who postulated the existence of several lost gospels as the sources for the Synoptic Gospels.[20] The proposal has not

---

[18]Full accounts of the history of the investigation may be found in Werner Georg Kümmel, *The New Testament: The History of the Investigation of Its Problems* (New York: Abingdon, 1970), pp. 74–88, 144–61; Stephen Neill and Tom Wright, *The Interpretation of the New Testament, 1861–1986* (Oxford: Oxford University Press, 1988), pp. 112–36.

[19]G. E. Lessing, *Neue Hypothese über die Evangelisten als blos menschichliche Geschichtschreiber betrachtet*, nos. 24–49 (1784).

[20]J. E. Eichhorn, *Einleitung in das Neue Testament* (1804).

Table 4
Order of Events in the Synoptics

Pericope	Matthew	Mark	Luke
Jesus and Beelzebub	12:22–37	3:20–30	**11:14–28**
The Sign of Jonah	12:38–45	—	11:29–32
Jesus' mother and brothers	12:46–50	3:31–35	**8:19–21**
Parable of the Sower	13:1–9	4:1–9	8:4–8
The Reason for Parables	13:10–17	4:10–12	8:9–10
Interpretation of Parable of the Sower	13:18–23	4:13–20	8:11–15
Parable of the Weeds	13:24–30	—	—
A Lamp on a Stand	—	4:21–25	8:16–18
Parable of the Seed growing secretly	—	4:26–29	—
Parable of the Mustard Seed	13:31–32	4:30–34	—
Parable of the Yeast	13:33	—	—
Jesus' Speaking in Parables	13:34–35	—	—
Interpretation of Parable of the Weeds	13:36–43	—	—
Parable of Hidden Treasure	13:44	—	—
Parable of the Pearl	13:45–46	—	—
Parable of the Net	13:47–50	—	—
The Householder	13:51–52	—	—
The Stilling of the Storm	**8:18, 23–27**	4:35–41	8:22–25
Healing of Gerasene Demoniac	**8:28–34**	5:1–20	8:26–39
Raising of Jairus's Daughter/ Healing of a Woman	**9:18–26**	5:21–43	8:40–56
Rejection at Nazareth	13:53–58	6:1–6a	**4:16–30**
Sending out of the Twelve	**10:1–15**	6:6b–13	9:1–6
Beheading of John the Baptist	14:1–12	6:14–29	[9:7–9]
Feeding of the Five Thousand	14:13–21	6:30–44	9:10–17
Walking on the Water	14:22–36	6:45–56	—

Note: Bold type indicates places where Matthew and Luke deviate from the order of events followed in Mark. A dash indicates that the incident does not appear in the gospel.

met with much favor in the twentieth century, although C. C. Torrey argued a form of it in 1933.[21]

Common dependence on oral sources. Shortly after Lessing had proposed an "Ur-gospel" as the solution to the synoptic problem, the German critic J. G. Herder argued that dependence of the Synoptic Gospels on a relatively fixed oral summary of the life of Christ explained the data better.[22] This approach was expanded and defended at length by J. K. L. Gieseler in 1818.[23] The view was more popular in the nineteenth century than today,[24] but it continues to be argued by a few scholars.[25]

[21]C. C. Torrey, *The Four Gospels* (New York: Harper, 1933). See also X. Léon-Dufour, "The Synoptic Gospels," in Robert/Feuillet, pp. 252–86. Léon-Dufour argues that the synoptic evangelists are independent on the literary level, all the similarities arising through dependence on an Aramaic Matthew and oral tradition.

[22]J. G. Herder, *Von der Regel der Zusammenstimmung unserer Evangelien* (1797).

[23]J. K. L. Gieseler, *Historisch-kritischer Versuch über die Entstehung und die frühesten Schicksale der schriftlichen Evangelien* (1818).

[24]B. F. Westcott was one of the better-known defenders of the view. See his *Introduction to the Study of the Gospels*, 8th ed. (London: Macmillan, 1895), pp. 165–212.

[25]John M. Rist has recently argued that the agreements between Matthew and Mark can be explained

Common dependence on gradually developing written fragments. The important and controversial theologian F. Schleiermacher suggested that several fragments of gospel tradition existed in the early church and that these gradually grew until they became incorporated into the Synoptic Gospels. This thesis is no longer argued in this form but remains significant as the first to argue that Papias's "logia" (see Eusebius, *H.E.* 3.39.16, and the discussion below and in chap. 1) refers to one of these fragments—a collection of the sayings of Jesus.[26]

Interdependence. The last basic solution to the synoptic problem maintains that two of the evangelists have used one or more of the other gospels in constructing their own. Without necessarily denying the use of other sources, now lost, advocates of this view argue that only borrowing at the final literary level can explain the degree of similarity among the Synoptic Gospels. This solution to the synoptic problem has been urged from early in the history of the church (e.g., Augustine; see below) and commands almost universal assent among contemporary New Testament scholars—and with good reason. While the ability of first-century Jews to transmit traditions with a remarkable degree of accuracy must not be minimized (see the discussion of form criticism above), it is unlikely that the degree of agreement *in the Greek text* such as is illustrated above can be explained by recourse to oral tradition alone.[27] Robert Stein draws attention to Mark 13:14 = Matthew 24:15 in this regard, where each of the evangelists directs a parenthetical remark to the *reader*.[28] Moreover, as quoted above, Luke makes clear that he, at least, used written sources in writing his gospel (1:1–4).

The hypothesis of a Semitic-language Ur-gospel encounters the same difficulty in explaining the remarkable agreement in the Greek text of the gospels. What is the likelihood that independent translators would come up with exactly the same wording in so many places? To be sure, we could propose a large *Greek* Ur-gospel as the source for all three gospels. But this hypothesis has three serious drawbacks. First, we would have expected so major a literary product in Greek to have been mentioned somewhere in early Christian literature, but it is not. Second, it is harder to explain the genesis of the three Synoptic Gospels if so significant a text already existed. And third, viewed as a comprehensive hypothesis, this theory has difficulty explaining the differences among the Synoptic Gospels.

Theories of Interdependence Only a theory that includes as a major component literary interdependence among the Synoptic Gospels is capable of explaining the data. One aspect of these data stands out as particularly determinative for the

by common use of oral tradition, without having to bring in written sources or to have one depending on the other (*On the Independence of Matthew and Mark*, SNTSMS 32 [Cambridge: Cambridge University Press, 1978]). Bo Reicke attributes the similarities among the Synoptic Gospels to a combination of shared (mainly) oral tradition and personal contacts among the authors (*The Roots of the Synoptic Gospels* [Philadelphia: Fortress, 1986]).

[26]See esp. F. Schleiermacher, "Über die Zeugnisse des Papias von unseren ersten beiden Evangelien," *TSK* 5 (1832): 335–68.

[27]F. Gerald Downing notes that Josephus rarely quoted his sources word-for-word. If this tendency can be assumed for the synoptic evangelists, it is the similarities, not the differences, that require explanation ("Redaction Criticism: Josephus' *Antiquities* and the Synoptic Gospels," *JSNT* 8 [1980]: 33).

[28]Robert Stein, *The Synoptic Problem: An Introduction* (Grand Rapids: Baker, 1987), p. 43. Stein's entire discussion of this matter, replete with many examples, gives a detailed defense of synoptic interdependence (pp. 29–44).

viability of proposed theories: the relationship among the gospels in the order of their recording of the events of the ministry. A study of the sequential parallelism of the Synoptic Gospels at this point reveals a significant fact: while Matthew and Mark frequently agree against Luke in the order of events, and Luke and Mark frequently agree against Matthew, Matthew and Luke almost never agree against Mark. This can be seen from the data in table 4 above. Note that Matthew and Mark agree, against Luke, in placing the accusation that Jesus casts out demons in the name of Beelzebub just before the so-called parables of the kingdom; and Luke and Mark agree, against Matthew, in putting the stilling of the storm and the healing of Gerasene demoniac just after these parables. At no point, however, do Matthew and Luke agree against Mark; to put it another way, at no point does Mark follow an order that disagrees with the other two (hence the lack of any bold type in the Mark column). This phenomenon has given rise to one of the most important arguments for the nature of synoptic relationships: the argument from order. It appears to require that Mark be the "middle term" in any scheme of relationships among Mark, Matthew, and Luke. In other words, Mark must have a relationship to *both* Matthew and Luke, whether he is earlier than both, comes between both, or is later than both. Figure 1 shows the four possibilities.

Figure 1
Synoptic Relations: Mark as Middle Term

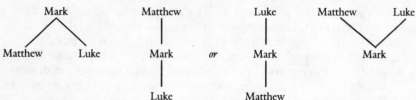

Each of these schemes can explain the phenomenon of order. Moreover, we cannot exclude the possibility that there is a relationship between Matthew and Luke independent of their use of Mark. The argument from order, in and of itself, does not exclude dependence of Matthew and Luke on one another, although it requires that the evangelist who wrote last would have deliberately chosen to follow the order of the other two gospels, whenever they agreed. We thus have the six additional possibilities shown in figure 2.

Figure 2
Synoptic Relations: Interdependence of Matthew and Luke

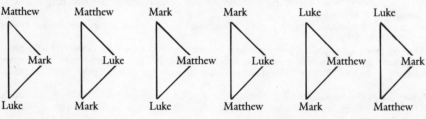

Of the ten schemes, only three have received significant support in the history of the study of the question.

The Augustinian Proposal. Taking its name from the famous North African theologian who first advocated it, this proposal holds that Matthew was the first gospel written. Mark then borrowed from Matthew, with Luke, finally, borrowing from both Matthew and Mark.[29] Until the nineteenth century, this was the standard view of those who saw a literary relationship among the Synoptic Gospels. At that time, however, many began to prefer alternative proposals. Augustine's proposal has not won many modern advocates, B. C. Butler being a notable exception.[30]

The "Two-Gospel" hypothesis. As part of his ground-breaking critical approach to the Synoptic Gospels, J. J. Griesbach, while agreeing that Matthew was the first gospel written, maintained that Luke was second and that Mark was dependent on both Matthew and Luke.[31] His proposal, dubbed the two-gospel hypothesis to contrast it with the two-source hypothesis, has enjoyed a considerable resurgence in popularity in the last thirty years.[32]

The "Two-Source" Hypothesis. While the two-gospel hypothesis views Matthew and Luke as the building blocks of Mark, the two-source hypothesis holds that Mark and "Q," a lost collection of Jesus' sayings, have been used independently by Matthew and Luke. Markan priority was first proposed in the 1830s, apparently independently, by Karl Lachmann and C. G. Wilke, while the full two-source hypothesis was advanced by C. H. Weisse in 1838.[33] It was given its classic expression in an 1863 monograph by H. J. Holtzmann.[34] Finally, in a work that stands as the high-water mark in source criticism, *The Four Gospels: A Study of Origins* (1924),[35] B. H. Streeter posited the existence of two other sources in addition to Mark and Q: "M," the material peculiar to Matthew's gospel, and "L," the material peculiar to Luke's gospel. This "four-source" hypothesis was an attempt to provide a comprehensive explanation of the origin of the Gospels through source criticism. Streeter even suggested dates and provenances for his sources. His resultant scheme may be diagramed as in figure 3.

---

[29]Augustine *The Harmony of the Gospels* 1.2, in NPNF Vol. 6.

[30]B. C. Butler, *The Originality of St. Matthew: A Critique of the Two-Document Hypothesis* (Cambridge: Cambridge University Press, 1951); see also D. J. Chapman, *Matthew, Mark, and Luke: A Study in the Order and Interrelation of the Synoptic Gospels,* ed. John M. T. Barton (London: Longmans, Green, 1937).

[31]J. J. Griesbach, *Commentatio qua Marci evangelium totum e Matthaei et Lucae commentariis decerptum esse monstratur* (Treatise in which is demonstrated that the gospel of Mark has been wholly derived from the commentaries of Matthew and Luke) (1789). Griesbach was anticipated in this proposal by H. P. Owen in 1764 (*Observations of the Four Gospels*).

[32]See esp. William Farmer, *The Synoptic Problem: A Critical Analysis* (New York: Macmillan, 1964); Hans-Herbert Stoldt, *History and Criticism of the Marcan Hypothesis* (Macon, Ga: Mercer University Press, 1980); William Farmer, ed., *New Synoptic Studies: The Cambridge Gospel Conference and Beyond* (Macon, Ga: Mercer University Press, 1983). A collection of significant essays for and against the hypothesis is found in Arthur J. Bellinzoni, Jr., ed., *The Two-Source Hypothesis: A Critical Appraisal* (Macon, Ga: Mercer University Press, 1985).

[33]Karl Lachmann, "De Ordine narrationum im evangeliis synopticis," TSK 8 (1835): 570–90; C. G. Wilke, *Der Urevangelist oder exegetisch-kritische Untersuchungen über das Verwandtschaftsverhältniss der drei ersten Evangelien* (1838); C. H. Weisse, *Die evangelische Geschichte kritisch und philosophisch bearbeitet* (1838).

[34]H. J. Holtzmann, *Die synoptische Evangelien: Ihr Ursprung und ihr geschichtlicher Charakter* (1863).

[35]B. H. Streeter, *The Four Gospels: A Study of Origins* (London: Macmillan, 1924).

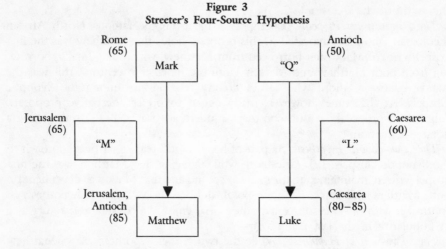

Figure 3
Streeter's Four-Source Hypothesis

Streeter took source criticism as far it could be taken (some would say beyond), and his was the last major work in the discipline to appear for some time. Not everyone agreed with the details of his scheme, and most contemporary gospel critics are skeptical about the existence of M and L as written documents and about the chronological and geographic conclusions he reached. (Some scholars use M and L simply to denote, respectively, material peculiar to Matthew and Luke.) But most scholars thought that Streeter and his predecessors had clearly proven the two-source hypothesis in general, and this explanation of gospel origins was generally assumed by those, such as the redaction critics, who were working on other aspects of the Gospels.

As noted above, however, this is no longer true. The two-source hypothesis has been subjected over the last thirty years to serious criticism, most notably by advocates of the two-gospel, or Griesbach, proposal, but by others also, some of whom maintain Markan priority, while questioning the existence or nature of Q. To the extent that these challenges have induced some caution into what was often an overly dogmatic and simplistic reconstruction of gospel origins, they have had a salutary effect. The two-source theory has been appropriately dethroned from the status of being an "assured result of scholarship." Nevertheless, properly nuanced, the two-source theory remains the best general explanation of the data. In the sections that follow, we will examine the evidence for and against each of the two sources of the two-source hypothesis.

Markan Priority Until the nineteenth century, most Christians assumed that Matthew was the first gospel to be written.[36] This tradition, which became the official position of the Roman Catholic Church, must be respected, particularly since it appears to be bolstered by the second-century testimony of Papias, as cited by Eusebius (see below). Nevertheless, it does not settle the issue. Many gave

---

[36]See the surveys in Zahn 2:392–96 and William Farmer, *Jesus and the Gospel* (Philadelphia: Fortress, 1982), pp. 13–110.

Matthew the priority on the inadequate grounds that he was the only apostle among the synoptic evangelists. Another, equally strong tradition holds that Mark wrote his gospel based on the preaching of Peter (see the introduction to Mark), and this makes Markan dependence on Matthew difficult. Since Lukan priority is rarely argued,[37] the main alternative to Matthean priority is Markan priority. Why have so many scholars been convinced that Mark is the gospel that lies at the basis of both Matthew and Luke? The following are the most important arguments.[38]

The brevity of Mark. Mark is considerably shorter than both Matthew and Luke: 11,025 words as against 18,293 and 19,376, respectively. It is not Mark's relative brevity per se that provides evidence for Mark's priority (it cannot be demonstrated that the shorter is necessarily the earlier), but its brevity taken in conjunction with its close relationship to Luke, and especially Matthew. Over 97 percent of Mark's words have a parallel in Matthew; over 88 percent in Luke.[39] It therefore makes more sense to think that Matthew and Luke have taken over much of Mark, expanding it with their own material, than that Mark has abbreviated Matthew and/or Luke with the omission of so much material. To be sure, it is possible to argue that Mark is a deliberate condensation of Matthew and Luke—as proponents of the two-gospel theory maintain.[40] But it would be a strange condensation that generally lengthens the narratives taken from these other gospels while omitting things like the Sermon on the Mount, the birth narratives, and the appearances of the risen Lord. Put simply, this argument runs: "Given Mark, it is easy to see why Matthew was written; given Matthew, it is hard to see why Mark was needed."[41]

The verbal agreements among the Gospels. As we illustrated earlier, at many places the three Synoptic Gospels manifest a remarkable degree of verbal parallelism. But careful study reveals that, while all three accounts sometimes agree (as in table 2), Matthew and Mark frequently agree, as do Mark and Luke, but Matthew and Luke only rarely agree. As with the argument from order, this phenomenon can be explained as long as Mark is the middle term of the three. It is much more difficult to explain if Mark is not the first, however, because on any other hypothesis, recourse must be had to the supposition of a deliberate and unlikely method of composition. With the Augustinian hypothesis, we would have to think that Luke almost always chose to use Mark's wording rather than Matthew's; with the two-gospel hypothesis, we would have to assume that Mark almost never introduced any wording of his own. While possible, both procedures are unlikely. (The minor agreements between Matthew and Luke are discussed below.)

---

[37]See, however, R. L. Lindsey, "A Modified Two-Document Theory of the Synoptic Dependence and Interdependence," *NovT* 6 (1963): 239.

[38]For further detail and other arguments, see esp. Kümmel, pp. 56–63; Stein, *Synoptic Problem*, pp. 45–88; Joseph A. Fitzmyer, "The Priority of Mark and the 'Q' Source in Luke," in *Jesus and Man's Hope* (Pittsburgh: Pittsburgh Theological Seminary, 1970), 1:131–70 (reprinted in Bellinzoni, *The Two-Source Hypothesis*).

[39]The statistics are from Stein, *Synoptic Problem*, p. 48, who is citing Joseph B. Tyson and Thomas R. W. Longstaff, *Synoptic Abstract*, The Computer Bible 15 (Wooster, Ohio: College of Wooster, 1978), pp. 169–71.

[40]E.g., David L. Dungan, "The Purpose and Provenance of the Gospel of Mark According to the Two-Gospel (Owen-Griesbach) Hypothesis," in *New Synoptic Studies*, pp. 411–40.

[41]G. M. Styler, "The Priority of Mark," in Moule, p. 231.

The order of events. We noted above that a comparison of the order of events in the Synoptic Gospels reveals a situation similar to what is observed about the verbal agreements: Matthew and Luke do not agree against Mark. This phenomenon was noted by Lachmann, who argued, furthermore, that this situation was best explained if Mark was the prior gospel. As with the verbal agreements, the phenomenon of order *can* be explained by other hypotheses; for example, Luke determined to follow Mark's order when he diverged from Matthew (on the Augustinian explanation), or Mark decided never to deviate from Matthew and Luke when they agreed. Again, the virtue of Markan priority is that it provides a natural explanation for this phenomenon, rather than having to postulate an unlikely compositional procedure on the part of one of the evangelists.

Mark's awkward and more primitive style. It is generally agreed that Mark has more grammatical irregularities and awkward constructions than do Matthew and Luke. This, it is argued, favors Markan priority, because the natural tendency would have been for later authors to smooth out such irregularities (a similar criterion is used in textual criticism). Similarly, Mark preserves more Aramaic expressions than does either Matthew or Luke in their parallels with Mark. It is easier to see, it is argued, why Matthew and Luke would eliminate or translate Aramaic expressions that would be unintelligible to their Greek-speaking readers than why Mark would have added such Aramaic expressions without a basis in his sources.

Mark's more primitive theology. Many scholars find many more theologically difficult statements in Mark than in Matthew and Luke, and this suggests (again, paralleling textual-critical principles) that Mark is the earliest. An example is Mark 6:5, where the evangelist claims that, because of the unbelief of the people in Nazareth, Jesus "*could not* do any miracles there." In the parallel verse, Matthew says that Jesus "*did not* do many miracles there" (13:58). It is argued that it is more likely that Matthew has removed the potentially troublesome implication that Jesus was incapable of working a miracle than that Mark has added it. This argument has some weight, but it is not as decisive as the ones above. Not only could one argue about which evangelist has the more difficult statements, but one also must take into account the effect of each evangelist's compositional purposes and theology. This makes it much harder to be sure about the direction of borrowing. The same objection applies to the related argument that redaction critics have found it more plausible to explain Matthew on the basis of Mark than vice versa. At least in some pericopes, there would be disagreement about this,[42] and the sparsity of redactional studies assuming Matthean priority means that most of the data will be on one side in any case.

While not all of equal weight, these arguments taken together make a strong case for thinking that Matthew and Luke have independently used Mark's gospel in writing their own.

"*Q.*" As we noted above, Schleiermacher was the first to posit the existence of a collection of Jesus' sayings as a source for the Gospels. His suggestion was taken

---

[42]See, e.g., David Wenham, "The Synoptic Problem Revisited: Some New Suggestions About the Composition of Mark 4:1–34," *TynB* 23 (1972): 3–38.

up by Weisse, as the second main source of the two-source hypothesis. Like Schleiermacher, some critics think that Papias refers to this document in his famous statement about the logia, but this is doubtful (see the discussion in the introduction to Matthew). At some point toward the end of the nineteenth century, the source became known as "Q," just how and where being a matter of debate.[43] Most proponents of Markan priority think that a sayings source such as Q must have been used by both Matthew and Luke.

The reason for positing the existence of such a written collection of Jesus' teaching is that there are approximately 250 verses common to Matthew and Luke that are not found in Mark. Most, though not all of this material, consists in teachings of Jesus. Many of these verses exhibit a degree of verbal parallelism that favors the existence of a common written source in Greek (see the example in table 3 above). The simplest explanation for this phenomenon would be dependence of one gospel on the other. Against this, however, is the lack of agreement between Matthew and Luke in their ordering of events and the general lack of verbal agreements between them. These factors strongly suggest that Matthew and Luke did not use one another; hence, the need to posit an additional source. Considerable effort has been expended in seeking to reconstruct this hypothetical source,[44] and the degree of certainty with which the hypothesis is entertained by some may be gauged from the fact that there has even been written a book entitled *A Theology of Q*.[45] Nevertheless, there is considerable debate about Q, and we must consider below some of main arguments for and against the hypothesis.

In addition to the argument from verbal agreement in non-Markan material, there are three main arguments for the existence of the Q source.

The agreement in order. A number of scholars have discerned in the non-Markan material common to Matthew and Luke (sometimes called the double tradition) a similar order.[46] Such a similar order would argue for a single written source. But the agreement in order is not all that clear, and this argument has limited force at best.[47]

Doublets in Matthew and Luke. "Doublets" are accounts that appear more than once in a single gospel. It is argued that these occur because the evangelist in question is following Mark at one point and Q at the other. An example is Luke 8:17 and 12:2, in both of which Jesus says "there is nothing hidden [concealed] that will not be disclosed, and [or] nothing concealed [hidden] that will not be known." The first is paralleled only in Mark 4:22 and the second in Matthew 10:26, the assumption then being that Luke has taken the first from Mark and the second from Q.[48] Such doublets suggest the existence of a common source in addition to Mark; they are insufficient to show, however, that Q must have been a single written source.

Different placement of Q material. The non-Markan material shared by Luke and

[43]The designation is often thought to be the first letter of the German word *Quelle*, "source." See the discussion in John J. Schmitt, "In Search of the Origin of the Siglum Q," *JBL* 100 (1981): 609–11.

[44]See esp. A. Polag, *Fragmenta Q: Texthelf zur Logienquelle*, 2d ed. (Neukirchen-Vluyn: Neukirchener, 1982). Guthrie provides a helpful outline (pp. 167–68).

[45]Richard A. Edwards, *A Theology of Q* (Philadephia: Fortress, 1976).

[46]See, e.g., Kümmel, pp. 65–66; Joseph A. Fitzmyer, *The Gospel According to Luke I–IX*, AB (Garden City, N.Y.: Doubleday, 1981), pp. 76–81.

[47]Stein, *Synoptic Problem*, p. 107.

[48]See, on this point, John C. Hawkins, *Horae Synopticae* (Oxford: Clarendon, 1909), pp. 80–107.

Matthew is put in different contexts, Matthew grouping much of it in his five great discourses, Luke generally leaving it scattered throughout the gospel (mainly in 6:20–8:3 and 9:51–18:14). This phenomenon is easier to explain if both were making independent use of a common source then if Luke was using Matthew.

These arguments have convinced most scholars that Matthew and Luke have access to a common non-Markan tradition. Probably most of these think of Q as a single written document, but there is considerable disagreement over this. Many prefer to think of Q as a series of written fragments or as a combination of written and oral traditions. But many scholars are not convinced that we need to posit the existence of any such tradition, arguing that it is far simpler to think that Luke has used Matthew. Since Luke's knowledge of Matthew would seriously undermine the evidence for Markan priority, most of those who deny the existence of Q also deny Markan priority. But some maintain both Markan priority and the use of Matthew by Luke.[49]

The strongest argument in favor of Luke's use of Matthew, and therefore against the two-source theory as a whole, is the existence of what have been called minor agreements between Matthew and Luke and against Mark. These consist both of agreements in the order of particular verses or sayings and of wording.[50] How can these be explained if Luke and Matthew have not used one another? Whether we even attempt such an explanation will depend on how convinced we are by the arguments above that Luke did not know Matthew. If we concede the strength of these earlier arguments, then several such explanations are possible: (1) Overlap of Mark and Q, with the agreement of Matthew and Luke being the result of their common use of Q; (2) coincidental redaction of Mark in the same way; (3) textual corruption, based on the known tendency of scribes to harmonize gospel accounts; and (4) common use of oral traditions that may have overlapped with Mark.[51]

These minor agreements demonstrate that the history of gospel origins was probably more complex than any single-source hypothesis can explain. But they do not overthrow the strength of the case in favor of the two-source hypothesis. A source like Q remains the best explanation for the agreements between Matthew and Luke in non-Markan material. Almost certainly some, if not a substantial portion, of Q was in written form. But we must probably allow for more than one written source, and some mixture of oral traditions as well.

Proto-Gospel Theories Partly in order to fill in some of the gaps left with the two-source hypothesis, partly because of early Christian testimony, and partly because of internal indications, various scholars have posited the existence of an earlier edition of each of the synoptic Gospels. Lachmann, one of the first proponents of the two-source theory, worked from the assumption of an original gospel, arguing that Mark was the closest to that original. Some modern scholars,

---

[49]Most notably, Austen Farrar, "On Dispensing with Q," in *Studies in the Gospels: Essays in Memory of R. H. Lightfoot*, ed. D. E. Nineham (Oxford: Blackwell, 1955), pp. 55–88.

[50]The number of these agreements is debated; see the tabulation and discussion in Franz Neirynck, *The Minor Agreements of Matthew and Luke Against Mark, with a Cumulative List*, BETL 37 (Louvain: Louvain University Press, 1974).

[51]For these suggestions, see Streeter, *Four Gospels*, pp. 293–331; Stein, *Synoptic Problem*, pp. 123–27; F. Neirynck, "Synoptic Problem," in *IDBSup*, p. 845.

noting the problem of the minor agreements and some elements in Matthew and Luke that are difficult to explain if these evangelists were using the canonical Mark, have suggested that one or both may have used an earlier edition of Mark.[52] This hypothesis must remain doubtful. The minor agreements are not all of the same kind; many cannot be explained by positing dependence on an "Ur-Mark."[53] More basically, we must question the assumption that dependence on a different source must be used to explain all the changes Matthew and Luke have made in their Markan source. Source criticism takes too much on itself when it presumes to explain every line in Matthew and Luke with reference to a written source. The influence of eyewitness accounts, various oral traditions, and the evangelists' own theological purposes must be allowed. When these factors are taken into account, the need for an Ur-Mark disappears.

Much more popular has been the thesis that Matthew wrote an earlier edition of his gospel. In this case, however, the motivation is only partly a more satisfactory explanation of synoptic relations; more important is the apparent reference to such an earlier edition in the second-century remark of Papias (quoted by Eusebius, H.E. 3.39.16): "Matthew collected the oracles [τὰ λόγια (ta logia)] in the Hebrew language, [Ἐβραΐδι διαλέκτῳ (Hebraidi dialektō)] and each interpreted [ἡρμήνευσεν (hērmēneusen)] them as best he could."[54] If Papias is referring to a gospel written in Aramaic or Hebrew, he must be referring to an earlier, Semitic edition of our Greek Matthew, since later church fathers appealed to Papias to prove the priority of canonical Matthew. It has been popular, then, to suppose that a Semitic Matthew was the first gospel written; that Peter, or Peter and Mark together, used that edition in composing Greek Mark; and that Greek Matthew then made use of Mark.[55] The stubborn tradition that Matthew was first written in Aramaic or Hebrew, along with the widespread belief in the early church that Matthew was the first gospel, renders the hypothesis of a Semitic "first edition" of Matthew attractive.

Clearly, however, if such an edition existed, the canonical Matthew is not simply a translation of this Semitic original. Matthew does not read like "translation Greek"; more important, Matthew has probably, as we have seen, used Greek Mark in composing his gospel. And there are other problems for the supposition that Mark has used a Semitic-language Matthew. Strong early tradition views Mark as composing his gospel on the basis of Peter's preaching (see the introduction to Mark's gospel). But then it is hard to imagine how Mark could also be using an earlier edition of Matthew. Moreover, Papias may not be referring to a gospel at all (see the discussion in the introduction to Matthew). All

---

52E.g., Günther Bornkamm, *Jesus of Nazareth* (London: Hodder & Stoughton, 1960), p. 217; Vincent Taylor makes such a suggestion, but very cautiously (*The Gospel According to St. Mark*, 2d ed. [London: Macmillan, 1966], pp. 67–77).

53Kümmel, p. 62.

54The translation is by Kirsopp Lake, from *Eusebius: Ecclesiastical History*, vol. 1, LCL (Cambridge: Harvard University Press, 1926). See further discussion of this passage in chap. 2 below, in the section "Author."

55E.g., Zahn 2:601–17. Others who maintain the existence of an Aramaic or Hebrew Matthew lying behind the Synoptic Gospels are Westcott, *Introduction to the Study of the Gospels*, pp. 188–89; Chapman, *Matthew, Mark, and Luke*, pp. 90–92; X. Léon-Dufour, "Synoptic Problem," pp. 283–86; and J. A. T. Robinson, *Redating the New Testament* (Philadelphia: Westminster, 1976), p. 97.

in all, the hypothesis of an earlier, Semitic-language edition of Matthew cannot be certainly proven or disproven.

The evidence for a proto-Luke comes from within Luke itself and rests on three considerations: (1) the greater amount of special material in Luke in comparison with Matthew and Mark; (2) Luke's tendency to "go his own way"; even in material shared with Matthew and Mark (esp. in the passion narrative); and (3) the fact that Luke includes material from Mark in blocks rather than scattered evenly throughout the gospel. These phenomena have suggested to many scholars that Luke had composed a first edition of this gospel with the use of Q and L (his special material) and then later integrated Mark into this initial work.[56] While the case remains unproven,[57] the hypothesis is an attractive one (see discussion in chap. 4).

Conclusion The two-source hypothesis provides the best overall explanation for the relationships among the Synoptic Gospels, but two caveats must be introduced in conclusion. First, the process through which the Gospels came into being was a complex one, so complex that *no* source-critical hypothesis, however detailed,[58] can hope to provide a complete explanation of the situation. Granted that at least one of the evangelists was an eyewitness, that various oral and written traditions unrecoverable to us were undoubtedly circulating, and that the evangelists may even have talked together about their work, the "scissors-and-paste" assumptions of some source critics are seen to be quite unfounded.[59] Recognizing this complexity, along with the stubborn persistence of phenomena that the two-source hypothesis cannot satisfactorily explain, we should treat this hypothesis more as a working theory than as a conclusion set in concrete. Especially important is the need to be open to the possibility that, in a given pericope, an explanation based on the two-source hypothesis may not fit the data. For a given text we thus may conclude that Matthew is more primitive than Mark, or that Luke has followed a special eyewitness source rather than Mark, or that Matthew has relied on his own remembrance or written notes rather than on Q.

The Stage of Final Composition: Redaction Criticism

In our account of gospel origins thus far, we have paid but scant attention to the evangelists themselves. We have looked at the earliest, mainly oral stage of transmission, where the apostles and other unknown Christian preachers and teachers preserved Jesus' teachings and the stories about him. And we have examined the written sources, known and unknown, that the evangelists used in composing their gospels. The evangelist Mark, we have argued, is the author of one of those basic sources. But our interest in Mark from a source-critical

---

[56]See esp. Streeter, *Four Gospels*, pp. 199–221; Vincent Taylor, *The Passion Narrative of St. Luke: A Critical and Historical Investigation*, ed. Owen E. Evans, SNTSMS 19 (Cambridge: Cambridge University Press, 1972); Friedrich Rehkopf, *Der lukanische Sonderquelle*, WUNT 5 (Tübingen: Mohr, 1959).

[57]See Fitzmyer, *Luke I–IX*, pp. 90–91, for criticisms.

[58]See, e.g., the complicated source-critical proposal of L. Vaganay, *Le problème synoptique: Une hypothèse de travail* (Paris: Desclée, 1954); note his summary on p. 444.

[59]Correctly emphasized by Robinson, *Redating*, pp. 93–94.

standpoint is not in his work as an author but in his gospel as a source for Matthew and Luke. So in both form criticism and source criticism, interest in the evangelists themselves recedes into the background. It is redaction criticism that brings the evangelists back onto center stage.

Description Redaction criticism seeks to describe the theological purposes of the evangelists by analyzing the way in which they use their sources. Without denying, then, the need for form critics to study the oral traditions or the need for source critics to scrutinize written sources, redaction critics insist that the evangelists must be given their rightful place as *authors*: people who, however much dependent on sources and traditions, have creatively and purposefully molded that tradition into a literary whole with a theology of its own. The evangelists have not simply collected traditions and sources and pasted them together. They have added their own modifications to those traditions and, in doing so, bring their own particular emphases to the story of Jesus.[60] Redaction criticism is therefore one method of gospel study, and it includes five basic elements.

1. Redaction criticism distinguishes between tradition and redaction. "Tradition," in this sense, is everything—from long written sources to brief orally transmitted stories and sayings—that the evangelist had before him as he wrote his gospel. "Redaction" refers to the process of modifying that tradition as the gospel was actually written. Because redaction criticism depends on our ability to identify the traditions on which the evangelist worked (so we can know what changes he made), it is accomplished most successfully on Matthew and Luke. We can compare their final edition with two extensive sources they have used: Mark and Q. For the same reason, redaction criticism of Mark is a much more difficult procedure, since we do not possess any sources that he has used.[61]

2. The redactional, or editorial, activity of the evangelists can be seen in several areas:

The material they have chosen to include and exclude. For instance, it is generally agreed that the roughly parallel sermons recorded by Matthew in chapters 5–7 and Luke in 6:20–49 are taken from Q. Luke's, however, is less than one-third the length of Matthew's, and it is evident that Luke has omitted almost all reference to the Old Testament and the law (e.g., Matt. 5:17–19, and the antitheses of Matt. 5:21–48). This suggests that Matthew has a serious interest in teaching the church in his day about Jesus' relationship to the law, while Luke has not.

The arrangement of the material. It can be seen from table 4 above that Matthew

---

[60]Good descriptions of redaction criticism are found in Norman Perrin, *What is Redaction Criticism?* (Philadelphia: Fortress, 1969); R. H. Stein, "What Is Redaktionsgeschichte?" *JBL* 88 (1969): 45–56; idem, *Synoptic Problem*, pp. 231–72; Joachim Rohde, *Rediscovering the Teaching of the Evangelists* (London: SCM, 1968). R. T. France provides an illuminating example of redaction criticism at work in his "Exegesis in Practice: Two Samples," in *New Testament Interpretation: Essays on Principles and Methods*, ed. I. Howard Marshall (Grand Rapids: Eerdmans, 1977), pp. 253–64.

[61]For the methodology of redaction criticism as applied to Mark, see E. J. Pryke, *Redactional Style in the Marcan Gospel: A Study of Syntax and Vocabulary as Guides to Redaction in Mark*, SNTSMS 33 (Cambridge: Cambridge University Press, 1978); Stein, *Synoptic Problem*, pp. 251–63. Skeptical of the whole enterprise of redaction criticism as applied to Mark is C. Clifton Black, *The Disciples in Mark: Markan Redaction in Current Debate*, JSNTSupp 27 (Sheffield: JSOT, 1989).

differs from Mark and Luke in the placement of three significant miracle stories: the stilling of the storm (8:18, 23–27), the healing of the Gerasene demoniac(s) (8:28–34), and the intertwined accounts of the raising of Jairus's daughter and the healing of the woman with a flow of blood (9:18–26). Since Mark is probably Matthew's main source for these stories, it is evident that Matthew has chosen to put them in a different order. When we find him doing the same thing with other miracle stories that end up in Matthew 8–9, we are justified in concluding that Matthew is deliberately arranging the material to make a point about Jesus as miracle worker. Such rearrangement takes place within pericopes also: does the change in order of the temptations (Matt. 4:1–11 = Luke 4:1–12) reveal different emphases of the respective evangelists?

The "seams" that the evangelist uses to stitch his tradition together. In order to fashion a continuous narrative from diverse sources, an evangelist has to supply transitions. These transitions, or seams, often reveal important concerns of the author. Matthew, for instance, alternates teaching and narrative in a very effective manner, and he signals the transition at the end of discourses with a repeated formula: "when Jesus had finished saying these things" (7:28; 19:1; see also 11:1; 13:53; 26:1).

Additions to the material. In Luke's account of Jesus' healing ministry and call of the Twelve (6:12–19), which appears to depend on Mark 3:7–18, he mentions the fact, not found in Mark, that "Jesus went out to a mountainside to pray, and spent the night praying to God" (6:12). Here, perhaps, we find evidence of a Lukan concern.

Omission of material. Where the redaction critic can be pretty sure that an evangelist has had access to a tradition that he does not include, it is important to ask whether the omission serves a theological interest. For instance, it is frequently argued that Luke has omitted the reference to Jesus "coming on the clouds of heaven" (found in both Mark and Matthew) in his reply to the high priest (22:29) because Luke wants to avoid the idea of an imminent parousia.

Change of wording. In a well-known beatitude, Jesus, according to Matthew, pronounces a blessing on "the poor in spirit" (5:3); according to Luke, on the poor (6:20). The redaction critic would note this difference as perhaps indicating Luke's relatively greater interest in socioeconomic issues.

3. Redaction critics look for patterns in these kinds of changes within a gospel. Where such a pattern emerges, we may conclude that we are dealing with a theological concern of the author. For instance, the addition of reference to Jesus praying (noted above) is of a piece with similar additions about prayer that Luke makes throughout his gospel. Prayer, we can surmise, was a theological concern of Luke. Following this procedure, a general picture of the theological stance of a particular gospel is eventually built up.

4. On the basis of this general theological picture, the redaction critic then seeks to establish a setting for the production of the gospel. Luke's alleged omission of references to an imminent parousia, for instance, is said to show that he was writing in a setting where the delay of the parousia had become a problem. To "the setting in the life of Jesus" and "the setting in the life of the church" (the form-critical concern) is added "the setting in the life of the evangelist and his community."

5. Some include within redaction criticism not only the study of the evangelists'

modification of tradition but the literary and theological characteristics of the Gospels, however discerned—what is sometimes called composition criticism. To some extent, this is a fruitless semantic quarrel, but it is perhaps better to maintain the narrower definition of redaction criticism so as to differentiate it from the composition criticism that good exegetes have always done.

Origins William Wrede, though not a redaction critic in the sense defined above, was something of a precursor of the emphasis typical of redaction criticism. Wrede wrote at a time when the Markan hypothesis reigned in scholarly study of the Gospels. This hypothesis was so named not just because it maintained Markan priority but because it also claimed that Mark gave a generally untheological, historically reliable portrait of Jesus. Wrede destroyed this assumption by demonstrating that Mark was as thoroughly theological as the other gospels. Specifically, Wrede argued that Mark had added the many references where Jesus urged silence about his messiahship. This "messianic secret" was designed to explain how it came about that so few people recognized Jesus to be the Messiah during his lifetime.[62] While Wrede's specific thesis is now generally discredited, his contention that Mark is as much theologian as historian (or theologian *instead of* historian) has been widely accepted.

The implications of Wrede's understanding of the evangelists as creative theologians were not immediately appropriated. Redaction criticism as an identifiable discipline did not develop until the 1950s. Three German critics were the pioneers in the field.[63] Günther Bornkamm's essay on the stilling of the storm, in which he sought to uncover Matthew's theological point by comparing his account with Mark's, was the earliest redaction-critical work.[64] More significant were two monographs that appeared later in the decade. Hans Conzelmann, in *The Theology of St. Luke*,[65] analyzed the theological standpoint of Luke, arguing that the evangelist imposed a threefold periodization of salvation history on the gospel material—the time of Israel, the time of Jesus, and the time of the church. In doing so, according to Conzelmann, Luke provided a basis for a continuing role of the Christian community in history, thereby defusing early Christian disappointment about the delay of the parousia, namely, the failure of Jesus to return as soon as expected. Willi Marxsen did for Mark what Conzelmann did for Luke. Mark, according to Marxsen, was also motivated by concern about the parousia, but Mark believed that the parousia was imminent and wrote his gospel

---

[62]William Wrede, *Das Messiasgeheimnis in den Evangelien* (Göttingen: Vandenhoeck & Ruprecht, 1901 [ET *The Messianic Secret in Mark*]).

[63]R. H. Lightfoot's 1934 Bampton Lectures, published as *History and Interpretation in the Gospels* (London: Hodder & Stoughton, 1935), anticipates many of the emphases of redaction criticism, as do Ned B. Stonehouse's *The Witness of Matthew and Mark to Christ* (1944) and *The Witness of Luke to Christ* (1951) (the two can be found in a one-volume edition from Baker Book House [1979]). On Stonehouse's work, see Moisés Silva, "Ned B. Stonehouse and Redaction Criticism. Part I: The Witness of the Synoptic Evangelists to Christ; Part II: The Historicity of the Synoptic Tradition," *WTJ* 40 (1977–78): 77–88, 281–303.

[64]It can be found in English translation in G. Bornkamm, G. Barth, and H. J. Held, *Tradition and Interpretation in Matthew* (Philadelphia: Westminster, 1974).

[65]Hans Conzelmann, *The Theology of St. Luke* (New York: Harper & Row, 1960). The German original, more revealingly titled *Die Mitte der Zeit* ("The center of time"), was published in 1954.

with the overarching purpose of gathering together Christians in Galilee to await the Lord.[66]

It would be impossible to select even the most outstanding redaction-critical works since these initial studies. The conclusions reached by Bornkamm, Marxsen, and Conzelmann are not widely held anymore, but the methodology they pioneered has won a secure place in the field of gospel studies.[67] Countless monographs, dissertations, and articles using redaction criticism analyze themes within a gospel or the gospel as a whole, or they compare and contrast the contribution of two or more evangelists to a theme. Hardly any serious study of the Gospels proceeds without considerable utilization of redaction criticism. This is not to say that redaction criticism has ousted form criticism or source criticism; contemporary scholars employ all three together as they seek to understand the final product, the Gospels (the redactional stage), in terms of the raw material that has gone into them (the stage of tradition).

Evaluation Popularity does not make anything right. As with any other method, we must take a critical look at redaction criticism before we endorse it as a method of gospel study. We begin with five criticisms of the discipline.[68]

1. Redaction criticism depends for its validity on our ability to distinguish tradition and redaction. We must have a pretty good idea about the sources that a given evangelist has used before we can begin speaking about his modifications to those sources. Almost all redaction critics have assumed the validity of the two-source hypothesis in their research—that Matthew and Luke both used Mark and another source, Q, in writing their gospels. Those who question the accuracy of that hypothesis will also, of course, have to establish a different basis on which to do redaction criticism. Advocates of the two-gospel hypothesis, for instance, will have to speak about Mark's modifications of Matthew and Luke rather than Matthew's modifications of Mark, and they will be able to do redaction criticism of Matthew only with great difficulty. But even if we assume the general reliability of the two-source hypothesis, our difficulties for redaction criticism are not eliminated.

First, as we have argued, in some places the direction of dependence hypothesized with the two-source theory may be reversed. Some places in Mark, let us say, may depend on a version of a story that found its way eventually almost intact into Matthew's gospel. In such a situation we would have to speak of Mark's changes of Matthew rather than Matthew's changes of Mark. Second, Matthew or Luke may sometimes depend on a version of a story independent of, but parallel to, Mark. Again, then, what a redaction critic would label "Matthean redaction" (of Mark) may be tradition that Matthew is simply passing on. Third, since we do

---

[66]Willi Marxsen, *Mark the Evangelist: Studies on the Redaction History of the Gospel* (Nashville: Abingdon, 1969); the German original appeared in 1956.

[67]Note particularly three monographs from conservative scholars that employ redaction-critical methods and that dissent from the conclusions of Marxsen, Conzelmann, and Bornkamm: Ralph Martin, *Mark: Evangelist and Theologian* (Grand Rapids: Zondervan, 1972); I. Howard Marshall, *Luke: Historian and Theologian*, new, enlarged ed. (Grand Rapids: Zondervan, 1989); R. T. France, *Matthew: Evangelist and Theologian* (Grand Rapids: Zondervan, 1989).

[68]For more detail on these points and others, see D. A. Carson, "Redaction Criticism: On the Legitimacy and Illegitimacy of a Literary Tool," in *Scripture and Truth*, ed. D. A. Carson and John D. Woodbridge (Grand Rapids: Zondervan, 1983), pp. 119–42, 376–81.

not possess a copy of Q, arguments about whether Matthew or Luke has redacted Q are necessarily uncertain. Scholars generally think that they can identify, by various factors, what the original of Q probably was, and they base their redactional judgments on that supposition. But the process is necessarily subjective and leaves room for much disagreement. For instance, with respect to the difference between "poor" (Luke) and "poor in spirit" (Matthew) already mentioned, can we be sure that Luke has socialized Q, rather than Matthew spiritualizing it? In this case, perhaps we can suspect that Luke is the one responsible, since his change conforms to an obvious emphasis in his gospel. But the decision is often much more difficult and is fraught with possibilities for error. All this goes to say that redaction critics often need to be much more cautious about claiming that one evangelist has changed his source. We may not be able to identify redactional elements as often as, or as certainly as, we might like.

2. Redaction critics too often assume that all the changes an evangelist makes to his tradition are theologically motivated. Many no doubt are; but many others, and particularly minor changes affecting one or two words, are stylistic in nature. In other cases, even major additions may be due not to theological concerns but to historical interest; we cannot omit simple historical purposes from the intentions of the evangelists.[69]

3. Redaction critics have sometimes equated "redactional emphases" with the evangelist's theology. What is determined to be redaction shows us what is distinct about a particular gospel in comparison with the others or with its sources. We may often legitimately conclude that what is redactional, since it is what an evangelist has deliberately changed, is particularly significant to that evangelist. But it is certainly not the whole of, or perhaps even representative of, his theology. To assume so would be to assume that the tradition an evangelist takes over is *not* of interest to him or part of his theology. This is manifestly absurd. It would be as if, in comparing the writings of Calvin and Beza, the theologies of each of these men were determined only on the basis of what was unique in each one. The common emphases of Matthew, Mark, and Luke far outweigh their distinctives, and a holistic picture of what each teaches must take both into account.

4. The identification of the setting of a particular gospel on the basis of the author's theology is often far more specific than the data allow. That the additions of Matthew to both Mark and Q involving the Mosaic law and Old Testament quotations demonstrate that Matthew was writing in a setting and to an audience that needed teaching on this matter is evident. And that the tenor of these additions may even allow us to make some guesses about the particular problems of the community in which Matthew was writing is also clear. But the details of setting that some redaction critics hypothesize are often castles built on sand. They usually depend on only part of the evidence (hence different critics working on the same gospel come up with conflicting settings) and draw conclusions far more specific than the evidence allows.

5. Redaction criticism is often pursued in such a way that the historical trustworthiness of the gospel material is called into question. It is not so much that redaction criticism seeks to prove the unhistorical nature of the changes

---

[69]See Graham N. Stanton, *Jesus of Nazareth in New Testament Preaching*, SNTSMS 27 (Cambridge: Cambridge University Press, 1974).

introduced by the evangelists. Rather, many redaction critics assume that the evangelists would have little concern about it. Thus, as Marxsen puts it, "Within this approach, the question as to what really happened is excluded from the outset."[70] In this sense, redaction criticism is a true descendant of radical form criticism. Mark, Matthew, and Luke, according to many redaction critics, had no more interest in historical accuracy than did the early Christian community as reconstructed by Bultmann and Dibelius. So typical is the antihistorical bias of many of the best-known redaction critics that redaction criticism, like form criticism, has earned for itself the reputation of being a method that attacks the historical reliability of the Gospels.

But this is an unfair generalization from the way many pursue redaction criticism to the method itself. Nothing about redaction criticism per se is antihistorical. Indeed, as we will argue below, redaction criticism has some very positive contributions to make to our interpretation of the Synoptic Gospels. Why, then, do so many redaction critics come to conclusions that question the historical credibility of the Gospels?

One major reason is an assumption among many redaction critics that an evangelist cannot be both theologically motivated and historically accurate. We are often presented, explicitly or implicitly, with the choice between historical and theological. Yet there is no reason why an evangelist cannot have both concerns. That Matthew, Mark, and Luke have redacted the gospel traditions that came to them is beyond doubt. And for some redaction critics, it appears, this is enough to justify the conclusion that, in tampering with the tradition, the evangelists have tampered with history. But this is not necessary at all. Rearranging, adding, omitting, and rewording need not detract from the historicity of the event or teaching concerned. For instance, newspapers will frequently rewrite for their own readers news-service reports that they receive, but their rewrites need not affect the accuracy of the report. Major speeches will sometimes be summarized in a few words, or excerpts will be taken from them. In doing so, different newspapers may focus on different emphases in the same speech. We do not accuse these newspapers of inaccuracy in doing this; nor should we accuse the evangelists of historical inaccuracies if they summarize, excerpt, or reword Jesus' own sayings. That they have done so seems clear, as a comparison among the evangelists at almost any page in a synopsis shows. But their failure to preserve the *ipsissima verba Jesu* (the authentic words of Jesus) does not mean that they have tampered with the *ipsissima vox Jesu* (the authentic voice of Jesus). As long as the evangelists' redactional modifications are consistent with what actually happened or with what Jesus actually said—even if they select, summarize, and reword—historical integrity is maintained.[71]

The question, then, boils down to the intentions of the evangelists as these can be determined from their express statements and their actual redactional work. Did they intend to write their gospels with a concern for historical accuracy? Or

---

[70]Marxsen, *Mark the Evangelist*, p. 23.

[71]The issue raised in this paragraph is very broad and important. For these points and others, see esp. R. T. France, "The Authenticity of the Sayings of Jesus," in *History, Criticism, and Faith*, ed. Colin Brown (Downers Grove, Ill.: IVP, 1976), pp. 101–41; Craig Blomberg, *The Historical Reliability of the Gospels* (Downers Grove, Ill.: IVP, 1987), esp. pp. 35–43, 113–52; I. Howard Marshall, *I Believe in the Historical Jesus* (Grand Rapids: Eerdmans, 1977).

did they theologize the message of Jesus with little interest in whether it really happened that way or not? Redaction criticism, in itself, cannot answer these questions. And redaction critics themselves come to radically different conclusions about this matter. Some are convinced that a careful study of the modifications introduced by the evangelists shows no tampering with historicity. They separate redaction from tradition in order to understand the message of the Gospels better, without supposing that the redaction has any less historical foundation than the tradition.[72] Thus, for instance, they may conclude that Luke has redacted Jesus' beatitude "Blessed are the poor" to include an economic focus by pairing it with his "Woe to you rich," while Matthew has redacted the same saying as "Blessed are the poor in spirit" to emphasize the spiritual dimension. But as long as Jesus intended both—and it is quite likely that he did, given the Old Testament concept of the poor—then it would be unfair to accuse either evangelist of an unhistorical tampering with the words of Jesus. Many instances are, of course, more difficult, and only a text-by-text scrutiny of the data is finally adequate to demonstrate the case one way or the other. Our point here is simply that redaction criticism need not be destructive to the historical accuracy of the Gospels and that redaction critics who assume that the evangelists had no concern for history in their redactional activity have not proven their point.

The problems of redaction criticism, then, are problems of exaggerated claims, false assumptions, and inappropriate applications. Pursued properly, redaction criticism offers the promise of real help in interpreting the Gospels. Specifically, the discipline of redaction criticism has several positive elements.

1. By focusing on the final, authorial stage in the production of the Gospels, it offers immediate help to the interpreter and theologian. In this respect it contrasts favorably with both form and source criticism, both of which, in their concern with the prehistory of the gospel tradition, are important for the historian of early Christianity but of only minimal help to the interpreter. Redaction criticism looks at the level that deserves most of our attention: the final literary product, the gospel.

2. Redaction criticism reminds us that the evangelists wrote with more than (though not less than) historical interest. They were preachers and teachers, concerned to apply the truths of Jesus' life and teaching to specific communities in their own day. This theological purpose of the evangelists has sometimes been lost, with a consequent loss of appreciation for the significance and application of the history that the evangelists narrate.

3. Redaction criticism recognizes, and increases our appreciation of, the multiplicity of the Gospels. The story of Jesus has come to us not in one super gospel but in four gospels, each with its own distinct and important contribution to make to our understanding of Jesus. While creating occasional problems at the historical level, this fourfold gospel should be appreciated for the richness of perspective it brings. "Jesus is such a gigantic figure that we need all four portraits to discern him,"[73] and redaction criticism helps us to appreciate the artistry and meaning of each of those portraits.

---

[72]See, e.g., Grant R. Osborne, "The Evangelical and Redaction Criticism: Critique and Methodology," *JETS* 22 (1979): 305–22.

[73]Leon Morris, *Studies in the Fourth Gospel* (Grand Rapids: Eerdmans, 1969), p. 107.

THE GOSPELS AS WORKS OF LITERATURE

We have sketched the process by which the Gospels have come into being. We now turn our attention to the final products, considered on their own as works of literature. Two matters call for specific consideration: the question of gospel genre and the new literary criticism.

The Genre of the Gospels

Nowhere in the New Testament is any of the four accounts of Jesus' ministry called a gospel (εὐαγγέλιον [*euangelion*]; on Mark 1:1, see the introduction to Mark). "Gospel" and the cognate verb "preach the gospel" (εὐαγγελίζομαι [*euangelizomai*]) are used in the New Testament, and especially frequently in Paul, to denote the message of God's saving act in his Son (see, e.g., Mark 1:14–15; Rom. 1:16; 1 Cor. 15:1; Gal. 1:6–7).[74] Perhaps some time toward the end of the first century or early in the second, titles were added to the church's authoritative accounts of Jesus' ministry. Certainly this was when "gospel" was first used to denote a work of literature.[75] These titles preserve the stress on the singleness of *the* gospel by the way they are phrased: not "the gospel *by* Mark," but "the [one] gospel, according to [the version of] Mark" (and Matthew and Luke and John). Justin, in the middle of the second century, is the first author to use the word "gospel" of the canonical accounts of Jesus' ministry (*Apol.* 1.66; *Dial.* .0.2). It was probably Mark's use of the word in prominent places in his gospel (e.g., 1:1, 14) that led to its use as a literary designation.[76] No books before our Gospels had ever been given this designation. What implications does this hold for the literary genre of the Gospels?

The question is an important one for the reader of the Gospels because accurate interpretation depends to some extent on accurate decisions about genre. The phrase "red rose" will signify something quite different in a botanical treatise than it does in Robert Burns's line "O, my luve is like a red, red rose." Similarly, Jesus' walking on the water will mean one thing for the reader who takes the Gospels to be straightforward history and a very different thing for the reader who is convinced he or she is reading a myth or a midrash.

Modern study of the genre of the Gospels began with K. L. Schmidt's decision to classify them as "popular literature" (*Kleinliteratur*) rather than "literary works" (*Hochliteratur*).[77] As popular literature, the Gospels could be expected to follow the rules of transmission typical of such literature—an important point for Schmidt, who was one of the pioneers of form criticism. This classification also meant that the Gospels were to be viewed as distinct from the more literary

---

[74]The New Testament use of εὐαγγέλιον (*euangelion*, "gospel") and εὐαγγελίζομαι (*euangelizomai*, "to preach good news") is taken from the Old Testament. These Greek words translate Hebrew words (from the root בשׂר [*bśr*, "bear tidings"]) that refer to the deliverance that God has promised his people (see esp. Isa. 40:9; 42:7; 52:7; 61:1; Ps. 95:1).

[75]See, e.g., G. Friedrich, "εὐαγγέλιον," in *TDNT* 2:721–35.

[76]E.g., Martin Hengel, "The Titles of the Gospels and the Gospel of Mark," in *Studies in the Gospel of Mark* (Philadelphia: Fortress, 1985), pp. 64–84.

[77]K. L. Schmidt, "Die Stellung der Evangelien in der allgemeinen Literaturgeschichte," in *EYXAPIΣTHPION: Studien zur Religion und Literatur des Alten und Neuen Testaments, Fs.* Hermann Gunkel, ed. K. L. Schmidt, FRLANT 19.2 (Göttingen: Vandenhoeck & Ruprecht, 1923), pp. 59–60.

biographies of various types prevalant in the ancient Greco-Roman world. From a slightly different perspective, C. H. Dodd viewed the Gospels (and especially Mark) as mirroring the early Christian preaching (kerygma) about Christ. As expansions of this kerygma, the Gospels were viewed rather more as the last stage in a continuous oral tradition than as self-conscious literary creations.[78] These approaches to the Gospels led to the view that they could be fit into no ancient literary genre but were unique. Without necessarily subscribing to either Schmidt's or Dodd's view of gospel origins, many (perhaps even a majority of) contemporary scholars think that the Gospels do not fit into any established literary category.[79]

But others are convinced that, while possessing some unique features, the Gospels share enough features with other works of the ancient world to be placed in the genre of these works. A number of specific genre identifications have been proposed, from Greek aretalogy (stories of the miraculous deeds of a godlike hero) to Jewish midrash. But the most popular suggestion, as well as the most defensible, is that the Gospels are biographies. True, the Gospels are quite different from the standard modern biography: they lack accounts of Jesus' childhood development and education, his character and motivations, and chronological precision. But ancient Greco-Roman biographies did not always contain such features either. Indeed, the biographical genre of antiquity was a very broad one, encompassing works of considerable diversity. It was certainly broad enough, it is argued, to include the Synoptic Gospels.[80]

If, however, we define the biographical genre as broadly as it must be in order to place the Gospels within it, the question as to whether the Gospels are biographies or are unique is little more than a question of semantics. It is clear that the Gospels share many elements with Greco-Roman biographies, the most important being that they portray the significant events in the life of an important person. But it is equally clear that the Gospels differ from most other Greco-Roman biographies: they are formally anonymous, which is rare for the biography; they lack the literary pretensions characteristic of most biographies; and, most of all, they combine teaching and action in a preaching-oriented work that stands apart from anything else in the ancient world.[81] We may, then, single

---

[78]See Robert Guelich, "The Gospel Genre," in *Das Evangelium und die Evangelien*, ed. Peter Stuhlmacher (Tübingen: Mohr, 1983), pp. 183–219.

[79]See, e.g., Kümmel, p. 37; Guthrie, pp. 16–19; Martin 1:20; Robert H. Gundry, "Recent Investigations into the Literary Genre 'Gospel,'" in *New Dimensions in New Testament Study*, ed. Richard N. Longenecker and Merrill C. Tenney (Grand Rapids: Zondervan, 1974), pp. 101–13; Graham N. Stanton, *The Gospels and Jesus* (Oxford: University Press, 1989), pp. 15–20.

[80]See esp. C. W. Votaw, "The Gospels and Contemporary Biographies," *AJT* 19 (1915), pp. 45–71; Charles H. Talbert, *What Is a Gospel? The Genre of the Canonical Gospels* (Philadelphia: Fortress, 1977); Philip L. Shuler, *A Genre for the Gospels: The Biographical Character of Matthew* (Philadelphia: Fortress, 1982); Detlev Dormeyer and Hubert Frankemölle, "Evangelium als literarische Gattung und als theologisches Begriff: Tendenzen und Aufgaben der Evangelienforschung im 20. Jahrhundert, mit einer Untersuchung des Markusevangeliums in seinem Verhältnis zur antiken Biographie," in *ANRW* 25.2, pp.1545–81; Albrecht Dihle, "Die Evangelien und die griechische Biographie," in *Das Evangelium und die Evangelien*, pp. 383–411; David E. Aune, *The New Testament in Its Literary Environment*, Library of Early Christianity 8 (Philadelphia: Westminster, 1987), pp. 17–76.

[81]Patricia Cox makes the important point that ancient biographies recounted the "deeds" (πράξεις [πραχεις]) of its subject only as a means of illuminating his or her "essence," or "manner of life" (ἔθος [ethos]) (*Biography in Late Antiquity* [Berkeley: University of California, 1983], p. 65). This does not match the intention of the evangelists.

out the similarities and call the Gospels biographies with unique aspects; or we may focus on the differences and put them into a unique genre, with points of contact with ancient biography (and with other genres as well). In either case, it will be important to recognize that the Gospels cannot simply be forced into the confines of an existing genre. The uniqueness of the Person on whom they focus has forced the evangelists to create a literary form that is without clear parallel.

The New Literary Criticism

Description "Literary criticism" is a catchall designation that embraces a wide variety of contemporary approaches to the Gospels. What binds these approaches together is an interest in applying contemporary literary theories to the interpretation of the Gospels. Many who employ such techniques are professedly reacting against what they perceive to be an excessive and unproductive preoccupation with historical concerns. Investigations of the prehistory of the Synoptic Gospels, such as dominate form and source criticism, have resulted, it is claimed, in a "critical distancing of the text" that "has transformed biblical writings into museum pieces without contemporary relevance."[82] Nor does redaction criticism escape censure, for it too, although concerned with the final stage in the process, is nevertheless rooted in the enterprise of tradition-history. What is needed, it is argued, is a new approach whereby the Gospels are read "as they are" and interpreted by means of contemporary literary theory.

In place of barren studies of tradition history, modern literary critics want to look at the text as it is. How it originated, what sources it incorporates, and even who wrote it are unimportant. With many modern literary critics, the text is considered to have, as it were, a life of its own. The meaning it conveys is not tied to its historical origin—whether we think of that origin as located in a community or an author—but to the way it functions as it is read by the modern interpreter. For many literary critics, then, we cannot speak of a true or false meaning of any given gospel text or of the gospel as a whole but only of *my* meaning and *your* meaning. Meaning is located not in an author's intention but in the encounter of text and reader. This meaning is often seen to be the product of certain so-called deep structures—basic, universal ways of putting things—that are found in the Gospels. Structuralism, a broad movement that incorporates several different approaches, seeks to identify these structures, classify them, and use them as an aid to interpretation.[83]

---

[82] Edgar V. McKnight, *Post-Modern Use of the Bible: The Emergence of Reader-Oriented Criticism* (Nashville: Abingdon, 1988), p. 14.

[83] A fine, brief survey of the movement generally, with competent critique, is Tremper Longman III, *Literary Approaches to Biblical Interpretation* (Grand Rapids: Zondervan, 1987). Some important studies that consider various approaches within this general movement are Norman R. Peterson, *Literary Criticism for New Testament Critics* (Philadelphia: Fortress, 1978); Edgar V. McKnight, *Meaning in Texts* (Philadelphia: Fortress, 1974); idem, *Post-Modern Use of the Bible*; Daniel Patte, *What Is Structural Exegesis?* (Philadelphia: Fortress, 1976); idem, *Structural Exegesis for New Testament Critics* (Philadelphia: Fortress, 1990); Robert W. Funk, *The Poetics of Biblical Narrative* (Somona, Calif.: Polebridge, 1989). See also Jack Dean Kingsbury, *Matthew as Story* (Philadelphia: Fortress, 1986).

Evaluation Literary criticism is rooted in a valid concern: study of the Gospels has too often focused on the history of the tradition behind them to the extent that the Gospels themselves become lost to sight. Focus on the text as we now have it is a welcome corrective to this tendency. Literary critics have also shed new light on the way different parts of the Gospels function within the larger literary unit. And exegetes can profit from the taxonomies of narrative structures that literary critics use in their intepretations. But there are severe problems with the general movement that seriously vitiate its usefulness.

First, there exists among many literary critics a reaction not only against excessive historical analysis but against history itself. It appears that literary criticism has sought to turn the problem of historical skepticism and uncertainty into a virtue. True, they say, we can know little for certain about Jesus, but by insisting that the truth of the Gospels lies within their own "narrative world," the literary critic can ignore the problem. Yet the problem will not go away so easily, for the evangelists are demonstrably *referring* to events in the real world. The failure of literary criticism to deal with this means that it can never get to the real heart of the Gospels.[84]

Second, the casting of the text loose from the author means—as many literary critics teach—that there can be no such thing as a correct meaning of the text. But the evangelists were individuals writing in specific circumstances and to specific audiences; this historical setting, not the individual reader, must set the context for interpretation.[85]

Third, the general tendency to derive categories of interpretation from modern literature, such as the novel, is a questionable procedure. Quite apart from the issue of the validity of modern theories of novel interpretation (and there is reason for skepticism), it is doubtful whether the Gospels can be compared to the modern novel.

Fourth, there are questions about the structuralism used in much literary criticism. These questions have to do with both the existence of the alleged deep structures as well as their usefulness for interpretation. Are we attributing to ancients modern structures of thinking and writing? Must all writing fall into such structures? These questions do not apply to all forms of structuralism, but they should make us very cautious about the usefulness of some of the more popular and far-reaching wings of the movement.

JESUS AND THE SYNOPTIC GOSPELS

The two previous questions we have examined—How did the Gospels come into being? How are they to be understood as literary works?—are important in their own right but become especially significant when we understand their ramifications for the historical issue. Do the Gospels tell us a great deal about the early church but almost nothing about Jesus (Bultmann)? Do they tell us mainly about different forms of early Christianity, with Jesus but a shadowy and uncertain figure at its inception (some redaction critics)? Do they introduce us

---

[84]See, for this point, Kevin Vanhoozer, "A Lamp in the Labyrinth: The Hermeneutics of 'Aesthetic' Theology," *TrinJ* 8 (1987): 25–56.

[85]See, e.g., E. D. Hirsch, Jr., *Validity in Interpretation* (New Haven, Conn.: Yale University Press, 1967).

into a narrative world in which Jesus becomes little more than a protagonist in a story (some literary critics)? What do the Gospels tell us of Jesus? This is a fundamental question for New Testament studies, and here we answer it only briefly by surveying some of the main approaches and indicating briefly our own position.

The Question of the "Historical" Jesus

Christians before the eighteenth century entertained few doubts that the Gospels were to be read as historically reliable accounts of the life of Jesus. The main problem to be faced was that of harmonization: explaining how the four gospels could be combined together to produce a smooth and coherent account of Jesus' life. Such attempts date from the earliest days of the church (e.g., Tatian in the second century) and continue to be popular in our own day. But this generally unquestioned confidence in the historical accuracy of the gospels' portrait of Jesus changed in the eighteenth century under the onslaught of the Enlightenment. A new, critically oriented historiography was less disposed to accept ancient accounts at face value. This attitude applied especially to miracles, which did not fit well into the deistic view of a mechanical and reliable universe. The most famous early attack on the historicity of the Gospels was that of Samuel Reimarus. His "Fragments," published by Lessing in 1774–78 after Reimarus's death, raised serious doubts about the gospel accounts. Among other things, Reimarus suggested that the resurrection did not occur; instead, the disciples stole the body.[86]

Skepticism about the miraculous element in the Gospels quickly became widespread. H. E. G. Paulus, for example, explained away the resurrection as a revival from a coma in the cold tomb, and Jesus' walking on the water was in reality his walking on a barely submerged sandbar. But a major break with this rationalistic approach came in the groundbreaking *Life of Jesus* by D. F. Strauss (1835–36). Strauss, while no more accepting of the historicity of the Gospels than were his rationalistic predecessors, insisted that the Gospels taught truth, but truth of a religious and philosophical nature. Much of the Gospels were made up of myths (stories with religious value) that were important witnesses to the "absolute spirit," a concept taken from the then-popular philosophy of Hegel. Reaction against Strauss and other such extreme skeptics took many forms. One was the Markan hypothesis, which viewed Mark as relatively untheological and therefore a generally reliable basis for a historical Jesus. Such a view fed into the many lives of Jesus, told from a liberal perspective, in which the theological and dogmatic layers of the Greek-influenced early church (and particularly Paul) were stripped off in order to get at the real Jesus: the humble teacher of Nazareth.

Three influential works ended such efforts. The most famous was Albert Schweitzer's *Quest for the Historical Jesus*, a chronicle of "lives of Jesus" from Reimarus to his own time (1906).[87] Schweitzer showed how each successive

---

[86]On Reimarus and other key figures in the debate about the "historical Jesus" through the middle of the nineteenth century, see esp. Colin Brown, *Jesus in European Protestant Thought, 1778–1860* (Grand Rapids: Baker, 1988). A broader survey is found in Charles C. Anderson, *Critical Quests of Jesus* (Grand Rapids: Eerdmans, 1969).

[87]Albert Schweitzer, *The Quest for the Historical Jesus* (New York: Macmillan, 1961). The German title is *Von Reimarus zu Wrede* (From Reimarus to Wrede).

"historical" Jesus was little more than the projection of the writer's own cultural and philosophical outlook back into the plane of history. Schweitzer, building on the work of Johannes Weiss,[88] saw eschatology as the key to understanding Jesus. Jesus proclaimed the impending world-ending entrance of the kingdom of God and died disappointed when it had not come. Two other books written a bit earlier called into question the possibility of a nontheological, untendentious picture of Jesus: Martin Kähler's *The So-Called Historical Jesus and the Historic, Biblical Christ*[89] and William Wrede's *The Messianic Secret in Mark*.[90] Thus, as E. E. Ellis puts it, "The Quest began with the supposition that history could be extracted from the Gospels like a kernel from the husk; it ended with the growing recognition that the process was more like peeling an onion with history and interpretation intermixed at every layer."[91]

Rudolf Bultmann kept peeling until there was almost nothing left. His form-critical studies of the Gospels convinced him that we could know very little for sure about Jesus himself: the accounts have simply been reinterpreted too thoroughly by the early church. But this did not concern Bultmann, for it is not what we can uncover about Jesus in history that matters for us but what we can experience of Jesus in personal encounter with him here and now. Historical facts cannot prove articles of faith: "Rather, the acknowledgment of Jesus as the one in whom God's word decisively encounters man, whatever title be given him . . . is a pure act of faith independent of the answer to the historical question. . . . Faith, being personal decision, cannot be dependent on a historian's labor."[92] Bultmann, using existentialist philosophy as a guide, pursues a program of "demythologization" in which the modern reader penetrates through the myths of the Gospels to find real truth. A "new quest for the historical Jesus" was initiated by pupils of Bultmann who worried that so complete a casting loose of Christian faith from historical moorings would leave the church adrift and helpless to make any claims for itself at all. Ernst Käsemann opened this new quest in 1953, and he has been followed by several other influential German theologians.[93] Nevertheless, what even the "new questers" decide can be reliably known about Jesus is so small a residue of the whole that little has been gained.

It would be impossible to catalog here the variety of interpetations of the life of Jesus that are current in scholarship in our own day;[94] nor have we done more than scratch the historical surface. Indeed, the picture we come away with from so

---

[88]Johannes Weiss, *Jesus' Proclamation of the Kingdom of God* (Philadelphia: Fortress, 1971); the German original was published in 1892.

[89]Martin Kähler, *The So-Called Historical Jesus and the Historic, Biblical Christ* (Philadelphia: Fortress, 1964); the German original was published in 1896.

[90]The German original, *Das Messiasgeheimnis in den Evangelien*, was first published in 1901.

[91]E. E. Ellis, "Gospels Criticism: A Perspective on the State of the Art," in *Das Evangelium und die Evangelien*, p. 30.

[92]Rudolph Bultmann, *Theology of the New Testament*, 2 vols. (New York: Charles Scribner's Sons, 1951–55), 1:26.

[93]Ernst Käsemann, "The Problem of the Historical Jesus," in *Essays on New Testament Themes* (Philadelphia: Fortress, 1964), pp. 15–47; Bornkamm, *Jesus of Nazareth*, esp. pp. 13–26; and note James M. Robinson, *A New Quest of the Historical Jesus*, SBT 25 (London: SCM, 1959). For a conservative appraisal, see Ralph P. Martin, "The New Quest of the Historical Jesus," in *Jesus of Nazareth: Savior and Lord*, ed. Carl F. H. Henry (Grand Rapids: Eerdmans, 1966), pp. 31–45.

[94]A helpful collection of essays on a variety of views current through 1969 is Harvey K. McArthur, ed., *In Search of the Historical Jesus* (New York: Charles Scribner's Sons, 1969).

cursory a survey can be seriously misleading, since it focuses on the new and the unusual at the expense of the many fine restatements of a more conservative approach. But at least it enables us to see the extent to which the Gospels have come to be considered exceedingly weak reeds for the historian's labors.

Yet such skepticism is not warranted. The evangelists certainly claim to be writing history. True, they write as passionate exponents of a certain interpretation of that history, and they select and arrange their facts accordingly. But as we have seen when discussing redaction criticism, there is no reason to think a person must be a bad historian because he or she is a strong partisan. As Martin Hengel points out, scholars have erred in thinking they had to choose between preaching and historical narration. "In reality the 'theological' contribution of the evangelist lies in the fact that he combines both these things inseparably: he preaches by narrating; he writes history and in so doing proclaims."[95] A truly open-minded approach is to listen sympathetically to the case the evangelists are arguing, trying to enter into their own world to see if it makes sense. We might find that it makes more sense than the worlds we have constructed for ourselves.[96]

The Possibility of a Historical Outline

We have made no attempt here to prove a position with respect to the historicity of the Gospels. But if we may grant that others have provided, not a proven position (there is no such thing as proof in such matters) but nonetheless solid grounds for accepting the Gospels as historically reliable,[97] what kind of information about Jesus can we expect to find in them? Is it possible to reconstruct a historically coherent "life of Jesus"? Some deny the validity of any such attempt. Brevard Childs, for instance, insists that the "canonical shape" of the fourfold gospel should be respected. He faults traditional harmonies for seeking the meaning of the Gospels in a historical construct that disregards this canonical shape.[98] While Childs is right to insist that meaning is to be found in the texts as we have them, rather than in some necessarily hypothetical pasting together of all four accounts, he is wrong to deny all significance to harmonies. For the truth of what the evangelists are saying is inevitably tied to the historical reality of what they narrate. The attempt to put together that historical reality—the life and ministry of Jesus of Nazareth—is both necessary and significant.

But is it really possible? A major barrier to the enterprise has always been the many places in which the Gospels appear to contradict themselves over historical details. The most troublesome texts have been the subject of many harmonizing interpretations, ranging from the ridiculous to the convincing. Our whole approach to this matter will depend greatly on what we think of the evangelists' accuracy generally. The more we are impressed by their accuracy—as the authors of this volume are—the further we will search for satisfactory explanations. Nevertheless, there are some places where fully satisfactory answers simply are not

[95]Martin Hengel, "Literary, Theological, and Historical Problems in the Gospel of Mark," in *Studies in the Gospel of Mark* (Philadelphia: Fortress, 1985), p. 41.

[96]Note, e.g., the approach advocated by Royce Gordon Gruenler, *New Approaches to Jesus and the Gospels: A Phenomenological and Exegetical Study of Synoptic Christology* (Grand Rapids: Baker, 1982).

[97]See, e.g., Marshall, *I Believe in the Historical Jesus*; Blomberg, *Historical Reliability of the Gospels*.

[98]Childs, pp. 154–56.

available. In such cases, it is better, as Luther put it, to just to let it alone than to force unlikely meanings on the text.[99]

These difficulties must not obscure the fact that the Synoptic Gospels exhibit a high degree of coherence about the general course of Jesus' ministry as well as about many of the incidents within that ministry. Some of the greatest divergences do not suggest contradictions, so much as accounts that have little in common with one another (such as the infancy narratives in Matthew and Luke). Coherence at the historical level in such situations is relatively easy to attain. Nevertheless, a fully satisfactory historical harmony of Jesus' life is impossible. It was simply not the evangelists' intention to provide us with the kind of data we would need for such an enterprise. They give few exact chronological indicators, and those we do have (general phrases such as "after these things," "when," and Mark's "immediately") are often too general to be of real use to the historian. The evangelists narrate historical facts, but they so select, arrange, and present these facts that little information of the kind needed to piece together a detailed life of Jesus is available.

The generally similar chronological sequence in the Synoptic Gospels is not always matched by agreement on individual episodes. In such cases, it is not a matter of chronological error, but of chronological indifference. The evangelists, and sometimes the sources the evangelists use, arrange their material topically at times, often making it impossible for us to know when in the ministry of Jesus a particular incident occurred. An example is the series of controversy stories that Mark narrates in 2:1–3:6. That Mark or his source has grouped these stories together because of their similarity in subject matter (Jesus in controversy with Jews) seems likely, particularly when we note that none of the episodes is given a specific chronological relation to any other. When, then, did Jesus heal the man's hand in the synagogue on the Sabbath (Mark 3:1–6)? Early in the ministry, as we might conclude if Mark's placement was chronological? Or later on, as the placement of the incident in Matthew might suggest (see 12:9–14)? We might venture some guesses, but we cannot know for sure: the evangelists simply have not given us enough information. The fact, then, that a detailed life of Jesus cannot be reconstructed on the basis of the Synoptic Gospels in no way discredits the Gospels as accurate historical sources. They should be judged for what they do tell us, not for what they do not tell us.

Gospel Chronology

The task of setting the events of the Gospels against the background of secular history is made easy by the references to well-known historical personages such as Herod the Great (Matt. 2), Caesar Augustus (Luke 2:1), Herod Antipas (Luke 23:6–12), and Pontius Pilate (Matt. 27). With such indicators, we can situate the Gospels generally within the history of first-century Palestine and the wider Roman Empire. But can we be any more exact? Several key incidents may yield more exact chronological data.

---

[99]On harmonizing, see esp. Craig L. Blomberg, "The Legitimacy and Limits of Harmonization," in *Hermeneutics, Authority, and Canon*, ed. D. A. Carson and John D. Woodbridge (Grand Rapids: Zondervan, 1986), pp. 135–74, 388–97.

Jesus' Birth Three data have been used to date Jesus' birth: the involvement of Herod the Great (Matt. 2); the decree of Caesar Augustus, issued when "Quirinius was governor of Syria" (Luke 2:1–2); and the appearance of the "star of Bethlehem" (Matt. 2:1–12). Herod the Great is undoubtedly the "king" of Matthew 2. It is almost certain that Herod died in late March or early April of 4 B.C.[100] Jesus must therefore have been born before 4 B.C.—but probably not much before 4 B.C., since Herod slays children only two years old and younger (2:16). Augustus ruled the Roman Empire from 31 B.C. to A.D. 14. Unfortunately, the census to which Luke refers cannot be identified from secular sources. Josephus refers to a local census that took place in A.D. 6, and some think that Luke has confused the census that brought Joseph and Mary to Bethlehem with this one. Adding fuel to the fire is the fact that we know of a Quirinius as a Syrian officeholder only in A.D. 6–8. But it is unlikely that Luke, proven so accurate in historical and geographic details in Acts, would have made so serious a blunder. We may surmise that Quirinius had held an earlier post in Syria,[101]or that Luke 2:2 should not be translated "this was the first census that took place while Quirinius was governer of Syria" (NIV), but "this census was before the census taken when Quirinius was governer of Syria."[102] In any case, the census does not help us date the birth of Jesus. Nor does the appearance of the star give us much help. Several identifications of the star with known astronomical phenomena have been proposed—a comet reported in 5 B.C. or a conjunction of Jupiter, Saturn, and Mars in 7–6 B.C.—but none is certain. Moreover, in light of Matthew's statement that the star "went ahead of [the magi] until it stopped over the place where the child was" (2:9), it is perhaps unlikely that the star can be identified with any natural astronomical phenomenon.

All things considered, then, we can only estimate that Jesus must have been born sometime during 6–4 B.C.

The Beginning of Jesus' Ministry According to Luke 3:1, Jesus began his public ministry "in the fifteenth year of the reign of Tiberius Caesar." Here, we might think, is an indication that should yield an exact date. But the matter is not so simple. Tiberius became emperor after the death of Augustus in August of A.D. 14. If this is when Luke begins his fifteen years, then the date of the beginning of Jesus' ministry would be either 28 or 29.[103] But Tiberius began a coregency with Augustus in A.D. 11/12. Counting from this date would place the beginning of Jesus' ministry in 25/26 or 26/27.[104] However, while we cannot be certain, the former way of reckoning the beginning of Tiberias's reign is the most natural, and it is therefore likely that Luke dates the beginning of Jesus' ministry in either 28 or

---

[100]See esp. Harold Hoehner, *Chronological Aspects of the Life of Christ* (Grand Rapids: Zondervan, 1977), pp. 12–13.

[101]E.g., William Ramsay, *The Bearing of Recent Discovery on the Trustworthiness of the New Testament*, reprint ed. (Grand Rapids: Baker, 1953), pp. 238–300.

[102]E.g., Nigel Turner, *Grammatical Insights into the New Testament* (Edinburgh: T. & T. Clark, 1965), pp. 23–24.

[103]Within this general span, there are several possibilities for the exact month and date, depending on which calendar may have been used. See, e.g., George Ogg, *The Chronology of the Public Ministry of Jesus* (Cambridge: Cambridge University Press, 1940), pp. 174–83.

[104]E.g., F. Godet, *A Commentary on the Gospel of St. Luke*, 2 vols. (Edinburgh: T. & T. Clark, n.d.), 1:166–67.

29. With any of these dates, justice is done to Luke's approximation that Jesus was "about thirty years old" at the beginning of his ministry (3:23).

The Length of Jesus' Ministry The synoptic evangelists provide little information that can be used to determine the length of the ministry. It has been proposed that the events in the synoptics could be packed into less than a year, but this compresses events too much. Moreover, Mark indicates that at the time of the feeding of the five thousand, the grass was green (6:39), which points to the Palestinian springtime. Yet since Jesus was crucified in the spring, Mark's gospel suggests a ministry of at least a year's duration.

John supplies us with more information. He mentions the Passover three times in his narration of Jesus' ministry: at the time of the cleansing of the temple (2:13), at the time of the feeding of the five thousand (6:4), and at the time of Jesus' crucifixion (11:55). He also mentions a "feast" in 5:1 that may have been, although probably was not, a Passover. If the three Passovers that John mentions were distinct in time,[105] then John's gospel requires a ministry of at least two years.[106]

The Death of Jesus On the basis of the previous two considerations, Jesus' death must have occurred in A.D. 30 or later. Two lines of evidence have been used to determine the precise year: astronomical/calendrical and historical. We know that Jesus was crucified on Friday ("the Preparation Day" [Mark 15:42 par.]) in the Jewish month of Nisan. The beginning of that month was fixed at the time when the new moon was sighted. Thus, if we knew the date of the crucifixion, we could use astronomical calculations to determine the years during which that date would have fallen on a Friday. Unfortunately, the date of Jesus' death continues to be a matter of considerable debate, Nisan 14 and 15 being the main possibilities. The uncertainty arises from apparently conflicting data from the Synoptic Gospels and from John. The synoptics appear to make the last supper a Passover meal (see, e.g., Mark 14:12), making Friday Nisan 15. But on one reading of the fourth gospel, John implies that the Passover meal had not yet been eaten at the time of Jesus' trial (18:28), which suggests that the day of Jesus' death was Nisan 14. Numerous harmonization attempts have been offered, the two most likely being that the synoptic evangelists and John were utilizing different calendars in use in first-century Palestine,[107] or that John in 18:28 does not really intend to suggest that the official Passover meal was still to be eaten.[108] In any case, we must remain

---

[105]Most evangelical scholars argue that John's cleansing of the temple is a different cleansing than the one narrated in the Synoptic Gospels. If, however, they are one and the same event, then John would refer to only two separate Passovers.

[106]Hoehner's claim that John's gospel, as it now stands, requires a ministry of at least three years, appears to depend on taking Jesus' reference in 4:35 as an indication that it was January or February (*Chronological Aspects*, pp. 56–63). But this is unlikely (see Leon Morris, *The Gospel According to John*, NICNT [Grand Rapids: Eerdmans, 1971], pp. 278–80); nor does Hoehner seriously consider the possibility that John's cleansing is the same as the one narrated in the synoptics. See particularly the discussion in C. H. Turner, "Chronology of the New Testament," in *A Dictionary of the Bible*, ed. James Hastings, 5 vols. (Edinburgh: T. & T. Clark, 1898–1904), 1:407–9; and G. B. Caird, "Chronology of the New Testament," in *IDB* 1:602.

[107]Morris, *John*, pp. 774–86.

[108]D.A. Carson, "Matthew," in *EBC* 8:528–32.

uncertain about the day of the month on which Jesus died. Nisan 14 may have occurred on a Friday in A.D. 30, and almost certainly did in 33; Nisan 15 may have occurred on a Friday in A.D. 30, and possibly also in 31.[109] However, since the calculation of the beginning of Nisan depended on human observation, with many possibilities for uncertainty, we must not depend too strongly on the results. Nevertheless, the two most likely candidates are Nisan 14 (= April 3), A.D. 33, and Nisan 15 (= April 7), A.D. 30.

The historical argument estimates the time at which it was most likely that Pilate, the Roman governor in Palestine, would have caved in to the pressure exerted on him by the Jewish leaders at the time of Jesus' trial. Hoehner, for instance, has argued that Pilate's desire to accommodate the Jewish leaders is credible only after A.D. 31, in October of which year the anti-Semitic Sejanus, ruler of the empire in fact under Tiberias, was executed.[110] Combined with the astronomical argument, this narrows the possibilities down to one year: A.D. 33.

But it may be doubted whether this set of circumstances is needed to explain Pilate's behavior, for the Roman administration, whoever was in charge, was concerned to maintain stability in the provinces, and Pilate had already given some indication of failure at this point. Quite apart from this argument, however, a growing number of scholars think that the astronomical data are more favorable to the A.D. 33 date. In contrast, the year 33 is virtually ruled out if Jesus was crucified on Nisan 15, as the synoptic evangelists appear to suggest. Moreover, a crucifixion as late as A.D. 33 might fail to leave enough time between the death of Jesus and Paul's conversion (see chap. 7).

The various data do not, then, allow us at this time to resolve the problem. Both April 7, A.D. 30, and April 3, A.D. 33, must be considered possible dates for the crucifixion.

BIBLIOGRAPHY

Charles C. **Anderson,** *Critical Quests of Jesus* (Grand Rapids: Eerdmans, 1969); David E. **Aune,** *The New Testament in Its Literary Environment,* Library of Early Christianity 8 (Philadelphia: Westminster, 1987); idem, *Prophecy in Early Christianity and the Ancient Mediterranean World* (Grand Rapids: Eerdmans, 1983); Arthur J. **Bellinzoni, Jr.,** ed., *The Two-Source Hypothesis: A Critical Appraisal* (Macon, Ga: Mercer University Press, 1985); C. Clifton **Black,** *The Disciples in Mark: Markan Redaction in Current Debate,* JSNTSupp 27 (Sheffield: JSOT, 1989); Craig **Blomberg,** *The Historical Reliability of the Gospels* (Downers Grove, Ill.: IVP, 1987); idem, "The Legitimacy and Limits of Harmonization," in *Hermeneutics, Authority, and Canon,* ed. D. A. Carson and John D. Woodbridge (Grand Rapids: Zondervan, 1986), pp. 135–74, 388–97; Günther **Bornkamm,** *Jesus of Nazareth* (London: Hodder & Stoughton, 1960); G. **Bornkamm, G. Barth,** and H. J. **Held,** *Tradition and Interpretation in Matthew* (Philadelphia: Westminster, 1974); Colin **Brown,** *Jesus in European Protestant Thought, 1778–1860* (Grand Rapids: Baker, 1988); Rudolf **Bultmann,** *The History of the Synoptic Tradition* (New York:

---

[109]The most recent calculations are found in Colin J. Humphreys and W. Graeme Waddington, "The Date of the Crucifixion," *JASA* 37 (1985): 2–10; See also J. K. Fotheringham, "The Evidence of Astronomy and Technical Chronology for the Date of the Crucifixion," *JTS* 35 (1934): 146–62; Joachim Jeremias, *The Eucharistic Words of Jesus* (London: SCM, 1966), pp. 36–41.

[110]Hoehner, *Chronological Aspects,* pp. 105–11.

Harper & Row, 1963); idem, *Theology of the New Testament*, 2 vols. (New York: Charles Scribner's Sons, 1951–55); B. C. **Butler,** *The Originality of St. Matthew: A Critique of the Two-Document Hypothesis* (Cambridge: Cambridge University Press, 1951); G. B. **Caird,** "Chronology of the New Testament," in *IDB* 1:599– 607; D. A. **Carson,** "Matthew," in *EBC* 8; idem, "Redaction Criticism: On the Legitimacy and Illegitimacy of a Literary Tool," in *Scripture and Truth*, ed. D. A. Carson and John D. Woodbridge (Grand Rapids: Zondervan, 1983), pp. 119– 42, 376–81; D. J. **Chapman,** *Matthew, Mark, and Luke: A Study in the Order and Interrelation of the Synoptic Gospels*, ed. John M. T. Barton (London: Longmans, Green, 1937); Hans **Conzelmann,** *The Theology of St. Luke* (New York: Harper & Row, 1960); Patricia **Cox,** *Biography in Late Antiquity* (Berkeley: University of California Press, 1983); Peter **Davids,** "The Gospels and Jewish Tradition: Twenty Years After Gerhardsson," in *GP* 1:75–79; Martin **Dibelius,** *From Tradition to Gospel* (New York: Charles Scribner's Sons, n.d.); Albrecht **Dihle,** "Die Evangelien und die griechische Biographie," in *Das Evangelium und die Evangelien*, ed. Peter Stuhlmacher, WUNT 2.28 (Tübingen: Mohr, 1983), pp. 383–411; C. H. **Dodd,** "The Framework of the Gospel Narrative," *ExpTim 43 (1932): 396–400;* Detlev **Dormeyer** and Hubert **Frankemölle,** "Evangelium als literarische Gattung und als theologisches Begriff: Tendenzen und Aufgaben der Evangelienforschung im 20. Jahrhundert, mit einer Untersuchung des Markuse- vangeliums in seinem Verhältnis zur antiken Biographie," in *ANRW* 25.2, pp. 1545–81; F. Gerald **Downing,** "Redaction Criticism: Josephus' *Antiquities* and the Synoptic Gospels," *JSNT* 8 (1980): 29–48; 9 (1980): 46–65; David L. **Dungan,** "The Purpose and Provenance of the Gospel of Mark According to the Two-Gospel (Owen-Griesbach) Hypothesis," in *New Synoptic Studies: The Cambridge Gospel Conference and Beyond*, ed. William Farmer (Macon, Ga: Mercer University Press, 1983), pp. 411–40; J. D. G. **Dunn,** "Prophetic 'I'-Sayings and the Jesus Tradition: The Importance of Testing Prophetic Utterances Within Early Christianity," *NTS* 24 (1978): 175–98; Richard A. **Edwards,** *A Theology of Q* (Philadephia: Fortress, 1976); J. G. **Eichhorn,** *Einleitung in das Neue Testament* (1804); E. E. **Ellis,** "Gospels Criticism: A Perspective on the State of the Art," in *Das Evangelium und die Evangelien*, pp. 27–54; William **Farmer,** *Jesus and the Gospel* (Philadelphia: Fortress, 1982); idem, *The Synoptic Problem: A Critical Analysis* (New York: Macmillan, 1964); Austen **Farrar,** "On Dispensing with Q," in *Studies in the Gospels: Essays in Memory of R. H. Lightfoot*, ed. D. E. Nineham (Oxford: Blackwell, 1955); Joseph A. **Fitzmyer,** *The Gospel According to Luke I-IX*, AB (Garden City, N.Y.: Doubleday, 1981); idem, "The Priority of Mark and the 'Q' Source in Luke," in *Jesus and Man's Hope* (Pittsburgh: Pittsburgh Theological Seminary, 1970), 1:131–70 (reprinted in Bellinzoni, *The Two-Source Hypothesis*); J. K. **Fotheringham,** "The Evidence of Astronomy and Technical Chronology for the Date of the Crucifixion," *JTS* 35 (1934): 146–62; R. T. **France,** "The Authenticity of the Sayings of Jesus," in *History, Criticism, and Faith*, ed. Colin Brown (Downers Grove, Ill.: IVP, 1976), pp. 101–41; idem, "Exegesis in Practice: Two Samples," in *New Testament Interpretation: Essays on Principles and Methods*, ed. I. Howard Marshall (Grand Rapids: Eerdmans, 1977), pp. 253–64; idem, *Matthew: Evangelist and Theologian* (Grand Rapids: Zonder- van, 1989); G. **Friedrich,** "εὐαγγέλιον," in *TDNT* 2:721–35; Robert W. **Funk,** *The Poetics of Biblical Narrative* (Somona, Calif.: Polebridge, 1989); Birger **Gerhardsson,** *Memory and Manuscript: Oral Tradition and Written Transmission in Rabbinic Judaism and Early Christianity*, ASNU 22 (Lund: Gleerup, 1964); J. K. L. **Gieseler,** *Historisch-kritischer Versuch über die Entstehung und die frühesten Schicksale der schriftlichen Evangelien* (1818); F. **Godet,** *A Commentary on the*

Gospel of St. Luke, 2 vols. (Edinburgh: T. & T. Clark, n.d.); J. J. **Griesbach,** *Commentatio qua Marci evangelium totum e Matthaei et Lucae commentariis decerptum esse monstratur* (Treatise in which is demonstrated that the gospel of Mark has been wholly derived from the commentaries of Matthew and Luke) (1789); Royce Gordon **Gruenler,** *New Approaches to Jesus and the Gospels: A Phenomenological and Exegetical Study of Synoptic Christology* (Grand Rapids: Baker, 1982); Robert **Guelich,** "The Gospel Genre," in *Das Evangelium und die Evangelien*, pp. 183–219; Robert H. **Gundry,** "Recent Investigations into the Literary Genre 'Gospel,' " in *New Dimensions in New Testament Study*, ed. Richard N. Longenecker and Merrill C. Tenney (Grand Rapids: Zondervan, 1974), pp. 101–13; Erhardt **Güttgemanns,** *Candid Questions Concerning Gospel Form Criticism: A Methodological Sketch of the Fundamental Problematics of Form and Redaction Criticism* (ET Pittsburgh: Pickwick, 1979); John C. **Hawkins,** *Horae Synopticae* (Oxford: Clarendon, 1909); Martin **Hengel,** "Literary, Theological, and Historical Problems in the Gospel of Mark," in *Studies in the Gospel of Mark* (Philadelphia: Fortress, 1985), pp. 221–65; idem, "The Titles of the Gospels and the Gospel of Mark," in ibid., pp. 64–84; J. G. **Herder,** *Von der Regel der Zusammenstimmung unserer Evangelien* (1797); David **Hill,** *New Testament Prophecy* (Richmond: John Knox, 1979); E. D. **Hirsch, Jr.,** *Validity in Interpretation* (New Haven, Conn.: Yale University Press, 1967); Harold **Hoehner,** *Chronological Aspects of the Life of Christ* (Grand Rapids: Zondervan, 1977); H. J. **Holtzmann,** *Die synoptische Evangelien: Ihr Ursprung und ihr geschichtlicher Charakter* (Leipzig: W. Engelmann, 1863); M. D. **Hooker,** "On Using the Wrong Tool," *Theol* 75 (1972): 570–81; Colin J. **Humphreys** and W. Graeme **Waddington,** "The Date of the Crucifixion," *JASA* 37 (1985): 2–10; Joachim **Jeremias,** *The Eucharistic Words of Jesus* (London: SCM, 1966); Martin **Kähler,** *The So-Called Historical Jesus and the Historic, Biblical Christ* (Philadelphia: Fortress, 1964); Ernst **Käsemann,** "The Problem of the Historical Jesus," in *Essays on New Testament Themes* (Philadelphia: Fortress, 1964), pp. 15–47; Werner H. **Kelber,** *The Oral and the Written Gospel* (Philadelphia: Fortress, 1983); Jack Dean **Kingsbury,** *Matthew as Story* (Philadelphia: Fortress, 1986); W. L. **Knox,** *The Sources of the Synoptic Gospels*, 2 vols. (Cambridge: Cambridge University Press, 1957); Werner Georg **Kümmel,** *The New Testament: The History of the Investigation of Its Problems* (New York: Abingdon, 1970); Karl **Lachmann,** "De Ordine narrationum im evangeliis synopticis," *TSK* 8 (1835): 570–90; G. E. **Lessing,** *Neue Hypothese über die Evangelisten als bloss menschliche Geschichtschreiber betrachtet* (1784); R. H. **Lightfoot,** *History and Interpretation in the Gospels* (London: Hodder & Stoughton, 1935); R. L. **Lindsey,** "A Modified Two-Document Theory of the Synoptic Dependence and Interdependence," *NovT* 6 (1963): 239–63; Tremper **Longman III,** *Literary Approaches to Biblical Interpretation* (Grand Rapids: Zondervan, 1987); Harvey K. **McArthur, ed.,** *In Search of the Historical Jesus* (New York: Charles Scribner's Sons, 1969); Edgar V. **McKnight,** *Meaning in Texts* (Philadelphia: Fortress, 1974); idem, *Post-Modern Use of the Bible: The Emergence of Reader-Oriented Criticism* (Nashville: Abingdon, 1988); Scot **McKnight,** *Interpreting the Synoptic Gospels* (Grand Rapids: Baker, 1988); I. Howard **Marshall,** *I Believe in the Historical Jesus* (Grand Rapids: Eerdmans, 1977); idem, *Luke: Historian and Theologian*, new, enlarged ed. (Grand Rapids: Zondervan, 1989); Ralph **Martin,** *Mark: Evangelist and Theologian* (Grand Rapids: Zondervan, 1972); idem, "The New Quest of the Historical Jesus," in *Jesus of Nazareth: Savior and Lord*, ed. Carl F. H. Henry (Grand Rapids: Eerdmans, 1966), pp. 31–45; Willi **Marxsen,** *Mark the Evangelist: Studies on the Redaction History of the Gospel* (Nashville: Abingdon,

1969); Ben F. **Meyer**, *The Aims of Jesus* (Philadelphia: Fortress, 1979); Leon **Morris**, *The Gospel According to John*, NICNT (Grand Rapids: Eerdmans, 1971); idem, *Studies in the Fourth Gospel* (Grand Rapids: Eerdmans, 1969); Stephen **Neill** and Tom **Wright**, *The Interpretation of the New Testament*, 1861–1986 (Oxford: Oxford University Press, 1988); Franz **Neirynck**, *The Minor Agreements of Matthew and Luke Against Mark, with a Cumulative List*, BETL 37 (Louvain: Louvain University Press, 1974); George **Ogg**, *The Chronology of the Public Ministry of Jesus* (Cambridge: Cambridge University Press, 1940); Grant R. **Osborne**, "The Evangelical and Redaction Criticism: Critique and Methodology," *JETS* 22 (1979): 305–22; H. P. **Owen**, *Observations of the Four Gospels* (1764); Daniel **Patte**, *Structural Exegesis for New Testament Critics* (Philadelphia: Fortress, 1990); idem, *What Is Structural Exegesis?* (Philadelphia: Fortress, 1976); Norman **Perrin**, *Rediscovering the Teaching of Jesus* (London: SCM, 1967); idem, *What Is Redaction Criticism?* (Philadelphia: Fortress, 1969); Norman R. **Peterson**, *Literary Criticism for New Testament Critics* (Philadelphia: Fortress, 1978); A. **Polag**, *Fragmenta Q: Texthelf zur Logienquelle*, 2d ed. (Neukirchen-Vluyn: Neukirchener, 1982); E. J. **Pryke**, *Redactional Style in the Marcan Gospel: A Study of Syntax and Vocabulary as Guides to Redaction in Mark*, SNTSMS 33 (Cambridge: Cambridge University Press, 1978); William **Ramsay**, *The Bearing of Recent Discovery on the Trustworthiness of the New Testament* (reprint, Grand Rapids: Baker, 1953); Friedrich **Rehkopf**, *Der lukanische Sonderquelle*, WUNT 5 (Tübingen: Mohr, 1959); Bo **Reicke**, *The Roots of the Synoptic Gospels* (Philadelphia: Fortress, 1986); Rainer **Riesner**, *Jesus als Lehrer*, WUNT 2.7 (Tübingen: Mohr, 1981); idem, "Jüdische Elementarbildung und Evangelienüberlieferung," in *GP* 1:209–23; John M. **Rist**, *On the Independence of Matthew and Mark*, SNTSMS 32 (Cambridge: Cambridge University Press, 1978); J. A. T. **Robinson**, *Redating the New Testament* (Philadelphia: Westminster, 1976); James M. **Robinson**, *A New Quest of the Historical Jesus*, SBT 25 (London: SCM, 1959); Joachim **Rohde**, *Rediscovering the Teaching of the Evangelists* (London: SCM, 1968); F. **Schleiermacher**, "Über die Zeugnisse des Papias von unseren ersten beiden Evangelien," *TSK* 5 (1832): 335–68; Karl Ludwig **Schmidt**, *Der Rahmen der Geschichte Jesu: Literarkritische Untersuchungen zur ältesten Jesusüberlieferung* (Berlin: Trowitzsch & Son, 1919); idem, "Die Stellung der Evangelien in der allgemeinen Literaturgeschichte," in ΕΥΧΑΡΙΣΤΗΡΙΟΝ: *Studien zur Religion und Literatur des Alten und Neuen Testaments*, Fs. Hermann Gunkel, ed. K. L. Schmidt, FRLANT 19.2 (Göttingen: Vandenhoeck & Ruprecht, 1923); John J. **Schmitt**, "In Search of the Origin of the Siglum Q," *JBL* 100 (1981): 609–11; Albert **Schweitzer**, *The Quest for the Historical Jesus* (New York: Macmillan, 1961); Philip L. **Shuler**, *A Genre for the Gospels: The Biographical Character of Matthew* (Philadephia: Fortress, 1982); Moisés **Silva**, "Ned B. Stonehouse and Redaction Criticism. Part I: The Witness of the Synoptic Evangelists to Christ; Part II: The Historicity of the Synoptic Tradition," *WTJ* 40 (1977–78): 77–88, 281–303; Graham N. **Stanton**, *The Gospels and Jesus* (Oxford: Oxford University Press, 1989); idem, *Jesus of Nazareth in New Testament Preaching*, SNTSMS 27 (Cambridge: Cambridge University Press, 1974); Robert **Stein**, "The 'Criteria' of Authenticity," in *GP* 1:225–63; idem, *The Synoptic Problem: An Introduction* (Grand Rapids: Baker, 1987); idem, "What Is Redaktionsgeschichte?" in *JBL* 88 (1969): 45–56; Hans-Herbert **Stoldt**, *History and Criticism of the Marcan Hypothesis* (Macon, Ga: Mercer University Press, 1980); Ned B. **Stonehouse**, *The Witness of the Synoptic Gospels to Christ* (Grand Rapids: Baker, 1979); B. H. **Streeter**, *The Four Gospels: A Study of Origins* (London: Macmillan, 1924); G. M. **Styler**, "The Priority of Mark," in *The Birth of the New Testament*, ed. C. F. D.

Moule, 3d ed. (San Francisco: Harper & Row, 1982), pp. 285–316; Charles H. **Talbert,** *What Is a Gospel? The Genre of the Canonical Gospels* (Philadelphia: Fortress, 1977); Vincent **Taylor,** *The Formation of the Gospel Tradition,* 2d ed. (London: Macmillan, 1935); idem, *The Gospel According to St. Mark,* 2d ed. (London: Macmillan, 1966); idem, *The Passion Narrative of St. Luke: A Critical and Historical Investigation,* ed. Owen E. Evans, SNTSMS 19 (Cambridge: Cambridge University Press, 1972); C. C. **Torrey,** *The Four Gospels* (New York: Harper, 1933); C. H. **Turner,** "Chronology of the New Testament," in *A Dictionary of the Bible,* ed. James Hastings, 5 vols. (Edinburgh: T. & T. Clark, 1898–1904), 1:403–25; Nigel **Turner,** *Grammatical Insights into the New Testament* (Edinburgh: T. & T. Clark, 1965); Joseph B. **Tyson** and Thomas R. W. **Longstaff,** *Synoptic Abstract,* The Computer Bible 15 (Wooster, Ohio: College of Wooster, 1978); L. **Vaganay,** *Le problème synoptique: Une hypothèse de travail* (Paris: Desclée, 1954); Kevin **Vanhoozer,** "A Lamp in the Labyrinth: The Hermeneutics of 'Aesthetic' Theology," *TrinJ* 8 (1987): 25–56; C. W. **Votaw,** "The Gospels and Contemporary Biographies," *AJT* 19 (1915): 45–71; Johannes **Weiss,** *Jesus' Proclamation of the Kingdom of God* (Philadelphia: Fortress, 1971); C. H. **Weisse,** *Die evangelische Geschichte kritisch und philosophisch bearbeitet* (1838); David **Wenham,** "The Synoptic Problem Revisited: Some New Suggestions About the Composition of Mark 4:1–34," *TynB* 23 (1972): 3–38; B. F. **Westcott,** *Introduction to the Study of the Gospels,* 8th ed. (London: Macmillan, 1895); C. G. **Wilke,** *Der Urevangelist oder exegetisch-kritische Untersuchungen über das Verwandtschaftsverhältniss der drei ersten Evangelien* (1838); William **Wrede,** *Das Messiasgeheimnis in den Evangelien* (Göttingen: Vandenhoeck & Ruprecht, 1901).

2

matthew

CONTENTS

That Matthew was a skilled literary craftsman no one denies. Disagreements over the structure of this gospel arise because there are so many overlapping and competing structural pointers that it appears impossible to establish a consensus on their relative importance.

If we consider the structure of the book as a whole, then, apart from several idiosyncratic proposals,[1] there are three dominant theories.

1. Some have detected a geographic framework that is related to Mark's gospel (see chap. 1 on the synoptic problem).[2] Matthew 1:1–2:23 is the prologue, and it is tied to 3:1–4:11 (Jesus' preparation for ministry) to constitute an introduction parallel to Mark 1:1–13. Matthew 4:12–13:58 finds Jesus ministering in Galilee (cf. Mark 1:14–6:13). This ministry is extended to other locales in the North (Matt. 14:1–16:12; Mark 6:14–8:26), before Jesus begins to move toward Jerusalem (Matt. 16:13–20:34; Mark 8:27–10:52). The confrontation in Jerusalem (Matt. 21:1–25:46; Mark 11:1–13:37) issues in his passion and resurrection (Matt. 26:1–28:20; Mark 14:1–16:8).

This sort of analysis rightly reflects the broad chronological development of Jesus' ministry and preserves some geographic distinctions. But it is based entirely on a selection of thematic considerations and does not reflect on the *literary* markers that Matthew has left us. Precisely because, with minor alterations, this sort of analysis could be applied to any of the Synoptic Gospels, it tells us very little of the purposes that are uniquely Matthew's.

2. Following suggestions made by Stonehouse, Lohmeyer, and Krentz,[3]

---

[1]E.g., C. H. Lohr proposes a giant chiasm ("Oral Techniques in the Gospel of Matthew," *CBQ* 23 [1961]: 403–35), but there are too many tenuous pairings to convince many scholars that Matthew had this in mind. M. D. Goulder attempts to tie the structure of this gospel to a lectionary cycle (*Midrash and Lection in Matthew* [London: SPCK, 1974]). So little is known about first-century lectionary cycles, however, that the proposal is long on speculation (cf. L. Morris, "The Gospels and the Jewish Lectionaries," in *GP* 1:129–56), quite apart from the extraordinary diversity of lection lengths that Goulder proposes.

[2]E.g., A. H. McNeile, *The Gospel According to St. Matthew* (London: Macmillan, 1915).

[3]Ned B. Stonehouse, *The Witness of Matthew and Mark to Christ* (Grand Rapids: Eerdmans, 1944), pp. 129–31; Ernst Lohmeyer, *Das Evangelium des Matthäus*, ed. W. Schmauck (Göttingen: Vandenhoeck & Ruprecht, 1956); E. Krentz, "The Extent of Matthew's Prologue," *JBL* 83 (1964): 409–14.

Kingsbury has argued for three large sections, tightly tied to Christological development.[4] The first he titles "The Person of Jesus Messiah" (1:1–4:16); the second, "The Proclamation of Jesus Messiah" (4:17–16:20); and the third, "The Suffering, Death, and Resurrection of Jesus Messiah" (16:21–28:20). Immediately after the two breaks come the decisive words ἀπὸ τότε (apo tote, "from that time on"), signalling progress in the plot. The last two of the three sections each contains three summary passages (4:23–25; 9:35; 11:1; and 16:21; 17:22–23; 20:17–19).

Though this outline has gained adherents (e.g., Kümmel), it suffers from several weaknesses. It is not at all clear that ἀπὸ τότε (apo tote) is so redactionally important for Matthew that his entire structure turns on it: after all, Matthew uses it at 26:16 without any break in the flow of the narrative. One could argue that there are four passion summaries in the third section, not three (add 26:2). At both structural transitions, Matthew may have been more influenced by his following of Mark than by other considerations. In any case, the outline breaks up the important Peter passage in Matthew 16 in an unacceptable way. Even the Christological development is not as clear as Kingsbury alleges: the person of Jesus (section 1) is still a focal point in sections 2 and 3 (e.g., 16:13–16; 22:41–46); the proclamation of Jesus can scarcely be restricted to section 2, for two of the discourses (chaps. 18 and 24–25) and several important exchanges (chaps. 21–23) are reserved for the third section.

3. The most frequently proposed structures turn on the observation that Matthew presents five discourses, each of which begins in a specific context and ends with a formula found nowhere else (lit. "And it happened, when Jesus had finished saying these things, that . . ." [Matt. 7:28–29; 11:1; 13:53; 19:1; 26:1]. It becomes attractive to link narrative with discourse in five pairs. Bacon proposed just such a scheme, calling the five sections "books."[5] Book 1 deals with discipleship (narrative, chaps. 3–4; discourse, chaps. 5–7); book 2 with apostleship (narrative, 8–9; discourse, 10); book 3 with the hiding of the revelation (narrative, 11–12; discourse, 13); book 4 with church administration (narrative, 14–17; discourse, 18); and book 5 with the judgment (narrative, 19–22; discourse, 23–25). This leaves Matthew 1–2 as a preamble and 26–28 as an epilogue. Bacon himself thought that this was Matthew's self-conscious response to and fulfillment of the five books of Moses.

Few today think that Matthew intended any link between these five sections and the five books of Moses: proposed connections are just too tenuous. The ties between each narrative and discourse pair are not always very strong, and any outline that relegates the entire passion and resurrection narrative to the status of an epilogue must be seriously questioned.

But something of the scheme can be salvaged. That Matthew reports extensive teaching of Jesus outside the five discourses is no criticism of the outline: the fivefold sequence of narrative and discourse does not assume that Jesus is not portrayed as speaking in the narrative sections. He may do so, even extensively (e.g., chaps. 11, 21). The point, rather, is that the five discourses are so clearly

---

[4]J. D. Kingsbury, *Matthew: Structure, Christology, Kingdom* (Philadelphia: Fortress, 1975).

[5]B. W. Bacon, "The 'Five Books' of Moses Against the Jews," *Exp* 15 (1918): 56–66. The idea is then worked out in detail in Bacon's *Studies in Matthew* (London: Constable, 1930).

marked, from a literary point of view, that it is well-nigh impossible to believe that Matthew did not plan them. Chapters 1–2 do constitute a preamble or prologue: all four canonical gospels preserve some kind of independent opening, before turning to the first step taken in common, namely, the ministry of John the Baptist (in Matthew, beginning at 3:1). Certainly Matthew 26–28 must not be taken as a mere epilogue. But it is just possible that Matthew thinks of these chapters as the climactic, sixth narrative section, with the corresponding "teaching" section laid on the shoulders of the disciples (28:18–20) and therefore open-ended.

Superimposing on these literary markers the transparent development of the plot, we arrive at a seven-part outline.

The prologue (1:1–2:23). This is divisible into six sections, treating the genealogy of Jesus (1:1–17), his birth (1:18–25), the visit of the Magi (2:1–12), the escape to Egypt (2:13–15), the massacre at Bethlehem (2:16–18), and the return to Nazareth (2:19–23). A quotation from the Old Testament, introduced by an appropriate fulfillment formula, dominates the last five of these sections.

The gospel of the kingdom (3:1–7:29). The narrative (3:1–4:25) includes the foundational steps (3:1–4:11)—including the ministry of John the Baptist (3:1–12), the baptism of Jesus (3:13–17), and the temptation of Jesus (4:1–11)—and Jesus' early Galilean ministry (4:12–25). The first discourse (5:1–7:29) is the Sermon on the Mount. After the setting is established (5:1–2), the kingdom of heaven is introduced, with its norms (5:3–12) and its witness (5:13–16). The great body of the sermon runs from 5:17 to 7:12, beginning and ending with the way in which the kingdom is related to the Old Testament Scriptures, "the Law and the Prophets." This is particularly the theme of 5:17–48, with its initial explanation (5:17–20) and dependent antitheses ("you have heard . . . but I say to you" [5:21–48]). The demand for perfection (5:48) introduces correlative warnings against rank hypocrisy (6:1–18), with particular attention devoted to the proper way to go about the three traditional manifestations of Jewish piety: alms (6:2–4), prayer (6:5–15), and fasting (6:16–18). To maintain such a stance it is necessary to pursue kingdom perspectives (6:19–34), including unswerving loyalty to kingdom values (6:19–24) and uncompromised trust in God (6:25–34). The demand for balance and perfection, fulfilling Old Testament expectations (7:1–12), is followed by a conclusion that sets forth two ways (7:13–14), two trees (7:15–20), two claims (7:21–23), and two builders (7:24–27): every reader must choose. The closing verses (7:28–29) not only offer the first instance of the formula that terminates the five discourses but reaffirm Jesus' authority, thus preparing for the series of authoritative miracles that dominate the next two chapters.

The kingdom extended under Jesus' authority (8:1–11:1). The narrative (8:1–10:4) includes not only a number of miracles, each symbol-laden to portray some facet of the kingdom and its king, but the calling of Matthew (9:9) and Jesus' insistence on eating with public sinners (9:10–13) while announcing that the dawning kingdom, manifest in his own presence, was a time for joy (9:14–17). The miracles and Jesus' audacity are pushing back the frontiers of darkness, but the narrative ends with the demand for prayer for more workers (9:35–38) and the commissioning of the Twelve (10:1–4). This naturally leads to the second discourse, on mission and martyrdom (10:5–11:1), which moves from the immediate project (10:5b–16) to warnings of future sufferings (10:17–25), a prohibition of fear in the light of the Father's providence (10:26–31), and a more general description of authentic discipleship (10:32–39). Response to such disciples, for good or ill, is equivalent to response to Jesus himself (10:40–42). The transitional conclusion (11:1) points to Jesus' expanding ministry.

Teaching and preaching the gospel of the kingdom: rising opposition (11:2–13:53). The narrative (11:2–12:50) not only establishes the relative roles of John the Baptist and of Jesus in the stream of redemptive history (11:2–19) but reverses public expectations by reporting Jesus' strong condemnation of the "good," Jewish, religious towns of Galilee (which are aligned in his mind with pagan cities such as Tyre and Sidon, or a proverbially wicked center such as Sodom), and by announcing relief and rest to the weary and broken—provided they find it in the context of the "yoke" of the Son (11:20–30). Tension mounts as Sabbath conflicts erupt (12:1–14), as Jesus proves to be rather more a meek and suffering servant than a visibly conquering king (12:15–21), and as confrontation develops not only between Jesus and the Pharisees (12:22–45) but between Jesus and his own family (12:46–50). The reversal of expectations is a major theme of the discourse that follows, which is a series of parables (13:1–53; see outline below).

The glory and the shadow: progressive polarization (13:54–19:2). The narrative (13:54–17:27) is a series of vignettes that reflect the rising polarization (e.g., rejection at Nazareth, 13:54–58; Herod and Jesus, 14:1–12; demands for a sign, 16:1–4) or, where they display the power of Jesus' ministry, nevertheless betray the profound misunderstanding of its nature and focus (e.g., the feeding of the five thousand, 14:13–21, and the walk on the water, 14:22–33; Jesus and the tradition of the elders, 15:1–20; the transfiguration, 17:1–13; the healing of the epileptic boy, 17:14–20[21]). The high point of the narrative is the confession of Jesus by Peter (16:13–20), but the aftermath—the first passion prediction (16:21–23; cf. the second in 17:22–23)—shows how little even he has understood. The fourth discourse (18:1–19:2) describes life under kingdom authority. Greatness is irrefragably tied to humility (18:3–4); few sins are more odious than causing believers, Jesus' "little ones," to sin (18:5–9); the saving of lost sheep is judged more important than the mere nurture of safe sheep (18:10–14); the priority of forgiveness and the importance of discipline in the messianic community are set forth (18:15–35). The transitional conclusion (19:1–2) serves as an introduction to the Judean ministry.

Opposition and eschatology: the triumph of grace (19:3–26:5). The narrative (19:3–23:39) leads through a number of exchanges and parables that stress the surprising conduct expected of those who would follow Jesus (19:3–20:34), leading up to the events of passion week (21:1–23:39). The triumphal entry (21:1–11), Jesus' cleansing of the temple (21:12–17) and his cursing of the fig tree (21:18–22) are preludes to a string of controversies in the temple court (21:23–22:46), increasingly pointed and focused on Jesus' messianic claims. Exasperated, Jesus pronounces his woes on the teachers of the law and the Pharisees (23:1–36) and utters his lament over Jerusalem (23:37–39). The Olivet (or eschatological) discourse that follows (24:1–25:46), notoriously difficult to interpret, begins with the setting overlooking the temple (24:1–3), describes the birth pains of the interadvent period (24:4–28) and the coming of the Son of Man (24:29–31), before reflecting on the significance of the birth pains (24:32–35) and urging the need to be prepared, since the day and hour of the coming of the Son are unknown (24:36–41). A series of parables presents variations on the theme of watchfulness (24:42–25:46). The transitional conclusion (26:1–5) includes this gospel's fourth major passion prediction and some details of the plot against Jesus, which prepares for the final section of the book.

The passion and resurrection of Jesus (26:6–28:20). The pace is now rapid. In the passion narrative, the anointing at Bethany (26:6–13) and Judas's betrayal agreement (26:14–16) are rapidly followed by the last supper (26:17–30), including the words of institution in vv. 26–30), prediction of abandonment and denial (26:31–35), Gethsemane (26:36–46), the arrest (26:47–56), Jesus before the Sanhedrin (26:57–68), Peter's denial of Jesus (26:69–75), the formal decision of the Sanhedrin (27:1–2) and the death of Judas Iscariot (27:3–10), Jesus before Pilate (27:11–26), the soldiers' treatment of Jesus (27:27–31), the crucifixion and mocking (27:32–44), Jesus' death (27:45–50) and its immediate impact (27:51–56), the burial of Jesus (27:57–61), and the guard at the tomb (27:62–66). The resurrection narratives (28:1–17) climax in the great commission, placing the job of spreading the gospel and the content of Jesus' teaching squarely on the shoulders of the small enclave of witnesses, who are assured of Jesus' presence with them to the end of the age (28:18–20).

No outline can do justice to the numerous ministructures that the text displays (cf. Kümmel, pp. 106–7). To take but one example: the third discourse, the parables of the kingdom, is constructed as a large chiasm:

To the crowds (13:3b–33)

1. the parable of the soils (13:3b–9)

   2. interlude (13:10–23)

   (a) on understanding parables (13:10–17)

   (b) interpretation of the parable of the soils (13:18–23)

      3. the parable of the weeds (13:24–30)

         4. the parable of the mustard seed (13:31–32)

            5. the parable of the yeast (13:33)

   Pause (13:34–43)

      —parables as fulfillment of prophecy (13:34–35)

      —interpretation of the parable of the weeds (13:36–43)

To the disciples (13:44–52)

            5´. the parable of the hidden treasure (13:44)

         4´. the parable of the expensive pearl (13:45–46)

      3´. the parable of the net (13:47–48)

   2´. interlude (13:49–51)

   (b´) interpretation of the parable of the net (13:49–50)

   (a´) on understanding parables (13:51)

1´. the parable of the teacher of the law (13:52)[6]

---

[6]See D. A. Carson, *Matthew*, EBC 8:303–4, 331–33, and sources cited there.

AUTHOR

It is frequently asserted that the gospel commonly designated as Matthew's, like the other three canonical gospels, is anonymous. That is formally correct, if the standard of comparison is, say, Paul's epistle to the Romans, where the opening lines of the agreed text designate both the author and the initial readers. There is nothing comparable in Matthew, Mark, Luke, or John. Nevertheless, we have no evidence that these gospels ever circulated without an appropriate designation, κατὰ Μαθθαῖον (*kata Matthaion*, "according to Matthew") or the like. How early are these titles?

Until recently, most scholars tacitly assumed that the four gospels first circulated anonymously and that the present titles were first attached to them about A.D. 125. There is little evidence to support this date as the decisive turning point; it is little more than an educated guess, based only on the presupposition that the Gospels were originally entirely anonymous and on the fact that by about 140, and perhaps earlier, the traditional attributions were widely known, without significant variation. Now, however, this consensus has been vigorously challenged by Martin Hengel.[7] Hengel examines the practice of book distribution in the ancient world, where titles were necessary to identify a work to which any reference was made. In this context he studies the manner in which second-century authors refer to the Gospels, calling to mind, among other things, Tertullian's criticism of Marcion for publishing his own gospel (a highly truncated version of Luke) without the author's name. Tertullian contends that "a work ought not to be recognized, which holds not its head erect . . . which gives no promise of credibility from the fulness of its title and the just profession of its author."[8] Hengel argues that as soon as two or more gospels were publicly read in any one church—a phenomenon that certainly occurred, he thinks, not later than A.D. 100—it would have been necessary to distinguish between them by some such device as a title. The unanimity of the attributions in the second century cannot be explained by anything other than the assumption that the titles were part of the works from the beginning. It is inconceivable, he argues, that the Gospels could circulate anonymously for up to sixty years, and then in the second century suddenly display unanimous attibution to certain authors. If they had originally been anonymous, then surely there would have been some variation in second-century attributions (as was the case with some of the second-century apocryphal gospels). Hengel concludes that the four canonical gospels were never even formally anonymous.

Objections have been raised against this proposal in four areas.

1. Some of Hengel's arguments are of the "what must have been the case" variety. That is a fair charge. Even so, "what must have been the case" in the church's reference to the gospels that were circulating is based on demonstrable second-century practices. Certainly Hengel's reconstruction makes more sense than any other theory that seeks to explain the unanimity of second-century attribution.

---

[7]Martin Hengel, *Studies in the Gospel of Mark* (Philadelphia: Fortress, 1985), pp. 64–84. Cf. the admirable discussion in R. T. France, *Matthew—Evangelist and Teacher* (Grand Rapids: Zondervan, 1989), pp. 50–80.

[8]Tertullian, *Against Marcion*. 4.2.

2. Hengel's arguments are no defense against pseudonymity. Again, that is correct. But most scholars think of the four canonical gospels as anonymous, not pseudonymous. In any case, not only was pseudonymity in the first century largely if not entirely restricted to apocalyptic works, but as soon as the church began to discuss the issue, there was unanimity in rejecting the authority of any work that fell under the suspicion of being a pseudonymous composition.

3. Anonymity was surely less threatening than Hengel intimates. Was not the epistle to the Hebrews, say, written anonymously? Certainly Tertullian overstates the argument. Nevertheless, the epistle to the Hebrews is distinguished from other epistles by a title, namely, its (assumed) addressees; and its adoption by the church into the canon was constrained in part by doubts as to the identity of its author. It is not an accident that it was first accepted in the East, where tradition associated it with the apostle Paul. Hengel himself has discussed this question at length.[9]

4. Hengel's interpretation assumes that κατὰ Μαθθαῖον (*kata Matthaion*, "according to Matthew") is an attribution of authorship, whereas parallels show that the phrase "according to" serves other purposes. For example, in the titles "Gospel According to the Hebrews" and "Gospel According to the Egyptians," the prepositional expression does not indicate authorship. Plummer says it "implies *conformity to a type*, and need not mean more than 'drawn up according to the teaching of.'"[10] Plummer and others acknowledge that by the time of Papias, κατά (*kata* "according to") is understood to indicate authorship, but they insist that the expression does not necessarily bear that weight. Hengel agrees that κατά plus the accusative is not *itself* a necessary indication of authorship and indeed is only rarely used in that way in contemporary Greek literature. But he draws attention to a telling analogy. In the Greek fathers, the *one* Old Testament is referred to as "according to the Seventy" or "according to Aquila" or "according to Symmachus," where the prepositional expression is used to introduce the person or group thought to be responsible for producing the version concerned. In the same way, the *one* gospel early circulated in four distinct forms, "according to Matthew," "according to Mark," and so forth, where the prepositional expression introduces the person understood to be the author.

In short, the argument that Matthew was understood to be the author of the first gospel long before Papias wrote his difficult words affirming such a connection seems very strong, even if not unassailable.

Before considering Papias's disputed words, it is important to recognize that the credibility of Papias himself is widely questioned. Although Ireneus, writing in the second half of the second century, insists that both Papias and Polycarp knew the apostle John personally, the fourth-century church historian Eusebius disputes the claim in the case of Papias (*H.E.* 3.39.). Largely on this ground, modern scholarship tends to date Papias to A.D. 140 or later; but if Ireneus is right and Eusebius is wrong, then there is no reason Papias could not have written twenty or more years earlier, and with excellent access to accurate information. In recent years it has been repeatedly shown that Eusebius misunderstood Papias on several points and tried his best to reduce his importance because he could not stand his

---

[9]Hengel, *Mark*, pp. 170–72 n. 57.

[10]Alfred Plummer, *An Exegetical Commentary on the Gospel According to S. Matthew* (London: Robert Scott, 1909), p. vii.

millenarian views. (The evidence and arguments are summarized in chap. 5 below.)[11] It is far more likely that Ireneus is correct in his assessment of Papias than that Eusebius is.

Whatever the date and knowledge of Papias, what he actually wrote is available to us only in quotations preserved by Eusebius. The five exegetical books of Papias, Λογίων Κυριακῶν Ἐξήγησις (Logiōn Kyriakōn Exēgēsis, Exegesis of the Dominical Logia), survived into the Middle Ages in some libraries in Europe, but they are no longer extant. It is from this work that Eusebius (H.E. 3.39.14–16) quotes Papias's two surviving comments on the authorship of the Gospels. The one that bears on the fourth gospel is discussed later in this volume; the one that bears directly on Matthew is notoriously difficult to translate, as indicated here. "Matthew συνετάξετο (synetaxeto, 'composed'? 'compiled'? 'arranged [in an orderly form]'?) τὰ λόγια (ta logia, 'the sayings'? 'the gospel'?) in Ἑβραΐδι διαλέκτῳ (Hebraïdi dialektō , 'the Hebrew [Aramaic] language'? 'Hebrew [Aramaic] style'?), and each ἡρμήνευσεν (hērmēneusen, 'interpreted'? 'translated' 'transmitted'?) them as best he could."[12]

There is no doubt that the early church understood this to mean that Matthew first wrote his gospel in Hebrew (or Aramaic; the same Greek word was used to refer to both cognate languages) and that it was then translated by others. But there are serious problems with this view. Although a few modern scholars argue that Matthew's entire gospel was first written in Aramaic,[13] substantial linguistic evidence is against them. In the first place, the many quotations from the Old Testament do not reflect a single text form. Some are unambiguously Septuagintal; others are apparently translations from a Semitic original; still others are so eccentric as to defy easy classification. Had the gospel first been written in Aramaic, one might have expected that the Old Testament quotations would be either the translator's own rendering of the Aramaic or standard quotations from the accepted Bible of the early church, the LXX. The mix of text forms suggests an author writing in Greek but knowledgeable in Semitic languages and therefore able to vary his form.

Second, assuming that Matthew depends on Mark (see chap. 1, on the synoptic problem), the detailed verbal connections between Matthew and Mark make it extremely unlikely that Matthew was first written in Aramaic. Of course, those who do not accept the priority of Mark or who propose that an Aramaic edition of

---

[11]In addition to the literature cited in connection with John, see the following discussions that focus on the Matthean connections, all of them arguing against Eusebius: C. Stewart Petrie, "The Authorship of 'The Gospel According to Matthew': A Reconsideration of the External Evidence," NTS 14 (1967–68): 15–32; France, Matthew—Evangelist and Teacher, pp. 53–56; Robert H. Gundry, Matthew: A Commentary on His Literary and Theological Art (Grand Rapids: Eerdmans, 1982), pp. 609ff. Gundry points out, among other things, that Eusebius had earlier (H.E. 3.36.1–2) associated Papias with Ignatius, who died not later than A.D. 110,

[12]For the bearing of this Papias passage on the synoptic problem, see chap. 1 above.

[13]E.g. C. F. Burney, The Poetry of Our Lord (Oxford: Oxford University Press, 1925); C. C. Torrey, Our Translated Gospels (London: Hodder & Stoughton, n.d.); A. Schlatter, Der Evangelist Matthäus: Seine Sprache, sein Ziel, seine Selbständigkeit, 6th ed. (Stuttgart: Calwer, 1963); P. Gaechter, Die literarische Kunst im Matthäusevangelium (Stuttgart: Katholisches Bibelwerk, 1966); J. W. Wenham, "Gospel Origins," TrinJ 7 (1978): 112–34. In very recent times, a small number have argued that Hebrew (not Aramaic) underlies the canonical gospels, but this proposal has been rightly dismissed by the overwhelming majority of those who have looked into the matter.

Matthew preceded the publication of Mark, which then served as the heart of our Greek Matthew, will perceive no problem here.

Finally, the Greek text of Matthew does not read like translation Greek. True, there are Semitisms and, more frequently, Semitic enhancements,[14] but these are largely restricted to the sayings of Jesus, and (arguably) they are introduced for effect by an author who is demonstrably capable of writing idiomatic Hellenistic Greek.[15] One could argue that a very good translator could have produced the same effect, but he would have had to be a very good translator indeed.

How, then, should the statement of Papias be taken? Among the dominant proposals are these (see also Guthrie, pp. 44–49):

1. Some identify the λόγια (*logia*, "sayings") with some independent collection of Jesus' sayings, perhaps Q (on which see chap. 1, on the synoptic problem).[16] That would make Matthew the author of a sayings source (if Q, about 250 verses common to Matthew and Luke). Papias confused this source with the canonical Matthew. But it is not at all clear how an apostolic source as important as this could have fallen so completely out of use as to be lost to posterity. Indeed, the entire Q-hypothesis, however reasonable, is still merely a hypothesis: however much one may speak of material common to Matthew and Luke, it is far from clear that such material was all drawn from one common source. Besides, as we shall see, Papias does not normally use λόγια to refer only to sayings.

2. Some of the same criticisms can be raised against the view that λόγια (*logia*) refers to Old Testament "testimonia" books, that is, a book of Old Testament proof texts compiled by Matthew from the Hebrew canon, used in Christian apologetics, and now incorporated in canonical Matthew.[17] It is not certain that such books ever existed independently. In any case, it does not explain the diversity of text forms in Old Testament quotations in Matthew, still less the fact that Matthew most closely follows the LXX where he is parallel to Mark.

3. J. Kürzinger,[18] followed by Gundry,[19] thinks that τὰ λόγια (*ta logia*) refers to canonical Matthew but that Ἑβραΐδι διαλέκτῳ (*Hebraïdi dialektō*) refers, not to the Hebrew or Aramaic language, but to Semitic style or literary form: Matthew arranged or composed (συνετάξετο [*synetaxeto*]) his gospel in Semitic (i.e. Jewish-Christian) literary form, dominated by Semitic themes and devices. This is an unlikely rendering, but certainly possible (see LSJ 1:401). In this view, the last clause of Papias's statement cannot refer to translation, since Semitic *language* is no longer in view: everyone simply *interpreted* the text to the world, as he was able. Kürzinger points out that immediately preceding this passage, Papias

---

[14]In modern linguistic theory, the term "Semitism" is rightly applied only to phenomena in the Greek New Testament where sense can be made of an expression only by appealing to a Semitic underlay. "Semitic enhancement" refers to literary phenomena that do occur elsewhere in purely Greek texts but whose *frequency* of occurrence in some New Testament book is most easily explained by observing that the construction or expression is common in one or more of the Semitic languages.

[15]See Moule, pp. 276–80.

[16]This view was made popular by T. W. Manson, *The Sayings of Jesus* (London: SCM, 1949), pp. 18ff.

[17]J. R. Harris, *Testimonies*, 2 vols. (Cambridge: Cambridge University Press, 1920); F. C. Grant, *The Gospels: Their Origin and Their Growth* (New York: Harper, 1957), pp. 65, 144.

[18]J. Kürzinger. "Das Papiaszeugnis und die Erstgestalt des Matthäusevangeliums," *BZ* 4 (1960): 19–38; idem, "Irenäus und sein Zeugnis zur Sprache des Matthäusevangeliums," *NTS* 10 (1963): 108–15.

[19]Gundry, *Matthew*, pp. 619–20.

describes Mark as the ἑρμηνευτής (*hermēneutēs*) of Peter; this, Kürzinger says, cannot mean that Mark was Peter's "translator," but that he "interpreted" Peter and thus "transmitted" his message to the world. If the same reasoning is applied to the cognate verb in Papias's statement about Matthew, Kürzinger's interpretation becomes possible.

But however possible, it is not the natural way to read the passage, and it is certainly not what later Fathers in the church understood. Without exception, they held that the apostle Matthew wrote canonical Matthew and that it was first written in Semitic. That is true, for instance, of Ireneus (*Adv. Haer.* 3.1.1, quoted in Eusebius, *H.E.* 5.8.2), Tertullian (*Against Marcion.* 4.2), Origen (quoted by Eusebius, *H.E.* 6.25.3–6), Eusebius himself (*H.E.* 3.24.5–6), and Jerome (*De vir. ill.* 3).[20]

There does seem to be increasing agreement as to what τὰ λόγια (*ta logia*) means. Although at this period it would be most natural to use this expression to refer either to Old Testament oracles of God, and thus derivatively to the entire Old Testament, or else to the sayings of Jesus, two bits of evidence suggest that Papias used the term to refer to the words *and deeds* of Jesus—in short, to the substance of what became our Gospels. First, although the title of his five-volume work is *Exegesis of the Dominical Logia*, enough is known of this work to know that it was not restricted in scope to an exposition of Jesus' *words*: it included exposition also of *deeds* alleged to have been performed by Jesus. Moreover, in the sequence preserved in Eusebius, just before Papias tells us of how Matthew wrote, he tells us that Mark recorded from Peter's teaching "the things said or done by the Lord." This teaching, however, was given as the occasion demanded; Peter was not speaking "as if he were making an ordered collection (σύνταξις [*syntaxis*]) of the Lord's oracles (τὰ κυριακὰ λόγια [*ta kyriaka logia*])." Clearly, what Mark was writing was the gospel that bears his name, with its collection of "things either said or done by the Lord," and the parallelism between this clause and τὰ κυριακὰ λόγια shows that the latter expression can include deeds as well as words. When a few lines later we read that Matthew τὰ λόγια συνετάξετο (*ta logia synetaxeto*, "composed the *logia*" or "put the *logia* in order"), it is most natural to conclude that what he was doing, at least in Papias's mind, was composing the gospel that bears his name. It is thus highly unlikely that τὰ λόγια should be understood to refer to Q or to a book of "testimonies."

In short, the evidence leads to a difficult conclusion. Unless we adopt the solution of Kürzinger, we are gently nudged to the conclusion that Papias was wrong when he claimed that Matthew was first written in Aramaic. And if he was wrong on this point, what prevents us from supposing that he was likely wrong in his ascription of authorship to the apostle Matthew?

Such skepticism, superficially plausible, seems a trifle extreme. The two issues are not integrally connected. Authors have been known to err on one point without erring on all points! Moreover, plausible reasons have been advanced to suggest why Papias may have been led astray on the question of a Semitic original. It may have been an intelligent, albeit erroneous, guess. The early Fathers assumed

---

[20]These and other passages are conveniently summarized in France, *Matthew—Evangelist and Teacher*, pp. 60–62. For the fullest account of the use of Matthew in the early church, see Edouard Massaux, *Influence de l'évangile de Saint Matthieu sur la littérature chrétienne avant Saint Irénée*, BETL 75 (Louvain: Louvain University Press, 1986).

that Matthew was the first gospel to be written. Since Jesus and his apostles lived and served among the Hebrews, it may well have been a natural conclusion that the first gospel to be written was produced "in the Hebrew [Aramaic] dialect"—the more so if Papias, living in the Hellenistic world, had no real knowledge of just how much Greek was spoken in first-century Palestine, especially in Galilee. Moreover, Papias may have confused canonical Matthew with another gospel, written in Aramaic or Hebrew, that was well known in the second century. Reports have come down to us of a "gospel according to the Hebrews," a "gospel of the Nazareans," and a "gospel of the Ebionites." It is uncertain whether these titles refer to three separate books or two or more of them refer to one book.[21] Epiphanius claims that the Ebionites, a group he regards as heretical, based their beliefs on a gospel of Matthew that they called "According to the Hebrews," written in Hebrew, but (as far as Epiphanius was concerned) falsified and mutilated: for a start, it eliminated the genealogy of Jesus and began with the ministry of John the Baptist. Similarly, Ireneus says that the Ebionites used only the gospel of Matthew but denied the virgin birth—which again suggests that their Matthew did not include Matthew 1–2. The great translator Jerome claims that he translated the "gospel according to the Hebrews" into both Greek and Latin. This book he associates with the Nazareans, who, he insists, gave him permission to copy the Hebrew original of the gospel according to Matthew. Yet as far as we can tell from his frequent references, the actual content is far removed from canonical Matthew. All this suggests that there was ample opportunity for confusion to arise between some "gospel according to the Hebrews" and Matthew, engendering the theory that the latter was originally written in Hebrew or Aramaic.

We note several other factors in the contemporary debate over the authorship of this Gospel.

1. Only this gospel refers to "Matthew the tax collector" (10:3). On the assumption of apostolic authorship, this is best seen as gentle self-deprecation, an allusive expression of gratitude for the freedom of grace (see 9:9–13). Those who deny apostolic authorship of this book are inclined to interpret the same evidence as the reason why the unknown author(s) chose to associate the book with Matthew as opposed to some other apostle.

2. In Mark 2:14 and Luke 5:27, the man whom Jesus calls from his role as tax collector is identified as Levi. In what is transparently the same story, Matthew 9:9–13 identifies the man as Matthew. All three Synoptic Gospels, in their respective lists of the apostles (Matt. 10:2–4; Mark 3:16–18; Luke 6:13–16; cf. Acts 1:13), name a "Matthew," and Matthew 10:3 identifies this Matthew as the tax collector. The reasonable assumption is that Matthew and Levi are one and the same person. But other suggestions are not lacking. Pesch,[22] followed by Beare,[23] has argued that the calling of the tax-collector concerned one Levi, but that the unknown first evangelist, choosing to identify this otherwise unknown disciple with an apostle, substituted the name of a relatively obscure apostle, Matthew, whom he then dubbed a tax collector. Albright and Mann suggest that "Matthew"

---

[21]For a competent treatment of the sources, see P. Vielhauer in Hennecke 1:118–39.

[22]R. Pesch, "Levi-Matthäus (Mc 2¹⁴/Mt 9⁹ 10³): Ein Beitrag zur Lösing eines alten Problems," *ZNW* 59 (1968): 40–56.

[23]F. W. Beare, *The Gospel According to Matthew* (Oxford: Blackwell, 1981), pp. 224–25.

is the personal name and that "Levi" refers to his tribe (i.e. that the original designation was "Matthew the Levite" but that at some early point in the tradition the designation was confused and became the common personal name Levi).[24] The theory has its attractions. It would explain why the author has such a detailed command of the Old Testament. As for the likelihood that a Levite would find employment as a disreputable tax collector, Albright and Mann argue that there were far more Levites than were needed to run the temple complex and that many therefore had to seek employment elsewhere. By taking on this task, Matthew the Levite forfeited the esteem of his tribe and his race, the most strict of whom viewed tax collectors not only as traitors (since they were indirectly serving the despised Herods; see Schürer 1:372–76) but as immoral and rapacious (since the tax-farming system ensured that a fair bit of corruption was bound up with the job). But the linguistic transformation of "Levite" to "Levi" is not very plausible, and no text preserves the designation "Matthew the Levite." On the whole, the most economical explanation still seems the best: "Matthew" and "Levi" are alternative Semitic names for one person—a phenomenon found not only in Simon/Cephas (= Peter) but also in inscriptional evidence.[25]

3. The assumption that Matthew was a tax collector (essentially a minor customs official collecting tariff on goods in transit) and was the author of this gospel makes sense of a number of details.[26] Not all the evidence cited is equally convincing. A number of peculiarly Matthean pericopes do depict financial transactions (17:24–27; 18:23–35; 20:1–16; 26:15; 27:3–10; 28:11–15), but none of them betrays an insider's knowledge of the customs system. Certainly a customs official in Matthew's position would have had to be fluent in both Aramaic and Greek, and such fluency must have been important when the gospel was first crossing racial barriers: indeed, it squares with the notion of a gospel written in Greek that nevertheless could draw on Semitic sources. C. F. D. Moule suggests that 13:52 is a subtle self-reference by the author: the "scribe" (γραμματεύς [grammateus], NIV "teacher of the law") who becomes a disciple should not be understood as a reference to a rabbinic scribe but to a "scribe in the secular sense," that is, a well-educated writer.[27] Goodspeed goes further yet: after compiling impressive evidence that shorthand was widely practiced in the Roman world, he suggests that Matthew's training and occupation would have equipped him to be a kind of notetaker or secretary for the group of disciples, even during Jesus' ministry.[28] The theory is plausible enough, but completely without hard evidence.

4. On the assumption of Markan priority, some think it unlikely that an apostle would so freely use the work of a secondary witness such as Mark and believe that this tells against any theory of apostolic authorship. But plagiarism in the modern sense, and the shame associated with it, developed in the wake of the invention of

---

[24]W. F. Albright and C. S. Mann, *Matthew*, AB 26 (Garden City, N.Y.: Doubleday, 1981), pp. clxxvii–clxxviii, clxxxiii–clxxxiv.

[25]See W. L. Lane, *The Gospel According to Mark*, NICNT (Grand Rapids: Eerdmans, 1974), pp. 100–101 n. 29.

[26]See Gundry, *Matthew*, pp. 620–21.

[27]C. F. D. Moule, "St. Matthew's Gospel: Some Neglected Features," *SE* 2 (1964): 90–99; Moule, pp. 94–95.

[28]E. J. Goodspeed, *Matthew: Apostle and Evangelist* (Philadelphia: J. C. Winston, 1959).

the printing press and the financial gain that could be associated with the mass production of some writing. The wholesale takeover, without acknowledgment, of someone else's literary work, with or without changes, was a common practice in the ancient world, and no opprobrium was connected with it. In that case it is hard to think of a reason why an apostle might not also find the practice congenial, the more so if he knew that behind Mark's gospel was the witness of Peter.

5. Among the reasons Kümmel advances (p. 121) for holding that apostolic authorship is "completely impossible" is the insistence that this gospel is "systematic and therefore nonbiographical." This is a double non sequitur, because (1) a topically ordered ("systematic") account can yield biographical information as easily as a strictly chronological account,[29] and (2) it is surely a false step to assume that apostles would for some reason prove incapable of choosing anything other than a chronological form.

6. The most powerful reason today for denying even the possibility of apostolic authorship is bound up with an entire array of antecedent judgments about the development of the gospel tradition, about the shape of the history of the church in the first century, about the evidence of redactional changes, and much more. The conclusion drawn from these prior judgments is that Matthew is too late and too theologically developed to be assigned to any of the first witnesses.

It is impossible here to address all of these issues. Some of them have been briefly discussed in the first chapter. We must recognize that these interlocking theories not only discount the external evidence, such as it is, but in fact rest on far less tangible support than is often thought. For instance, how far the theology reflected in this gospel has developed is often judged on the basis of Matthew's Christology. But a high Christology developed very early, as the so-called Christ-hymns in the Pauline corpus (e.g., Phil. 2:5–11; Col. 1:15–20) testify, and it has been shown that Matthew is quite careful to distinguish, at point after point, what the first disciples understood during the time of Jesus' ministry and what he himself knows to be the case some decades later.[30] Such evidence might almost better be taken to *support* apostolic authorship: only those present at the beginning would be as likely to preserve such distinctions and point out with such sharpness how much the first disciples did *not* understand at the beginning (e.g., Matt. 16:21–23). Other factors alleged to demonstrate the lateness of Matthew's gospel are briefly mentioned in the next section.

7. Several scholars have argued that the author could not have been a Jew, let alone an apostle, on one of two grounds: (1) it is alleged that there are too many signs of a profound ignorance of Jewish customs and culture; (2) some have argued that the work is too anti-Jewish (some prefer the more emotionally laden term "anti-Semitic") to have been written by a Jew.[31] But the alleged ignorance of

---

[29]Even contemporary biographies commonly treat certain parts of their subject's life in topical arrangements; see, e.g., Antonia Fraser, *Cromwell: Our Chief of Men* (St. Albans: Panther, 1975), pp. 455ff.

[30]D. A. Carson, "Christological Ambiguities in the Gospel of Matthew," in *Christ the Lord, Fs. Donald Guthrie*, ed. Harold Rowdon (Leicester: IVP, 1982), pp. 97–114.

[31]E.g. John P. Meier, *The Vision of Matthew: Christ, Church, and Morality in the First Gospel* (New York: Paulist, 1979), pp. 17–23; G. Strecker, *Der Weg der Gerechtigkeit* (Göttingen: Vandenhoeck & Ruprecht, 1962), p. 34; Sjef van Tilborg, *The Jewish Leaders in Matthew* (Leiden: Brill, 1972), p. 17.

Jewish culture is sharply disputed. For example, it is alleged that Matthew lumps together the teaching of the Pharisees and the teaching of the Sadducees as if there were no difference between the two (16:12). But Matthew himself elsewhere highlights some of the differences (22:23–33). All that Matthew 16:12 requires us to hold is that in certain respects, allied with their joint failure to recognize the Messiah when he came, the Pharisees and the Sadducees were at one. Groups that differ do not have to differ on everything; compared with some other group—in this case, the group of nascent Christians—they may hold more in common than they themselves at first suspect. Common enemies make strange bedfellows. Many alleged errors (e.g., the use of Zech. 9:9 in Matt. 21:4–5, where Matthew has two animals) are better treated in the commentaries.[32]

As for the anti-Jewishness of Matthew, it must be remembered that this book depicts Jesus as being sent only to Israel (15:24) and recalls Jesus forbidding his disciples from extending their ministry beyond Israel (10:5–6), while at the same time it reports a commission to spread the gospel to all nations (28:18–20) and looks forward to people from every point on the compass participating in the Jewish messianic banquet (8:11–12). Arguably, the tension in presentation stems from two factors: (1) Matthew attempts to distinguish what happened "back then," during Jesus' ministry, from what is happening in his own day; (2) Matthew's ambivalent treatment of the Jews may well be shaped in part by the confusing cross-currents between Christianity and Judaism at the time of writing. Some Jews were still being converted, and Matthew wants to woo them and stabilize the faith of new Jewish converts; others, especially more conservative leaders, were appalled by this upstart faith and opposed it, ensuring that Matthew would warn his readers against their views, and especially against their rejection of Jesus the Messiah.[33]

It must be said that at one level very little hangs on the question of the authorship of this gospel. By and large, neither its meaning nor its authority are greatly changed if one decides that its author was not an apostle. What changes, however, is the matrix of thought in which these and related questions are evaluated. We have seen that strong commitments to the view that this gospel reflects late traditions that cannot possibly be tied directly to any apostle inevitably casts a hermeneutical shadow on how the evidence, including the external evidence, will be evaluated. Conversely, the judgment that in all probability the apostle Matthew was responsible for the work casts a hermeneutical shadow on the reconstruction of early church history. The web of interlocking judgments soon affects how one weighs evidence in other parts of the New Testament. Such problems can be addressed both as large-scale theoretical challenges and at the level of their constituent details. All that can be attempted in this short *Introduction* is a rather perfunctory statement of how we read the evidence and of why we weight things as we do.

---

[32]On this particular passage, see Barnabas Lindars, *New Testament Apologetic* (London: SCM, 1961), p. 114; Carson, *Matthew*, pp. 436–40.
[33]See France, *Matthew—Evangelist and Teacher*, pp. 70–73.

PROVENANCE

From the time of the influential work of Kilpatrick,[34] many have held that this book is not the work of an individual author but the product of a Christian community. Whoever wrote it was simply putting down the materials, liturgical and otherwise, that were circulating in his church. Doubtless this unknown writer ordered the material in various ways, but the book as a whole is best seen as the product of community thought and catechesis, rather than the theological and literary contribution of a single author. Indeed, Kilpatrick argues that the community deliberately and pseudonymously assigned the work to Matthew in order to ensure its wider acceptance in the Christian church.

On the basis of form criticism (see chap. 1 above), Stendahl argues that the conception of individual authorship must be relegated to an entirely subsidiary role. Unlike Kilpatrick, however, he thinks the group that produced Matthew is not some church as a whole but a school, a group within the community devoted to study and instruction, and particularly interested in the way the ancient Hebrew Scriptures are to be related to Christian life and thought.[35]

These proposals no longer have the influence they once did. In part, this owes something to redaction criticism (see chap. 1), with its insistence that the evangelists, even if they took over traditional material, so presented it and shaped it that they gave it a distinctive theological cast. Reasons for a more traditional ascription of authorship were outlined in the last section. But whether this gospel is understood to be the product of a single author or a community of thought, one must try to hazard a guess as to its *geographic* provenance.[36]

Because the Fathers held the work to have been written first in Aramaic, quite naturally they also presupposed that it was written in Palestine. Indeed, Jerome specifically ties it to Judea (*De vir. ill.* 3). Certainly a Palestinian origin makes sense of many features: the inclusion of Aramaic words without translation (see 5:22; 6:24; 27:6), the assumption of some Jewish customs, the bilingual character of the text forms when the Old Testament is cited, and the adoption for literary purpose of forms of speech that are more typically Semitic than Greek.

Most scholars today, however, opt for Syria as the place of origin. This choice depends primarily on two factors: (1) the adoption of a date after A.D. 70, by which time most of Palestine was destroyed; (2) the influence of Streeter,[37] who argued for Antioch as the provenance of this gospel. The first factor, we shall argue, is too subjective; the second is far more important. Not all of Streeter's arguments are weighty. But Antioch did boast a very large Jewish population yet was the first center for outreach to the Gentile world; these two realities come together rather forcefully in Matthew, "which breathes a Jewish atmosphere and yet looks upon the Gentile mission in a most favorable light."[38] Moreover, the gospel of Matthew has its first convincing external attestation in the writings of Ignatius, bishop of Antioch in the early years of the second century (see *Eph.*

---

[34]G. D. Kilpatrick, *The Origins of the Gospel According to St. Matthew* (Oxford: Clarendon, 1946).
[35]K. Stendahl, *The School of St. Matthew*, 2d ed. (Philadelphia: Fortress, 1968).
[36]For an excellent survey, see W. D. Davies and Dale C. Allison, Jr., *The Gospel According to Saint Matthew*, ICC 1 (Edinburgh: T. & T. Clark, 1988), pp. 138–47.
[37]B. H. Streeter, *The Four Gospels* (London: Macmillan, 1930), pp. 500–23.
[38]Davies and Allison, *Matthew*, p. 144.

19:1–3 and Matt. 2; *Smyr.* 1:1 and Matt. 3:15; *Polyc.* 2:2 and Matt. 10:16). Neither argument is conclusive, still less so others that have been adduced, but Syria, if not necessarily Antioch, is an entirely plausible suggestion.

Other centers have been suggested: Alexandria, Caesarea Maritima, Edessa, and Phoenicia all have their champions. The most plausible alternative to Syria is the Transjordan, defended by Slingerland,[39] who notes that both 4:25 and 19:1 seem to view Jesus' presence in Palestine from the east side of the Jordan. That is possible, though Davies and Allison cautiously argue against such a reading of the text.[40]

In short, we cannot be certain of the geographic provenance of this gospel. Syria is perhaps the most likely suggestion, but nothing of importance hangs on the decision.

DATE

The quotations of Matthew in Ignatius (referred to above) put an upper limit on the date that can be assigned to the publication of this gospel. The modern consensus approaches that limit: most hold that Matthew was written during the period A.D. 80–100. Yet most of the reasons advanced in defense of this date depend on a network of disputed judgments.

1. Most scholars today hold that Matthew borrowed from Mark. Dates for Mark commonly vary from about A.D. 55 to 70, with opinion generally favoring the high end. Hence a date of Matthew before 80 seems impracticable. There are several disputed points in this chain of reasoning. Some scholars continue to uphold the unanimous or virtually unanimous opinion of the early church that Matthew was written first.[41] Although in this *Introduction* we have argued that Markan priority is most likely, it is probably too simplistic, and in any case we recognize that the arguments are sufficiently fragile that we are reluctant to let too much rest on them. Moreover, even if Markan priority prevails and if Mark is dated to, say, A.D. 60, there is plenty of time for Matthew to be published before 70, when Jerusalem and its temple were destroyed.

2. Many aver that anachronisms in Matthew point to a date of writing after A.D. 70. The two most commonly cited are the reference to the destruction of a city and the references to the church. In the parable of the wedding feast, we are told that the king "sent his army and destroyed those murderers and burned their city" (22:7). This must be seen as an oblique reference to the destruction of Jerusalem at the end of the Jewish War (A.D. 66–70), and the mention of the burning suggests knowledge of what had already happened at the time of writing. The utterance is cast as a prophecy but depends on historical knowledge. This judgment, it is thought, is confirmed by the fact that such sweeping destruction of an entire city seems wildly disproportionate to the offense—namely, lame excuses for turning down a wedding invitation. But quite apart from the question as to whether Jesus *could* predict the future, most scholars who think that Mark was

---

[39]H. D. Slingerland, "The Transjordanian Origin of St. Matthew's Gospel," *JSNT* 3 (1979): 18–29.
[40]Davies and Allison, *Matthew*, pp. 142, 420.
[41]"Virtually unanimous" because some have suggested that the fact Papias treats Mark before he treats Matthew (at least as Eusebius represents Papias) indicates that Papias thought Mark was written first.

written before A.D. 70 concede that he predicts the fall of Jerusalem (Mark 13:14; cf. Matt. 24:15). They argue that if Mark wrote about 65, he was so close to the events that he could see how political circumstances were shaping up. But on this reasoning, Matthew, even if he borrowed from Mark, could have done the same thing in 66. More to the point, the language of Matthew 22:7, including the reference to the burning of the city, is the standard language of both the Old Testament and the Roman world describing punitive military expeditions against rebellious cities. Granted that Jesus foresaw the destruction of Jerusalem (as did many prophets before him), the language he used does not in any detail depend on specific knowledge as to how things actually turned out in A.D. 70.[42] In fact, Robinson goes so far as to argue that the synoptic prophecies about the fall of Jerusalem, including Matthew 22:7, are so restrained that they must have been written *before* 70.[43] Otherwise, he insists, we should expect to see some indication that the prophecies had actually been fulfilled. True, the punishment in this particular parable seems extravagant if the offense was nothing more than the social gaffe of turning down the wedding invitation of a petty monarch. But there is reason to think this offense is more serious: in the first-century world, it smacks of rebellion against one's lord. More important, many of Jesus' parables begin with the commonplace and then introduce elements that destroy the listeners' world of expectations. The monarch represented by the king in this parable is God himself; the wedding is the wedding of God's own Son. To refuse *his* invitation—indeed, his command—is dangerous rebellion that invites catastrophic retribution.

Explicit references to "church" (ἐκκλησία [*ekklēsia*], Matt. 16:18; 18:17–18.) are often taken to betray an interest in church order that developed only later. But these texts say nothing about church order. Bishops and deacons are not mentioned (though Phil. 1:1, written *before* A.D. 70, does!). The church envisaged is simply the messianic community. The discipline pictured in Matthew 18 is cast in broad principles applicable even in the earliest stages of Christianity. And Meyer has mounted an admirable defense of the authenticity of Matthew 16:18.[44]

3. The references in Matthew to the effect that something or other has continued "to this [very] day" (Matt. 27:8; 28:15)[45] are frequently taken as evidence that there was a long interval between the events of Jesus' day and the time of writing. But how long is a long interval? Would not three decades suffice? If we were to say that the effects of President Kennedy's assassination continue "to this day," would that be thought an inappropriate judgment on the ground that the assassination took place some thirty years ago?

4. Tensions between Jews and Christians must have been high when this book was written, and the most plausible date for such tensions, it is argued, is either just before or just after the Council of Jamnia (c. A.D. 85), which allegedly

---

[42]See K. H. Rengstorf, "Die Stadt der Mörder (Mt 22⁷)," in *Judentum Urchristentum, Kirche, Fs.* J. Jeremias, ed. Walther Eltester (Berlin: Töpelmann, 1960), pp. 106–29; B. Reicke, "Synoptic Prophecies on the Destruction of Jerusalem," in *Studies in New Testament and Early Christian Literature, Fs.* A. P. Wikgren, ed. D. E. Aune (Leiden: Brill, 1972), pp. 121–34.

[43]J. A. T. Robinson, *Redating the New Testament* (Philadelphia: Westminster, 1976), chap. 2.

[44]Ben F. Meyer, *The Aims of Jesus* (Philadelphia: Fortress, 1979), pp. 189–91. See also France, *Matthew—Evangelist and Teacher*, pp. 242ff.

[45]Some add Matt. 11:12, but that passage is relevant only if an anachronism is read into the text; see Carson, *Matthew*, pp. 265–68.

introduced the so-called *Birkath ha-Minim* into the Jewish synagogue liturgy. This was a clause in the Eighteen Benedictions which were supposed to be recited three times a day by all pious Jews. In the version found in the Cairo Geniza,[46] it reads, "Let Nazarenes [= Christians] and *minim* [= heretics] perish in a moment; let them be blotted out of the book of the living, and let them not be written with the righteous." This had the effect (it is argued) of expelling Christians from the synagogues and was the climax of mutual antipathy between Jews and Christians in the first century. But mutual suspicions between Jews and Christians have much longer roots, as both Acts and the epistles of Paul testify. It is far from clear that such antipathy followed a straight line of development, enabling us to plot its apex; it must have varied enormously from place to place and from time to time. Moreover, there is now very strong evidence that the circumstantial reconstruction that locates the *Birkath ha-Minim* at the time of Jamnia is to be questioned at every level (see discussion in chap. 5, the section "Date").

It appears, then, that arguments for a relatively late date of Matthew depend on a network of antecedent judgments, each of which can be questioned in turn. Theological developments that many scholars think must have taken at least two generations of believers may well have occurred more rapidly (after all, Romans was written within twenty-five years of the resurrection).[47] And some of the arguments, such as the contention that the prophecy of Matthew 22:7 is in reality a prophecy after the fact, can be turned on their head to argue for a date before A.D. 70. Indeed, five other arguments point in the same direction.

1. The question of date is marginally bound up with the question of authorship. If the apostle Matthew is judged, on balance, to be the evangelist, a date before A.D. 70 is more plausible (though certainly not necessary; there is excellent evidence that the apostle John was active for at least two decades after 70).

2. The early church fathers are unanimous in assigning Matthew an early date. Because this is tied to Matthean priority, a view discounted by most scholars today, patristic evidence is given little weight in the contemporary debate. But the two issues do not have to be tied together. Whether Mark was written shortly after Peter's death, in the mid-sixties, as Ireneus claims (see *H.E.* 3.1.1),[48] or while Peter was still alive, as Clement of Alexandria assumes (*H.E.* 2.15.1–2; 6.14.6–7), there is time for Matthew to write before A.D. 70. More can be said for Clement's dating than is sometimes thought.[49]

3. Some sayings of Jesus might be taken to indicate that the temple was still standing when Matthew wrote (Matt. 5:23–24; 12:5–7; 23:16–22; cf. 26:60–61). It might be objected that Matthew is simply being historically accurate: these things were said during Jesus' days, regardless of whether the temple was still standing when Matthew wrote. But one must at least inquire why Matthew would include so many utterances cast in terms no longer relevant to his readers. The story about the payment of the temple tax (17:24–27) is stronger evidence yet.

---

[46]Probably this version was in use in Palestine at the end of the first century. For discussion of the various versions, including the Babylonian version still in use today (in which the "doers of wickedness" are not identified), see Schürer 2:455–63.

[47]See Moule who argues that the period before A.D. 70 is "the most plausible dating" of Matthew's gospel (p. 242).

[48]Taking the ἔξοδος (*exodos*) of Peter and Paul to refer to their death.

[49]See Robinson, *Redating*, pp. 107–15; contra Hengel, *Mark*, pp. 2–6.

Before A.D. 70, the episode, whatever else it meant, would be taken as a gesture reinforcing solidarity with Israel. After 70, when the tax still had to be paid by Jews but was collected on behalf of the temple of Jupiter in Rome,[50] the same episode might suggest solidarity with idolatry. Even if for other reasons Matthew had wanted to preserve this pericope, it is hard to see how, if he was writing after 70, he could have permitted such an implication without comment.

4. While many assign Matthew to the period A.D. 70–100, we actually have few primary sources from that period, so it is difficult to check the claims. By contrast, Gundry has compiled a list of passages in Matthew that, he thinks, suggest a date before 70, on the basis of features known to have existed during that period.[51] Not all of his suggestions are equally convincing, but many carry considerable weight (e.g., insertion of the Sabbath day alongside winter as an undesirable time to flee from Jerusalem [24:20]; baptism before teaching [28:19; cf. *Didache* 7:1 and other later sources]).

5. Arguing for a date earlier than A.D. 90, Kilpatrick draws attention to the fact that although the apostolic fathers demonstrate their knowledge of many epistles from the Pauline corpus, in Matthew there is no undisputed instance of dependence on Paul.[52] Indeed, Kilpatrick argues that some passages in Matthew would not have been written as they are if certain passages in Paul were known (e.g., Matt. 28, with respect to the list of resurrection appearances in 1 Cor. 15). Kilpatrick concludes that a church unaffected by Paulinism and apparently unacquainted with Paul's epistles cannot possibly be dated after 90. We are inclined to agree, but wonder why this terminus ad quem must be so late. If Matthew was written before 70, this complete independence from Paul would be still easier to understand.

None of the arguments presented is conclusive. Other arguments tend to be even less decisive, owing to additional imponderables. For example, Gundry specifies a date not later than A.D. 63, but this depends on his view that Luke borrowed from Matthew and that Luke-Acts was published while Paul was still alive. We may agree with the latter point (though many do not); fewer yet will agree with the former. But the preponderance of evidence suggests that Matthew was published before 70, most probably during the sixties.

DESTINATION

The usual assumption is that the evangelist wrote this gospel to meet the needs of believers in his own area. There is a prima facie realism to this assumption if we hold that Matthew was working in centers of large Jewish population, whether in Palestine or Syria (see the section "Provenance" above), since the book betrays so many Jewish features; it is not easy to imagine that the author had a *predominantly* Gentile audience in mind. But it is not implausible to suggest that Matthew wrote his gospel with certain *kinds* of readers in mind, rather than their geographic location.

---

[50]Josephus *Wars* 7.218; Dio Cassius, 65.7.2; Suetonius, *Domitian Hist. Rom.* 12. Cf. E. M. Smallwood, *The Jews Under Roman Rule* (Leiden: Brill, 1976), pp. 371–76.

[51]Gundry, *Matthew*, pp. 602–6.

[52]Kilpatrick, *Origins*, pp. 129–30.

PURPOSE

Because Matthew includes no direct statement of his purpose in writing, all attempts at delineating it are inferences drawn from his themes and from the way he treats certain topics as compared with the way the other gospels treat similar topics. This forces us to recognize several limitations that must be imposed on quests to uncover his purpose. Matthew's dominant themes are several, complex, and to some extent disputed. Attempts to delineate a single, narrow purpose are therefore doomed to failure. It is always possible for other scholars to emphasize complementary themes and correspondingly shift the purpose to another area. Students of the New Testament are well aware how difficult it is to achieve consensus on the purpose of some of Paul's letters, even though most of them were written with occasional purposes in mind that may actually be articulated in the text. How much more difficult is it to isolate the purpose of a gospel! The challenge increases when we recognize that Matthew, like any gospel writer but unlike the writer of an epistle, is committed to describing what happened during the ministry and passion of the historical Jesus, while nevertheless addressing issues that are contemporary to his own ministry. This leads some commentators to try to infer what kind of situation might prompt Matthew to include this or that pericope (e.g., the transfiguration) and to present it as he does. But it is always possible that he sees no direct connection between what happened formerly and what is happening currently in his own congregation(s). For instance, he may at times be interested in explaining the basis in Jesus' ministry for beliefs and practices that are accepted (or disputed) in the evangelist's time. That means inferences must be more remote, and therefore more speculative.

Because Matthew devotes so much space to Old Testament quotations, some have suggested that he wrote his gospel to teach Christians how to read their Bibles—what we refer to as the Old Testament. Others appeal to the same evidence to infer that he was trying to evangelize Jews. Or perhaps he wrote to train Christians to sharpen their apologetics as they wrestled with the Pharisaic Judaism of their own day. Because Matthew devotes many passages to Jesus' teaching on the law, some have thought he was aiming to confute incipient antinomianism, or even Paulinism. Others have appealed to the same evidence to argue that Matthew was a master churchman, struggling to develop a distinctively Christian ethical structure, and to do so in a way that retains the unique place assigned to Jesus without offending too many Jewish sensitivities over the law. Conversely, others suppose that Matthew was trying to head off too rapid an institutionalization of the church, returning to an earlier, more charismatic emphasis while retaining some of the gains that a few decades of church experience had brought. Or did he write his work to train leaders, or as a catechesis for new converts?

These and many more suggestions have been put forward as *the* purpose of Matthew's gospel. Still others find contradictory strands in Matthew—for example, between Jewish exclusivism and worldwide mission, or between recognition of the place of law and the assumption that the law has been fulfilled in Christ—and conclude that no unitary purpose is possible: the conflicting emphases reflect different strands of tradition that have been brought together by incompetent redactors.

All these divisions of opinion do not prevent us from saying anything about Matthew's purpose. If we restrict ourselves to widely recognized themes, it is surely fair to infer that Matthew wishes to demonstrate, among other things, that (1) Jesus is the promised Messiah, the Son of David, the Son of God, the Son of Man, Immanuel, the one to whom the Old Testament points; (2) many Jews, especially Jewish leaders, sinfully failed to recognize Jesus during his ministry (and, by implication, are in great danger if they continue in that stance after the resurrection); (3) the promised eschatological kingdom has already dawned, inaugurated by the life, death, resurrection, and exaltation of Jesus; (4) this messianic reign is continuing in the world, as believers, both Jews and Gentiles, submit to Jesus' authority, overcome temptation, endure persecution, wholeheartedly embrace Jesus' teaching, and thus demonstrate that they constitute the true locus of the people of God and the true witness to the world of the "gospel of the kingdom"; and (5) this messianic reign is not only the fulfillment of Old Testament hopes but the foretaste of the consummated kingdom that will dawn when Jesus the Messiah personally returns.

Doubtless this complex array of themes (and more could be enumerated) was designed to meet diverse needs. Such themes would effectively instruct and perhaps catechize the church (the latter facilitated by the carefully crafted, topical arrangement of many sections). They would also be effective in equipping Christians in the task of Jewish evangelism and might prove to be an effective evangelistic tool in their own right.

TEXT

Compared with Acts, for example, the text of Matthew is relatively stable. But as with all the Synoptic Gospels, Matthew's text is afflicted with many variants that are tied to the synoptic problem. This provides many opportunities for harmonizing or disharmonizing alterations in the transmission (e.g., variants at 12:47; 16:2–3; 18:10–11). But not every instance of possible harmonization should be taken as such and assumed to be secondary (12:4, 47; 13:35 may well be examples where caution is required). Davies and Allison provide an excellent bibliography on these textual matters.[53]

ADOPTION INTO THE CANON

The gospel of Matthew was universally received as soon as it was published and continued to be the most frequently cited gospel for centuries. The refusal of Marcion to accept it carries no weight, since his antipathy to all things Jewish is well known. So far as our sources go, the book never divided the Eastern and Western wings of the church, as did, say, the epistle to the Hebrews.

---

[53]Davies and Allison, *Matthew*, pp. 147–48 n. 127, to which must be added C. M. Martini, "La problématique générale du texte de Matthieu," in *L'évangile selon Matthieu: Rédaction et Théologie*, BETL 29, ed. M. Didier (Gembloux: Duculot, 1972), pp. 21–36.

MATTHEW IN RECENT STUDIES

Until the last few years, English-language commentators ignored Matthew more than any other of the canonical gospels. This has been partly redressed by six commentaries,[54] with several more on the way. Two of these six, however, are mildly eccentric. The bibliography and discussion in Beare (1981) was fifteen years out of date the day it was published. Gundry's work (1982) is a detailed redaction-critical study of the Greek text but comes to so many conclusions that scholars of all stripes find implausible that it has not been well received. In particular, several of his contentions—(1) that Q (see chap. 1 above) embraces far more than the 250 or so verses normally assigned to it, (2) that the changes and additions Matthew makes in his sources are entirely motivated by theological concerns and are without historical referent (including, e.g., the birth narratives in Matt. 1–2), and (3) that the genre of literature he was writing (which Gundry labels "midrash") would have been recognized as a mixture of history and ahistorical reflection by the first readers—have all come in for considerable criticism. On the third point, it has repeatedly been observed that in the first century, "midrash" could refer to many different kinds of commentary: it was not a well-defined genre that readers would instantly recognize, thereby enabling them to draw conclusions about its nonreferential nature. Extending well beyond the commentaries, excellent surveys in English of recent Matthean studies are provided by Stanton[55] and France.[56]

Much scholarly energy during the last three decades has been devoted to redaction-critical studies of Matthew. Beginning with the groundbreaking work of Bornkamm, Barth, and Held,[57] many scholars have focused on differences between Matthew and Mark, and between Matthew and what can be retrieved of Q, in order to determine what is distinctive in Matthew's gospel. Although many of these have proved suggestive, not a few are so narrowly based as to be somewhat eccentric. Rolf Walker thinks that Matthew was written to show that Israel has been entirely rejected: the great commission authorizes that the gospel be preached exclusively to Gentiles.[58] Only rarely is Walker exegetically convincing. His treatment of πάντα τὰ ἔθνη (panta ta ethnē, "all nations") in 28:19 has persuaded almost no one; nowhere does he adequately struggle with the fact that all the disciples and early converts were Jews. Hubert Frankemölle argues that Matthew is so unlike Mark that it cannot meaningfully be called a gospel at all;[59] it is, rather, like Deuteronomy and Chronicles, a book of history—the history not of Jesus but of the community, since in this "literary fiction," "Jesus" is an idealized figure intentionally fused with Matthew the theologian. But Frankemölle overemphasizes formal differences between Mark and Matthew and neglects substantial differences between Matthew and Deuteronomy or Chronicles.

[54]See the commentaries by Albright and Mann (1981), Beare (1981), Gundry (1982), Carson (1984), France (1985), and vol. 1 of Davies and Allison (1988).

[55]Stanton, "Origin and Purpose."

[56]France, *Matthew—Evangelist and Teacher.*

[57]G. Bornkamm, G. Barth, and H. J. Held, *Tradition and Interpretation in Matthew* (ET London: SCM, 1963).

[58]R. Walker, *Die Heilsgeschichte im ersten Evangelium* (Göttingen: Vandenhoeck & Ruprecht, 1967).

[59]Hubert Frankemölle, *Jahwebund und Kirche Christi: Studien zur Form- und Traditionsgeschichte des "Evangeliums" nach Matthäus* (Münster: Aschendorff, 1974).

Although he is right to read Matthew as a unified book, he does not adequately reflect on the fact that for most of his gospel, Matthew heavily depends on Mark and Q (however Q is understood).

Some studies have been widely accepted, not least the work of Bornkamm.[60] He holds that whereas in Mark the disciples do not understand what Jesus says until Jesus explains things to them in secret, Matthew attributes large and instant understanding to the disciples. In fact, this is what sets the disciples off from the crowds: the disciples understand. The faltering of the disciples at various points stems from their lack of faith, not from any lack of understanding. Yet one is tempted to qualify this thesis. Apart from the fact that he relies rather too heavily on the so-called Messianic secret in Mark, Bornkamm does not adequately deal with the disciples' request for private instruction (13:36), their failure to understand Jesus' teaching about his passion even after his explanations (e.g. 16:21–26; 17:23; 26:51–56), or the passages that deal with "stumbling" and "falling away." This is not a peripheral failure; at bottom, Bornkamm does not wrestle with the degree to which the failure of the disciples turns on their location in the stream of redemptive history. They were unprepared before the passion and resurrection to conceive of a Messiah who could be defeated, who could die the ignominious and odious death of the scum of Roman society. To this extent, the disciples' coming to deeper understanding *and* faith was unique: it was in part a function of their place in salvation history, a place rendered forever obsolete by the triumph of Jesus' resurrection. Our coming to faith and understanding today, or even in Matthew's day, therefore cannot be exactly like the coming to faith and understanding of the first disciples. In numerous ways Matthew makes this clear, but Bornkamm is so interested in reading Matthew's church into Matthew's description of the first disciples that the exegesis becomes skewed.[61]

Some recent studies, however, have manifested an increasing concern to read Matthew holistically—that is, to read Matthew in his own right, even while keeping an eye cocked on the synoptic (and other) parallels. Where the first gospel is studied as a book on its own and not simply as a modified Mark, its themes, unity, and essential power more easily come into focus. This is not to deny the validity of both approaches; it is to insist that the traditional historical-critical method be complemented by greater literary sensitivity.

THE CONTRIBUTION OF MATTHEW

Because of the tight relationships among the Synoptic Gospels, the contribution made by any one of them must be evaluated in light of the contribution made by all three. If Matthew suddenly disappeared, much of its material would still be found, more or less intact, in Mark and Luke. In that sense Matthew cannot be said to make the same sort of independent contribution that Hebrews or the Apocalypse does, for example.

But the Synoptic Gospels as a whole make an irreplaceable contribution. Alongside John, they constitute the foundational witness to the person, ministry,

---

[60]Bornkamm, Barth, and Held, *Tradition and Interpretation*, pp. 105–16.

[61]See esp. Andrew H. Trotter, "Understanding and Stumbling: A Study of the Disciples' Understanding of Jesus and His Teaching in the Gospel of Matthew" (Ph.D. diss., Cambridge University, 1987).

teaching, passion, and resurrection of Jesus the Messiah. Nor are the three Synoptic Gospels to be seen as merely redundant testimony. Each provides its own slant, together providing a kind of stereoscopic depth that would otherwise be almost entirely missing. And at a secondary level, each provides a window onto the life of the church at the time each was written. But this window, it must be insisted, is never transparent: it is at best translucent, and the shadows one sees through it have to be interpreted with some care.

Within this framework, we may highlight some of Matthew's emphases, and therefore some of the peculiar contributions this gospel makes to the canon.

1. Matthew preserves large blocks of Jesus' teaching, in the discourses already enumerated. Doubtless that was one of the major reasons this gospel was so popular in the early church. However they came to be preserved in this form, there can be no doubt that the church would be greatly impoverished without the sermon on the Mount, Matthew's list of parables, his version of the eschatological discourse, and so forth.

2. Matthew complements the other gospels, Luke in particular, by giving an alternative account of Jesus' virginal conception, cast in Joseph's perspective. Quite apart from other stories in the birth narrative of which there is no other record (e.g., the visit of the Magi, the flight into Egypt), the whole account is strongly tied to the antecedent revelation in what we now call the Old Testament.[62]

3. More generally, Matthew's use of the Old Testament is particularly rich and complex. The most noticeable peculiarity is the number of Old Testament quotations (variously estimated between ten and fourteen) found only in Matthew and introduced by a fulfillment formula characterized by a passive form of πληρόω (*plēroō*, "to fulfill"). These "formula quotations" are all asides of the evangelist, his own reflections (hence the widely used German word for them, *Reflexionszitate*), and characteristically they adopt a text form rather more Semitic and rather less like the LXX than most of the other Old Testament quotations in Matthew. The precise significance of these features is disputed.[63] What is clear is that Matthew's appreciation for the links between the old covenant and the new is characterized by extraordinarily evocative nuances. For instance, his notion of prophecy and fulfillment cannot be reduced to mere verbal prediction and historical fulfillment in raw events (though it sometimes includes such a notion). He employs various forms of typology and a fortiori arguments and adopts a fundamentally Christological reading of the Old Testament. Thus, Jesus' temptations, for instance (Matt. 4:1-11), are in some sense a reenactment of the temptations confronted in the wilderness by the Israelites, God's "son" (Exod. 4:22-23)— except that Jesus the Son of God is entirely victorious in them because he is determined by God's Word.

4. In the same way, Matthew's treatment of the law is especially suggestive. Although many think Matthew internalizes the law, radicalizes it, subsumes it under the love command, absolutizes only its moral dimensions, or treats it (in

---

[62]The most detailed study is that of Raymond E. Brown, *The Birth of the Messiah* (Garden City, N.Y.: Doubleday, 1977).

[63]See among other studies the bibliographical entries under Doeve, France (*Jesus and the Old Testament*), Gundry, McConnell, Moo, Rothfuchs, Soarés Prabhu, Stanton ("Matthew"), Stendahl, and Westerholm.

Pauline fashion) as a schoolmaster that conducts people to Christ, it is better to utilize Matthew's own category: Jesus comes to "fulfill" the law (5:17). In Matthew's usage, that verb presupposes that even the law itself enjoys a teleological, prophetic function.[64]

5. Matthew's gospel is foundational not only as one looks backward to the Scriptures of the old covenant but as one looks forward to what the church became. The later debates on the relation between Israel and the church find much of their genesis in Matthew, John, Romans, and Hebrews. Not a little of this debate, as far as Matthew is concerned, has focused on his treatment of the Jewish leaders.[65]

6. Finally, there are shadings to Matthew's portrait of Jesus—surely the heart of his gospel—that are unique. It is important to say, again, that much of what is central in Matthew's thought in this regard is *not* unique:[66] it is not just in Matthew that Jesus is the Christ, the Son of David, the Son of God, the Son of Man, the Servant of the Lord, and so forth. Whatever special coloring these titles take on in Matthew, their semantic overlap with their usage in other gospels is even more striking. Nor is it justifiable to try to isolate one Christological title as that which explains or hermeneutically controls all the others in this gospel.[67] But having entered these caveats, Matthew's shadings are important. He may achieve such shading by associating a particular title with some theme, as when he repeatedly links "Son of David" with Jesus' healing ministry (and he is not alone in this association).[68] He may also do it by introducing titles of which the other evangelists make no mention, as when he insists that Jesus is Immanuel, "God with us" (1:23).

BIBLIOGRAPHY

W. F. **Albright** and C. S. **Mann,** *Matthew,* AB 26 (Garden City, N.Y.: Doubleday, 1981); Willoughby C. **Allen,** *A Critical and Exegetical Commentary on the Gospel According to S. Matthew,* ICC (Edinburgh: T. & T. Clark, 1912); B. W. **Bacon,** "The 'Five Books' of Moses Against the Jews," *Exp* 15 (1918): 56–66; idem, *Studies in Matthew* (London: Constable, 1930); Robert **Banks,** *Jesus and the Law in the Synoptic Tradition* (Cambridge: Cambridge University Press, 1975); F. W. **Beare,** *The Gospel According to Matthew* (Oxford: Blackwell, 1981); Pierre **Bonnard,** *L'evangile selon Saint Matthieu* (Neuchâtel: Delachaux et Niestlé, 1970); G. **Bornkamm,** G. **Barth,** and H. J. **Held,** *Tradition and Interpretation in Matthew* (ET London: SCM, 1963); Raymond E. **Brown,** *The Birth of the Messiah: A Commentary on the Infancy Narratives* (Garden City, N.Y.: Doubleday, 1977); C. F. **Burney,** *The Poetry of Our Lord* (Oxford: Oxford University Press, 1925); D. A. **Carson,** "Christological Ambiguities in the Gospel of Matthew," in *Christ the*

---

[64]See esp. the bibliographical entries under Meier (*Law*), Banks, and Carson (*Matthew*, pp. 140ff.).

[65]See discussion of the options in D. A. Carson, "Jewish Leaders in Matthew's Gospel: A Reappraisal," *JETS* 25 (1982): 161–74.

[66]A point perhaps not sufficiently observed in the important article by G. M. Styler, "Stages in Christology in the Synoptic Gospels," *NTS* 10 (1963–64): 398–409.

[67]The best-known instance is the argument of Kingsbury (*Matthew*) that "Son of God" is for Matthew the controlling title, under which all others must be subsumed. See the important response by David Hill, "Son and Servant: An Essay on Matthean Christology," *JSNT* 6 (1980): 2–16.

[68]See David Duling, "The Therapeutic Son of David: An Element in Matthew's Christological Apologetic," *NTS* 24 (1978): 392–410.

Lord, *Fs*. Donald Guthrie, ed. Harold Rowdon (Leicester: IVP, 1982), pp. 97–114; idem, "Jewish Leaders in Matthew's Gospel: A Reappraisal," *JETS* 25 (1982): 161–74; idem, *Matthew*, in *EBC* 8 (Grand Rapids: Zondervan, 1984); W. D. **Davies** and Dale C. **Allison, Jr.**, *The Gospel According to Saint Matthew*, ICC 1 (Edinburgh: T. & T. Clark, 1988); J. W. **Doeve,** *Jewish Hermeneutics in the Synoptic Gospels and Acts* (Assen: Van Gorcum, 1954); David **Duling**, "The Therapeutic Son of David: An Element in Matthew's Christological Apologetic," *NTS* 24 (1978): 392–410; R. T. **France,** *Jesus and the Old Testament: His Application of Old Testament Passages to Himself and His Mission* (London: Tyndale, 1971); idem, *Matthew*, TNTC (Grand Rapids: Eerdmans, 1985); idem, *Matthew—Evangelist and Teacher* (Grand Rapids: Zondervan, 1989); Hubert **Frankemölle,** *Jahwebund und Kirche Christi: Studien zur Form- und Traditionsgeschichte des "Evangeliums" nach Matthäus* (Münster: Aschendorff, 1974); P. **Gaechter,** *Die literarische Kunst im Matthäusevangelium* (Stuttgart: Katholisches Bibelwerk, 1966); E. J. **Goodspeed,** *Matthew: Apostle and Evangelist* (Philadelphia: J. C. Winston, 1959); M. D. **Goulder,** *Midrash and Lection in Matthew* (London: SPCK, 1974); F. C. **Grant,** *The Gospels: Their Origin and Their Growth* (New York: Harper, 1957); Robert H. **Gundry,** *Matthew: A Commentary on His Literary and Theological Art* (Grand Rapids: Eerdmans, 1982); idem, *The Use of the Old Testament in St. Matthew's Gospel* (Leiden: Brill, 1967); J. R. **Harris,** *Testimonies*, 2 vols. (Cambridge: Cambridge University Press, 1920); Martin **Hengel,** *Studies in the Gospel of Mark* (Philadelphia: Fortress, 1985); David **Hill,** *The Gospel of Matthew*, NCB (Grand Rapids: Eerdmans, 1972); idem, "Son and Servant: An Essay on Matthean Christology," *JSNT* 6 (1980): 2–16; G. D. **Kilpatrick,** *The Origins of the Gospel According to St. Matthew* (Oxford: Clarendon, 1946); J. D. **Kingsbury,** *Matthew: Structure, Christology, Kingdom* (Philadelphia: Fortress, 1975); E. **Krentz,** "The Extent of Matthew's Prologue," *JBL* 83 (1964): 409–14.; J. **Kürzinger,** "Irenäus und sein Zeugnis zur Sprache des Matthäusevangeliums," *NTS* 10 (1963): 108–15; idem, "Das Papiaszeugnis und die Erstgestalt des Matthäusevangeliums," *BZ* 4 (1960): 19–38; M.-J. **Lagrange,** *Evangile selon Saint Matthieu* (Paris: Lecoffre, 1948); W. L. **Lane,** *The Gospel According to Mark*, NICNT (Grand Rapids: Eerdmans, 1974); B. **Lindars,** *New Testament Apologetic* (London: SCM, 1961); Ernst **Lohmeyer,** *Das Evangelium des Matthäus*, ed. W. Schmauck (Göttingen: Vandenhoeck & Ruprecht, 1956); C. H. **Lohr,** "Oral Techniques in the Gospel of Matthew," *CBQ* 23 (1961): 403–35; Richard S. **McConnell,** *Law and Prophecy in Matthew's Gospel* (Basel: Friedrich Reinhardt, 1969); A. H. **McNeile,** *The Gospel According to St. Matthew* (London: Macmillan, 1915); T. W. **Manson,** *The Sayings of Jesus* (London: SCM, 1949); C. M. **Martini,** "La problématique générale du texte de Matthieu," in *L'évangile selon Matthieu: Rédaction et Théologie* , BETL 29, ed. M. Didier (Gembloux: Duculot, 1972); Edouard **Masseaux,** *Influence de l'évangile de Saint Matthieu sur la littérature chrétienne avant Saint Irénée*, BETL 75 (Louvain: Louvain University Press, 1986); John P. **Meier,** *Law and History in Matthew's Gospel: A Redactional Study of Mt. 5:17–48* (Rome: BIP, 1976); idem, *Matthew* (Wilmington, Del.: Glazier, 1980); idem, *The Vision of Matthew: Christ, Church, and Morality in the First Gospel* (New York: Paulist, 1979); Ben F. **Meyer,** *The Aims of Jesus* (Philadelphia: Fortress, 1979); Douglas J. **Moo,** *The Old Testament in the Gospel Passion Narratives* (Sheffield: Almond, 1983); L. **Morris,** "The Gospels and the Jewish Lectionaries," in *GP* 1:129–56; C. F. D. **Moule,** "St. Matthew's Gospel: Some Neglected Features," *SE* 2 (1964): 90–99; Daniel **Patte,** *The Gospel According to Matthew* (Philadelphia: Fortress); R. **Pesch,** "Levi-Matthäus (Mc 2[14]/Mt 9[9] 10[3]): Ein Beitrag zur Lösing eines alten Problems,"

ZNW 59 (1968): 40–56; Alfred **Plummer**, *An Exegetical Commentary on the Gospel According to S. Matthew* (London: Robert Scott, 1909); B. **Reicke**, "Synoptic Prophecies on the Destruction of Jerusalem," in *Studies in New Testament and Early Christian Literature*, Fs. A. P. Wikgren, ed. D. E. Aune (Leiden: Brill, 1972); K. H. **Rengstorf**, "Die Stadt der Mörder (Mt 22[7])," in *Judentum, Urchristentum, Kirche*, Fs. J. Jeremias, ed. Walther Eltester (Berlin: Töpelmann, 1960), pp. 106–29; H. N. **Ridderbos**, *Matthew* (Grand Rapids: Zondervan, 1987); J. A. T. **Robinson**, *Redating the New Testament* (Philadelphia: Westminster, 1976); Wilhelm **Rothfuchs**, *Die Erfüllungszitate des Matthäus-Evangeliums* (Stuttgart: Kohlhammer, 1969); Alexander **Sand**, *Das Gesetz und die Propheten: Untersuchungen zur Theologie des Evangeliums nach Matthäus* (Regensburg: Friedrich Pustet, 1976); A. **Schlatter**, *Der Evangelist Matthäus: Seine Sprache, sein Ziel, seine Selbständigkeit*, 6th ed. (Stuttgart: Calwer, 1963); Eduard **Schweizer**, *The Good News According to Matthew* (Atlanta: John Knox, 1975); H. D. **Slingerland**, "The Transjordanian Origin of St. Matthew's Gospel," *JSNT* 3 (1979): 18–29; E. M. **Smallwood**, *The Jews Under Roman Rule* (Leiden: Brill, 1976); George M. Soarès **Prabhu**, *The Formula Quotations in the Infancy Narrative of Matthew* (Rome: BIP, 1976); G. N. **Stanton**, "Matthew," in *It Is Written: Scripture Citing Scripture*, Fs. Barnabas Lindars, ed. D. A. Carson and H. G. M. Williamson (Cambridge: Cambridge University Press, 1988), pp. 205–19; idem, "The Origin and Purpose of Matthew's Gospel: Matthean Scholarship from 1945 to 1980," in H. Temporini and W. Haase, eds., *ANRW* II.25.3, pp. 1889–1951; K. **Stendahl**, *The School of St. Matthew*, 2d ed. (Philadelphia: Fortress, 1968); Ned B. **Stonehouse**, *The Witness of Matthew and Mark to Christ* (Grand Rapids: Eerdmans, 1944); G. **Strecker**, *Der Weg der Gerechtigkeit* (Göttingen: Vandenhoeck & Ruprecht, 1962); B. H. **Streeter**, *The Four Gospels* (London: Macmillan, 1930); G. M. **Styler**, "Stages in Christology in the Synoptic Gospels," *NTS* 10 (1963–64): 398–409; C. C. **Torrey**, *Our Translated Gospels* (London: Hodder & Stoughton, n.d.); Wolfgang **Trilling**, *Das wahre Israel: Studien zur Theologie des Matthäus-Evangeliums* (Munich: Kösel, 1964); Sjef van **Tilborg**, *The Jewish Leaders in Matthew* (Leiden: Brill, 1972); R. **Walker**, *Die Heilsgeschichte im ersten Evangelium* (Göttingen: Vandenhoeck & Ruprecht, 1967); J. W. **Wenham**, "Gospel Origins," *TrinJ* 7 (1978): 112–34; Stephen **Westerholm**, *Jesus and Scribal Authority* (Lund: Gleerup, 1978).

3

mark

CONTENTS

Mark's story of Jesus' ministry is action oriented. Recounting little extended teaching of Jesus, Mark shifts scenes rapidly (εὐθύς [*euthys*], "immediately," is almost a standard linking word in Mark). Jesus is constantly on the move, healing, exorcising demons, confronting opponents, and instructing the disciples. This fast-paced narrative is punctuated by six transitional paragraphs or statements, which divide Mark's account into seven basic sections.

1) *Preliminaries to the ministry (1:1–13).* While it could be the title of the entire gospel, Mark 1:1 is probably the heading for 1:1–13, the preliminaries to the ministry: the "beginning" (ἀρχή, [*archē*]) of the "good news" about Jesus Christ consists in the ministry of John the Baptist, the eschatological forerunner (1:2–8), Jesus' baptism by John (1:9–11), and Jesus' temptation by Satan in the wilderness (1:12–13).[1]

2) *First part of the Galilean ministry (1:16–3:6).* The important summary in 1:14–15—Jesus' entrance into Galilee, proclaiming the good news that the time of fulfillment had come and that the kingdom was near—is the first of the six transitional sections. It introduces Jesus' ministry in Galilee (1:16–8:26) and, more immediately, the opening events in that period of ministry (1:16–3:6). After Jesus' call of four disciples (1:16–20), Mark gives us a glimpse of a typical day in Jesus' ministry, including teaching in the synagogue, exorcisms, and healings (1:21–34). The extraordinary nature of these events attracts great crowds of people, but Jesus insists on moving from Capernaum, on the Sea of Galilee (where these events took place), to other towns in Galilee (1:35–39). After another healing story (1:40–45), Mark narrates five events that focus on Jesus' controversy with Jewish leaders: controversies over his claim to be able to forgive sins (2:1–12), over his fellowship with "tax collectors and 'sinners'" (2:13–17), over his disiciples' failure to fast regularly (2:18–22), and over the Sabbath (2:23–28 and 3:1–6). The section climaxes with the plot of the Herodians to take Jesus' life.

Second part of the Galilean ministry (3:13–5:43). Mark's second transitional

---

[1]For this view of Mark 1:1, along with nine others, see C. E. B. Cranfield, *The Gospel According to Saint Mark*, CGTC (Cambridge: Cambridge University Press, 1966), pp. 34–35.

passage focuses on Jesus' immense popularity and emphasizes Jesus' ministry of healing and exorcism (3:7–12). It introduces the third major section of the gospel, in which Jesus continues the Galilean ministry. Mark here focuses especially on the kingdom (3:13–5:43). Like the second section, this one also begins with a narrative about the disciples—in this case, Jesus' appointment of twelve of them to be "apostles" (3:13–19). There follow further stories about the growing opposition to Jesus on the part of both Jesus' family (3:20–21, 31–34) and "the teachers of the law" (3:22–30). Jesus uses parables to explain this opposition as part of "the mystery of the kingdom of God" (4:1–34). The section comes to a climax with four miracles, each of them representing a type of Jesus' miracles: the calming of the storm (a nature miracle, 4:35–41); the casting out of a "legion" of demons from a man in the region of the Gerasenes (an exorcism, 5:1–20); the healing of a woman with a flow of blood (a healing, 5:25–34); and the raising of the daughter of Jairus from the dead (a resurrection, 5:21–24, 35–43).

The concluding phase of the Galilean ministry (6:7–8:26). The story of Jesus' movement away from the region of the Sea of Galilee, where so much of the action of 1:16–5:43 takes place, to his hometown of Nazareth in the hill country of Galilee (6:1–6) is Mark's third transitional text. In the ensuing fourth section of his gospel (6:7–8:26), Mark amplifies notes that he has sounded in the two previous sections—Jesus' amazing feats of power, his criticism of certain Jewish customs, and the growing opposition to him. He also initiates what will become an important theme in the gospel: the disciples' lack of understanding. The disciples are again featured at the beginning of this section, as Jesus sends the Twelve out on a mission (6:7–13). The rumor that Jesus is John the Baptist returned from the dead, mentioned along with other popular estimates of his person, leads Mark to include here a flashback explanation of John's death at the hands of Herod Antipas (6:14–29). After the return of the Twelve, the press of the crowds forces Jesus and his disciples into the wilderness, where the five thousand are fed (6:30–44). This is followed by Jesus' miraculous walking on the water, as he meets the disciples crossing the Sea of Galilee (6:45–52). At Gennesaret, on the western shore of the Sea, Jesus heals many people (6:53–56) and, shortly afterward, explains the real nature of impurity in response to Jewish criticism (7:1–23). Jesus then leaves Galilee (and Israel) for the regions of Tyre and Sidon to the North, where he commends the faith of a Gentile woman (7:24–30). Very quickly, however, we find him back in the regions around the Sea of Galilee, healing (7:31–37), feeding the four thousand (8:1–13), teaching without much success the "blinded" disciples (8:14–21), and, with considerably greater success, healing a physically blinded man (8:22–26).

The way of glory and suffering (8:27–10:52). Mark's gospel reaches its climax with Peter's recognition of Jesus' messiahship (8:27–30). It forms the fourth major transition in the gospel, as the emphasis shifts from the crowds and the power of Jesus displayed in miracles to the disciples and the cross. The ensuing fifth section of the gospel (8:27–10:52) has at its heart the thrice-repeated sequence of (1) Jesus' prediction of his death, (2) the disciples' failure, and (3) teaching about the cost of discipleship (8:31–38; 9:30–37; 10:32–45). In addition, we have in this section the transfiguration (9:1–13), the driving of a demon out of a young lad (9:14–29), and teaching about putting others first

(9:38–50), divorce (10:1–12), humility (10:13–16), and the difficulty of combining wealth with discipleship (10:17–31). The section concludes, as Jesus nears Jerusalem, with his giving sight to Bartimaeus in Jericho (10:46–52).

Final ministry in Jerusalem (11:1–13:37). Jesus' entrance into Jerusalem marks the beginning of the next major stage in the gospel: the days of confrontation with various Jewish groups and authorities preceding the passion (11:1–13:37). Jesus' public entry into the city, with its messianic overtones (11:1–11), sets the stage for the confrontation; and the cleansing of the temple (11:12–19), a strike at the heart of Judaism, forces the issue. The withering of the fig tree, in addition to being a lesson in faith, is also an acted parable of judgment upon Israel (11:20–25). It is thus no surprise that we find "the chief priests, the teachers of the law and the elders" challenging Jesus' authority (11:27–33), or Jesus telling a parable in which the Jewish leaders' rebelliousness to God is a prominent theme (12:1–12). Jesus is further questioned about the appropriateness of paying taxes to a Gentile ruler by "the Pharisees and Herodians" (12:13–17), about implications of the doctrine of resurrection by the Sadducees (12:18–27), and about the greatest commandment in the law by a teacher of the law (12:28–34). Finally, Jesus takes the initiative, asking about the interpretation of Psalm 110:1 in an effort to force the Jews to consider his claims to be Messiah (12:35–40). After Jesus' commending of a widow's sacrificial giving (12:41–44) comes the Olivet discourse, in which Jesus encourages the disciples to be faithful in light of coming suffering and as they look toward his triumphant return in glory (13:1–37).

The passion and empty-tomb narratives (15:1–16:8). The last section of Mark's gospel has two parts: the passion narrative (chaps. 14–15) and the story of the empty tomb (chap. 16). Mark leads into the passion narrative with his only mention of a definite date: it is two days before the Passover when the chief priests and teachers of the law plot Jesus' death (14:1–2). The narrative of Jesus' anointing in Bethany is found here for topical reasons (for it took place "six days before the Passover"; see John 12:1–8), namely, the anointing of Jesus' head points to his royal dignity (14:3–9). As Judas provides a means of arresting Jesus quietly, Jesus arranges for himself and the disciples to celebrate Passover together (14:12–26). After this meal, during which he uses elements of the Passover ritual to refer to his death, Jesus and the disciples leave the city for Gethsemane on the Mount of Olives, where Jesus agonizingly prays and is then arrested (14:27–52). There follows the series of judicial proceedings and trials: a nighttime hearing before the supreme Jewish council, the Sanhedrin (14:53–65), during which Peter denies the Lord (14:66–72), a quick morning trial before the Sanhedrin (15:1), and the decisive trial before the Roman procurator, Pontius Pilate (15:2–15). Pilate sentences Jesus to death by crucifixion; he is mocked by the soldiers and executed at Golgotha (15:16–41). The burial takes place that same day (15:42–47). But the despair of the women who saw him buried gives way to awe at the empty tomb and the angel's announcement of the resurrection (16:1–8).

AUTHOR

Like the other three gospels, Mark is anonymous. The title, "According to Mark" (κατὰ Μάρκον [*kata Markon*]),[2] was probably added when the Gospels were collected and there was need to distinguish Mark's version of the gospel from the others. The gospel titles are generally thought to have been added in the second century but may have been added much earlier.[3] Certainly we may say that the title indicates that by A.D. 125 or so an important segment of the early church thought that a person named Mark wrote the second gospel.

Mark's connection with the second gospel is asserted or assumed by many early Christian writers. Perhaps the earliest (and certainly the most important) of the testimonies is that of Papias, who was bishop of Hierapolis in Phrygia of Asia Minor until about A.D. 130. His statement about the second gospel is recorded in Eusebius's *History of the Church* (*Historia Ecclesiastica*), written in 325.

> And the presbyter used to say this, "Mark became Peter's interpreter [*hermēneutēs*] and wrote accurately all that he remembered, not indeed, in order, of the things said or done by the Lord. For he had not heard the Lord, nor had he followed him, but later on, as I said, followed Peter, who used to give teaching as necessity demanded but not making, as it were, an arrangement of the Lord's oracles, so that Mark did nothing wrong in writing down single points as he remembered them. For to one thing he gave attention, to leave out nothing of what he had heard and to make no false statements in them." (*H.E.* 3.39.15)[4]

Three important claims about the second gospel emerge from this statement:
1. Mark wrote the gospel that, in Eusebius's day, was identified with this name.
2. Mark was not an eyewitness but obtained his information from Peter.[5]
3. Mark's gospel lacks "order", reflecting the occasional nature of Peter's preaching.[6]

The importance of these claims is magnified when we realize that the presbyter whom Papias is quoting is the presbyter John, probably the apostle John himself. If Papias is to be trusted, the identification of Mark as the author of the second gospel goes back to the first generation of Christians.

Later Christian writers confirm that Mark was the author of the second gospel and that he depended on Peter for his information: Ireneus, *Adv. Haer.* 3.1.2 (A.D. 180); Tertullian, *Adv. Marc.* 4.5 (c. 200); Clement of Alexandria, *Hypotyposes* (c. 200), according to Eusebius (*H.E.* 6.14.5–7); Origen, *Comm. on Matt.* (early

---

[2]Or "The Gospel According to Mark"—the manuscript tradition makes it hard to be sure whether the longer or shorter form is the original. NA[26] prints the shorter, but Hengel argues for the longer ("The Titles of the Gospels and the Gospel of Mark," in *Studies in the Gospel of Mark* [Philadelphia: Fortress, 1985], pp. 66–67).

[3]Ibid., pp. 64–84.

[4]The quotation is taken from the translation by Kirsopp Lake in *Eusebius: Ecclesiastical History*, vol. 1, LCL (Cambridge: Harvard University Press, 1926).

[5]In identifying Mark as Peter's *hermēneutēs* Papias may mean that he was Peter's "translator" (from Aramaic into Greek) (see H. E. W. Turner, "The Tradition of Mark's Dependence upon Peter," *ExpTim* 71 [1959–60]: 260–63) or, more probably, his "interpreter," one who repeated and transmitted Peter's preaching (Zahn 2:442–44).

[6]This may mean that Mark, in the judgment of the presbyter, lacked chronological order (Martin Hengel, "Literary, Theological, and Historical Problems in the Gospel of Mark," in *Studies in the Gospel of Mark*, p. 48) or, more probably, that it lacked rhetorical/artistic order (Robert A. Guelich, *Mark 1–8:26*, WBC [Waco, Tex.: Word, 1989], p. xxvii).

third century), again according to Eusebius (*H.E.* 6.25.5); and, probably, the Muratorian Canon (a list of New Testament books drawn up c. 190 and so named because the sole manuscript to preserve the list, an incomplete Latin manuscript of the seventh or eighth century, was discovered and published by Cardinal L. A. Muratori in 1740).[7] Some scholars dismiss these testimonies as secondhand evidence going back to Papias, believing that Papias invents his claim about Mark's connection with Peter in order to defend the gospel against its detractors.[8] But Papias does not appear to be defending Mark's authorship or his connection with Peter but only the reliability of the gospel, against the charge that it lacked "order." Moreover, no dissenting voice from the early church regarding the authorship of the second gospel is found. This is surprising, since the tendency in the early church was to associate apostles with the writing of the New Testament books. While we must not uncritically accept everything that early Christian writers say about the origins of the New Testament, we should not reject what they say without good reason. The early and uncontested claim that Mark wrote the second gospel based on Peter's teaching can be overturned only by rather clear indications to the contrary from the gospel itself.

To assess this internal evidence, we must first identify the "Mark" intended by Papias and the other early Christian writers. That they refer to the (John) Mark mentioned in Acts (12:12, 25; 13:5, 13; 15:37) and in four New Testament epistles (Col. 4:10; Philem. 24; 2 Tim. 4:11; 1 Peter 5:13) is almost certain.[9] No other early Christian Mark would have been so well known as to be mentioned without further description.[10] Son of a woman prominent in the early Jerusalem church (Christians had gathered at her home during Peter's imprisonment [Acts 12:12]) and cousin of Barnabas (Col. 4:10), "John, also called Mark," accompanied Paul and Barnabas as far as Pamphylia, in Asia Minor, on the first missionary journey (Acts 13:5, 13). For whatever reason (and speculation has been rampant), Mark left Paul and Barnabas before the first journey ended, and Paul therefore refused to take him along on his second extended preaching trip. Barnabas disagreed with Paul's decision and separated himself from Paul, taking Mark along with him (Acts 15:36–40). Yet Paul and Mark were eventually reconciled: Paul mentions Mark's presence with him during his Roman imprisonment (Philem. 24; Col. 4:10). Peter, writing from Rome, also mentions that Mark was with him, calling him his son (1 Peter 5:13), perhaps implying that Mark had been converted through his ministry.[11] Mark has also been identified as the "young man" who "fled naked" from Gethsemane when Jesus was arrested (Mark 14:51–52): it has been argued that this enigmatic reference, peculiar to Mark's gospel, is an autobiographical reminiscence.[12] This may be the case, but the identification may call into question Papias's claim that Mark was not an eyewitness.[13]

---

[7]Justin Martyr mentions the "reminiscences of Peter" in conjunction with a quotation from Mark's gospel (*Dial.* 106).

[8]E.g. Kümmel, p. 95; Rudolf Pesch, *Das Markusevangelium*, 2 vols., HTKNT (Freiburg: Herder, 1976–80), 1:4–7.

[9]A few scholars think that an unknown Mark wrote the gospel (see, e.g., Pesch, *Markusevangelium*, 1:9–11).

[10]Jerome is the first explicitly to identify the Mark of the second gospel with the John Mark mentioned in the New Testament.

[11]See Zahn 2:427.

[12]E.g. A. B. Bruce, "The Synoptic Gospels," in *EGT* 1:441–42. Early tradition also identified the home of Mark and his mother as the location of the last supper.

Does the little we know of John Mark from the New Testament present any difficulty to identifying him as the author of the second gospel? Some scholars think so, pointing to Mark's alleged ignorance of Jewish customs and errors about Palestinian geography.[14] But neither difficulty stands up to scrutiny; careful and sympathetic interpretation of the alleged problem passages reveals no errors in such matters. In contrast, two features of Mark and his career as they are presented in the New Testament fit the author of the second gospel. The Greek style of Mark's gospel is simple and straightforward and full of the kind of Semitisms that one would expect of a Jerusalem-bred Christian.[15] And Mark's connection with Paul may help explain what many scholars have found to be a Pauline theological influence in the second gospel. Both features are far too general to offer any positive evidence toward an identification. But the important point is that nothing in the second gospel stands in the way of accepting the earliest tradition that identifies John Mark as its author. Our decision, then, will rest almost entirely on external evidence, and especially on the tradition handed down through Papias and Eusebius from the unnamed presbyter. Those who are skeptical of the reliability of Papias conclude that the author of the gospel is unknown.[16] Yet, as we have seen, there is nothing in the New Testament that is inconsistent with Papias's claim that Mark wrote the second gospel. And since we have no indication that anyone in the early church contested Papias's claim, we see no reason not to accept it.

But can we also accept the tradition that Mark is dependent on the preaching of Peter? Here, again, skepticism is rampant. Modern approaches to the Gospels consider the gospel material to be the product of a long and complex process of traditions-history, a view that has difficulty accommodating the direct connection between Mark and Peter suggested by Papias.[17] While recognizing this as something of a problem, two factors may mitigate its force. First, we must question whether the assuredness with which critics identify the origins and growth of traditions is always justified. In many cases the basis for such judgments does not appear to be strong, and we may well think that the derivation of a given pericope from Peter himself may satisfy the evidence equally well. Only a doctrinaire form critic would insist that all the gospel tradition must have been transmitted through the faceless "community."[18] Second, we must probably allow for Mark to have used sources other than Peter. As long as the apostle was a central source for the gospel, Papias's claim stands.

On the other side of the ledger are factors that could be taken to point to Peter's connection with the gospel. The vividness and detail of the second gospel is said to point to an eyewitness. Only Mark, for instance, mentions that the grass on

[13]Kümmel calls the identification "a strange and wholly improbable conjecture" (p. 95), but he gives no better explanation for the inclusion of these verses in Mark's gospel.

[14]E.g. ibid., pp. 96–97.

[15]Note Martin Hengel's judgment: "I do not know any other work in Greek which has so many Aramaic or Hebrew words and formulae in so narrow a space as does the second gospel" ("Literary, Theological, and Historical Problems," p. 46).

[16]E.g. Kümmel, pp. 95–97; Joachim Gnilka, Das Evangelium nach Markus, EKKNT, 2 vols. (Neukirchen-Vluyn: Neukirchener, 1978; Zürich: Benziger, 1979), 1:32–33.

[17]Thus, for instance, Guelich concludes that Papias is right in identifying Mark as the author but wrong in thinking that the gospel is based on the preaching of Peter (Mark 1–8:26, pp. xxvi–xxix).

[18]Martin 1:204–5.

which the five thousand sat was green (6:39). But even if valid (and some scholars insist that there was a tendency to *add* such detail to the tradition), this feature would do no more than show that there was some eyewitness testimony behind Mark's gospel.

This focus may be narrowed by another feature of the gospel: the especially critical light in which the Twelve are displayed. While found in all four gospels, the picture of the disciples as cowardly, spiritually blind, and hard of heart is particularly vivid in Mark. This, it is held, points to an apostolic viewpoint, for only an apostle would have been able to criticize the Twelve so harshly. Two other factors suggest that this apostolic witness may be Peter's. First, Peter figures prominently in Mark, and some of the references are most naturally explained as coming from Peter himself (e.g. the references to Peter "remembering" [11:21; 14:72]).[19] Second, C. H. Dodd has pointed out that Mark's gospel follows a pattern very similar to that found in Peter's rehearsal of the basic kerygma, the evangelistically oriented recitation of key events in Jesus' life, found in Acts 10:36–41.[20] We might add, finally, that Peter's reference to Mark as "my son" in his first letter fits nicely with the relationship between Peter and Mark mentioned by Papias; it discourages one from thinking Papias simply invented such a relationship.

Each of these factors is commensurate with the tradition that Mark is based on Peter's preaching, and one or two of them may even point slightly in that direction, but none of them, nor all of them together, is sufficient to establish the connection. Again, however, there seems to be no compelling reason to reject the common opinion of the early church on this matter.

PROVENANCE

Early tradition is not unanimous about the place where Mark wrote his gospel, but it favors Rome. The anti-Marcionite prologue to Mark (late second century?) claims that Mark wrote the gospel "in the regions of Italy." Both Ireneus (*Adv. Haer.* 3.1.2) and Clement of Alexandria (according to Eusebius, *H.E.* 6.14.6–7) suggest the same thing. Several considerations are said to confirm a Roman provenance: (1) the large number of Latinisms in the gospel;[21] (2) the incidental mention of Simon of Cyrene's sons, Alexander and Rufus, at least one of whom may have been known to Mark in Rome (when writing to the Roman church, Paul greets a Rufus [16:13]); (3) the apparently Gentile audience of the gospel; (4) the many allusions to suffering, which would be appropriate if the gospel was written under the shadow of persecutions of the church in Rome; (5) the fact that 1 Peter 5:13 locates Mark in Rome with Peter in the early sixties; and (6) the connection with an important early center of Christianity, which would have explained the gospel's quick acceptance.

---

[19]Ibid., 1:204.

[20]C. H. Dodd, "The Framework of the Gospel Narrative," *ExpTim* 43 (1932): 396–400.

[21]See esp. Mark's explanation of the widow's two copper coins as equaling a κοδράντης (*kodrantēs*), a Roman coin (12:42), and of the "courtyard" (αὐλή, [*aulē*]) as being a πραιτώριον (*praitōrion*), another distinctively Roman/Latin name (15:16). Readers in the eastern part of the Roman Empire would almost certainly have known these Greek terms. For a complete list of Mark's Latinisms, see Kümmel, pp. 97–98.

None of these points, however, carries much weight: numbers 1 and 3 could fit a provenance anywhere that boasted Gentiles and Latin influence; number 6 is of questionable validity and, even if accepted, could point to several possible locations (Jerusalem, Antioch, Ephesus); numbers 4 and 5 are valid only if Mark was written in the middle sixties (we will argue for an earlier date, in the middle or late fifties); and number 3 assumes that there was only one Rufus in the early church. Nevertheless, there is nothing in the gospel that is incompatible with a Roman provenance, and Mark may well have been in Rome with Peter for some years prior to the writing of 1 Peter.

The only other provenance that finds support in early tradition is Egypt (Chrysostom, *Hom. in Matt.* 1.3 [c. A.D. 400]). If Morton Smith is right, Clement of Alexandria may also have connected Mark with the church in Alexandria. According to Smith, a letter he discovered in the monastery of Mar-Saba in Egypt is an authentic letter of Clement, in which he says that Mark, after writing his gospel in Rome with Peter, came to Alexandria, where he composed a "deeper," Gnostic-oriented gospel.[22] But the authenticity of the letter is disputed, and in any case, it simply corroborates a Roman provenance for the canonical Mark. Chrysostom's identification of Egypt as the place of Mark's composition may even be a mistaken inference from Eusebius.[23]

Two other specific provenances have gained support from modern scholars. J. Vernon Bartlet argues for Antioch, noting, among other things, its proximity to Palestine (which explains why Mark assumes his readers will know Palestinian place-names), its large Roman colony, Peter's connection with Antioch, and the fact that the presbyter whom Papias quotes comes from the East.[24] Other scholars, while less specific, are inclined to think that Mark was written somewhere in the East.[25] In his groundbreaking redactional study of Mark, Willi Marxsen argues for a Galilean provenance. Noting the positive significance accorded to Galilee in Mark, Marxsen theorizes that Galilee, for Mark, was the place of revelation and that the references to Jesus "going before" the disciples into Galilee (14:28; 16:7) were a summons to Christians to gather in Galilee and await the return of Christ.[26] Marxsen's theory, however, is fraught with problems, and there is no convincing reason to locate Mark in Galilee. While certainty is impossible, a Roman provenance is the best alternative, granted the strength of the early tradition and the lack of any evidence from within the New Testament to the contrary.

DATE

Mark has been dated in four different decades: the forties, the fifties, the sixties, and the seventies.

---

[22]Morton Smith, *The Secret Gospel: The Discovery and Interpretation of the Secret Gospel According to Mark* (New York: Harper & Row, 1973).

[23]*H.E.* 2.16.1: "Mark is said to have been the first man to set out for Egypt and preach there the gospel which he had himself written down." See, e.g., Vincent Taylor, *The Gospel According to St. Mark*, 2d ed. (London: Macmillan, 1966), p. 32; Martin 1:215.

[24]J. Vernon Bartlet, *St. Mark* (London: Thomas Nelson & Sons, n.d.), pp. 5–6.

[25]E.g. Kümmel, p. 98. Bo Reicke suggests Caesarea, its Palestinian location fitting his theory of gospel origins, and its Roman flavor (it was the Roman admininistrative center) explaining the large number of Latinisms (*The Roots of the Synoptic Gospels* [Philadelphia: Fortress, 1986], pp. 165–66).

[26]Willi Marxsen, *Mark the Evangelist* (Nashville: Abingdon, 1969).

A Date in the Forties

A date in the forties has been proposed on the basis of historical and papyrological considerations. C. C. Torrey argues that Mark's "abomination that causes desolation" (13:14) is a reference to the attempt in A.D. 40 of the Emperor Caligula to have his image set up in the Jerusalem temple, and he contends that the gospel was written shortly after this.[27] But the identification is unlikely. José O'Callaghan bases his early dating of Mark on three papyrus fragments found at Qumran (7Q5; 7Q6,1, 7Q7), dated c. 50, which he claims contain, respectively, Mark 6:52–53, 4:28, and 12:17.[28] But most scholars have contested the identification;[29] even if it were valid, it would prove only the existence at this date of tradition that came to be incorporated into Mark. Another theory holds that Peter may have journeyed to Rome in the 40s after being freed from prison (see Acts 12:17) and that Mark may have written the gospel at that time.[30] But so early a date for Mark's gospel makes it hard to explain the silence of Paul and other New Testament writers about it, and it does not perhaps allow sufficient time for the development of the tradition behind Mark.

A Date in the Fifties

Another problem in the way of dating Mark as early as the forties arises if we give credence to the traditions that the gospel was written in Rome on the basis of the preaching of Peter. Although possible, it is not likely that Peter came to Rome in the early forties.[31] But there is evidence that Peter was in Rome in the middle fifties, making it possible to date Mark in the later fifties without contradicting the well-established tradition of the origin of the gospel.[32] The strongest case for this dating comes not from Mark directly but from the relationship of Mark to Luke-Acts. The argument assumes that Acts ends where it does, with Paul languishing in a Roman prison, because Luke published the work at that time—that is, in about A.D. 62. This would require that the gospel of Luke, the first volume of Luke's literary effort, be dated sometime before 62. If we then accept the

[27]C. C. Torrey, *The Four Gospels*, 2d ed. (New York: Harper, 1947), pp. 261–62. Moreover, Torrey's theory assumes an early Aramaic gospel of Mark. A similar proposal has recently been defended by Günther Zuntz ("Wann wurde das Evangelium Marci geschrieben?" in *Markus-Philologie: Historische, literargeschichtliche, und stilistische Untersuchungen zum zweiten Evangelium*, ed. Herbert Cancik, WUNT 33 [Tübingen: Mohr, 1984], pp. 47–71).

[28]José O'Callaghan, "Papiros neotestamentarios en la cuere 7 de Qumran," *Bib* 53 (1972): 91–100. See William Lane, *The Gospel According to Mark*, NICNT (Grand Rapids: Eerdmans, 1974), pp. 18–21, for a summary and discussion.

[29]See, e.g., Pierre Benoit, "Note sur les fragments grecs de la Grotte 7 de Qumran," *RevBib* 79 (1972): 321–24; Lane, *Mark*, pp. 19–21.

[30]J. W. Wenham, "Did Peter Go to Rome in A.D. 42?" *TynB* 23 (1972): 97–102.

[31]Wenham is representative of those who think that Peter may have come to Rome after his miraculous release from prison, recorded in Acts 12 ("Did Peter Go to Rome?" pp. 97–99). Yet Peter is back in Palestine by the time of the Jerusalem Council in A.D. 48 or 49 (Acts 15), and it is difficult to think that Paul and Barnabas would have taken on the first missionary journey one who had worked closely with Peter in Rome for some years. For a discussion of Peter's movements, see Oscar Cullmann, *Peter: Disciple, Apostle, Martyr*, 2d ed. (Philadelphia: Westminster, 1962), pp. 38–39.

[32]Peter was probably in Corinth before A.D. 55, when Paul wrote 1 Corinthians (see 1:12; 2:22), and in Rome in about 63 (the probable date of 1 Peter). Eusebius implies that Peter was in Rome during the reign of Claudius, who died in 54 (*H.E.* 2.14.6). The absence of any reference to Peter in Romans suggests that Peter was not in Rome in 57.

prevailing scholarly opinion that Luke used the canonical Mark as one of his key sources, Mark must have been written by 60, at the latest.[33] This argument is based on two key assumptions: that Acts is to be dated in the early 60s, and that Luke has used canonical Mark. Yet these assumptions are well founded (on Luke's use of canonical Mark, see chap. 1, and on the date of Acts, see chap. 6), and there is much to be said for this dating of Mark.

A Date in the Sixties

The majority of contemporary scholars date Mark in the sixties, for three reasons. First, the earliest traditions favor a date for Mark after the death of Peter.[34] Second, and perhaps more important for most, the internal evidence of Mark is said to favor a date during, or shortly after, the onset of persecution in Rome. Mark has much to say about the importance of disciples' following the "road to the cross" walked by our Lord. This emphasis best fits a situation when Christians were facing the grim prospect of martyrdom, a setting that would have obtained in Rome at the time of, or after, Nero's famous persecution of Christians in A.D. 65.[35] Third, Mark 13 is said to reflect the situation in Palestine during the Jewish revolt and just before the Roman entrance into the city, and thus it must be dated between 67 and 69.[36]

A Date in the Seventies

The main argument for dating Mark as late as the seventies rests on the assumption that Mark 13 reflects the actual experience of the sacking of Jerusalem by the Romans.[37] But the argument is seriously flawed. As several scholars have shown, Mark 13 shows very little evidence of being influenced by the course of events in A.D. 70. Jesus' predictions reflect stock Old Testament and Jewish imagery having to do with the beseiging of cities rather than the specific circumstances of the siege of Jerusalem.[38] Even more damaging to this argument is the assumption on the part of these critics that Jesus could not accurately have

---

[33]See esp. Adolf Harnack, *The Date of Acts and of the Synoptic Gospels* (New York: Putnam's, 1911). Reicke's argument is similar, although he thinks Mark was written at about the same time as Luke (*Roots of the Synoptic Gospels*, pp. 177–80). C. S. Mann thinks that Mark composed a first draft of his gospel in A.D. 55 (*Mark*, AB [Garden City, N.Y.: Doubleday, 1986], pp. 72–83).

[34]The anti-Marcionite prologue (late second century?), Irenaeus (A.D. 185; see *Adv. Haer.* 3.1.2), and perhaps Papias's citation of the presbyter (note the tense: "Mark, who *had been* Peter's interpreter").

[35]For this case, see esp. Cranfield, *Mark*, p. 8; Hugh Anderson, *The Gospel of Mark*, NCB (London: Marshall, Morgan & Scott, 1976), p. 26; Martin 1:213. Martin Hengel cites other arguments in support of a late date: (1) the clarity of Mark's writing; (2) Mark's lateness in comparison with Q; (3) the assumption in Mark of the existence of a worldwide mission (see 13:10; 14:9); and (4) the prophecy of the martyrdom of James and John ("The Gospel of Mark: Time of Origin and Situation," in *Studies in the Gospel of Mark*, pp. 12–28).

[36]Hengel, "Time of Origin," pp. 2–28; Augustine Stock, *The Method and Message of Mark* (Wilmington, Del.: Glazier, 1989), pp. 6–8; Guelich, *Mark* 1–8:26, pp. xxi–xxxii.

[37]See Kümmel, p. 68; Pesch, *Markusevangelium* 1:14; Gnilka, *Das Evangelium nach Markus* 1:34.

[38]See esp. Bo Reicke, "Synoptic Prophecies of the Destruction of Jerusalem," in *Studies in New Testament and Early Christian Literature*, ed. David E. Aune, SuppNovT 33 (Leiden: Brill, 1972), pp. 121–33; John A. T. Robinson, *Redating the New Testament* (Philadelphia: Westminster, 1976), pp. 13–30.

predicted the course of events in 70. As long as we grant Jesus the ability to do so, Mark 13 will offer no help in dating the gospel.

Conclusion

Mark, then, is to be dated either in the late fifties or the middle sixties. While the latter is the majority view, we favor the late fifties. Indeed, we are required to date Mark before A.D. 60 if our assumptions about the ending of Acts and the priority of Mark are valid. Mark's emphasis on persecution need not reflect a situation in which his readers are actually undergoing such persecution. Persecution, as the New Testament makes clear, is always a possibility for the believer, and Mark's inclusion of so much of Jesus' teaching on the subject is perfectly understandable on such a basis. Dating Mark in the fifties does go against the earliest traditions about Mark having been written after the death of Peter. But other traditions affirm that Mark wrote while Peter was still alive, so the early evidence is by no means unanimous on the subject.[39]

AUDIENCE AND PURPOSE

Mark is a self-effacing narrator. He tells his story with a minimum of editorial comments and says nothing about his purpose or his intended audience. We must depend, then, on the early testimonies about Mark and on the character of the gospel itself for information about his readers and his purpose.

Audience

The extrabiblical sources point to a Gentile Christian audience, probably in Rome. The Roman destination of Mark's gospel is simply an inference from its Roman provenance. If Mark wrote in Rome, he probably wrote to Romans. This is either stated or implied in the early traditions about the gospel, which have Mark recording the preaching of Peter for those who had heard the great apostle in Rome. As we have noted above, the many Latinisms of the gospel are compatible with, if not conclusive for, a Roman audience. That Mark writes to Gentiles seems clear from his translation of Aramaic expressions, his explanation of Jewish customs (such as the washing of hands before eating [7:3–4]), and, in the few texts he includes on the subject, his interest in the cessation of the ritual elements in the Mosaic law (see 7:1–23, esp. v. 19; 12:32–34).

---

[39]Clement of Alexandria says: "When Peter had preached the word publicly in Rome and announced the gospel by the Spirit, those present, of whom there were many, besought Mark, since for a long time he had followed him and remembered what had been said, to record his words. Mark did this, and communicated the gospel to those who made request of him. When Peter knew of it, he neither actively prevented nor encouraged the undertaking" (recorded by Eusebius in *H.E.* 6.14.6–7; the translation is from Taylor, *Mark*, pp. 5–6.) Tertullian may also witness to this tradition (see *Against Marcion* 4.5.3). It has even been argued that the key early traditions can be reconciled by understanding the word ἔξοδος (*exodos*) in Ireneus (e.g. "after the 'exodos' of these [Peter and Paul]") to refer not to their death but to their departure from Rome (so T. W. Manson, *Studies in the Gospels and Epistles*, ed. Matthew Black [Philadelphia: Westminster, 1962], pp. 34–40). Others reconcile the conflicting traditions by assuming that Mark began his gospel during Peter's lifetime but published it after his death (Zahn 2:433–34; Guthrie is favorable to the suggestion [p. 86]).

Purpose

Mark's purpose is much harder to determine. Interest in this question has been high because of its importance in redaction criticism, the most popular contemporary method of interpreting the Gospels. Redaction criticism of Mark is hampered by our inability to isolate the sources Mark has used, but this has not stood in the way of the quest for Mark's purpose. Redaction critics typically stress theological purposes in the writing of the Gospels, and this has certainly been the case with respect to Mark. The large number of specific proposals forbids our giving anything close to a complete survey. We mention here three representative intepretations, the first focusing on eschatology, the second on Christology, and the third on apologetics.

Willi Marxsen, who initiated the modern redactional study of Mark, thought that Mark wanted to prepare Christians for Jesus' imminent parousia in Galilee.[40] He argued that Mark focuses on Galilee, as the place where Jesus meets with his disciples, at the expense of Jerusalem, where Jesus is rejected and killed. Jesus' command to his disciples to meet him in Galilee (14:28; cf. 16:7) was taken by Marxsen as a prediction to Mark's community of Jesus' glorious return to them. But the meeting with Jesus to which these verses refer is clearly a postresurrection meeting, not the parousia.[41] Moreover, the geographic contrast that Marxsen (and some before him) discerns is much better explained as a reflection of the actual course of Jesus' ministry than as a theologically motivated invention of Mark's.

Theodore Weeden found in Mark a polemic against a "divine man" (*theios anēr*) Christology, a way of viewing Jesus that saw him as a wonder-working hero but denied or neglected his suffering and death.[42] To counter this tendency, Mark wrote a gospel that emphasized the humanity and suffering of Jesus. Weeden is correct to see in Mark a focus on Jesus' suffering, but he goes too far in identifying Mark's opponents as people who held to a divine-man Christology. For one thing, evidence for a polemical stance in Mark is not at all clear—he probably does not have any opponents in view at all.[43] For another, the very existence of a Hellenistic divine-man concept as a category into which early Christians would have put Jesus is open to question.[44]

A specific kind of apologetic was discerned in Mark by S. G. F. Brandon. He thought that Mark had attempted to mask the political implications of Jesus' life and, especially, his death. According to Brandon, Jesus was a sympathizer with the Jewish revolutionaries, the Zealots. For this reason he was crucified by the Romans, a method of execution generally reserved for political criminals. By branding Jesus as a rebel against Rome, his crucifixion made it very difficult for Christians to win a hearing from the Roman public—particularly in the aftermath of the Jewish revolt in Palestine, when, according to Brandon, Mark wrote his gospel. To overcome this difficulty, Mark transferred as much of the blame for Jesus' death from the Romans to the Jews as he could, a process revealed by the

---

[40]Marxsen, *Mark the Evangelist.*
[41]See, e.g., Robert H. Stein, "A Short Note on Mark XIV.28 and XVI.7," *NTS* 20 (1974): 445–52.
[42]Theodore Weeden, *Mark: Traditions in Conflict* (Philadelphia: Fortress, 1971).
[43]See Jack Dean Kingsbury, *The Christology of Mark's Gospel* (Philadelphia: Fortress, 1983).
[44]See, e.g., David Tiede, *The Charismatic Figure as Miracle Worker* (Missoula, Mont.: SP, 1972).

disciples, and his ascension. This long ending is printed as verses 9–20 in the KJV; in modern English versions, it usually appears in the margin or with a notation. Since it is found in the bulk of the manuscripts and can be traced to as early as the first half of the second century, this long ending can lay some claim to be considered as the original ending of Mark's gospel.[54]

But the arguments against this ending being original are very strong. First, it is missing from what are generally considered the two most important manuscripts (the uncials ℵ and B), as well as several others. Second, Jerome and Eusebius both state that the best manuscripts available to them did not contain this longer ending. Third, two other endings to the gospel exist: a shorter ending (attested in the uncials L, Ψ, 099, 0112, and some other witnesses), and the longer ending combined with an interpolation (attested in the uncial W and mentioned by Jerome). The presence of these alternative endings suggests that there was uncertainty about the ending of Mark for some time. Fourth, the longer ending contains several non-Markan words and expressions. Fifth, the longer ending does not flow naturally after 16:8: Jesus is presumed to be the subject in verse 9 (the Greek does not have an expressed subject), although "the women" was the subject in verse 8; Mary is introduced in verse 9 as if she has not been mentioned in verse 1; and "when Jesus rose early on the first day of the week" (v. 9) sounds strange after "very early on the first day of the week"(v.2). With the great majority of contemporary commentators and textual critics, then, we do not think that verses 9–20 were written by Mark as the ending for his gospel. The resemblances between what is narrated in these verses and the narrative of Jesus' resurrection appearances in the other gospels suggest that this longer ending was composed on the basis of these other narratives to supplement what was felt to be an inadequate ending to the gospel.[55]

If verses 9–20 were not the original ending to Mark's gospel, what was? Three main possibilities exist. First, Mark may have intended to write more but been prevented from doing so (by his death or arrest?).[56] Second, Mark may have written a longer ending to his gospel, including one or more resurrection appearances, and this ending may have been lost in the course of transmission. It has been suggested, for instance, that the last leaf of Mark's gospel—presuming the gospel was in the form not of a scroll but of a codex, or many-paged book—may have been accidentally torn off.[57] Third, Mark may have intended to end his gospel with verse 8. This third possibility is becoming more popular and is perhaps the most likely. Mark's gospel is typified by a degree of secrecy and understatement. For him to conclude his gospel with a plain announcement of the fact of the resurrection (v. 7) and the resulting astonishment and fear (perhaps to

---

[54]William R. Farmer has recently argued that Mark composed vv. 9–20 before writing his gospel and then added it at the end of this gospel as he finished (*The Last Twelve Verses of Mark*, SNTSMS 25 [Cambridge: Cambridge University Press, 1974]).

[55]The secondary character of the longer ending has been argued in the monograph by Joseph Hug, *La finale de l'évangile de Marc*, EBib (Paris: Gabalda, 1978).

[56]E.g. Zahn 2:479–80.

[57]C. F. D. Moule speculates that the loss of the "bottom sheet" could have resulted in both the ending and the beginning of the gospel being lost, and that 1:1, as 16:9–20, is a later attempt to fill in the resulting gaps (pp. 131–32n.).

be understood in the biblical sense as reverential awe) of the women would not be out of keeping with his purposes.[58]

RECENT STUDY

For many centuries, little attention was paid to Mark's gospel.[59] The early church quickly saw Matthew come to pride of place among the Gospels, with Mark considered to be a rather inferior and inconsequential extract from Matthew. It was only in the nineteenth century that Mark came into a position of prominence. The liberal school of interpretation, pioneered by scholars such as H. J. Holtzmann, found in Mark's simplicity of style and relative paucity of theological embellishment evidence of an earlier and more factual account of the life of Jesus than was presented in the other gospels. This isolation of Mark was destroyed by the work of W. Wrede. Specifically, Wrede argued that Mark had imposed on the tradition the notion of the messianic secret. Jesus' many commands for silence about his status in the gospel, argued Wrede, were invented by Mark in order to explain how it was that Jesus was not recognized to be the Messiah during his lifetime.[60] Today few hold to this notion of the messianic secret.[61] The motif itself is more likely to reflect the actual situation in the life of Jesus than it does a later invention.[62] But at the time, Wrede's work was taken to indicate that Mark wrote with just as much theological interest and bias as did the other evangelists.

The dominance of the form-critical approach during most of the first half of the twentieth century resulted in little interest in Mark as a gospel as such—attention was focused on the tradition before Mark. With the advent of redaction criticism in the 1950s, this changed, and the last three decades have witnessed an avalanche of studies on Mark's theology, purposes, and community. The contributions of Willi Marxsen, Theodore Weeden, S. G. F. Brandon, and Ralph Martin have been described above. To these could be added numerous other studies, devoted either to the gospel as a whole or to specific themes within the gospel. Two themes that receive considerable attention in recent studies are Mark's Christology[63] and his portrait of the disciples.[64]

The methodology of interpreting the Gospels, and Mark in particular, has also been the subject of debate. Some scholars are attempting to refine the technique of redaction criticism as it may be applied to Mark,[65] while at least one recent study

---

[58]See, e.g., Ned B. Stonehouse, *The Witness of Matthew and Mark to Christ*, reprint ed., with *The Witness of Luke to Christ* (Grand Rapids: Baker, 1979), pp. 86–118; Kümmel, pp. 100–01; Lane, *Mark*, pp. 590–92; Pesch, *Markusevangelium*, 1:40–47.

[59]For a history of interpretation of Mark's gospel, see Sean Kealy, *Mark's Gospel: A History of Its Interpretation from the Beginning Until 1979* (New York: Paulist, 1982); Martin, *Mark*, pp. 29–50.

[60]William Wrede, *The Messianic Secret* (London: J. Clarke, 1971); the German original was published in 1901.

[61]See David E. Aune, "The Problem of the Messianic Secret," *NovT* 11 (1969): 1–31.

[62]See, e.g., Hengel, "Literary, Historical, and Theological Problems," pp. 41–45.

[63]E.g. Kingsbury, *Christology*.

[64]E.g. Ernest Best, *Following Jesus: Discipleship in the Gospel of Mark*, JSNTSupp 4 (Sheffield: JSOT, 1981).

[65]E.g. E. J. Pryke, *Redactional Style in the Marcan Gospel: A Study of Syntax and Vocabulary as Guides to Redaction in Mark*, SNTSMS 33 (Cambridge: Cambridge University Press, 1978).

questions the fruitfulness of the whole approach for the study of Mark.[66] In this respect, we might mention two other methods that are being used in recent study of Mark. The first is sociological analysis, exhibited in Howard Clark Kee's *Community of the New Age*.[67] Kee analyzes Mark's community, suggesting that it was molded by an apocalyptic perspective and that Mark was seeking to redefine and encourage the community in light of God's purposes in history. Another direction is determined by the recent interest in the application of modern literary techniques to the Gospels. These studies focus on the way in which Mark, as a narrative, is put together and how it may be understood by the contemporary reader.[68] Mark's significance is then often seen to lie not in what he actually says but in the deeper structures created by his "narrative world." Older questions and methods continue to crop up in the recent literature as well. Notable in this respect is the series of articles by Martin Hengel, which show that Mark must be taken seriously as a historian of early Christianity and that his obvious theological interests do not force us to abandon his material as historically worthless.[69]

THE CONTRIBUTION OF MARK

One might be tempted to mimic the early church and wonder why one should bother with Mark at all. Those who do not consider the gospel an inferior extract of Matthew and/or Luke may well find Mark's significance to lie almost entirely in his supplying to these more verbose evangelists the basic raw material of their own gospels. On this view, Mark's significance could be considered mainly historical: he was the first to compose a gospel, the first to set forth an account of the ministry of Jesus in this peculiar and largely unparalleled genre.

But that accomplishment in itself should not be underrated. Mark is the creator of the gospel in its literary form—an interweaving of biographical and kerygmatic themes that perfectly conveys the sense of meaning of that unique figure in human history, Jesus of Nazareth, the Son of God. Furthermore, by tying the significance of Jesus for the church so tightly to a specific series of historical occurrences in Palestine in the the third decade of the first century, Mark has ensured that the church, if it is to be true to its canonical documents, never abandons the real humanity of the Christ whom it worships. By reminding Christians that their salvation depends on the death and resurrection of Christ, Mark has inextricably tied Christian faith to the reality of historical events.

Mark's very organization of this history makes a point in this regard. The structure of the gospel has been understood in various ways. Philip Carrington suggested that a synagogue lectionary sequence lies at the basis of its structure,[70]

[66]C. Clifton Black, *The Disciples According to Mark: Markan Redaction in Current Debate*, JSNTSupp 27 (Sheffield: JSOT, 1989).
[67]Howard Clark Kee, *Community of the New Age* (Philadelphia: Westminster, 1977).
[68]See, e.g., Elizabeth Struthers Malbon, *Narrative Space and Mythic Meaning in Mark* (San Francisco: Harper & Row, 1986); B. L. Mack, *A Myth of Innocence: Mark and Christian Origins* (Philadelphia: Fortress, 1988); Mary Ann Tolbert, *Sowing the Gospel: Mark's World in Literary-Historical Perspective* (Minneapolis: Augsburg/Fortress, 1989).
[69]Hengel's essays have been collected in *Studies in the Gospel of Mark* (Philadelphia: Fortress, 1985).
[70]Philip Carrington, *The Primitive Christian Calendar* (Cambridge: Cambridge University Press, 1952).

Table 5
Parallels between Peter's Preaching and Mark

Acts 10	Mark
"good news" (v. 36)	"the beginning of the gospel" (1:1)
"God anointed Jesus of Nazareth with the Holy Spirit" (v. 38)	the coming of the Spirit on Jesus (1:10)
"beginning in Galilee" (v. 37)	the Galilean ministry (1:16–8:26)
"He went around doing good and healing all who were under the power of the devil" (v. 38)	Jesus' ministry focuses on healings and exorcisms
"We are witnesses of everything he did . . . in Jerusalem" (v. 39)	the ministry in Jerusalem (chaps. 11–14)
"They killed him by hanging him on a tree" (v. 39)	focus on the death of Christ (chap. 15)
"God raised him from the dead on the third day" (v. 40)	"He has risen! He is not here." (16:6)

but this is most unlikely.[71] Equally improbable is the complicated series of Old Testament correspondences discerned by Austin Farrer.[72] Most think that geography plays a significant role in the gospel's structure, and there is truth to this. But the significance of the geography lies not in some particular theological scheme of Mark's but in the actual sequence of the ministry of Jesus. As C. H. Dodd has noted, the sequence of Mark's gospel follows the same sequence revealed in the early church's preaching.[73] In table 5 note the parallels between the preaching of Peter in Acts 10:36–40 and the structure of Mark.

While the sequence in table 5 is to a considerable extent dictated by the actual course of events, Mark's straightforward, action-oriented account preserves the sequence more clearly than do the other gospels. The kerymatic structure of Mark helps the readers of the gospel understand the basic salvation events and prepares them to recite those events in their own evangelism.

This same bare-bones narrative sequence also throws into prominence the structural divide of Caesarea Philippi. Though often differing on the structure of Mark, commentators find in this incident the hinge on which the gospel turns. The material in 1:1–8:26, with its stress on Jesus' miracles, leads up to Peter's divinely given insight into the true nature of the man Jesus of Nazareth. But immediately after the confession, and dominating the remainder of the gospel, is the focus on the suffering and death of Jesus. As we have noted, this combination of emphases reveals a major Christological purpose of Mark's: Jesus is the suffering Son of God and can truly be understood only in terms of this suffering.

As we also noted above when discussing the purpose of the gospel, another

---

[71]On the issue of Jewish lectionaries and the Gospels, see Leon Morris, *The New Testament and the Jewish Lectionaries* (London: Tyndale, 1964).

[72]Austin Farrer, *A Study in St. Mark* (Westminster: Dacre, 1951).

[73]Dodd, "Framework of the Gospel Narrative." Dodd's scheme was criticized by D. E. Nineham (*Studies in the Gospels* [Oxford: Blackwell, 1955], pp. 223–39) but has been accepted by others (e.g. Lane, *Mark*, pp. 10–12).

central theme in Mark is discipleship. The Twelve figure very prominently in Mark and serve in general as a pattern for the disciples whom Mark addresses in his gospel. To be sure, the Twelve are not always presented as models to be emulated: their conspicuous failure, though present to some degree in the other gospels, is especially prominent in Mark. Mark portrays the disciples as hard of heart (e.g. 6:52), spiritually weak (e.g. 14:32–42), and incredibly dim-witted (e.g. 8:14–21). As Guelich puts it, Mark presents the disciples as both "privileged and perplexed."[74] Perhaps in both these ways they are models for the disciples of Mark's day and of ours: privileged to belong to the kingdom, yet perplexed about the apparent reverses suffered by that kingdom when Christians suffer. In another way, Mark perhaps wants implicitly to contrast the situation of the Twelve, seeking to follow Jesus before the cross and the resurrection, with that of Christian disciples at his time of writing: the latter, however, follow Jesus with the help of the powers of the new age of salvation that has dawned.

BIBLIOGRAPHY

Hugh **Anderson**, *The Gospel of Mark*, NCB (London: Marshall, Morgan & Scott, 1976); David E. **Aune**, "The Problem of the Messianic Secret," *NovT* 11 (1969): 1–31; J. Vernon **Bartlet**, *St. Mark* (London: Thomas Nelson, n.d.); Pierre **Benoit**, "Note sur les fragments grecs de la Grotte 7 de Qumran," *RevBib* 79 (1972): 321–24; Ernest **Best**, *Following Jesus: Discipleship in the Gospel of Mark*, JSNT 4 (Sheffield: JSOT, 1981); idem, "Mark's Narrative Technique," *JSNT* 37 (1989): 43–58; Gilbert **Bilezikian**, *The Liberated Gospel: A Comparison of the Gospel of Mark and Greek Tragedy* (Grand Rapids: Baker, 1977); C. Clifton **Black**, *The Disciples According to Mark: Markan Redaction in Current Debate*, JSNT 27 (Sheffield: JSOT, 1989); Josef **Blinzler**, *Der Prozess Jesu*, 2d ed. (Regensburg: Pustet, 1955); A. B. **Bruce**, "The Synoptic Gospels," in *EGT* 1; T. A. **Burkill**, *Mysterious Revelation: An Examination of the Philosophy of St. Mark's Gospel* (Ithaca, N.Y.: Cornell University Press, 1963); Herbert **Cancik**, "Die Gattung Evangelium: Das Evangelium des Markus in Rahmen der antiken Historiographie," in *Markus-Philologie*, ed. H. Cancik, WUNT 33 (Tübingen: Mohr, 1984); Philip **Carrington**, *The Primitive Christian Calendar: A Study in the Making of the Marcan Gospel* (Cambridge: Cambridge University Press, 1952); David R. **Catchpole**, *The Trial of Jesus: A Study in the Gospels and Jewish Historiography from 1770 to the Present Day* (Leiden: Brill, 1971); C. E. B. **Cranfield**, *The Gospel According to St. Mark*, CGTC (Cambridge: Cambridge University Press, 1966); Oscar **Cullmann**, *Peter: Disciple, Apostle, Martyr*, 2d ed. (Philadelphia: Westminster, 1962); Martin **Dibelius**, *From Tradition to Gospel* (New York: Charles Scribner's Sons, n.d.); C. H. **Dodd**, "The Framework of the Gospel Narrative," *ExpTim* 43 (1932): 396–400; William **Farmer**, *The Last Twelve Verses of Mark's Gospel*, SNTSMS 25 (Cambridge: Cambridge University Press, 1974); Austin **Farrer**, *A Study in St. Mark* (Westminster: Dacre, 1951); Joachim **Gnilka**, *Das Evangelium nach Markus*, 2 vols., EKKNT (Neukirchen-Vluyn: Neukirchener, 1978; Zürich: Benziger, 1979); Robert A. **Guelich**, *Mark 1–8:26*, WBC (Waco, Tex.: Word, 1989); Ernst **Haenchen**, *Der Weg Jesu: Eine Erklarung des Markusevangelium und der kanonischen Parallelen* (Berlin: Töpelmann, 1966); Adolf **Harnack**, *The Date of Acts and of the Synoptic Gospels* (New York: Putnam, 1911); Martin **Hengel**, *Studies in the Gospel of Mark* (Philadelphia: Fortress,

---

[74]Guelich, *Mark* 1–8:26, p. xlii.

1985); Joseph **Hug**, *La finale de l'évangile de Marc*, EBib (Paris: Gabalda, 1978); Sean **Kealy**, *Mark's Gospel: A History of Its Interpretation from the Beginning Until 1979* (New York: Paulist, 1982); Howard Clark **Kee**, *Community of the New Age: Studies in Mark's Gospel* (Philadelphia: Westminster, 1977); Werner H. **Kelber**, *Mark's Story of Jesus* (Philadelphia: Fortress, 1979); idem, ed., *The Passion in Mark: Studies in Mark 14–16* (Philadelphia: Fortress, 1976); Jack Dean **Kingsbury**, *The Christology of Mark's Gospel* (Philadelphia: Fortress, 1983); William L. **Lane**, *The Gospel According to Mark*, NICNT (Grand Rapids: Eerdmans, 1974); Eta **Linnemann**, *Studien zur Passionsgeschichte*, FRLANT 102 (Göttingen: Vandenhoeck & Ruprecht, 1970); Ernst **Loymeyer**, *Galiläa und Jerusalem*, FRLANT 34 (Göttingen: Vandenhoeck & Ruprecht, 1936); B. L. **Mack**, *A Myth of Innocence: Mark and Christian Origins* (Philadelphia: Fortress, 1988); Elizabeth Struthers **Malbon**, *Narrative Space and Mythic Meaning in Mark* (San Francisco: Harper & Row, 1986); C. S. **Mann**, *Mark*, AB (Garden City, N.Y.: Doubleday, 1986); T. W. **Manson**, *Studies in the Gospels and the Epistles*, ed. Matthew Black (Philadelphia: Westminster, 1962); Ralph P. **Martin**, *Mark: Evangelist and Theologian* (Grand Rapids: Eerdmans, 1972); Willi **Marxsen**, *Mark the Evangelist* (Nashville: Abingdon, 1969); Frank J. **Matera**, *What Are They Saying About Mark?* (New York: Paulist, 1987); Leon **Morris**, *The New Testament and the Jewish Lectionaries* (London: Tyndale, 1964); D. E. **Nineham**, *Studies in the Gospels* (Oxford: Blackwell, 1955); José **O'Callaghan**, "Papiros neotestamentarios en la cuere 7 de Qumran," *Bib* 53 (1972): 91–100; David Barrett **Peabody**, *Mark as Composer* (Macon, Ga.: Mercer University Pres⸱ 1987); Rudolf **Pesch**, *Das Markusevangelium*, 2 vols., HTKNT (Freiburg: Herder, 1976–80); E. J. **Pryke**, *Redactional Style in the Marcan Gospel*, SNTSMS 33 (Cambridge: Cambridge University Press, 1978); Quentin **Quesnell**, *The Mind of Mark: Interpretation and Method Through the Exegesis of Mark 6,52*, AnBib 38 (Rome: Pontifical Biblical Institute, 1969); Gottfried **Rau**, "Das Markusevangelium: Komposition und Intention der ersten Darstellung christliches Mission," *ANRW* 25.3 (1985): 2036–2257; Bo **Reicke**, *The Roots of the Synoptic Gospels* (Philadelphia: Fortress, 1986); idem, "Synoptic Prophecies of the Destruction of Jerusalem," in *Studies in New Testament and Early Christian Literature*, ed. David E. Aune, SuppNovT 33 (Leiden: Brill, 1972), pp. 121–33; J. A. T. **Robinson**, *Redating the New Testament* (Philadelphia: Westminster, 1976); Eduard **Schweizer**, *The Good News According to Mark* (Richmond: John Knox, 1970); Morton **Smith**, *The Secret Gospel* (New York: Harper & Row, 1973); Robert H. **Stein**, "A Short Note on Mark XIV.28 and XVI.8," *NTS* 20 (1974): 445–52; Augustine **Stock**, *The Method and Message of Mark* (Wilmington, Del: Glazier, 1989); Ned B. **Stonehouse**, *The Witness of Matthew and Mark to Christ*, reprint ed., with *The Witness of Luke to Christ* (Grand Rapids: Baker, 1979); Vincent **Taylor**, *The Gospel According to St. Mark*, 2d ed. (London: Macmillan, 1966); David **Tiede**, *The Charismatic Figure as Miracle Worker* (Missoula, Mont.: SP, 1972); G. Minette de **Tillesse**, *Le secret messianique dans l'évangile de Marc* (Paris: Cerf, 1968); Mary Ann **Tolbert**, *Sowing the Gospel: Mark's World in Literary-Historical Perspective* (Minneapolis: Augsburg/Fortress, 1989); C. C. **Torrey**, *The Four Gospels* (New York: Harper, 1947); Étienne **Trocmé**, *The Formation of the Gospel According to Mark* (London: SPCK, 1975); H. E. W. **Turner**, "The Tradition of Mark's Dependence upon Peter," *ExpTim* 71 (1959–60): 260–63; Theodore J.

Weeden, *Mark: Traditions in Conflict* (Philadelphia: Fortress, 1971); J. W. **Wenham**, "Did Peter Go to Rome in A.D. 42?" *TynB* 23 (1972): 97–102; William **Wrede**, *The Messianic Secret* (London: J. Clarke, 1971); Günther **Zuntz**, "Wann wurde das Evangelium Marci geschrieben?" in *Markus-Philologie*, ed. H. Cancik, WUNT 33 (Tübingen: Mohr, 1984).

4

Luke

CONTENTS

Luke's Gospel is the longest book in the New Testament, and it includes a good deal of material not found elsewhere. We may see something of the movement Luke discerns if we look at five principal sections in his story.

Christian beginnings (1:1–4:13). After a short preface (1:1–4), Luke has a section peculiar to himself on the infancy of John the Baptist and of Jesus. He tells us that the angel Gabriel foretold the birth of John the Baptist (1:5–25) and that of Jesus (1:26–38). He writes of a visit Mary paid Elizabeth (1:39–45) and gives the text of the song of Mary (1:46–56). The birth and naming of John follow (1:57–66), and then comes the song of Zechariah (1:67–80). He goes on to the birth of Jesus, together with the story of the angels and the shepherds (2:1–20), the presentation of the baby Jesus in the temple (2:21–40), and the one story we have of the boy Jesus (2:41–52). The ministry of John the Baptist follows (3:1–20), and then his baptism of Jesus (3:21–22), Jesus' genealogy (3:23–38), and the temptation narrative (4:1–13).

Jesus in Galilee (4:14–9:50). Jesus' public ministry in Galilee begins with his sermon at Nazareth (4:14–30) and accounts of his healings (4:31–41) and of a preaching tour (4:42–44). He brings about a miraculous catch of fish, ending in a call of Simon to catch men (5:1–11), and then heals a leper (5:12–16) and a paralytic (5:17–26). He calls Levi (5:27–32) and deals with a question about fasting (5:33–39). The right use of the Sabbath (6:1–11) and the calling of the Twelve (6:12–16) are presented. Now comes the Sermon on the Plain, with its important teachings on love (6:17–49), then the healing of the centurion's slave (7:1–10) and the raising from the dead of the son of a widow at Nain (7:11–17). John the Baptist's questions follow (7:18–35) and then the anointing of Jesus by a sinful woman (7:36–50). Luke goes on to speak of women who helped Jesus (8:1–3) and to narrate the parable of the sower (8:4–15), which he follows with teaching about the lamp and the cover (8:16–18) and about his mother and brothers (8:19–21). Next come the stilling of the storm (8:22–25), the healing of the Gerasene demoniac (8:26–39), and the twin story of the healing of the woman with the hemorrhage and the raising of the daughter of Jairus (8:40–56). In chapter 9 we have the mission of the Twelve (9:1–6), the perplexity of Herod (9:7–9), the feeding of the five thousand (9:10–17), the recognition that Jesus is the Christ and its consequence for discipleship (9:18–27), the transfiguration (9:28–36), the healing of the boy with an evil spirit (9:37–45), and teaching about discipleship (9:46–50).

Jesus' journey to Jerusalem (9:51–19:44). In this long section about Jesus' journey from Galilee to Jerusalem, it is not easy to follow the course of the journey or to determine at most points of the narrative just where on the journey Jesus is. Luke seems more intent on stressing the journey motif than in giving precise locations. He is making the point that Jesus moved consistently forward on his way to Jerusalem for the consummation of the work he came on earth to accomplish.[1] The section begins with more lessons on discipleship (9:51–62) and with Jesus sending out seventy-two preachers to the towns he was about to visit and with his response to their report (10:1–24). The parable of the Good Samaritan follows (10:25–37), then Jesus' visit to the home of Martha and Mary (10:38–42). Luke goes on to the Lord's Prayer (11:1–4) and teaching about prayer (11:5–13). An important passage about evil spirits makes it clear that Jesus is too strong for the powers of evil (11:14–26), after which there is a long section on Jesus' teaching the people, with warnings, encouragement, worry, watchfulness, and divisions coming in for attention (11:27–12:59). Repentance is stressed (13:1–9) before Jesus heals a crippled woman in a synagogue on a sabbath (13:10–17). There is teaching about the kingdom of God (13:18–30) and a lament over Jerusalem (13:31–35). There is interesting teaching a a meal in the house of a prominent Pharisee, including the parable of the excuses (14:1–24) and a statement of the cost of discipleship (14:25–35). Luke follows with three parables about the lost sheep, the lost coin, and the lost son (15:1–32), another about an unjust manager (16:1–9), and further teaching, mostly about money, that includes the parable of the rich man and Lazarus (16:10–31). There is teaching about service (17:1–10), the healing of ten men with leprosy (17:11–19), the coming of God's kingdom (17:20–37), and two parables about prayer (18:1–14). Luke reports the bringing of children to Jesus (18:15–17) and the story of the rich young ruler (18:18–30). Jesus prophesies his passion (18:31–34), and Luke proceeds to two stories situated in Jericho and its vicinity: the healing of a blind beggar (18:35–43) and Jesus' visit to Zaccheus (19:1–10). He narrates the parable of the pounds (19:11–26) and Jesus' triumphal entry into Jerusalem (19:28–44).

Jesus in Jerusalem (19:45–21:38). This section is devoted to what Jesus did and taught in Jerusalem. Luke reports the cleansing of the temple (19:45–46) and Jesus' teaching (19:47–48), including teaching about his authority (20:1–8). The parable of the wicked tenants (20:9–18) is followed by a series of attempts to trap Jesus (20:19–44) and by a warning about the teachers of the law (20:45–47). Luke tells us of the widow's gift (21:1–4) and moves into Jesus' eschatological discourse (21:5–36). The section ends with further teaching in the temple (21:37–38).

Jesus' crucifixion and resurrection (22:1–24:53). Luke begins his crucifixion narrative with Judas's betrayal of Jesus (22:1–6) and goes on to the last supper and related teaching in the upper room (22:7–38). He speaks of Jesus' agony and

---

[1]"He deemphasizes all topographical data except those relating to Jerusalem, and the result is striking" (Robert/Feuillet, p. 230).

prayer (22:39–46) and of his arrest (22:47–54). Peter's denials and the soldiers' mockery follow (22:55–65), and then we see Jesus before the Sanhedrin (22:66–71), before Pilate (23:1–5), and before Herod (23:6–12). Jesus is sentenced (23:13–25) and crucified (23:26–49), then buried by Joseph of Arimathea (23:50–56). The resurrection narrative begins with two men in gleaming clothes telling the women that Jesus has risen (24:1–11) and with Peter at the tomb (24:12). There is the beautiful story of Jesus' appearance to the two as they walk to Emmaus (24:13–35), followed by his appearance to the disciples (24:36–49). Luke concludes his gospel with a brief account of the ascension (24:50–53).

AUTHOR

Most critics agree that Luke and Acts are from the same author. Acts 1:1 refers to Theophilus and to the "former book," so that Acts appears to be the second volume of a two-volume work. The style and the vocabulary are what we would expect from the same author, and no good reason has been brought forward for disputing this. That Luke was this author is affirmed by the heretic Marcion about the middle of the second century, by an ancient prologue to this gospel (often called the anti-Marcionite prologue),[2] apparently written toward the end of the second century, and by the Muratorian Canon. Authors such as Ireneus and Tertullian write as though there was no doubt about the Lukan authorship of these books. The oldest MS of Luke, Bodmer Papyrus XIV, cited as p^{75} and dated A.D. 175–225, ascribes the book to Luke.[3] The tradition attaches no other name to these writings.[4] We should bear in mind the point made by M. Dibelius that a book bearing the name of the person to whom it was dedicated is unlikely to have lacked the author's name (it would have been on an attached tag).[5] It is not easy to see how some other name would have been completely suppressed, or why the name Luke should have been attached to the writings if he had not produced them. In patristic discussions apostolicity receives a good deal of emphasis as a criterion for acceptance of books, so if the author was not known, it would have been much more likely that an apostle or someone like Mark would have been credited with them. As far as we know, Luke was not such an eminent member of the early church as to have writings like these attributed to him without reason. The preface shows that the author was not an eyewitness of Jesus' ministry but that he had made careful inquiries, and this agrees with what tradition says about Luke.

In four passages of Acts the writer uses "we" in such a way as to suggest that he

---

[2]Both the Greek and the Latin forms of the prologue are printed in Kurt Aland, *Synopsis Quattuor Evangeliorum* (Stuttgart: Württembergische Bibelanstalt, 1964), p. 533. R. G. Heard cites the Greek text and an English translation ("The Old Gospel Prologues," *JTS* 6 [1955]: 7).

[3]Joseph A. Fitzmyer, *The Gospel According to Luke* I–IX, 2d ed. (New York: Doubleday, 1983), pp. 35–36. Kirsopp Lake said, of the titles of all four Gospels, "Why should this testimony not be accepted? No reason has ever been shown, for the view that antiquity tended to anonymous books is contrary to evidence" (Lake, p. 4).

[4]E. Earle Ellis calls the view that before the middle of the second century someone used "shrewd detective work" to discover a previously unknown author of this gospel "an exercise in improbabilities" (*The Gospel of Luke* [London: Nelson, 1966], p. 42).

[5]M. Dibelius, *Studies in the Acts of the Apostles* (London: SCM, 1956), p. 148. He also says forthrightly, "Both writings, Gospel and Acts, were offered to the literary reading public from the very beginning under the name of Luke as author" (p. 89).

was present on those occasions (Acts 16:10–17; 20:5–16; 21:1–18; 27:1–28:16). The use of the first-person singular in the openings of both Luke and Acts perhaps supports these passages, showing as it does that the author took a personal interest in what he was writing. The last "we" passage locates the writer in Rome at the time of Paul's imprisonment there, so the author is one of those mentioned as being with Paul at that time and is probably not mentioned in Acts. This leaves us with Titus, Demas, Crescens, Jesus Justus, Epaphras, Epaphroditus, and Luke. No good reason seems ever to have been adduced for ascribing the authorship of Luke-Acts to any of the others, so we come back to Luke. The objection that no one who had been a companion of Paul would show as little interest in his letters as Luke-Acts does or would be so un-Pauline in his theology is without foundation, for we have no means of knowing how much Paul's travel companions knew about his correspondence or how deeply they entered into his theology. Those who argue for a late date suggest that the author was not the diarist but someone who had access to the diary of a travel companion of the apostle. But the style of the "we" sections is the same as that of the rest of Luke-Acts, so this demands that the writer be clever enough to rewrite the original so thoroughly that its initial style has disappeared and at the same time so carelessly that he did not always change "we" to "they." This is highly improbable.

From the "we" passages we learn that the author stayed at the house of Philip the Evangelist in Caesarea (Acts 21:8) and that it was not until a couple of years later that Paul and his entourage sailed for Rome (Acts 24:27; 27:1). There was clearly abundant opportunity for the writer to glean a good deal of information about Jesus and about the life of the early church.

Rendel Harris developed an argument that the original Western text of Acts 20:13 read, "But I Luke, and those who were with me, went on board," and F. F. Bruce reasons that, if this can be accepted, we have testimony to the Lukan authorship c. A.D. 120, for this is "the probable date of the 'Western' recension." He further points out that the Mechitarist Fathers published an Armenian translation of Ephrem's commentary on Acts and that it contains these very words in Acts 20:13.[6] If this can be accepted, it is very early evidence indeed of Lukan authorship.

In earlier days a good deal was made of the medical language of Luke-Acts,[7] but H. J. Cadbury has shown that there is not much in this, for medical writers seem by and large to have used much the same language as other people, and Cadbury maintains that in any case Luke's language is not particularly medical.[8] But if the medical language is no longer a strong proof that the author was "our dear friend Luke, the doctor" (Col. 4:14), at least it is not inconsistent with that hypothesis. Some passages indicate a medical interest, for example, when Luke speaks of a "high" fever, where Matthew and Mark speak only of a fever (Luke 4:38; Matt. 8:14; Mark 1:30). Other such examples could be adduced.[9]

---

[6]F. F. Bruce, *The Acts of the Apostles* (London: Tyndale, 1951), p. 5.

[7]This was argued by W. K. Hobart, *The Medical Language of St. Luke* (Dublin: Hodges, Figgis, 1882), and less strongly by A. Harnack, *Luke the Physician* (New York: Putnam, 1907).

[8]H. J. Cadbury, *The Style and Literary Method of Luke*, HTS 6 (Cambridge: Harvard University Press, 1919).

[9]Alfred Wikenhauser agrees that the language does not prove a medical author, but then adds, "Nevertheless the tradition need not be abandoned, and it may still be sustained, for the author

The strongest objection to Luke as the author is the contention that the author of Acts cannot have been a companion of Paul's, partly on account of the difficulties in reconciling some statements in Acts with what Paul says in his letters (e.g. in references to Paul's visits to Jerusalem, cf. Acts 9:26; 11:30; 15:2 and Gal. 1:18; 2:1), partly because of the theology Acts attributes to Paul.[10] Such objections do not seem valid; it may be sufficient to refer to the chapter in this book on Acts.

Luke is usually held to have been a Gentile Christian. In Colossians 4:10-14. Paul refers to Aristarchus, Mark, and Jesus Justus as "the only Jews among my fellow workers" and a little later sends greetings from Luke, which seems clearly to place Luke among the Gentile believers. This is denied by some, but the denial is not convincing. He may have been a Greek, but this does not itself suggest he sprang from Greece. The ancient prologue referred to earlier says that he was a native of Antioch;[11] we cannot be sure. He was quite clearly an educated man, and he writes very good Greek (note his reference to "their language" in Acts 1:19; Aramaic was not Luke's language). He starts with a paragraph in classical style (1:1–4). The remainder of his first two chapters has a strongly Hebraic strain,[12] while the remainder of the book is in a good Hellenistic Greek that constantly reminds the reader of the Septuagint. This versatility points to a writer of no mean competence.[13]

PROVENANCE

According to the anti-Marcionite prologue Luke came from Antioch and wrote his gospel "in the regions of Achaea."[14] It would fit in with what we know if Luke remained in Rome until Paul was released from prison (or executed if we hold that he was not released), then went to Greece and wrote his gospel. But it must be emphasized that this is speculation. In some late MSS Rome is given as the place of composition, but it is not known on what basis. A few scholars stress the connection of Luke with Antioch. Eusebius says he was "by race an Antiochian" (*H.E.* 3.4.6), but this is not the same as saying that he wrote his gospel in that city. In the end we must say that there is not sufficient evidence to link the gospel

---

displays familiarity with medical terminology (cf. e.g. Lk. 4,38; 5,12; 8,44; Acts 5,5 10; 9,40), and he indisputably describes maladies and cures from the point of view of a medical man (e.g. Lk. 4,35; 13,11; Acts 3,7; 9,18)" (*New Testament Introduction* [ET New York: Herder, 1963], p. 209); his conclusion is only slightly softened in the latest (German) edition (Wikenhauser, pp. 254–55).

[10]Robert M. Grant points out that such a claim "neglects the extent to which it is possible to associate and work with others without necessarily sharing all their concerns; in other words, it fails to do justice either to the variety to be found within the unity of modern Christianity or to that within the early Church" (Grant, p. 135).

[11]This is supported by the fact that D and a few other authorities make Acts 11:28, locating events at Antioch, a "we" passage.

[12]On the significance of the Semitic flavor of the language in chaps. 1–2, esp. in the so-called hymns, see Stephen Farris, *The Hymns of Luke's Infancy Narratives: Their Origin, Meaning, and Significance*, JSNTSupp 9 (Sheffield: JSOT, 1985).

[13]"He composed his narrative (*diēgēsis*) not merely as an ancient historian of the Hellenistic mode, nor merely as a theologian of the early church writing in a biblical mold, but also as a conscious littérateur of the Roman period" (Fitzmyer, *Luke* I-IX, p. 92). X. Léon-Dufour thinks that Luke "to a Greek ear was at once refined and often vulgar" (Robert/Feuillet, p. 223).

[14]Cited from R. G. Heard, "Old Gospel Prologues," p. 7.

definitely with any particular area. Achaia is a reasonable conjecture, but we cannot say more.

DATE

The date of Acts must be considered along with that of Luke, for the gospel cannot be later than its second volume. Some considerations favor a date for the gospel in the early 60s.

1. In Acts there is no mention of the Neronian persecution or events such as the destruction of Jerusalem or the deaths of Paul or James (A.D. 62). No event later than 62 is mentioned.

2. Luke would probably have mentioned Paul's release or execution if it had happened. But he leaves the apostle in prison in Rome at the end of Acts.

3. It is recorded that Agabus's prophecy was fulfilled (Acts 11:28), but not Jesus' prophecy of the fall of Jerusalem (Luke 21:20). The inference is that it had not yet taken place.

4. Second Timothy 1:18 records a visit of Paul to Ephesus, but Acts 20:25, 38 records Paul's words that he would not see the Ephesians again. It is argued that if this later visit had taken place, Luke would have made a suitable comment.

5. The Pauline Epistles were evidently treasured in the early church, but they are ignored in Acts. The later we put Acts, the more difficult it is to account for this.

6. It is unlikely that a Christian writer would give as friendly a picture of Rome as we find in Luke-Acts after the Neronic persecution.

To some scholars such evidence is compelling, and they date the gospel in the early 60s. Others point out that the arguments depend to some extent on what we think Luke would or would not have written, and they prefer a later date. They may argue for A.D. 75–85 on grounds such as the following:

1. That the fall of Jerusalem must precede the writing of this gospel is held to be self-evident (see Luke 19:43; 21:20, 24). But are we really in a position to deny that Jesus had prophetic gifts? In any case, the passages to which attention is drawn contain very little in the way of detail and certainly nothing that demands it be written after the event.[15] Such things as "Jerusalem being surrounded by armies" (21:20) or building "an embankment" (19:43) are no more than references to normal seige technique and cannot be held to be prophecies after the event.[16] Those who argue that they are such prophecies should take notice of the words about "the Son of Man coming in a cloud with power and great glory" (21:27). To be consistent, they should argue that this too must be after the event. We should also bear in mind the flight of the Christian community to Pella on

---

[15]Bo Reicke sees the view that this is a prophecy after the event as "an amazing example of uncritical dogmatism in New Testament studies" and points out that in none of the synoptists does the prophecy conform exactly to what we know about the destruction of Jerusalem("Synoptic Prophecies of the Destruction of Jerusalem," in *Studies in New Testament and Early Christian Literature*, ed. D. E. Aune [Leiden: Brill, 1972], p. 121).

[16]Fitzmyer holds that such allusions "make it clear" that Luke is writing after the destruction of Jerusalem, and again he says, "It is beyond comprehension how one can say that there is no reference in the Lucan Gospel to the destruction of Jerusalem" *Luke* I–IX, pp. 54, 56). It is curious that such a scholar should be so dogmatic.

account of a revelation,[17] which looks like a knowledge of Jesus' words in 21:21 before the seige.

2. Since Luke used Mark, he must be later, which puts him into the 70s at least. But if Mark is earlier than these critics allow, Luke may also be earlier than they say. Both Mark and Luke were in the group associated with Paul, so it is probable that Luke obtained a copy of Mark's gospel quite early.

3. It is urged that Luke must be dated somewhere near Matthew. Because Matthew is commonly dated in the 80s, Luke should be put there too. But it is not clear why Luke should be dated near Matthew, and in any case Matthew's date is disputed.

4. Many had written before Luke (1:1), and this would take time. A good number, however, could try their hand in thirty years, and thirty years brings us only to the early 60s (Paul was writing in the 50s, perhaps as early as the 40s).

It thus seems that the arguments adduced are mostly subjective. There is no really convincing reason for a date in the 80s. Even less probable is the view that Luke was written in the second century. Somewhere about 140 Marcion took an expurgated Luke into his canon of Scripture as his only gospel, which suggests already by Marcion's time this book was regarded as authoritative. A date in the second century does not leave much time for this to take place. Some claim support for a late date for Luke by claiming that this evangelist made use of Josephus (whose *Antiquities* was published c. A.D. 93). If so, Luke must have written in the second century. But there is little in Josephus that would have been of any use to Luke, and in both the passages alleged to come from that author, there are significant differences. In particular, if he depended on Josephus, Luke used him twice and got him wrong both times. The argument is of little weight.[18]

The evidence for an early date seems more convincing than that for a later time, and while it comes short of complete proof, it should be accepted.

ADDRESSEE(S)

As it stands, this gospel is addressed to "most excellent Theophilus" (1:3). The most natural way of understanding this is that Theophilus was a real person and that he was Luke's patron, probably paying the costs of the publication of the book thus addressed to him. The adjective probably means that Theophilus was a person of rank. It is sometimes used as a courtesy title, but in the New Testament it is applied to two governors, Felix (Acts 24:3) and Festus (Acts 26:25). However, the name itself means "lover of God," and some have thought that Luke is using it in a symbolic way, thereby addressing his book to godly people everywhere. This cannot be disproved, but it seems unlikely.

If we take Theophilus as a real person and the first recipient of the book, this does not mean that Luke meant it for his eyes only. The literary preface means that

---

[17]Eusebius, *H.E.* 3.5.3. This is supported by Epiphanius. William L. Lane notices S. G. F. Brandon's rejection of this testimony and S. Sowers's refutation of Brandon's position (*The Gospel According to Mark* [Grand Rapids: Eerdmans, 1974], p. 468 and n. 79).

[18]Hans Conzelmann argues that Luke belongs to "the third generation" of Christians, but he agrees that dependence on Josephus "cannot be shown" ("Luke's Place in the Development of Early Christianity," in *Studies in Luke-Acts*, ed. Leander E. Keck and J. Louis Martyn [Nashville: Abingdon, 1966], pp. 299, 305).

from the first the book was meant to be read, and presumably by a wide audience, not a small group of believers.[19] The care with which Luke has set out such a large amount of information seems to indicate that he had a wider public in view. His two volumes were written to give valuable information to the Christian public (and any others who might be interested) about the life, death, resurrection, and ascension of Jesus and about the history of parts of the Christian church up until Paul's imprisonment in Rome. He had in mind predominantly Gentile Christians, as we see from (1) the dedication to someone with a Greek name, (2) his clear showing of the relevance of salvation to people outside the commonwealth of Israel, and (3) the Greco-Roman style of his preface. He mostly avoids Aramaic words such as "Rabbi" (Mark 9:5) and "Abba" (Mark 14:36);[20] what he says is of interest to Jewish Christians but apparently was not intended for them in the first instance.

THE COMPOSITION OF LUKE'S GOSPEL

The first three gospels exhibit many similarities. This fact, coupled with some striking differences, sets the students of these gospels a problem that has so far defied solution (though much may be learned from a study of the relationships; see chap. 1 above). It seems highly probable that in writing his gospel Luke made use of Mark and a source or sources he shared with Matthew (the so-called Q; this may have been a single document but more probably was a group of documents), together with material not used by either of the others, a source or sources that may have been written or oral (the so-called L).

In the use of his sources, Luke makes alterations that improve the style of passages in Mark and probably also in Q. He does not wholly rewrite such passages, retaining enough for us to see that he is using a source. But his superior literary ability means that he inevitably takes the opportunity of improving the form of expression. He also abbreviates what Mark has written by omitting details that are not essential for his purpose. For example, in the parable of the sower Luke has 90 words where Mark has 151 (Luke 8:4–8; Mark 4:1–9), and there are similar abbreviations in a number of places. Luke's omissions often involve incidents he has included elsewhere, apparently derived from one of his other sources. This is a somewhat complicated subject, for he sometimes does include matter from two stories, or "doublets." Thus 9:23–24 seems to come from Mark 8:34–35 and the similar 14:27; 17:33 resembles Matthew 10:38–39 and may well have come from Q.

What seems rather curious to people of our day is that, while he sometimes speaks of Jesus as showing feeling (e.g. 7:13), Luke now and then omits references to Jesus' emotions, whether of compassion (5:13; cf. Mark 1:41), anger and grief (6:10; cf. Mark 3:5), or love (18:22; cf. Mark 10:21); he concentrates

---

[19] "The formal dedication of this work to Theophilus, whose title ('Your Excellency') shows that he held high office in the Roman government, strongly suggests that it was intended for publication and was therefore directed primarily to the outside world" G. B. Caird (*The Gospel of St Luke* [Harmondsworth: Penguin, 1963], p. 14).

[20] He does include a few Aramaic words in Greek transliteration, such as ἀμήν (*amēn*, 4:24, etc.), Βεελζεβούλ (*Beelzeboul*, 11:15–19), γέεννα (*geenna*, 12:5), μαμωνᾶς (*mamōnas, 16:9–13*), πάσχα (*pascha*, 22:1, etc.), σάββατον (*sabbaton*, 4:16, etc.), Σατανᾶς (*Satanas*, 10:18, etc.), and σίκερα (*sikera*, 1:15).

on what Jesus did and said, rather than on what he felt. Perhaps he wanted his readers to be clear that Jesus was not unduly swayed by emotions but was always in command of the situation. A curious feature of Luke's writing, which is very good Greek, is his inclusion of several expressions more common in Semitic languages than Greek (e.g. "it came to pass . . ."). This may be due to his faithfulness to his sources or to a desire to write in "biblical" language.

It is sometimes held that before he came across a copy of Mark and began his work, Luke produced what is called proto-Luke. It is pointed out that about 60 percent of Luke is not contained in Mark, that about 30 percent of Mark is not found in Luke, that Luke's passion narrative is apparently quite independent of Mark's,[21] and that some of Luke's parallels to Mark contain significant differences. Some have advocated the hypothesis that Luke combined matter from Q and his own sources (L) and worked it into a document.[22] It could be argued that this was meant as a gospel, for the total length of Q + L is greater than the length of Mark.[23]

There are various reasons for postulating a proto-Luke document. One is that Luke's Q material is *combined* with L, not simply inserted by itself, while his Markan material is not combined in this way. In the Lukan manner, Mark's material may be worked over with stylistic improvements and the like, but it is not combined with Q or L. Again, 3:1 looks like the opening of a book (the infancy stories are thought not to belong to proto-Luke), and the genealogy of Jesus would then come at a very natural point, following the first mention of his name. There is a short section, 6:20–8:3, and a longer one, 9:51–18:14, where Luke seems to make no reference to Mark, which is most curious if Mark gave him his basic framework. Throughout this gospel the Markan and non-Markan matter come in alternate blocks, and Luke's passion narrative seems to be for the most part independent of that in Mark. Furthermore, in the passages where he is following Mark, Luke sometimes omits an incident that he then places in another context. For example, Mark has Jesus' rejection at Nazareth between the stories of Jairus's daughter and the sending out of the Twelve (Mark 6:1–5); Luke has these two stories in the same sequence (8:40–9:6), but the rejection at Nazareth is at 4:16–30.[24]

Another relevant fact is the way Luke uses "the Lord" to refer to Jesus in

---

[21]Kümmel holds that Mark's passion story is the basis of that in Luke (pp. 131ff.). But Caird points out that of 163 verses in Luke's passion narrative, there are "only 20 in which there is the sort of verbal similarity which is normally regarded as evidence of dependence." He adds, "When Luke is indisputably following Mark, he uses 53 per cent of Mark's words, but here he uses only 27 per cent, and many of the words which he shares with Mark are words without which the Passion story could not have been told at all" (*Gospel of St Luke*, p. 25). It cannot be said that the case for dependence on Mark in the passion story has ever been convincingly made.

[22]E.g. Vincent Taylor, *The Gospel According to St. Mark*, 2d ed. (London: Macmillan, 1966); B. H. Streeter, *The Four Gospels* (London: Macmillan, 1930). Neither, of course, originated the idea; Streeter notices something very like it in a work of E. R. Buckley in 1912 (p. ix n.1), and others have likewise advocated it. Pullan for example, has something very like it (p. 26). But it is to Taylor and Streeter that it owes its later popularity.

[23]Streeter estimates the non-Markan matter in Luke at about 806 verses (Mark itself contains about 660 verses). (*Four Gospels*, p. 209).

[24]Reginald H. Fuller sees it as "most unlikely" that Luke "deliberately shifted the rejection at Nazareth to the beginning of the ministry for theological purposes." He sees Luke as "opposed to rearrangements" and holds that he "follows Mk, Q and Special material in turn," (p. 119 n. 1).

narrative, a usage not found in Matthew or Mark. This does not occur in Luke's Markan material, but it is found fifteen times in the rest of Luke, in more or less the same proportion in L and Q. He also has the address Κύριε (*Kyrie*, "O Lord") sixteen times, as against once in Mark, and fourteen of these are in the proto-Luke passages (eight in L and six in Q). Some urge that the use of the term does not belong to the final writing of the gospel, else it would be in the Markan passages as much as in the others, and the conclusion is drawn that it belongs to an earlier stage in the production of the book. It is further pointed out that whereas Luke retains about 53 percent of Mark's actual words in the Markan passages in the body of the gospel, in the passion narrative he has only 27 percent, and this includes words necessary for telling a passion story. There are many variations in order. Luke has the resurrection appearances in Jerusalem, whereas most agree either that Mark had no such appearances at all or, if he did, that he located them in Galilee (see Mark 16:7). Many conclude that Luke did not depend on Mark in this part of his book.[25]

If this hypothesis is correct, we have identified a very old document indeed, for proto-Luke would have preceded the writing of both Matthew and Luke (as Q does). For a variety of reasons, most scholars remain unconvinced, but it is an interesting hypothesis. Those who reject it have not satisfactorily explained two facts: (1) Luke habitually combines his L with Q but never with Mark, and (2) he departs radically from Mark in his passion narrative. If Luke had Mark as one of his principal sources, it seems strange that he should desert it at the high point of the book. Against the hypothesis, many scholars point out that if we take out the Markan sections from Luke, what is left does not read like a book. Perhaps the best solution is to think of Luke as having been busy with such sources as Q and L before he came across Mark. When he received a copy of that gospel, he inserted most of it into the narrative he had been working on but had not yet completed. It is unlikely that Luke took any one document and made that his foundation; he seems rather to have selected his material from a variety of sources. While this seems the most likely solution, it is clearly no more than a hypothesis, and much remains uncertain.[26]

An interesting feature of this gospel is the amount of material it shares with the fourth gospel (far more than does either Matthew or Mark). For example, both Luke and John mention Martha and Mary, Annas, and a disciple named Judas in addition to Judas Iscariot. Both have an interest in Jerusalem generally and in the temple. Both speak of Satan as being active in the betrayal of Jesus (Luke 22:3; John 13:27), say that the ear that Peter cut off the slave in Gethsemane was the *right* ear (Luke 22:50; John 18:10), and tell us that Pilate three times declared that Jesus was innocent (Luke 23:4, 14, 22; John 18:38; 19:4, 6). Most agree

---

[25]B. H. Streeter counted the non-Markan material in Luke 3:1–22:14 as 671 verses, with another 135 in the passion narrative—a total of 806 verses. From such facts as Luke's use of only about 30 verses from Mark in his passion narrative compared to 135 from elsewhere, Streeter reasoned that he preferred his non-Markan to his Markan source (*Four Gospels*, p. 209).

[26]See Fitzmyer, I–IX, pp. 90–91, for seven reasons for rejecting proto-Luke, and Caird, *St Luke*, pp. 23–27, for seven reasons for accepting it! J. M. Creed sees Mark as "a determining factor in the construction of the existing book from the outset" but does not see this as "necessarily inconsistent with the hypothesis that Q and some of Luke's peculiar material may have been already combined, and may have lain before Luke as a single document."(*The Gospel According to St. Luke* [London: Macmillan, 1950], p. lviii n. 1). Martin is respectful of the proto-Luke hypothesis (1:153–56).

that it is highly unlikely either that John used Luke or that Luke used John. The best explanation is that they used a common source or sources.

TEXT

In most New Testament books textual variation is comparatively minor, but in Luke and Acts there are major differences in the so-called Western text, a text whose principal representatives are Codex Bezae (D) and the Old Latin manuscripts. In Luke, for example, D includes the story of the man working on the Sabbath (6:4), the words "And he said, 'You do not know what kind of spirit you are of, for the Son of Man did not come to destroy men's lives, but to save them'" (9:55); additional clauses in the Lord's Prayer (11:2–4); Jesus' agony in the garden (22:43); the languages used in the inscription on the cross (23:38); and the information that the stone before Jesus' tomb was one "which twenty men could scarcely roll" (23:53). The Western text is certainly old, for it was used by Justin and Tatian and others in the second century. It sometimes omits passages found in other text types, but more characteristically it has additions (as we have just seen is the case in Luke). Its changes and additions clarify passages that the scribe evidently thought were unclear. Its tendency is to harmonize passages and generally to try to remove difficulties.

In a notable series of passages in Luke and Acts, the Western text omits readings that are well attested elsewhere. Notably is this the case with a series of passages that Westcott and Hort called "Western non-interpolations," a cumbersome expression referring to passages lacking in the Western text that they thought must be interpolations in the so-called neutral text. They saw the neutral text as far and away the most trustworthy, but they made exceptions here. They reasoned that since the Western text so consistently includes additional material and longer readings, special attention must be given to it when it omits passages. In Luke some of these Western omissions are as follows: the words to Martha, "You are worried and upset about many things, but only one thing is needed" (10:41–42), the command to repeat the Lord's Supper together with the words about the cup following those about the bread (22:19–20), the prayer for forgiveness of those who crucified Jesus (23:34), the words "he is not here; he has risen" (24:6), Peter's visit to the tomb (24:12), Jesus' showing his hands and feet (24:40), and the ascension (24:51).

Some of the differences between the Western text and other authorities are clearly very significant. But in estimating them, most recent scholars think it likely that Westcott and Hort put too great a weight on Western omissions. The principal reason for this is the discovery of a number of papyri that show that the neutral text of Westcott and Hort, which these days is generally called Alexandrian, is not a fourth-century creation but goes back to the second. Particularly important are the great p^{75} (the oldest MS of this gospel, which dates from the end of the second century or the beginning of the third) and p^{45} (about much the same date). The text type they represent is thus very old, and its preservation in MSS such as Codex Vaticanus (B) shows that it was copied faithfully through the years. It is an austere form of text, tending to eschew picturesque elaborations such as those we find in the Western text. It still seems to most textual critics the best form of the text, although they do not regard it in the same way as did Westcott and Hort, and they recognize that there are mistakes in it, so that each variant must be judged on its merits. The tendency in recent discussions is indeed to take the Western text into consideration but not to give it veto power. Especially is this the case where D is the only Greek MS to support a reading (which happens with quite a few Western readings; the strength of supporting evidence is with the Old Latin). There will still remain uncertainty about some readings, but there is considerable agreement about most. There is no reason for doubting that we have Luke's text substantially as he wrote it.[27]

ADOPTION INTO THE CANON

We often cannot tell when one of the Fathers is quoting from Luke. Certainly Luke made use of oral tradition, and he used sources; but neither of these disappeared when he wrote his gospel. Luke explicitly says that many had written before him (1:1), and some of what he did not use may have contained material similar to that which he took up. Thus when an early Christian writes words that we find in the third gospel, we cannot always be sure that he is quoting Luke. He may have taken the words from the oral tradition that meant so much to many early believers; he may have taken them from a source that Luke used; he may have taken them from an early Christian writing that has perished. We must also allow for the fact that first-century memories were not infallible. While people developed their capacity to memorize rather more than we do and thus were able to quote longer passages with exactitude, they also seem often to have given the sense without trying to give the exact words. This means that a passage that merely resembles a part of Luke may yet come from that gospel. It is not easy to be sure in every case whether we are dealing with a quotation from Luke or not.

This kind of uncertainty confronts us as we face a number of passages in Clement of Rome (*1 Clem.* 13:2; 48:4), Polycarp (*Phil.* 2:3), and Ignatius (*Magn.* 10). These resemble Luke, but we cannot be sure that they are quotations from this source. We can be more certain that the *Didache* and the *Gospel of Peter* used Luke, the former being of uncertain date but quite early, and the latter possibly the middle of the second century.[28] Justin Martyr certainly used Luke (or a harmony based on it), and *2 Clement* seems to have done the same. Marcion, of course, had an expurgated Luke as the one gospel in his canon. Some have argued that it was not our Luke that Marcion used, but an earlier source that both he and Luke employed, but evidence for this is lacking, and there seems no real doubt that it was the third gospel that formed the basis of Marcion's work. In any case, from this time onward there is no real doubt: Luke is universally accepted in the church as authoritative and part of the canon of sacred books.

LUKE IN RECENT STUDY

Traditionally Luke has been seen as a historian, perhaps the greatest historian of the early church, and discussion has centered on just how good a historian he was.

---

[27]There is a useful summary of the position in Metzger, pp. 191–93. See also Klyne Snodgrass, "Western Non-Interpolations," *JBL* 91 (1972): 369–79. Snodgrass concludes that "it now appears doubtful that any of the readings supported only by D and its non-Greek allies are the genuine text" (p. 379).

[28]So C. Maurer in Hennecke 1:180.

Comparisons have been made between his gospel and the others and between what he says in Acts and what may be gleaned from the Pauline Epistles and from our information about the first-century Roman Empire. There is still, of course, something to be done along these lines, for there is indeed a good deal of history in Luke's two volumes. But the tendency in recent discussions has been to see Luke as a theologian. It is recognized that he was not primarily concerned with history: his main concern was with what God had done in Christ. So Luke is now seen as one of the three great theologians of the early church. He may be thought of as not reaching the intellectual and spiritual stature of Paul and of John; like them, however, he produced writings that show something of the way God was active in the life, death, resurrection, and ascension of Jesus and again in the life of the early church.

Hans Conzelmann set the agenda for a good deal of recent discussion by his treatment of Luke's understanding of history and of salvation. He put a good deal of emphasis on a difficult text, Luke 16:16, which he regards as "the key to the topography of redemptive history."[29] Conzelmann argues that we should see three stages in what he calls the story of salvation.

1. The period of Israel (16:16).

2. The period of Jesus' ministry (not of his "life"); see Luke 4:16ff.; Acts 10:38.

3. The period since the ascension, a period in which the church by looking back to the period of Jesus also looks forward to the parousia.[30]

This outline highlights the ministry of Jesus and sees it as absolutely central to the working out of salvation. The German title of his book, *Die Mitte der Zeit* (The Middle of Time), well captures his argument. Such an emphasis is surely unexceptionable, and Conzelmann's emphasis on the meaningfulness of history as Luke saw it is surely to be welcomed. Not so acceptable, however, is his treatment of Luke's geographic references. He refuses to take them seriously as geography, for he doubts whether Luke knew Palestine. Rather, they are essentially symbolic, merely a function of Lukan theology. Thus the Jordan is simply "the region of the Baptist, the region of the old era."[31] The desert in which Jesus' temptations took place symbolizes the separation between the Jordan and Galilee; it is "pointless to attempt to locate it."[32] This approach to geography is so important to Conzelmann that he devotes to it the first of the five parts into which his book is divided. But it is difficult to take seriously the idea that Luke did not mean his geography to be accurate, as is clear from his use of geographic references throughout Acts.[33]

Conzelmann sees Luke as profoundly affected by the delay of the parousia. Whereas previously the imminence of the End was what mattered, Luke sees it as far away. Therefore instead of thinking of a short period of awaiting the parousia, he has more in mind the "Christian life" and gives attention, for example, to the

---

[29]Hans Conzelmann, *The Theology of St Luke* (London: Faber & Faber, 1960), p. 23.
[30]Ibid., pp. 16−17.
[31]Ibid., p. 20.
[32]Ibid., p. 27.
[33]For examples, see Leon Morris, *Luke: An Introduction and Commentary*, 2d ed. (Leicester: IVP; Grand Rapids: Eerdmans, 1988), pp. 34−35.

importance of endurance (ὑπομονή, [hypomonē]).[34] Where the first Christians had their eyes firmly fixed on the future with their emphasis on Jesus' imminent return, Luke preferred to think of an ongoing historical process.[35] He saw the life of Jesus as a historical event of the past and as the anchor or the foundation of the continuing life of the church. With the End so far in the distance, Luke introduces a more reflective attitude.

All this is difficult to reconcile with some of the sayings Luke records, for example, the nearness of judgment in the teaching of John the Baptist (3:9, 17) and the nearness of the kingdom in the teaching of Jesus (10:9, 11), not to mention his promise of speedy judgment (18:7–8). So also Jesus said, "This generation will certainly not pass away until all these things have happened" (21:32; there are problems in interpreting this verse, but it is as clear in teaching an imminent parousia as any other saying in the Gospels). With this we should take into consideration Luke's deep interest in eschatology. As we shall see a little later, there is no real reason for thinking of Luke as essentially different from other New Testament writers in his attitude to eschatology. Conzelmann has done us a service in drawing attention to many features of Luke's writing, but it can scarcely be denied that he has overplayed his hand.

The great interest of many recent writers on Luke-Acts stems from their conviction that Luke is one of the foremost exponents of *Frühkatholizismus*, or "early Catholicism." This is not always defined, and there is no agreement as to exactly what the term connotes. But most who write about it think of the first Christians as caught up in the enthusiasm that ensued on being saved through faith in Jesus. They lived in a charismatic freedom that gave no thought to the trammels of institutionalism. In particular, they lived in the daily expectation of the return of Christ. As E. Käsemann puts it, "You do not write the history of the Church, if you are expecting the end of the world to come any day."[36] It was the proclamation of the kerygma and the awaiting of the parousia that preoccupied the first Christians. Only when time went by without the return of the Lord did believers begin to give serious attention to institutional Christianity. Luke says that Jesus taught a certain parable because "the people thought that the kingdom of God was going to appear at once" (19:11), and this is held to support the view that this evangelist had no thought of an imminent parousia. Luke, then, is seen as a man who has lost the keen expectation that Christ would soon return. His main interest is in establishing the life of the church as an institution.

For all its popularity in some circles, this viewpoint is far from having been established. That the early church lived in the daily expectation of the parousia has been pressed too far. Too much reliance has been put on confident interpretations of passages such as "we who are still alive, who are left till the coming of the Lord" (1 Thess. 4:15). These words are taken to mean that Paul held that he would still be alive when the Lord returned. But the words do not necessarily mean this. Greek scholar J. B. Lightfoot gave the meaning as "When I say 'we,' I mean those

---

[34]Ibid., pp. 231ff.

[35]Marxsen has a similar view: "The eschatological element present in the proclamatory character of the pre-Lucan tradition is eliminated. Luke's 'historicizing' is therefore at the same time a process of 'de-eschatologizing'"; "the expectation of an imminent *parousia* is abandoned" (pp. 157–58). For a useful evaluation of this view, see Rowland, pp. 285–94.

[36]E. Käsemann, *Essays on New Testament Themes* (London: SCM, 1964), p. 28.

who are living, those who survive to that day."[37] And people who insist that Paul expected the parousia during his lifetime take little notice of passages in which he says that he will be dead—for example, "God raised the Lord from the dead, and he will raise us also" (1 Cor. 6:14). Paul tends to class himself with the people of whom he is writing (see Rom. 6:1; 13:12; 1 Cor. 10.22); we should therefore not press 1 Thessalonians 4:15 beyond what is legitimate. Moreover, Paul's interest in the institution is seen in his directions for disciplining an offender (1 Cor. 5:1–5), and in his references to the ministry (2 Cor. 11:28; Phil. 1:1; 1 Thess. 5:12–13; etc.).

To this we should add that Luke's interest in eschatology should not be minimized. In addition to teaching he shares with the other synoptists, he has references to the coming of the kingdom in Jesus' ministry that the other evangelists do not record (10:11). He alone records these words of Jesus: "Be dressed ready for service and keep your lamps burning, like men waiting for their master to return from a wedding banquet" (12:35–36). In the great eschatological discourse he makes a clearer distinction than either Matthew or Mark between what applies to the fall of Jerusalem and what refers to the parousia.[38] Charles E. Talbert sees Luke as making a distinctive contribution to the church's understanding of eschatology. He holds that some in the early church thought that the parousia had already taken place, perhaps by seeing it as identical with Jesus' being "received up," perhaps by seeing it as identical with the coming of the Spirit at Pentecost. He thinks that Luke, in common with other early Christians, proclaims that the End is near, but that he also attempts "to prevent a misinterpretation of the Jesus-tradition by someone in the Lucan sphere of influence to the effect that the eschaton had been and could be fully experienced in the present."[39] That such a position can be taken up shows clearly that it is erroneous to say that Luke has no interest in eschatology. He may express himself differently, and he may put emphasis on different aspects,[40] but it simply ignores the facts to say that he has no interest in eschatology.

We should also bear in mind that Luke says little about the ordained ministry or about the sacraments, two topics that have always been central in the "catholic" tradition. In Acts he mentions elders but says nothing about ordination and gives no certain example of the Holy Communion. In his gospel, he tells us of its institution, but in Acts all the occurrences of "the breaking of bread" could be understood as referring to ordinary meals. We would not contend that all must be taken that way; the sacraments are very important to a "catholic," however, and it is unthinkable that the identification of sacramental observances would be left to

---

[37]J. B. Lightfoot, *Notes on Epistles of St Paul* (London: Macmillan, 1904), p. 66.

[38]Caird (*St. Luke*, p. 229) finds here Luke's "own peculiar contribution to New Testament eschatology." Kümmel asserts, "The persecution of the disciples and the destruction of Jerusalem (21:12ff., 20ff.) as inner-historical events are clearly distinguished . . . from the signs of the parousia and from the parousia itself (21:25ff. par. Mk. 13:24ff.)" (p. 101).

[39]Charles E. Talbert in *Jesus and Man's Hope*, ed. Donald G. Miller (Pittsburgh: Perspective Books, 1970), p. 191.

[40]Childs thinks that "Luke has not de-eschatologized the promise, but reshaped it and made it conform more closely to the traditional Old Testament pattern"; not least among the factors that influenced Luke was "the sense of continuity between the old and the new Israel as the people of God among the nations" (p. 113).

chance. A "catholicism" without an ordained ministry and regular sacraments would be very strange indeed.

This is all the more important in view of Luke's emphasis on the Word. In part we see this in the strong note of promise and fulfillment that runs through his writing. He is speaking about God's Chosen One in language reminiscent of the Old Testament (1:32–35, 68–75). From the beginning, Scripture may be quoted of him (2:23) and seen to be fulfilled in his forerunner (3:4–6). A further fulfillment in John the Baptist really points to the divine plan in Jesus (7:27); Jesus is the One who fulfills the messianic hope of the Scriptures (4:16ff.). Indeed, in him "everything that is written by the prophets about the Son of Man will be fulfilled" (18:31; cf. 20:17; 22:37). Furthermore, every such thing "must be fulfilled" (24:44, 46).[41] This teaching must be taken together with Luke's emphasis on the Spirit; he is not writing of a rigid pattern that must be fulfilled with a wooden literalism, but of one with the freedom of God's Holy Spirit. The fulfillment of what is written sometimes takes place in ways that people would never have expected.[42]

Luke begins his gospel by informing the reader that he is writing "so that you may know the certainty of the things you have been taught" (1:4). Just as the Word of God in the ancient Scripture is important, so also the authentic tradition about Jesus is important. Luke is writing to Theophilus so that he will be in no doubt about what that tradition is. As Childs points out, "The great events transpired in history, indeed in a series of acts which now lie in the historical past. Yet these events are not moored in past history but continue to be fulfilled time 'for us.'"[43]

These days there is a good deal of discussion about Luke's placing of Acts after his gospel (in distinction from the practice of the other three evangelists), but we should not overlook the importance of the fact that he prefixed his gospel to Acts. The early church is inexplicable without authentic knowledge of who Jesus was and what he did. The speeches in Acts are surely meant, in part at least, to place on record what the apostolic preaching was. With this before them, local church officials would not be able to manufacture teachings and claim them to be authentically Christian. It may well be that the appointment of elders (Acts 14:23 etc.) was meant in part at least to secure adherence to the apostolic tradition.[44]

---

[41]Luke's appeal to Scripture is particularly significant. He joins other New Testament writers in detecting in the Old Testament not only verbal predictions of Jesus the Messiah but *patterns* of saving events that predict the dawning of the age of salvation—as is suggested by the title by Darrell Bock, *Proclamation from Prophecy and Pattern: Lucan Old Testament Christology*, JSNTSupp 12 (Sheffield: Sheffield Academic Press, 1987).

[42]See further the essay by Leon Morris, "Luke and Early Catholicism," in *Studying the New Testament Today, I*, ed. John H. Skilton (Nutley, N.J.: Presbyterian & Reformed, 1974), pp. 60–75 and the literature there cited.

[43]Childs, p. 106. He further says, "Luke thus confirms the authoritative quality of the apostolic tradition which he attempts to render in its most accurate form for the sake of the church, and which he sharply sets apart from all later teachings" (ibid.).

[44]According to Talbert: "It is clear that in the Lucan succession the elders are appointed in order to serve the tradition. The church and its ministry are brought under the judgment of the apostolic word. It is the Word which legitimizes the church and its ministry and not *vice versa*. It would appear, then, that for Luke the apostolic tradition was, by his act of writing, crystallized in Luke-Acts" (*Jesus and Man's Hope*, p. 206). Conzelmann says that Luke "offers not a contribution to the tradition but *the* tradition" ("Luke's Place," p. 305).

C. K. Barrett comments, "Luke's stress on the proclamation of the Word . . . shows that the Word itself was the decisive factor," and that the church is an agency of salvation "only in so far as it provides the framework within which the preaching of the Word takes place."[45] We should not miss this emphasis. Talbert goes so far as to suggest that Luke might well be thought of as "proto-Protestant" rather than "early Catholic."[46]

THE CONTRIBUTION OF LUKE

We owe to Luke a good deal of our information about Jesus. His first two chapters, for example, tell us almost all we know about the birth of John the Baptist and most of what we know about the birth and boyhood of Jesus. He alone tells us of the miraculous catch of fish and of its effect on Peter (5:1–11), the anointing of Jesus by a sinful woman (7:36–50), the women who helped Jesus (8:1–3), Jesus' rejection by some Samaritans (9:51–56), the mission of the seventy (10:1–12, 17–20), Jesus' visit with Martha and Mary (10:38–42), teaching on repentance (13:1–5), healing the crippled woman (13:10–17), Jesus' teaching about Herod (13:31–33), the man with dropsy (14:1–6), the invitation to a banquet (14:7–14), Jesus' teaching about unprofitable servants (17:7–10), the healing of ten lepers (17:11–19), Zaccheus (19:1–10), the lament over Jerusalem (19:41–44), the words about two swords (22:35–38), Jesus before Herod (23:6–12), the words to the daughters of Jerusalem (23:27–31), three of the "words" from the cross (23:34, 43, 46), and the whole section on the resurrection after the women at the tomb (24:12–53). Several of the parables are found in this gospel only: the Good Samaritan (10:25–37), the friend at midnight (11:5–8), the barren fig tree (13:6–9), the lost sheep, the lost coin, and the lost son (15:1–32), the unjust manager (16:1–9), the rich man and Lazarus (16:19–31), the unjust judge (18:1–8), and the Pharisee and the publican (18:9–14).

The sheer volume of what we owe to Luke is impressive. So is the beauty of his writing, such that Renan called this gospel the most beautiful book in the world. Luke has a good deal of what we might call human-interest material, which none of the other evangelists includes, such as the infancy stories of both Jesus and John the Baptist. We are fortunate Luke included parables such as those of the good man from Samaria and the prodigal son.

But we should not exclusively concentrate on material that no one else includes. When Luke is writing about stories we find elsewhere, he has his own way of going about it, and we owe a good deal to his presentation. He tells us in his opening words that he is writing about things that "have been fulfilled" (1:1), not simply things that have happened. He is concerned with the purpose of God that is worked out in the events he records and with the way those events impinge on the present. His theological interest leads him to bring out truths that are of permanent significance in the life of the church. This is the case with the point made at the close of the preceding section, Luke's insistence on the primacy of the

---

[45]C. K. Barrett, *Luke the Historian in Recent Study* (London: Epworth, 1961), pp. 72, 74.

[46]Talbert, *Jesus and Man's Hope*, p. 220. He adds, "*Sola Scriptura* is a major plank in the Lucan theological platform."

Word. Although he does not develop a theology of inspiration or say how the writings of the New Testament relate to those of the Old, Luke leaves the reader in no doubt that there is an authentic deposit of Christian truth and that this must be guarded zealously.

Luke has a good deal to say about salvation; he is the theologian of *Heilsgeschichte*, the linkage of salvation with historical events.[47] It is a new and significant idea for Luke to see God's salvation as worked out in the life, death, resurrection, and ascension of Jesus also in the ongoing life of the church.[48] He sets his story firmly in the context of secular history (2:1–2; 3:1), and he sees God at work in all that Jesus said and did. It was in Jesus that God worked out salvation for sinners. Conzelmann has pointed to an important truth in calling his book *Der Mitte der Zeit*: all history pivots on Christ, and in the coming of Jesus we see the action of the love of God. This gospel is a tender gospel, one in which it is impossible to miss the truth that God loves the sinners Jesus came to save. In the frequency of Luke's use of words such as "today" (eleven times, vs. eight times in Matthew and once in Mark) and "now" (fourteen times, vs. four in Matthew and three in Mark), he unobtrusively brings out the truth that salvation has become a present reality with the coming of Jesus. Almost alone among the four gospels, Luke uses nouns translated "salvation": four times he uses σωτηρία (*sōtēria*; used in the other gospels only once in John), and twice he alone uses σωτήριον (*sōtērion*), with another seven examples of the two words in Acts. Twice he calls Jesus "Savior" (with two more in Acts), and he has the verb "to save" more often than any other book in the New Testament. Salvation matters for Luke.[49]

This salvation is open to all. While there is a deep interest in the Jews,[50] there is nothing like Jewish particularism or a most-favored nation of any kind. Simeon sang of the Christ child as one who was "a light for revelation to the Gentiles" (2:32). In another significant early passage (3:4–6), Luke quotes from Isaiah 40. Matthew also quotes this passage, but Luke includes the words, "And all mankind will see God's salvation" (3:6). There is a marked interest in a wide variety of people, including Samaritans (10:30–37; 17:16), the widow of Zarephath, and Naaman the Syrian (4:25–27). People will come from all directions to sit in God's kingdom (13:29). The angels who announced the birth of Jesus spoke of peace to human beings in general, not specifically to Jews (2:14). Luke's universalism is often commented on, though this should not be understood in the sense that all people will be saved. There remains a difference between "the people

---

[47]Ellis thinks Luke "is properly called a 'theologian of redemptive history,'" which he explains in these terms: "That is, he regards history to be the realm of God's redemptive activity and interprets the movement and goal of history by this fact" (*Luke*, p. 15).

[48]"Luke grasps the meaning of Jesus and the church for the world in a single vision, and he tells that story so that what happens with Jesus foreshadows the church's experience and what happens in the church finds meaning as the continuation of Jesus' story" (Johnson, p. 199).

[49]Small wonder that I. Howard Marshall says, "It is our thesis that the idea of salvation supplies the key to the theology of Luke" (*Luke: Historian and Theologian* [Exeter: Paternoster, 1970], p. 92).

[50]Martin brings this out in this manner: "Luke's intention may be stated in a sentence: to demonstrate the continuous line in salvation-history between the two covenants"(1:250). We should not forget that Luke tells of the conversion of large numbers of Jews (Acts 2:41, 47; 4:4; 5:14; 6:1, 7; 9:42; 12:24; 13:43; 14:1; 17:10–12; 21:20); his deep interest in the Gentiles does not mean that he is unmindful of the place of the Jews in the plan of God.

of this world" and "the people of the light," and judgment is a reality (10:14; 11:31–32; 19:22; 20:47; 22:30).

J. Jervell has produced a novel view of the relation of Christians to the Old Testament people of God in this gospel. He sees Luke as differing from other New Testament writers in seeing the law as binding new believers, just as it bound ancient Israel. There is but one people of God; Jervell denies that Luke sees believers as "the new Israel." For Jervell there is "only one Israel, one people of God, one covenant,"[51] so that when Gentiles are evangelized, in some sense they join Israel. Jervell thinks of a "people" and an "associate people." This idea has been subjected to searching criticism by M. M. B. Turner, who makes it clear that Jervell is not being fair to Luke. Luke certainly sees Christians as more than simply associates of the Jews. As Turner puts it, "The focus of redemptive revelation has shifted from the Torah to Jesus; adherence to His teaching and leading is the necessary condition of belonging to the Israel of fulfillment (Acts 3:22–23). By the Spirit, in His disciples, Jesus continues the rule announced in Luke 4:16–21. All of this amounts to a new kind of relationship between God and His people, mediated through Jesus."[52] Jervell is scarcely fair to this new relationship that Jesus established.

We should not overlook the fact that Luke's gospel is the first part of a two-volume work. It is the one story of salvation that Luke tells, a salvation that rests on who Jesus was and what he did, but one that did not cease when Jesus died. It went right on in the life of the church, and through the church it went out to the Gentiles. The continuity of the work of salvation in God's plan is a most important part of what Luke is telling his readers.[53]

A notable feature of Luke's gospel is its interest in those who were generally held as of no account in the first century: women, children, the poor, and the disreputable. The rabbis regarded it as a sin to teach a woman, but Jesus taught women as freely as he taught men. He brings out something of the importance of womankind with his infancy stories and his references to Martha and Mary (10:38–42), Mary Magdalene, Joanna, and Susanna (8:2–3). There are also women he does not name, such as the widow of Nain, to whom he restored her dead son (7:11–12), the crippled lady whom he healed (13:11), the sinner who anointed Jesus' feet (7:37–50) and others (he refers to ten women others do not mention and has another three in parables).[54] Luke does not engage in overt propaganda as though he were presenting some great new insight; he simply takes it for granted that women will feature largely in God's plan, and that attitude is striking. So with children. This is seen in the infancy stories and also in references

---

[51]J. Jervell, *Luke and the People of God: A New Look at Luke-Acts* (Minneapolis: Augsburg, 1973), p. 141.

[52]M. M. B. Turner, "The Sabbath, Sunday, and the Law in Luke/Acts," in *From Sabbath to Lord's Day*, ed. D. A. Carson (Grand Rapids: Zondervan, 1982), p. 120.

[53]Marxsen points out that such a continuation as Acts would have been impossible for Matthew and Mark. "Of course Matthew (and—with certain reservations—Mark) could have written a Church history; however, this would not have been a continuation of their original works, but a history of the continuing influence of these works, which is something quite different" (p. 156). But Luke's two volumes belong together.

[54]The ten are Elizabeth, Anna, the widow of Sarepta, the widow of Nain, the crippled woman, the sinner who anointed Jesus' feet, Joanna, Susanna, the woman who called from the crowd, and the daughters of Jerusalem.

to "the only son" or "the only daughter" in some of his stories (7:12; 8:42; 9:38). He also tells us that when Jesus wanted to rebuke pride in the disciples, he "took a little child" (9:47; is it relevant that he did not have to send for one, that one was apparently there, where Jesus was?) and taught them to welcome little ones. He spoke of children a number of times as he taught the people (10:21; 17:2; 18:16). He had watched children at play and could use what he had observed when he wanted to make a point about the attitude of the people to John the Baptist and himself (7:31–35). Did any other of the world's great religious teachers have such an interest in children?

A noteworthy feature of Luke's presentation is his interest in the poor. This is evident at the beginning, for the offering made at the birth of the baby Jesus was that prescribed for poor people (2:24; see Lev. 12:8), which indicates that the family at Nazareth was poor. Then, at the beginning of his ministry in his programmatic sermon at Nazareth, Jesus quotes the prophecy of Isaiah to show that he was sent "to preach good news to the poor" (4:18; there are, of course, other facets to his ministry). The message of Jesus to John the Baptist outlining his ministry includes the clause "the good news is preached to the poor" (7:22; for other references to the poor, see 1:53; 6:30; 14:11–13, 21; 16:19–31). This aspect of Luke's contribution has aroused a good deal of interest in modern discussions, and it is seen more clearly now than has always been the case that Jesus had a deep concern for the poor. Liberation theology and other movements pay a good deal of attention to Luke's teaching on the poor. This is as it should be, but we must exercise care. Jesus is concerned for the poor because of their greater need and their general helplessness, not because there is any particular virtue in poverty. Normally, nobody chooses to be poor; poverty is a condition forced on people against their will. It is impossible to hold that Jesus pronounces as blessed those in a socioeconomic situation not of their own choosing and from which they would escape if they could.[55] But there is no doubting that the poor were generally despised in antiquity or that Luke shows a great interest in them and a deep compassion for them.

Luke also warns against riches, a very important part of his gospel for those who live in an affluent society. In the song of Mary we find that God has sent the rich away empty (1:53). Just as he records a blessing on Jesus' poor followers (6:20), so Luke records a woe for the rich (6:24). Luke has parables full of warning for the wealthy: the rich fool (12:16–21), the unjust manager (16:1–12), and the rich man and Lazarus (16:19–35). There is an example of what a rich man might do in the story of Zaccheus (19:1–10), another example from a poor widow (21:1–4), and a warning in the case of the rich young ruler (18:18–27). Luke is far from accepting an order of society in which riches are esteemed as such and poverty despised. God has a way of upsetting our sociological distinctions and finding his saints in unexpected places.

We see this too in Luke's interest in the disreputable. The shepherds who were the recipients of the angels' message at the birth of Jesus (2:8–20) came from a despised class. Their job prevented them from paying much attention to the

---

[55]Charles H. Talbert examines the question of whether "poor," "hunger," "weep," "rich," "full," and "laugh" are to be understood "sociologically or religiously." He concludes, "It must be the latter because the gospel canonizes no sociological state" (*Reading Luke* [New York: Crossroad, 1984], p. 70).

requirements of ceremonial cleanness, and as they moved round the country they had a distressing habit of pilfering. They were regarded as untrustworthy[56] and were not permitted to give testimony in courts of law.[57] There were "tax collectors and 'sinners'" at the banquet Levi gave for Jesus (5:30), and Luke tells of the sinful woman who anointed Jesus' feet after washing them with her tears (7:37– 50). He has many references to the unrighteous in the parables (7:31–32; 12:13–21; 16:1–12, 19–31; 18:1–8, 9–14; the prodigal son should perhaps be included here). Clearly Luke had a deep interest in the fact that Jesus came to save sinners, and he records contacts with sinful people that shocked the respectable citizens of his day.

Luke has a deep interest in the Holy Spirit. We see this most clearly in Acts, but we should also notice it in his gospel, which has more references to the Holy Spirit than do Matthew and Mark combined. The Spirit was to be on John the Baptist "even from birth" (1:15), and both his parents on occasion were filled with the Spirit (1:41, 67). The Spirit was on Simeon, and the Spirit both revealed that he would see the Lord's Christ and brought him into the temple courts at the appropriate time (2:25–27).

The Holy Spirit is linked with Jesus' ministry in a variety of ways. The Spirit was active in bringing about Mary's conception (1:35). Before Jesus began his work, the Baptist said that Jesus would baptize with the Holy Spirit and with fire (3:16). At Jesus' baptism the Spirit came on him (3:22), and the Spirit both filled him and led him into the desert at the temptation (4:1). In due course Jesus "returned to Galilee in the power of the Spirit" (4:14), and he began his sermon at Nazareth by reading the passage beginning "the Spirit of the Lord is on me" (4:18). Once Jesus was "full of joy through the Holy Spirit" (10:21), and his teaching that the Spirit would give his followers what they needed to say (12:12) implies that the Spirit did the same for him. He taught that the Father gives the Spirit to those who ask (11:13), and the very end of the gospel includes the promise that the disciples would be "clothed with power from on high" (24:49), which surely refers to the coming of the Spirit at Pentecost.

The people of God should constantly look to God for the supply of their need; Luke emphasizes the place of prayer. He records nine times when Jesus prayed (seven found only in this gospel); our Lord's example is prominently brought home to the reader. There are parables about prayer, some teaching about the right kind of prayer, and one warning against the wrong kind of prayer (the Pharisee and the publican; see also 20:47). Luke leaves his readers in no doubt about the importance of prayer in Christian living.

The third gospel is one of song and of joy. It is to Luke that we owe the preservation of some of the great Christian songs, such as the songs of Mary (1:46–55)), Zechariah (1:68–79) and Simeon (2:29–32). Luke has more occurrences of the joy words (the verb χαίρειν, [*chairein*], together with the noun χαρά [*chara*]) than any other book in the New Testament. People are often found rejoicing or giving glory to God or praising him (e.g. 1:14, 44, 47; 2:20; 7:16; 10:21; 13:13). Luke speaks of laughter (6:21), of an exuberant leaping for joy

---

[56]Herdsmen are included in a list of people whose craft a man should not teach his son, "for their craft is the craft of robbers" (*m. Qidd.*4:14).

[57]Talmud, *b. Sanhedrin* 25b.

(6:23), of joy in the encounter Zaccheus has with Jesus (19:6), of joy in the finding of what was lost (15:6–7, 9–10), of merrymaking (15:23, 32), and much more. There can be no doubt that the Christianity Luke knew was a wonderfully joyful affair.

Even so, this is a gospel with emphasis on the passion.[58] Quite early there is a reference to "God my Savior" (1:47), and the gospel proceeds to develop this thought. It is not uncommon for some contemporary scholars to miss this theme. They concentrate on the fact that Luke has omitted some striking sayings such as the ransom saying (Mark 10:45); they observe that he does not have some of the characteristic Pauline emphases on the way of atonement. Thus Conzelmann says that in this gospel there is no "direct soteriological significance drawn from Jesus' suffering or death. There is no suggestion of a connection with the forgiveness of sins."[59] This gives a misleading impression. Although Luke does not specify the purpose of the cross in the way the other evangelists do, he devotes a good deal of space to the cross and its predictions (see 5:35; 9:22, 43–45; 12:50; 13:32–33; 17:25; 18:31–33). As we saw earlier, he uses terms such as "Savior" and "salvation" much more than the other evangelists. Salvation from what? If he did not see the cross as soteriological, then what was its meaning? He certainly does not describe it as a martyrdom or as setting us an example. He records Jesus' words, "The Son of Man came to seek and to save what was lost" (19:10), activities that involved the overcoming of the powers of evil. At the time of his arrest Jesus said, "This is your hour—when darkness reigns" (22:53), which means that the cross is the climax of the struggle. Elsewhere Luke views Jesus as accomplishing the new exodus (9:31, where "departure" renders ἔξοδος [exodos]; 22:15–16). Luke is no pale shadow of Mark or of Paul; he has his own way of bringing out the importance of the cross. He makes it clear that the purpose of God is in it, and this surely points to soteriological significance.

All that the objections seem to prove is that Luke has his own way of making the point that the cross is central. We see this in the structure of the gospel, with the space it devotes to the passion narrative and to its foreshadowings. Note the time reference: "As the time approached for him to be taken up to heaven, Jesus resolutely set out for Jerusalem" (9:51). Luke records Jesus as saying, "I have a baptism to undergo, and how distressed I am until it is completed!" (12:50). There are repeated predictions of the passion; 17:25 records a Q saying in which Luke, but not Matthew, has the reference to Jesus' suffering. Another Lukan touch is the information that at the transfiguration the subject of the conversation between Jesus and the heavenly visitors was his coming death (9:31), the inclusion of which shows something of Luke's interest in the cross. Luke brings out the purpose of God by referring to fulfillments of prophecy accomplished in the passion (e.g. 18:31; 20:17; 22:37; 24:26–27, 44, 46). All in all, he makes it quite clear that the passion effects God's will for our salvation.

In all this there is nothing triumphalist. Luke is sure that there is victory in the cross, but he usually does not emphasize this. He says simply, "On the third day he will rise again" (18:33). Here there is nothing at all about triumph. Doubtless

---

[58]The point is clearly made by Robert J. Karris (*Luke: Artist and Theologian: Luke's Passion Account as Literature* [New York: Paulist, 1985]), even if one must demur at some of Karris's findings as to how and why Luke emphasizes Jesus' passion.

[59]H. Conzelmann, *Theology of St. Luke*, p. 201.

it is implied, but the point is that Luke does not stress it.[60] For him the important truth is that Jesus died for sinners, even if he does not add things that would help those who are trying to formulate a theory of the atonement. It is enough for Luke that God saves through the work of Christ; he does not go into detail as to how this is worked out.

BIBLIOGRAPHY:

C. K. **Barrett**, *Luke the Historian in Recent Study* (London: Epworth, 1961); O. **Betz**, "The Kerygma of Luke," *Int* 22 (1968): 131–46; Darrell L. **Bock**, *Proclamation from Prophecy and Pattern: Lucan Old Testament Christology*, JSNTSupp 12 (Sheffield: Sheffield Academic Press, 1987); F. **Bovon**, *Luc le théologien: Vingt-cinq ans de recherches (1950-75)* (Neuchâtel: Delachaux & Niestlé, 1978); Schuyler **Brown**, *Apostasy and Perseverance in the Theology of Luke*, AnBib 36 (Rome: Pontifical Biblical Institute, 1969); F. F. **Bruce**, *The Acts of the Apostles* (London: Tyndale, 1951); Henry J. **Cadbury**, *The Making of Luke-Acts* (London: SPCK, 1958); idem, *The Style and Literary Method of Luke* (Cambridge: Harvard University Press, 1919); G. B. **Caird**, *The Gospel of St Luke* (Harmondsworth: Penguin, 1963); J. Bradley **Chance**, *Jerusalem, the Temple, and the New Age in Luke-Acts* (Macon, Ga.: Mercer University Press, 1988); Hans **Conzelmann**, "Luke's Place in the Development of Early Christianity," in *Studies in Luke-Acts*, ed. Leander E. Keck and J. Louis Martyn (Nashville: Abingdon, 1966), pp. 298–316; idem, *The Theology of St Luke* (London: Faber & Faber, 1961); J. M. **Creed**, *The Gospel According to St. Luke* (London: Macmillan, 1950); M. **Dibelius**, *Studies in the Acts of the Apostles* (ET London: SCM, 1956); J. **Drury**, *Tradition and Design in Luke's Gospel* (London: Darton, Longman & Todd, 1976); E. Earle **Ellis**, *Eschatology in Luke* (Philadelphia: Fortress, 1972); idem, *The Gospel of Luke* (London: Nelson, 1966); Stephen **Farris**, *The Hymns of Luke's Infancy Narratives: Their Origin, Meaning, and Significance*, JSNTSupp 9 (Sheffield: JSOT, 1985); Joseph A. **Fitzmyer**, *The Gospel According to Luke*, 2 vols. (New York: Doubleday, 1983–85); Helmut **Flender**, *St Luke, Theologian of Redemptive History* (London: SPCK, 1967); E. **Franklin**, *Christ the Lord: A Study in the Purpose and Theology of Luke-Acts* (London: SPCK, 1975); David **Gooding**, *According to Luke: A New Exposition of the Third Gospel* (Grand Rapids: Eerdmans, 1987); A. **Harnack**, *Luke the Physician* (New York: Putnam, 1907); R. G. **Heard**, "The Old Gospel Prologues," *JTS* 6 (1955): 1–16; W. K. **Hobart**, *The Medical Language of St. Luke* (Dublin: Hodges, Figgis, 1982); J. **Jervell**, *Luke and the People of God: A New Look at Luke-Acts* (Minneapolis: Augsburg, 1973); Luke T. **Johnson**, *The Literary Function of Possessions in Luke-Acts*, SBLDS 39 (Missoula, Mont.: SP, 1977); Donald **Juel**, *Luke-Acts: The Promise of History* (Atlanta: John Knox, 1985); Robert J. **Karris**, *Luke: Artist and Theologian. Luke's Passion Account as Literature* (New York: Paulist, 1985); E. **Käsemann**, *Essays on New Testament Themes* (London: SCM, 1964); Leander E. **Keck** and J. Louis **Martyn**, *Studies in Luke-Acts* (Nashville: Abingdon, 1966); A. F. J. **Klijn**, *A Survey of the Researches in the Western Text of the Gospel and Acts: Part Two (1949–1969)*, SuppNovT 21

---

[60]Alfred Plummer draws attention to the fact that Luke was somewhat differently evaluated in earlier days. When symbols were allotted to the gospels, there were some differences, but Luke was always symbolized by the ox (*A Critical and Exegetical Commentary on the Gospel According to S. Luke* [Edinburgh: T. & T. Clark, 1928], p. xxii). Quoting Isaac Williams, Plummer adds: "This sacerdotal animal implies Atonement and Propitiation; and this exactly corresponds with what is supposed to be the character of St. Luke's Gospel."

(Leiden: Brill, 1969); William L. Lane, *The Gospel According to Mark*, NICNT (Grand Rapids: Eerdmans, 1974); A. R. C. Leaney, *The Gospel According to St Luke*, BNTC, 2d ed. (London: Black, 1966); J. B. Lightfoot, *Notes on Epistles of St Paul* (London: Macmillan, 1904); R. Maddox, *The Purpose of Luke-Acts* (Edinburgh: T. & T. Clark, 1982); I. Howard Marshall, *Commentary on Luke: A Commentary on the Greek Text*, NIGTC (Grand Rapids: Eerdmans, 1978); idem, *Luke: Historian and Theologian* (Exeter: Paternoster, 1970); idem, "The Present State of Lucan Studies," *Themelios*, 14 (January/February 1989): pp. 52–57; Donald G. Miller, ed., *Jesus and Man's Hope* (Pittsburgh: Perspective Books, 1970); Leon Morris, "Luke and Early Catholicism," in *Studying the New Testament Today, I*, ed. John H. Skilton (Nutley, N.J.: Presbyterian & Reformed, 1974), pp. 60–75; idem, *Luke: An Introduction and Commentary*, 2d ed., TNTC (Leicester: IVP; Grand Rapids: Eerdmans, 1988); Alfred Plummer, *A Critical and Exegetical Commentary on the Gospel According to S. Luke* (Edinburgh: T. & T. Clark, 1928); Bo Reicke, "Synoptic Prophecies of the Destruction of Jerusalem," in *Studies in New Testament and Early Christian Literature*, ed. D. E. Aune (Leiden: Brill, 1972), pp. 121–33; M. Rese, *Alttestamentliche Motive in der Christologie des Lukas* (Gütersloh: Gerd Mohn, 1969); Leopold Sabourin, *The Gospel According to St Luke: Introduction and Commentary* (Bombay: St. Paul, 1984); David Peter Seccombe, *Possessions and the Poor in Luke-Acts* (Linz: SNTU, 1982); Robert B. Sloan, Jr., *The Favorable Year of the Lord: A Study of Jubilary Theology in the Gospel of Luke* (Austin, Tex.: Schola Press, 1977); Klyne Snodgrass, "Western Non-Interpolations," *JBL* 91 (1972): 369–79; B. H. Streeter, *The Four Gospels* (London: Macmillan, 1930); Charles H. Talbert, *Literary Patterns, Theological Themes, and the Genre of Luke-Acts*, SBLMS 20 (Missoula, Mont.: SP, 1974); idem, *Reading Luke* (New York: Crossroad, 1984); idem, ed., *Perspectives on Luke-Acts* (Edinburgh: T. & T. Clark, 1978); V. Taylor, *Behind the Third Gospel* (Oxford: Clarendon, 1926); idem, *The Gospel According to St. Mark*, 2d ed. (London: Macmillan, 1966); M. M. B. Turner, "The Sabbath, Sunday, and the Law in Luke/Acts," in *From Sabbath to Lord's Day*, ed. D. A. Carson (Grand Rapids: Zondervan, 1982), pp. 99–157; Michael Wilcock, *Savior of the World: The Message of Luke's Gospel* (Leicester: IVP, 1979).

5

John

CONTENTS

Like the other canonical gospels, John's gospel sets out to tell the story of Jesus' origins, ministry, death, and resurrection. Like them, it does not purport to be neutral. The evangelist sets out to engender faith (20:30–31), and to that end he shapes his witness with the needs of his readers in mind.[1]

Like many other facets of the gospel of John, its basic structure seems fairly simple until one starts to think more deeply about it. Doubtless this complexity wrapped in simplicity is the reason why scores of studies on John's structure have been published during the last two or three decades.

On the face of it, the fourth gospel offers a prologue (1:1–18) and an epilogue, or appendix (21:1–25), between which are the two central sections, 1:19–12:50 and 13:1–20:31. Under the influence of two or three influential scholars, these are now frequently designated, respectively, Book of Signs and Book of Glory,[2] or Book of Signs and Book of the Passion.[3]

Nevertheless, the designation "Book of Signs" makes it sound as if the signs are restricted to 1:19–12:50, whereas 20:30–31 makes it clear that from the evangelist's perspective the *entire* gospel is a book of signs: the passion and resurrection of Jesus is the greatest sign of all. Moreover, although Jesus' passion is related in chapters 13–20, the passion narrative itself does not begin until chapter 18. If chapters 13–17 can be included on the ground that they are thematically tied to the passion, so also are many passages in chapters 1–12 (e.g., 1:29, 36; 6:35ff.; 11:49–52).

Others have advocated a quite different structure. Wyller,[4] for example, holds that 10:22–29 is the "structural summit" of the work, the "change of fate" of the hero, around which the rest of the material is organized. Despite the superficial

---

[1]At several points this chapter has used, with permission, material from D. A. Carson, *The Gospel According to John* (Grand Rapids: Eerdmans, 1990)—sometimes verbatim, more frequently in condensed form.

[2]R. E. Brown, *The Gospel According to John* (Garden City, N.Y.: Doubleday, 1966–70), pp. cxxxviii–cxxxix.

[3]C. H. Dodd, *The Interpretation of the Fourth Gospel* (Cambridge: Cambridge University Press, 1953), p. 289.

[4]Egil A. Wyller, "In Solomon's Porch: A Henological Analysis of the Architectonic of the Fourth Gospel," *ST* 42 (1988): 151–67.

plausibility of his argument, it is difficult to believe, on thematic grounds, that these verses have quite the structural importance Wyller assigns to them, and almost impossible to believe that Plato's simile of the cave is the most plausible model for the structure of a gospel. Another scholar has detected a massive concentric structure patterned to have the concentric structure of the prologue.[5] However, structures that are so complex and disputed as not to be *intuitively* obvious should not be assigned much credibility.

Trying to account for all the complexity in John, one recent and important discussion of the structure of John's gospel finds major chiasms and what the author calls bridge-pericopes and bridge-sections—sections that fit into two or more structured units and that tie them together.[6] For instance, he suggests that 2:1–12:50 might be called the Book of Jesus' Signs, that 11:1–20:29 is the Book of Jesus' Hour, and that the overlapping chapters, 11–12, constitute a bridge-section. Although this or that detail may be disputed, he does succeed in showing how unified and tightly organized the fourth gospel is. Many have pointed out, for instance, that individual sections of various length are neatly brought to a close (e.g., 1:18; 4:42; 4:53–54; 10:40–42; 12:44–50; 20:30–31; 21:25).

One of the reasons why critics find so many mutually exclusive structures in John is that his repeated handling of only a few themes makes it possible to postulate all kinds of parallels and chiasms. Another is that various structures seem to serve as overlays to other structures. For instance, it has often been noted that the section 2:1–4:54 reflects a geographic *inclusio* (i.e. a literary device that both introduces and concludes a passage by the same literary feature): the action moves from Cana to Cana. But although that device helps us see the boundaries of this unit, it is less than clear that Cana per se is so important in Johannine thought that it should be accorded paramount *theological* significance, beyond its minor role in helping readers to follow the movement of the text.

Following the prologue (1:1–18), Jesus' discloses himself in word and deed (1:19–10:42). This large unit begins with a prelude to Jesus' public ministry (1:19–51). As in the synoptic tradition, John the Baptist is first introduced: his relation to Jesus is articulated (1:19–28), as is his public witness concerning Jesus (1:29–34). The prelude ends with reports as to how Jesus gains his first disciples (1:35–51).

The rest of this first large unit (1:19–10:42) may be divided into three sections. The first reports Jesus' early ministry: his signs, works, and words (2:1–4:54). This includes the first sign, namely, the changing of the water into wine (2:1–11), the clearing of the temple (2:12–17), and the utterance about Jesus' replacing the temple (2:18–22). The inadequate faith of many who trust him at this juncture (2:23–25) sets the stage for the exchange between Jesus and Nicodemus (3:1–15), the dialogue rapidly turning to monologue. Twice in this chapter the evangelist himself apparently offers his own extended comment, the first at this point (3:16–21), and the second after his description of John the Baptist's continuing witness concerning Jesus (3:22–30, followed by 3:31–36). On his way to Galilee, Jesus stops in Samaria and leads both a Samaritan woman and

---

[5]Jeffrey Lloyd Staley, *The Print's First Kiss: A Rhetorical Investigation of the Implied Reader in the Fourth Gospel*, SBLDS 82 (Atlanta: SP, 1985).

[6]George Mlakushyil, *The Christocentric Literary Structure of the Fourth Gospel*, AnBib 117 (Rome: Pontifical Biblical Institute, 1987).

many of her countrymen to faith in himself (4:1–42). The section is capped by the second sign, the healing of the official's son (4:43–54).

In the next section (5:1–7:53), there are more signs, works, and words, but now in the context of rising opposition. The healing of the paralytic at the pool of Bethesda (5:1–15), which connects sin and illness, is performed on the Sabbath, and this triggers some opposition, which Jesus quickly transforms into a *Christological* question, especially regarding the nature of his sonship to the Father (5:16–30). These central Christological claims give rise to treatment of the witnesses concerning Jesus (5:31–47). The feeding of the five thousand (6:1–15) and the walking on the water (6:16–21) serve to introduce the bread of life discourse (6:22–58), where Jesus' claims that he is himself the true manna (esp. 6:27–34), the bread of life (6:35–48) that must be eaten. This gives rise to more hesitations: opinion is divided over him, and even some of his disciples turn against him, while he himself retains the initiative in determining who truly are his followers (6:59–71). Skepticism and uncertainty regarding him continue, even among members of his own family (7:1–13). This means that the first round of exchange at the Feast of Tabernacles (7:14–44), climaxing in his promise to pour out the eschatological Spirit consequent on his own glorification (7:37–44), is frankly confrontational and leads to the first organized opposition from the Jewish authorities (7:45–52).

After the pericope of the woman caught in adultery (7:53–8:11), which we believe was not part of the original text (see discussion below in the section "Text"), the last section (8:12–10:42) reports climactic signs, works, and words in the context of radical confrontation. The second round of exchanges at the Feast of Tabernacles (8:12–59) ends with Jesus telling the authorities they are children of the Devil, while he himself is none less than the "I am"—and this sparks off a futile attempt to stone him to death. The healing of the man born blind (9:1–41), in which no connection between sin and the man's condition is allowed, comes to its climax with the denunciation of those who think they see. In chapter 10, Jesus presents himself as the good shepherd of the sheep. The effect is to make his own messianic flock the one locus of the people of God, with predictable reactions from the Jews (10:1–21). At the Feast of Dedication, Jesus' claims to be both Messiah and Son of God engender open opposition (10:22–39), prompting Jesus to make a strategic retreat to the area where John the Baptist had earlier baptized—a retreat that prompts the reader to recall John's true witness and that is nevertheless accompanied by growing numbers of people who are placing their faith in Jesus (10:40–42).

Although many include the next unit, 11:1–12:50, as part of the Book of Signs, there appear to be good reasons for treating these chapters as something of a transition. The account of the death and resurrection of Lazarus (11:1–44) is both a foil and an anticipation of Jesus' death and resurrection and directly leads to the judicial decision to kill Jesus (11:45–54). In the next section (11:55–12:36), set during the "Jewish Passover" (11:55–57) in anticipation of the death of the true Passover lamb, Mary anoints Jesus in anticipation of his death, thereby displaying sacrificial love for him—the only kind of any value (12:1–11); the triumphal entry announces Jesus' kingship, but the ominous signs are already present that this kingship will be unlike any other (12:12–19); and the arrival of the Gentiles triggers Jesus' announcement of the dawning "hour" of his death and exaltation (12:20–36). This transitional unit concludes with a theology of unbelief, that is, theological reflections that reveal the nature and inevitability of unbelief (12:20–36).

The final major unit of the book depicts Jesus' self-disclosure in his cross and exaltation (13:1–20:31). It opens with the last supper (13:1–30), but instead of preserving any report of the institution of Holy Communion, John recalls how Jesus washed his disciples' feet (13:1–17), an act that simultaneously anticipated the unique cleansing effected by his impending death and left an example for his disciples to emulate. Jesus' prediction of the betrayal (13:18–30) leaves no doubt that he remains in charge of his own destiny, in submission to his Father's will. The so-called farewell discourse that follows—partly dialogue and partly monologue—is conveniently broken up into two parts (13:31–14:31 and 15:1–16:33). In some ways, this farewell discourse explains the significance of the last sign—Jesus' own death and exaltation—*before* the sign itself takes place and thus becomes a theology of the place of Jesus and his death and glorification in the stream of redemptive history, including the role and function of the promised Paraclete, the Holy Spirit whom Jesus bestows on believers in consequence of his exaltation. There follows the prayer of Jesus (17:1–26), in which Jesus prays for his own glorification (17:1–5), for his disciples (17:6–19), for those who will later believe (17:20–23), and, climactically, for the perfection of all believers so as to see Jesus' glory (17:24–26). The trial and passion of Jesus follow (18:1–19:42), with particular emphasis on the nature of Jesus' kingship. The resurrection of Jesus (20:1–31) includes not only several resurrection appearances but the remarkable saying regarding the gift of the Spirit and the forgiveness of sins (20:19–22) and the equally remarkable confession of Thomas, "My Lord and my God!" (20:28). This large unit ends with a concise statement of the fourth gospel's purpose (20:30–31).

The epilogue (21:1–25) not only ties up several loose ends (e.g., Peter's restoration to service) but, in symbolic ways, points to the growth of the church and the diversity of gifts and callings within the church. Appropriately, it ends with the greatness of Jesus (21:25).

AUTHOR

It is commonly held that the fourth gospel does not bear its author's name: like the synoptics, it is formally anonymous. As far as we can prove, the title "According to John" was attached to it as soon as the four canonical gospels began to circulate together as "the fourfold gospel," in part, no doubt, to distinguish it from the rest of the collection; but it may have served as the title from the beginning (see chap. 2 above, on Matthew). But even if the attribution "According to John" was added two or three decades after the book was published, the observation of Bruce is suggestive: "It is noteworthy that, while the four canonical Gospels could afford to be published anonymously, the apocryphal Gospels which began to appear from the mid-second century onwards claimed (falsely) to be written by apostles or other persons associated with the Lord."[7]

---

[7]F. F. Bruce, *The Gospel of John* (Basingstoke: Pickering & Inglis, 1983), p. 1.

External Evidence

Although there are several earlier documents, both within the orthodox stream and within Gnosticism, that allude to the fourth gospel or quote it (see the discussion below), the first writer to quote unambiguously from the fourth gospel and to ascribe the work to John is Theophilus of Antioch (c. A.D. 181). Before this date, however, several writers, including Tatian (a student of Justin Martyr), Claudius Apollinaris (bishop of Hierapolis), and Athenagorus, unambiguously quote from the fourth gospel as from an authoritative source. This pushes us back to Polycarp and Papias, information about whom derives primarily from Ireneus (end of the second century) and Eusebius, the historian of the early church (fourth century). Polycarp was martyred in 156 at the age of eighty-six. There is no reason therefore to deny the truth of the claims that he associated with the apostles in Asia (John, Andrew, Philip) and was "entrusted with the oversight of the Church in Smyrna by those who were eye-witnesses and ministers of the Lord" (*H.E.* 3.36).

Ireneus knew Polycarp personally, and it is Polycarp who mediates to us the most important information about the fourth gospel. Writing to Florinus, Ireneus recalls:

> I remember the events of those days more clearly than those which have happened recently, for what we learn as children grows up with the soul and becomes united to it, so I can speak even of the place in which the blessed Polycarp sat and disputed, how he came in and went out, the character of his life, the appearance of his body, the discourse which he made to the people, how he reported his converse with John and with the others who had seen the Lord, how he remembered their words, and what were the things concerning the Lord which he had heard from them, including his miracles and his teaching,[8] and how Polycarp had received them from the eyewitnesses of the word of life, and reported all things in agreement with the Scriptures (*H.E.* 5.20.5–6).

Most scholars recognize that this "John," certainly a reference to John the apostle, the son of Zebedee, is (so far as Ireneus is concerned) none other than the John whom he emphatically insists is the fourth evangelist. For Ireneus, that the gospel should be fourfold (in the sense already described) was as natural as that there should be four winds. As for the fourth gospel itself, he wrote, "John the disciple of the Lord, who leaned back on his breast, published the Gospel while he was resident at Ephesus in Asia" (*Adv. Haer.* 2.1.2). In other words, the name of the fourth evangelist is John and is to be identified with the beloved disciple of John 13:23.

The evidence of Papias similarly depends on secondary sources. Papias was a contemporary of Polycarp and may himself have been a student of John (Ireneus, *Adv. Haer.* 5.33.4, affirms it; Eusebius, *H.E.* 3.39.2, denies it). That Eusebius does not mention that Papias cited the fourth gospel is irrelevant: Eusebius's stated purpose was to discuss the disputed parts of the New Testament, as well as some of those people who linked the first century with what follows, rather than to provide a list of citations regarding "acknowledged" books.[9]

---

[8]The translation is from the Loeb edition of Eusebius, except for this clause, where the Loeb edition clearly errs.

[9]In this connection, however, it is rather remarkable that 1 John should be mentioned, since it *was*

Another piece of evidence regarding Papias is harder to evaluate. About A.D. 140 an eccentric follower of the writings of Paul, Marcion by name, who had become convinced that only this apostle had truly followed the teachings of Jesus while all the others had relapsed into Judaism, went to Rome to try to convince the church there of his views. He argued, unsuccessfully, that the proper New Testament canon comprised ten letters of Paul and one gospel, a mutilated version of Luke. Marcion was so dangerous that he succeeded in arousing responses. In particular, the so-called anti-Marcionite prologues to the Gospels have been viewed as part of these reponses (though it must be admitted that some scholars think they emerged at a later period). The anti-Marcionite prologue to John has come down to us in a rather corrupt Latin version. It tells us that the gospel of John was published while John was still alive and was written down at John's dictation by Papias, a man from Hierapolis and one of John's near disciples. As for Marcion, he had been expelled by John himself. This information, the prologue argues, derives from the five exegetical books of Papias himself: the reference is to his *Exegesis of the Dominical Logia*, which survived into the Middle Ages in some libraries in Europe but, which is regrettably no longer extant.

Some of the information provided by the anti-Marcionite prologue is clearly mistaken. It is extremely doubtful that John excommunicated Marcion: the chronology is stretched too thin. Moreover, it has been suggested that Papias for his part may have said that the churches or certain disciples "wrote dow 1" what John said and was subsequently misquoted as meaning "I wrote down," since in Greek the latter may be formally indistinguishable from "they wrote down."[10] Even so, there is no doubt in this document that John himself was responsible for the fourth gospel.

Not only Ireneus but Clement of Alexandria and Tertullian provide firm, second-century evidence for the belief that the apostle John wrote this gospel. According to Eusebius (*H.E.* 6.14.7), Clement wrote, "But that John, last of all, conscious that the outward facts had been set forth in the Gospels, was urged on by his disciples, and, divinely moved by the Spirit, composed a spiritual Gospel." A more enigmatic and, in its details, less believable version of the same development is preserved in the Muratorian Canon, the earliest orthodox list of New Testament books to come down to us, probably from c. A.D. 170–80. It tells us not only that John's fellow disciples and bishops urged him to write but that by a dream or prophecy it was revealed to Andrew that John should in fact take up the task, writing in his own name, but that the others should review his work and contribute to it. Most scholars take this to be someone's deduction from John 21:24.

Some indirect evidence is in certain respects much more impressive. Tatian, a student of Justin Martyr, composed the first harmony of the fourfold gospel: he took the books apart and wove them together into one continuous narrative

---

universally accepted. Perhaps, as some have suggested, it is because it belongs to the so-called General, or Catholic, Epistles, which constituted a rather exceptional group of writings.

[10]In the imperfect tense, ἀπέγραφον (*apegraphon*) means either "I wrote down" or "they wrote down"; in the aorist tense, there is normally a formal distinction: "I wrote down" is ἀπέγραψα (*apegrapsa*), while "they wrote down" is ἀπέγραψαν (*apegrapsan*). But even this distinction could be blurred; see J. B. Lightfoot, *Essays on the Work Entitled "Supernatural Religion"* (London: 1889), p. 214.

known as the *Diatessaron*. First prepared in Greek, this harmony exerted an enormous influence in its Syriac translation. But the crucial point to observe is that it is the gospel of John that provides the framework into which the other three gospels are fitted. This could not have been the case had there been questions about the authenticity of the book.

Indeed, by the end of the second century the only people who denied Johannine authorship to the fourth gospel were the so-called *Alogoi*—a substantivized adjective meaning "witless ones," used by the orthodox as a pun to refer to those who rejected the Logos (the "Word" of John 1:1) doctrine expounded in the fourth gospel, and therefore the fourth gospel itself. (Epiphanius gave them this name in *Haer.* 51.3; they are probably the same group mentioned by Ireneus in *Adv. Haer.* 3.11.9.) Even here, there were sometimes competing forces at work. For instance, Gaius, an elder in the Roman church who was one of the Alogoi, maintained orthodoxy at every point except in his rejection of John's gospel and the Apocalypse. At least part of his motivation, however, was his virulent opposition to Montanism, an uncontrolled charismatic movement arising in the middle of the second century that claimed that its leader, Montanus, was the mouthpiece of the promised Paraclete. Since all of the Paraclete sayings that refer to the Spirit are found in John's gospel (14:16, 26; 15:26; 16:7–15), Gaius did not need much persuading to side with the Alogoi on this point.

Certainly from the end of the second century on, there is virtual agreement in the church as to the authority, canonicity, and authorship of the gospel of John. An argument from silence in this case proves impressive: "It is significant that Eusebius, who had access to many works which are now lost, speaks without reserve of the fourth Gospel as the unquestioned work of St. John."[11] The silence is most significant precisely because it was Eusebius's concern to discuss the doubtful cases.

The external evidence that maintains the fourth evangelist was none other than the apostle John, then, is virtually unanimous, though not impressively early. But even if we must turn to Ireneus, toward the end of the second century, to find one of the first totally unambiguous witnesses, his personal connection with Polycarp, who knew John, means the distance in terms of personal memories is not very great. Even Dodd, who discounts the view that the apostle John wrote the fourth gospel, considers the external evidence formidable, adding, "Of any external evidence to the contrary that could be called cogent I am not aware."[12]

The fact remains that, despite support for Johannine authorship by a few front-rank scholars in this century and by many popular writers, a large majority of contemporary scholars reject this view. As we shall see, much of their argumentation turns on their reading of the *internal* evidence. Nevertheless, it requires their virtual dismissal of the external evidence. This is particularly regrettable. Most historians of antiquity, other than New Testament scholars, could not so easily set aside evidence as plentiful and as uniform.

One way of circumventing the force of the external evidence is by appealing to the words of Papias, as reported and interpreted by Eusebius, in support of the

---

[11]B. F. Westcott, *The Gospel According to St John: The Greek Text with Introduction and Notes*, 2 vols. (London: John Murray, 1908), 1:lix.

[12]C. H. Dodd, *Historical Tradition in the Fourth Gospel* (Cambridge: Cambridge University Press, 1963), p. 12; cf. J. A. T. Robinson, *The Priority of John* (London: SCM, 1985), pp. 99–104.

hypothesis that there were two Johns. Papias writes (according to Eusebius): "And if anyone chanced to come who had actually been a follower of the elders, I would enquire as to the discourses of the elders, what Andrew or what Peter said, or what Philip, or what Thomas or James, or what John or Matthew or any other of the Lord's disciples; and things which Aristion and John the elder, disciples of the Lord, say." Eusebius then comments: "Here it is worth noting that twice in his enumeration he mentions the name of John: the former of these Johns he puts in the same list with Peter and James and Matthew and the other apostles, clearly indicating the evangelist; but the latter he places with the others, in a separate clause, outside the number of the apostles, placing Aristion before him; and he clearly calls him 'elder' " (H.E. 3.39.4–5).[13] From this passage, many have inferred that it was this second John, a disciple of John the son of Zebedee, who wrote the fourth gospel. Perhaps, indeed, Ireneus and Theophilus and other early Fathers confused their Johns.

But recent study has shown that this appeal to Papias is precarious, for four reasons.

1. It is now widely recognized that whereas Eusebius makes a distinction between apostles and elders, understanding that the latter are disciples of the former and therefore second-generation Christians, Papias himself makes no such distinction. In the terms of Papias, "the discourses of the elders" means the teaching of Andrew, Peter, and the other apostles. It is Eusebius who el ewhere writes, "Papias, of whom we are now speaking, acknowledges that he received the discourses of the apostles from those who had been their followers" (H.E. 3.39.7). Transparently, that is not what Papias said.[14]

2. In the Papias quotation John is designated "the elder" precisely because he is being grouped with the elders just mentioned, that is, with the apostles. It is worth noting that "apostle" and "elder" come together with a common referent in 1 Peter 5:1. Indeed, the Greek syntax Papias employs favors the view that "Aristion and John the elder" means something like "Aristion and the aforementioned elder John."[15]Not only here but in H.E. 3.39.14 it is John and not Aristion who is designated "the elder." In choosing to refer to the apostles as elders, Papias may well be echoing the language of 3 John (on the assumption that Papias thought that epistle was written by the apostle John).

3. It appears that the distinction Papias is making in his two lists is not between apostles and elders of the next generation but between first-generation witnesses who have died (what they *said*) and first-generation witnesses who are still alive (what they *say*). Aristion, then, can be linked with John, not because neither is an apostle, but because both are first-generation disciples of the Lord. And this supports the witness of Ireneus, who says that Papias, not less than Polycarp, was "a hearer of John."

4. In any case, Eusebius had his own agenda. He so disliked the apocalyptic language of Revelation that he was only too glad to find it possible to assign its

---

[13]In this instance we have followed the translation of H. J. Lawlor and J. E. L. Oulton, *Eusebius: The Ecclesiastical History and the Martyrs of Palestine*, 2 vols. (1927; reprint, London: SPCK, 1954), 1:89, since it observes distinctions in the Greek text overlooked by the more popular Loeb edition.

[14]See J. B. Lightfoot, *Biblical Essays* (London: Macmillan, 1893), pp. 58ff.

[15]So C. S. Petrie, "The Authorship of 'The Gospel According to Matthew': A Reconstruction of the External Evidence," *NTS* 14 (1967–68): 21.

authorship to a John other than the apostle, and he seizes on "John the elder" as he has retrieved him from Papias.[16]

Martin Hengel has recently devoted an entire monograph to the thesis that it was John the elder, not John the apostle, who was the author of the penultimate draft of the fourth gospel (which then, after his death, was lightly edited, with 21:24–25 also being added).[17] But Hengel's "elder" is not the second-century disciple of the aged apostle that many modern scholars have reconstructed. Hengel argues that "John the elder" is none other than the "beloved disciple" (13:23; 19:26–27; 20:2–9; 21:24), a Palestinian Jew who was a contemporary of Jesus and an eyewitness of at least some events in Jesus' life, but not John the son of Zebedee. Even Hengel admits his "hypothesis may sound fantastic."[18] He is forced to concede that "the figures of John son of Zebedee and the teacher of the school [i.e. his hypothesized 'John the elder'] . . . are deliberately superimposed in a veiled way" and therefore admits that "it would be conceivable that with the 'beloved disciple' 'John the elder' wanted to point more to the son of Zebedee, who for him was an ideal, even *the* ideal disciple, in contrast to Peter, whereas in the end the pupils impress on this enigmatic figure the face of *their* teacher by identifying him with the author in order to bring the Gospel as near to Jesus as possible."[19] It is hard to imagine how one could get closer than this to affirming apostolic authorship while still denying it!

Why Hengel prefers his hypothesis of an otherwise unknown first-century Palestinian Jew by the name of John who was a contemporary of the apostle John, to the apostle himself, is far from clear. He thinks, for instance, that the Judean focus of the fourth gospel argues for an author who was not a Galilean, as John the apostle was. He judges that the verbal link between "elder" (sometimes rendered "presbyter") in Papias and the same expression in 2 John 1 and 3 John 1 is very significant (though in fact apostles were known to refer to themselves as elders on occasion; see 1 Peter 5:1).[20] He hypothesizes that there may have been unambiguous evidence in Papias to the effect that this "John the elder" wrote the fourth gospel and holds that one must "reckon with the possibility that Eusebius sometimes concealed information which seemed disagreeable to him or omitted it through carelessness";[21] on this view the early church simply repeated the error.

All of this is exceedingly weak. From the evidence of Eusebius, it is far from certain that there ever was an "elder John" independent of the apostle, and if there was, it is still less certain that he wrote anything. If against the evidence we accept Eusebius's interpretation of Papias, we will assign the fourth gospel to the apostle John and the Apocalypse to the elder John—while mainstream biblical scholarship assigns neither book to the apostle. Meanwhile, Hengel's objections to identifying the beloved disciple with the apostle John are not at all weighty. Because they turn on an evaluation of the internal evidence, to that we must turn.

---

[16]Cf. G. M. Lee, *SE* 6:311–20.
[17]Martin Hengel, *The Johannine Question* (ET Philadelphia: Trinity Press International, 1989).
[18]Ibid., p. 130.
[19]Ibid., pp. 131–32.
[20]Ibid., p. 132.
[21]Ibid., p. 21.

Internal Evidence

The classic approach of Westcott, updated by Morris,[22] was to establish five points: the author of the fourth gospel was (1) a Jew, (2) of Palestine, (3) an eyewitness, (4) an apostle (i.e. one of the Twelve), and (5) the apostle John. The first two points are today rarely disputed and need not detain us here, except to make three observations.

1. The discovery of the Dead Sea Scrolls compels us to recognize that it is unnecessary to resort to a period of expansion into the Hellenistic world to account for John's characteristic expressions. See further discussion below in the section "Provenance." Moreover, the evangelist's detailed knowledge of Palestinian topography and of features in conservative Jewish debate probably reflects personal acquaintance, not mere dependence on reliable Jewish sources.

2. To this we must add the widely accepted fact, already appealed to by Lightfoot in the last century,[23] that at least in some instances John's quotations are closer in form to the Hebrew or Aramiac than to the Greek (esp. 12:40; 13:18; 19:37).

3. The recent attempt of Margaret Pamment to argue that the beloved disciple is a Gentile believer turns on her argument that 21:1ff. is concerned with the Gentile mission (in this she is partly right), and this, she says, "suggests the beloved disciple [who appears in this chapter] is a gentile."[24] This is a classic non sequitur. Granted that all the first believers were Jews, at least *some* of the first witnesses to Gentiles had to be Jews!

The other three points, however, are all disputed and turn in large part on the identity of the "beloved disciple," the now-standard way of referring to the one whom the NIV more prosaically describes as "the disciple whom Jesus loved" (e.g., 13:23). The raw information is quickly canvassed. The beloved disciple first appears as such at the last supper, where he is reclining next to Jesus and mediating Peter's question to the Master (13:23). He is found at the cross, where he receives a special commission having to do with Jesus' mother (19:26–27), and at the empty tomb, where he outstrips Peter in speed but not in boldness (20:2–9). In the epilogue (chap. 21), he is said to be the one who wrote "these things." If "wrote" means that he wrote the material himself (and did not simply cause the material to be written, as some have suggested) and "these things" refers to the entire book and not just to chapter 21, then the beloved disciple is the evangelist. If that is correct, then it is natural to identify the eyewitness who saw the blood and water flow from Jesus' side as the beloved disciple, even though he is not so described.

But who is the beloved disciple? The traditional view, that he is John the son of Zebedee, has been advanced for reasons of quite different weight. That the beloved disciple was at the last supper is not disputed (13:23). The synoptics insist that only the apostles joined Jesus for this meal (Mark 14:17 par.), which places the beloved disciple within the band of the Twelve (and coincidentally speaks against Hengel's hypothesis, described above). He is repeatedly distinguished from Peter (John 13:23–24; 20:2–9; 21:20), and by the same token should not

[22]Leon Morris, *Studies in the Fourth Gospel* (Grand Rapids: Eerdmans, 1969), pp. 218ff.
[23]Lightfoot, *Biblical Essays*, pp. 20–21.
[24]Margaret Pamment, "The Fourth Gospel's Beloved Disciple," *ExpTim* 94 (1983): 367.

be confused with any of the other apostles named in John 13–16. That he is one of the seven who go fishing in chapter 21 and, by implication, is not Peter, Thomas, or Nathanael suggests he is one of the sons of Zebedee or one of the other two unnamed disciples (21:2). Of the sons of Zebedee, he cannot be James, since James was the first of the apostolic band to be martyred (probably toward the end of the reign of Herod Agrippa I, A.D. 41–44; see Acts 12:1–2), while the beloved disciple lived long enough to give weight to the rumor that he would not die (21:23). The fact that neither John nor James is mentioned by name in the fourth gospel, which nevertheless has place not only for prominent apostles such as Peter and Andrew but also for relatively obscure members of the apostolic band such as Philip and "Judas (not Judas Iscariot)" (14:22) is exceedingly strange, unless there is some reason for it. The traditional reason seems most plausible: the beloved disciple is none other than John, and he deliberately avoids using his personal name. This becomes more likely when we remember that the beloved disciple is constantly in the company of Peter, while the synoptics (Mark 5:37; 9:2; 14:33; par.) and Acts (3:1–4:23; 8:15–25), not to mention Paul (Gal. 2:9), link Peter and John in friendship and shared experience. It has also been noted that in this gospel most of the important characters are designated with rather full expressions: Simon Peter; Thomas Didymus; Judas, son of Simon Iscariot; Caiaphas, the high priest that year. Strangely, however, John the Baptist is simply called John, even when he is first introduced (1:6; cf. Mark 1:4 par.). The simplest explanation is that John the son of Zebedee is the one person who would *not* feel it necessary to distinguish the other John from himself.

The evidence is not entirely conclusive. For instance, it is just possible that the beloved disciple is one of the unnamed pair of disciples in John 21:2. But once the logical possibility has been duly noted, it seems to be a rather desperate expedient that stands against the force of the cumulative internal evidence and the substantial external evidence.

Other identifications have been advanced. Some, for instance, have suggested Lazarus, on the grounds that "beloved disciple" would be an appropriate form of self-reference for one of whom it is said that Jesus loved him (11:5, 36). One or two have suggested the rich young man of Mark 10:21, on much the same ground. Still others argue for the owner of the upper room, arguing that the reason he could lay his head on Jesus' breast was that, as the host, he was placed in a position of honor next to Jesus; perhaps he was John Mark.

None of this is convincing, and all of it notoriously speculative. According to the synoptic evidence, only the Twelve were present at the last supper: that alone rules out all three suggestions. There is nothing to be said for the first two, other than that Jesus loved them; but that is surely an insufficient ground for identifying the beloved disciple, presupposing as it does that the circle of those whom Jesus loved was extremely limited. As for the second suggestion, to appeal to the gospel of Mark to sort out the identity of the beloved disciple in John seems to be a dubious procedure. And if the owner of the upper room was present as host in any sense, why is it that all four gospels present Jesus taking the initiative at the meal, serving, in fact, as the host? Moreover, there is no patristic evidence that John the son of Zebedee and John Mark were ever confused.

In his commentary, Brown strongly argues that the beloved disciple is John the son of Zebedee (though he does not identify him with the evangelist), largely along the lines just taken. By the time of his more popular book, outlining his understanding of the history of the Johannine community, however, Brown has changed his mind,[25] without answering his own evidence. He now thinks the beloved disciple is an outsider, not one of the Twelve, but a Judean with access to the high priest's court (18:15–16), possibly the unnamed disciple in 1:35–40. Others have advanced extensive lists of reasons why the beloved disciple could not be John the son of Zebedee.[26] These vary considerably in quality, but they include such entries as these: John the son of Zebedee was a Galilean, yet much of the narrative of the fourth gospel takes place in Judea; John and Peter are elsewhere described as "unschooled, ordinary men" (Acts 4:13), so John could not be expected to write a book of subtlety and depth; John and James are elsewhere described as "Sons of Thunder" (Mark 3:17), presumably suggesting impetuosity, intemperance, and anger, yet this book is the most placid, even mystical, of the canonical gospels; John was vengeful against the Samaritans (Luke 9:54), so it is hard to imagine him writing a book that treats them so kindly (John 4).

None of these arguments seems to carry much weight against the mass on the other side.

1. Although John the son of Zebedee was a Galilean, by the time he wrote, he had not only lived for years in Judea (during the earliest period of the church) but (in any traditional view) in the great metropolitan center of Ephesus. To restrict John's focus of interest to the place of his origin, when at the time of writing he had not lived there for decades, seems rather unrealistic.

2. It has long been pointed out that the expression in Acts 4:13 does not mean that Peter and John were illiterate or profoundly ignorant but, from the point of view of contemporary theological proficiency, "untrained laymen" (NEB), not unlike Jesus himself (John 7:15). The astonishment of the authorities was in any case occasioned by the competence of Peter and John when they should have been (relatively) ignorant, not by their ignorance when they should have been more competent. Jewish boys learned to read. Since John sprang from a family that was certainly not poor (they owned at least one boat [Luke 5:3, 10] and employed others [Mark 1:20]), he may well have enjoyed an education that was better than average. And surely it would not be surprising if some of the leaders of the church, decades after its founding, had devoted themselves to some serious study.

3. The suggestion that a "son of thunder" could not have become the apostle of love, or that a man steeped in racial bias against the Samaritans could not have written John 4, is an implicit denial of the power of the gospel and the mellowing effect of years of Christian leadership in an age when the Spirit's transforming might was so largely displayed. The argument is as convincing as the view that Saul the persecutor of the church could not have become the apostle to the Gentiles.

4. Although the "other disciple" who arranges for Peter to be admitted to the high priest's courtyard (18:15–16) is not explicitly said to be the beloved disciple and may be someone else, yet the connection with John has more to be said for it than some think. It appears that this "other disciple" was in the band of those who

---

[25]R. E. Brown, *The Community of the Beloved Disciple* (New York: Paulist, 1979), pp. 33–34.

[26]E.g., Pierson Parker, "John the Son of Zebedee and the Fourth Gospel," *JBL* 81 (1962): 35–43; see also Domingo León ("¿Es el apóstol Juan el discípulo amado?" *EstBib* 45 [1987]: 403–92), who raises the objections in order to rebut them.

were with Jesus when he was arrested and therefore one of the Eleven who had emerged from the upper room and had accompanied Jesus up the slopes of the Mount of Olives. His close association with Peter supports (though it does not prove) the view that he is none other than John. That a Galilean fisherman could have access to the high priest's court is frequently dismissed on the ground that a fishmonger could not enter unquestioned into the waiting room of the prime minister. In fact, the social model is all wrong. We have already seen that John's family enjoyed some substance; it may have been rich, and in many societies money breaks down social barriers. The relevant social barriers of first-century Palestine may not have been that strong in any case; rabbis were expected to gain a skilled trade apart from their study (thus Paul was a leatherworker), so that the stratification that divided teacher from manual laborer in Stoic and other circles of the Hellenistic world was not a significant factor in much of Palestine. Galilee supplied the fish for all of the country except for the coast and was brought into Jerusalem through the Fish Gate (see Neh. 3:3; Zeph. 1:10). As Robinson comments, the tradition may not be entirely fanciful that says that John's acquaintance with the girl at the gate and with the high priest's household stemmed from familiarity with the tradesman's entrance.[27] He may have had a place in the city (19:27) and served on occasion as his father's agent (a role that crops up in the saying of 13:16). It has been pointed out that the peculiar term for cooked fish ($\dot{o}\psi\acute{a}\rho\iota o\nu$ [*opsarion*]), the form in which much of the trade would be conducted, occurs five times in the fourth gospel (6:9, 11; 21:9, 10, 13) and not elsewhere in the New Testament.

5. Although in the past it has been argued that a Palestinian could not write such fluent Greek, the argument no longer stands. There is now a powerful consensus that at least in Galilee, and perhaps elsewhere in first-century Palestine, the populace was at least bilingual, and in some cases trilingual. Aramaic was used for everyday speech, at least in the villages. (Hebrew may have been used for some formal and cultic occasions, but how many people could *speak* it is uncertain.) And judging by the number of Greek coins and the amount of Greek inscriptional evidence uncovered, Greek was common enough as an alternative language that linked the Jews not only to the Mediterranean world in general but to the Jewish Diaspora and (in Galilee) to the Decapolis in particular. Some whose work brought them into close relationship with the army may also have attained a working knowledge of Latin. In any case, if John lived abroad for years before writing, he had ample time to practice his Greek. Moreover, although the Greek of John's gospel is reasonably competent, it is not elegant, and it betrays a fair number of Semitizing "enhancements."[28] It is, "with little exception, the language of the Septuagint."[29] This sort of evidence is perfectly consonant with what little we know of the background of John the son of Zebedee.

In short, the internal evidence is very strong, though not beyond dispute, that

---

[27]Robinson, *Priority*, p. 117.

[28]On the difference between Semitisms and Semitic enhancements, see n. 14 in chap. 2 above. John's gospel undoubtedly betrays both Aramaic and Hebraic enhancements; whether it betrays any Aramaisms or Hebraisms is disputed.

[29]G. D. Kilpatrick, "The Religious Background of the Fourth Gospel," in *Studies in the Fourth Gospel*, ed. F. L. Cross (London: Mowbray, 1957), p. 43.

the beloved disciple is John the apostle, the son of Zebedee. What, then, is the relationship between the beloved disciple and the fourth evangelist?

The traditional answer is that they are one and the same. Today this is commonly denied. Some think that John the son of Zebedee probably in some way stands behind the tradition in the fourth gospel but that the material went through lengthy adaptations. It finally wound up in the hands of the evangelist (whose identity is unknown—unless he is the "elder" John), whose work was subsequently touched up by a redactor, whose hand is perhaps betrayed in 21:24– 25. Others think that the influence of John the son of Zebedee is more immediate and pervasive: he did not actually write the book but caused it to be written, perhaps through an amanuensis who enjoyed certain liberties of expression and who might appropriately be called the evangelist. Important factors to be assessed are these:

1. Perhaps the most frequently advanced reason for denying that the beloved disciple is the evangelist lies in the expression "beloved disciple" itself. It is argued that no Christian would call *himself* "the disciple whom Jesus loved": the expression smacks of exclusivism and is better thought of as something someone else would say *about* another disciple, than as something any believer would say about himself. Similarly, it is argued, the person who wrote (lit.) that Jesus was in the bosom of the Father (εἰς τὸν κόλπον τοῦ πατρός [*eis ton kolpon tou patros*], 1:18) would be loath to say *of himself* that he reclined in the bosom of Jesus (ἐν τῷ κόλπῳ τοῦ Ἰησοῦ [*en tō kolpō tou Iēsou*], 13:23).

But these arguments, often repeated, should be abandoned. When a New Testament writer thinks of himself as someone whom Jesus loves, it is *never* to suggest that other believers are *not* loved or are somehow loved less. Thus Paul, in describing the saving work of the Son of God, can suddenly make that work personal: he "loved me and gave himself for me" (Gal. 2:20). In no way does this imply that Paul thinks the Galatians are loved less. The suggestion betrays a profound ignorance of the psychological dynamics of Christian experience: those who are most profoundly aware of their own sin and need, and who in consequence most deeply feel the wonders of the grace of God that has reached out and saved them, *even them*, are those who are most likely to talk about themselves as the objects of God's love in Christ Jesus. Those who do not think of themselves in such terms ought to (Eph. 3:14–21). If a "son of thunder" has become the apostle of love, small wonder he thinks of himself as the peculiar object of the love of Jesus. But that is scarcely the mark of arrogance; it is, rather, the mark of brokenness.

Thus, if we are to hear overtones of 1:18 in the description of John lying on Jesus' bosom (13:23), it is no more than a suggestive example of a pattern that is constantly *prescribed* in the fourth gospel: Jesus is the mediator of his Father's love, his Father's judgment, his Father's redemption, his Father's knowledge, his Father's covenant.

2. The same sort of reasoning probably explains why the evangelist does not name himself. He prefers to refer to himself obliquely, the better to focus on the One whom he serves; to achieve his purposes in writing, he does not need to stand explicitly on his apostolic dignity. He is already well known by his intended readership (21:24–25) and, like Paul when he is writing without strong polemical intent, does not need to call himself an apostle (Phil. 1:1; cf. Gal.1:1). As most

scholars agree, the beloved disciple is no mere idealization but a historical figure; yet even so, in certain respects he serves as a model for his readers to follow. They too are to serve as witnesses to the truth and to make much of the love of Jesus in their lives.

Even if someone protested that this sort of reasoning does not seem to provide an adequate reason for the refusal of the beloved disciple to identify himself, it must surely be admitted that if the evangelist is someone other than John the son of Zebedee, his failure to mention the apostle John by name, when he mentions so many others, is even more difficult to explain. The point may be pressed a little further. The suggestion that the expression "the disciple whom Jesus loved" is something one is more likely to say about someone else than about oneself is not only without merit, it is self-defeating. It implies that the evangelist (someone other than the beloved disciple, on this view) thought Jesus loved certain disciples and not others. Whatever the reason that Jesus nurtured an inner three (Peter, James, and John) according to the synoptic witness, it is very doubtful that it had much to do with arbitrarily dispensed love on Jesus' part.

3. Some think the "these things" that the beloved disciple is said to have written (21:24) refers only to the contents of chapter 21, not to the book as a whole. Quite apart from the fact that this view depends on a certain reading of chapter 21, it results in an anomaly: the beloved disciple, apparently the apostle John, wrote only this chapter, but someone else wrote the rest—even though "beloved disciple" occurs much earlier than chapter 21.

4. It is frequently argued that wherever John appears with Peter, the superiority of his insight is stressed. In John 13, for instance, Peter merely signals to the beloved disciple, who in turn actually asks Jesus the fateful question; in John 20, not only does the beloved disciple reach the tomb before Peter, but only he is said to believe. Would John have said such things about himself?

But more careful expositors have argued, rightly, that there is no question of inferiority or superiority in these descriptions, but of different gifts and characters. Barrett, for instance, quite convincingly argues that 21:24 must be read with the verses that precede it: it is given to Peter to feed the flock of God and to glorify God by his death, while it is given to the beloved disciple to live a long time and to serve as the one who writes this book, serving as witness to the truth.[30] If the beloved disciple arrives at the tomb first, Peter enters first. If the beloved disciple is said to believe, it is not said that Peter fails to believe; the statement is part of the description that is moving toward his authentication as the author of this book.

5. Some think that 21:22–23 must be taken to mean that the beloved disciple has died by the time the fourth gospel was published and that one of the reasons for publication was to alleviate the crisis that had consequently arisen. But it is as easy to suppose that the widely circulating rumor had come to the ears of the aging apostle, who consequently feared what might happen to the faith of some after he died, since their faith was resting on a false implication of something Jesus had actually said.

6. The suggestion that the beloved disciple merely caused these things to be written, apparently through a disciple who served as an amanuensis of sorts (Tertius is commonly cited; see Rom. 16:22), receives minor support from John

---

[30]C. K. Barrett, *The Gospel According to St John* (London: SPCK, 1978), pp. 118–19, 587–88.

19:19–22. Pilate himself probably did not write the *titulus* on the cross but simply caused it to be written. Certainly it is far from clear just how much freedom an amanuensis in the ancient world might be permitted.[31] Nevertheless, the example of Pilate suggests that what he caused to be written was *exactly* what he wanted written, and the verb "testifies" in 21:24 suggests that the influence of the beloved disciple is not remote. This is not to argue that John could not have used an amanuensis; nor is it to argue that only authorship by the apostle John can be squared with the internal and external evidence. It is to say, however, that this rather traditional view squares most easily with the evidence and offers least tortuous explanations of difficulties that all of the relevant hypotheses must face.

Over against Brown, then, who (at least in his commentary) sees the beloved disciple as the apostle John but not as the evangelist, and Cullmann,[32] who sees the beloved disciple as the evangelist but not the apostle John, the evidence seems to favor Robinson, who writes, "I believe that both men are right in what they assert and wrong in what they deny."[33]

The fact remains that Kümmel (p. 245) insists that Johannine authorship is "out of the question," while Barrett insists it is a "moral certainty" that John the son of Zebedee did not write the fourth gospel.[34] One is frankly puzzled by their degree of dogmatism. Barrett writes:

> Apostolic authorship has been defended at length and with learning by L. Morris . . . and his arguments should be carefully considered. It must be allowed to be not impossible that John the apostle wrote the gospel; this is why I use the term "moral certainty". The apostle may have lived to a very great age; he may have seen fit to draw on other sources in addition to his own memory; he may have learnt to write Greek correctly; he may have learnt not only the language but the thought-forms of his new environment (in Ephesus, Antioch, or Alexandria); he may have pondered the words of Jesus so long that they took shape in a new idiom; he may have become such an obscure figure that for some time orthodox Christians took little or no notice of his work. These are all possible, but the balance of probability is against their having all actually happened.[35]

This is a mixed list. Apart from the acquisition of Greek language skills, already discussed, the other challenges do not seem insuperable.

1. Assessment of the "very great age" turns on one's dating of the book. If one opts for about A.D. 80 (see discussion below in the section "Date"), John need only have been, say, seventy-five. Dodd published *Historical Tradition in the Fourth Gospel* when he was in his eighties; Goodspeed wrote his work on Matthew when he was ninety; Sir Norman Anderson is still writing books at eighty. One of the three authors of this *Introduction* is in his seventies. And in any case it is not impossible that the fourth gospel was written before 70.

2. Why it should be thought at all improbable that an apostle should "draw on other sources in addition to his own memory" is hard to imagine. In any case, the

---

[31]R. N. Longenecker, "On the Form, Function, and Authority of the New Testament Letters," in *Scripture and Truth*, ed. D. A. Carson and John D. Woodbridge (Grand Rapids: Zondervan, 1983), pp. 101–14.

[32]O. Cullmann, *The Johannine Circle* (London: SCM, 1976), pp. 74–85.

[33]J. A. T. Robinson, *Redating the New Testament* (Philadelphia: Westminster, 1976), p. 310.

[34]Barrett, *St John*, p. 132.

[35]Ibid., p. 132 n. 2.

question of the identification of sources in John's gospel is extremely problematic (see the following section, "Stylistic Unity and the Johannine 'Community'").

3. As for making Jesus' words come home in his own idiom, that is the preacher's métier, especially if involved in cross-cultural ministry. One of the strengths of the commentary by Lindars is his suggestion that various parts of the fourth gospel are simply the skeletons of sermons polished and preached on various occasions over years of Christian ministry.[36] We need not adopt all of his detailed suggestions to appreciate the plausibility of the basic thesis.

4. The suggestion that the author of the fourth gospel was obscure or unknown is somewhat overstated. Scholars differ as to whether John is alluded to in the *Epistle of Barnabas*, the *Didache*, and the *Shepherd* of Hermas(all early second century). Probably a majority find echoes of the fourth gospel in Ignatius (c. A.D. 110). Justin Martyr wrote: "Christ indeed said, 'Unless you are born again you shall not enter into the kingdom of heaven.' It is evident to all that those who have once been born cannot re-enter their mothers' wombs" (*First Apology* 61.4–5). This is almost certainly a reference to John 3:3–5; it seems unduly skeptical to think that Justin simply found this as an independent saying in the oral tradition, the more so in the light of the reference to the mothers' wombs. The pattern of recognition is not too surprising if the gospel of John was published toward the end of the first century. We should not then expect to find traces of it in, say, Clement of Rome (c. 95). There is more of a problem if the fourth gospel was published before 70 (as Morris and Robinson think). Even so, especially if the evidence of Ireneus regarding Papias and Polycarp is read sympathetically, it is hard to credit the view that "orthodox Christians took little or no notice" of this gospel.

Moreover, Christians then as now had their favorite books. Matthew was an early favorite; John was not. In John's case, this may have had a little to do with the fact that the fourth gospel was early used (and abused) by the Gnostics. The Gnostic Basilides (c. A.D. 130) cites John 1:9 (though this information depends on Hippolytus's *Refutation of Heresies* 7.22.4); the first commentary on a gospel that we know about is the the treatment of John by the Gnostic Heracleon. It takes a little while to get a counterpolemic going—arguably, the first sign of it is found in the epistles of John.

But perhaps the largest stumbling block to acceptance of Johannine authorship is the amorphous assumption that the gospel was composed by a Johannine school or circle or community; so to this we must turn.

Stylistic Unity and the Johannine "Community"

Although Bultmann[37] and Fortna[38] and others have in the past attempted detailed source-critical analyses of the fourth gospel, it has increasingly been recognized that the retrieval of sources from this gospel is an extremely problematic endeavor.[39] There is no reason to doubt that John used sources: his

---

[36]Barnabas Lindars, *The Gospel of John* (London: Oliphants, 1972).

[37]R. Bultmann, *The Gospel of John* (ET London: Blackwell, 1971).

[38]R. T. Fortna, *The Gospel of Signs*, SNTSMS 11 (Cambridge: Cambridge University Press, 1970).

[39]For a useful survey of the application of source criticism to the fourth gospel, see D. Moody Smith,

fellow evangelist Luke certainly did (Luke 1:1–4), and there is no need to think that the fourth evangelist followed some different course. Even here, however, caution is needed: Luke does not purport to be the result of eyewitness testimony, while John does. But regardless of who wrote the fourth gospel, the presumption that the evangelist used written sources is quite different from the assumption we can retrieve them. One of the features of John's gospel on which virtually all sides now agree is that stylistically it is cut from one cloth. There are minor differences between, say, the vocabulary of Jesus' speech and the vocabulary of the rest of the fourth gospel, but they are so minor that they present us with a quite different problem: How accurate is John's presentation of Jesus if Jesus sounds so much like John? We shall address that problem in a moment; meanwhile, the fact that it is a problem should also serve as a warning flag against those who think they can distinguish separate sources buried in the text. The stylistic unity of the book has been demonstrated again and again as concrete evidence against this or that source theory.[40] Even the prologue (1:1–18) and the epilogue (chap. 21) exhibit a style remarkably attuned to the rest of the book.[41]

Even the delineation of the so-called signs source has fallen on hard times.[42] Several scholars have postulated the existence of such a source of signs stories, suggested, it is argued, by the enumeration of the first two (2:11; 4:54), and climaxed by 20:30–31. But the enumeration ("first," "second") has been plausibly accounted for as a rhetorical feature within the text as it stands. Even if there were documents relating signs stories circulating in the early church, it is very doubtful that any of them was regarded as a "gospel of signs,"[43] since in the first century the gospel form, so far as we know, was rapidly associated with a balanced account of Jesus' ministry, including some of his teaching, and climaxing in his death and resurrection. Hengel rightly questions the likelihood that the evangelist took over something like the alleged signs source, which all sides admit (if it ever existed) boasted a theology radically different from that of the evangelist, and incorporated it so mechanically that it can be retrieved by contemporary scholarship.[44]

One of the more recent and creative attempts to use stylistic features to probe the unity of the fourth gospel is the statistically informed and understated study by

---

Johannine Christianity: Essays on Its Setting, Sources, and Theology (Columbia: University of South Carolina Press, 1984), pp. 39–93.

[40]E.g., E. Schweizer, *Ego Eimi: Die religionsgeschichtliche Bedeutung der johanneischen Bildreden, zugleich ein Beitrag zur Quellenfrage des vierten Evangeliums* (Göttingen: Vandenhoeck & Ruprecht, 1939); E. Ruckstuhl, *Die literarische Einheit des Johannesevangeliums* (Freiburg: Paulus, 1951; slightly enlarged ed., Freiburg: Universitätsverlag, 1987); idem, "Johannine Language and Style," in *L'évangile de Jean: Sources, rédaction, théologie,* ed. M. de Jonge (Louvain: Louvain University Press, 1977), pp. 125–47; G. van Belle, *De semeia-bron in het vierde evangilie: Ontstaan en groei van een hypothese* (Louvain: Louvain University Press, 1975); D. A. Carson, "Current Source Criticism of the Fourth Gospel: Some Methodological Questions," *JBL* 97 (1978): 411–29; Hans-Peter Heekerens, *Die Zeichen-Quelle der johanneischen Redaktion* (Stuttgart: KBW, 1984).

[41]On the former, see Jeff Staley, "The Structure of John's Prologue: Its Implications for the Gospel's Narrative Structure," *CBQ* 48 (1986): 241–63; on the latter, see Paul S. Minear, "The Original Functions of John 21," *JBL* 102 (1983): 85–98.

[42]It is therefore all the more surprising that in his more recent work, Robert T. Fortna simply assumes the validity of his postulated source, not even interacting with the numerous criticisms that have been raised against it (see his *Fourth Gospel and Its Predecessor* [Philadelphia: Fortress, 1988]).

[43]Cf. Fortna, *The Gospel of Signs.*

[44]Martin Hengel, "The Wine Miracle at Cana," in *The Glory of Christ in the New Testament, Fs.* G. B. Caird, ed. L. D. Hurst and N. T. Wright (Oxford: Clarendon, 1987), p. 92.

Poythress of the Greek conjunctions δέ (de), καί (kai), and οὖν (oun), along with the syntactic phenomenon of asyndeton.[45] The frequency of the conjunctions is abnormally low in John; the frequency of asyndeton is unusually high. He demonstrates, as far as such evidence will take him (and he is aware of the pitfalls of small samples and the like), that this test argues for unified authorship of the fourth gospel and common authorship between the fourth gospel and the Johannine Epistles.

It is this sort of evidence that has convinced commentators such as Brown, Lindars, and Haenchen that the pursuit of separable sources in the fourth gospel is a lost cause.[46] That is why Brown prefers his pursuit of separable *traditions* that have allegedly evolved over the length of a certain trajectory of theological development, and Lindars prefers to think of a series of homilies that were collected, published, edited, and added to over a period of time. But as influential as is, say, the five-step theory of Brown, it is important to see that it too is a kind of source theory, compounded with speculation about the "setting in life" (*Sitz im Leben*) of each source—only in his case the sources are much fuzzier around the edges than the source postulated by Fortna. Brown prefers to talk about the development of traditions rather than the delineation of sources. Still, someone has to enter John's text with a literary scalpel and retrieve those traditions. Some of these lie on the surface and are tied to certain words and expressions (which make them very similar indeed to literary sources), while others are the reconstructions Brown offers to explain what he thinks must have generated this or that bit of text.

In other words, the source criticism of Bultmann and Fortna has fallen on hard times because their hard evidence turns out to be patient of far simpler explanations, while the tradition probing of Brown (for example), which is far more speculative and much less controlled than Fortna's work, has exerted wide influence—presumably, one has to say, because it is self-coherent and therefore satisfying, but also utterly untestable. It must be remembered that the six groups Brown thinks the gospel of John is confronting are mere inferences from the gospel's text. Again and again, other inferences are possible. And all of Brown's six groups, inferences as they are, are based on a prior inference, namely, that it is relatively easy to read off from a text that purports to be about *Jesus* the life and circumstances and opponents of the *group* that produces the document. Small wonder that Kysar concludes, "If the gospel evolved in a manner comparable to that offered by Brown and Lindars, it is totally beyond the grasp of the johannine scholar and historian to produce even tentative proof that such was the case."[47]

It is this stack of inferences heaped on inferences that bedevils most discussions of Johannine authorship. A consensus has arisen that the history of the Johannine community can largely be delineated by the careful analysis of differentiable Johannine "traditions," each of which has its easily inferred setting-in-life. In the dominant view, these culminate in a situation toward the end of the first century

---

[45]Vern Poythress, "The Use of the Intersentence Conjunctions *De, Oun, Kai,* and Asyndeton in the Gospel of John," *NovT* 26 (1984), pp. 312–40; idem, "Testing for Johannine Authorship by Examining the Use of Conjunctions," *WTJ* 46 (1984): 350–69.

[46]The commentaries by Brown and Lindars have already been mentioned; see E. Haenchen, A *Commentary on the Gospel of John,* 2 vols. (ET Philadelphia: Fortress, 1984).

[47]R. Kysar, *The Fourth Evangelist and His Gospel* (Minneapolis: Augsburg, 1975), p. 53.

when the church is locked in debate with the synagogue, and John's gospel, as we have it, more or less reflects that debate. We discuss this view further in the next section. For the moment it is sufficient to say that if this reconstruction is adopted, it is hard to see how the reader can take seriously the claims of this book to be the *witness* of the beloved disciple, most plausibly the apostle John himself, to Jesus Christ. Thus the harder literary and historical evidence is displaced by the softer inferential evidence of interlocking reconstructions. One should not object to historical reconstructions; one worries, however, when they are used to set aside large swaths of the actual literary and historical evidence.

For at least some contemporary scholars, this matrix of inherited beliefs, judgments, and commitments about the provenance of the fourth gospel makes it difficult to postulate apostolic authorship without abandoning the inherited web. As we have seen, this matrix turns on the existence of a Johannine circle or school,[48] the core of a Johannine community whose existence and history can to some extent be delineated by inferences drawn from layers of tradition that are peeled back. But attempts to place this chain of inferences on a secure footing by positing ostensible parallels are not reassuring. For example, Culpepper attempts to delineate various schools in the ancient world: the Pythagorean school, the Greek academy, the lyceum, the school at Qumran, the house of Hillel, Philo's school, and so forth. But Culpepper's understanding of "school" is undifferentiable from that of "sect," except that a school has the additional characteristic of being preoccupied with studying, learning, teaching, and writing.[49] Even here, of course, his model runs into difficulty. Culpepper is forced to admit, for instance: "Nothing is known of the history of the synagogue-school in which Philo worked, and none of the names of his students has survived. The inference that his writings continued to be studied arises from the use made of them by the later Christian school in Alexandria and the evident popularity of allegorical exegesis there. . . . Perhaps the reason for the complete silence of our sources on the history of Philo's school is that he actually exerted little influence on his community."[50]

Here, then, is speculation on the reason for the silence of the sources regarding a school the existence of which is an inference drawn from the later use of an earlier Jewish writer! Out of this model emerges the construct of a Johannine school, with the beloved disciple serving as its head, functioning for the community as the Paraclete does in the gospel of John.[51] But Culpepper offers no criteria whatsoever to distinguish how this school could be distinguished from a group of Christians who simply cherish the evangelist's writings and commend them to others. The history of the Johannine community (he now flips back and forth between "community" and "school") will, he assures us, be traced when there is greater consensus on the "composition-history" of the fourth gospel.[52] The assumption is massive. He adds that the Johannine Epistles constitute evidence for the existence of "more than one community of believers which shared the same traditions, vocabulary, doctrines, and ethical principles"—though on the

---

[48]Cullmann, *Johannine Circle*; Alan R. Culpepper, *The Johannine School* (Missoula, Mont.: SP, 1975).
[49]Culpepper, *Johannine School*, p. 213.
[50]Ibid.
[51]Ibid., pp. 261–90.
[52]Ibid., p. 279.

face of it this too invokes a major assumption about community participation in the writing, for the simpler inference is that the Johannine Epistles constitute evidence that their author wrote several pieces to several communities that were known to him. They *may* have constituted a collegial grouping of churches around one authority figure; it is entirely plausible to suppose that they did. But that is still a long way from delineating a school of writers and students who were responsible for *the composition* of the fourth gospel. Even the "we" in John 21:24, a difficult pronoun on any view,[53] does not unambiguously argue for a school of writers. It could as easily refer to a group of attesting elders.

This is not to argue that there is no self-conscious recognition of development *within the fourth gospel itself.* From the perspective of the evangelist, there was a remarkable development in the disciples' *understanding* of who Jesus was, and much of this took place after the resurrection and exaltation of their Lord. But it is a development of understanding (e.g., 2:22; 20:9), not a fresh theological invention. By constantly drawing attention to the *mis*understandings of observers and disciples alike during the days of Jesus' ministry, John shows he is able to distinguish what he and others understood originally and what he came to understand only later. Indeed, he *insists* on the distinction,[54] and this fact constitutes a remarkably strong piece of evidence that the evangelist was self-consciously aware of the possibility of anachronism and, for his own reasons, studiously avoided it. It flies in the face of such evidence to suppose that the evangelist happily cast the circumstances of his own church and situation back into the third decade, projecting them onto Jesus and his teaching, whether wittingly or unwittingly ignoring the anachronisms this generated.

None of this is meant to suggest that all problems in the fourth gospel are purely in the eye of the beholder. It is merely to suggest that comprehensive source and tradition theories are unacceptably speculative and too frequently end up contradicting the only textual evidence we actually have. Some of the most prominent theories of textual dislocation (such as the view that chaps. 5 and 6 have somehow become inverted) solve some problems—in this case, quick geographic movement—only to introduce others. All things considered, it seems least difficult to believe that the evangelist, himself a Christian preacher, proclaimed the gospel for years. Doubtless he made notes; doubtless he learned from others and incorporated the work of others. But whatever he took from other sources, he made his own. Eventually he put the material together and published it as a book. It is quite conceivable that he produced the work in stages; it is unlikely that the work was released in stages, at least in stages with long delays between them, since there is no textual evidence of a distinction between earlier and later editions. There is in any case a sureness of touch, a simplicity of diction, and a unity of theme and development that rhetorical criticism rightly applauds and that testifies to a mature Christian witness and theologian.

There is, of course, a converse problem. Why should the evangelist impose so uniform a stamp on his work that there is so *little* distinction between what he

---

[53]See discussion of this passage in Carson, *John.*

[54]See D. A. Carson, "Understanding Misunderstandings in the Fourth Gospel," *TynB* 33 (1982): 59–89.

writes and what he ascribes to Jesus during the days of his flesh? Several observations may be helpful.

1. Although the style of the fourth gospel is remarkably uniform, the point must not be overstated. Reynolds lists about 150 words that are placed on Jesus' lips in John but are never used elsewhere by the evangelist.[55] Not a few of these are sufficiently general that they would have been as appropriate in the evangelist's narrative as in Jesus' discourse.

2. Many have argued, rightly, that fair reporting can be accomplished with other than verbatim quotations. A many-sided writer who is also an advocate will wisely choose the form of the reportage, especially if the communication is cross-cultural. If we also suppose that much of this material was first of all sermonic, the general point is strengthened. A number of features are probably best explained by supposing we are listening to a preacher's revised sermons. The doubled "Amen!" on Jesus' lips, for instance, found only in John, is just such a homiletic device and causes no umbrage unless for some strange reason we suppose that preachers in the ancient world could appeal only to verbatim quotations. Some of what is included in or excluded from John's gospel is much better accounted for by reflecting on the evangelist's situation *as a Christian preacher*, so far as we can reconstruct it from both internal and external evidence, than by supposing that the evangelist is including all he knows, or is attempting to correct some other gospel, or is simply ignorant of some vital fact preserved elsewhere. The absence of narrative parables, especially parables about the kingdom, suggests this preacher's audience is not steeped in apocalyptic and not linguistically Semitic. The prevalence of so much terminology that has almost *universal* religious appeal (see comments below) suggests the evangelist is trying to use language that will present the fewest barriers.

This does not mean that John is uninterested in, say, the kingdom of God. Quite apart from the few crucial places where he does use the expression (3:3, 5; cf. 18:36), the *theme* of the kingdom is very powerfully presented in certain passages (e.g., it dominates the plot line of chaps. 18–19). Moreover, the kingdom in the Synoptic Gospels is often a "tensive symbol" that can bear an extraordinary number of overtones.[56] This ensures that in some passages, for instance, "entering the kingdom" is indistinguishable from "entering into life" (e.g., Matt 7:14, 21)—and John certainly has a great deal to say about life. In short, the fourth evangelist is interested in presenting certain truths to certain people, and he exercises the preacher's prerogative of shaping his message accordingly.

It has often been remarked that John's gospel, however profound it may be, is narrower in focus than the synoptics. When this narrowness of focus fills the entire page, certain things come to light that would not otherwise be seen, but a certain sense of dislocation in the reader is understandable. Once what the preacher (i.e.

---

[55]H. R. Reynolds, *The Gospel of St. John*, 2 vols. (London: Funk & Wagnalls, 1906), pp. cxxiii–cxxv.

[56]See J. Jeremias, *New Testament Theology I: The Proclamation of Jesus* (London: SCM, 1971), pp. 32–34; Norman Perrin, *Jesus and the Language of the Kingdom* (Philadelphia: Fortress, 1976), esp. pp. 29–34; R. T. France, "The Church and the Kingdom of God: Some Hermeneutical Issues," in *Biblical Interpretation and the Church: Text and Context*, ed. D. A. Carson (Exeter: Paternoster, 1984), pp. 30–44.

the evangelist) is doing becomes clear—that is, when the *scale* of his vision is clarified—the sense of dislocation largely evaporates.

3. Of course, this preacher is not *just* a preacher. He presents himself as an eyewitness, a reliable intermediary between the events themselves and the people who now need to hear them. Nor is he alone: he is conscious of the continuity of Christian truth (1:14–18) and especially of the Spirit's role in equipping him for this task (15:26–27; 16:12–15). So far as John's understanding of his task goes, we may speak of the liberty he felt to use his own language, of the principles of selection that governed his choices of material, of the nature of the audience that he envisioned, of the focus of his interests, of his remarkable habit of getting to the heart of an issue. But we may not glibly suppose that one who felt so strongly about the importance of fidelity in witnesses (10:40–42) could simply invent narrative and dialogue and pass them off as history.

4. Several of the discourses have been shown, with some degree of plausibility, to be modeled on midrashim, or the rabbinic commentaries of the day. These discourses are so tightly knit that it is very difficult to believe they are nothing more than a pastiche of isolated (and retrievable!) sayings of Jesus onto which Johannine commentary has been patched. This leads to one of two conclusions. Borgen, who has demonstrated the finely wrought nature of the bread of life discourse (6:26–59) as in part an exposition of Exodus 16, argues for the unity of the discourse but does not attribute it to Jesus.[57] Hunter likewise recognizes the unity but thinks there is no evidence to prevent us from concluding the discourse is authentic.[58] What must be added is that, granted its essential authenticity, the discourse has been cast into its shape and place in the gospel by the evangelist, whose style so largely stamps the whole. Similar things could be said about the midrashic nature of parts of John 12, the chiastic structure of 5:19–30, the cohesiveness of the dialogue with Nicodemus, and much more.

In short, the most straightforward reading of the evidence is still the traditional one: it is highly probable that John the son of Zebedee wrote the fourth gospel. In itself, this makes no difference whatsoever to the authority of the book (after all, Luke's gospel does not purport to be by an eyewitness; the epistle to the Hebrews is anonymous). It does, however, make a considerable difference to how we think the book came to be written and therefore to the situation to which it was addressed, the purpose of the writing.

PROVENANCE

Discussion of the provenance of the fourth gospel can usefully be divided into two spheres.

Geographic Provenance

Four places are commonly proposed. *Alexandria* is championed by some, on the ground that John has certain affinities to Philo. These are considerably overstated

---

[57]P. Borgen, *Bread from Heaven*, SuppNovT 10 (Leiden: Brill, 1965).
[58]A. M. Hunter, *According to John* (London: SCM, 1968).

(see e.g., the major commentaries on 1:1), and in any case one must assume that Philo was read outside Alexandria.

Antioch has been put forward, on the ground that the fourth gospel has some affinities with the Syriac *Odes of Solomon*, presumed to come from this region, and with Ignatius, who served Antioch as its bishop. Again, however, the assumption that literary influence is possible only in the place of literary origin is seen to be unconvincing as soon as it is stated.

3. The view that the fourth gospel must have been written in *Palestine* because of its close familiarity with cultural and topographical details peculiar to the region entails the view, strange on its very surface, that any book about the historical Jesus must have been written in Palestine. Both then and now, authors have been known to move around.

4. The traditional view is that the fourth gospel was written in *Ephesus*. In large part this view depends on the weight given to the uniform but sometimes difficult patristic evidence. Eusebius (*H.E.* 3.1.1) says that Asia (i.e. Asia Minor, approximately the western third of modern Turkey) was allotted to John when the apostles were dispersed at the outbreak of the Jewish War (A.D. 66–70). Some of the allotments or assignments that Eusebius lists are likely legendary, but perhaps this one is reliable, since it agrees with other sources, for example, Ireneus (*Adv. Haer.* 3.1.2), who says that "John, the disciple of the Lord . . . published the gospel while living at Ephesus in Asia." Some hold, however, that Ireneus confuses John the apostle with another John, the John who writes the Apocalypse (see discussion in chap. 24, below). The fact that the Montanists, who were largely based on Phrygia, not too far from Ephesus, used John is often taken to support the case for Ephesian provenance; but again, John's gospel could have been circulating in Phrygia half a century and more after it was written, regardless of where it was first published. What must be acknowledged is that no other location has the support of the church Fathers: rightly or wrongly, they point to Ephesus.

Conceptual Provenance

John's Religious World The wealth of suggestions that various scholars have offered as to the background of the fourth gospel has an important bearing on how we view John's ostensible setting, the Palestine of Jesus' day, and how we understand his message. From the end of the last century until about the 1960s, the history-of-religions movement tied John's gospel to the Hellenistic world. As the gospel stretched outward from Jerusalem through the Jewish Diaspora and into the broader streams of Hellenistic culture, it was progressively transformed both in vocabulary and in substance. Typically, this Hellenistic culture was judged to be some combination of four influences.

Philo. Scholars have seen an influence from Philo, especially with respect to John's use of λόγος (*logos*, "word") in 1:1. Philo borrows the Stoic concept of the word as the principle of reality, the medium of creation and governance. Numerous other parallels can be observed.

The Hermetic writings. Alleged to be the instruction of Hermes Trismegistos (= the Egyptian god Thoth), these writings in the Gnostic tradition display some distinctive features by mitigating the dualism of Gnosticism. The cosmos is related to God and may be called the son of God. Regeneration is an important theme in some Hermetic tractates: a person is born again when he or she gains the proper knowledge of God and thereby becomes divine. Dodd was the greatest defender of the pervasive influence of the Hermetic literature on John.

Gnosticism. Sometimes (and rightly) described as an amorphous "theosophical hotchpotch," Gnosticism sprang out of neoplatonic dualism that tied what is good to the ideal, to the spiritual, and what is bad to the material. In full-blown Gnosticism, the Gnostic redeemer comes to earth to inform those with ears to hear of their true origins. This "knowledge" (γνῶσις [*gnōsis*]) brings release and salvation to those who accept it.

Mandaism. This is a peculiar form of Gnosticism whose origins are much disputed. Probably it originated in one of the Jewish baptizing sects, but the form in which it has come down to us, in which the rite of baptism, oft repeated, is the key step by which the myth of the descent of the "knowledge of life" (*Manda d'Hayye*) is reenacted and release from the demonic powers secured, is exceedingly late.[59]

Quite apart from considerations of dating (all but the first of these are attested by sources that come from the second or third century or later), the conceptual differences between John and these documents are very substantial. Moreover, the discovery of the Dead Sea Scrolls in 1947 and their subsequent publication has shown that the closest religious movement to the fourth gospel, in terms of vocabulary at least, was an extremely conservative hermitic *Jewish* community. This is not to say that John springs from the Essenes, thought to be represented by the Dead Sea Scrolls, but that the appeal to strongly Hellenistic sources is now much less convincing than it was half a century ago. Thus another stream of scholarship has attempted to plot the connections between John and various Palestinian movements, including rabbinic thought, Samaritan religion, the Essenes, and various apocalyptic movements. Whatever parallels can be drawn, it is now virtually undisputed that both John and these movements drew their primary inspiration from what we today call the Old Testament Scriptures.

John's indebtedness to this primary wellspring is profound, much more profound than the mere number of Old Testament quotations might suggest. The countless allusions to the Old Testament (e.g., references to the tabernacle, Jacob's ladder, Jacob's well, manna, the serpent in the wilderness, Sabbath, and various feasts) presuppose both a writer and envisioned readers who are steeped in the Scriptures.[60]

Even so, many scholars would be comfortable with the approaches displayed in the commentaries of, say, Barrett and Schnackenburg, who argue that a rich diversity of non-Christian influences was incorporated into the very substance of this gospel, providing it with its peculiar emphases and form. This is surely partly right, yet potentially misleading. One reason why interpreters are able to find

---

[59]For useful coverage of these and other movements, see G. R. Beasley-Murray, *John*, WBC 36 (Waco, Tex.: Word, 1987), pp. liiiff. One of the best assessments of Gnosticism in general and Mandaism in particular is still that of E. Yamauchi, *Pre-Christian Gnosticism: A Survey of the Proposed Evidence* (London: Tyndale, 1973).

[60]See D. A. Carson, "The Use of the Old Testament in John and the Johannine Epistles," in *It Is Written: Scripture Citing Scripture,. Fs.* Barnabas Lindars, ed. D. A. Carson and H. G. M. Williamson (Cambridge: Cambridge University Press, 1988), pp. 245–64.

parallels to John in so diverse an array of literature lies in John's vocabulary and pithy sayings. Words such as light, darkness, life, death, spirit, word, love, believing, water, bread, clean, birth, and children of God can be found in almost any religion. Frequently they have very different referents as one moves from religion to religion, but the vocabulary is as popular as religion itself. Nowhere, perhaps, has the importance of this phenomenon been more clearly set forth than in a little-known essay by Kysar.[61] He compares the studies of Dodd and Bultmann on the prologue (John 1:1–18), noting in particular the list of possible parallels each of the two scholars draws up to every conceivable phrase in those verses. Dodd and Bultmann each advance over three hundred parallels, but the overlap in their lists is only 7 percent. The dangers of what Sandmel calls parallelomania become depressingly obvious.[62]

This does not mean that there is no influence at all on the fourth gospel from other religious forms. The early Christians were certainly aware that they were expanding outward into a frequently hostile set of world views. The evangelist's efforts to communicate the truth of the gospel to men and women far removed from Palestine ensured that, if he was at all thoughtful in his task, he would not simply parrot the received traditions but try to cast them in ways that would make them most easily understood. The question to be asked, then, is whether his attempt has succumbed, wittingly or unwittingly, to a syncretism that has admitted strands of thought essentially alien to the historic gospel or, better, has simply transposed the good news, as it were, to another key. It is surely here that John has proved to be not only a faithful witness but a gifted preacher.

John's Relation to the Synoptics One cannot long speak of the conceptual provenance of the fourth gospel without weighing the relations between this gospel and the synoptics. How much does John owe to the synoptists?

The differences between John and the synoptics have often been detailed. John omits many things that are characteristic of the synoptics: narrative parables, the account of the transfiguration, the record of the institution of the Lord's Supper, and many of Jesus' pithy sayings. Themes central to the synoptics have all but disappeared (esp. the theme of the kingdom of God/heaven). Conversely, John includes a fair bit of material of which the synoptists make no mention: virtually all the material in John 1–5, Jesus' frequent visits to Jerusalem and what takes place there, the resurrection of Lazarus, extended dialogues and discourses, and much more.

Doubtless some of this can be accounted for by the different geographic focus: John reports far more of Jesus' ministry in the South, in Judea and Samaria, than in Galilee, while the focus of the synoptists is the opposite. But one cannot legitimately reduce all distinctions to questions of geography. In John, Jesus is *explicitly* identified with God (1:1, 18; 20:28). Here, too, is a series of important "I am" statements, sometimes with predicates (e.g., 6:35; 8:12; 15:1–5), sometimes absolute (e.g., 8:28, 58). There are passages not superficially easy to integrate with other New Testament texts, such as John the Baptist's denial that he

---

[61]Robert Kysar, "The Background of the Prologue of the Fourth Gospel: A Critique of Historical Methods," *CJT* 16 (1970): 250–55.

[62]Samuel Sandmel, "Parallelomania," *JBL* 81 (1962): 2–13.

is Elijah (1:21; cf. Mark 9:11–13 par.) and the apparent bestowal
(John 20:22; cf. Acts 2). John 1 begins with the disciples confessing Je
of God, Son of Man, Messiah, Rabbi, and King of Israel; in the synop
confession of Jesus as the Messiah is a great turning point at Caesarea Ph.
about halfway through Jesus' ministry (Mark 8:27–30 par.). Nor have we
considered the chronological difficulties that the fourth gospel introduces: its da
for the passion, for instance, is not easily squared with that of the synoptics. The
last line of 14:31 strikes many as the evidence of an awkward edit; the threat of
synagogue excommunication (9:22) strikes others as desperately anachronistic,
reflecting a situation in the late 80s, not in the ministry of the historical Jesus.

On the other hand, there are many notable points of comparison.[63] Parallel
incidents include the Spirit's anointing of Jesus as testified by John the Baptist
(Mark 1:10 par. and John 1:32), the contrast between the Baptist's baptism with
water and the Messiah's anticipated baptism with the Spirit (Mark 1:7–8 par. and
John 1:23), the feeding of the five thousand (Mark 6:32-44 par. and John 6:1-
15), and the walking on the water (Mark 6:45–52 par. and John 6:16–21).
Many sayings are at least partially parallel, though not dicisively attesting literary
dependence (Matt. 9:37–38 par. and John 4:35; Mark 6:4 par. and John 4:44;
Matt. 25:46 and John 5:29; Matt. 11:25–27 par. and John 10:14–15; Mark
4:12 par. and John 12:39–40; and many more). More significant yet are the
subtle parallels: both John and the synoptists describe a Jesus given to colorful
metaphors and proverbs, many drawn from the world of nature (e.g., 4:37; 5:19–
20a; 8:35; 9:4; 11:9–10; 10:1ff.; 12:24; 15:1–16; 16:21). All four gospels
depict Jesus with a unique sense of sonship to his heavenly Father; all of them
note the distinctive authority Jesus displays in his teaching; all of them show Jesus
referring to himself as the Son of Man, with no one else using that title to refer to
him or to anyone else (John 12:34 is no real exception).

More impressive yet are the many places where John and the synoptics represent
an *interlocking* tradition, that is, where they mutually reinforce or explain each
other, without betraying overt literary dependence.[64]A very incomplete list
includes the following items: John's report of an extensive Judean ministry helps
to explain the assumption in Mark 14:49 that Jesus had constantly taught in the
temple precincts (NEB "day after day"), the trepidation with which the final trip
southward was viewed (Mark 10:32), and Jesus' ability to round up a colt (Mark
11:1–7) and secure a furnished upper room (Mark 14:12–16). The charge
reported in the synoptics that Jesus had threatened the destruction of the temple
(Mark 14:58 par.; 15:29 par.) finds its only adequate explanation in John 2:19.
Mark gives no reason as to why the Jewish authorities should bother bringing
Jesus to Pilate; John provides the reason (18:31). Only John provides the reason
(18:15–18) why Peter can be placed within the high priest's courtyard (Mark
14:54, 66–72 par.). Even the call of the disciples in the synoptics is made easier to
understand (Matt. 4:18–22 par.) if we presuppose, with John 1, that Jesus had
already had contact with them and that their fundamental shift in allegiance had
already occurred.

[63]See Craig Blomberg, *The Historical Reliability of the Gospels* (Leicester: IVP, 1987), pp. 156–57.
[64]See esp. Morris, *Studies*, pp. 40–63; Robinson, *John*, chaps. 4–6; Carson, *John*, "Introduction,"
III(3).

Conversely, numerous features in John are explained by details reported only by the synoptists. For instance, in John 18–19 the trial plunges so quickly into the Roman court that it is difficult to see just what judicial action the Jews have taken, if any, to precipitate this trial; the synoptics provide the answer. It is quite possible that the reason Philip apparently hesitates to bring the Gentiles to Jesus in John 12:21–22, consulting with Andrew before actually approaching Jesus, is that Jesus had earlier issued his prohibition against going among the Gentiles (Matt. 10:5)—a point not reported by John.

We summarize here the complex scholarly debates on the relation between John and the synoptics and offer some tentative conclusions.

1. Although the majority of contemporary scholars side with the magisterial work of Dodd,[65] who argues that there is no good evidence for any literary dependence of John on any of the Synoptic Gospels, a number of scholars[66] and at least one major commentator[67] argue that John had read at least Mark, perhaps Luke, and (one or two have argued) perhaps also Matthew—or, at the very least, substantial synoptic tradition. All agree that if John made use of any of the synoptics, the dependency is quite unlike that between, say, Mark and Matthew, or Jude and 2 Peter. The fourth evangelist chose to write his own book.

2. The question of the relationship between John and the synoptics is inextricably tied to complex debates about the authorship and dates of composition of all four gospels. For example, if, as is commonly the case, scholars think of the Gospels as the products of anonymous faces in Christian communities that are more or less independent of other Christian communities—indeed, as the products of long streams of tradition largely free from the constraints of eyewitnesses—then the only means of weighing whether the author(s) of one gospel (in this case John) had read any of the other gospels would be by testing for direct literary dependence. If that is the case, most scholars think the evidence is not strong enough to prove dependence, and one must either assume independence or leave the question open. A minority of scholars, as we have seen, think that a case for dependence can be made out.

But if on the sorts of grounds that have already been canvassed here, we come to think that John the son of Zebedee wrote the fourth gospel and that Mark wrote the gospel that bears his name, with Peter behind him, then additional factors must be considered. Granted the close friendship that Peter and John enjoyed, would it be very likely that either of them would long remain ignorant of a publication for which the other was responsible? Considerations of date then become important. If Mark, say, was written about A.D. 64, and John within a year

---

[65]Dodd, *Historical Tradition*.

[66]E.g., F. Neirynck in M. de Jonge, *L'évangile de Jean*, pp. 73–106; idem, in collaboration with Joël Delobel, Thierry Snoy, Gilbert Van Belle, and Frans Van Segbroeck, *Jean et les synoptiques: Examen critique de l'exégèse de M.-E. Boismard* (Louvain: Louvain University Press, 1979); Mgr. de Solages, *Jean et les synoptiques* (Leiden: Brill, 1979); J. Blinzler, *Johannes und die Synoptiker* (Stuttgart: KBW, 1965); E. F. Seigman, "St. John's Use of the Synoptic Material," *CBQ* 30 (1968): 182–98; M. E. Glasswell, "The Relationship Between John and Mark," *JSNT* 23 (1985): 99–115; Gerhard Maier, "Johannes und Matthäus—Zweispalt oder Viergestalt des Evangeliums?" in *GP* 2:267–91; Thomas M. Dowell, "Jews and Christians in Conflict: Why the Fourth Gospel Changed the Synoptic Tradition," *LouvStud* 15 (1990): 19–37. For a summary of the literature, see Smith, *Essays*; Blomberg, *Historical Reliability*, p. 159.

[67]Barrett, *John*.

or two of that date, then the likelihood of mutual independence is enhanced. But if Mark was written sometime between 50 and 64, and the fourth gospel not until about 80, it is very difficult to believe that John would not have read it. The idea of hermetically sealed communities is implausible in the Roman Empire anyway, where communications were as good as at any time in the history of the world until the nineteenth century. It becomes doubly implausible while the apostles were still alive, living with friendships and the memory of friendships. In this case, tests for direct, literary dependence are too narrow if they are meant to answer the question whether or not John had read Mark. On balance, it appears likely that John had read Mark, Luke, and possibly even Matthew but that in any case he chose to write his own book.

3. The incidental nature of the interlocking patterns between John and one or more of the synoptics cannot be used to prove dependency but for the same reason turns out to be of inestimable value to the historian. It is not that the theological thrusts connected with, say, John's passion narrative cannot be appreciated without reading the synoptics, or that the theological points the individual synoptists make when they describe the call of the disciples cannot be grasped without referring to what John has to say on the matter. Rather, the implication of the interlocking patterns is that *at the historical level* what actually took place was much bigger and more complex than any one gospel intimates. Something of that complexity can be sketched in by sympathetically examining the interlocking nature of the diverse gospel presentations. The result makes good historical sense of many passages that have too quickly been written off by those prone to disjunctive thinking.

4. This has considerable practical bearing on the evaluation of some of the differences between John and the synoptics. For example, the lengthy list of Christological confessions in John 1 is, as we have seen, often set against the rising Christological awareness pictured in the Synoptic Gospels, which reaches its climax at Caesarea Philippi. It has been argued that the reason for this difference is that John, writing at the end of the first century, *presupposes* the appropriateness of the Christological titles he introduces in his first chapter but is now concerned to move the church to adopt one further confession: Jesus is God. This interpretation of the evidence simultaneously assumes that the ascription of deity to Jesus is exceedingly late and that the ostensible setting in John 1 is entirely fictional.

Yet if we listen to John and to the synoptics with both theological *and historical* sympathy, a simpler resolution presents itself. On its own, John's account makes good historical sense. For disciples of the Baptist to dissociate themselves from him while he is at the height of his power and influence and to transfer their allegiance to someone from Galilee, still unknown and unsought, is most readily explained as the evangelist explains it: John the Baptist himself pointed out who Jesus was, insisting that he came as Jesus' precursor, or forerunner. Those most in tune with the Baptist and most sympathetic to his message would then prove most likely to become the followers of Jesus, and for the reason given: they believed him to be the promised Messiah, the king of Israel, the Son of God (a category that our sources show could serve as a designation of the messiah). None of this means that Jesus' fledgling followers enjoyed a full, Christian understanding of these titles: of all four evangelists, it is John who most persistently catalogues how much the early disciples did *not* understand, how much they actively *mis*understood. All of this makes good intrinsic sense.

But so does the synoptic presentation. It is only to be expected that Jesus' disciples grew in their understanding of who he was. Constantly astonished by the kind of messiah he was turning out to be, they nevertheless came with time to settled conviction: he was none less than the Messiah, the hope of Israel. Even this was less than full, Christian belief. Peter's next step (Mark 8:31–34 par.) was to tell Jesus that predictions about his imminent death were inappropriate to the messiah they were following. Thus, the synoptics portray rising understanding but still expose the massive *mis*understanding that stood at the core of all belief in Jesus that was exercised before his death and resurrection.

Superimposing both views of reality also makes good intrinsic sense. The evangelist who most quickly introduces the Christological titles most heavily stresses the lack of understanding and the sheer misunderstanding of Jesus' followers; the evangelists who track their rising comprehension say less about the disciples' initial false steps but soon point out the profundity of their lingering misapprehensions. John's presentation no longer appears unhistorical; it is merely part of the undergirding historical realities.

5. But this does not mean we must constantly refer to the synoptics to make sense of John. Superimposing the two visions gives us access to certain *historical* realities. Rightly handled, it may also enable us to discern what is peculiarly Johannine and thus to understand with greater sensitivity just what the evangelist is saying. His decision to structure his presentation this way, with the evangelist himself constantly drawing attention to the misunderstanding of the disciples and of others and explaining what was understood only later (e.g., 2:19–22; 3:3–5, 10; 6:32–35, 41, 42; 7:33–36; 8:18–20, 27–28; 10:1–6; 11:21–44, 49–53; 12:12–17; 13:6–10, 27–30; 16:1–4, 12–15; 18:10–11; 19:14; 20:3–9), enables him to operate at two levels, utilizing irony to make his readers see, again and again, that the disciples believed better than they knew, that Caiaphas prophesied better than he thought, that Pilate gave verdicts more just than he could have imagined. The narrative unfolds like a Greek tragedy, every step followed by the reader even when the participants cannot possibly understand what they rightly confess. And then, unlike the Greek tragedy, there is triumph and glorification: the supreme irony is that in the ignominy and defeat of the cross, the plan of God achieved its greatest conquest, a conquest planned before the world began.

6. More generally, though the Christological distinctiveness of John's gospel should not be denied, it should not be exaggerated. True, only this gospel explicitly designates Jesus "God" (1:1, 18; 20:28); but this gospel also insists not only on Jesus' humanity but on his profound subordination to the Father (see esp. 5:16–30).[68] Conversely, the synoptists, for all their portrayal of Jesus as a man, portray him as the one who has the right to forgive sins (Mark 2:1–12 par.—and

---

[68]On the humanity of Jesus in John's gospel, see D. A. Carson, *Divine Sovereignty and Human Responsibility* (Atlanta: John Knox, 1981), pp. 146–60; Marianne M. Thompson, *The Humanity of Jesus in the Fourth Gospel* (Philadelphia: Fortress, 1986); Leon Morris, *Jesus Is the Christ: Studies in the Theology of John* (Grand Rapids: Eerdmans, 1989), pp. 43–67; cf. E. Käsemann, *The Testament of Jesus* (ET London: SCM, 1968), who argues that the evidence for Jesus' humanity in John is nothing more than the trappings necessary to secure a docetic Christology.

who can forgive sins but God alone?) and relate parables in which Jesus transparently takes on the metaphoric role most commonly assigned to God in the Old Testament. The Synoptic Gospels present in seed form the full flowering of the incarnational understanding that would develop only later; but the seed is there, the entire genetic coding for the growth that later takes place.[69] If John lets us see a little more of the opening flower, it is in part because he indulges in more explanatory asides that clarify for the reader what is really going on.

Even the "I am" statements constitute less of a historical problem than at first meets the eye. The statements themselves are quite varied.[70] Jesus' plain affirmation of his messianic status in 4:26 ("I who speak to you am he"), contrasting sharply with the circumlocutions and symbol-laden language of so many synoptic sayings, may turn on the identity of his interlocutor: she is a Samaritan woman and unlikely to harbor exactly the same political expectations bound up with ideas of messiahship in many strands of first-century Judaism. After all, John reports that Jesus resorts to circumspect language when he is in Judea (e.g., 7:28–44; 10:24–29). The majority of the "I am" statements in John have some sort of completion: bread of life, good shepherd, vine, or the like (6:35; 10:11; 15:1). They are plainly metaphoric, and although they are reasonably transparent to later readers, they were confusing and difficult for the first hearers (e.g., 6:60; 10:19; 16:30–32): religious leaders did not customarily say that sort of thing.[71] As for the occurrences of an absolute form of "I am," which can ultimately be traced back to Isaiah's use of the same expression as a reference for God (e.g., Isa. 43:10; 47:8, 10, esp. LXX), they are mixed in their clarity and are in any case partly paralleled by Mark 6:50; 13:6. And if the most dramatic of the sayings in John, "Before Abraham was born, I am" (8:58), is without explicit synoptic parallel, it is hard to see how it makes a claim fundamentally superior to the synoptic portrayal of a Jesus who not only can adjudicate Jewish interpretations of the law but can radically abrogate parts of it (Mark 7:15–19) while claiming that all of it is fulfilled by him (Matt. 5:17ff.), who forgives sin (Matt. 9:1ff.) and insists that an individual's eternal destiny turns on obedience to him (Matt. 7:21-23), who demands loyalty that outstrips the sanctity of family ties (Matt. 10:37-39; Mark 10:29–30) and insists that no one knows the Father except those to whom the Son discloses him (Luke 10:22), who offers rest for the weary (Matt.11:28–30) and salvation for the lost (Luke 15), who muzzles nature (Mark 4:39) and raises the dead (Matt. 9:18–26). Individual deeds from such a list may in some cases find parallels in the prophets or in the apostles; the combination finds its only adequate parallel in God alone.[72]

---

[69]For a responsible treatment of this organic growth of Christology, see I. Howard Marshall, *The Origins of New Testament Christology* (Leicester: IVP, 1976); C. F. D. Moule, *The Origin of Christology* (Cambridge: Cambridge University Press, 1977); and many of the essays in H. H. Rowdon, ed., *Christ the Lord, Fs.* D. Guthrie (Leicester: IVP, 1982).

[70]See Philip B. Harner, *The "I Am" of the Fourth Gospel* (Philadelphia: Fortress, 1970).

[71]Most of the alleged parallels are from second- and third-century (or even later) Gnostic and Hermetic sources. Those closest in time to John, drawn from the first half of the first century, are claims of the mythical Egyptian goddess Isis, who was popular in the Greek-speaking world: "I am the one who discovered fruit for men"; "I am the one who is called the goddess among women" (see *NewDocs* 1.2). These are, however, remarkably *un*metaphorical and, in any case, do not bear the Old Testament resonances of the utterances in John.

[72]For a useful defense of the authenticity of the "I am" sayings in John, see E. Stauffer, *Jesus and His Story* (London: SCM, 1960), pp. 142–59.

Limitations of space preclude detailed treatment of other well-known difficulties in John and their relation to the synoptic tradition. They are in any case sympathetically treated in the stream of commentaries that seeks to keep history and theology together (e.g., Westcott, Morris, Carson) and in the longer New Testament introductions (e.g., Guthrie, pp. 248ff.).

DATE

During the past 150 years, suggestions as to the date of the fourth gospel have varied from before A.D. 70 to the final quarter of the second century. Dates in the second century are now pretty well ruled out by manuscript discoveries (see discussion below in the section "Text"). But apart from this limitation, none of the arguments is entirely convincing, and almost any date between about 55 and 95 is possible. Probably John 21:23 "suggests it was probably nearer the end of that period than the beginning."[73]

Some dates seem implausibly early. Probably the inference to be drawn from 21:19 is that Peter had by his death glorified God when chapter 21 was composed. Peter died in A.D. 64 or 65; dates earlier than that for the composition of the fourth gospel seem unlikely. Those who hold to a date before 70 (but after 65) point to details of Palestine presented as if Jerusalem and its temple complex were still standing; for example, "Now there is in Jerusalem near the Sheep Gate a pool" (John 5:2), the evangelist writes. The argument would be conclusive, except that John frequently uses the Greek present tense to refer to something in the past. The silence of the fourth gospel on the destruction of the temple is considered powerful evidence for a pre-70 date by some authors. Arguments from silence, however, are tricky things. At first glance there is some force to this one, since the theme of the evangelist in, say, 2:19–22, could have been strengthened if the overthrow of the temple had been mentioned. But the evidence is far from compelling. How prominent the temple was in the thinking of Jews in the Diaspora varied a great deal. If some time had elapsed, perhaps a decade, between the destruction of the temple and the publication of this gospel, so that the initial shock of the reports had passed, there is no reason to think that the evangelist should have brought it up. Indeed, John is a writer who loves subtle allusions. If he wrote in, say, 80, he may have taken the destruction of the temple as a given and let this fact make its own contribution to his theological argument. Other arguments for a date before 70 do not seem any more convincing.

Those who defend a date toward the end of the first century, say between A.D. 85 and 95, commonly resort to four arguments:

1. Many theologians appeal to the tradition that the fourth gospel was written under the reign of Emperor Domitian (ruled A.D. 81–96). But Robinson has shown that this tradition rests on very little.[74] There is good, early tradition that the apostle John lived to a great age, surviving even into the reign of Emperor Trajan (98–117; see Ireneus, *Adv. Haer.* 2.22.5; 3.3.4; quoted by Eusebius, *H.E.* 3.23.3–4). Jerome, admittedly in the fourth century, places John's death in the

---

[73]J. Ramsey Michaels, *John* (San Francisco: Harper & Row, 1983), p. xxix.
[74]Robinson, *Redating*, pp. 256–58.

sixty-eighth year "after our Lord's passion" (*De vir. ill.* 9), or about 98.[75] There is also good patristic evidence that John was the last of the evangelists to write his book (Ireneus, *Adv. Haer.* 3.1.1; Clement, as cited by Eusebius, *H.E.* 6.14.7; Eusebius himself, *H.E.* 3.24.7). "But that he wrote as a very old man is an inference which only appears late and accompanied by other statements which show that it is clearly secondary and unreliable."[76]

2. A strong contingent of scholars argue that both the concept and the term meaning "put out of the synagogue" (9:22; 12:42; 16:2; ἀποσυνάγωγος [*aposynagōgos*]) betray a period after the decision of the Council of Jamnia to ban Christians from the synagogue.[77] In other words, they find in this expression an irreducible anachronism that dates the gospel of John to a period after A.D. 85. Yet at every point this thesis has been challenged,[78] and today it is beginning to wield less influence than it did a few years ago.

3. Numerous details are often taken to indicate a late date. For instance, this gospel makes no mention of the Sadducees, who contributed much to the religious life of Jerusalem and Judea before A.D. 70 but who withered and became of marginal importance after that date. The argument would be weighty, except that John is similarly silent on the scribes, whose influence actually increased after 70. And John does make it clear that the priests, with rapidly diminishing influence after 70, were largely in control of the Sanhedrin in the time up to Jesus' passion. Other matters of detail are no more convincing.

4. Perhaps the most pervasive reason for a late date is that in the prevailing reconstruction of early Christian history, John's gospel best fits into a date toward the end of the first century. For example, the ready ascription of deity to Jesus and the unapologetic insistence on his preexistence are said to fit a later date.

The issue turns in part on countless exegetical and historical details that cannot be canvassed here. Nevertheless it must be noted that the New Testament passages closest in theology to John 1:1–18 are probably the so-called Christ-hymns (e.g., Phil.2:5–11; Col. 1:15–20; see Rom. 9:5), which were doubtless already circulating in the mid-fifties. Moreover, no gospel stresses the functional subordination of Jesus to his Father more strongly than does John. In other words, the emphasis in the fourth gospel on the deity of Christ must not be allowed to eclipse complementary emphases. Attempts to date the fourth gospel by charting Christological trajectories do not appear very convincing.

If a date for the publication of the fourth gospel must be suggested, we may very tentatively advance A.D. 80–85, for these reasons:

1. There is no convincing pressure to place the gospel of John as early on the

---

[75]On the very slight evidence that the apostle John was early martyred, almost universally dismissed, see Guthrie, pp. 272–75. Astonishingly, Hengel (*Johannine Question*) entertains the suggestion.

[76]Robinson, *Redating*, p. 257.

[77]Dominated by J. Louis Martyn, *History and Tradition in the Fourth Gospel* (Nashville: Abingdon, 1979).

[78]See R. Kimelman, "*Birkat ha-Minim* and the Lack of Evidence for an anti-Christian Jewish Prayer in Late Antiquity," in *Jewish and Christian Self-Definition*, vol. 2 of *Aspects of Judaism in the Greco-Roman Period*, ed. E. P. Sanders (Philadelphia: Fortress, 1981), pp. 226–44, 391–403; W. Horbury, "The Benediction of the *Minim* and Early Jewish-Christian Controversy," *JTS* 33 (1982): 19–61; Robinson, *John*, pp. 72ff.; Beasley-Murray, *John*, pp. lxxvi–lxxviii; H. Ridderbos, *Het evangelie naar Johannes*, 2 vols. (Kampen: J. H. Kok, 1987–), 1:395–98; and discussion in Carson, *John*.

spectrum as possible, but there is a little pressure to place John rather later on it, namely, the relatively late date at which it is cited with certainty by the Fathers.

2. Although the arguments from theological trajectories are, as we have seen, rather weak, yet if any weight is to be given to them at all, at several points John's gospel uses language that is on its way toward the less restrained language of Ignatius—in particular the ease and frequency with which Ignatius refers to Jesus as God, his sacramental language (where in our view he has misunderstood John rather badly), and his sharp antitheses.

3. Although the fall of the temple may not have had as much impact in the Diaspora as in Palestinian Judaism, yet it is hard to believe that, if the fourth gospel was written after A.D. 70, the date was *immediately* after 70, when the reverberations around the empire, in both Jewish and Christian circles, were still being felt.

4. If, as is argued later in this book, the Johannine Epistles are concerned in part to combat an incipient form of Gnosticism, predicated in part on a Gnostic misunderstanding of the fourth gospel, then some time must be allowed between the publication of the gospel and the publication of the epistles of John. That tends to rule out a date in the nineties.

DESTINATION

No destination is specified by the fourth gospel itself. Inferences are largely controlled by conclusions drawn in the areas of authorship and purpose. If John the son of Zebedee wrote this book while residing in Ephesus, then it might be inferred that he prepared this book for readers in this general part of the empire. But he may have hoped for the widest possible circulation; in any case, the inference cannot be more certain than the assumption of authorship. Some general things may be inferred from the purposes John displays in the writing of his gospel. However, since these purposes are disputed, we must turn to them.

PURPOSE

Much of the discussion on this topic during the twentieth century has turned on questionable assumptions or procedures, of which four are particularly common.

1. Many treatments at the beginning of the century depended on the assumption that John is parasitic on the Synoptic Gospels.[79] That means the governing purpose of John should be uncovered by contrasting what John does with what the synoptists do. He wrote a "spiritual" gospel, it is argued; or he wrote to supplement the earlier efforts, or even to supersede or to correct them. These theories refuse to let John be John; he must be John-compared-with-Mark, say, or with another synoptist. This approach has faded in recent decades, largely owing to the revised estimate of John's relation to the synoptics.

2. Many modern proposals have sprung from a reconstruction of the Johannine community that is alleged to have called this book forth. Inevitably a degree of circularity is set up: the community is reconstructed by drawing inferences from

---

[79]In one form, the theory is as old as Clement of Alexandria (Eusebius, *H.E.* 6.14.7). In this century it was made famous by Hans Windisch, *Johannes und die Synoptiker* (Leipzig: J. C. Hinrichs'sche Buchhandlung, 1926).

the fourth gospel; once this background is sufficiently widely accepted, the next generation of scholars tends to build on it, or to modify it slightly, by showing how the fourth gospel achieves its purpose by addressing that situation so tellingly. The circularity is not necessarily vicious, but the final picture is much less well substantiated than is often assumed, owing to the very high number of merely possible but by no means compelling inferences that are invoked to delineate the community in the first place.

Meeks, for instance, argues that the Johannine community is sectarian, an isolated conventicle struggling in opposition against a powerful synagogue.[80] The fourth gospel, then, is a summary of these polemics, possibly even a handbook for new converts, certainly something to strengthen the community in its continuing conflict. Martyn's reconstruction is a modification of this: the church is aggressively evangelizing the Jews, and this book not only reports the conflict but helps the church in its task.[81] But at least some components of these reconstructions may be called into question. To think of the Johannine community as isolated and sectarian is to miss the grand vision of John 17, not to mention the fact that John's Christology finds its closest parallels in the New Testament in the so-called hymns (e.g., Phil. 2:5–11; Col. 1:15–20), which suggests that the evangelist is thoroughly in touch with the wider church.

3. Many statements of John's purpose depend rather narrowly on a single theme, feature, or even literary tool. Mussner, for instance, examines all expressions dealing with knowledge, hearing the word of Jesus, and the like, and suggests that the evangelist is effecting a transfer of reference from the time of Jesus to his own time.[82] In this merged vision, the past is not annulled, but the angle of vision is from the present. This merging of visions, however, is so strong, in Mussner's view, that the distinctive word of the historical Jesus cannot be distinguished at all.

Whence, then, the evangelist's constant distinction between what Jesus' disciples understood at the time and what they understood only later? What starts off as a suggestive entry point for considering the purpose of the fourth gospel ends up disowning too many features integral to the book.

In the same way, Freed wonders if John 4 does not constitute evidence that the fourth gospel was written, at least in part, to win Samaritan converts.[83] One may well ask what methodological steps warrant the leap from circumstances ostensibly set in Jesus' day to identical circumstances set in the evangelist's day. Again, Malina attempts to locate the Johannine community by reading the fourth gospel in the framework of two models provided by sociolinguistics.[84] However, as subsequent debate demonstrated, not only the adequacy of the sociolinguistic models may be questioned, but also the extent to which data on the Johannine community are obtained to feed into the models by "mirror-reading" the text and

---

[80]Wayne A. Meeks, *The Prophet-King: Moses Traditions and the Johannine Christology*, SuppNovT 14 (Leiden: Brill, 1967).

[81]Martyn, *History and Theology*.

[82]F. Mussner, *The Historical Jesus and the Gospel of St. John* (ET London: Burns & Oates, 1967).

[83]E. D. Freed, "Did John Write His Gospel Partly to Win Samaritan Converts?" *NovT* 12 (1970): 241–56.

[84]Bruce J. Malina et al., *The Gospel of John in Sociolinguistic Perspective*, ed. Herman C. Waetjen, Protocol of the Forty-Eighth Colloquy (Claremont: Center for Hermeneutical Studies in Hellenistic and Modern Culture, 1984).

seeing only what is being projected onto it. In David Rensberger's reading, the fourth evangelist is a kind of prototypical liberation theologian.[85] At some point, the text of the gospel is swamped by the rush of inferences.[86]

4. Finally, several commentators adopt what might be called a synthetic, or additive, approach. What appear to be the best suggestions of others are blended together, so that the purpose of John's gospel is to evangelize Jews, to evangelize Hellenists, to strengthen the church, to catechize new converts, to provide materials for the evangelization of Jews, and so forth.[87]Part of the problem is the confusion between purpose and plausible effect. Just because John's gospel can be used to offer comfort to the bereaved in the twentieth century does not mean that is why the evangelist wrote it. In the same way, just because this gospel could help Jewish Christians witnessing to unconverted Jews and proselytes in the nearby synagogue does not itself mean that is why the evangelist wrote it. To think through all the plausibly good effects various parts of this book could have does not provide adequate reasons for thinking that any one of them, or all of them together, was the purpose the evangelist had in mind when he put pen to paper.

Other purposes have been suggested; the proper place to begin, however, is with John's own statement of his purpose: "Jesus did many other miraculous signs in the presence of his disciples, which are not recorded in this book. But these are written that you may believe that Jesus is the Christ, the Son of God, and that by believing you may have life in his name" (20:30–31). The words rendei ·d "that you may believe" hide a textual variant: either ἵνα πιστεύητε (hina pisteuēte, present subjunctive) or ἵνα πιστεύσητε (hina pisteusēte, aorist subjunctive). Some have argued that the latter expression supports an evangelistic purpose: that you may come to faith, come to believe. The former, then, supports an edificatory purpose: that you may continue in faith, continue to believe. In fact, it can easily be shown that both tenses are used in John for both initial faith and continuing in faith, so that nothing can be resolved by the appeal to one textual variant or the other.

It is worth comparing these verses with the stated purpose of 1 John: "I write these things to you who believe in the name of the Son of God so that you may know that you have eternal life" (1 John 5:13). This verse was clearly written to encourage Christians; by the contrasting form of its expression, John 20:30–31 sounds evangelistic.

This impression is confirmed by the firm syntactic evidence that the first purpose clause in 20:31 must be rendered "that you may believe that the Christ, the Son of God, is Jesus." Thus the fundamental question the fourth gospel addresses is not Who is Jesus? but Who is the Messiah, the Christ, the Son of God?[88] In its context, the latter is a question of identity, not of kind: that is, the question Who is the Christ? should not here be taken to mean "What kind of Christ are you talking about?" but "So you claim to know who the Christ is. Prove it, then: Who is he?"

---

[85]David Rensberger, *Overcoming the World: Politics and Community in the Gospel of John* (London: SPCK, 1988).

[86]For a summary and critique of Rensberger, see the review in *Themelios*, forthcoming.

[87]Beasley-Murray, *John*, pp. lxxxvii–xc, comes close to this range.

[88]See D. A. Carson, "The Purpose of the Fourth Gospel: John 20:30–31 Reconsidered," *JBL* 108 (1987): 639–51.

Christians would not ask that kind of question, because they already knew the answer. The most likely people to ask that sort of question would be Jews and Jewish proselytes who know what "the Christ" means, have some sort of messianic expectation, and are perhaps in dialogue with Christians and want to know more. In short, John's gospel not only is evangelistic in its purpose (which was a dominant view until this century, when relatively few have defended it)[89] but aims in particular to evangelize Diaspora Jews and Jewish proselytes. This view is gradually gaining influence,[90] and much can be said for it. It may even receive indirect support from some recent studies that try to interpret the fourth gospel as a piece of mission literature. The best of these[91] display generally excellent exegesis but give no attention to the fact that with very little adaptation the same exegesis could justify the thesis that the gospel of John was not written to believers *about* mission but to outsiders to *perform* mission.

It goes beyond the limits of a brief introduction to show how this stated purpose of the evangelist sheds a great deal of light on the rest of his gospel: that is the work of an entire commentary. The constant allusions to the Old Testament show that John's intended readership is biblically literate; his translation of Semitic expressions (e.g., 1:38, 42; 4:25; 19:13, 17) shows he is writing to those whose linguistic competence is in Greek. His strong denunciation of "the Jews" cannot be taken as a mark against this thesis: John may well have an interest in driving a wedge between ordinary Jews and (at least) some of their leaders. The fourth gospel is not as anti-Jewish as some people think anyway: salvation is still said to be "from the Jews" (4:22), and often the referent of "the Jews" is "the Jews in Judea" or "the Jewish leaders" or the like. "Anti-Semitic" is simply the wrong category to apply to the fourth gospel: whatever hostilities are present turn on theological issues related to the acceptance or rejection of revelation, not on race. How could it be otherwise, when all of the first Christians were Jews and when, on this reading, both the fourth evangelist and his primary readers were Jews and Jewish proselytes? Those who respond to Jesus, whether Jews, Samaritans, or "other sheep" (10:16) to be added to Jesus' fold, are blessed; those who ignore him or reject him do so out of unbelief, disobedience (3:36), and culpable blindness (9:29–41).

Within some such a framework as this, further inferences can usefully be drawn from the content of his gospel about the people to whom John was writing and

---

[89]E.g., W. Oehler, *Das Johannesevangelium, eine Missionsschrift für die Welt* (Gütersloh: Bertelsmann, 1936); idem, *Zum Missionscharackter des Johannesevangeliums* (Gütersloh: Bertelsmann, 1941); Dodd, *Interpretation*, p. 9; Moule, pp. 136–37; Morris, *John*, pp. 855–57. See the discussion in Guthrie, pp. 283ff.

[90]K. Bornhäuser, *Das Johannesevangelium: Eine Missionsschrift für Israel* (Gütersloh: Bertelsmann, 1928); W. C. van Unnik, "The Purpose of St. John's Gospel," in *SE* 1:382–411; J. A. T. Robinson, *Twelve New Testament Studies* (London: SCM, 1962), pp. 107–25; David D. C. Braine, "The Inner Jewishness of St. John's Gospel as the Clue to the Inner Jewishness of Jesus," *SNTU* 13 (1988): 101–55, esp. pp. 105–11; George J. Brooke, "Christ and the Law in John 7–10," in *Law and Religion: Essays in the Place of the Law in Israel and Early Christianity*, ed. Barnabas Lindars (London: SPCK, 1988), pp. 102–12; Carson, *John*.

[91]See esp. Teresa Okure, *The Johannine Approach to Mission*, WUNT 2.31 (Tübingen: J. C. B. Mohr [Paul Siebeck], 1988). Something similar could be said for Miguel Rodrigues Ruiz, *Das Missionsgedanke des Johannesevangeliums: Ein Beitrag zur johanneischen Soteriologie und Ekklesiologie* (Würzburg: Echter Verlag, 1987). For a survey of recent studies of John along this vein, see R. Schnackenburg, *Das Johannesevangelium*, 4 vols. (Freiburg: Herder, 1965–84), 4:58–72.

the topics that interested them. But these inferences are secondary, always in principle to be challenged by other (and possibly competing) inferences and never capable of more than confirming John's purpose, which we must establish on other grounds.

TEXT

The earliest New Testament fragment known to us is a fragment of John, p^{52}, dating from about A.D. 130 and containing a few words from John 18. Two other papyrus witnesses, both codices, spring from the end of the second century: p^{66} includes most of John 1–14 and parts of the remaining chapters, while p^{75} contains most of Luke, followed by John 1–11 and parts of chapters 12–15. From the beginning of the third century comes p^{45}, which contains parts of all four gospels plus Acts, though the mutilated state of the manuscript ensures that no book is complete. Thereafter the manuscript evidence becomes richer, capped by the great fourth-century uncials (manuscripts written in capital letters) and followed by the many minuscules in succeeding centuries.

There is an excellent list of the most important textual witnesses, including versional and patristic evidence, along with a summary of scholarly discussion, in Schnackenburg.[92] On the whole, the text is in good shape, but there are a few passages where notorious difficulties are still disputed. Perhaps the most famous of these is 1:18. It appears likely that the original reading was μονογενὴς θεὸς (monogenēs theos), the second word probably understood appositionally: "[the] unique one, [himself] God," rather than "the only begotten God."

Despite the best efforts of Zane Hodges to prove that the narrative of the woman caught in adultery (John 7:53–8:11) was originally part of John's Gospel,[93] the evidence is against him, and modern English versions are right to rule it off from the rest of the text (NIV) or to relegate it to a footnote (RSV). These verses are present in most of the medieval Greek minuscule manuscripts, but they are absent from virtually all early Greek manuscripts that have come down to us, representing great diversity of textual traditions. The most notable exception is the Western uncial D, known for its independence in numerous other places. They are also missing from the earliest forms of the Syriac and Coptic Gospels, and from many Old Latin, Old Georgian, and Armenian manuscripts. All the early church fathers omit this narrative; in commenting on John, they pass immediately from 7:52 to 8:12. No Eastern Father cites the passage before the tenth century. Didymus the Blind (a fourth-century exegete from Alexandria) reports a variation on this narrative,[94] not the narrative as we have it here. Moreover, a number of (later) manuscripts that include the narrative mark it off with asterisks or obeli, indicating hesitation as to its authenticity, while those that do include it display a rather high frequency of textual variants. Although most of the manuscripts that include the story place it at 7:53–8:11, some place it instead after Luke 21:38, and others variously after John 7:44, John 7:36, or John 21:25 (see Metzger, pp.

[92]R. Schnackenburg, *The Gospel according to St John*, 3 vols. (London: Burns & Oates, 1968–82), 1:173–91.

[93]Zane Hodges, "The Woman Taken in Adultery (John 7:53–8:11)," *BS* 136 (1979): 318–72; 137 (1980): 41–53.

[94]See Bart D. Ehrman, "Jesus and the Adulteress," *NTS* 34 (1988): 24–44.

219–22, for a summary of the evidence). The diversity of placement confirms (though it cannot establish) the inauthenticity of the verses. Finally, even if someone should decide that the substance of the narrative is authentic—a position plausible enough—it would be very difficult to justify the view that the material is authentically Johannine: it includes numerous expressions and constructions that are found nowhere in John but that are characteristic of the Synoptic Gospels, Luke in particular.

ADOPTION INTO THE CANON

By the end of the second century, all four canonical gospels were accepted not only as authentic but as Scripture on a par with Old Testament Scripture. Even earlier, the fact that Tatian's *Diatessaron* (see discussion above) could use John as the chronological framework for the other three testifies to the authority that it enjoyed. Outside of Marcion and the Alogoi, the early church nowhere questioned either the authenticity or, once it began to address the subject, the canonicity of the fourth gospel.

JOHN IN RECENT STUDY

The overwhelming majority of scholarly energy on John during the last twenty or thirty years has been devoted to some theme in the fourth gospel as a means of access to the ostensible Johannine community.[95] Enough has been said on this approach.

A second focus has been a perennial one: the examination, from fresh standpoints, of particular themes in John's gospel. For instance, the role of the Paraclete, the Holy Spirit, in the fourth gospel continues to call forth books and articles.[96] There are similar treatments of many Johannine themes.

A third emphasis has been the study of a variety of historical matters—the trial of Jesus, the relation between John and the synoptics, or this or that topographical detail.[97]

But by far the most important development in recent studies on John is the application of various forms of literary criticism to the fourth gospel. This may be a structuralist approach to certain chapters,[98] an examination of the asides in

[95]For surveys of recent literature on John, one might usefully consult R. Schnackenburg, "Entwicklung und Stand des johanneischen Forschung seit 1955," in *L'évangile*, pp. 19–44; H. Thyen, "Aus der Literatur des Johannesevangeliums," *ThR* 39 (1974): 1–69, 222–52, 289–330; 42 (1977): 211–70; 44 (1979): 97–134; Jürgen Becker, "Aus der Literatur des Johannesevangeliums," *ThR* 47 (1982): 279–347; James McPolin, "Studies in the Fourth Gospel—Some Contemporary Trends," *IBS* 2 (1980): 3–26; D. A. Carson, "Recent Literature on the Fourth Gospel: Some Reflections," *Themelios* 9 (1983): 8–18; 14 (1989): 57–64.

[96]See the books by Johnston, Franck, and Burge in the Bibliography.

[97]Here it must be said, with regret, that few recent scholars have interacted in any detail with such valuable and detailed earlier works as J. Armitage Robinson, *The Historical Character of the Fourth Gospel* (London: Longmans-Green, 1908); E. H. Askwith, *The Historical Value of the Fourth Gospel* (London: Hodder & Stoughton, 1910); H. Scott Holland, *The Fourth Gospel* (London: John Murray, 1923); or A. C. Headlam, *The Fourth Gospel as History* (Oxford: Blackwell, 1948).

[98]B. Olsson, *Structure and Meaning of the Fourth Gospel* (Lund: Gleerup, 1974), on John 2–4; Hendrikus Boers, *Neither on This Mountain nor in Jerusalem*, SBLMS 35 (Atlanta: SP, 1988), on John 4.

John,[99] or a consideration of some such literary device as irony.[100] The tendency in all of these approaches is to treat the text synchronically, that is, to treat the text as a finished product and to ask virtually no questions about its historical development or its referents. Nowhere is this better seen than in the magisterial and provocative work of Culpepper,[101] which analyzes the gospel of John in the categories reserved for modern novels.

There have been both a gain and a loss in these studies. Some of them have said not much more than the obvious, with the heavy weight of the formal categories of structuralism or the new literary criticism to drag them down. The most creative have in their favor that they treat the gospel of John as a single text, a unified piece of work. This is both refreshing and something of a relief from older approaches whose primary goal was to detach sources or traditions from the text as we have it.

But there is a loss as well. These studies often ignore the rootedness of the gospels, including this Gospel, in history—their passionate concern to bear witness, not simply to pass on abstract ideas. The genuine insights of these studies are sometimes offset by an air of unreality, of merely esoteric textual formality.

THE CONTRIBUTION OF JOHN

John's thought is so wonderfully integrated that attempts to compartr..entalize it by itemizing its components are destined in some measure to misrepresent it. The best theological summaries are provided by Barrett and Schnackenburg.[102] Among John's more important contributions are the following:

1. John adds stereoscopic depth to the picture we might gain of Jesus and his ministry, death, and resurrection from the synoptic accounts alone. By telling the same story from another angle, with many things omitted that they include and with many emphases that they scarcely treat, the total portrait is vastly richer than what would otherwise have been achieved.

2. John's presentation of who Jesus is lies at the heart of all that is distinctive in this gospel. It is not just a question of the shading assigned to certain Christological titles—whether those found only in the fourth of the gospels (e.g., Lamb of God, Word, I Am), or those found in all four (e.g., Son of Man, Christ, King). Rather, fundamental to all else that is said of him, Jesus is peculiarly the Son of God, or simply the Son. Although "Son of God" can serve as a rough synonym for "Messiah," it is enriched by the unique manner in which Jesus as God's Son relates to his Father: he is functionally subordinate to him and does and says only those things the Father gives him to do and say, but he does *everything* that the Father does, since the Father shows him everything that he himself does (5:19ff.). The perfection of Jesus' obedience and the unqualified nature of his dependence thereby become the loci in which Jesus discloses nothing less than the words and deeds of God.

---

[99]G. van Belle, *Les parenthèses dans l'évangile de Jean: Aperçu historique et classification* (Louvain: Louvain University Press, 1985).

[100]P. Duke, *Irony in the Fourth Gospel* (Atlanta: John Knox, 1985).

[101]R. A. Culpepper, *Anatomy of the Fourth Gospel: A Study in Literary Design* (Philadelphia: Fortress, 1983).

[102]Barrett, *John*, pp. 67–99; Schnackenburg, *John*, esp. in the many excursuses.

3. Despite the heavy emphasis on Jesus as the one who reveals his Father, salvation does not come (as in Gnosticism) merely by revelation. John's work is a gospel: all the movement of the plot is toward the cross and the resurrection. The cross is not merely a revelatory moment:[103] it is the death of the shepherd for his sheep (John 10), the sacrifice of one man for his nation (John 11), the life that is given for the world (John 6), the victory of the Lamb of God (John 1), the triumph of the obedient Son, who in consequence bequeaths his life, his peace, his joy, his Spirit (John 14–16).

4. John's distinctive emphasis on eschatology is bound up with his use of the "hour" theme (often rendered "time" in the NIV: e.g., 2:4; 7:6). All the major New Testament corpora display the tension of trying simultaneously (1) to express the wonderful truth that in the ministry, death, resurrection, and exaltation of Jesus, God's promised "last days" have already arrived, and (2) to insist that the fullness of hope is still to come. Different authors set out the tension in different ways. In John, the hour "is coming and has now come" (4:23; 5:25); Jesus has bequeathed his peace, but in this world we will have trouble (16:33). Above all, in the wake of Jesus' exaltation and his gift of the Spirit, we can possess eternal life even now: that is characteristic of John, who tilts his emphasis to the *present* enjoyment of eschatological blessings. But this is never at the expense of all future hope: the time is coming when those who are in the graves will come out to face the judgment of the One to whom all judgment has been entrusted by the Father (5:28–30). If John asserts that Jesus even now makes himself present among his followers in the person of his Spirit (14:23), he also insists that Jesus himself is coming back to gather his own to the dwelling he has prepared for them (14:1–3).

5. Although John's teaching on the Holy Spirit has important similarities to synoptic emphases (e.g., cf. John 3:34 and Luke 4:14–21), there are numerous strands that are unique. Jesus not only bears and bestows the Spirit, but by bequeathing the eschatological Spirit, he discharges his role as the one who introduces what is characteristic under the new covenant (3:5; 7:37–39). In the farewell discourse (John 14–16), the Spirit, the Counselor, is clearly given in consequence of Jesus' death and exaltation. The elements of what came to be called the doctrine of the Trinity find their clearest articulation, within the New Testament, in the gospel of John.

6. Although John does not cite the Old Testament as frequently as, say, Matthew, his use of the Old Testament is characterized by an extraordinary number of allusions, and above all by his insistence that Jesus in certain respects replaces revered figures and institutions from the old covenant (e.g. temple, vine, tabernacle, serpent, passover). The underlying hermeneutic assumed deserves close study.

7. No gospel better preserves the ways in which Jesus was misunderstood by his contemporaries, including his own followers. This feature not only provides an entrance into various historical questions, as we have seen, but is itself a reflection on the relation between the old covenant and the new. For the same gospel that insists that Jesus fulfills and in certain respects replaces many Old Testament

---

[103]Contra J. T. Forestell, *The Word of the Cross: Salvation as Revelation in the Fourth Gospel*, AnBib (Rome: BIP, 1974).

features equally insists that most of these points were not grasped by Jesus' disciples until after his exaltation.

8. Not a little attention is devoted to what it means to belong to the people of God. Although there is nothing on church order per se, there is much on the election, life, origin, nature, witness, suffering, fruit-bearing, prayer, love, and unity of the people of God.

9. We have seen that John in certain respects provides greater depth than do the Synoptic Gospels, but on relatively restricted topics. That is a major reason why his vocabulary is relatively small, with certain words and expressions occurring again and again. This repetition becomes an index of some of the things that are important to him. For instance, he uses the verb πιστεύω (pisteuō, "to believe") 98 times; the "love" words 57 times; κόσμος (kosmos, "world") 78 times, the "to send" verbs (πέμπω [pempō] and ἀποστέλλω [apostellō]) 60 times, "Father" 137 times (mostly with reference to God). However tricky it is to approach an author's theology through word studies, in John's case such studies constitute an important entrée.

10. The complexities that bind together election, faith, and the function of signs are repeatedly explored. If faith bursts forth in consequence of what is revealed in the signs, well and good: signs legitimately serve as a basis for faith (e.g., 10:38). In contrast, people are excoriated for their dependence on signs (4:48). It is a better faith that hears and believes rather than sees and believes (20:29). Put in the last analysis, faith turns on sovereign election by the Son (15:16), on being part of the gift from the Father to the Son (6:37–44). This truth is at the heart of a book that is persistently evangelistic.

BIBLIOGRAPHY

Mark L. **Appold**, *The Oneness Motif in the Fourth Gospel*, WUNT 2.1 (Tübingen: J. C. B. Mohr [Paul Siebeck], 1976); E. H. **Askwith**, *The Historical Value of the Fourth Gospel* (London: Hodder & Stoughton, 1910); C. K. **Barrett**, *The Gospel According to St John* (London: SPCK; Philadelphia: Westminster, 1978); G. R. **Beasley-Murray**, *John*, WBC 36 (Waco, Tex.: Word, 1987); J. **Becker**, "Aus der Literatur des Johannesevangeliums," *ThR* 47 (1982): 279–347; idem, *Das Evangelium des Johannes*, 2 vols. (Gütersloh: G. Mohn, 1979–81); J. H. **Bernard**, *The Gospel According to St John*, 2 vols., ICC (Edinburgh: T. & T. Clark, 1928); Josef **Blank**, *Krisis: Untersuchungen zur johanneischen Christologie und Eschatologie* (Freiburg: Lambertus, 1964); J. **Blinzler**, *Johannes und die Synoptiker* (Stuttgart: KBW, 1965); Craig L. **Blomberg**, *The Historical Reliability of the Gospels* (Leicester: IVP, 1987); Hendrikus **Boers**, *Neither on This Mountain nor in Jerusalem*, SBLMS 35 (Atlanta: SP, 1988); P. **Borgen**, *Bread from Heaven*, SuppNovT 10 (Leiden: Brill, 1965); K. **Bornhäuser**, *Das Johannesevangelium: Eine Missionsschrift für Israel* (Gütersloh: C. Bertelsmann, 1928); David D. C. **Braine**, "The Inner Jewishness of St. John's Gospel as the Clue to the Inner Jewishness of Jesus," *SNTU* 13 (1989): 101–55; George J. **Brooke**, "Christ and the Law in John 7–10," in *Law and Religion: Essays in the Place of the Law in Israel and Early Christianity*, ed. Barnabas Lindars (London: SPCK, 1988), pp. 34–43; R. E. **Brown**, *The Community of the Beloved Disciple* (New York: Paulist, 1978); idem, *The Gospel According to John*, 2 vols. (Garden City, N.Y.: Doubleday, 1966–70); F. F. **Bruce**, *The Gospel of John* (Basingstoke: Pickering & Inglis, 1983); R. **Bultmann**, *The Gospel of John: A Commentary* (ET Oxford: Blackwell, 1971); G.

M. **Burge**, *The Anointed Community: The Holy Spirit in the Johannine Tradition* (Grand Rapids: Eerdmans, 1987); D. A. **Carson**, "Current Source Criticism of the Fourth Gospel: Some Methodological Questions," *JBL* 97 (1978): 411–29; idem, *Divine Sovereignty and Human Responsibility* (Atlanta: John Knox, 1981); idem, *The Gospel According to John* (Grand Rapids: Eerdmans, 1990); idem, "The Purpose of the Fourth Gospel: John 20:30–31 Reconsidered," *JBL* 108 (1987): 639–51; idem, "Recent Literature on the Fourth Gospel: Some Reflections," *Themelios* 9 (1983): 8–18; 14 (1989): 57–64; idem, "Understanding Misunderstandings in the Fourth Gospel," *TynB* 33 (1982): 59–89; idem, "The Use of the Old Testament in John and the Johannine Epistles," in *It Is Written: Scripture Citing Scripture*, Fs. Barnabas Lindars, ed. D. A. Carson and H. G. M. Williamson SSF Cambridge: Cambridge University Press, 1988), pp. 245–64; D. A. **Carson** and John D. **Woodbridge**, eds., *Scripture and Truth* (Grand Rapids: Zondervan, 1983); O. **Cullmann**, *The Johannine Circle* (ET London: SCM, 1976); R. A. **Culpepper**, *Anatomy of the Fourth Gospel: A Study in Literary Design* (Philadelphia: Fortress, 1983); idem, *The Johannine School* (Missoula, Mont.: SP, 1975); M. **de Jonge**, "The Beloved Disciple and the Date of the Gospel of John," in *Text and Interpretation*, Fs. Matthew Black, ed. E. Best and R. M. Wilson (Cambridge: Cambridge University Press, 1979), pp. 99–114; I. **de la Potterie**, *La vérité dans Saint Jean*, 2 vols. (Rome: BIP, 1977); Mgr. **de Solages**, *Jean et les synoptiques* (Leiden: Brill, 1979); C. H. **Dodd**, *Historical Tradition in the Fourth Gospel* (Cambridge: Cambridge University Press, 1963); idem, *The Interpretation of the Fourth Gospel* (Cambridge: Cambridge University Press, 1953); Thomas **Dowell**, "Jews and Christians in Conflict: Why the Fourth Gospel Changed the Synoptic Tradition," *LouvStud* 15 (1990): 19–37; P. **Duke**, *Irony in the Fourth Gospel* (Atlanta: John Knox, 1985); Bart D. **Ehrman**, "Jesus and the Adulteress," *NTS* 34 (1988): 24–44; J. T. **Forestell**, *The Word of the Cross: Salvation as Revelation in the Fourth Gospel*, AnBib 57 (Rome: BIP, 1974); R. **Fortna**, *The Fourth Gospel and Its Predecessor* (Philadelphia: Fortress, 1988); idem, *The Gospel of Signs*, SNTSMS 11 (Cambridge: Cambridge University Press, 1970); R. T. **France**, "The Church and the Kingdom of God: Some Hermeneutical Issues," in *Biblical Interpretation and the Church: Text and Context*, ed. D. A. Carson (Exeter: Paternoster, 1984), pp. 30–44; E. **Franck**, *Revelation Taught: The Paraclete in the Gospel of John* (Lund: Gleerup, 1985); E. D. **Freed**, "Did John Write His Gospel Partly to Win Samaritan Converts?" *NovT* 12 (1970): 241–56; M. E. **Glasswell**, "The Relationship Between John and Mark," *JSNT* 23 (1983): 99–115; E. **Haenchen**, *A Commentary on the Gospel of John*, 2 vols. (ET Philadelphia: Fortress, 1984); Philip B. **Harner**, *The "I Am" of the Fourth Gospel* (Philadelphia: Fortress, 1970); A. E. **Harvey**, *Jesus on Trial: A Study in the Fourth Gospel* (London: SPCK, 1976); A. C. **Headlam**, *The Fourth Gospel as History* (Oxford: Blackwell, 1948); Hans-Peter **Heekerens**, *Die Zeichen-Quelle der johanneischen Redaktion* (Stuttgart: KBW, 1984); W. **Hendriksen**, *Exposition of the Gospel According to John*, 2 vols. (Grand Rapids: Baker, 1953–54); Martin **Hengel**, *The Johannine Question* (Philadelphia: Trinity Press International, 1989); Zane **Hodges**, "The Woman Taken in Adultery (John 7:53–8:11)," *BS* 136 (1979): 318–72; 137 (1980): 41–53; W. Scott **Holland**, *The Fourth Gospel* (London: John Murray, 1923); W. **Horbury**, "The Benediction of the *Minim* and Early Jewish-Christian Controversy," *JTS* 33 (1982): 19–61; E. C. **Hoskyns**, *The Fourth Gospel*, ed. F. N. Davey (London: Faber & Faber, 1954); A. M. **Hunter**, *According to John* (London: SCM, 1968); J. **Jeremias**, *New Testament Theology I: The Proclamation of Jesus* (London: SCM, 1971); G. **Johnston**, *The Spirit-Paraclete in the Gospel of John*, SNTSMS 12 (Cambridge: Cambridge University Press, 1970); E.

Käsemann, *The Testament of Jesus: A Study of the Gospel of John in the Light of Chapter 17* (ET London: SCM, 1968); G. D. **Kilpatrick**, "The Religious Background of the Fourth Gospel," in *Studies in the Fourth Gospel*, ed. F. L. Cross (London: Mowbray, 1957), pp. 36–44; R. **Kimelman**, "*Birkat ha-Minim* and the Lack of Evidence for an anti-Christian Jewish Prayer in Late Antiquity," in *Jewish and Christian Self-Definition*, vol. 2 of *Aspects of Judaism in the Greco-Roman Period*, ed. E. P. Sanders (Philadelphia: Fortress, 1981), pp. 226–44, 391–403; Joachim **Kügler**, *Der Jünger, dem Jesus liebte* (Stuttgart: KBW, 1988); Robert **Kysar**, "The Background of the Prologue of the Fourth Gospel: A Critique of Historical Methods," *CJT* 16 (1970): 250–55; idem, *The Fourth Evangelist and His Gospel: An Examination of Contemporary Scholarship* (Minneapolis: Augsburg, 1975); M.-J. **Lagrange**, *Evangile selon Saint Jean* (Paris: Gabalda, 1925); Domingo **León**, "¿Es el apóstol Juan el discípulo amado?" *EstBib* 45 (1987): 403–92; B. **Lindars**, *The Gospel of John*, NCB (London: Oliphants, 1972); R. N. **Longenecker**, "On the Form, Function, and Authority of the New Testament Letters," in *Scripture and Truth*, ed. D. A. Carson and John D. Woodbridge (Grand Rapids: Zondervan, 1983), pp. 101–14; James **McPolin**, "Studies in the Fourth Gospel—Some Contemporary Trends," *IBS* 2 (1980): 3–26; Gerhard **Maier**, "Johannes und Matthäus—Zweispalt oder Viergestalt des Evangeliums?" in *GP* 2:267–97; I. Howard **Marshall**, *The Origins of New Testament Christology* (Leicester: IVP, 1976); J. L. **Martyn**, *History and Theology in the Fourth Gospel* (Nashville: Abingdon, 1979); Wayne A. **Meeks**, *The Prophet-King: Moses Traditions and the Johannine Christology*, SuppNovT 14 (Leiden: Brill, 1967); J. Ramsey **Michaels**, *John* (San Francisco: Harper & Row, 1983); Paul S. **Minear**, "The Original Functions of John 21," *JBL* 102 (1983): 85–98; George **Mlakushyil**, *The Christocentric Literary Structure of the Fourth Gospel*, AnBib 117 (Rome: Pontifical Biblical Institute, 1987); L. **Morris**, *The Gospel According to John* (Grand Rapids: Eerdmans, 1971); idem, *Jesus Is the Christ: Studies in the Theology of John* (Grand Rapids: Eerdmans, 1979); idem, *Studies in the Fourth Gospel* (Grand Rapids: Eerdmans, 1969); C. F. D. **Moule**, *The Birth of the New Testament* (London: Black, 1982); idem, *The Origin of Christology* (Cambridge: Cambridge University Press, 1977); F. **Mussner**, *The Historical Jesus in the Gospel of St John* (ET London: Burns & Oates, 1967); F. **Neirynck** et al., *Jean et les synoptiques* (Louvain: Louvain University Press, 1979); W. **Oehler**, *Das Johannes-evangelium, eine Missionsschrift für die Welt* (Gütersloh: Bertelsmann, 1936); idem, *Zum Missioncharackter des Johannesevangeliums* (Gütersloh: Bertelsmann, 1941); Teresa **Okure**, *The Johannine Approach to Mission*, WUNT 2.31 (Tübingen: J. C. B. Mohr [Paul Siebeck], 1988); B. **Olsson**, *Structure and Meaning of the Fourth Gospel* (Lund: Gleerup, 1974); Margaret **Pamment**, "The Fourth Gospel's Beloved Disciple," *ExpTim* 94 (1983): 363–67; Pierson **Parker**, "John the Son of Zebedee and the Fourth Gospel," *JBL* 81 (1962): 35–43; Norman **Perrin**, *Jesus and the Language of the Kingdom* (Philadelphia: Fortress, 1976); C. S. **Petrie**, "The Authorship of 'The Gospel According to Matthew': A Reconsideration of the External Evidence," *NTS* 14 (1967–68): 15–32; David **Rensberger**, *Overcoming the World: Politics and Community in the Gospel of John* (London: SPCK, 1988); H. R. **Reynolds**, *The Gospel of St. John*, 2 vols. (London: Funk & Wagnalls, 1906); H. **Ridderbos**, *Het evangelie naar Johannes*, 2 vols. (Kampen: J. H. Kok, 1987-); J. A. T. **Robinson**, *The Priority of John* (London: SCM, 1985); idem, *Redating the New Testament* (Philadelphia: Westminster, 1976); idem, *Twelve New Testament Studies* (London: SCM, 1962); J. Armitage **Robinson**, *The Historical Character of the Fourth Gospel* (London: Longmans-Green, 1948); H. H. **Rowdon**, ed., *Christ the Lord*, Fs. D. Guthrie (Leicester: IVP, 1982); Samuel

Sandmel, "Parallelomania," *JBL* 81 (1962): 2–13; R. **Schnackenburg**, *The Gospel According to St John*, 3 vols. (ET London: Burns & Oates, 1968–82), vol. 4 only in German, subtitled *Ergänzende Auslegungen und Exkurse* (Freiburg: Herder, 1984); E. F. **Seigman**, "St. John's Use of the Synoptic Material," *CBQ* 30 (1968): 182–98; S. S. **Smalley**, *John: Evangelist and Interpreter* (Exeter: Paternoster, 1978); D. M. **Smith**, *Johannine Christianity: Essays on Its Setting, Sources, and Theology* (Columbia: University of South Carolina Press, 1984); Jeffrey Lloyd **Staley**, *The Print's First Kiss: A Rhetorical Investigation of the Implied Reader in the Fourth Gospel*, SBLDS 82 (Atlanta: SP, 1988); idem, "The Structure of John's Prologue: Its Implications for the Gospel's Narrative Structure," *CBQ* 48 (1986): 241–63; E. **Stauffer**, *Jesus and His Story* (London: SCM, 1960); Marianne M. **Thompson**, *The Humanity of Jesus in the Fourth Gospel* (Philadelphia: Fortress, 1988); H. **Thyen**, "Aus der Literatur des Johannesevangeliums," *ThR* 39 (1974): 1–69, 222–52, 289–330; 42 (1977): 211–70; 44 (1979): 97–134; G. **van Belle**, *Johannine Bibliography, 1966–1985*, BETL 82 (Louvain: Louvain University Press, 1988); idem, *Les parenthèses dans l'évangile de Jean: Aperçu historique et classification* (Louvain: Louvain University Press, 1985); W. C. **van Unnik**, "The Purpose of St. John's Gospel," in *SE* 1:382–411; Herman C. **Waetjen**, ed., *The Gospel of John in Sociolinguistic Perspective*, Protocol of the Forty-Eighth Colloquy (Claremont: Center for Hermeneutical Studies in Hellenistic and Modern Culture, 1984); B. F. **Westcott**, *The Gospel According to St John: The Greek Text with Introduction and Notes*, 2 vols. (London: John Murray, 1908); Hans **Windisch**, *Johannes und die Synoptiker* (Leipzig: J. C. Hinrichs'sche Buchhandlung, 1926); Egil A. **Wyller**, "In Solomon's Porch: A Henological Analysis of the Architectonic of the Fourth Gospel," *ST* 42 (1988): 151-67.

6

acts

CONTENTS

The book we know as the Acts of the Apostles belongs with the gospel of Luke as the second volume in a history of Christian beginnings. Luke probably did not give this second book a title of its own; only when his gospel was separated from its companion volume and placed with the other gospels was there need to give the second part of his story a title. Second- and third-century authors made various suggestions, such as "The Memorandum of Luke" (Tertullian) and "The Acts of All the Apostles" (Muratorian Canon). The name that would eventually stick, "The Acts of the Apostles," is first used in the anti-Marcionite prologue to Luke (late second century?)[1] and in Ireneus (*Adv. Haer.* 3.13.3).[2] The word "Acts" (πράξεις [*praxeis*]) denoted a recognized genre, or subgenre, in the ancient world, characterizing books that described the great deeds of people or of cities. In that Acts narrates the founding events of the church and ascribes most of them to apostles, the title is not inappropriate. Yet, judging from Luke's own emphases, he may have preferred a title such as "The Acts of the Holy Spirit" or "What Jesus Continued to Do and to Teach" (see 1:1).

In Acts, Luke conducts the reader on a whirlwind tour of three decades of church history. We visit Jerusalem, Judea, Samaria, Syria, Cyprus, many cities in Asia Minor, Macedonia, Greece, and, finally, Rome. We witness everything from preaching and miracles to jailbreaks and shipwrecks. And, while many individuals accompany us on our tour, two are rather constant companions: Peter, who is often with us in Jerusalem, Judea, and Samaria; and Paul, who is our almost constant companion from Syria to Rome. We can, in fact, divide our tour into two major parts based on the prominence of these two individuals: chapters 1–12 and chapters 13–28. Each of these major sections can be subdivided further into three parts, which are marked off by key summary statements. In these brief notes, Luke sums up a series of events by telling us that they have led to the growth of

---

[1] For the date of this prologue to the third gospel, traditionally thought to be directed against Marcion (hence its name), see F. F. Bruce, *The Book of Acts*, rev. ed., NICNT (Grand Rapids: Eerdmans, 1988), p. 5 n. 6. For a summary of current scholarly views about these prologues, see esp. Joseph A. Fitzmyer, *The Gospel According to Luke I–IX*, AB (New York: Doubleday, 1982), p. 39.

[2] See Frederick Fyvie Bruce, "The Acts of the Apostles: Historical Record or Theological Reconstruction?" *ANRW* 25.3 (1985): 2571.

the Word of God or of the church (6:7; 9:31; 12:24; 16:5; 19:20). Each section carries us to a new geographic and/or cultural stage in the itinerary of the gospel, as Luke portrays the fulfillment of Jesus' command to the apostles that they be his witnesses "in Jerusalem, and in all Judea and Samaria, and to the ends of the earth" (1:8).[3]

Prologue: Foundations for the church and its mission (1:1–2:41). Luke begins by rooting the church and its mission in Jesus' acts and words. It is the risen Jesus who prepares the apostles for the coming of the Spirit (1:4–5) and charges them with their worldwide missionary mandate (1:8). Jesus' earthly ministry is then brought to a close with Luke's second narrative of his ascension into heaven (1:9–11; cf. also Luke 24:50–51), a narrative that serves as a hinge between the gospel and Acts. Luke then describes the choosing of Matthias to replace Judas (1:12–26), the coming of the Spirit on the Day of Pentecost (2:1–13), and the first missionary sermon (2:14–41).

The church in Jerusalem (2:42–6:7). Luke begins this section with a summary of the characteristics of the early church in Jerusalem (2:42–47). He then describes Peter's healing of a crippled man in the temple precincts (3:1–10), a notable and public miracle that gains Peter a hearing for another missionary sermon (3:13–26). Opposition arises from the Sanhedrin, but Peter and John boldly resist its request that they cease speaking "in the name of Jesus" (4:1–22). The church as a whole, infused with the power of the Spirit, follows the lead of the apostles, preaching the Word of God boldly after having prayed that God would grant them such opportunity (4:23–31). But all is not perfect, even in these early and exciting days in the life of the church. The lie of a married couple, Ananias and Sapphira, about their participation in the early community's voluntary sharing program (4:32–37) brings swift judgment upon them (5:1–11). The popular healing and preaching ministry of the apostles (5:12–16) again sparks opposition from the Jewish leaders, and again the apostles are arrested and brought before the Sanhedrin. Gamaliel, an important rabbi of his day, counsels moderation, and the apostles are released (5:17–42). In order to give themselves fully to the preaching of the Word, the apostles appoint seven men to regulate the distribution of food among the community (6:1–6). In his first summary statement, Luke concludes that in this way "the word of God spread" (6:7).

Wider horizons for the church: Stephen, Samaria, and Saul (6:8–9:31). To this point in his narrative, Luke has portrayed the early believers as loyal, if somewhat unusual, Jews. The stories in this next section show how the church began to strain the bounds of traditional Judaism. Stephen is a pivotal figure in this respect. A charismatic figure who attracted a considerable following, Stephen was falsely accused of speaking against the temple and the law (6:8–15). When brought before the Sanhedrin to answer charges about his teaching, Stephen uses a sketch of Israel's history to suggest that God's revelation cannot be confined to one place and to charge the Sandedrin members themselves with resisting the Holy Spirit (7:1–53). So bold a charge does not go unanswered: Stephen is condemned to be stoned (7:54–60).

---

[3]The division of Acts into six sections based on these summary statements was proposed by C. H. Turner, "The Chronology of the New Testament," in *A Dictionary of the Bible*, ed. James Hastings, 5 vols. (Edinburgh: T. & T. Clark, 1898–1904), 1:421, and is adopted by, among others, McNeile, pp. 97–98, and Richard N. Longenecker, "The Acts of the Apostles," in *EBC* 9:234.

Stephen's radical stance sparks opposition to the young Christian movement, and "all except the apostles" are forced to leave Jerusalem (8:1–3). One of those who leaves, Philip, brings the gospel to Samaria, a territory to the north of Judea inhabited by people considered by most Jews to be renegade Jews at best. The Samaritans believe the message of Philip, and Peter and John are sent to confirm that the Samaritans had indeed been accepted into the kingdom of God (8:4–25). Philip, directed by an angel, travels south, where he meets and converts a court official of the queen of Ethiopia (8:26–40). Finally, Luke tells us of the conversion and early ministry of the one chosen by God to be the pioneer in the mission to the Gentiles—Saul of Tarsus (9:1–30). Again Luke summarizes: "The church . . . was strengthened; and encouraged by the Holy Spirit, it grew in numbers, living in the fear of the Lord" (9:31).

Peter and the first Gentile convert (9:32–12:24). This section focuses on Peter, and especially on Peter's role in opening the way for Gentiles to become Christians. Peter performs miracles in Lydda and Joppa, cities in Judea to the northwest of Jerusalem (9:32–43). He is then used by God to bring Cornelius, a Gentile Roman soldier, into the church. Through visions and the direct command of the Spirit, God brings Cornelius and Peter together (10:1–23). At Cornelius's house, Peter's preaching of the gospel is interrupted by the sovereign action of God, bestowing the Spirit upon Cornelius in so evident a manner that Peter had to recognize that God had truly accepted a Gentile into his church (10:24–48).

The importance of so clear a witness is revealed in the next narrative, in which Peter is able to reassure Jewish-Christian skeptics in Jerusalem about the reality of Cornelius's conversion (11:1–18). It is surely significant that here Luke tells us of the church at Antioch, where the mixture of Jews and Gentiles required that believers in Jesus be given a new name: Christian (11:19–30). The section concludes with the story of Peter's miraculous escape from prison (12:1–19) and the death of Herod Agrippa I, who had initiated the persecution that led to Peter's arrest (12:20–23). Here again occurs Luke's transitional summary: "The word of God continued to increase and spread" (12:24).

Paul turns to the Gentiles (12:25–16:5). From Peter, Luke turns now to Paul, who dominates the remainder of the book. Paul's significance for Luke lies in his being used by God to pioneer an extensive ministry to Gentiles, to carry the gospel to the ends of the earth, and to show that the gospel was no direct threat to the Roman government. The vibrant Christian community at Antioch, to which Paul had been brought by Barnabas, is led by the Spirit to send Paul, along with Barnabas and John Mark, on the first missionary journey (12:25–13:3). The journey takes them first to Barnabas's home, Cyprus, where a Roman official is converted (13:4–12). The band then sails to the south coast of Asia Minor, where they quickly head inland to the important city of Pisidian Antioch. Paul delivers an evangelistic sermon in the synagogue there, a sermon that Luke summarizes, giving us a sample of the way Paul preached to a Jewish audience (13:13–43). Here also what becomes a typical pattern is first enacted: general Jewish rejection of the gospel, leading Paul and his companions to turn directly to the Gentiles, followed by Jewish persecution that forces them to move on (13:44–52).

They move on to Iconium (14:1–7), to Lystra, where Paul is stoned (14:8–20), and to Derbe, planting churches in each city and strengthening the new believers as they retrace their steps again to the coast (14:21–28). Upon arriving back in Antioch, the missionaries are confronted with a serious dispute about their outreach to the Gentiles. A council convened in Jerusalem to discuss the matter endorses the law-free offer of the gospel to the Gentiles, a decision that was of vital importance in establishing the character of the church and enabling its further growth (15:1–29). Paul and Barnabas bring the good news back to Antioch and begin planning a new missionary trip. But their inability to agree about taking along John Mark, who had turned for home before the first journey was complete, leads them to split, Barnabas taking Mark with him back to Cyprus, Paul taking Silas with him overland to Syria, Cilicia, and on to the churches established on the first journey (15:30–41). Here Paul also recruits Timothy for the cause (16:1–4). And thus, Luke again concludes, "the churches were strengthened in the faith and grew daily in numbers" (16:5).

Further Penetration into the Gentile world (16:6–19:20). It seems a bit odd that we should divide Luke's story at this point. Yet Luke implies that we have reached a decisive stage by the care with which he shows how Paul was directed by God's Spirit step-by-step to take the gospel into Macedonia (16:6–10). (This is also the beginning of the first "we" passage—see v. 10.) The first stop is Philippi, a Roman colony in Macedonia, where an exorcism lands Paul and Silas in jail. They (like Peter before them—one of the many parallels Luke draws between Peter and Paul) are miraculously rescued, and Paul turns his Roman citizenship to good account in order to be set free (16:16–40). Paul and Silas move on to Thessalonica, but persecution forces them to flee by night to the relatively insignificant town of Berea (17:1–9). Trouble follows them even here, so Paul is sent away to Athens (17:10–15).

Here we are treated to a second sample of Paul's preaching, this time to a sophisticated, skeptical, Gentile audience on so-called Mars' Hill in Athens (17:16–34). The results in Athens seem to be meager, however, so Paul travels across the narrow isthmus to Corinth, the chief city in the Peloponnese. Here Paul spends a year and a half, preaching, defending himself before the Roman official Gallio, and enlisting the Roman Jewish couple Priscilla and Aquila in the work of the gospel (18:1–17). The three leave Corinth for Ephesus, where Paul leaves the other two as he proceeds on to Caesarea, Antioch, and the churches of southern Asia Minor (18:18–23). In Ephesus, meanwhile, Priscilla and Aquila establish more firmly in the faith a gifted young man from Alexandria, Apollos (18:24–28). Paul himself arrives in Ephesus for a stay of two and a half years. We are given glimpses of Paul converting some disciples of John the Baptist (19:1–7), preaching in the synagogue and in his own hired hall (19:8–10), working miracles (19:11–12), and confronting the strong current of demonism for which the city was known (19:13–19). "In this way," Luke informs us, "the word of the Lord spread widely and grew in power" (19:20).

On to Rome (19:21–28:31). Again we may feel that it is rather artificial to insert a major break in the midst of Paul's stay in Ephesus. But Luke again suggests such a break with his first indication that Paul was determined to go to Rome (19:21–22). This determination drives Luke's narrative from this point on, but it takes Paul some time to get there. He leaves Ephesus only after a serious public uprising forces him to go (19:23–41). He revisits the churches in Macedonia and Greece and decides to return to Judea by the same route because of a plot against his life (20:1–6). On his way back, Paul stops to preach in Troas and stops again in

Miletus to meet with the elders of the church of Ephesus (20:7–38). He arrives in Jerusalem via Tyre and Caesarea, with warnings about his impending arrest in Jerusalem ringing in his ears (21:1–16). The warning quickly becomes reality.

Paul's willingness to "fly his Jewish flag" for the sake of the Jewish Christians in Jerusalem by paying for, and joining in, some purification rites in the temple backfires (21:17–26). Certain Jews think that Paul has brought Gentiles into the temple with him, and the ensuing riot forces the Romans to intervene (21:27–36). Paul is arrested but is allowed to address the crowd before being taken away (21:37–22:22). Paul's Roman citizenship again stands him in good stead, and he is allowed to state his case before the Jewish Sanhedrin (22:30–23:10). The Lord assures Paul that he will live to testify about him in Rome (23:11), despite a plot of the Jews to kill him (23:12–15). Paul is moved to Caesarea because of this threat, where he again defends himself, this time before the Roman governor, Felix (23:16–24:27). After Paul has languished in prison in Caesarea for two years, Festus replaces Felix, and Paul forces the issue by appealing to Caesar to hear his case (25:1–12). Before leaving, however, Paul again defends himself before Festus and his guests King Agrippa II and his sister Bernice (25:13–26:32). Paul is then sent on to Rome. The trip, however, is interrupted by a severe storm, stranding Paul and his sailing companions for three months on the island of Malta (27:1–28:10). Paul finally arrives in Rome, where he is able to live in his own house, under guard, and preach the gospel freely (28:11–31). Here, with Paul in Rome for two years under house arrest, Luke's tour of the expansion of the gospel comes to an end.

AUTHOR

The Traditional Case

Both Luke and Acts are, strictly speaking, anonymous. From the preface to Luke, which is probably intended to introduce both the gospel and Acts, we can conclude that the author was well educated (the Greek of Luke 1:1–4 is good, literary Greek), not an original apostle or disciple of Christ (he writes about those things "handed down to us by those who from the first were eyewitnesses and servants of the word"), yet one who may have been a participant in some of the events he narrates ("fulfilled *among us*"). He knows his Old Testament in the Greek Septuagint version, has an excellent knowledge of political and social conditions in the middle of the first century, and thinks a great deal of the apostle Paul.[5]

Further inferences about the author come from the "we" passages in Acts. These

---

[4]There has been considerable debate over the meaning of the word παρηκολουθηκότι (*parēkolouthēkoti*) in v. 3 of the prologue. Cadbury insists that it must mean "having kept in touch with" and implies the author's personal involvement in at least some of the events narrated ("The Tradition," in *The Beginnings of Christianity*, Part 1: *The Acts of the Apostles*, by F. J. Foakes Jackson and Kirsopp Lake, 5 vols. [London: Macmillan, 1920–33], 2:501–3). Others, probably correctly, argue that the word means simply "having investigated," with no implication of personal involvement (e.g., Fitzmyer, *Luke I–IX*, pp. 297–98).

[5]The claim that the Greek of Luke-Acts indicates that the author is a medical doctor (W. K. Hobart, *The Medical Language of St. Luke* [Dublin: Hodges, Figgis, 1882]) is not valid (H. J. Cadbury, *The Style and Literary Method of Luke*, HTS 6 [Cambridge: Harvard University Press, 1919]). The most that can be said is that the Greek is consistent with the author's being a medical doctor.

are four passages in which the author shifts from his usual third-person narration to a first person plural narration. Note the beginning of the first such passage: "So *they* [Paul, Silas, and Timothy] passed by Mysia and went down to Troas. During the night Paul had a vision of a man of Macedonia standing and begging him, 'Come over to Macedonia and help us.' After Paul had seen the vision, *we* got ready at once to leave for Macedonia, concluding that God had called *us* to preach the gospel to them" (16:8–10). The author continues with his first person plural style through 16:17, and then uses it again in 20:5–15, 21:1–18, and 27:1–28:16. The most natural explanation for this style is that the author of Acts accompanied Paul at these times during his ministry. On this showing, he was with Paul on the trip from Troas to Philippi and during the initial evangelization of Philippi on the first missionary journey (16:10–17). Joining Paul again as the apostle came through Philippi at the end of the third missionary journey, he then accompanied him to Miletus, and from Miletus to Jerusalem (20:5–15; 21:1–18). Finally, he was with Paul on his voyage to Rome (27:1–28:16).

The author could not have been any of the companions of Paul who are mentioned in these passages. Furthermore, since the author accompanied Paul to Rome and was probably with him during Paul's two-year house arrest in Rome, we might expect Paul to mention him in the letters he wrote during that period of time: Colossians, Philemon, Ephesians, and, perhaps, Philippians.[6] Those companions who are named in these letters are Mark, Jesus Justus, Epaphras, Demas, Luke, Tychicus, Timothy, Aristarchus, and Epaphroditus. This line of reasoning is certainly not foolproof: the author of Acts may have left Paul after their arrival in Rome, or Paul may not have mentioned him in his letters, but it is suggestive. At least, this is as far as the internal evidence of Luke and Acts can take us.

External evidence takes over at this point and singles out Luke from the list of possible candidates. The tradition that Luke, a companion of Paul, was the author of the third gospel and of Acts is early and unchallenged: the Muratorian Canon (A.D. 190), Ireneus (*Adv. Haer.* 3.1; 3.14.1–4), the anti-Marcionite prologue (end of second century), Clement of Alexandria (*Strom.* 5.12), Tertullian (*Adv. Marc.* 4.2), and Eusebius (*H.E.* 3.4; 3.24.15). Luke's authorship of these two books went virtually unchallenged until the onset of critical approaches to the New Testament at the end of the eighteenth century. Since then, doubt about the tradition has been widespread. We now examine the reasons for these doubts.

The Case Against the Tradition

The external evidence. Critics of the tradition question the value of the testimony of the early church. Early Christians, Cadbury alleges, produced many fanciful theories about the origin of New Testament books.[7] Moreover, in an argument echoed again and again in the literature, it is said that the tradition itself is probably no more than an inference from the text of the New Testament itself and has no independent historical value.[8] But as we saw above in our examination of

---

[6]We assume here, as is argued in the relevant chapters, that Colossians, Philemon, and Ephesians were written during Paul's Roman imprisonment; the provenance of Philippians is not so clear.
[7]Cadbury, "The Tradition," pp. 250–64.
[8]See, e.g., Gerhard Schneider, *Die Apostelgeschichte*, 2 vols., HTKNT (Freiburg: Herder, 1980–82), 1:108–10.

the internal evidence, the New Testament does not furnish enough data to single out Luke as the author of Acts. Fitzmyer's criticism of the idea that the external evidence can be dismissed because it depends on the reasoning of early Christians is fair. "That an individual in the second century—or even several individuals—might have so reasoned is certainly possible; but that such inferences from the NT text are the sole basis of an otherwise uncontested or unambiguous tradition . . . is difficult to accept."[9] We must, then, attach importance to the testimony of the early church—particularly since this testimony runs against form in singling out a nonapostle as the author.

The "we" passages. The traditional argument (given above) is that the "we" passages reveal the presence of the author of Acts. Some think that the author depends on an itinerary or diary that he himself wrote in the first person plural at the time of the events and that he incorporates into his literary product; others that the author has lapsed into the first person plural at these points as he writes. In either case, however, the "we" passages are thought to point to the author of the book.

But two other explanations for the phenomenon are advanced that would remove the value of this datum for the question of authorship. One is that the author has incorporated into his history a source written by another person in the first person plural.[10] But why would the author leave his source in that form? As critics never tire of pointing out, Luke has consistently reworded his sources, putting the stamp of his own style on everything he writes. And Harnack has shown that the style of the "we" passages is no different than the style of the text around these passages.[11] Why, then, would the author have left these several sections in this first person plural style, especially since it could hardly escape being misunderstood?

A second alternative explanation is that the use of the first person plural is a stylistic device, intended to make a rhetorical rather than a historical point.[12] But the evidence for such a rhetorical use of "we" is not strong, nor is it clear why the author would have used such a device at the points where he does.[13] The attempts to explain the use of "we" in these four texts as anything other than an indication of the presence of the author are failures.

Acts and Paul. These first two points are not so much arguments against the traditional view of authorship as they are attempts to make the data conform to the view that Luke did not write Acts. The reason why so many scholars now conclude that Luke could not have written Acts lies in the picture the book gives us of the apostle Paul. This picture, it is alleged, distorts the "historical Paul" at a number of key points; so serious is this distortion that they find it impossible to think that a companion of Paul could have produced the picture. The alleged distortions are of two kinds: historical and theological.

One of the most frequently cited historical discrepancies is the disagreement

---

[9]Fitzmyer, *Luke I–IX*, p. 41.

[10]E.g., Kümmel, p. 184.

[11]Adolf Harnack, *The Date of the Acts and of the Synoptic Gospels* (New York: Putnam, 1911), pp. 1–89.

[12]Vernon K. Robbins, "The We-Passages in Acts and Ancient Sea Voyages," *BR* 20 (1975): 5–18.

[13]See esp. Colin J. Hemer, *The Book of Acts in the Setting of Hellenistic History*, WUNT 2.49 (Tübingen: Mohr, 1989), pp. 316–21.

between Acts and Paul about the number of trips the apostle made to Jerusalem. But this matter has a plausible solution, which we consider briefly toward the end of this chapter. Other historical discrepancies, such as the claim of Paul in Acts that he had been educated in Jerusalem (22:3), in contrast with Paul's own silence on the matter in his letters, can be resolved through a recognition of the different purposes of Acts and the letters of Paul. Paul tells us very little about his background in his letters, and his failure to mention items that Luke includes should not surprise us.

More serious are the alleged theological discrepancies. Philipp Vielhauer, whose essay on the subject is something of a classic,[14] points out four key areas of contrast between the Paul of Acts and the Paul of the Epistles.

1. In the Areopagus speech of Acts 17, the Paul of Acts liberally uses Stoic notions about God, the world, and the relationship of human beings to God to make a case for natural theology. Nature and the world are so constituted, Paul here argues, that they serve as a preparation for the gospel. The Paul of the Epistles, on the other hand, as Romans 1 reveals, viewed natural revelation as having only a negative purpose: to confirm the responsibility of people for their sins.

2. The Paul of Acts is utterly loyal to the law: he agrees to impose ritual requirements on Gentile Christians (15:22–35); he circumcises Timothy, who had a Gentile father (16:3); he claims to be a loyal Pharisee (23:6); he even goes so far as to participate in Jewish purification rites in the temple in Jerusalem (21:17–26). Contrast this picture with the Paul of the letters, the Paul who claimed that Christians should not impose ritual restrictions on one another (1 Cor. 8–10; Col. 2), who told the Galatians that their circumcision would mean their being severed from Christ (Gal. 5:2–4), who viewed his Pharisaic background as so much refuse to be discarded (Phil. 3:5–8), and who proclaimed loudly and often that Christians were no longer "under the law."

3. The Paul of Acts lacks the emphasis on union with Christ and the expiatory benefits of Christ's death that is so central in the Paul of the letters.

4. The preaching of the Paul of Acts is uneschatological. Missing is the focus on fulfillment in Christ with the sense of imminence that is so typical of the "authentic Paul." Related to this lessening of eschatological intensity is the concern for orderly church government manifested by the Paul of Acts (e.g., on the first missionary journey he and Barnabas very quickly appoint elders in the newly founded churches [14:23]). Contrast the Paul of the Epistles, who insists that the Spirit should have sovereign freedom in ruling the churches (1 Cor. 12).

To answer these objections fully would require monographs on both Paul's theology and the theology of Acts. We will content ourselves with a few remarks on each of these points, along with some general comment.

The attitude toward natural revelation that emerges from Acts 17 and Romans 1 is certainly different, but the question is whether they are contradictory. Could not the Paul who wrote Romans 1, when arguing with sophisticated pagans in Athens, have used as many contacts with their culture as possible in order to establish some common ground as preparation for the gospel? Nothing in the

---

[14]Philipp Vielhauer, "On the 'Paulinism' of Acts," in *Studies in Luke-Acts*, ed. Leander E. Keck and J. Louis Martyn (Nashville: Abingdon, 1966), pp. 33–50.

theology of Romans 1 suggests that he could not. True, in Romans 1 Paul teaches that the ultimate effect of natural revelation *by itself* is wholly negative: people cannot be saved by it, only judged by it. But Paul never suggests in Acts 17 that knowledge of "an unknown god" could be saving—it is only by repentance in that God as now revealed in the resurrection of Jesus Christ that salvation can come (see v. 30). Moreover, we should probably view Paul's speech in Acts 17 more as a preparation for the gospel than his preaching of the gospel as such. The text suggests that Paul's mention of the resurrection led to a premature conclusion to his sermon.[15]

Two things must be said about the issue of the law. First, Paul's view of the law as found in his epistles has frequently been caricatured as being far more negative than it really is. Serious revision in the teaching of Paul on the law is now underway; while much of that revision is going too far in the other direction, it does serve to caution us about assuming a certain view of the law in Paul's letters that is at least unbalanced. Second, and more important, the practices of Paul in Acts are by no means incompatible with the standard interpretation of his teaching on the law. Paul's agreement with the decree of the apostolic council, which probably applied to mixed Jewish-Gentile Christian communities, is quite in keeping with his principle that a Christian should not be a stumbling block to others (see 1 Cor. 8–10 and Rom. 14:1–15:13). Timothy, whose Jewish mother gave him rights as a Jew, is circumcised not to enable him to be part of God's people (the issue in Galatia) but to enable him to carry out his mission more effectively. This is quite in keeping with Paul's claim that circumcision is a thing indifferent (Gal. 6:15). Paul's claim to be a Pharisee must be understood in its context to be a claim to adhere to the Pharisaic doctrine of resurrection, over against the Sadducean rejection of the doctrine. And Paul's willingness to participate in a Jewish purification rite is in keeping with his expressed willingness to be all things to all people (1 Cor. 9:19–22). Nothing in Paul's letters suggests that he was opposed to participating in Jewish rites—as long as they were neither being imposed as necessary to salvation nor causing a stumbling block to other believers.[16]

Some of the distinctive Pauline Christological and eschatological motifs are indeed missing in Acts. But this may be because the preaching of Paul that we have in Acts is almost entirely evangelistic, and we would not expect to see some of these motifs in such a context. Moreover, the picture of the Paul of the letters that Vielhauer and others set in contrast to the Paul of Acts is itself distorted and lacking in balance. In denying (in our opinion, wrongly) the Pauline authorship of Ephesians and the Pastoral Epistles, they eliminate a significant and distinctive part of Paul's own teaching—teaching that, if integrated into our total picture of Paul, would bring the Paul of the Epistles much closer to the Paul of Acts.

Distortion of the Paul of the Epistles takes place in another way as well. As Ulrich Wilckens has pointed out, many of those who find a great gulf between the Paul of the Epistles and the Paul of Acts do so because they are committed to an

---

[15]A treatment of the speech that is more sympathetic to the possibility that it stems from Paul himself is Bertil Gärtner, *The Areopagus Speech and Natural Revelation*, ASNU 21 (Uppsala: Gleerup, 1955).

[16]On the subject of this paragraph, see esp. Richard N. Longenecker, *Paul, Apostle of Liberty*, reprint ed. (Grand Rapids: Baker, 1976), pp. 245–63.

existential interpretation of Paul.[17] It is this narrow and distorted understanding of Paul that creates a significant amount of the distance with the Paul of Acts.

The great distance between the Paul of Acts and the Paul of the Epistles that so many find is, in reality, a distance between a caricature of the supposedly authentic Paul and a one-sided interpretation of the Paul of Acts. To be sure, some distance between the two remains, but no more than we might find between one's self-portrait and a portrait drawn by a sympathetic friend for a specific purpose.[18]

Conclusion

We have shown that there is no convincing reason to deny that the author of Acts was a companion of Paul. That he was his companion is the natural implication of the "we" passages. That this companion was none other than Luke "the beloved physician" is the unanimous opinion of the early church. We have good reason, then, to conclude that Luke was the author of Acts.

We know almost nothing about Luke's background. That he was a Gentile seems clear from Colossians 4:10–14, where Luke is not included among Paul's Jewish fellow workers. That he had not been a follower of Christ from the beginning is clear from the prologue to the gospel. William Ramsay speculated that Luke may have been the "man of Macedonia" who appeared to Paul in a vision (Acts 16:9).[19] On the basis of theological parallels between Acts and Roman documents, others have suggested that Luke was from Rome.[20] But the oldest and most respected tradition associates Luke with Syrian Antioch,[21] and several scholars are inclined to accept the tradition as probably authentic.[22] But the evidence is far from conclusive, and we would perhaps do better simply to admit that we do not know very much specific about Luke's background.

DATE

Suggested dates for the book of Acts range across almost a century, from A.D. 62, the date at which the last event of the book takes place, to the middle of the second century, when the first clear reference to Acts occurs.[23] Most scholars locate Acts in one of three periods of time within this range: 62–70, 80–95, or 115–30.

---

[17]Ulrich Wilckens, "Interpreting Luke-Acts in a Period of Existentialist Theology," in *Studies in Luke-Acts*, pp. 60–83.

[18]To use the analogy employed by F. F. Bruce, *Paul: Apostle of the Heart Set Free* (Grand Rapids: Eerdmans, 1977), p. 17. See further Bruce's article "Is the Paul of Acts the Real Paul?" *BJRL* 58 (1975–76): 282–305.

[19]William Ramsay, *St. Paul, the Traveller and the Roman Citizen* (London: Hodder & Stoughton, 1897), pp. 200–205.

[20]The editors of *Beginnings of Christianity*, in "The Internal Evidence of Acts," 2:200–204.

[21]The anti-Marcionite prologue to the gospel of Luke (late second century), Eusebius, *H.E.* 3.4, Jerome, *De vir. ill.* 7. The western text of Acts may indirectly suggest the same tradition by making Acts 11:28, which mentions an incident that takes place in Antioch, the first "we" passage in Acts.

[22]E.g., Zahn 3:2–3; Fitzmyer, *Luke I–IX*, pp. 45–47.

[23]In Justin's *Apology* 1.50.12 (see Ernst Haenchen, *The Acts of the Apostles: A Commentary* [Philadelphia: Westminster, 1971], pp. 3–8).

A Second-Century Date

A second-century date for the Acts is associated especially with the Tübingen School, a number of like-thinking scholars from the famous German university, whose best-known member was F. C. Baur. These scholars attributed to Acts a definite theological tendency—a desire to reconcile the opposing early Christian factions of Jewish Christianity, whose representative was Peter, and Gentile Christianity, whose representative was Paul. The author of Acts plays down the differences between these factions, making Peter more Gentile and Paul more Jewish than they really were. He thus prepares the way for a middle-of-the-road position, the position of the "old catholic church." This attempt at reconciliation could have been made only after sufficient time had elapsed for these factions to have mellowed, and so the Tübingen School dated Acts in the middle of the second century.[24]

While remnants of its approach remain, the Tübingen interpretation of early Christian history and the place of the book of Acts within this history are no longer defended. Scholars such as J. B. Lightfoot demonstrated that the apostolic fathers of the late first century reveal none of the factionalism and polemics that Baur and his disciples attributed to this period in the history of the church. An impressive ideological synthesis, the Tübingen approach was without historical underpinnings. But there are still some who date Acts in the second century. One reason for doing so has been the belief that the author of Acts depended on Josephus's *Antiquities* (written c. A.D. 94).[25] But dependence of Acts on Josephus is most unlikely.[26] J. C. O'Neill argues on the basis of theological parallels to *1 Clement*, the Pastoral Epistles, and especially Justin that Acts must be dated in the period 115–30.[27] But the parallels O'Neill finds are both questionable and susceptible of a different interpretation. Few scholars now think that Acts is a second-century document.

A Date of 80–95

Most scholars now date Acts in the 80s, or a bit later.[28] Acts cannot be dated any earlier than this, it is argued, because it shows signs of having been written some years after the first volume of Luke's work, the gospel,[29] which cannot be dated before A.D. 70. Furthermore, Acts cannot be dated much later than 95 or so because of its optimistic attitude toward the Roman government—an attitude that would have been inconceivable after the persecution of Domitian in the middle 90s—and because the author of Acts does not know about the letters of

---

[24]On this approach to the book of Acts, see W. Ward Gasque, *A History of the Criticism of the Acts of the Apostles*, BGBE 17 (Tübingen: Mohr, 1975), pp. 21–54.

[25]E.g., F. C. Burkitt, *The Gospel History and Its Transmission*, 3d ed. (Edinburgh: T. & T. Clark, 1911), pp. 105–10.

[26]This has been argued convincingly in Zahn 3:94–100; F. F. Bruce, *The Acts of the Apostles: The Greek Text, with Introduction and Commentary* (Grand Rapids: Eerdmans, 1952), pp. 24–25.

[27]J. C. O'Neill, *The Theology of Acts in Its Historical Setting* (London: SPCK, 1961).

[28]E.g., Kümmel, pp. 185–87; Schneider, *Apostelgeschichte* 1:118–21.

[29]A few scholars have suggested that Acts was written only after the first edition of Luke's gospel— what they claim to be a proto-Luke—but there is little to commend the suggestion.

Paul, which were collected and made generally available at the end of the first century.

None of these reasons is convincing. A date after A.D. 70 for Luke's gospel is based on two assumptions: that the gospel reflects the actual circumstances of the Roman sack of Jerusalem in 70, and that the gospel of Mark, which Luke has probably used, must be dated in the middle or late 60s. But neither of these assumptions is valid (see above, respectively, the section "Date" in chap. 4 and in chap. 7). Acts does not mention the letters of Paul, and the author probably has not used them in writing the book. But this may be because Acts is early, rather than late, or because it was simply not Luke's purpose to refer to the letters. Acts is indeed generally optimistic about Rome's attitude toward the church. Yet one could argue on this basis that Acts must be dated before the infamous persecution of Christians by the Emperor Nero in Rome in 64–65. So while the arguments for dating Acts after 80 are not persuasive, the arguments for dating Acts before 100 suggest, in fact, a date long before the turn of the century—indeed, a date in the early or middle 60s.

A Date Before 70

Arriving at a firm date for books within the New Testament is not easy—there are few solid data to go by, and many of the arguments cancel each other or are so subjective that they can only confirm a conclusion reached on other grounds. But a significant number of scholars have thought that the book of Acts furnishes one piece of evidence that determines a relatively firm and exact date for the book: its abrupt ending.

Acts ends with Paul languishing for two years under house arrest in Rome. This conclusion seems to be rather lame and unfulfilling. Is not the best explanation for this ending that Luke had decided it was necessary at this point to publish his work? After all, Luke has spent eight chapters detailing the course of Paul's judicial proceedings. Is it likely that he would have left us in suspense about the outcome of these proceedings? It is almost certain that Paul was not executed at the end of this two-year period. Why, if Luke knew this, did he not tell us that Paul was released from prison, as a final, climactic indication of the innocence of the Christian movement in the eyes of the Romans? Alternatively, if Luke was writing late enough to know of Paul's execution in A.D. 64 or 65, why did he keep this from the reader? Would not Paul's execution have made a fitting parallel to the execution of James earlier in Acts (12:2) and brought Acts to a similar climax as the gospel of Luke, with its narrative of Jesus' death? And would Luke have left as it is Paul's solemn assurance to the elders of Ephesus that he would never see them again (20:25, 38) if he had known that Paul had returned and ministered in Ephesus (as 1 Timothy assumes that he did, probably in the years 63–64)? Our difficulty in answering these questions satisfactorily suggests that the simplest and most natural explanation for the abrupt ending of Acts is that Luke finished writing the book when Paul had been in Rome for two years—in 62, according to the most probable chronology.[30]

---

[30]The most important defenders of this line of argument are Harnack, *Date of Acts*, esp. pp. 90–116; Richard Belward Rackham, *The Acts of the Apostles* (London: Methuen, 1901), pp. l-lv (and see the

This line of argument appears to be objective, simple, and persuasive. But there are other possible explanations for the ending of Acts that claim to invalidate this argument. One explanation is that Luke may have intended to write a third volume and that Acts ends where it does to keep the reader in suspense until he or she can begin that third volume.[31] Indication that Luke intended a third volume has been found in his use of the word πρῶτος (prōtos, "first") in Acts 1:1 to describe the gospel of Luke. This word is technically a superlative adjective and would thus refer to the first of three or more books rather than to the former of two. But Hellenistic Greek tended to confuse the degrees of comparison in adjectives, and little can be built on the use of this word here. We have no other indication that Luke intended another volume, and this explanation for the ending must be considered purely speculative.

The explanation of the ending of Acts that is most popular today is that Paul's arrival in Rome and his unhindered preaching of the gospel in the capital of the empire bring the book to its intended conclusion.[32] Luke's focus is not biographical but theological—he is not interested in a life of Paul but in the expansion of the gospel. To have the gospel being preached in Rome "without hindrance" (Acts 28:31) brings Luke's epic account of the growth and expansion of the Christian movement to its natural terminus. To argue, then, that Acts is strangely incomplete because it does not tell us the outcome of Paul's appeal to the emperor or the ultimate fate of the apostle is to assume that Luke was more interested in Paul per se than he really was. Perhaps, indeed, Luke knew that the outcome of Paul's trial in Rome was a negative one or that Paul had been executed by the Romans, but he deliberately refrained from giving us this information because it would have spoiled his upbeat conclusion. Perhaps Luke knew that Paul had been freed after this first Roman trial and did not want to get Paul in trouble by publishing the details of his further ministry.[33] Or perhaps—and this is the most probable explanation—Luke knew that Paul was continuing to minister in the churches of the East but did not include this information because it did not make as neat a climax as did Paul's preaching in Rome. In any case, it is argued, the ending of Acts, being the natural climax of the narrative, gives no help at all in dating the book.

This argument carries considerable weight. Further substantiating it is Luke's mention of a specific period of time—"two whole years"—during which Paul preached in Rome. This suggests that Luke knew that Paul's circumstances changed after this two-year period. Nevertheless, doubts linger about Luke's failure to mention the results of Paul's trial in Rome. Luke's interest in Paul may be exaggerated, but he does spend a considerable amount of time telling us of the apostle's own circumstances and history. The space devoted to Paul's trials in the

updating of Rackham's arguments by A. J. Mattill, Jr., "The Date and Purpose of Luke-Acts: Rackham Reconsidered," *CBQ* 40 [1978]: 335–50); and J. A. T. Robinson, *Redating the New Testament* (Philadelphia: Westminster, 1976), pp. 88–92.

[31]Zahn 3:57–61; Ramsay, *St. Paul*, pp. 23, 27–28.

[32]See, e.g., Bruce, *Book of Acts*, p. 11; Longenecker, "Acts," pp. 234–35; Floyd V. Filson, "The Journey Motif in Luke-Acts," in *Apostolic History and the Gospel: Biblical and Historical Essays Presented to F. F. Bruce on His Sixtieth Birthday*, ed. W. Ward Gasque and Ralph P. Martin (Grand Rapids: Eerdmans, 1970), pp. 68–77.

[33]Hemer, *Book of Acts*, pp. 406–8.

latter part of the book makes Luke's failure to tell us the outcome of those trials somewhat unexpected.

While it is difficult to be certain, then, we are inclined to think that the most natural explanation for the ending of Acts is that Luke decided to publish the book at that particular point in history. This leaves unanswered the question, Why did Luke not wait to learn the outcome of Paul's trial before publishing the book? One answer is that Luke wrote Acts as a defense brief to be used by Paul at this trial. But this explanation is unlikely, and we must admit that we do not not know what prompted Luke to finish his work at this point. Nevertheless, a failure to answer this question does not invalidate the general line of reasoning.

The ending of Acts, we have argued, suggests a date of about A.D. 62 for the book. But since this argument is by no means certain, we should seek for other grounds on which to establish a date. In fact, several other factors point to a date of about the same time (e.g., 62–64): (1) Luke's apparent ignorance of the letters of Paul; (2) Luke's portrayal of Judaism as a legal religion, a situation that would have changed abruptly with the outbreak of the Jewish rebellion against Rome in 66; (3) Luke's omission of any reference to the Neronian persecution, which, if it had occurred when Luke was writing, would surely have affected his narrative in some way; (4) the vivid detail of the shipwreck = voyage narrative (27:1–28:16), which suggests very recent experience.[34]

GENRE, ADDRESSEES, AND PURPOSE

Genre

The earliest identification of the genre of Acts may be reflected in the second-century authors who began calling Luke's second volume the Acts. As noted abbove, several ancient historians used the word "acts" to describe the narratives in which they recounted the heroic deeds of individuals or cities (e.g., Polybius, 1.1.1; Diodorus Siculus, 1.1.1), and the early church may then have thought that this was the category into which Luke's narrative fit. But "acts" was not the name of a technical genre as such,[35] so the title does not help much in establishing a well-defined literary classification for the book of Acts. Most scholars agree that Acts should be put into the category "history."[36] This identification has recently been challenged by some who find the differences between Acts and other ancient works of history too great to admit of their common categorization. C. H. Talbert has styled Acts a "succession narrative,"[37] while Richard Pervo suggests that Acts be read as a historical novel.[38] Both these scholars remind us of important features in Acts—Talbert the relationship of Acts to Luke's gospel, Pervo the element of

---

[34]See esp. ibid., pp. 376–90, and also Longenecker, "Acts," pp. 236–38.

[35]See David E. Aune, *The New Testament in Its Literary Environment*, Library of Early Christianity 8 (Philadelphia: Westminster, 1987), p. 78.

[36]E.g., Martin Hengel, *Acts and the History of Earliest Christianity* (Philadelphia: Fortress, 1979), pp. 36–37; W. Ward Gasque, "A Fruitful Field: Recent Study of the Acts of the Apostles," *Int* 42 (1988): 129.

[37]Charles H. Talbert, *Literary Patterns, Theological Themes, and the Genre of Luke-Acts*, SBLMS 20 (Missoula, Mont.: SP, 1974).

[38]Richard I. Pervo, *Profit with Delight: The Literary Genre of the Acts of the Apostles* (Philadelphia: Fortress, 1987).

storytelling in Acts—but neither of their proposed genre identifications has much to be said for it.[39] Others, noting these same differences, argue that Acts is unique and cannot be fit into any known genre.[40] However, while the features unique to Acts (e.g., its theological perspective and its relationship to the gospel of Luke) should not be minimized, we doubt that they are sufficient to take Acts out of the category of ancient history. Ancient historical works differ a great deal among themselves, with most—perhaps all of them—possessing some features unique to themselves.[41]

Addressees and Purpose

Acts, like the gospel of Luke, is addressed to Theophilus (1:1), who was probably Luke's patron, the person who was putting up the money for the publication of Luke's literary effort. But we learn, and can infer, almost nothing more about him from either book. Moreover, it is almost certain that Luke had a broader audience than one individual in mind. Just who made up Luke's intended audience can be determined only after we have identified his purpose in writing.

Identifying Luke's purpose in writing Acts is complicated by the relationship between Acts and the gospel of Luke. With only a few exceptions,[42] scholars have rightly seen these two books to be a literary unity—"Luke-Acts." Most also think that Luke intends the prologue of the first of these books (Luke 1:1–4) to cover his second volume as well.[43] Ancient writers were severely limited in their verbosity by the need to compress their work into the space of a papyrus scroll. The gospel of Luke and Acts each would have occupied a full-sized papyrus roll. The division of Luke's work into two volumes was therefore dictated by physical limitations, and like other ancient writers, he has used the opening of this second volume to tie it to the first and to the prologue of that first volume.[44] Any estimation of Luke's purpose in Acts must thus take into account the information Luke himself furnishes us in the gospel's prologue. But recognizing the applicability of the prologue to the matter in hand does not solve all our problems. It is not certain, for instance, how much of the prologue applies to Acts. At least some of its statements—such as Luke's reference to the many who had written before him—seem to apply only to the gospel. Nevertheless, we are safe in concluding that the purpose stated in Luke 1:4, namely, to communicate the "certainty of the things you have been taught," applies equally to the gospel and to Acts. This, the author's own statement, must be considered basic to any discussion of the purpose of Acts. But instilling certainty in his readers is a very broad aim and may not cover all the purposes that Luke had. We need, then, to examine

---

[39]See Aune, *The New Testament in Its Literary Environment*, pp. 78–80.

[40]Wikenhauser, pp. 351–52; Kümmel, p. 165; Schneider, *Apostelgeschichte* 1:73–76.

[41]Aune, *The New Testament in its Literary Environment*, p. 80.

[42]Albert C. Clark argued on the basis of stylistic differences that Luke and Acts were written by different people (*The Acts of the Apostles: A Critical Edition with Introduction and Notes on Selected Passages* [Oxford: Clarendon, 1933], pp. 393–408), while Wikenhauser thinks that Luke wrote Acts so long after the gospel that they can be considered separately (pp. 352–54).

[43]E.g., Fitzmyer, *Luke I–IX*, p. 9; I. Howard Marshall, "Luke and His Gospel,' " in *Das Evangelium und die Evangelien*, ed. Peter Stuhlmacher, WUNT 2.28 (Tübingen: Mohr, 1983), pp. 289–308.

[44]A. J. B. Higgins, "The Preface to Luke and the Kerygma in Acts," in *Apostolic History and the Gospel*, pp. 78–83.

some of the suggested purposes for Acts and test them against Luke's own claim and against the data of the text.

Conciliation As we noted above, the Tübingen School viewed the book of Acts as a second-century attempt to create a synthesis out of the supposed antitheses of Jewish Christianity and Gentile Christianity. The author of Acts seeks to accomplish this particularly through his portrayals of the two key figures in Acts, Peter and Paul. Texts such as 1 Corinthians 1:10–17 and Galatians 2:11–14 show that there was a sharp division between Peter and Paul, a division between a conservative Jewish theological outlook and a liberal Gentile-oriented outlook that was perpetuated in warring church factions into the late first and early second centuries. But the antagonism between Peter and Paul disappears in Acts. The author of Acts "Gentilizes" Peter, turning him into the initiator (chap. 10) and defender (11:1–18; 15:6–11) of the outreach to the Gentiles. Paul, on the other hand, is "Judaized": he accepts the council decree (15:22–35), circumcises Timothy (16:3), takes Jewish vows (18:18; 21:17–26), and claims to be a loyal Pharisee (23:6). By thus rewriting the history of the early church, the author of Acts hopes to conciliate the factions in his second-century context.

The Tübingen approach to the book of Acts did not survive the criticisms of scholars such as J. B. Lightfoot and Albrecht Ritschl. The assumption that the late-first-century and early-second-century church was torn by factions was shown to be unfounded. More important, the Tübingen critics were guilty of seriously overemphasizing the differences between Peter and Paul. That they differed occasionally is clear (e.g., Gal. 2:11–14). But that they were leaders of opposing theological tendencies in the early church is an idea that finds no basis in the New Testament text. We therefore have no grounds on which to accuse the author of Acts of creating an unhistorical and tendentious scenario, and as little reason to think that the second-century church was in need of conciliation. We may still, however, think that conciliation was Luke's subsidiary purpose; perhaps he knew of continuing tensions between Jewish Christians and Gentile Christians and wanted to show that Peter and Paul were in essential agreement over the basics of the faith.

Evangelism/Apologetics Luke's inclusion of a number of evangelistic speeches and his emphasis on the miraculous accrediting of the early preachers suggest that he may have written in order to awaken faith. Many scholars think that evangelism was, then, at least a subsidiary purpose of (Luke-) Acts. Particularly influential is the notion that Acts is intended to create an apologetic for Christianity in the eyes of Romans.

One of the puzzling features of Acts is the amount of time that Luke spends describing in detail the trials and defenses of Paul. Almost one-fourth of the whole book of Acts (chaps. 22–28) is occupied with this topic. Why is this, when undoubtedly Luke could have told us much else about evangelistic outreaches in various parts of the world, or about Paul's missionary work? The traditional answer has been that Luke wanted to prove to Roman citizens that Christianity was a religion to be tolerated—a *religio licita* in the official terminology. Rome had become quite skeptical about Oriental religions, even fearful of their harmful effects on the population. For Christian missionaries to work effectively with Roman citizens, it was necessary to stifle these fears and to make Christianity a religion that Romans could embrace without being considered traitors to their country. This Luke does by showing how Roman official after Roman official refuses to stand in the way of the new movement. The city officers in Philippi apologize to Paul for imprisoning him (16:38–39); Gallio, the Roman official in charge of the province of Achaia, declines to forbid Christian preaching in Corinth (18:12–17); King Agrippa II and Festus, the Roman procurator of Judea, agree that Paul had done nothing wrong and could have been released had he not appealed to Caesar (26:31–32).

Most scholars think that this kind of apologetic plays some role in Acts, but a few elevate this to the central concern of the book.[45] As mentioned, some have suggested that Luke intended Acts to be used as a brief for Paul at his trial in Rome, a document that Paul could submit to a Roman magistrate (Theophilus?) or even to the emperor himself as part of his defense. This last suggestion, at least, is most unlikely. Luke would hardly have written as much as he did, had this been his purpose. A few scholars go further and question whether apologetic to Romans plays any role at all in Luke's purpose. They argue that Luke-Acts must be considered as a whole and that apologetic to a Roman audience is not very clear in the gospel. Moreover, Luke gives many indications that he is writing to a Christian rather than to a non-Christian audience.[46] One writer, in fact, reverses the traditional understanding, arguing that Luke was not trying to legitimize the church before Rome, but Rome before the church.[47] These scholars make some good points: Luke-Acts is primarily directed to Christians, and it is easy to overemphasize the theme of Roman apologetic at the expense of other themes. Nevertheless, the way in which Luke goes out of his way to bring out Roman acceptance of the church, seen particularly in the latter chapters of Acts, strongly suggests that apologetic to Romans is one of Luke's purposes. Perhaps, while writing mainly for Christians, Luke knew that Acts would also be read by non-Christian Romans and so included this material. Or perhaps Luke wanted to help new converts from a Roman background understand better the relationship between their new faith and their Roman political and social identity.

A rather different apologetic purpose is discerned in the book of Acts by A. J. Mattill, Jr. Reviving the thesis of Matthias Schneckenburger, he argues that Acts is directed to Jewish Christians in Rome and has as its central purpose an apology for the apostle Paul. Luke wanted to scotch rumors to the effect that Paul was an apostate Jew by emphasizing the parallels between Peter and Paul and by selecting incidents that revealed Paul's continuing allegiance to his "kinsmen according to the flesh."[48] There is much to be said for this proposal, for there is no doubt that Paul is Luke's hero and that his emphasis on Paul's Jewishness would be most appropriate for a Jewish Christian audience. In contrast, many other features of

---

[45]E.g., Johannes Weiss, *Absicht und literarischer Charakter der Apostelgeschichte* (Marburg: Vandenhoeck & Ruprecht, 1897); O'Neill, *Theology of Acts*, pp. 166–177; cf. Bruce, *Book of Acts*, pp. 8–13.
[46]See Schneider, *Apostelgeschichte* 1:139–45.
[47]Paul W. Walaskay, *"And So We Came to Rome": The Political Perspective of St. Luke*, SNTSMS 49 (Cambridge: Cambridge University Press, 1983).
[48]A. J. Mattill, Jr., "The Purpose of Acts: Schneckenburger Reconsidered," in *Apostolic History and the Gospel*, pp. 108–122.

Luke-Acts imply a Gentile Christian audience. Apologetic to Jewish Christians may, then, be one of Luke's purposes, but it is not his main purpose.

Theological Polemics That Luke writes with theological purposes is clear. But some scholars think that he has a definite theological ax to grind and that this theological polemic is his central purpose. Charles Talbert, for instance, suggests that Luke is writing to oppose Gnosticsm.[49] But it is unlikely that Gnosticism existed as a movement requiring refutation at this stage in history, and there is far too much in both Luke and Acts that would be immaterial for this purpose. Hans Conzelmann and others think that Luke is propagating a new conception of salvation history in response to the problem of the delay of the parousia.[50] More will be said about this theological issue below; we note here simply that while Luke indeed has much to contribute to our understanding of salvation history, there is little evidence that he was the initiator of such a view or that his writing was occasioned by the delay of the parousia. In general, then, we may conclude that Luke was writing with theological purposes and that he has many specific theological points to make but that the evidence for a particular theological polemic as central to his purpose is lacking. Such proposals are reductionistic: they oversimplify Luke's complex and many-faceted work.

Edification We agree with a growing number of scholars who think that Luke wrote with a variety of specific purposes and that these purposes are part of a larger, general purpose—the edification of Christians.[51] Luke tells us in the prologue to his gospel that confirmation of the gospel is his overriding purpose[52] and implies by using the word κατηχέω (katēcheō, ["to teach"]) that this confirmation is directed to a Christian, perhaps a recent convert. Perhaps, indeed, we should view this intended reader as a former God-fearer, a Gentile, like Cornelius (Acts 10), who had been an active worshiper of the God of Israel without becoming a Jew.[53] Luke accomplishes this purpose by describing the historical foundation for Christian faith and by showing, through this historical survey, that the church of his, and Theophilus's, day is the culmination of biblical history. God's salvation was revealed in, and made available through, his Son, Jesus Christ. The message of that salvation was entrusted by Christ himself to his apostles, and through the empowering and directing of the Holy Spirit, they have now brought that message, and the salvation it mediates, to "the ends of the earth."[54] Only so broad a purpose is able to accommodate the richness of Luke-Acts. (For we must not forget that Luke wrote two books, bound together with a

---

[49]Charles H. Talbert, *Luke and the Gnostics: An Examination of the Lucan Purpose* (Nashville: Abingdon, 1966).

[50]See esp. Hans Conzelmann, *The Theology of St. Luke* (New York: Harper & Row, 1961).

[51]See, e.g., Ernst Haenchen, "The Book of Acts as Source Material for the History of Earliest Christianity," in *Studies in Luke-Acts*, pp. 258–278; I. Howard Marshall, *The Acts of the Apostles*, TNTC (Grand Rapids: Eerdmans, 1980), pp. 20–21; idem, "Luke and His 'Gospel,' " pp. 289–308; Fitzmyer, *Luke I–IX*, p. 9.

[52]See esp. the essay by W. C. van Unnik, "The Book of Acts' the Confirmation of the Gospel," *NovT* 4 (1960): 26–59.

[53]See Walter L. Liefeld, "Luke," in *EBC* 8:802.

[54]This theme is stressed by C. K. Barrett, *Luke the Historian in Recent Study* (London: Epworth, 1961), pp. 56–61; Marshall, *Acts of the Apostles*, pp. 20–21; Gasque, "Recent Study," pp. 120–21.

single overall plan and purpose.) As part of this general purpose, of course, Luke pursues many subsidiary purposes—legitimation of the church in the eyes of Romans, vindication of Paul in the eyes of Jewish Christians, evangelism, and others.

SOURCES

The search for the sources of Luke's material in Acts is important for the light it might shed both on Luke's literary techniques as well as on the historical trustworthiness of his narrative. In the prologue to his gospel, Luke tells us that he has "carefully investigated everything from the beginning" (1:3) and mentions both written records (1:1) and oral transmission (1:2, "handed down"). Luke may be thinking here mainly of the gospel, but we can assume that he would have made the same careful investigation, and used all the sources he could lay his hands on, in writing his second volume. And in any case, the question of the extent to which written sources stand behind Acts naturally arises. The "we" passages that surface in Acts 16 and following, as well as the general shift from a Palestinian to a wider Mediterranean setting that occurs at this point, makes it necessary to separate Acts 1–15 from Acts 16–28 in the investigation of the sources for Acts.

Acts 1–15

At the end of the nineteenth and beginning of the twentieth centuries, scholars working on Acts shared with their colleagues working on the Synoptic Gospels a preoccupation with written sources. Adolf Harnack's source proposal for Acts 1–15 stands as a climax to this development. Harnack recognized, along with most scholars of his day and ours, that Luke has so uniformly imposed his own style on whatever sources he has used as to make it impossible to distinguish his sources through style and language.[55] Harnack appealed rather to geographic setting, theological tendency, and, especially, the presence of doublets to dissect Acts 1–15 into its component sources. Doublets are apparent duplicate narratives of the same story, and there are five of them, claimed Harnack, in Acts 1–5: two sermons of Peter (2:14–39; 3:12–26), two arrests of the apostles (4:3; 5:18), two appearances of the apostles before the Sanhedrin (4:8–20; 5:27–40), two estimates of the number of converts (2:41; 4:4), and two accounts of the sharing of material goods in the Jerusalem church (2:44–45; 4:32). Source critics often think that such doublets point to an amalgamation of two different sources, each with its own particular version of such incidents. Using these doublets in Acts 1–5 as his starting point, Harnack postulated the existence of three written sources in Acts 1–15: a "Jerusalem A" source, standing behind 3:1–5:16, 8:5–40, and 9:31–11:18; a "Jerusalem B" source, represented in 2:1–47 and 5:17–42; and an "Antiochene" source, which shows up in 6:1–8:4, 11:19–30, and 12:25–15:35.[56] Harnack's scheme has been very influential and has been adopted, sometimes with modifications, by a significant number of scholars.

---

[55]E.g., Cadbury, *Making of Luke-Acts*, pp. 65–70; Jacques Dupont, *The Sources of the Acts* (New York: Herder & Herder, 1964), p. 88; Haenchen, *Acts*, p. 81.
[56]Adolf Harnack, *The Acts of the Apostles* (London: Williams & Norgate, 1909), pp. 162–202.

Despite its popularity, Harnack's proposal is unlikely. Its foundation is shaky in that the evidence for doublets in Acts 1–5 is not strong. The narratives concerned are either so different from one another (e.g., the speeches of Peter), so integral to the progression of events (e.g., the two arrests and hearings of the apostles), or so integral to Luke's plan (e.g., the references to the community of goods and the numbers of the converted) that they are unlikely to be duplicates.[57] Beyond that, there is little basis for differentiating the material in Acts 1–15, beyond the obvious matter of setting, and this can be explained in any number of ways. We simply do not have enough data to identify written sources of this sort behind Acts 1–15.

A source proposal of a very different sort was advanced by C. C. Torrey. He argued from the presence of Semitisms that Acts 1:1–15:35 is the translation of a single Aramaic source.[58] Torrey's theory is now universally rejected. Although it is recognized that his proposal goes far beyond the available evidence, the discussion continues of the Semitic element in this first part of Acts and of its implications for Luke's sources. There is some reason to think that the distribution of Semitisms in these chapters points to the use, at places, of Aramaic sources,[59] but the evidence is not clear enough to justify firm conclusions or the identification of specific sources.

The sources behind Acts 1–15 cannot, then, be definitely pinpointed. It is likely that Luke depends on Aramaic sources for parts of these chapters, particularly for some of the speeches, and other written sources that we now have no means of isolating were perhaps used as well. But we should probably place as much if not more emphasis on oral reports as the basis for Luke's narrative.[60] Certainly Luke's two-year stay in Palestine during Paul's Caesarean imprisonment (his stay is a fair inference from the "we" passages) would have given him ample opportunity to interview people such as Philip, Mark, and Peter himself.[61] And if Luke was a native of Antioch, he could have had firsthand knowledge of the planting and growth of the church there, as well as of the labors of the missionaries Paul and Barnabas, sent out from that church.

Acts 16–28

Attention in these chapters is focused on the significance of the "we" passages. Dibelius thought that these passages indicated the existence of an "itinerary" source (perhaps a travel diary) that Luke used for much of this narrative.[62] We have argued above that the best explanation of the "we" in these texts is that Luke himself was with Paul on these occasions. His own eyewitness recollection

---

[57]See Joachim Jeremias, "Untersuchungen zum Quellenproblem der Apostelgeschichte," *ZNW* 36 (1937): 205–21; Bruce, *Acts of the Apostles*, p. 23.

[58]Charles Cutler Torrey, *The Composition and Date of Acts*, HTS 1 (Cambridge: Harvard University Press, 1916), pp. 3–41.

[59]See esp. Max Wilcox, *The Semitisms of Acts* (Oxford: Clarendon, 1965).

[60]Haenchen, *Acts*, p. 82.

[61]See Hemer, *Book of Acts*, pp. 336–64.

[62]Martin Dibelius, "Style Criticism of the Book of Acts," in *Studies in the Acts of the Apostles*, ed. Heinrich Greeven (London: SCM, 1956), p. 4 (the original German essay was published in 1923); see also Kümmel, pp. 184–85.

(combined perhaps with notes he may have taken), along with close personal contact with Paul himself, fully accounts for the material in Acts 16–28.

TEXT

The text of Acts presents as interesting a problem as the text of any New Testament book. This is because the text has been preserved in two distinct forms: the form that is represented by the great uncials Sinaiticus (א) and Vaticanus (B), which is the basis for all modern Greek texts and English translations; and the form represented by the uncial Bezae Cantabrigiensis (D). The latter form of the text, often called Western because of its alleged geographic origin, is about 10 percent longer than the usually accepted text. These additions are of various kinds, extending from single words to whole sentences.

Some of these additions are very interesting. As we noted above, it is the Western text that identifies Luke as a native as Antioch by inserting in 11:28 the words, "And there was much rejoicing. And as *we* were gathered together. . . ." The Western text furnishes the wholly likely information that Paul used the rented quarters of Tyrannus in Ephesus "from 11 A.M. to 4 P.M.," that is, during the hot hours of the day when Tyrannus himself was not using the hall. An ethicizing tendency can be observed in the Western version of the apostolic decree. In place of the shorter text's prohibition of food polluted by idols, sexual immorality, meat of strangled animals, and "blood"—a mixture of ritual and ethical points—Codex D and its allies list idolatry, sexual immorality, and "blood," and adds after the list, "and not to do to others what they would not like to be done to themselves."

Scholars take three basic standpoints in their assessment of this Western text in Acts. A few have argued that it represents the original Lukan text, which א, B, and others have abbreviated.[63] Others have thought that it might represent a completely separate recension that could have come from Luke himself.[64] The great majority, however, view the Western form of the text in Acts as a secondary modification of the generally accepted text.[65] This is almost certainly right. A comparison between the Western text and the text of א and B shows generally that the Western text tends to smooth out grammatical difficulties, clarify ambiguous points, expand references to Christ, and add notes of historical detail and interest.[66] Accepted canons of textual criticism state that such features are typical of secondary texts. This is not, of course, to say that the Western text may not at points preserve the original reading. But the text, as a whole, must be considered a third- or fourth-century revision of the original, shorter text of Acts.[67]

---

[63]Most notably, Clark, *Acts of the Apostles.*

[64]F. Blass, "Die Textüberlieferung in der Apostelgeschichte," *TSK* 67 (1894): 86–119; Zahn 3:8–41.

[65]E.g., James Hardy Ropes, *The Text of Acts*, vol. 3 of *Beginnings of Christianity*, pp. ccxv–ccxlvi; Bruce, *Acts of the Apostles*, pp. 40–47; Kümmel, pp. 187–88.

[66]Eldon Jay Epp also discerns an anti-Jewish bias in Bezae, (*The Theological Tendency of Codex Bezae Cantabrigiensis in Acts*, SNTSMS 3 [Cambridge: Cambridge University Press, 1966]).

[67]On the date of the text, see Kurt Aland and Barbara Aland, *The Text of the New Testament*, rev. ed. (Grand Rapids: Eerdmans, 1989), p. 69.

ACTS IN RECENT STUDY

Survey of Research

Recent study of Acts must be understood against nineteenth- and early-twentieth-century background.[68] The assumption that Acts gives to us a straightforward historical narrative of the beginnings of the church was first seriously questioned at the beginning of the nineteenth century by the German critic W. M. L. de Wette.[69] He was followed by F. C. Baur and his disciples (the Tübingen School), who argued that Acts pursues a definite theological "tendency" (*Tendenz*; hence *Tendenzkritik*). This tendency, formulated with the purpose of reconciling second-century church factions, determines what is contained in Acts. Luke does not, then, simply tell us about things "as they really happened."[70] Predictably, so new and radical a thesis stimulated a strong reaction, and numerous objections to the Tübingen approach from scholars of widely varying theological commitments appeared during the course of the nineteenth century. The turn of the century witnessed the work of two great Acts scholars, both of whom made a strong case for the essential historicity of Acts. In a series of books, the famous German historian and theologian Adolf Harnack argued, among other things, that Acts was written at an early date by Luke the physician and must be considered a serious work of history.[71] William Ramsay went further. Ramsay, an archaeologist, started out as a skeptic but became firmly convinced ot Luke's historical reliability as he discovered detail after detail in Acts that demonstrated firsthand acquaintance with conditions in the Roman Empire in the middle of the first century. Luke, Ramsay concluded, belongs in the first rank of ancient historians.[72]

At about the same time, scholars were showing considerable interest in the sources of Acts. Harnack himself, as we have seen above, was in the forefront of this development. As Ernst Haenchen puts it, scholarly attention had shifted from the question of what Luke was *willing* to say ("tendency criticism") to what he was *able* to say (source criticism).[73] Shortly after this, in the 1920s, the new discipline of form criticism began to be applied to Acts. The most prominent practitioner of form criticism in Acts was Martin Dibelius, who, in a series of articles, established influential methodological points and conclusions.[74] Dibelius argued that criticism of Acts must focus on the style of the narrative, since, in contrast to the Gospels, one does not have written sources with which to make comparison. By analyzing the style of Acts, Dibelius believed we could isolate certain forms, or narratives

---

[68]This history is thoroughly surveyed in Gasque, *History*. See also Haenchen, *Acts*, pp. 14–50.

[69]See Gasque, *History*, pp. 24–26.

[70]The fullest treatment of Acts from the Tübingen approach is that of Eduard Zeller, *The Contents and Origin of the Acts of the Apostles, Critically Investigated*, 2 vols. (London: Williams & Norgate, 1875–76); the German original was published in 1854.

[71]Adolf Harnack, *Luke the Physician* (New York: Putman, 1907), *The Acts of the Apostles* (London: Wiliams & Norgate, 1909), and *Date of Acts*.

[72]See esp. Ramsay's *Bearing of Recent Discovery on the Trustworthiness of the New Testament*, reprint ed. (Grand Rapids: Baker, 1953), and *St. Paul: The Traveller and Roman Citizen* (London: Hodder & Stoughton, 1897).

[73]Haenchen, *Acts*, p. 24.

[74]The relevant essays are collected in Martin Dibelins, *Studies in the Acts of the Apostles*, ed. Heinrich Greeven (London: SCM, 1956).

that Luke had used in his composition, from the rest of Acts, which was the product of Luke's own creativity. The speeches of Acts, Dibelius particularly emphasized, showed every sign of Luke's own creativity. The unique features of Acts rendered the shift from form-critical approaches to redaction-critical approaches to Acts less obvious than in the case of the Synoptic Gospels. Thus, the work of Hans Conzelmann and Ernst Haenchen builds directly on that of Dibelius, with perhaps slightly more interest in Luke's theology as a whole.[75] Both writers are quite skeptical about the historicity of Acts, arguing that Luke's desire to edify the church (Haenchen) or to explain the delay of the parousia (Conzelmann) has virtually erased any concern on his part with what really happened.

Recent Contributions

Recent study of the Acts has tended to focus on three areas: historicity, literary phenomena, and theological tendencies.

Historicity Acts is the New Testament book that most nearly resembles historical narration, and it is the only source for most of what it narrates. Scholars have therefore long debated its historical accuracy, some doubting whether we can learn much at all of "what really happened" from Acts,[76] others insisting that Acts deserves to be considered as a serious and generally reliable historical source.[77] The same division of opinion is evident in contemporary scholarship. Gerd Lüdemann, while by no means dismissing Acts as a historical source, is generally skeptical.[78] He acknowledges the importance of the theological approach to Acts that has reigned supreme in recent studies but insists that the study of Acts as a historical source needs to be reopened. He attempts to distinguish Luke's redactional touches from the traditions he has inherited, and from this basis to assess the historical reliability of Acts.

But Lüdemann's generally negative conclusions are more than balanced by the contributions of two scholars who are much more positive toward the historical accuracy of Acts. Martin Hengel, while finding historical errors in Acts, is critical of the tendency in modern scholarship to dismiss Luke as a serious historian. "The radical 'redaction-critical' approach so popular today, which sees Luke above all as a freely inventive theologian, mistakes his real purpose, namely that as a Christian 'historian' he sets out to report the events of the past that provided the foundation for the faith and its extension. He does not set out primarily to present his own

---

[75]See esp. Conzelmann, *Theology of St. Luke*, and also his commentary *Acts of the Apostles*, Hermeneia (Philadelphia: Fortress, 1987); Haenchen's major work is his commentary *The Acts of the Apostles*.

[76]E.g., the Tübingen School and many contemporary redactional approaches (e.g., Conzelmann, *Acts*).

[77]E.g., Harnack, Ramsay; and note also two of the classic treatments from this perspective: Eduard Meyer, *Ursprung und Anfänge des Christentums*, 3 vols. (Stuttgart: J. G. Cotta, 1921–23); and Alfred Wikenhauser, *Die Apostelgeschichte und ihr Geschichtswert*, NTAbh 8.3–5 (Münster: Aschendorff, 1921).

[78]Gerd Lüdemann, *Early Christianity According to the Traditions in Acts: A Commentary* (Philadelphia: Fortress, 1989).

'theology.'"[79] Hengel concludes that Luke deserves to be considered as trustworthy as any ancient historian.

Far more detailed than Hengel is Colin Hemer's *The Book of Acts in the Setting of Hellenistic History*, a magisterial and definitive defense of the historicity of Acts. Hemer compares Luke favorably with the highest standards of ancient historiography. He updates and expands the list of points at which Luke demonstrates his knowledge of, and accuracy about, first-century political, social, and geographic details. He also defends Luke at those points where he has been considered to be inaccurate and contests the scholars who think that Luke's theological concerns must have overridden his historical reliablity. Hemer's work puts the defense of Luke's historical reliablity on firmer ground than ever before.

Literary Approaches The last twenty years have witnessed an explosion of studies on literary aspects of the Bible. Scholars have been particularly interested in fitting the biblical books into ancient literary genres and in using contemporary literary techniques to open up new approaches to, and understandings of, the text of Scripture. Luke-Acts has been the focus of many such studies, although more have focused on the gospel than on Acts. Charles H. Talbert, however, has scrutinized Luke-Acts as a whole.[80] He emphasizes the parallels that Luke draws between the gospel on the one hand and Acts on the other and between Acts 1–12 and Acts 13–28. Luke has selected and ordered events in such a way that the h story of Jesus parallels the history of the church, while the "acts" of Peter parallel the "acts" of Paul. These patterns bind Luke's two works together and serve to emphasize the unity of the salvation-historical drama that is at the heart of Luke-Acts. Talbert also suggests that Luke-Acts may be compared with Diogenes Laertius's *Lives of Eminent Philosophers*. Comparison of Acts with other ancient literature is not new, but in the past comparison was usually made with historical works. Recent scholarship has emphasized the dramatic and novelistic aspects of the book of Acts, with its travel narratives, stories of miracles, and accounts of dangers on the high seas. Richard Pervo takes these characteristics as indications that Luke was not intending to write history, but a historical novel.[81] While this is certainly going too far, the reminder from such scholars that Luke has written Acts in such a way that it makes for exciting reading is a salutary one.

Theological Themes In the middle 1960s, W. C. van Unnik noted that Luke-Acts had suddenly become a storm center in contemporary scholarship.[82] This was largely owing, he noted, to the new interest in Luke as a theologian, sparked by the application of redaction-critical techniques to the gospel. It was the proposal of Hans Conzelmann that led the way, and came to dominate, in the new theological approach to Luke.[83] Conzelmann argued that "Luke" (he did not think that Luke the physician was the author) wrote largely in order to explain to the church of his day the delay of the parousia. For some time after Jesus' death, the

---

[79]Martin Hengel, *Acts and the History of Earliest Christianity*, pp. 67–68.
[80]Talbert, *Literary Patterns*.
[81]Richard Pervo, *Profit with Delight*; see also Vernon K. Robbins, "The We-Passages in Acts."
[82]W. C. van Unnik, "Luke-Acts, a Storm Center in Contemporary Scholarship," in *Studies in Luke-Acts*, pp. 15–32.
[83]Conzelmann, *The Theology of St. Luke*.

early church believed that Jesus would return in glory to bring an end to this earth in their own lifetimes. At some point, however, as time went by and Jesus did not return, the church came to realize that Jesus would not be coming back in the immediate future. So basic a shift in eschatological expectation demanded a massive reinterpretation of Christian theology. It is this reinterpretation that Luke provides. The heart of Luke's scheme is the replacement of the early Christian eschatological expectation with salvation history. In place of a church waiting for the Lord from heaven, Luke offers a historical outline of the course of saving events, divided into three periods: the period of Israel, the period of Jesus' ministry, and the period of the church. It is this segmentation of salvation history into its separate stages that the very structure of Luke's two-volume work provides. Luke writes to encourage Christians in his day to endure the pressures of living as believers in an indefinitely continuing world order. He thus tries to establish a role for the church. He stresses its authority by locating its establishment in apostles accredited by Jesus himself. He provides for its effective working by organizing it, with elders and bishops. This attention to the church, its authority and organization, has come to be called "early Catholicism" (*Frühkatholizismus*), because it is seen as leading on to the organized "universal" (catholic) church of the second century.

Reaction to Conzelmann's proposal has been vigorous and varied. Three points may be singled out as particularly important. First, as Oscar Cullmann and others have shown, "salvation history," in the sense of a series of stages through which God has brought his salvation to the world, is integral to the New Testament and to the message of Jesus himself.[84] It is not something invented by Luke. Second, it is questionable whether there was at any time in the early church a broadly held conviction that Jesus was *certain* to come back within a few short years. Those sayings of Jesus in which he is thought to have said that he would return in glory within the lifetime of the first apostles (e.g., Matt. 10:23; Mark 9:1 par.; Mark 13:30 par.) probably do not mean that at all.[85] It can be demonstrated that the early Christians were strongly imbued with a sense of the Lord's *imminence* (that Jesus *could* return at any time) but not that they held to a notion of the *immediacy* of the Lord's return (that he definitely *would* return within a short period of time). The third important response to the scenario drawn by Conzelmann and others is to question the existence of "early Catholicism" in Luke. Luke has not, as these scholars claim, abandoned a doctrine of imminence: the church has not simply settled down into the world but exists in "the last days," eagerly awaiting the return of Jesus from heaven.[86]

While Luke's salvation history and "early Catholicism" continue to be debated, two other theological issues are attracting more attention and debate in contemporary scholarship. The first is Luke's social and political teaching. It is well known that Luke's gospel evinces a special interest in the problems of the

---

[84]Oscar Cullman, *Christ and Time: The Primitive Christian Conception of Time and History* (Philadelphia: Westminster, 1950).

[85]See, e.g., A. L. Moore, *The Parousia in the New Testament* (Leiden: Brill, 1966).

[86]See, e.g., Kümmel, pp. 170–73, and on this and the subject of this paragraph, see esp. E. Earle Ellis, *Eschatology in Luke* (Philadephia: Fortress, 1972); A. J. Mattill, Jr., *Luke and the Last Things* (Dillsboro, N.C.: Western North Carolina Press, 1979); I. Howard Marshall, *Luke: Historian and Theologian*, rev. ed. (Grand Rapids: Zondervan, 1989), esp. pp. 77–88.

poor and the outcasts and that Jesus has more to say about the economic aspects of discipleship in Luke's gospel than in any other. Stimulated by the agenda of liberation theology and by a new awareness of the materialistic preoccupations of Western society, scholars have devoted considerable attention to Luke's teaching on these matters. Many of the studies focus exclusively on the gospel, but several important ones bring Acts into the picture as well.[87]

Perhaps the most debated issue in Luke's theology in recent years has been his view of the Mosaic law and of the relationship between Israel and the church. The stimulus of the discussion has come above all from the writings of Jacob Jervell.[88] In opposition to those scholars who have seen in Luke-Acts the theme of the church as the new Israel—the new people of God that *replaces* Israel—Jervell insists that it is repentant Jews who constitute Israel in Luke-Acts and that Gentile Christians belong to this Israel as an "associate people." In keeping with this stress on the continuity of Israel, Jervell also argues that Luke has "the most conservative outlook within the New Testament" on the Mosaic law.[89] Jewish Christians are required to keep the law, while Gentile Christians must keep the part of the law that concerns them (see the apostolic decree). Jervell's thesis has met with considerable approval,[90] but also with some serious criticisms.[91] His view of the Mosaic law is particularly vulnerable to criticism, several scholars showing that Luke-Acts takes a far more discontinuous view of the law than Jervell thinks.[92]

THE CONTRIBUTION OF ACTS

Historical

Without denying that Acts has as its main purpose the edification of believers and that its theological contributions are significant, we must not lose sight of the fact that Acts purports to narrate historical events. This narrative of historical events—the founding and growth of the church, with its particular emphasis on the career of Paul—is without parallel and therefore invaluable as a source for our knowledge of these events. Without Acts we would know nothing of the pouring out of the Spirit at Pentecost, the martyrdom of Stephen, the life of the early Jerusalem church, or the way in which the gospel first came to Samaritans and Gentiles. We would have little knowledge of the life and missionary journeys of Paul against which to understand his letters and theology. But can we trust the information that Acts gives us on these matters? As we noted above, the historical

---

[87]L. T. Johnson, *The Literary Function of Possessions in Luke-Acts*, SBLDS 39 (Missoula, Mont.: SP, 1977); Richard J. Cassidy and Philip J. Scharper, eds., *Political Issues in Luke-Acts* (Maryknoll, N.Y.: Orbis, 1983); P. F. Esler, *Community and Gospel in Luke-Acts: The Social and Political Motivations of Lucan Theology* (Cambridge: Cambridge University Press, 1987).

[88]See particularly Jacob Jervell, "The Divided People of God" and "The Law in Luke-Acts," in *Luke and the People of God* (Minneapolis: Augsburg, 1972), pp. 41–74 and 133–51.

[89]Jervell, "The Law in Luke-Acts," p. 141.

[90]See Robert L. Brawley, *Luke-Acts and the Jews: Conflict, Apology, and Conciliation*, SBLMS 33 (Atlanta: SP, 1987); Fitzmyer, *Luke I–IX*, pp. 58–59.

[91]See particularly Jack T. Sanders, "The Jewish People in Luke-Acts," in *Luke-Acts and the Jewish People: Eight Critical Perspectives*, ed. Joseph B. Tyson (Minneapolis: Augsburg, 1988), pp. 51–75.

[92]S. G. Wilson, *Luke and the Law*, SNTSMS 50 (Cambridge: Cambridge University Press, 1983); Craig L. Blomberg, "The Law in Luke-Acts," *JSNT* 22 (1984): 53–80; M. A. Seifrid, "Jesus and the Law in Acts," *JSNT* 30 (1987): 39–57.

reliability of Acts has been widely questioned. The doubts about Luke's accuracy concentrate on three main issues: Luke and ancient historical standards, the comparison of Acts with other sources of information, and the speeches of Acts.

Ancient Historical Standards It is often suggested that we should not expect Luke to give us an accurate, true-to-life record of the facts because ancient historians were not careful to stick to the facts. They wrote to edify or to draw moral lessons and felt at liberty to play fast and loose with the way things really happened if it suited their purpose or if they did not have access to the facts. To insist on historical accuracy would be unfairly to impose modern standards of history on an ancient historian.

Standards for historical writing in the ancient world were certainly not as uniformly insistent on factual accuracy as those in our day. Many writers who claimed the name "historian" wrote more fiction than fact. But the best ancient historians were concerned with the facts and did not differ very much from the modern historian in this regard. Polybius, for instance, criticizes other historians for making up dramatic scenes in the interest of moral lessons or sensationalism and insists that the historian should "simply record what really happened and what really was said, however commonplace" (2.56.10).[93] A similar position is taken by Lucian in his essay "On Writing History." To be sure, the words of Thucydides are often quoted to substantiate a different position. Describing his procedure in writing his history of the Peloponnesian War, Thucydides says:

> As to the speeches that were made by different men, either when they were about to begin the war or when they were already engaged therein, it has been difficult to recall with strict accuracy the words actually spoken, both for me as regards that which I myself heard, and for those who from various other sources have brought me reports. Therefore the speeches are given in the language which, as it seemed to me, the several speakers would express, on the subjects under consideration, the sentiments most befitting the occasion, though at the same time I have adhered as closely as possible to the general sense of what was actually said. (1.22)

While Thucydides, who is generally highly regarded as an ancient historian, admits that not all his speeches are verbatim reports, two things also need to be noted about this statement. First, he resorted to giving the general sense "befitting the occasion" only when he did not have firsthand data. Second, he did not make up rhetorical flights to match his own purposes but stuck to what was appropriate to the actual occasion.

We will come back to the issue of the speeches in Acts.[94] Here we want simply to point out that ancient authors testify to very high standards of historical reporting, standards that are not much different at all from those with which we are familiar. It is not fair, then, to conclude that a concern for the way things actually happened was foreign to ancient historians.

---

[93]Quoted from the translation of W. R. Paton, *Polybius: The Histories*, vol. 1, LCL (Cambridge: Harvard University Press, 1922). On these points, see esp. A. W. Mosley, "Historical Reporting in the Ancient World," *NTS* 12 (1965–66): 10–26; Hemer, *Book of Acts*, pp. 43–44, 75–79. See also W. C. van Unnik, "Luke's Second Book and the Rules of Hellenistic Historiography," in *Les Actes des Apôtres: Traditions, rédaction, théologie*, ed. J. Kremer, BETL 48 (Louvain: Louvain University Press, 1979), pp. 37–60.

[94]On Thucydides, see Hemer, *Book of Acts*, pp. 421–26.

Comparison Between Acts and Other Sources Luke, then, had available to him standards of historiography as rigorous as those in our day. The question is whether he successfully met them or not. Only a careful comparison of Luke with other ancient sources for the same data can answer this question. Because of the lack of parallels to Acts, we do not have available to us a great deal of material for comparison. But we can test Luke at three points: his knowledge of first-century society, politics, and geography; his reporting of events recorded by other ancient historians; and his accuracy in depicting the history and theology of Paul.

William Ramsay,[95] A. N. Sherwin-White,[96] and Colin Hemer[97] have demonstrated the accuracy of Luke's knowledge about detail after detail of Roman provincial government, first-century geographic boundaries, social and religious customs, navigational procedures,[98] and the like. This accuracy shows not only that Luke knew the first-century Roman world but that he was intimately acquainted with the specific areas and regions in which his narrative is set.

Luke does not often record events that are also mentioned by other historians, and when he does, he does not usually give us enough detail to enable us to make comparisons. In the book of Acts, Luke's mention of the death of Herod Agrippa I (12:19–23), of a serious famine in the middle 40s (11:27–30), of the edict of Claudius expelling Jews from Rome (18:2), of the replacement of the Judean procurator Felix with Festus, and of an Egyptian terrorist active in the middle 50s are all confirmed in secular historical sources. Only at two places ha: it been claimed that such a comparison finds Luke to be inaccurate. In 5:36–37, Luke has Gamaliel, the Jewish rabbi, mention the false messianic claims of a Theudas and, after him, of "Judas the Galilean." Josephus, however, also mentions a rebel named Theudas but places his activity in the years A.D. 44–46, about forty years after Judas and at least ten years after the setting of Acts 5 (*Ant.* 20.5.1). But Gamaliel may be referring to a different Theudas entirely, and in any case, as F. F. Bruce remarks, "where we have simply the one author's word against the other's, Luke is at least as likely to be right as Josephus."[99] The other problem is the Roman officer's reference to the "four thousand" men whom "the Egyptian" had led in revolt (Acts 21:38); Josephus, however, refers to thirty thousand (*Ant.* 20.8.6). But again, we should certainly prefer Luke to Josephus, especially since Josephus's numbers are often impossibly large.

The most serious challenge to Luke's accuracy involves a comparison between his story of Paul and the apostle's own accounts. We have examined some of the alleged discrepancies above and have concluded that there is no reason to drive a wedge between the Paul of Acts and the Paul of the Epistles. The alleged historical contradictions almost all involve matters on which Paul's own evidence is incomplete or ambiguous. This is not surprising, for, granted the nature and purpose of Paul's letters, it is not to be expected that the apostle would have gone into the historical detail that we find in Acts.

[95]Ramsay, *Bearing of Recent Discovery and St. Paul.*
[96]A. N. Sherwin-White, *Roman Society and Roman Law in the New Testament* (London: Oxford, 1963).
[97]Hemer, *Book of Acts.*
[98]On the shipwreck voyage, see James Smith, *The Voyage and Shipwreck of St. Paul,* 4th ed. (London: Longman, Brown, Green & Longmans, 1880; reprint, Grand Rapids: Baker, 1978).
[99]Bruce, *Acts of the Apostles,* p. 18.

Perhaps we should say something further here about one of the most famous problems in a comparison with Paul and Acts: the number of trips Paul made to Jerusalem after his conversion. Paul's own epistles mention only three such trips: three years after his conversion (Gal. 1:18); fourteen years after his conversion, or, perhaps, after his first visit (Gal. 2:1); and a projected visit at the time of the writing of Romans (15:24). In Acts, however, we are told of five visits: the postconversion visit (9:26), the famine-relief visit (11:27–30), the visit for the apostolic council (chap 15), a visit between the second and third missionary journeys (18:22), and a visit at the end of the third missionary journey (21:17). Now, it is clear that the first visit in Acts corresponds to the one Paul mentions in Galatians 1:18, and the last to the one mentioned in Romans. But it is common to accuse Luke of fabricating one or more of the other visits, particularly because, it is usually argued, the visit in Galatians 2:1 must be the visit for the apostolic council (Acts 15), leaving no place for the famine relief visit of Acts 11:27–30. But it is, in fact, more likely that Galatians 2:1 describes the famine-relief visit (see the introduction to Galatians, chap. 10 below). There would then be no contradiction between Paul and Acts, only a difference over the number of trips mentioned. But we have no reason to expect that Paul has told us of all his journeys to Jerusalem, so the problem disappears entirely. A similar situation prevails with respect to the other, less serious alleged discrepancies between the history of Paul in Acts and the details of his life furnished in his letters.

The Speeches of Acts Many scholars think that Luke is most untrustworthy in the speeches of Acts. They point out that the speeches are all in the same general style, a style that is found in the narrative portions of Acts. And they claim that the theology of the speeches is distinctively Lukan, rather than Petrine, Pauline, or whatever. It is therefore concluded that Luke has followed the Thucydidean model (see the quotation above) and put on the lips of his speakers the sentiments that he felt were appropriate for the occasion.[100]

Several responses to this accusation are necessary. First, as we noted above, Thucydides claims that only when he did not have information available did he not report what was actually said. Some other ancient historians were far more free in inventing speeches, but there is no a priori reason to compare Luke with them instead of with those who did seek accuracy in recording speeches (e.g., Polybius; see 12.25b.1, 4). Second, uniformity of style in the speeches means only that Luke has not given us verbatim reports but has paraphrased in his own words. This is likely in any case, since any of the speeches were probably translated by Luke from Aramaic. It is also likely that almost all the speeches Luke reports were much longer than the summaries he has given us. But paraphrases and summaries of speeches can still accurately convey their contents. Third, it is alleged there are differences in the theology of the speeches. Peter's speeches in Acts 2 and 3, for instance, contain formulations of Christology (e.g., 2:36) and eschatology (e.g., 3:19–20) that fit very well the early days of the church and that differ from

---

[100]See esp. Dibelius, "The Speeches of Acts and Ancient Historiography," in *Studies in the Acts of the Apostles*, pp. 138–85; Cadbury, "The Speeches in Acts," in *The Beginnings of Christianity*, 5:405–27; Ulrich Wilckens, *Die Missionsreden der Apostelgeschichte*, WMANT 5 (Neukirchen-Vluyn: Neukirchener, 1961); Eduard Schweizer, "Concerning the Speeches in Acts," in *Studies in Luke-Acts*, pp. 208–16.

the formulations found in the speeches of Paul in Acts 13 and 17.[101] In no case can it be shown that the theology or sentiments expressed in the speeches are inappropriate for the occasion or impossible for the speaker. On the positive side, the fidelity of Luke to his sources in the gospel (Mark, Q) suggests that he has been equally faithful to his sources in Acts. This argument is often contested. It is argued that Luke would have much greater respect for the words of Jesus than for the words of the apostles. But there is little to suggest that Luke would have made such a distinction. He claims to have the intention of instilling in his readers "the certainty of the things you have been taught" (Luke 1:4), and there is every reason to think that he has sought for accuracy in recording what people actually said, in Acts as much as in the gospel.[102]

Theological and Pastoral

As we argued above, Luke's primary purpose is to edify Christians by recounting how God's plan, coming to fulfillment in Jesus, had continued to unfold in the history of the early church. Perhaps Luke's most important contribution is precisely this careful linking of the apostolic proclamation of the Word of God with the word that Jesus both taught and fufilled. The "Word of God" thus binds together Luke's two volumes,[103] as the salvation that the angel first announced on the night of Jesus' birth on a Judean hillside (Luke 2:10–12) is brought finally to the capital of the Roman Empire. Luke thus presents "the things that have been fulfilled among us" (Luke 1:1) as a continuation of the salvific history of the Old Testament, showing how this history reaches its culmination in Christ and flows from him through the Spirit-led apostles into a new phase, the church as the eschatological people of God.[104] By doing so, Luke gave to Theophilus, and continues to give to every Christian who reads his two volumes, an assurance that faith is solidly grounded in the acts of God in history and that the message we believe is the same message sent from God.

While Luke makes clear the continuity in the message of salvation, he also reveals the progressive unfolding of new implications from that message. The historical veracity of Luke is seen in the way he makes clear the differences between the early Jerusalem community of believers and the later Gentile churches founded by Paul. The earliest Christians, Jews who believed that Jesus was the promised Messiah and that the messianic age had therefore dawned, continued to worship in the temple and were apparently loyal to the law and its institutions. Only by stages did the church move away from this Jewish orientation to a more universal orientation, as God made clear that he was doing a new work in which the law would no longer play a central role and in which Gentiles would share equally with the Jews in the blessings of God. A major contribution of Acts is the way in which the progress of this movement is portrayed, coming to a climax with

---

[101]See, on Christology, C. F. D. Moule, "The Christology of Acts," in *Studies in Luke-Acts*, pp. 159–85; and Richard N. Longenecker, *The Christology of Early Jewish Christianity* (London: SCM, 1970).
[102]See, again, on the speeches, Hemer, *Book of Acts*, pp. 415–26.
[103]Haenchen, *Acts*, p. 98; Longenecker, "Acts," p. 218.
[104]On this theme, see particularly Marshall, *Luke, Historian and Theologian*; idem, *Acts*, pp. 20–21; Gasque, "Recent Study," pp. 120–21.

Paul's announcement of judicial obduracy on the part of unbelieving Israel and the offer of salvation to the Gentiles (28:25–29).

Paul is the chief instrument through which this universalizing of the church takes place, and there is no doubt that he is Luke's hero.[105] Childs has suggested that Luke thus portrays a "canonical Paul," a figure who does not necessarily match the historical Paul but who can function as the representative apostle for a later age.[106] But it is questionable whether Luke presents Paul as a representative of the future. Rather, Luke suggests that Paul plays a decisive role in the foundation of a new period of salvation history, and in this sense, his significance is more for the past of the church than for its present or future. And as we have already argued, there is little reason to think that the apostle portrayed in Acts is different from the apostle as he really was.

BIBLIOGRAPHY.

Kurt **Aland** and Barbara **Aland**, *The Text of the New Testament*, rev. ed. (Grand Rapids: Eerdmans, 1989); David E. **Aune**, *The New Testament in Its Literary Environment*, Library of Early Christianity 8 (Philadelphia: Westminster, 1987); idem, *Studies in New Testament and Early Christian Literature* (Leiden: Brill, 1972); C. K. **Barrett**, *Luke the Historian in Recent Study* (London: Epworth, 1961); F. **Blass**, "Die Textüberlieferung in der Apostelgeschichte," *TSK* 67 (1894): 86–119; Craig L. **Blomberg**, "The Law in Luke-Acts," *JSNT* 22 (1984): 53–80; François **Bovon**, *Luke the Theologian: Thirty-three Years of Research* (1950–1983) (Allison Park, Pa.: Pickwick, 1987); Robert F. **Brawley**, *Luke-Acts and the Jews: Conflict, Apology, and Conciliation*, SBLMS 33 (Atlanta: SP, 1987); F. F. **Bruce**, *The Acts of the Apostles: The Greek Text, with Introduction and Commentary*, 2d ed. (Grand Rapids: Eerdmans, 1952); idem, "The Acts of the Apostles: Historical Record or Theological Reconstruction?" *ANRW* 25.3 (1985): 2569–2603; idem, *The Book of Acts*, rev. ed., NICNT (Grand Rapids: Eerdmans, 1988); idem, "Is the Paul of Acts the Real Paul?" *BJRL* 58 (1975–76): 282–305; idem, *Paul: Apostle of the Heart Set Free* (Grand Rapids: Eerdmans, 1977); F. C. **Burkitt**, *The Gospel History and Its Transmission*, 3d ed. (Edinburgh: T. & T. Clark, 1911); Henry J. **Cadbury**, *The Making of Luke-Acts* (New York: Macmillan, 1927); idem, *The Style and Literary Method of St. Luke*, HTS 6 (Cambridge: Harvard University Press, 1919); Richard **Cassidy** and Philip J. **Scharper**, eds., *Political Issues in Luke-Acts* (Maryknoll, N.Y.: Orbis, 1983); Albert C. **Clark**, *The Acts of the Apostles: A Critical Edition, with Introduction and Notes on Selected Passages* (Oxford: Clarendon, 1933); Hans **Conzelmann**, *Acts of the Apostles*, Hermeneia (Philadelphia: Fortress, 1987); idem, *The Theology of St. Luke* (New York: Harper & Row, 1961); Oscar **Cullmann**, *Christ and Time: The Primitive Christian Conception of Time and History* (Philadelphia: Westminster, 1950); Martin **Dibelius**, *Studies in the Acts of the Apostles*, ed. Heinrich Greeven (London: SCM, 1956); Jacques **Dupont**, *The Sources of the Acts* (New York: Herder & Herder, 1964); E. Earle **Ellis**, *Eschatology in Luke* (Philadelphia: Fortress, 1972); Eldon Jay **Epp**, *The Theological Tendency of Codex Bezae Cantabrigiensis in Acts*, SNTSMS 3 (Cambridge: Cambridge University Press, 1966); P. F. **Esler**, *Community and Gospel in Luke-Acts: The Social and Political Motivations of Lucan Theology* (Cambridge: Cambridge University Press, 1987); Floyd V. **Filson**, "The Journey Motif in

---

[105]E.g., Martin Hengel, *Between Jesus and Paul* (Philadelphia: Fortress, 1983), p. 2.
[106]Childs, pp. 225–27.

Luke-Acts," in *Apostolic History and the Gospel: Biblical and Historical Essays Presented to F. F. Bruce on His Sixtieth Birthday*, ed. W. Ward Gasque and Ralph P. Martin (Grand Rapids: Eerdmans, 1970), pp. 68–77; idem, *Three Crucial Decades: Studies in the Book of Acts* (London: Epworth, 1964); F. J. Foakes Jackson and Kirsopp Lake, eds., *The Beginnings of Christianity*, Part 1: *The Acts of the Apostles*, 5 vols. (London: Macmillan, 1920–33); Bertil Gärtner, *The Areopagus Speech and Natural Revelation*, ASNU 21 (Uppsala: Gleerup, 1955); W. Ward Gasque, "A Fruitful Field: Recent Study of the Acts of the Apostles," *Int* 42 (1988): 117–31; idem, *A History of the Criticism of the Acts of the Apostles*, BGBE 17 (Tübingen: Mohr, 1975); M. D. Goulder, *Type and History in Acts* (London: SPCK, 1964); Ernst Haenchen, *The Acts of the Apostles* (Philadelphia: Westminster, 1971); idem, "The Book of Acts as Source Material for the History of Earliest Christianity," in *Studies in Luke-Acts*, ed. Leander E. Keck and J. Louis Martyn (Nashville: Abingdon, 1966), pp. 258–78; Adolf Harnack, *The Acts of the Apostles* (London: Williams & Norgate, 1909); idem, *The Date of Acts and of the Synoptic Gospels* (New York: Putman, 1911); idem, *Luke the Physician* (New York: Putman, 1907); Everett F. Harrison, *Interpreting Acts* (Grand Rapids: Zondervan, 1986); Colin J. Hemer, *The Book of Acts in the Setting of Hellenistic History*, WUNT 2.49 (Tübingen: Mohr, 1989); Martin Hengel, *Acts and the History of Earliest Christianity* (Philadelphia: Fortress, 1979); idem, *Between Jesus and Paul: Studies in the Earliest History of Christianity* (Philadelphia: Fortress, 1983); A. J. B. Higgins, "The Prologue to Luke and the Kerygma of Acts," in *Apostolic History and the Gospel*, pp. 78–91; W. K. Hobart, *The Medical Language of St. Luke* (Dublin: Hodges, Figgis, 1882); Joachim Jeremias, "Untersuchungen zum Quellenproblem der Apostelgeschichte," *ZNW* 36 (1937): 205–21; Jacob Jervell, *Luke and the People of God* (Minneapolis: Augsburg, 1972); L. T. Johnson, *The Literary Function of Possessions in Luke-Acts*, SBLDS 39 (Missoula, Mont.: SP, 1977); Walter L. Liefeld, "Luke," in *EBC* 8; Richard N. Longenecker, "Acts," in *EBC* 9;. idem, *The Christology of Early Jewish Christianity* (London: SCM, 1970); idem, *Paul, Apostle of Liberty*, reprint ed. (Grand Rapids: Baker, 1976); Gerd Lüdemann, *Early Christianity According to the Traditions in Acts: A Commentary* (Minneapolis: Fortress, 1989); Robert Maddox, *Commentary on Acts* (Minneapolis: Fortress, 1989); idem, *The Purpose of Luke-Acts*, FRLANT 126 (Göttingen: Vandenhoeck & Ruprecht, 1982); I. Howard Marshall, *The Acts of the Apostles*, TNTC (Grand Rapids: Eerdmans, 1980); idem, *Luke: Historian and Theologian*, new, enlarged ed. (Grand Rapids: Zondervan, 1989); idem, "Luke and His 'Gospel,' " in *Das Evangelium und die Evangelien*, ed. Peter Stuhlmacher, WUNT 2.28 (Tübingen: Mohr, 1983), pp. 289–308; A. J. Mattill, Jr., "The Date and Purpose of Luke-Acts: Rackham Reconsidered," *CBQ* 40 (1978): 335–50; idem, *Luke and the Last Things* (Dillsboro, N.C.: Western North Carolina Press, 1979); idem, "The Purpose of Acts: Schneckenburger Reconsidered," in *Apostolic History and the Gospel*, pp. 108–22; Eduard Meyer, *Ursprung und Anfänge des Christentums*, 3 vols. (Stuttgart: J. G. Cotta, 1921–23); A. L. Moore, *The Parousia in the New Testament* (Leiden: Brill, 1966); A. W. Mosley, "Historical Reporting in the Ancient World," *NTS* 12 (1965–66): 10–26; C. F. D. Moule, "The Christology of Acts," in *Studies in Luke-Acts*, pp. 159–85; J. C. O'Neill, *The Theology of Acts in Its Historical Setting* (London: SPCK, 1961); Richard I. Pervo, *Profit with Delight: The Literary Genre of the Acts of the Apostles* (Philadelphia: Fortress, 1987); Eduard Plümacher, *Lukas als hellenistischer Schriftsteller*, SUNT 9 (Göttingen: Vandenhoeck & Ruprecht, 1972); Richard Belward Rackham, *The Acts of the Apostles*, WC (London: Methuen, 1901); William Ramsay, *The Bearing of Recent Discovery on the Trustworthiness of the New*

Testament, reprint ed. (Grand Rapids: Baker, 1983); idem, *St. Paul, the Traveller and the Roman Citizen* (London: Hodder & Stoughton, 1897); Vernon K. **Robbins**, "The We-Passages in Acts and Ancient Sea Voyages," *BR* 20 (1975): 5–18; J. A. T. **Robinson**, *Redating the New Testament* (Philadelphia: Westminster, 1976); Gerhard **Schneider**, *Die Apostelgeschichte*, 2 vols., HTKNT (Freiburg: Herder, 1980–82); Eduard **Schweizer**, "Concerning the Speeches in Acts," in *Studies in Luke-Acts*, pp. 208–16; M. A. **Seifrid**, "Jesus and the Law in Acts," *JSNT* 30 (1987): 39–57; A. N. **Sherwin-White**, *Roman Society and Roman Law in the New Testament* (London: Oxford, 1963); Joseph **Smith**, *The Voyage and Shipwreck of St. Paul*, 4th ed. (London: Longman, Brown, Green & Longmans, 1880); Charles H. **Talbert**, *Literary Patterns, Theological Themes, and the Genre of Luke-Acts* (Missoula, Mont.: SP, 1974); idem, *Luke and the Gnostics: An Examination of the Lucan Purpose* (Nashville: Abingdon, 1966); Charles Cutler **Torrey**, *The Composition and Date of Acts*, HTS 1 (Cambridge: Harvard University Press, 1916); C. H. **Turner**, "The Chronology of the New Testament," in *Dictionary of the Bible*, ed. James Hastings, 5 vols. (Edinburgh: T. & T. Clark, 1898–1904), 1:403–25; Joseph B. **Tyson**, ed., *Luke-Acts and the Jewish People: Eight Critical Perspectives* (Minneapolis: Augsburg, 1988); W. C. van **Unnik**, "The 'Book of Acts' the Confirmation of the Gospel," *NovT* 4 (1960): 26–59; idem, "Luke-Acts, a Storm Center in Contemporary Scholarship," in *Studies in Luke-Acts*, pp. 15–32; idem, "Luke's Second Book and the Rules of Hellenistic Historiography," in *Les Actes des Apôtres: Traditions, rédaction, théologie*, ed. J. Kremer, BETL 48 (Louvain: Louvain University Press, 1979); Philipp **Vielhauer**, "On the 'Paulinism' of Acts," in *Studies in Luke-Acts*, pp. 33–50; Paul W. **Walaskay**, *"And So We Came to Rome": The Political Perspective of St. Luke*, SNTSMS 49 (Cambridge: Cambridge University Press, 1983); Johannes **Weiss**, *Absicht und literarischer Charakter der Apostelgeschichte* (Marburg: Vandenhoeck & Ruprecht, 1897); Alfred **Wikenhauser**, *Die Apostelgeschichte und ihr Geschichtswert*, NTAbh 8.3–5 (Münster: Aschendorff, 1921); Ulrich **Wilckens**, "Interpreting Luke-Acts in a Period of Existentialist Theology," in *Studies in Luke-Acts*, pp. 60–83; idem, *Die Missionsreden der Apostelgeschichte: Form- und Traditionsgeschichtliche Untersuchungen*, 2d ed., WMANT 5 (Neukirchen-Vluyn: Neukirchener, 1961); Max **Wilcox**, *The Semitisms of Acts* (Oxford: Clarendon, 1965); David John **Williams**, *Acts* (San Francisco: Harper & Row, 1985); S. G. **Wilson**, *Luke and the Law*, SNTSMS 50 (Cambridge: Cambridge University Press, 1983); Eduard **Zeller**, *The Contents and Origin of the Acts of the Apostles Critically Investigated*, 2 vols. (London: Williams & Norgate, 1875–76).

7

paul: the man and his letters

Paul is so significant a figure in the New Testament and in the church's history that he has been called the second founder of Christianity. This, of course, is not true, for it ignores the continuity between Jesus and Paul and diminishes unfairly the contributions of men such as Peter, John, and Luke. But there is no question that Paul played a vital role in the growth and establishment of the church and in the interpretation and application of God's grace in Christ. And Paul continues to minister to us today through the thirteen epistles of his that have become part of the canon of the New Testament. These epistles make up almost one-fourth of the New Testament, putting Paul just behind Luke in the percentage of the New Testament written by a single individual. And if one adds the sixteen chapters of Acts (13–28) that are almost entirely devoted to Paul, Paul figures in almost one-third of the New Testament.

PAUL'S BACKGROUND

Who was this man Paul? Exploring his background will help us to understand him better and to interpret his words more accurately. Paul himself provides a rough outline of his own background, but in his epistles this material is scattered. The basic historical details are conveniently grouped in the speeches Paul gave (as reported by Luke) to a hostile crowd of Jews on the steps of the temple (Acts 22:1–21) and to King Agrippa II and the Roman procurator Festus (Acts 26:2–23). (On the historical value of such material in Acts, see below on the chronology of Pauls's missionary career, and chap. 6 above.)

"Born in Tarsus of Cilicia" (Acts 22:3)

Tarsus was the major city in Cilicia, a region in the extreme southeastern part of Asia Minor.[1] In Paul's day, the city was the capital of the Roman province Syria-Cilicia (see Gal. 1:21). It was prosperous, privileged (it was exempt from Roman

---

[1] On Tarsus generally, see William M. Ramsay, *The Cities of St. Paul: Their Influence on His Life and Thought* (London: Hodder & Stoughton, 1907), pp. 85–244; Colin J. Hemer, "Tarsus," in *ISBE* 4:734–36.

taxation), and cultured, being famous for its schools.[2] Not only was Paul born in Tarsus, he was a citizen of this "no ordinary city" (Acts 21:39).

More important, however, was the fact that Paul was a citizen of Rome. The Romans did not confer citizenship on just anyone; only a small percentage of people who lived within the Roman Empire possessed this privilege. Paul's Roman citizenship was inherited from his family (Paul claims, "I was born a citizen" [Acts 22:28]), perhaps because of some deed of service performed by his father or grandfather for the Romans.[3] However achieved, Paul's Roman citizenship was an important and providential qualification for his role as missionary to the Roman Empire. It enabled him to escape detainment when his preaching brought disfavor (Acts 16:37–39), to avoid punishment (Acts 22:23– 29), and to plead his case before the emperor's court in Rome (Acts 25:10–12).

As a Roman citizen, Paul had three names: a first name (*praenomen*), family name (*nomen*), and surname (*cognomen*). Of these, we know only his *cognomen*, Παῦλος (*Paulos*). Paul's native town may also have led him into his trade. A local product, *cilicium*, was used to make tents, and Luke tells us that Paul was himself a "tentmaker" (Acts 18:3).[4] This is presumably the trade that Paul pursued during his missionary work in order not to burden the churches with his support (e.g., 1 Thess. 2:9).

"Brought up in this city" (Acts 22:3)

This phrase in Paul's speech on the temple steps has given rise to a debate about whether Paul's early years were spent in Tarsus or Jerusalem. The issue has attracted so much attention because it figures in the debate about Paul's thought world: was he indebted more to the Greek world or to the Jewish world for his teaching? The contribution of this phrase to the debate depends on two issues. First, does "this city" refer to the city in which Paul is speaking (Jerusalem) or to the city he has just mentioned (Tarsus)? Nigel Turner has argued for the latter,[5] but the former is more likely, considering the setting of the speech. The second issue is the punctuation of the verse, the two possibilities being clearly represented in the NIV and RSV:

NIV: I am a Jew, born in Tarsus of Cilicia, but brought up in this city. Under Gamaliel I was thoroughly trained in the law of our fathers. . . .

RSV: I am a Jew, born at Tarsus in Cilicia, but brought up in this city at the feet of Gamaliel, educated according to the strict manner of the law of our fathers. . . .

The NIV, by putting a period after "this city," separates "brought up" from "under Gamaliel," and this suggests that "brought up" refers to Paul's parental nurturing as a young child. Paul would then be implying that, although born in Tarsus, he was raised in Jerusalem.[6] The RSV rendering, on the other hand, by

---

[2]Strabo, *Geog.* 14.5.14.

[3]F. F. Bruce, *Paul: Apostle of the Heart Set Free* (Grand Rapids: Eerdmans, 1977), pp. 37–38.

[4]This is probably the meaning of the word σκηνοποιοί (*skēnopoioi*), although Ronald F. Hock has argued that it means simply "leatherworker" (*The Social Context of Paul's Ministry* [Philadelphia: Fortress, 1980]).

[5]Nigel Turner, *Grammatical Insights into the New Testament* (Edinburgh: T. & T. Clark, 1965), pp. 83–84.

[6]See particularly W. C. van Unnik, *Tarsus or Jerusalem: The City of Paul's Youth* (London: Epworth, 1962).

linking "brought up" with "at the feet of Gamaliel," requires that "brought up" refer to Paul's rabbinic education, a process that would have begun in his early teens. On this interpretation of the verse, Paul would perhaps be suggesting that he was brought up in Tarsus, moving to Jerusalem only when he went away to school.[7]

But the punctuation represented by the NIV should probably be adopted. The three-stage sequence—born/brought up/educated—was a natural autobiographical pattern. Nevertheless, this does not solve the matter, nor is it the decisive point in the debate about Paul's background. On the one hand, Paul would have had ample opportunity to pick up Hellenistic ideas during his education in Jerusalem (Hellenism was by no means unknown in Jerusalem) or during his decade-long ministry in Tarsus after his conversion. On the other hand, even if Paul did spend the first ten or so years of his life in Tarsus, he need not have been imbued with Hellenistic ideas. Paul himself stresses that he was a "Hebrew of Hebrews" (Phil. 3:5), apparently meaning that both his parents and he himself were, linguistically and culturally, Jewish and Palestinian in their orientation (see 2 Cor. 11:22, and the contrast between Hebrew and Hellenist in Acts 6:1). The home in which he was raised, whether located in Tarsus or in Jerusalem, was one in which Aramaic was spoken and in which traditional Palestinian Jewish customs were preserved.[8] So to the extent that Paul's background influenced his theology, that influence was mainly Palestinian and Jewish. But having said this, we must also be careful not to erect rigid distinctions between "Hellenistic" and "Palestinian" or "Hellenistic" and "Jewish." That there was a difference is clearly implied by Paul's own claims. But that the difference can be exaggerated has been revealed by the extent to which Hellenistic ideas had penetrated Palestine and Judaism in the first century.[9] "In antiquity ideas did not flow in pipes,"[10] and Paul's world was one in which he was exposed to many different influences and combinations of influences.

"Thoroughly trained in the law of our Fathers ... zealous for God" (Acts 22:3)

Not only was Paul by birth a "Hebrew of Hebrews," but as he never tired of emphasizing (see also Acts 26:5; Gal. 1:14; Phil. 3:5–6), he was by conviction a serious and zealous follower of Judaism, a member of its "strictest sect" (Acts 26:5), the Pharisees. Although scholars disagree considerably over many aspects of first-century Pharisaism, several things are relatively clear. They paid a great deal of attention to the "oral law," "the traditions of the elders" (Mark 7:3 par.), a body of regulations designed to interpret and supplement the written, Mosaic law. They had a number of fundamental disagreements with the Sadducees, stemming from the Pharisees' greater willingness to accept doctrines not clearly stated in the Pentateuch (e.g., the resurrection of the body; see Acts 23:6–8). They exercised great influence over the common people, who respected their zeal for their beliefs

---

[7]E.g., Richard N. Longenecker, *Paul, Apostle of Liberty*, reprint ed. (Grand Rapids: Baker, 1976), pp. 25–27.
[8]Ibid., pp. 21–64; Bruce, *Paul: Apostle of the Heart Set Free*, p. 42.
[9]See esp. Martin Hengel, *Judaism and Hellenism*, 2 vols. (Philadelphia: Fortress, 1974).
[10]Leander E. Keck, *Paul and His Letters*, Proclamation Commentaries (Philadelphia: Fortress, 1979), p. 11.

and their desire to sanctify all aspects of life.[11] Paul was trained under Gamaliel I (see Acts 26:3), a Pharisee of the school of Hillel. Hillel and his followers were generally known for their liberality, an attitude revealed in Gamaliel's advice to the Sanhedrin about the early church (Acts 5:34–39). Paul seems to have differed from his teacher at this point. By his own repeated admission, Paul's zeal for Judaism led him to persecute the early Christian movement (e.g., Acts 22:4a; 26:9–11; Gal. 1:13; Phil. 3:6). But Paul may not, after all, have differed much from his teacher. Gamaliel's advice is given before the Stephen incident revealed the extent to which at least some of the Christians were willing to do without the law and the temple. It may very well have been this development that turned Paul, and perhaps other Pharisees, against the fledging Christian movement.[12]

"As I came near Damascus" (Acts 22:6)

The persecutor of Christians was turned into the foremost preacher of Christ by a sudden confrontation with the risen Jesus on the road to Damascus. Paul's Damascus-road experience is described once by Luke (Acts 9:3–6), twice by Paul in Acts (22:6–11 and 26:12–15) and once by Paul in his epistles (Gal. 1:15–16). In addition to these clear descriptions, other allusions to this event are probably to be found in many places in Paul.[13] Several scholars have suggested that the event and its implications played a basic role in the formation of much of Paul's theology.[14] Paul's encounter with Christ was no merely psychological experience, nor was it even a divinely given vision. Paul's companions saw the blaze of light, although they did not see Jesus himself (see Acts 9:7 with 22:9), and heard, but did not understand, the voice (cf. Acts 9:7 with 22:9).[15] Moreover, Paul makes clear that this appearance to him of the resurrected Jesus was fully on a par with the appearances to Peter and the others in the days between Jesus' resurrection and ascension (1 Cor.15:5–8; see also 9:1).

The "revelation" (ἀποκάλυψις [apokalypsis]) of Christ to Paul came without any preparation. Paul gives no hint that before this point he was at all dissatisfied with his Jewish convictions or searching for a deeper experience of God. The texts that have sometimes been thought to indicate such a preparatory period are better interpreted otherwise. When Paul is warned by the heavenly voice that "it is hard for you to kick against the goads" (Acts 26:14), the meaning is not that Paul has been resisting the Spirit's wooing but that he should not now resist the will of God expressed in the revelation from heaven.[16] Neither does Romans 7:14–25

---

[11]For a succinct orientation to the discussion, see R. J. Wyatt, "Pharisees," in ISBE 3:822–29.
[12]See Longenecker, Paul, pp. 33–37.
[13]Seyoon Kim, The Origin of Paul's Gospel (Tübingen: Mohr, 1981), pp. 3–31.
[14]Especially Kim, Origin, and Christian Dietzfelbinger, Die Berufung des Paulus als Ursprung seiner Theologie, WMANT 58 (Neukirchen-Vluyn: Neukirchener, 1985).
[15]This difference is probably signaled by the shift from the genitive τῆς φωνῆς (tēs phōnēs, "the sound" [NIV]) in 9:7 to the accusative τὴν φωνήν (tēn phōnēn, "the voice" [NIV]) in 22:9, although the significance of the change is debated (see Maxmillian Zerwick, Biblical Greek [Rome: Pontifical Biblical Institute, 1963], §69; C. F. D. Moule, An Idiom Book of New Testament Greek [Cambridge: Cambridge University Press, 1971], p. 36).
[16]See Johannes Munck, Paul and the Salvation of Mankind (London: SCM, 1959), pp. 20–21. "Kicking against the goads" was a popular proverb meaning to resist the Deity (see Longenecker, Paul, pp. 98–101).

refer to a preconversion psychological struggle.[17] Rather, the descriptions of the experience in Acts, as well as Paul's allusions to it in Philippians 3:3–11, suggest a sudden and dramatic turn from zealous Jew and persecutor of the church to a follower of Jesus.

The Damascus-road encounter turned Paul into more than a follower of Jesus: it turned him into a preacher of Jesus. Although the relationship between the two is not stated the same way in all the accounts, each one makes clear that Paul's conversion was also a call to ministry (Acts 9:15; 22:15; 26:15–18 and Gal. 1:16). Indeed, some have gone so far as to argue that this revelation was properly a "call" experience and not a "conversion" experience at all.[18] But whatever the continuity between Judaism and Christianity, the New Testament makes clear that the two are distinct, that only within Christianity is salvation found. The change from one to the other is, then, appropriately called a conversion. For Paul, however, conversion and call were bound up together. As Johannes Munck has emphasized, Paul viewed himself as a peculiar instrument in God's hands, one who, like the Old Testament prophets Isaiah and Jeremiah, would have an important role to play in salvation history.[19] It is significant in this light that, whereas ministry to Jews is certainly included in Paul's call (see Acts 9:15), Paul himself often emphasizes that his call was particularly a call to preach to Gentiles (Gal. 1:16; 1 Thess. 2:4; Rom. 1:1, 5; 15:15–16). The mission of carrying the gospel to the Gentiles was fundamental to Paul's call and to his being chosen as a vessel for God's use.

PAUL'S AUTHORITY AND THE SOURCES FOR HIS THOUGHT

Paul's Authority

Fundamental to Paul's ministry was his consciousness of being an apostle. Like the other apostles, he had seen the Lord (1 Cor. 9:1), and the Lord himself, not any human being, had called Paul to his apostleship (e.g., Gal. 1:1). Because Paul was an apostle by God's call, he could claim an authority equal to that of Peter, James, John, and the rest of the twelve—those whom some of Paul's opponents had labeled "super-apostles" (2 Cor. 11:5). Paul writes from the consciousness of this apostolic authority in every one of his letters. True, Paul can sometimes distinguish between his teaching and the teaching of the Lord (e.g., 1 Cor. 7:6, 10, 12; 2 Cor. 11:17), and nowhere does Paul make it clear that he thought his letters to be inspired Scripture. Nevertheless, in differentiating his teaching from the Lord's, Paul does not suggest that his carries any less authority. And, while not perhaps conscious of writing inspired Scripture, Paul's apostolic stance enables him to interpret with sovereign freedom the Old Testament Scriptures and to make demands on his people that he considered to be as binding as anything in Scripture.

---

[17]Paul is probably referring either to his experience as a regenerate person or to his experience as a Jew under the law, as typical of all Jews under the law.

[18]E.g., Krister Stendahl, *Paul Among Jews and Gentiles, and Other Essays* (Philadelphia: Fortress, 1976), pp. 7–12.

[19]Munck, *Paul*, pp. 24–33.

The Sources of Paul's Teaching

Revelation Versus Tradition Any discussion of the sources to which Paul is indebted for his teaching must reckon with Paul's claim that his gospel came "by revelation from Jesus Christ"(δἰ ἀποκαλύψεως Ἰησοῦ Χριστοῦ [di' apokalypseōs Iēsou Christou], Gal. 1:12). This "revelation" refers to the appearance of Christ to Paul on the Damascus road (see 1:16). Paul makes clear that the gospel he had taught the Galatians came through this means, *not* through any human being. Paul's was a supernatural gospel, and we must never forget this claim. Without taking anything away from this point, however, we must recognize that Paul on other occasions indicates his indebtedness to Christians before him for his teaching. In 1 Corinthians 15:1–3, for instance, Paul asserts of the gospel that he preached to the Corinthians, "what I received [παρέλαβον (parelabon)] I passed on [παρέδωκα (paredōka)] to you. " The word Paul uses here, παραλαμβάνω (paralambanō, "receive"), corresponds to language that the rabbis used to describe their transmission of traditions. What Paul seems to be asserting is that elements of his gospel teaching, such as the truth of Christ's death, burial, and resurrection (1 Cor. 15:3–5), were handed down to him by other people.

Some have found a contradiction in these claims of Paul, but a resolution is not hard to find. We need to distinguish between essence and form. The *essence* of the gospel, that Jesus of Nazareth was truly the Son of God, was revealed to Paul in one life-changing moment on the Damascus road. And this truth carried far-reaching implications. For one thing, those Christians whom Paul had been persecuting must be right after all. For another, now that Messiah had come, the law could no longer be at the center of God's purposes. Especially was this true because the law itself pronounced a curse upon Jesus, since he had been "hung on a tree" (see Gal. 3:13 and Deut. 21:23). So Paul was led to conclude that the law could no longer be imposed as a condition of membership upon the people of God (see Galatians).[20] The *form* of the gospel, however, including the historical undergirding of the gospel events, certain phraseology used to express the new truth, and doubtless many other things, were passed on to Paul by those before him.[21]

Early Christian Traditions We have no means of identifying just what early Christian traditions about Jesus were available to Paul, although we could certainly assume that many of the historical facts and theological emphases found in the speeches of Acts 1–8 were passed on to Paul by Peter and by other believers during Paul's fifteen-day stay with him three years after his conversion (Gal. 1:18). First Corinthians 15:3ff., as we have seen, uses language that refers to the receiving and passing on of traditions.

Paul's letters themselves may, however, provide us with more information about the traditions he has used. Through stylistic and theological analysis, it is argued,

---

[20]See Peter Stuhlmacher, " 'The End of the Law': On the Origin and Beginnings of Pauline Theology," in *Reconciliation, Law, and Righteousness: Essays on Biblical Theology* (Philadelphia: Fortress, 1986), pp. 134–54.

[21]See the discussion, e.g., in F. F. Bruce, *Tradition Old and New* (Grand Rapids: Zondervan, 1970); George Eldon Ladd, *A Theology of the New Testament* (Grand Rapids: Eerdmans, 1974), pp. 386–94; Kim, *Origin*, pp. 67–70.

we can identify within Paul's letters various early Christian creedal formulations, hymns, and traditional catechetical material. Unusual vocabulary, rhythmic and poetic patterns, and un-Pauline theological emphases are the criteria used to identify early Christian traditions that Paul may have quoted.[22] Philippians 2:6–11, to cite one of the most famous of these alleged quotations, has several unusual words (e.g., ἁρπαγμός [*harpagmos*], "snatching," v. 6), falls into lines of similar length that are capable of being arranged in a hymnic pattern, and introduces Christological ideas not found in Paul elsewhere.[23]

Philippians 2:6–11 is probably, then, an early Christian hymn that Paul has quoted (though it is just possible that Paul himself is its author). It is also probable that there are other similar quotations in the Pauline letters. It would be quite natural for Paul, both to build common ground with his readers and to show his agreement with the early Christian teaching generally, to quote from such sources—just as a preacher today will quote from early Christian creeds, hymns, and the like. But we must register two cautions with respect to these sources. First, we must be careful not to overemphasize our ability to identify such passages. The line between quotation of a preexisting tradition and the use of traditional language in one's own composition is difficult, and often impossible, to draw. Second, we must be careful not to use inevitably speculative data about these traditions, such as the place of origin or theological tendency, to draw exegetical and theological conclusions. We simply do not know enough to justify such procedures.

The Earthly Jesus Behind the early Christian tradition lay the teaching of Jesus himself. To what extent did the earthly Jesus constitute a source for Paul's teaching? Some have suggested that he contributed nothing at all. The most famous advocate of this view is Rudolf Bultmann, who interprets 2 Corinthians 5:16 to mean that Paul had no interest in the "Jesus of history."[24] Clearly this is not what the verse means. Rather, Paul is asserting that he no longer views Christ "from a worldly point of view." Still, the fact remains that Paul only rarely mentions an event (other than Jesus' death and resurrection) from Jesus' ministry and equally rarely quotes from Jesus' teaching. This does not always mean, however, that Paul's teaching is not influenced by Jesus' teaching. A good case can be made, for instance, for thinking that Paul's eschatological teaching in 1 Thessalonians 4–5 and 2 Thessalonians 2 depends to some extent on the Olivet discourse (Mark 13 par.).[25] It has long been recognized that the ethical teaching of Romans 12 has many similarities to the Sermon on the Mount. Paul, then, certainly knew and used more of the teaching of Jesus than a mere count of

---

[22]A good overview is found in Martin 2:248–75.

[23]The most comprehensive recent treatment in English is Ralph P. Martin, *Carmen Christi: Philippians 2:5–11 in Recent Interpretation and in the Setting of Early Christian Worship*, rev. ed. (Grand Rapids: Eerdmans, 1983). Considerably superior in its careful exegesis and accurate interpretation is the important essay by N. T. Wright, "ἁρπαγμός and the Meaning of Philippians 2:5–11," *JTS* 37 (1987): 321–52.

[24]Rudolf Bultmann, "The Significance of the Historical Jesus for the Theology of Paul," in *Faith and Understanding* (New York: Harper & Row, 1969), p. 241.

[25]See David Wenham, *The Rediscovery of Jesus' Eschatological Discourse*, in GP 4:372–73; idem, "Paul's Use of the Jesus Tradition: Three Samples," in GP 5:7–37.

his quotations suggests.[26] More important, essential aspects of Paul's theology can be shown to be compatible with, and perhaps dependent on, Jesus' teaching.[27]

The Old Testament That Paul was heavily indebted to the Old Testament in the formulation of his teaching is revealed by the more than ninety quotations from the Old Testament in his letters.[28] Perhaps even more important, however, are the many allusions to the Old Testament—places where Paul uses Old Testament language without clearly quoting—and the inestimable degree to which the Old Testament has formed Paul's conceptual world. Paul, of course, uses the Old Testament selectively and interprets it in a definite context, reading it through the lens of Jesus' fulfillment of "the Law and the Prophets."

The Greek World Nineteenth-century scholars frequently read Paul against the background of their own considerable knowledge of classical Greek literature and philosophy. Paul's indebtedness to the Greek world in which he grew up and in which he worked was assumed. Early in the twentieth century, the focus was narrowed, as the history-of-religions school stressed Paul's dependence on the Hellenistic mystery religions. These religions, which were very popular in Paul's day, stressed one's ability to be joined in a mystic relationship with a deity, secret mystery rites, and frequently a religious enthusiasm or ecstasy. Scholars such as Richard Reitzenstein, Wilhelm Bousset, and Rudolf Bultmann found many of these features in the letters of Paul and concluded that, to varying degrees, Paul had cast his teaching of Christ into the categories provided by these religions.[29] In its most extreme form, Paul was thought to have drastically transformed the simple, ethically oriented message of Jesus into a speculative and mystical religion.

Wherever he was raised (see above), Paul must have known the Greek world well, and it is to be expected that he would use the language of that world to express the significance of Christ and even borrow its concepts where they could help illuminate aspects of the gospel. But it is unlikely that we should consider the Greek world a source for Paul's teaching in the strict sense. It sometimes provided the clothing, but rarely, if ever, the body of teaching that was clothed. Particularly unlikely is the hypothesis that Paul borrowed from the mystery religions.[30] The parallels are simply not very close, and every one of the alleged cases of borrowing can be explained more satisfactorily in other terms.[31]

---

[26]Arnold Resch counts 1,158 allusions to Jesus' teaching in Paul (*Der Paulinismus und die Logia Jesu*, TU 27 [Leipzig: Akademie, 1904]). The number is greatly exaggerated but helps put the matter in perspective.

[27]See, e.g., F. F. Bruce, *Jesus and Paul* (Grand Rapids: Baker, 1974), pp. 55–67.

[28]The exact number depends on how "quotation" is defined. E. Earle Ellis gives a figure of ninety-three (*Paul's Use of the Old Testament*, reprint ed. [Grand Rapids: Baker, 1981], p. 11).

[29]The most famous name in this history-of-religions school is Richard Reitzenstein (*Hellenistic Mystery Religions: Their Basic Ideas and Significance* [ET Pittsburgh: Pickwick, 1978]; the final edition of the German original is dated 1927). See also Wilhelm Bousset, *Kyrios Christos*, reprint ed. (Nashville: Abingdon, 1970); Rudolf Bultmann (e.g., *Theology of the New Testament*, 2 vols. [New York: Charles Scribner's Sons, 1951–55], 1:187–352).

[30]A classic on this point is J. Gresham Machen, *The Origin of Paul's Religion* (London: Hodder & Stoughton, 1921). See also H. A. A. Kennedy, *St. Paul and the Mystery Religions* (London: Hodder & Stoughton, 1913).

[31]To cite only one example, see the study of Romans 6 by Günter Wagner, *Pauline Baptism and the Pagan Mysteries* (Edinburgh: Oliver & Boyd, 1967).

Judaism In reaction against the tendency to interpret Paul against the Greek or Hellenistic world, many scholars have insisted that Paul's world was a Jewish one and that Judaism must have exerted the most influence on his teaching. C. G. Montefiore suggests that the Hellenistic Judaism of Paul's childhood in Tarsus was a key factor.[32] (Even if Paul was not raised in Tarsus, he spent most of his adult life in the Diaspora.) Albert Schweitzer thinks that apocalyptic Judaism is the key to Paul's teaching,[33] while W. D. Davies stresses rabbinic Judaism and Pharisaism.[34] Contemporary scholars are less willing than before to make clear-cut distinctions between, say, Palestinian Judaism and Hellenistic Judaism, or between apocalyptic Judaism and Pharisaic Judaism. Without justifying such distinctions when they are made absolute, we may say that it is now generally agreed that Paul's own thought world was decisively formed by his Jewish upbringing. Paul's own claim to be a "Hebrew of the Hebrews" and a Pharisee must be allowed decisive weight on this matter. Paul's basic concepts are drawn, as we have seen, from the Old Testament, and Paul had learned the Old Testament in the context of the Judaism of his day. Paul's conversion, however, forced upon him a thoroughgoing reappraisal of his beliefs; the debt his teaching undoubtedly has to Judaism is the result of a deliberate choice and not of an unconscious carrying over of his Judaism into his new faith.

PAUL'S MISSIONARY CAREER AND ITS CHRONOLOGY

The Problem of Sources

While referring occasionally to his early life, past travels, and future plans, Paul's letters do not provide us with the kind of information necessary to reconstruct a "life of Paul." This is no more than what should be expected. Paul wrote his letters to deal with specific issues, and only where it was important to those issues, or where Paul was requesting prayer for a certain situation, does he mention his own history. Traditionally, then, an outline of Paul's missionary career has been built on the more detailed and sequential data provided by Acts, with Paul's letters fit into the general scheme given by Luke. But several scholars contest the legitimacy of such an approach. They argue that the Pauline letters provide the primary data for reconstructing a life of Paul and that Acts, because its historical accuracy is questionable, should be used only in those specific places where its accuracy can be validated or where it corroborates data attained from a study of the letters.[35]

Outlines of Paul's career and its chronology constructed on the basis of these constraints look quite different from traditional models. There are two particular points at which most revisionist models disagree with the usual chronology developed on the basis of Acts. The first is the placement of the apostolic council. Luke places it before the second missionary journey, but the data of the Epistles, it is argued, suggest that the council followed the second journey. The second major

---

[32]C. G. Montefiore, *Judaism and St. Paul* (London: Goschen, 1914).

[33]Albert Schweitzer, *The Mysticism of Paul the Apostle* (New York: H. Holt, 1931).

[34]W. D. Davies, *Paul and Rabbinic Judaism*, 4th ed. (Philadelphia: Fortress, 1980).

[35]See esp. John Knox, *Chapters in a Life of Paul* (London: Adam & Charles Black, 1954), pp. 13–43; Robert Jewett, *A Chronology of Paul's Life* (Philadelphia: Fortress, 1979), pp. 7–24; Gerd Lüdemann, *Paul, Apostle to the Gentiles: Studies in Chronology* (Philadelphia: Fortress, 1984), pp. 21–29.

area of difference is the number of visits Paul made to Jerusalem. The letters of Paul refer to only three: three years after Paul's conversion, the convening of the apostolic council, and the occasion when he delivered the collection money at the end of the third missionary journey. The two additional visits mentioned in Acts—the famine-relief visit of 11:27–30 and the visit between the second and third missionary journeys in 18:22—are therefore deemed to be unhistorical. Some revisionist schemes differ at many more points from the traditional outline of Paul's life based on the sequence of Acts.[36]

It is questionable, however, whether such revisions are helpful, let alone necessary. Paul's own writings are indeed the primary material for a study of his life. But since his own writings simply do not provide the necessary data for the piecing together of a chronology of his life, it is entirely legitimate to turn to other sources. Acts must be considered to be a reliable source of such data. It was written, as we have argued (see chap. 6 above), by Luke, a companion of Paul, and we can expect his information about the apostle's movements to be quite good. Moreover, we have found good reason to respect Luke's historical accuracy. This does not mean that we should prefer Acts to Paul's letters when they differ. But many of the differences that have been found are the product of certain specific interpretations that are by no means the only ones possible. A careful comparison of Paul's statements about his movements with the movements of Paul recorded in Acts reveals an amazing degree of correspondence.[37] The relegation of Acts to a secondary status in the construction of a life of Paul is simply not legitimate. We will therefore use Acts as a key source in the following sketch of Paul's missionary career and its chronology. Having established a relative sequence of movements based on both Acts and the Epistles, we will then work toward an absolute chronology.

An Outline of Paul's Missionary Career

From Paul's Conversion to the First Missionary Journey The decisive data in establishing a relative chronology for this earlier period come from Galatians 1:13–2:10. In this passage, Paul recounts his relationship with the Jerusalem apostles in order to demonstrate that his apostolic authority does not derive from them. He tells us that he first visited Jerusalem, as a Christian, three years after his conversion to "get acquainted with" Peter (1:18), and then visited Jerusalem again "fourteen years later" (2:1) to set before the Jerusalem apostles the gospel that he was preaching among the Gentiles. There are two key issues raised by this sequence: To which visits in Acts do the two visits Paul mentions here correspond? And how are we to understand the sequence of "after three years" and "fourteen years later"?

The first Jerusalem visit Paul mentions is clearly the same as the one Luke

---

[36]Lüdemann, for instance, relying a great deal on Paul's statements about the collection and the theology expressed in the letters, puts Paul's founding visit to the churches of Macedonia (e.g., Thessalonica) very early, in the early or middle 40s and has Paul returning to Jerusalem with the collection as early as A.D. 52 (see *Paul*, pp. 262–63). On the issue of the Jerusalem visits and the apostolic council, see also Charles Buck and Greer Taylor, *Saint Paul: A Study of the Development of His Thought* (New York: Charles Scribner's Sons, 1969), pp. 7–8.

[37]See T. H. Campbell, "Paul's 'Missionary Journeys' As Reflected in His Letters," *JBL* 74 (1955): 80–87.

mentions in Acts 9:26–30. But is the visit of Galatians 2:1 to be identified with the famine-relief visit of Acts 11:27–30 or with the apostolic-council visit of Acts 15? Many scholars have argued for the latter equation. It is pointed out that Paul's characterization of this visit as involving questions about his gospel to the Gentiles fits the circumstances of the council of Acts 15. But there are details in Paul's description that do not correspond very well with the Acts 15 situation, and the circumstances of the letter to the Galatians suggest that it was written *before* the apostolic council (see chap. 10 below). This would require that Galatians 2:1 refer to the famine-relief visit of Acts 11:27–30.

Assuming these identifications, the specific temporal indicators Paul gives in this passage should be invaluable in constructing a relative chronology of Paul's life. But these indicators are not as clear as might at first seem. It is generally agreed that the "three years" in Galatians 1:18 is the interval between Paul's conversion (1:15–16) and his first Jerusalem visit.[38] But do the "fourteen years" in 2:1 also begin with Paul's conversion, or do they begin with his first Jerusalem visit?[39] The former interpretation results in sequence A, the second in sequence B (see fig. 4).

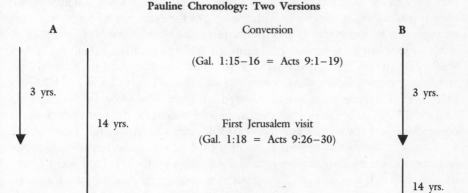

Figure 4
Pauline Chronology: Two Versions

A	Conversion	B
	(Gal. 1:15–16 = Acts 9:1–19)	
3 yrs.		3 yrs.
14 yrs.	First Jerusalem visit	
	(Gal. 1:18 = Acts 9:26–30)	
		14 yrs.
	Second Jerusalem visit	
	(Gal. 2:1–10 = Acts 11:27–30)	
14 years	Total time	17 years

For two reasons, sequence A should probably be preferred. First, the prominence of Paul's conversion in Galatians 1 suggests that he is thinking of this event in his temporal indications. Second, this sequence fits better with other chronological indications that we will note below.

There is one more issue that must be decided: whether Paul is here counting years inclusively or exclusively. The exclusive method is the one with which we are familiar: the interval between event X and event Y is the interval *between* the years

---

[38]Lüdemann, however, takes the "three years" to refer back to what immediately precedes: Paul's return to Damascus (1:17) (*Paul*, p. 63).

[39]Here, also, Lüdemann reckons the "fourteen years" from Paul's trip to Syria and Cilicia (1:21) (ibid.).

in which the events occur. If Paul's conversion was in A.D. 33, then his first Jerusalem visit "after three years" (Gal. 1:18) would be in 36. The inclusive method of reckoning an interval between event X and event Y includes the years in which both these events took place, as well as the years between. This would mean that the interval between Paul's conversion and his first Jerusalem visit could be as little as one and a third years (if, for instance, the conversion was late in 33 and the visit early in 35), and the interval between his conversion and his second Jerusalem visit as little as twelve and a third years. Although the point is debated, it is generally thought that the inclusive method was more typical in the ancient world, and so we may prefer it in interpreting Galatians 1–2.

Using the data from Galatians 1–2, supplemented by Acts 9–11, we can reconstruct the early years of Paul's missionary work. After his conversion, he stayed in Damascus a short time (Acts 9:19b) before leaving for "Arabia" (Gal. 1:17). Paul here refers not to the Arabian Peninsula but to the Nabataean Kingdom, northeast of the Dead Sea. Some think that Paul spent his time in Arabia meditating and hammering out his theology, and it is likely, considering the drastic change in perspective occasioned by his Damascus-road experience, that some of his time was so spent. But it is unlikely that this was simply a period of retreat. Paul's later difficulties with the king of the Nabataeans, Aretas, suggests strongly that he was engaged in active ministry during this time (2 Cor. 11:32).[40] After an indeterminate period, Paul returned again to Damascus (Gal. 1:17; Acts 9:20–22?), where his ministry was cut short by an attempt on the part of Jews and "the governor under King Aretas" to arrest or kill him (2 Cor. 11:32; Acts 9:23–24). Escaping in a basket lowered through a window in the city wall (2 Cor. 11:33; Acts 9:25), Paul then visited Jerusalem for the first time since his conversion, perhaps a litle more than two full years after that happy event. While at first suspicious of this famous persecutor of the church, the Jerusalem disciples were persuaded by Barnabas to receive Paul (Acts 9:26–27). Paul spent fifteen days getting acquainted with Peter, without meeting any of the other apostles except James, the brother of the Lord (Gal. 1:18–19). Accepted by his Christian brothers, Paul was rejected by his old associates: certain "Grecian Jews" tried to kill him, and he was forced to flee to Tarsus (Acts 9:28–30; see Gal. 1:21).

Some time after this, Barnabas, who had been sent from Jerusalem to investigate the reports of great numbers of Greeks becoming Christians in Antioch, called Paul from Tarsus to join in the work at Antioch (Acts 11:25–26a). Since Luke tells us that Barnabas and Paul spent a year with the church there (Acts 11:26b), and since during this year the famine-relief visit took place (Acts 11:27–30), Paul's arrival in Antioch must have been about twelve or thirteen years after his conversion. This means that Paul spent almost a decade in Tarsus, and it was perhaps during these years that some of the things took place that Paul mentions but that are not narrated in Acts (see 2 Cor. 11:22–27).[41]

[40]See, e.g., Kirsopp Lake, "The Conversion of Paul," in *The Beginnings of Christianity*, Part 1: *The Acts of the Apostles*, ed. F. J. Foakes Jackson and Kirsopp Lake, 5 vols. (London: Macmillan, 1920–33), 5:192–94.

[41]Bruce, *Paul, Apostle of the Heart Set Free*, pp. 127–28.

From Paul's First Missionary Journey to His Death Paul gives us no sequence of events or chronological indicators for the second stage of his missionary career—from the first missionary journey to the end of his life—comparable to what he provides for us in Galatians 1-2 for the first stage of his career. We are almost wholly dependent on Acts for this information. Unfortunately, while Luke provides us with a relatively straightforward account of this stage of Paul's life— and one that in no way contradicts Paul's own scattered autobiographical remarks—he is, with certain important exceptions, notoriously vague about chronology. Luke is fond of using phrases such as "a long time," "after some days," and "about this time," which provide little help is estimating elapsed time.

For instance, Luke introduces the first missionary journey in Acts 13:1–3 with no indication about its relationship in time to the other events he has been narrating. Nevertheless, we should probably view the narrative as a continuation of the Antiochian story that was begun in 11:19–30. If so, we can presume that the period of "a whole year" of ministry in Antioch mentioned in 11:26 is the time between Paul's joining of Barnabas and their setting out on the first missionary journey. This journey took Barnabas, Paul, and—for part of the way— John Mark to Barnabas's home, the island of Cyprus, and several cities in southern Galatia, namely, Pisidian Antioch, Iconium, Lystra, and Derbe (Acts 13:4– 14:26). Estimates of the time necessary for this trip of about 1,400 miles[42] vary from one year to five years.[43] The best guess is about eighteen months,[44] but we simply have no way of knowing for sure.

Following the first journey, Paul and Barnabas spent "a long time" in Antioch (Acts 14:28; cf. Gal. 2:11–14), before going to Jerusalem for the apostolic council (15:29). They then returned to Antioch for a period of time (15:30–33), where a dispute over John Mark's qualifications for continued missionary service led the two to go their separate ways (15:36–41). Paul's second missionary journey took him to southern Galatia, quickly through Asia Minor, and on to Macedonia—in particular the cities of Philippi (see 1 Thess. 2:2), Thessalonica (see 1 Thess. 2:2; Phil. 4:15–16), and Berea (Acts 17:10–15)—and then Achaia, including Athens (see 1 Thess. 3:1) and Corinth (see 2 Cor. 11:7–9). Luke provides no specific time references until Paul comes to Corinth: he mentions that Paul stayed there for a period of eighteen months (Acts 18:11). This reference may indicate only the length of time spent in Corinth before the Gallio incident (18:12–17),[45] but probably indicates the total time spent in Corinth.[46] Once again, the total amount of time required for the second journey— about 2,800 miles—is hard to estimate, but the indications are that Paul did not spend much time in any place before Corinth, so two years may be about right.

After returning to Jerusalem (implied in Acts 18:22, with its reference to "the church"), Paul went to Antioch, where he spent "some time" (18:23). This stay,

---

[42]All the mileage estimates for Paul's journeys come from Barry J. Beitzel, *The Moody Atlas of Bible Lands* (Chicago: Moody, 1985), p. 177.

[43]See the discussion in Jewett, *Chronology*, pp. 57–62. He opts for forty-six months. It is estimated that in Paul's day one could travel about one hundred miles a day by ship, and no more than fifteen or twenty by foot (Wayne A. Meeks, *The First Urban Christians: The Social World of the Apostle Paul* [New Haven, Conn.: Yale University Press, 1983], p. 18).

[44]George Ogg, *The Odyssey of Paul* (Old Tappan, N.J.: Fleming H. Revell, 1968), pp. 65–71.

[45]Ogg, *Odyssey*, pp. 114–15.

[46]Richard Longenecker, "Acts," in *EBC* 9:484.

however, was probably not a long one, for Paul would have been anxious to return to Ephesus, where he had left Priscilla and Aquila (18:19). Nevertheless, he traveled "from place to place throughout the region of Galatia and Phrygia"(18:23; the reference is probably to the Phrygian part of Galatia) before arriving in Ephesus (19:1; see 1 Cor. 16:8). How long Paul spent here is not clear. In Acts 20:31, Paul tells the elders of the Ephesian church that he had spent "three years" with them. But this could be a rounding off (counting inclusively) of the period of two years and three months specified in 19:8, 10. Luke, however, may not intend these two verses to summarize the entire stay in Ephesus. It is safest to conclude that Paul spent anywhere from two years and three months to three years in Ephesus. From Ephesus Paul moved north into Macedonia, where he met Titus returning from Corinth (Acts 20:1; cf. 2 Cor. 2:12–13). Some scholars speculate that it may have been at this time that Paul ministered in Illyricum (modern Albania and Yugoslavia; see Rom. 15:19), although neither Acts nor Paul's letters describe such a trip. Paul probably wintered in Corinth (his three-month stay in Greece [Acts 20:2–3; cf. 2 Cor. 9:4]), before retracing his steps to Caesarea and Jerusalem (20:3–21:16). This journey, of approximately 2,700 miles, must have taken at least three and a half years, and probably four or five.

Very shortly after his arrival in Jerusalem, Paul was imprisoned by the Roman authorities under suspicion that he had fomented a riot in the temple (Acts 21:27–36). Paul was shortly thereafter transferred to Caesarea, where he spent two years (Acts 24:27). Paul was then sent on to Rome, on a voyage that began in the autumn (the "Fast" in 27:9 is almost certainly the Day of Atonement) and ended in the spring, after three months shipwrecked on the island of Malta (28:11). Luke's account closes with Paul under house arrest for two years in Rome (28:30–31).

Many think that Paul's life ended at this point, but two considerations point decisively to a longer interval before his death. First, apparently reliable early church accounts associate Paul's death with Nero's persecution of Christians in A.D. 64–65. But it is unlikely that Paul's two-year stay in Rome brings us to this late a date (see below). Second, the evidence of the Pastoral Epistles points to a period of further ministry in the eastern Mediterranean after the Roman imprisonment of Acts 28:30–31 (see chap. 15 below). Almost certainly, then, Paul was released from this first Roman imprisonment for a period of further ministry. Whether this ministry took Paul to Spain, as he had originally planned (see Rom. 15:24), is uncertain.[47]

The Chronology of Paul's Missionary Career

Combining the evidence of Acts with indications in the letters of Paul enables us to establish a relative chronology of the life of Paul. But since neither Luke nor

---

[47]The key reference is in 1 Clement. 5:1–7, where it is claimed that Paul reached "the limit of the West" (τὸ τέρμα τῆς δύσεως [to terma tēs dyseōs]). Many think that Clement, a Roman, can mean by this only regions west of Rome (see also the Muratorian Canon) and that Paul probably did preach in Spain (e.g., John J. Gunther, Paul: Messenger and Exile [Valley Forge, Pa.: Judson, 1972], pp. 141–50). Others, however, think that Clement might be referring to Rome itself, or otherwise doubt the reliability of the tradition, and question whether Paul ever reached Spain (Ogg, Odyssey, pp. 188–92). The time required for ministry in the East in the Pastoral Epistles may make it unlikely that Paul reached Spain.

Paul furnishes us with any absolute dates in the career of Paul, the determination of absolute dates depends on the correlation of events mentioned in Acts and Paul with externally verifiable dates. The most important such event is Paul's appearance before the Roman proconsul of Achaia, Gallio, while he was in Corinth on the second missionary journey.[48] Inscriptions enable us to determine that Gallio was proconsul of Achaia from July 51 to July 52.[49] Luke suggests that Paul left Corinth rather quickly after the encounter with Gallio—"some time" (18:18) always denotes a rather short time in Acts (see also 9:23, 43; 27:7). This means that the extreme possibilities for Paul's eighteen-month stay in Corinth are spring 49 to autumn 51, and spring 50 to autumn 52. If, as many surmise, the Jews took advantage of a new proconsul to press their case against Paul, the former dates are slightly more likely. Either sequence of dates also fits Luke's reference to the edict of Claudius (18:2), which was probably issued in 49.[50]

This relatively secure date in the middle of Paul's missionary career is a fixed point from which we can work both backward and forward. Working backward first, an arrival of Paul in Corinth in the spring of A.D. 49 would place the beginning of the second missionary journey sometime in the summer or autumn of 48. The apostolic council must have been shortly before this, probably also in 48, with the first missionary journey in 46–47 or 47–48. This in turn puts Paul's famine-relief visit to Jerusalem in 45–47. This date fits Josephus's references to a severe famine in 45 or 46.[51] One problem with this date for the famine relief visit is that the death of Herod Agrippa I, narrated by Luke in the following chapter (12:19b–23), took place in 44. But there is every reason to think that Luke has arranged his material here topically and that the description of Agrippa's death is placed here simply because it is a natural sequel to the story of his persecution of believers (12:1–19a).

If the famine relief visit was in A.D. 45–47 and the "fourteen years" of Galatians 2:1 is to be reckoned inclusively and from the time of Paul's conversion (see above), then Paul's conversion could be dated anywhere from 32 to 35. Two other considerations impinge on the date for Paul's conversion. First, a certain amount of time, probably at least a year, must have elapsed between Jesus' crucifixion and Paul's conversion, to allow for the events of Acts 1–8.[52] If the crucifixion is dated in A.D. 30, then the entire range of dates—32 to 35—is still open. But if Jesus was

---

[48]Because he doubts the historicity of the incident, Lüdemann does not use the chronological implications of the Gallio incident in his reconstruction (*Paul*, pp. 157–64).

[49]See, e.g., Jewett, *Chronology*, pp. 38–40; Bruce, *Paul: Apostle of the Heart Set Free*, p. 253. There is a remote possiblity that Gallio's tenure should be put a year later.

[50]The edict is mentioned by Suetonius in his *Life of Claudius* 25.4 but first dated in A.D. 49 by the historian Orosius (*Hist.* 7.6.15–16). Some dispute this date, favoring the date of 41 given by Dio Cassius, *Hist. Rom.* (40.6.6) (e.g., Lüdemann, *Paul*, pp. 164–71), but Orosius is probably correct (see E. Mary Smallwood, *The Jews Under Roman Rule* [Leiden: Brill, 1976], pp. 210–15).

[51]Jos., *Ant.* 20.2.5. On the date, see Kirsopp Lake, "The Chronology of Acts," in *Beginnings of Christianity*, 5:452–55. Because there was no single, world-wide famine during these years, Luke's reference to a famine that affected "the entire Roman world" (ὅ λὴν τὴν οἰκουμένην [*holēn tēn oikoumenēn*]) has been considered an exaggeration or an outright fabrication. But the several famines throughout the Roman world during these years justify Luke's generalization (K. S. Gapp, "The Universal Famine Under Claudius," *HTR* 28 [1935]: 258–65).

[52]An early Gnostic tradition held that Jesus' resurrection appearances—up to and including Paul's—lasted for eighteen months (see Ireneus, *Adv. Haer.* 1.30.14; *Ascension of Isaiah* 9:16), and some scholars are inclined to respect this tradition (e.g., Ogg, *Odyssey*, pp. 24–30).

crucified in 33, then we are limited to the latter part of the range only. Second, Paul's reference to the involvement of King Aretas in seeking his arrest in Damascus (2 Cor. 11:32) may favor a date for this event after 37, since it is thought that only after this date would Aretas have had any influence over Damascus.[53] And Paul's escape from Damascus, as we have seen, must have taken place about two years or so after his conversion. Though there is considerable uncertainty about the date of Jesus' crucifixion, these two factors slightly favor the latter end of our range of dates for Paul's conversion—perhaps 34 or 35. The difficulties involved in interpreting Paul's reference to Aretas do not allow for any dogmatism,[54] so an earlier date for Paul's conversion cannot be excluded.

Working forward from the Gallio date, we find Paul ending the second missionary journey in the late summer or autumn of A.D. 51, and beginning the third probably relatively quickly, perhaps in the spring of 52. It is uncertain how long it would have taken Paul to reach Ephesus, but we can assume he was in that city from about mid or late 52 to mid or late 55. After leaving Ephesus, Paul may have spent considerable time in Macedonia or traveled to Illyricum;[55] at any rate, it is likely that he did not begin his return trip to Palestine until the spring of 57. This conclusion rests on the growing consensus among scholars that Festus must have replaced Felix as governor of Judea in 59.[56] Since we know that Paul's two-year imprisonment in Caesarea ended shortly after Festus replaced Felix (Acts 25:1–12), then he must have returned to Palestine in the spring of 57. (We know that Paul's return to Jerusalem occurred in the spring because the Feast of Unleavened Bread took place during the trip [Acts 20:6] and because Paul was anxious to reach Jerusalem before Pentecost [20:16].)

If this reasoning is correct, Paul began his voyage to Rome in the autumn of 59 (Acts 27:9, stating that "sailing had already become dangerous because by now it was after the Fast," shows that it was autumn),[57] and he arrived in Rome in the

---

[53]See esp. Ogg, Odyssey, pp. 16–23, and Jewett, Chronology, pp. 30–33; W. P. Armstrong and J. Finegan, "Chronology of the New Testament," in ISBE 1:689–90.

[54]Bruce, for instance, offers the attractive suggestion that the "governor" who sought to arrest Paul was the head of the Jewish citizens of Damascus rather than a direct underofficial of Aretas (Paul: Apostle of the Heart Set Free, pp. 81–82).

[55]See, e.g., Colin J. Hemer, The Book of Acts in the Setting of Hellenistic History, WUNT 2.49 (Tübingen: Mohr, 1989), pp. 258–61.

[56]See, e.g., Gunther, Paul: Messenger and Exile, pp. 140–41; G. B. Caird, "Chronology of the New Testament," in IDB, 1:604–5; Jewett, Chronology, pp. 40–44; Hemer, Book of Acts, p. 171; F. F. Bruce, New Testament History, 2d ed. (Garden City, N.Y.: Doubleday, 1971), pp. 345–46. Some scholars argue for a much earlier date, 55 or 56, based on the fact that Pallas, a Roman official who was removed from office in 55 or 56, was instrumental in Felix's recall (see Lake, "Chronology," pp. 464–67). But it is impossible to squeeze all that Josephus records as happening under Felix while Nero was emperor (A.D. 54 and later) into so short a time; and Pallas probably continued to exercise influence even after being removed from office. (For these points, see Emil Schürer, The History of the Jewish People in the Age of Jesus Christ [175 B.C.–A.D. 135], new ed., vol. 1, rev. and ed. by Geza Vermes and Fegus Millar [Edinburgh: T. & T. Clark, 1973], pp. 465–66n). In contrast, Schürer argues that Felix was recalled in A.D. 60 (History, pp. 465–66n) and Ogg in 61 (Odyssey, pp. 146–70).

[57]This reference may also corroborate the date of A.D. 59 for Paul's departure for Rome. W. P. Workman argued that the syntax of Acts 27:9 suggests that the date of the "Fast"—the Day of Atonement—in this year followed the date for the closing of sailing ("A New Date-Indication in Acts," ExpTim 11 [1899–1900]: 316–19). If, as is likely, September 24 was the traditional date for the end of safe navigation, then Paul must have sailed in a year when the Day of Atonement came later than September 24. This was true in the years 57, 59, and 62, and most scholars agree that 62 is too

Table 6
Chronology of Paul's Missionary Career

Event	Probably date
Conversion	A.D. 34–35 (or earlier)
Ministry in Damascus and Arabia	35–37
First Jerusalem Visit	37
Ministry in Tarsus and Cilicia	37–45
Famine-Relief Visit	45, 46, or 47
First Missionary Journey	46–47 or 47–48
Apostolic Council	48 or 49
Second Missionary Journey	48 or 49–51
Third Missionary Journey	52–57
Caesarean Imprisonment	57–59
Voyage to Rome	59–60
Roman Imprisonment	60–62
Ministry in the East	62–64
Death	64–65

spring of 60. On the assumption that Paul was released after the two-year period Luke mentions in Acts 28:30–31, he engaged in further ministry in the East (e.g., Ephesus [see 1 Timothy] and Crete [see Titus]) during the years 62–64. Paul was probably rearrested at the time of Nero's persecution and executed shortly thereafter (64 or 65). Table 6 summarizes our suggestions for the chronology of Paul's missionary career.

PAUL'S LETTERS
(AND NEW TESTAMENT LETTERS GENERALLY)

Twenty-one of the twenty-six New Testament books are letters, composing 35 percent of the New Testament text. Paul is the most famous letter writer, with thirteen authentic epistles.[58] Why have Paul, James, Peter, John, Jude, and the unknown author of Hebrews chosen to communicate in this form? The question is particularly apropos when we recognize that the letter was not a typical method of religious instruction among Jews.

The answer is probably twofold. First, the early Christian movement, with its fast growth and peripatetic missionaries, demanded a means of communication at a distance. The letter was the obvious solution. The abiding religious significance of the letters, in the sense of canonical, authoritative documents, was the product of later decision rather than intention at the time of writing. The early apostles,

---

late, while 57 is too early. But Workman's date for the close of sailing may be too late; Vegetius (*De re Militari* 4.39) gives September 14 (Ogg, *Odyssey*, p. 174).

[58]We here assume the Pauline authorship of the so-called disputed letters—Ephesians, Colossians, 2 Thessalonians, and the Pastorals. See the relevant chapters on these letters for argument.

then, communicated their teaching in letters because it was convenient and necessary; they were not deliberately creating a new means of religious instruction. A second reason the letter may have been chosen by the apostles is its sense of personal immediacy. People in Paul's day saw the letter as a means of establishing personal presence from a distance,[59] and this perfectly served the needs of the apostles in pastoring their flocks from a distance.

New Testament Letters Against Their Greco-Roman Background

While letters were by no means unknown in the world of the ancient Near East (see, e.g., 2 Sam. 11:14–15; Ezra 4–5), it was in the Greco-Roman world that the letter became an established and popular method of communication. Scholars have therefore turned to the ancient theory and practice of letter writing to illuminate the New Testament letters.

The typical Greco-Roman letter was composed of an address and greeting, a body, and a conclusion.[60] The address and greeting were usually very short, typically taking the form, "A to B, greetings [χαίρειν (chairein]." This simple formula is found in the letter sent by the apostolic council to the churches (Acts 15:23) and in James 1:1. Some New Testament letters (Hebrews, 1 John) have no epistolary opening at all, raising questions about their genre. But most New Testament letters expand—sometimes considerably (see Rom. 1:1–7)—the address and change the simple greeting into a so-called grace-wish (e.g., all the Pauline letters, 1 and 2 Peter, and 2 John). This change is undoubtedly related to the purpose of the letters and was facilitated by the similarity between χαίρειν (chairein, "greeting") and χάρις, (charis, "grace"). Ancient letters also often opened with a health-wish (see 3 John); perhaps the New Testament penchant for putting a thanksgiving (all the pauline letters except Galatians, 2 Corinthians, 1 Timothy, and Titus) or blessing (2 Corinthians, Ephesians, 1 Peter) at the beginning of letters reflects this practice.

Several scholars have suggested that we can identify standardized formulas that were used to make the transition between the opening of the letter and its body.[61] These attempts have not, however, commanded universal assent, and it is unlikely that any formula became standard enough to justify our drawing conclusions along these lines. Attempts to identify a typical sequence in the body of the Greco-Roman letter have not been successful.[62] The varying purposes for which letters were written led, naturally enough, to many different kinds of letter bodies. However, many of the New Testament letters stand out from their contemporary secular models in length. (Cicero wrote 776 letters, ranging in length from 22 to 2,530 words; Seneca 124 letters, from 149 to 4,134 words in length; Paul averages 1,300 words in length, and Romans has 7,114.) Ancient letters tended to

---

[59]E.g., Seneca, *Epist. Mor.* 75.1–2; and Robert W. Funk, "The Apostolic Parousia: Form and Significance," in *Christian History and Interpretation*, ed. W. R. Farmer, C. F. D. Moule, and R. R. Niebuhr (Cambridge: Cambridge University Press, 1966), pp. 249–68.

[60]Examples of ancient letters have been collected by Stanley K. Stowers, *Letter Writing in Greco-Roman Antiquity* (Philadelphia: Westminster, 1986), pp. 58–173. On the ancient theory of letter writing, see Abraham J Malherbe, *Ancient Epistolary Theorists* (Atlanta: SP, 1988).

[61]E.g., John Lee White, *The Form and Function of the Body of the Greek Letter*, SBLDS 2, 2d ed. (Missoula, Mont.: SP, 1972).

[62]See Stowers, *Letter Writing*, p. 22.

close with greetings, and this is typical of New Testament letters also. New Testament letters usually add a doxology or benediction.

This brief survey reveals that New Testament letters resemble ancient letters but that the similarities are of a very general nature. Indeed, most of the widespread parallels involve elements that would need to be present in any letter. There are also differences between New Testament letters and other ancient letters, and these are probably the product of Jewish influence[63] and especially the special situation and purpose of their writing. These differences are perhaps most numerous in the letters of Paul. According to David Aune, "Paul in particular was both a creative and eclectic letter writer."[64]

Classifications of ancient letters have their beginning in Adolf Deissmann's famous distinction between "epistles" (carefully composed, public pieces of literature) and "letters" (unstudied, private communications). Deissmann put all the letters of Paul into the latter category, arguing that they bore the same signs of hasty composition and lack of literary pretensions as are found in the Greek papyri letters.[65] Deissmann's distinction was an artificial one, and it is now generally agreed that one cannot erect such rigid distinctions between a private letter and a public one. Greco-Roman letters range from careful rhetorical masterpieces designed for wide dissemination to short, simple "send money" notes. The New Testament letters as a whole fall somewhere in the middle of this range, with some tending more toward the more literary end (e.g., Romans and Hebrews) and others more toward the common end (e.g., Philemon and 3 John). Many scholars have attempted more exact classification, often working from categories established through a study of Greco-Roman letters generally.[66] Such studies, however, have so far not led to solid conclusions.[67] We should probably content ourselves with identifying some of the particular aspects of each individual New Testament letter and draw parallels at specific points with other Greco-Roman letters.

The Use of Amanuenses

The value of papyrus and the low level of literacy meant that many ancient letters were dictated to trained scribes. The use of such scribes (or amanuenses) by New Testament authors is clearly indicated in Romans 16:22, where Tertius identifies himself as the one who "wrote down" the letter. It was typical, when an amanuensis had composed the letter, for the writer to add a final greeting in his own hand (see 2 Thess. 3:17 and Gal. 6:11). While we have no way of knowing for sure, it seems likely that most of the New Testament letters were produced in this way.

A crucial and debated question is the degree of freedom that a letter writer

---

[63]Ibid., p. 25.

[64]David E. Aune, *The New Testament in Its Literary Environment* (Philadelphia: Westminster, 1987), p. 203.

[65]Adolf Deissmann, "Prolegomena to the Biblical Letters and Epistles," in *Bible Studies* (Edinburgh: T. & T. Clark, 1901), pp. 1–59.

[66]See, e.g., Stowers, *Letter Writing*, pp. 51–173.

[67]For instance, after establishing his categories in the Greco-Roman letters, Stowers finds no New Testament letter that exactly conforms to any of the categories; he finds, rather, parallels within the New Testament letters to various categories. Aune recognizes the difficulty in classifying the New Testament letters (*Literary Environment*, p. 203).

might give to his or her scribe in the choice of wording.[68] A reasonable conclusion is that the freedom given to an amanuensis would have differed depending on the skill of the amanuensis and the nature of the relationship between the writer and the amanuensis.[69] It may be, for instance, that when Paul used a close and trusted companion for his amanuensis, he gave to that person some degree of freedom to choose the exact wording of the letter—Paul always, we can assume, checking the letter over and attesting to its accurate representation of his thoughts with his closing greeting. Many scholars think that the differences between the Greek of the Pastoral Epistles and Paul's Greek elsewhere could be explained by such a hypothesis (Luke, perhaps, being the amanuensis in this case; see 2 Tim. 4:11).

The Collection of Paul's Letters

Paul wrote his letters over a period of at least fifteen years, and to churches and individuals separated by thousands of miles. How and when were they gathered together into a single group, and what are the implications of that process for the canonical shape of the letters? Two basic theories about this process may be identified.

Theories of a sudden collection Many scholars think that Paul's letters were neglected after they had been sent to their addressees and that it was only at at certain point that someone took the initiative to gather them together. Since the first clear references to an actual corpus of the letters of Paul comes from Marcion, some suggest that he may have had something to do with the process. Marcion had a Pauline corpus of ten letters (he did not include the Pastorals). Marcion was perhaps the first to collect Paul's letters together. Later "orthodox" collection of the letters (see, e.g., the Muratorian Canon, at the end of the second century) may have been a reaction to Marcion.

Another popular theory puts the time of the first collection about fifty years earlier. Goodspeed, followed by John Knox and C. L. Mitton, argues that Paul's letters were neglected by the church after they were written and that the publication of Acts (which he dates c. A.D. 90) led a devoted follower of Paul to initiate a collection. According to Goodspeed, this follower was none other than Onesimus (the runaway slave of Philemon), who wrote Ephesians as a covering letter for the collected corpus.[70]

Goodspeed's theory is open to objection at a number of points. Ephesians was probably written by Paul (see chap. 11 below); Acts was probably published much earlier than A.D. 90; and, most seriously, there is good reason to think that Paul's letters circulated among the churches long before the end of the century. Paul himself encouraged some of his letters to be read in other churches (see Col.

---

[68]Otto Roller argued that amanuenses were almost always given a great deal of freedom (*Das Formular der paulinischer Briefe: Ein Beitrag zur Lehre vom antiken Briefe* [Stuttgart: Kohlhammer, 1933]), esp. p. 333); but his conclusions have been seriously questioned (e.g., Kümmel, p. 251).

[69]Richard N. Longenecker, "On the Form, Function, and Authority of the New Testament Letters," in *Scripture and Truth*, ed. D. A. Carson and John D. Woodbridge (Grand Rapids: Zondervan, 1983), pp. 101–14.

[70]Goodspeed, pp. 210–21; C. Leslie Mitton, *The Formation of the Pauline Corpus of Letters* (London: Epworth, 1955); John Knox, *Philemon Among the Letters of Paul* (London: Collins, 1960), pp. 63–93.

4:16), and it is certainly likely, granted the mobility of the early Christians, that exchanges of letters began at a fairly early date.[71] Another indication in the same direction is 2 Peter 3:16, which, while not necessarily speaking of a completed corpus of the letters of Paul, does refer to a number of Pauline letters. Despite the weight of scholarly opinion that dates 2 Peter in the beginning of the second century, there is good reason to date it as early as 64 or 65 (see chap. 20 below). It is possible, then, that another figure, earlier in the course of the church's history, was responsible for the collection. Guthrie, for instance, suggests that it may have been Timothy.[72]

Theories of a gradual growth Any identification of an individual as responsible for the collection of Paul's letters remains completely speculative; it may be, rather, that no one person had a large role in the process. In fact, if Paul's letters began circulating shortly after they were written, it is perhaps more likely that the process was a gradual one. We simply do not have enough information to know. How soon this collection was complete is also impossible to know. Some scholars think that *1 Clement* (c. A.D. 96) assumes a completed collection; others just as emphatically think it does not. But Zahn has made a solid case for dating the collection sometime between the death of Paul and the end of the first century.[73] Whatever the date, the process we envisage here leaves little room for the extensive editorial work that some think went on as the Pauline letters were gathered. Instead of an editor or editors piecing letters of Paul together and generally rearranging the corpus, we should think rather of a simple process of collection and, eventually, copying.

BIBLIOGRAPHY

W. P. **Armstrong** and J. **Finegan**, "Chronology of the New Testament," in *ISBE* 1:689–90; David E. **Aune**, *The New Testament in Its Literary Environment* (Philadelphia: Westminster, 1987); Barry J. **Beitzel**, *The Moody Atlas of Bible Lands* (Chicago: Moody, 1985); Wilhelm **Bousset**, *Kyrios Christos*, reprint ed. (Nashville: Abingdon, 1970); F. F. **Bruce**, *Jesus and Paul* (Grand Rapids: Baker, 1974); idem, *New Testament History*, 2d ed. (Garden City, N.Y.: Doubleday, 1971); idem, *Paul: Apostle of the Heart Set Free* (Grand Rapids: Eerdmans, 1977); idem, "Paul the Apostle," in *ISBE* 3:706; idem, *Tradition Old and New* (Grand Rapids: Zondervan, 1970); Charles **Buck** and Greer **Taylor**, *Saint Paul: A Study of the Development of His Thought* (New York: Charles Scribner's Sons, 1969); Rudolf **Bultmann**, "The Significance of the Historical Jesus for the Theology of Paul," in *Faith and Understanding* (New York: Harper & Row, 1969), idem, *Theology of the New Testament*, 2 vols. (New York: Charles Scribner's Sons, 1951–55); G. B. **Caird**, "Chronology of the New Testament," in *IDB*, 1:604–5; T. H. **Campbell**, "Paul's 'Missionary Journeys' as Reflected in His Letters," *JBL* 74 (1955): 80–87; W. D. **Davies**, *Paul and Rabbinic Judaism*, 4th ed. (Philadelphia: Fortress, 1980); Adolf **Deissmann**, "Prolegomena to the Biblical Letters and Epistles," in

---

[71]F. F. Bruce, "Paul the Apostle," in *ISBE* 3:706.

[72]Guthrie, pp. 998–1000. C. F. D. Moule hypothesizes that Luke could have collected the letters of Paul and written the Pastoral Epistles to augment the collection (pp. 264–65).

[73]Theodor Zahn, *Geschichte des neutestamentlichen Kanons*, 4 parts in 2 vols. (Erlangen: A. Deichert, 1888–92), 2:811–39.

Bible Studies (Edinburgh: T. & T. Clark, 1901), pp. 1–59; Christian **Dietzfel-binger**, *Die Berufung des Paulus als Ursprung seiner Theologie*, WMANT 58 (Neukirchen-Vluyn: Neukirchener, 1985); E. Earle **Ellis**, *Paul's Use of the Old Testament*, reprint ed. (Grand Rapids: Baker, 1981); Robert W. **Funk**, "The Apostolic Parousia: Form and Significance," in *Christian History and Interpretation*, ed. W. R. Farmer, C. F. D. Moule, and R. R. Niebuhr (Cambridge: Cambridge University Press, 1966), pp. 249–68; K. S. **Gapp**, "The Universal Famine Under Claudius," *HTR* 28 (1935): 258–65; John J. **Gunther**, *Paul: Messenger and Exile* (Valley Forge, Pa.: Judson, 1972); Colin J. **Hemer**, *The Book of Acts in the Setting of Hellenistic History*, WUNT 2.49 (Tübingen: Mohr, 1989); idem, "Tarsus," in *ISBE* 4:734–36; Martin **Hengel**, *Judaism and Hellenism*, 2 vols. (Philadelphia: Fortress, 1974); Ronald F. **Hock**, *The Social Context of Paul's Ministry* (Philadelphia: Fortress, 1980); A. M. **Hunter**, *Paul and His Predecessors*, rev. ed. (Philadelphia: Westminster, 1961); Robert **Jewett**, *A Chronology of Paul's Life* (Philadelphia: Fortress, 1979); Leander E. **Keck**, *Paul and His Letters*, Proclamation Commentaries (Philadelphia: Fortress, 1979); H. A. A. **Kennedy**, *St. Paul and the Mystery Religions* (London: Hodder & Stoughton, 1913); Seyoon **Kim**, *The Origin of Paul's Gospel* (Tübingen: Mohr, 1981); John **Knox**, *Chapters in a Life of Paul* (London: Adam & Charles Black, 1954); idem, *Philemon Among the Letters of Paul* (London: Collins, 1960); George Eldon **Ladd**, *A Theology of the New Testament* (Grand Rapids: Eerdmans, 1974); Kirsopp **Lake**, "The Chronology of Acts," in *The Beginnings of Christianity*, Part 1: *The Acts of the Apostles*, ed. F. J. Foakes Jackson and Kirsopp Lake, 5 vols. (London: Macmillan, 1920–33), 5:452–55; idem, "The Conversion of Paul," in ibid., pp. 192–94; Richard **Longenecker**, "Acts," in *EBC* 9; idem, "On the Form, Function, and Authority of the New Testament Letters," in *Scripture and Truth*, ed. D. A. Carson and John D. Woodbridge (Grand Rapids: Zondervan, 1983), pp. 101–14; idem, *Paul, Apostle of Liberty*, reprint ed. (Grand Rapids: Baker, 1976); Gerd **Lüdemann**, *Paul, Apostle to the Gentiles: Studies in Chronology* (Philadelphia: Fortress, 1984); J. Gresham **Machen**, *The Origin of Paul's Religion* (London: Hodder & Stoughton, 1921); Abraham J. **Malherbe**, *Ancient Epistolary Theorists* (Atlanta: SP, 1988); Ralph P. **Martin**, *Carmen Christi: Philippians 2:5–11 in Recent Interpretation and in the Setting of Early Christian Worship*, rev. ed. (Grand Rapids: Eerdmans, 1983); Wayne A. **Meeks**, *The First Urban Christians: The Social World of the Apostle Paul* (New Haven, Conn.: Yale University Press, 1983); C. Leslie **Mitton**, *The Formation of the Pauline Corpus of Letters* (London: Epworth, 1955); C. G. **Montefiore**, *Judaism and St. Paul* (London: Goschen, 1914); Johannes **Munck**, *Paul and the Salvation of Mankind* (London: SCM, 1959); George **Ogg**, *The Odyssey of Paul* (Old Tappan, N.J.: Revell, 1968); William M. **Ramsay**, *The Cities of St. Paul: Their Influence on His Life and Thought* (London: Hodder & Stoughton, 1907); idem, *Saint Paul, the Traveller and Roman Citizen* (London: Hodder & Stoughton, 1897); Richard **Reitzenstein**, *Hellenistic Mystery Religions: Their Basic Ideas and Significance* (Pittsburgh: Pickwick, 1978); Arnold **Resch**, *Der Paulinismus und die Logia Jesu*, TU 27 (Leipzig: Akademie, 1904); Herman **Ridderbos**, *Paul: An Outline of His Theology* (Grand Rapids: Eerdmans, 1975); Otto **Roller**, *Das Formular der paulinischer Briefe: Ein Beitrag zur Lehre vom antiken Briefe* (Stuttgart: Kohlhammer, 1933); Emil **Schürer**, *The History of the Jewish People in the Age of Jesus Christ (175 B.C–A.D. 135)*, new ed., vol. 1, rev. and ed. Geza Vermes and Fegus Millar (Edinburgh: T. & T. Clark, 1973); Albert **Schweitzer**, *The Mysticism of Paul the Apostle* (New York: H. Holt, 1931); E. Mary **Smallwood**, *The Jews Under Roman Rule* (Leiden: Brill, 1976); Krister **Stendahl**, *Paul Among Jews and Greeks, and Other Essays* (Philadelphia: Fortress,

1976); Stanley K. **Stowers**, *Letter Writing in Greco-Roman Antiquity* (Philadelphia: Westminster, 1986); Peter **Stuhlmacher**, " 'The End of the Law': On the Origin and Beginnings of Pauline Theology," in *Reconciliation, Law and Righteousness: Essays on Biblical Theology* (Philadelphia: Fortress, 1986), pp. 134–54. W. C. **van Unnik**, *Tarsus or Jerusalem: The City of Paul's Youth* (London: Epworth, 1962); Günter **Wagner**, *Pauline Baptism and the Pagan Mysteries* (Edinburgh: Oliver & Boyd, 1967); David **Wenham**, "Paul's Use of the Jesus Tradition: Three Samples," in *GP* 5:7–37; idem, *The Rediscovery of Jesus' Eschatological Discourse, GP* 4; John Lee **White**, *The Form and Function of the Body of the Greek Letter*, SBLDS 2, 2d ed. (Missoula, Mont.: SP, 1972); idem, *Light from Ancient Letters* (Philadelphia: Fortress, 1986); W. P. **Workman**, "A New Date-Indication in Acts," *ExpTim* 11 (1899–1900): 316–19; N. T. **Wright**, "ἁρπαγμός and the Meaning of Philippians 2:5–11," *JTS* 37 (1987): 321–52; R. J. **Wyatt**, "Pharisees," in *ISBE* 3:822–29; Theodor **Zahn**, *Geschichte des neutestamentlichen Kanons*, 4 parts in 2 vols. (Erlangen: A. Deichert, 1888–92).

8

ROMANS

CONTENTS

Romans is the longest and most theologically significant of the letters of Paul, "the very purest gospel" (Luther). The letter takes the form of a theological treatise framed by an epistolary opening (1:1–17) and closing (15:14–16:27). The opening contains the usual prescript (1:1–7) and thanksgiving (1:8–15) and is concluded with a transitional statement of the theme of the letter: the gospel as the revelation of God's righteousness, a righteousness that can be experienced only by faith (1:16–17).

The gospel as the righteousness of God by faith (1:18–4:25). Righteousness of God by faith is the theme of the first major section of the letter. Paul paves the way for this theme by explaining why it was necessary for God to manifest his righteousness and why humans can experience this righteousness only by faith. Sin, Paul affirms, has gained a stranglehold on all people, and only an act of God, experienced as a free gift through faith, can break that stranglehold (1:18–3:20). God's wrath, the condemning outflow of his holy anger, stands over all sinners (1:18–19). And justly so. For God has made himself known to all people through creation; their turning from him to gods of their own making renders them "without excuse" (1:20–32). Even less excusable are Jews, for they have a clear and detailed statement of God's will in their law. Mere possession of that law or bearing the outward mark of God's covenant (circumcision) does not suffice to protect the Jews from God's wrath (2:1–3:8). So, Paul concludes, all people, both Jews and Gentiles, are helpless slaves of sin and cannot be brought into relationship with God by anything they might do (3:9–20).

Only God can change this tragic state of affairs, and this he has done by making available through the sacrifice of his Son a means of becoming righteous, or innocent, before God (3:21–26). This justification, Paul insists, can be gained only by faith (3:27–31), as is illustrated clearly in the case of Abraham (4:1–25).

The gospel as the power of God for salvation (5:1–8:39). Having shown how sinful human beings can be declared right before God through faith, Paul in the second major section of the letter draws out the significance of this act both for the future judgment and for the present earthly life. Being justified means "peace with God," or reconciliation to God, and especially a secure hope for vindication on the day of judgment (5:1–11). The ground for this hope is the believer's relationship to

Christ, who, undoing the effects of Adam's sin, has won eternal life for all who belong to him (5:12–21). Nevertheless, although transferred into the new realm, where Christ, righteousness, grace, and life reign, the Christian still must battle the powers of this present realm: sin, the law, death, and the flesh. But we battle with confidence, knowing that Christ has set us free from the tyranny of these powers. Therefore sin can no longer dictate terms to us (6:1–14); God is now our master, which our lives must reflect (6:15–23). Likewise the law, which, because of sin, made the situation of people worse instead of better, no longer holds sway over the believer (7:1–25). Through the agency of God's Spirit, the Christian is assured of final victory over death and the power of the flesh (8:1–13). That same Spirit, making us God's children (8:14–17), provides additional assurance that the work God has begun in us will be brought to a triumphant conclusion: justification will assuredly lead to glorification (8:18–39).

The Gospel and Israel (9:1–11:36). A key motif throughout Romans 1–8 is the question of the relationship between law and gospel, Jew and Gentile, God's old-covenant people with his new-covenant people. This is the theme of the third major section of the letter. Does the transfer of covenant privileges from Israel to the church mean that God has spurned his promises to Israel (9:1–6a)? Not at all, Paul answers. First, God's promises were never intended to guarantee salvation to every Israelite by birth (9:6b–29). Second, the people of Israel themselves are to blame for failing to embrace God's righteousness in Christ, despite God's clear word to them (9:30–10:21). Furthermore, some Israelites, like Paul, are being saved, and in them God's promises are being fulfilled (11:1–10). Finally, in the climax to his argument, Paul counters the arrogant boasting of some Gentile Christians by reminding them that it is only through Israel that salvation has come to them and that there awaits a day when God's promise to Israel will come to full realization and "all Israel will be saved" (11:12–36).

The gospel and the transformation of life (12:1–15:13). The last major section of Paul's theological treatise is devoted to the practical outworking of God's grace in the gospel. In an initial summary statement, Paul reminds his readers that this grace of God should stimulate sacrificial giving of themselves in service to God (12:1–2). This service can take various forms, as the manifold gifts God has given his people are exercised (12:3–8). The many detailed aspects of this service to God are to be permeated by love (12:9–21). Serving God does not mean, Paul cautions, that the Christian can ignore the legitimate claims that government makes on us (13:1–7). Nor, though free from the law, can Christians ignore the continuing validity of the commandment that summarizes the law: loving our neighbor as ourselves (13:8–10). The Christian is to serve God in this way, recognizing that the day of salvation is already casting the rays of its light on our path, and our lives must reflect that light (13:11–14). Finally, Paul tackles an issue that was apparently a very divisive one in the church at Rome and, no doubt, elsewhere: the observance of certain dietary codes and rituals (14:1–15:13). Some of the Christians in Rome prided themselves on being strong in faith and looked down on others who were not convinced that their faith allowed them to eat any kind of food or to ignore set days of worship. They in turn condemned the so-called strong in faith as compromisers. Paul, while aligning himself with the strong, demands that each side respect the opinions of the other side and learn to live in mutual tolerance.

The epistolary conclusion (15:14–16:27) contains information about Paul's situation and travel plans (15:14–29), a request for prayer as he prepares to bring the collection to Christians in Jerusalem (15:30–33), a commendation of a sister in Christ and a long series of greetings (16:1–16), and a final warning about false teachers, followed by personal notes and a benediction (16:17–27 [vv. 25–27 are textually uncertain]).

AUTHOR

Romans claims to have been written by Paul (1:1), and there has been no serious challenge to this claim. Tertius, identified in 16:22, was probably Paul's amanuensis or scribe. While Paul may sometimes have given his amanuensis some freedom in choosing the wording of his letters, there is little evidence that this was the case in Romans. A few have wondered whether parts of Romans may have been written by someone else and incorporated into the letter by Paul, but none of these theories has proved convincing (see section "Integrity" below).

PROVENANCE AND DATE

If there is little debate about whether Paul wrote Romans, neither is there about the general situation in which he wrote. According to 15:22–29, three localities figure in Paul's travel plans: Jerusalem, Rome, and Spain. Paul's immediate destination is Jerusalem. As his prayer in 15:30–33 reveals, Paul looks upon this trip to Jerusalem with considerable trepidation. Paul is bringing to the impoverished Jewish Christians in Jerusalem an offering gathered from the Gentile-Christian churches he has planted (15:25–27), and he is uncertain how the offering will be received. It is his hope that the offering will be acceptable to the Jewish believers and that this will help to cement relations between Jewish and Gentile Christians. But Paul is unsure about this and requests the Roman Christians to pray for this outcome.

The second stop Paul plans to make is in Rome, but only as a stopping-off point on his way to Spain (15:24, 28). This is not to minimize the strategic importance of Rome but reflects Paul's sense of calling to "preach the gospel where Christ [is] not known" (15:20). Paul's gaze is fixed on faraway Spain because the task of initial church planting in the eastern Mediterranean has been completed: "From Jerusalem all the way around to Illyricum, I have fully proclaimed the gospel of Christ" (15:19). As a result of his first three missionary journeys, thriving churches have been planted in major metropolitan centers throughout this region. These churches can carry on the task of evangelism in their respective areas while Paul pursues his calling in virgin territory.

When we compare these indications with the details of Paul's career from Acts, it is clear that Paul must be near the end of his third missionary journey as he writes Romans. It was then that Paul was preparing to return to Jerusalem, with Rome as his next destination (see Acts 19:21; 20:16). Corinth is the most likely place of writing. When Luke tells us that Paul spent three months in Greece (Acts 20:3), it was most likely Corinth where Paul stayed (see 2 Cor. 13:1, 10). Confirmation that Corinth was the place of composition comes from Paul's commendation of a woman who lived in Cenchrea, a neighboring city to Corinth

(16:1-2); and the Gaius who sends greetings in 16:23 may be the same Gaius whom Paul baptized in Corinth (1 Cor. 1:14). Some have also thought that the city treasurer Erastus (16:23) can be identified with the Erastus mentioned on an inscription found at Corinth.[1]

The date at which Paul wrote Romans will accordingly depend on the date of Paul's three-month stay in Greece; fixing this date depends, in turn, on the chronology of Paul's life and ministry as a whole. While we cannot be certain within a year or two, A.D. 57 is the best alternative (see table 6 in chap.7).[2]

ADDRESSEES

Assuming that the text printed in our Greek and English Bibles is correct (for which see the next section), the letter is addressed to "all in Rome who are loved by God and called to be saints" (1:7; cf. also 1:15). We have no definite evidence about the origin of the church in Rome or about its composition at the time when Paul wrote to it. In about A.D. 180, Ireneus identified Peter and Paul together as founders of the Roman church (*Adv. Haer.* 3.1.2), while later tradition names Peter as the founder and first bishop of the church (e.g., the *Catalogus Liberianus* [A.D. 354]). But neither tradition can be accepted. The letter itself makes clear that Paul was a stranger to the church in Rome (see 1:10, 13; 15:22), and it is unlikely that Paul would be planning the kind of visit described in 1:8–15 to a church founded by Peter. Nor is it likely that Peter went to Rome early enough to have established a church there.[3] Since no other apostle is associated with the founding of the church in Rome, we may agree with the assessment of the fourth-century "Ambrosiaster" that the Romans "have embraced the faith of Christ, albeit according to the Jewish rite, without seeing any sign of mighty works or any of the apostles."[4] If, then, we are to speculate, the most likely scenario is that Jews converted on the Day of Pentecost (see Acts 2:10) were the first to bring the gospel to the great capital.

"Ambrosiaster" is probably also correct in thinking that Christianity in Rome began among Jews ("according to the Jewish rite"). Jews made up a significant part of the citizenry of Rome by the end of the first century B.C.[5] Here, as Paul found, was the most fertile seedbed for the planting of the gospel—especially if returned pilgrims from Pentecost first planted the seed. That there were Jewish Christians in Rome by (probably) A.D. 49 is attested by the statement of Suetonius

---

[1]See the disscusion in David W. J. Gill, "Erastus the Aedile," *TynB* 40 (1989): 293–302.

[2]Most introductions and commentaries agree on this approximate date. Minimizing the historical value of Acts, Charles Buck and Greer Taylor date Romans in A.D. 47 (*Saint Paul: A Study of the Development of His Thought* [New York: Charles Scribner's Sons, 1969], pp. 170–71), Gerd Lüdemann in 51/52 or 54/55 (*Paul, Apostle to the Gentiles: Studies in Chronology* [Philadelphia: Fortress, 1984], p. 263), while J. R. Richards puts it in 52–54 because he thinks on internal grounds that Romans must precede 1 Corinthians ("Romans and I Corinthians: Their Chronological Relationship and Comparative Dates," *NTS* 13 [1966–67]: 14–30).

[3]See the discussion in Oscar Cullmann, *Peter: Disciple, Apostle, Martyr* (Philadelphia: Westminster, 1962), pp. 72–157.

[4]Ambrosiaster, *PL* 17, col. 46.

[5]See, e.g., Philo's *Embassy to Gaius*; and note the discussions in Harry J. Leon, *The Jews of Ancient Rome* (Philadephia: Jewish Publication Society, 1960), pp. 4–9; and Wolfgang Wiefel, "The Jewish Community in Ancient Rome and the Origins of Roman Christianity," in *The Romans Debate*, ed. Karl Donfried (Minneapolis: Augsburg, 1977), pp. 101–8.

that Claudius the Roman emperor "expelled the Jews from Rome because they were constantly rioting at the instigation of Chrestus" (*Life of Claudius* 25.2). It is generally agreed that "Chrestus" is a corruption of the Greek Χριστός (*Christos*, "Christ") and that Suetonius's remark refers to violent debates within the Jewish community in Rome over the claims of Jesus to be the Christ. That this incident occurred in 49, as the fifth-century writer Orosius claims, is less certain, although the date receives indirect confirmation from Acts 18:2, where Luke says that Aquila and Priscilla had recently come to Corinth from Italy "because Claudius had ordered all the Jews to leave Rome."[6]

Since the Romans at this point would not have distinguished Jews from Jewish Christians, both would have been affected by Claudius's expulsion. But as with similar expulsions on other occasions, the edict probably did not stay in force for long, and less than a decade later we find Aquila and Priscilla back in Rome (Rom. 16:3). During its enforcement, however, the edict must have had a profound impact on the church in Rome. In the absence of Jewish Christians, those Gentiles who had been attracted to Christianity would have taken over the church, and Jewish Christians who then returned would probably be in a minority, and perhaps viewed with some condescension by the now-dominant Gentile wing.[7]

When Paul writes his letter, then, we may be certain that there were both Gentile and Jewish Christians in Rome, probably meeting in several house churches rather than in one large gathering.[8] Does Paul write to this mixed community as a whole? Or does he address himself to one segment of the community only? Only the evidence of the letter itself can answer these questions.

In turning to the letter, however, we are confronted with apparently conflicting data. On the one hand, there are indications that Paul had a Jewish-Christian audience in mind: (1) he greets the Jewish Christians Priscilla and Aquila and his "kinsmen" Andronicus, Junias, and Herodion (16:3, 7, 11); (2) he addresses himself to a Jew in chapter 2 (e.g., v. 17); (3) he associates his readers with the Mosaic law: they are "not under law" (6:14, 15) because they have "died to the law" (7:4); and note 7:1: "I am speaking to those who know the law"; (4) Paul calls Abraham "our forefather" (4:1); and (5) much of the letter is devoted to issues that would be of particular interest to Jewish Christians: the sin of the Jews (2:1–3:8); the Mosaic law, seen in terms both of its inadequacy (3:19–20, 27–31; 4:12–15; 5:13–14, 20; 6:14; 7:1–8:4; 9:30–10:8) and of its establishment in Christ (3:31; 8:4; 13:8–10); the significance of Abraham, the fountainhead of Israel (chap. 4); and the place of Israel in salvation history (chaps. 9–11).

On the other hand, indications of a Gentile-Christian audience are equally evident: (1) in his address of the letter as a whole, Paul includes his readers among the Gentiles to whom he has been called to minister (1:5–6; cf. also 1:13 and 15:14–21); (2) he directly addresses "you Gentiles" in 11:13 (continued in

---

[6]See esp. E. Mary Smallwood, *The Jews Under Roman Rule*, SJLA 20 (Leiden: Brill, 1976), pp. 210–16; and F. F. Bruce, "The Romans Debate—Continued," *BJRL* 64 (1982): 338–39. For a dissenting opinion, see Leon, *Jews*, pp. 23–27.

[7]See esp. Wiefel, "Jewish Community," pp. 109–13.

[8]It is noted, e.g., that the word "church" is absent from Romans; see F. F. Bruce, *Paul: Apostle of the Heart Set Free* (Grand Rapids: Eerdmans, 1977), pp. 385–89. The Christian community may then have reflected the lack of centralization that characterized the Jewish community in Rome; see Romano Penna, "Les Juifs à Rome au temps de l'apôtre Paul," *NTS* 28 (1982): 327–28; Leon, *Jews*, pp. 135–70.

the second person plural throughout 11:14–24); and (3) Paul's plea that the Christians in Rome "accept one another" (15:7) appears to be directed especially to Gentiles (see vv. 8–9).

We must consider several options in trying to reconcile these apparently conflicting indications of Paul's audience in the epistle to the Romans. First, we could downplay the evidence of a Gentile-Christian audience and conclude that the letter is addressed entirely or mainly to Jewish Christians.[9] It has been argued, for instance, that 1:6 simply designates the Roman Christians as being "among those who are called to belong to Jesus Christ" or that τὰ ἔθνη (ta ethnē) in verse 5 means "nations" rather than "Gentiles" (see RSV). But neither alternative is convincing. In a context dealing with Paul's apostleship, τὰ ἔθνη almost certainly means "Gentiles," and the connection between verses 5 and 6 (ἐν οἷς ἐστε καὶ ὑμεῖς [en hois este kai hymeis], "among whom you also") is most naturally construed as numbering the readers of the letter among these Gentiles.[10]

In light of these verses, then, we might be inclined to the opposite conclusion: that Romans is directed only to Gentile Christians.[11] Indeed, there is more to be said for a Gentile-Christian audience than for a Jewish-Christian one. Not only is 1:5–6 very significant, coming in the address of the letter as a whole, but the evidence for a Jewish-Christian readership is not all that strong. The direct address to "a Jew" in chapter 2 is a literary device and implies nothing about the intended audience. Calling Abraham our father (4:1) would suggest a Jewish audience only if Paul was including all his readers in the designation. But this is not clear: he may be thinking only of himself and other Jewish Christians. Paul certainly suggests that his readers have had some experience with the Mosaic law (6:14; 7:4), but there is a sense in which even Gentiles, according to Paul, have been under the law. Moreover, many of the Gentiles in the Christian community in Rome were probably former God-fearers—worshipers of the God of Israel who had not been circumcised and thus had not been made members of the covenant community. As such, they would have learned much of the Mosaic law in the synagogue.[12] Finally, while much of Romans is indeed a debate with Judaism, it is not at all clear that such a debate would have been irrelevant to a Gentile audience. Quite the contrary. Gentiles as much as Jews needed to understand how the fulfillment of God's plan in Christ related to the Old Testament people of God and his promises to them, and to the historical continuation of that people in contemporary Judaism. In this regard, it is important to observe that Paul's teaching about the future of Israel in 11:12–24 is specifically directed to Gentiles.

While there is much to be said for confining Paul's audience to Gentile Christians, it is doubtful that we can exclude Jewish Christians entirely. Paul addresses himself to "all in Rome who are loved by God and called to be saints"

---

[9]This view was first made popular by F. C. Baur ("Über Zweck und Veranlassung des Römerbriefes und die damit zusammenhängenden Verhältnisse der römischen Gemeinde," in *Historisch-kritische Untersuchungen zum Neuen Testament*, 2 vols. [Stuttgart: Friedrich Fromman, 1963], 1:147–266). See also Zahn 1:421–34.

[10]See Douglas J. Moo, *Romans*, vol. 1, WEC (Chicago: Moody, 1991), pp. 10–13, 44–46.

[11]See esp. Johannes Munck, *Paul and the Salvation of Mankind* (London: SCM, 1959), pp. 200–209; Walter Schmithals, *Der Römerbrief als historisches Problem*, SNT 9 (Gütersloh: Gerd Mohn, 1975), pp. 9–89; Jülicher, pp. 112–15.

[12]Schmithals, *Römerbrief*, pp. 69–82; J. D. G. Dunn, *Romans 1–8*, WBC (Waco, Tex.: Word, 1988), pp. xlvii–xlviii.

(1:7), and it is certain that there were Jewish Christians in Rome. If, as we maintain (see below), chapter 16 is part of Paul's original letter to the Romans, at least those Jewish Christians mentioned there must be included within Paul's audience. Moreover, the "weak in faith" whom Paul addresses in 14:1–15:13 are quite possibly to be identified with a Jewish-Christian faction.

So it appears that Paul is addressing both Jewish and Gentile Christians in Romans. This might mean that Paul addresses Gentile Christians in some passages and Jewish Christians in others. The most detailed attempt to understand the letter in this way is that of Paul Minear. He discerns no fewer than five separate groups in the Christian community in Rome and thinks each section of Romans has one of these groups specifically in view.[13] But Paul does not say enough to make clear the existence of so many distinct groups. Nor, with the exception of one or two passages (e.g., 11:12–24), does this epistle hint at an audience restricted to only some of the Roman Christians. We must thus conclude that Paul addresses in Romans a mixed community of Jewish and Gentile Christians.[14] Almost certainly, however, Gentile Christians were in a majority large enough to justify Paul's including the Christian community in Rome within the sphere of those Gentiles to whom his apostleship was especially directed.

INTEGRITY, LITERARY HISTORY, AND TEXT

Thus far we have been discussing Romans on the supposition that the letter Paul sent to the Roman Christians was composed of the entire sixteen chapters printed in our Bibles. But this supposition must now be examined, for a significant number of scholars doubt that this is the case. A few confine their argument to internal considerations. They claim that there are inconsistencies within the canonical Romans and that they can be explained only on the hypothesis that the letter is actually a combination of two or more original letters or that a redactor has inserted various interpolations into the text of Paul's original letter.[15] Not only are such theories bereft of any textual evidence, their proponents have manufactured inconsistencies in a letter that has been lauded through the centuries for its logical rigor and clarity of argument.[16]

There are, however, a number of other theories about the original form and literary history of Romans that deserve more serious consideration, for they arise from difficulties within the text of the letter. Central to these theories is the place of the doxology that is included at the very end of the letter in most modern texts and translations (16:25–27). It is omitted in some manuscripts and appears at

---

[13]Paul Minear, *The Obedience of Faith: The Purposes of Paul in the Epistle to the Romans* (London: SCM, 1971).

[14]This is the conclusion of most introductions and commentaries; see, e.g., Kümmel, pp. 309–11.

[15]Schmithals posits a "Romans A" made up of chaps. 1–11 and 15:8–13 and a "Romans B" made up of 12:1–15:7; 15:14–32; 16:21–23 and 15:33, with various other minor interpolations and fragments (see his summary in *Römerbrief*, pp. 180–211). J. Kinoshita also discerns two separate original letters in our Romans; significantly, however, he divides things very differently than does Schmithals ("Romans—Two Writings Combined," *NovT* 7 [1964]: 258–77). Another tack is taken by J. C. O'Neill, who identifies numerous editorial insertions in the text of Romans. (*Paul's Letter to the Romans*, PNTC [Baltimore: Penguin, 1975]).

[16]See the review of O'Neill's commentary by Nigel M. Watson, "Simplifying the Righteousness of God: A Critique of J. C. O'Neill's *Romans*," *SJT* 30 (1977): 464–69.

different places in others. The following sequences are found in the Greek manuscript tradition:

1. 1:1–14:23; 15:1–16:23; 16:25–27 p^{61}(?), B, C, D, 1739, et al

2. 1:1–14:23; 16:25–27; 15:1–16:23; A, P, 5, 33, 104
   16:25–27

3. 1:1–14:23; 16:25–27; 15:1–16:24 Ψ, the "majority" text, sy^h

4. 1:1–14:23; 15:1–16:24 F, G, 629, [archetype of D?]

5. 1:1–15:33; 16:25–27; 16:1–23 p^{46}

Since a doxology generally closes a letter, the presence of the doxology after chapter 14 or chapter 15 could indicate that the letter at one time ended at one or the other of these points. And this possibility is increased by other evidence.

1. Several MSS of the Latin Vulgate omit 15:1–16:23 entirely.
2. Another codex of the Vulgate (Amiatinus), while containing 15:1–16:24, omits the section summaries from this section.
3. Tertullian, Ireneus, and Cyprian fail to refer to chapters 15 and 16 in places where they may have been expected to, if they had a sixteen-chapter form of the text.

These data suggest that a fourteen-chapter form of Romans was extant in the early church, which some scholars conclude was the original version. Noting that a few MSS (G and the OL g) omit reference to Rome in 1:7 and 1:15 (and Paul never mentions a particular destination elsewhere in chaps. 1–14), they argue that Paul first wrote chapters 1–14 as a general doctrinal treatise and later added chapters 15–16 when he sent this treatise to Rome.[17] This reconstruction is unlikely. The close connection between chapters 14 and 15 makes it impossible to think that 14 ever existed without at least the first part of 15.[18] How, then, did the fourteen-chapter recension of Romans come into existence? Lightfoot suggests that Paul himself may have abbreviated his letter to the Romans in order to universalize the epistle.[19] But this still fails to explain the abrupt break between chapters 14 and 15.[20] The same objection applies to Gamble's theory that the text was shortened after Paul's time in order to make the letter more univerally applicable.[21] Perhaps the best explanation is also the earliest: that Marcion was responsible for cutting off the last two chapters of the letter.[22] Given his biases against the Old Testament, Marcion may been unhappy with the Old Testament quotations in 15:3 and 15:9–12 and considered that 15:1 was the most convenient place to make the break.

---

[17]E.g., Kirsopp Lake, *The Earlier Epistles of St. Paul* (London: Rivingstons, 1919), pp. 350–66.
[18]See, e.g., William Sanday and Arthur C. Headlam, *A Critical and Exegetical Commentary on the Epistle to the Romans*, ICC (Edinburgh: T. & T. Clark, 1902), p. xci; Harry Gamble, Jr., *The Textual History of the Letter to the Romans: A Study in Textual and Literary Criticism* (Grand Rapids: Eerdmans, 1977), p. 84.
[19]J. B. Lightfoot, "The Structure and Destination of the Epistle to the Romans," in *Biblical Essays* (London: MacMillan, 1893), pp. 287–320, 352–74; see also James Denney, "St. Paul's Epistle to the Romans," in *EGT* 2:576–82.
[20]See the criticisms of Lightfoot's view by Hort in *Biblical Essays*, pp. 321–51.
[21]Gamble, *Textual History*, pp. 115–24.
[22]See, e.g., Kümmel, p. 316; Guthrie, pp. 421–22; Sanday and Headlam, *Romans*, p. lxvi.

In recent decades, however, some scholars have thought that Paul's letter to the Romans did not include chapter 16. The placement of the doxology after chapter 15 in the early and important MS p^{46} suggests that some form of the letter may have ended there, and the contents of chapter 16, it is alleged, make it unlikely that it could have been addressed to the church in Rome. Nothing in chapters 1–15 has prepared us for the warning about false teachers in 16:17–20. But more important is the fact that Paul in chapter 16 greets twenty-five individuals by name, two families, one house church and an unspecified number of "brothers" and "saints." All this to a church he has never visited! Surely, it is argued, we must conclude that chapter 16 was originally an independent letter—perhaps a commendatory letter for Phoebe[23]—or was tacked on when Paul sent his Romans letter to the church in Ephesus.[24]

This thesis rests on rather shaky ground. There is no direct textual evidence at all for a fifteen-chapter form of the letter. Warnings about false teachers are by no means out of keeping with passages such as 3:8, and Paul often includes such a last-minute reminder in his letters.[25] Nor are the number of greetings in chapter 16 incompatible with a Roman destination. Many of those greeted may have been, like Priscilla and Aquila, Jewish Christians who had been forced to flee Rome and who met Paul in the course of his travels. What more natural than that believers from Rome would have spent their enforced exile in the kind of Roman-influenced cities of the East in which Paul was busy establishing churches?

We have, then, good grounds for concluding that Paul's letter to the Roman Christians contained all sixteen chapters.[26] Whether the doxology should be included at the end of chapter 16 is another question. Although omitted entirely in only a few MSS, its varied placement suggests that it may have been added to round off one of the recensions of the letter in the early church.[27] Moreover, a concluding doxology is unparalleled in the letters of Paul, and the language of this one is said to be un-Pauline. But these arguments are not conclusive,[28] and we think it likely that 16:25–27 was Paul's own conclusion to this letter.

NATURE AND GENRE

Romans has occasionally been viewed as a timeless treatise, a "compendium of Christian doctrine" (Melanchthon) that transcends time. However, while it

---

[23]E.g., Edgar J. Goodspeed, "Phoebe's Letter of Introduction," *HTR* 44 (1951): 55–57; Schmithals, *Römerbrief*, pp. 125–51; Moffat, pp. 135–39; Jülicher, pp. 109–12. J. I. H. McDonald has shown that so compact a letter of introduction is possible ("Was Romans XVI a Separate Letter?" *NTS* 16 [1969–70]: 369–72).

[24]This view is associated esp. with T. W. Manson; see his "Letter to the Romans—and Others," *BJRL* 31 (1948): 224–40. Some who adopt a similar view include G. Zuntz, *The Text of the Epistles: A Disquisition upon the Corpus Paulinum* (London: British Academy, 1953), pp. 276–77; McNeile, pp. 154–58; and Martin 2:194–96.

[25]Gamble, *Textual History*, p. 52. Ollrog, who thinks that chap. 16 belongs to the original letter, argues that 16:17–20a is a post-Pauline interpolation ("Die Abfassungsverhältnisse von Röm 16," in *Kirche, Fs.* Günther Bornkamm, ed. D. Lührmann and G. Strecker [Tübingen: Mohr, 1980], pp. 221–44).

[26]In addition to other works cited in these notes, see Bruce N. Kaye, " 'To the Romans and Others' Revisited," *NovT* 18 (1976): 37–77.

[27]See, e.g., Lake, *Earlier Epistles*, pp. 343–46; Manson, "To the Romans and Others," p. 8.

[28]See Larry W. Hurtado, "The Doxology at the End of Romans," in *New Testament Textual Criticism: Its Significance for Exegesis, Fs.* Bruce M. Metzger, ed. E. J. Epp and G. D. Fee (Oxford: Clarendon, 1981), pp. 185–99.

certainly speaks to every generation of Christians, the message of Romans is embedded in a document written to a particular audience in a definite situation. To put it simply, Romans is a letter.

But what kind of letter? There were many types of letters in the ancient world, ranging from brief requests for money from children away from home to long essays intended to reach a wide audience.[29] Paul's letters generally fall somewhere between these extremes, but Romans is further toward the latter end of the spectrum than any other letter of Paul's (with the possible exception of Ephesians). To be sure, Romans is written within a set a definite circumstances that are enumerated in the epistolary opening and closing of the book (1:1–17; 15:14–16:27). But within this framework, Paul pursues an argument that develops according to the inner logic of the gospel. This stands in marked contrast to, say, 1 Corinthians, where Paul's agenda is set by the needs and questions of the Corinthians. The questions that occur in Romans (e.g., 3:1, 5, 27; 4:1; 6:1, 15) are literary devices by which Paul moves his own argument along.[30] Not once in chapters 1–13 does Paul allude to a specific circumstance or individual within the Roman Christian community. When he addresses his audience, he does so with terms that could be applied to any Christian group: "brothers" (7:4; 8:12; 10:1; 11:25); those "who know the law" (7:1); "you Gentiles" (11:13). Not even chapters 14–15 need have a specific situation at Rome in mind.[31]

We may, then, describe Romans as a tractate letter, one that has as its main component a theological argument or series of arguments.[32] Attempting a more definite genre identification is perilous. Bultmann and others have compared Romans to the diatribe, an argumentative genre popular with Cynic-Stoic philosophers.[33] Features of the diatribe found in Romans are the direct address of an opponent or interlocutor (see 2:1, 17), rhetorical questions, and the use of μὴ γένοιτο (mē genoito, "may it never be!") to reject the inference found in such questions (see 3:3–4, 5–6; 6:1–2, 15; 7:7, 13; 9:14; 11:1, 11). Bultmann viewed the diatribe as polemical in orientation, but recent study has focused rather on its educative role and has raised the question whether the diatribe should be considered a genre at all.[34] In any case, while sharing some features of the diatribe, Romans as a whole cannot be classified as such.

Other attempts have been made to fit Romans into ancient literary categories: it has been labeled a memorandum,[35] an "epideictic" letter,[36] an ambassadorial

---

[29]See the section "Paul's Letters" in chap. 7 above.

[30]See esp. Günther Bornkamm, "The Letter to the Romans as Paul's Last Will and Testament," in The Romans Debate, p. 28.

[31]See Robert J. Karris, "Romans 14:1–15:13 and the Occasion of Romans," in The Romans Debate, pp. 75–99.

[32]See Richard N. Longenecker, "On the Form, Function, and Authority of the New Testament Letters," in Scripture and Truth, ed. D. A. Carson and John D. Woodbridge (Grand Rapids: Zondervan, 1983), p. 104; Lightfoot, Biblical Essays, p. 315.

[33]Rudolf Bultmann, Der Stil der paulinischen Predigt und die kynisch-stoische Diatribe, FRLANT 13 (Göttingen: Vandenhoeck & Ruprecht, 1910).

[34]Stanley K. Stowers, The Diatribe and Paul's Letter to the Romans, SBLDS 57 (Chico, Calif.: SP, 1981).

[35]Klaus Haacker, "Exegetische Probleme des Römerbriefs," NovT 20 (1978): 2–3.

[36]Wilhelm Wuellner, "Paul's Rhetoric of Argumentation in Romans: An Alternative to the Donfried-Karris Debate over Romans," in The Romans Debate, pp. 160–65.

letter,[37] a "protreptic" letter,[38] and a letter essay,[39] to name only a few. But Romans does not quite fit. To be sure, Romans has similarities to all of these genres. But this proves nothing more than that Paul has utilized various literary conventions of his day in getting his message across.[40]

PURPOSE

The treatise style of the letter to the Romans gives rise to one of the most debated questions about the letter: What was Paul's purpose in sending so heavy a theological exposition to the Christians in Rome? If we first turn to explicit statements of purpose in the letter itself, we find little to help answer this question. Paul writes about his reasons for visiting Rome, but not about his reason for writing to Rome. The only statement he makes on this latter point is too general to be of any real help: "I have written you quite boldly on some points, as if to remind you of them again" (15:15).

The only remaining method of determining Paul's purpose is to fit the contents of the letter to its occasion. The general occasion of the letter is sketched above (see the section "Provenance and Date"). But it is the particular occasion, Paul's motivations in writing, that will lead to conclusions about purpose. Opinions on this question tend to move in two different directions: those that focus on Paul's own circumstances and needs as the occasion for the letter, and those that stress the circumstances of the Christian community in Rome as its immediate occasion. Few solutions ignore one or the other of these factors entirely; the differences come in the importance accorded to each one.

1. We begin with those views that single out Paul's own circumstances as decisive. For the sake of convenience, these may be divided according to the location that is seen as central to Paul's concerns.

Spain. Paul's missionary-campaign plan is to travel to Spain in order to plant new churches in virgin territory (15:24–29). He is stopping in Rome on the way, and one of his undoubted purposes is to enlist the support of the church in Rome for his outreach there. Paul alludes to these hopes in 15:24 with the verb προπέμπω (*propempō*), which connotes "help on the way with material support." One of Paul's purposes in writing, then, may have been to introduce himself to the Roman Christians as a way of preparing for his visit and for his request for sponsorship. Indeed, some find this to be Paul's chief reason for writing.[41] They claim that the general theological tenor of the letter is due to Paul's desire to prove that he is orthodox and worthy of support.

Preparation for the mission in Spain was probably a major reason for the writing of Romans. But it cannot stand alone as a reason for the letter. Had this been Paul's overriding purpose, we would have expected mention of Spain long

---

[37]Robert Jewett, "Romans as an Ambassadorial Letter," *Int* 36 (1982): 5-20.

[38]Stanley K. Stowers, *Letter Writing in Greco-Roman Antiquity* (Philadelphia: Westminster, 1986), pp. 113–14.

[39]Martin Luther Stirewalt, Jr., "Appendix: The Form and Function of the Greek Letter-Essay," in *The Romans Debate*, pp. 175–206.

[40]According to James Dunn, "The distinctiveness of the letter far outweighs the significance of its conformity with current literary or rhetorical custom" (*Romans 1–8*, p. lix).

[41]E.g., Thorlief Boman, "Die dreifache Würde des Völke-apostels," *ST* 29 (1975): 63–69; Leon Morris, *The Epistle to the Romans* (Grand Rapids: Eerdmans, 1988), pp. 7–17.

before chapter 15. Furthermore, the contents of Romans, while theological in nature, focus on a limited number of topics, treating these from a certain perspective: the salvation-historical disjunction of law and gospel, Jew and Greek. Something more definite than a desire to introduce himself is required to explain Paul's purpose in Romans.

Corinth/Galatia Paul's concern with Jewish issues in Romans may be explained as stemming from his reflection on the struggle with the Judaizers that occupied him in Galatia and Corinth (see Galatians; 2 Cor. 3, 10–13). On this understanding of Romans, Paul's purpose in writing to Romans is to set forth his mature views on these issues as they have emerged from the rough-and-tumble of theological polemics. Paul's three-month stay in Corinth affords him the perfect opportunity to sum up these issues before he launches forth on a new stage of missionary activity with its own problems and challenges. Lending support to this view is the relatively neutral stance that Paul in Romans takes on such issues as the law, circumcision, and Judaism.[42]

There is much to be said for this view, and probably it has captured part of the truth. But it leaves one crucial question unanswered: Why send this theological monograph to Rome?[43]

Jerusalem. This same objection applies to the view that Paul's letter to Rome embodies the speech he anticipates giving in Jerusalem when he arrives there with the collection.[44] That this upcoming visit and its consequences were on Paul's mind as he wrote Romans is clear (see 15:30–33). Moreover, this understanding of Paul's purpose would explain his preoccupation with issues pertaining to the relationship between Jews and Gentiles, since this was his underlying concern as he looked ahead to Jerusalem. But in addition to its failure to explain the Roman destination of the letter, this view shares with the previous one the problem of leaving the purpose of the letter separate from Paul's desire to visit Rome. His stress on this last point in both the introduction and the conclusion implies that the purpose for the letter must be related to the purpose for his visit.

At the beginning of the eighteenth century, F. C. Baur initiated a new way of looking at Romans. He rejected the then-popular "timeless treatise" approach to Romans and insisted that it be treated like any other letter of Paul's—one directed to issues arising from the church to which it was written.[45] Baur's general approach has enjoyed a resurgence in the last few decades. Unlike Baur, however, who thought Romans was a polemic against Jewish Christians, most modern scholars who share his approach think that other concerns are primary. Attention in this regard is directed particularly to the one text in Romans in which it appears that Paul has in mind a problem in the community at Rome: 14:1–15:13. This

---

[42]For this approach, see particularly Bornkamm, "Last Will and Testament," p. 29; Munck, *Paul and the Salvation of Mankind*, p. 199; Kümmel, pp. 312–13 (with some modifications); Manson, "To the Romans—and Others," p. 2; Kaye, " 'To the Romans and Others' Revisited," pp. 41–50.

[43]Bernhard Weiss suggested that it was the significance of Rome as the "capital of the world" that led Paul to send this tractate there (1:300–307), but nothing in Paul suggests this attitude toward Rome.

[44]See esp. Jacob Jervell, "The Letter to Jerusalem," in *The Romans Debate*, pp. 61–74; note also Nils Alstrup Dahl, *Studies in Paul: Theology for the Early Christian Mission* (Minneapolis: Augsburg, 1977), p. 77.

[45]Baur, "Zweck und Veranlassung des Römerbriefes," pp. 153–60.

text rebukes two groups—the "weak in faith" and the "strong in faith"—for their intolerance of each other. It is likely that the weak are mainly Jewish Christians, and the strong are Gentile Christians. Here, it is argued, is the center of Romans. The treatise that precedes these chapters provides the necessary theological groundwork for this rebuke. And the rebuke, as the letter as a whole, focuses on the Gentile Christians, who are becoming arrogant toward the increasingly smaller minority of Jewish Christians.[46]

To be sure, this interpretation has been rejected on the grounds that 14:1–15:13 is general paraenesis, ethical guidance that has no basis in a specific circumstance.[47] But this is not convincing: the section is more naturally interpreted as arising from known divisions in the community in Rome.[48] One of Paul's purposes was to heal this division in the Christian community in Rome. But we doubt whether this was his primary purpose. Were this so, it is hard to understand why Paul would have waited until chapter 14 to make a practical application of his theology. Moreover, much of what Paul says in chapters 1–11 cannot serve as a basis for the exhortations in 14:1–15:13. Nor is it necessary that Romans be directed to the needs of the church addressed in just the same way that some of his other letters are. After all, Romans stands apart from all the other letters Paul wrote to churches (except perhaps Colossians), as being the only one not written to a community that Paul had founded or been closely related to. Moreover, we have too few letters from Paul to justify any dogmatic judgments about the kinds of letters Paul could or could not have written. Finally, we must insist that even a theological treatise without specific reference to problems in Rome could still be directed to the needs of the church there—what church is without need of clear theological guidance?

Paul's purpose in Romans cannot be confined to any of these specific suggestions. It may be better to speak of Paul's several purposes in Romans.[49] Several intersecting factors come together to form what we might call Paul's missionary situation, and it is out of that situation that he writes to the Romans. The past battles in Galatia and Corinth, the coming crisis in Jerusalem, the need to secure a missionary base for the work in Spain, the importance of unifying the divided Christian community in Rome around the gospel—these circumstances led Paul to write a letter in which he carefully set forth his understanding of the gospel, particularly as it related to the salvation-historical question of Jew and Gentile, law and gospel, continuity and discontinuity between the old and the new.[50]

---

[46]Some important exponents of this general approach are Marxsen, pp. 92–104; W. S. Campbell, "Why Did Paul Write Romans?" *ExpTim* 85 (1974): 264–69; Hans-Werner Bartsch, "The Historical Situation of Romans, with Notes by W. Gray," *Encounter: Creative Theological Scholarship* 33 (1972): 329–38; Karl P. Donfried, "A Short Note on Romans 16," in *The Romans Debate*, pp. 58–59.

[47]Karris, "Occasion," pp. 75–99.

[48]Donfried, "False Presuppositions," pp. 137–41.

[49]Note the title of the recent monograph on the subject by A. J. M. Wedderburn: *The Reasons for Romans* (Edinburgh: T. & T. Clark, 1989).

[50]For this general approach, see Wikenhauser, pp. 456–58; John Drane, "Why Did Paul Write Romans?" in *Pauline Studies, Fs.* F. F. Bruce, ed. D. A. Hagnar and M. J. Harris (Grand Rapids: Eerdmans, 1980), pp. 212–23; A. J. M. Wedderburn, "The Purpose and Occasion of Romans Again," *ExpTim* 90 (1979): 137–41; C. E. B. Cranfield, *A Critical and Exegetical Commentary on the Epistle to the Romans*, ICC, 2 vols. (Edinburgh: T. & T. Clark, 1975–79), 2:814; Dunn, *Romans 1–8*, pp. lv–lviii.

We should note another factor that probably influenced Paul to focus on these questions: polemic against his theology as being antilaw, and perhaps anti-Jewish. Paul's need to combat Judaizers in Galatia and Corinth could very well have led to this false picture of the apostle to the Gentiles; and 3:8, where Paul mentions some who are slandering his teaching, suggests that Paul knew he had to defend himself against such accusations at Rome.[51]

ROMANS IN RECENT STUDY

Recent scholarship on Romans has focused on three issues: its nature/genre, its purpose, and its treatment of the Jews and the Mosaic law. We have considered the first two in previous sections; here something must be said about the last.

Study of Romans in this regard must be seen against the background of what has been hailed as the new perspective on Paul.[52] This way of looking at Paul is the result of a new understanding of the Judaism that Paul opposed, and against which he hammered out so much of his theology. In the past, it is argued, most Christian scholars assumed that Paul was dealing with legalistic Jews who counted up their good works in order to get into heaven. But many modern scholars are convinced that first-century Judaism was nothing like this. While this case has been argued in the past, E. P. Sanders's 1977 monograph *Paul and Palestinian Judaism* is the touchstone for the contemporary discussion.[53] The heart of Sanders's argument is that the Judaism Paul knew was not a religion in which works were the means of becoming saved, or justified. Rather, in a pattern Sanders calls "covenantal nomism," first-century Jews believed that they were saved by means of their corporate election as a covenant people. Works or obedience to the law in this scheme does not save the Jew but maintains his or her status in the saving covenant relationship. If Paul's Jewish opponents were covenantal nomists rather than legalists, quite a different picture of Paul's teaching on fundamental issues such as justification and the law emerges. In fact, contemporary scholarship witnesses several different, and sometimes mutually exclusive, pictures of Paul's teaching about this covenantal nomism. And since Romans from beginning to end contains teaching about justification, Jews, and the law, these revised pictures of Paul are evident in many recent studies of Romans.[54]

While Sanders's view of Judaism is a necessary corrective to unfair caricatures of Jewish theology in some Christian circles, his own reconstruction has not met with universal acceptance. Questions about sources, method, and his interpretation of key documents have been raised.[55] It has been pointed out that his own

---

[51] Jülicher, pp. 115–18; Bruce, "Romans Debate," pp. 334–35; Peter Stuhlmacher, "The Apostle Paul's View of Righteousness," in *Reconciliation, Law and Righteousness: Essays in Biblical Theology* (Philadelphia: Fortress, 1986), pp. 76–77.

[52] See James Dunn, "The New Perspective on Paul," *BJRL* 65 (1983): 95–122.

[53] E. P. Sanders, *Paul and Palestinian Judaism* (Philadelphia: Fortress, 1977).

[54] This can be seen most readily and in greatest detail in James Dunn's commentary on Romans. See also Sanders, *Paul and Palestinian Judaism*; idem, *Paul, the Law and the Jewish People* (Philadelphia: Fortress, 1983); Heikki Räisänen, *Paul and the Law* (Tübingen: Mohr, 1983); Francis Watson, *Paul, Judaism, and the Gentiles: A Sociological Approach*, SNTSMS 56 (Cambridge: Cambridge University Press, 1986).

[55] See, e.g., G. B. Caird, "Review of *Paul and Palestinian Judaism*," by E. P. Sanders, *JTS* 29 (1978): 539–40; D.A. Carson, *Divine Sovereignty and Human Responsibility* (Atlanta: Knox, 1981), pp. 86–95.

covenantal nomism continues to give such a role to works that they are still, in some sense, necessary for salvation.[56] And we may justly question whether Sanders has ruled out the possibility that there were some Jews in the first century who were more legalistic than nomistic.[57]

Second, and most important, is a methodological point: Sanders's reconstruction (or any other reconstruction, for that matter) of the background against which Paul wrote should not *dictate* our exegesis of Romans. That it might, and should (if we accept it), *influence* our exegesis is acknowledged. But when all is said and done, we must interpret the text as we have it, not force unnatural meanings on it in order to conform to Sanders's reconstruction. Some current exegesis, in our opinion, succumbs to this error. When Paul, for instance, insists that justification is by faith and not by works of the law, the Reformers and most of their heirs have taken him to mean that a person is declared right before God only by faith and not by anything that that person might do. This interpretation, which is now often criticized as assuming a view of Judaism out of keeping with Sanders's Judaism, still seems to be the most natural way to read the relevant texts.[58] Similar things could be said about other passages and issues, such as the nature of Paul's criticism of the Jews in chapter 2, and the contrast between "the righteousness of God/of faith" and "the righteousness of their own/of the law" in 10:1–8.

THEME AND CONTRIBUTION

Opinions about the theme of Romans have tended over time to move the center of attention from the beginning to the end of the letter. The Reformers, following the lead of Luther, singled out justification by faith, prominent especially in chapters 1–4, as the theme of the letter. At the beginning of this century, however, Albert Schweitzer argued that justification by faith was no more than a "battle" doctrine—a doctrine Paul used only to fight against Judaizers—and that the true theme of Romans is to be found in the teaching of Romans 6–8 about union with Christ and the work of God's Spirit.[59] Romans 9–11 was the next section to take center stage in the debate. Far from the excursus that some have found in these chapters, scholars such as Krister Stendahl think that the central theme of Romans is to be found here: the history of salvation and of the two peoples, Jews and Gentiles, within this history.[60] Finally, it has been argued that the practical exhortation to unity in 14:1–15:13 is the true heart of the letter (see the previous section).

Each of these positions is alive in current scholarship, though sometimes in

[56]See particularly R. H. Gundry, "Grace, Works, and Staying Saved in Paul," *Bib* 66 (1985): 1–38.

[57]The suggestion of Richard Longenecker in his *Paul, Apostle of Liberty* (1964; reprint, Grand Rapids: Baker, 1976), pp. 65–85 that Judaism probably featured at least two tendencies—"acting legalism" and "reacting nomism"—has (despite Sanders's criticism) much to be said for it.

[58]See, in this regard, Stephen Westerholm, *Israel's Law and the Church's Faith* (Grand Rapids: Eerdmans, 1989).

[59]Albert Schweitzer, *The Mysticism of Paul the Apostle* (London: A. & C. Black, 1931), the first draft of which was finished in 1904. For this general approach, see also W. Wrede, *Paul* (London: Philip Green, 1907).

[60]See particularly Stendahl, "The Apostle Paul and the Introspective Conscience of the West," *HTR* 56 (1963): 199–215.

modified form. For example, the centrality of justification by faith is upheld by Ernst Käsemann—but only as one facet of the larger category "righteousness of God," interpreted to mean God's intervention in history to reclaim his creation for himself and to bring salvation to his people.[61] E. P. Sanders has followed Schweitzer in putting the stress on the "participationist" language of Romans 5– 8.[62] A large number of scholars think that Romans is about the role of Israel in salvation history.[63] And other themes have also been singled out: God,[64] hope,[65] and salvation,[66] to name only a few.

It is possible that Romans does not have a single theme, that the most we can do is note recurring motifs within several distinct topics. But if we are to single out one theme, a good case can be made for the "gospel." This word and its cognate verb "to evangelize" are prominent in the introduction and in the conclusion of Romans, that is, in its epistolary frame, where we might expect to encounter any overarching topic. It is the word "gospel" that has pride of place in 1:16–17, which is so often (and probably rightly) taken to be the statement of the letter's theme. Moreover, as we have seen, Romans grows out of Paul's missionary situation, which makes natural a focus on that gospel with which Paul had been entrusted by his Lord. Romans, then, is Paul's statement of his gospel.[67]

This summary of the gospel in tractate form has rightly furnished theologians throughout the centuries with prime material for their work. While not a timeless summary of Paul's theology, Romans is nevertheless much less tied to specific first-century circumstances than almost any other book of the New Testament. Less translation from first-century culture to ours is needed than is usually the case. As James Denney says, "Is it not manifest that when we give [the conditions under which Paul wrote] all the historical definiteness of which they are capable, there is something in them which rises above the casualness of time and place, something which might easily give the epistle not an accidental or occasional character, but the character of an exposition of principles?"[68] On this point, Augustine, Luther, and Calvin have seen more clearly than their latter-day critics.[69]

Nevertheless, as we have seen, this statement of the the gospel is made against a first-century background. The most important element in this background is also the most important issue that the early church had to face: the nature of the continuity between God's first "word" and his second, and between the people of

---

[61]See esp. Ernst Käsemann, " 'The Righteousness of God' in Paul," in *New Testament Questions of Today* (Philadelphia: Fortress, 1969), pp. 168–82, as well as ibid., *Commentary on Romans* (Grand Rapids: Eerdmans, 1980).

[62]Sanders, *Paul and Palestinian Judaism*, pp. 434–42.

[63]See, e.g., H. Boers, "The Problem of Jews and Gentiles in the Macro-Structure of Romans," *Neot* 15 (1981): 1–11; Jervell, "Letter to Jerusalem," p. 69; R. David Kaylor, *Paul's Covenant Community: Jew and Gentile in Romans* (Atlanta: John Knox, 1988), pp. 18–19; Dunn, *Romans 1–8*, pp. lxii–lxiii ("the intergrating motif").

[64]Leon Morris, "The Theme of Romans," in *Apostolic History and the Gospel*, ed. W. Ward Gasque and Ralph P. Martin (Grand Rapids: Eerdmans, 1970), pp. 249–63.

[65]John Paul Heil, *Romans: Paul's Letter of Hope*, AnBib 112 (Rome: BIP, 1987).

[66]J. Cambier, *L'évangile de Dieu selon l'épître aux Romains: Exégèse et théologie biblique*, vol. 1: L'évangile de la justice et de la grace (Brussels: Desclée de Brouwer, 1967), p. 34.

[67]For the theme "gospel" as central, see also Ulrich Wilckens, *Der Brief an die Römer*, 3 vols., EKKNT (Neukirchen-Vluyn: Neukirchener, 1978–82), 1:91.

[68]Denney, "Romans," p. 570.

[69]See Westerholm, *Israel's Law*, p. 222.

that first word, Israel, and the people of that second word, the church. At this point in particular, Romans makes its contribution to the formulation of New Testament faith. For the way in which the relationship between the Old Testament and the New Testament, between law and gospel, Israel and church, is expressed—the degree of continuity and discontinuity—is fundamental to the construction of any *Christian* theology. Romans supplies the basic building blocks for the construction of that foundation.

BIBLIOGRAPHY

C. K. **Barrett**, *A Commentary on the Epistle to the Romans* (San Francisco: Harper & Row, 1957); Karl **Barth**, *The Epistle to the Romans* (London: Oxford, 1933); Hans-Werner **Bartsch**, "The Historical Situation of Romans, with Notes by W. Gray," *Encounter: Creative Theological Scholarship* 33 (1972): 329–38; F. C. **Baur**, "Über Zweck und Veranlassung des Römerbriefes und die damit zusammenhängenden Verhältnisse der römischen Gemeinde," in *Historisch-kritische Untersuchungen zum Neuen Testament*, 2 vols. (Stuttgart: Friedrich Fromman, 1963), 1:147–266; H. **Boers**, "The Problem of Jews and Gentiles in the Macro-Structure of Romans," *Neot* 15 (1981): 1–11; Thorlief **Boman**, "Die dreifache Würde des Völkerapostels," *ST* 29 (1975): 63–69; Günther **Bornkamm**, "The Letter to the Romans as Paul's Last Will and Testament," in *The Romans Debate*, ed. Karl Donfried (Minneapolis: Augsburg, 1977), pp. 17–31; F. F. **Bruce**, *Paul: Apostle of the Heart Set Free* (Grand Rapids: Eerdmans, 1977); idem, "The Romans Debate—Continued," *BJRL* 64 (1982): 334–59; Charles **Buck** and Greer **Taylor**, *Saint Paul: A Study of the Development of His Thought* (New York: Charles Scribner's Sons, 1969); Rudolf **Bultmann**, *Der Stil der paulinischen Predigt und die kynisch-stoische Diatribe*, FRLANT 13 (Göttingen: Vandenhoeck & Ruprecht, 1910); John **Calvin**, *Commentaries on the Epistle of Paul the Apostle to the Romans*, reprint ed. (Grand Rapids: Eerdmans, 1947); J. **Cambier**, *L'évangile de Dieu selon l'épître aux Romains: Exégèse et théologie biblique*, vol. 1: *L'évangile de la justice et de la grace* (Brussels: Desclée de Brouwer, 1967); W. S. **Campbell**, "Why Did Paul Write Romans?" *ExpTim* 85 (1974): 264–69; D. A. **Carson**, *Divine Sovereignty and Human Responsibility* (Atlanta: John Knox, 1981); C. E. B. **Cranfield**, *A Critical and Exegetical Commentary on the Epistle to the Romans*, ICC, 2 vols. (Edinburgh: T. & T. Clark, 1975–79); Oscar **Cullmann**, *Peter: Disciple, Apostle, Martyr* (Philadelphia: Westminster, 1962); Nils Alstrup **Dahl**, *Studies in Paul: Theology for the Early Christian Mission* (Minneapolis: Augsburg, 1977); James **Denney**, "St. Paul's Epistle to the Romans," in *EGT* 2; Karl P. **Donfried**, "A Short Note on Romans 16," in *The Romans Debate*, pp. 50–60; John **Drane**, "Why Did Paul Write Romans?" in *Pauline Studies, Fs.* F. F. Bruce, ed. D. A. Hagnar and M. J. Harris (Grand Rapids: Eerdmans, 1980), pp. 212–23; James D. G. **Dunn**, "The New Perspective on Paul," *BJRL* 65 (1983): 95–122; idem, *Romans 1–8, Romans 9–16*, WBC (Waco, Tex.: Word, 1988); Harry **Gamble, Jr.**, *The Textual History of the Letter to the Romans: A Study in Textual and Literary Criticism* (Grand Rapids: Eerdmans, 1977); David W. J. **Gill**, "Erastus the Aedile," *TynB* 40 (1989): 293–302; F. L. **Godet**, *Commentary on Romans*, reprint ed. (Grand Rapids: Kregel, 1977); Edgar J. **Goodspeed**, "Phoebe's Letter of Introduction," *HTR* 44 (1951): 55–57; R. H. **Gundry**, "Grace, Works, and Staying Saved in Paul," *Bib* 66 (1985): 1–38; Klaus **Haacker**, "Exegetische Probleme des Römerbriefs," *NovT* 20 (1978): 1–21; John Paul **Heil**, *Romans: Paul's Letter of Hope*, AnBib 112 (Rome: BIP, 1987); Larry W. **Hurtado**, "The

Doxology at the End of Romans," in *New Testament Textual Criticism: Its Significance for Exegesis, Fs.* Bruce M. Metzger, ed. E. J. Epp and G. D. Fee (Oxford: Clarendon, 1981), pp. 185–99; Jacob **Jervell**, "The Letter to Jerusalem," in *The Romans Debate*, pp. 61–74; Robert **Jewett**, "Romans as an Ambassadorial Letter," *Int* 36 (1982): 5–20; Robert J. **Karris**, "Romans 14:1– 15:13 and the Occasion of Romans," in *The Romans Debate*, pp. 75–99; Ernst **Käsemann**, *Commentary on Romans* (Grand Rapids: Eerdmans, 1980); idem, "'The Righteousness of God' in Paul," in *New Testament Questions of Today* (Philadelphia: Fortress, 1969), pp. 168–82; Bruce N. **Kaye**, "'To the Romans and Others' Revisited," *NovT* 18 (1976): 37–77; David **Kaylor**, *Paul's Covenant Community: Jew and Gentile in Romans* (Atlanta: John Knox, 1988); J. **Kinoshita**, "Romans—Two Writings Combined," *NovT* 7 (1964): 258–77; Otto **Kuss**, *Der Römerbrief*, 3 vols. (Regensburg: Pustet, 1963–78); Kirsopp **Lake**, *The Earlier Epistles of St. Paul* (London: Rivingstons, 1919); Harry J. **Leon**, *The Jews of Ancient Rome* (Philadelphia: Jewish Publication Society, 1960); J. B. **Lightfoot**, "The Structure and Destination of the Epistle to the Romans," in *Biblical Essays* (London: MacMillan, 1893); Richard N. **Longenecker**, "On the Form, Function, and Authority of the New Testament Letters," in *Scripture and Truth*, ed. D. A. Carson and J. Woodbridge (Grand Rapids: Zondervan, 1983), pp. 101–14; idem, *Paul, Apostle of Liberty*, reprint ed. (Grand Rapids: Baker, 1976); Gerd **Lüdemann**, *Paul, Apostle to the Gentiles: Studies in Chronology* (Philadelphia: Fortress, 1984); J. I. H. **McDonald**, "Was Romans XVI a Separate Letter?" *NTS* 16 (1969–70): 369–72; T. W. **Manson**, "The Letter to the Romans—and Others," *BJRL* 31 (1948): 224–40; Paul **Minear**, *The Obedience of Faith: The Purposes of Paul in the Epistle to the Romans* (London: SCM, 1971); Douglas J. **Moo**, *Romans*, vol. 1, WEC (Chicago: Moody, 1991); Leon **Morris**, *The Epistle to the Romans* (Grand Rapids: Eerdmans, 1988); idem, "The Theme of Romans," in *Apostolic History and the Gospel*, ed. W. Ward Gasque and Ralph P. Martin (Grand Rapids: Eerdmans, 1970), pp. 249–63; Johannes **Munck**, *Paul and the Salvation of Mankind* (London: SCM, 1959); John **Murray**, *The Epistle to the Romans*, 2 vols., NICNT (Grand Rapids: Eerdmans, 1959–65); W.-H. **Ollrog**, "Die Abfassungsverhältnisse von Röm 16," in *Kirche, Fs.* Günther Bornkamm, ed. D. Lührmann and G. Strecker (Tübingen: Mohr, 1980), pp. 221–44; J. C. **O'Neill**, *Paul's Letter to the Romans*, PNTC (Baltimore: Penguin, 1975); Romano **Penna**, "Les Juifs à Rome au temps de l'apôtre Paul," *NTS* 28 (1982): 321–47; Heikki **Räisänen**, *Paul and the Law* (Tübingen: Mohr, 1983); J. R. **Richards**, "Romans and I Corinthians: Their Chronological Relationship and Comparative Dates," *NTS* 13 (1966–67): 14–30; William **Sanday** and Arthur C. **Headlam**, *A Critical and Exegetical Commentary on the Epistle to the Romans*, ICC (Edinburgh: T. & T. Clark, 1902); E. P. **Sanders**, *Paul and Palestinian Judaism* (Philadelphia: Fortress, 1977); idem, *Paul, the Law and the Jewish People* (Philadelphia: Fortress, 1983); Walter **Schmithals**, *Der Römerbrief als historisches Problem*, SNT 9 (Gütersloh: Gerd Mohn, 1975); Albert **Schweitzer**, *The Mysticism of Paul the Apostle* (London: A. & C. Black, 1931); E. Mary **Smallwood**, *The Jews Under Roman Rule*, SJLA 20 (Leiden: Brill, 1976); Krister **Stendahl**, "The Apostle Paul and the Introspective Conscience of the West," *HTR* 56 (1963): 199–215; Martin Luther **Stirewalt, Jr.**, "Appendix: The Form and Function of the Greek Letter-Essay," in *The Romans Debate*, pp. 175–206; Stanley K. **Stowers**, *The Diatribe and Paul's Letter to the Romans*, SBLDS 57 (Chico, Calif.: SP, 1981); idem, *Letter Writing in Greco-Roman Antiquity* (Philadelphia: Westminster, 1986); Peter **Stuhlmacher**, "The Apostle Paul's View of Righteousness," in *Reconciliation, Law and Righteousness: Essays in Biblical Theology* (Philadelphia:

Fortress, 1986), pp. 68–93; Francis **Watson** *Paul, Judaism, and the Gentiles: A Sociological Approach*, SNTSMS 56 (Cambridge: Cambridge University Press, 1986); Nigel M. **Watson**, "Simplifying the Righteousness of God: A Critique of J. C. O'Neill's *Romans,*" *SJT* 30 (1977): 464–69; A. J. M. **Wedderburn**, "The Purpose and Occasion of Romans Again," *ExpTim* 90 (1979): 137–41; idem, *The Reasons for Romans* (Edinburgh: T. & T. Clark, 1989); Stephen **Westerholm**, *Israel's Law and the Church's Faith* (Grand Rapids: Eerdmans, 1989); Wolfgang **Wiefel**, "The Jewish Community in Ancient Rome and the Origins of Roman Christianity," in *The Romans Debate*, pp. 100–19; Ulrich **Wilckens**, *Der Brief an die Römer*, 3 vols., EKKNT (Neukirchen-Vluyn: Neukirchener, 1978–82); W. **Wrede**, *Paul* (London: Philip Green, 1907); Wilhelm **Wuellner**, "Paul's Rhetoric of Argumentation in Romans: An Alternative to the Donfried-Karris Debate over Romans," in *The Romans Debate*, pp. 152–74; G. **Zuntz**, *The Text of the Epistles: A Disquisition upon the Corpus Paulinum* (London: British Academy, 1953).

9

1 and 2 corinthians

CONTENTS

Both Corinthian epistles are occasional letters, that is, they are real letters addressed to specific people and occasioned by concrete issues; the letter form is not a mere literary device by which the author shapes his views for general publication. Questions have been raised about the cohesiveness and the authenticity of parts of these epistles, especially the second. These will be discussed below (see section "Occasion"). As the texts stand, however, the letters fall into two books.

1 Corinthians

Following the proem, or salutation (1:1–3), and the thanksgiving for God's enriching work in the believers of the Corinthian church (1:4–9), Paul begins the first main division of the epistle (1:10–4:21), which deals with the church's profound internal divisions and fundamental misapprehensions as to the nature of Christian leadership. On the basis of reports brought to Paul by "some from Chloe's household" (1:11), Paul has learned of the party spirit by which various sectors of the church identified themselves with particular leaders, apparently boasting of the superior wisdom of their self-identification in each case (1:10-17). Paul despises such so-called wisdom: its categories are inimical to all that Paul holds dear—so much so that if its categories were to prevail, the gospel itself could be dismissed as God's folly (1:18–25), to become a Christian would mean to become a fool (1:26–231, and to preach the gospel without manipulative and self-promoting eloquence but with simple dependence on the truthfulness and power of the message of the crucified Messiah would be the essence of ignorance (2:1–5). Conversely, if God's folly is wiser than the world's wisdom, if Christians rejoice that God has chosen the "foolish" in order to shame the "wise" and to make it clear that Christ alone is our "wisdom from God," if Paul's priorities in preaching are foundational, then the Corinthians' pursuit of the world's wisdom implicitly contradicts their own Christian profession.

This does not mean that there is no sense in which the Christian gospel is wise. Far from it: God's wisdom is revealed by the Spirit (2:6–16). But Paul could not address the Corinthian believers as if they were in fact spiritual, because they were not living up to their calling: they were still divided along party lines associated with well-known leaders (3:1–4) and were thus, at best, "infants." So Paul must clarify the nature of Christian leadership. In the rest of this chapter, he removes false impressions in this regard, first by two metaphors—one agricultural (3:5–9a) and one drawn from the construction industry (3:9b–15)—in order to stress the complementary nature of the leaders' work and their accountability to God for its quality. That leads to a warning against all who destroy the church (3:16–17). Returning to the contrast between wisdom and folly, Paul directly assaults any remaining misconceptions about Christian leadership: the Corinthians are deceiving themselves if they think their partisan spirit is a mark of wisdom, when the Scriptures promote humility and when genuine Christian maturity recognizes that in Christ *all* Christian leaders—and everything else—have become part of the Christians' inheritance (3:18–23). Paul concludes by showing that Christian leaders and those who follow them must alike recognize that God alone is the One who makes the distinctions, and he alone rightly assesses performance (4:1–7). Indeed, the Corinthians should learn this lesson by the simple contrast between their own self-vaunting pretensions and the way the apostles are treated as the scum of the earth (4:8–11). They should learn to imitate the Christian conduct of their own father in Christ, the apostle Paul himself, and thus align themselves with what is normative in other churches (4:14–17). The prospect of Paul's impending visit constitutes both a final appeal and a scarcely veiled threat (4:18–21).

Whether the further reports that Paul deals with in chapters 5–6 also came from Chloe's people or from some other source—perhaps from Stephanas, Fortunatus, and Achaicus (16:17)—is unclear. Three issues dominate these chapters. The first is a case of incest (5:1–13), resulting in Paul's clarifying what he had meant in an earlier letter to the Corinthians (5:9–13); the second deals with the problem of litigation between believers (6:1–11); and the third addresses some men in the Corinthian congregation who so misunderstood their supposed spirituality that they thought they were free to frequent prostitutes, presumably on the ground that this involved merely the body.

In response to a written inquiry from the Corinthians (7:1), probably brought to Paul by Stephanas, Fortunatus, and Achaicus (16:17), Paul sets himself to address the topics they raise. The first has to do with marriage and related matters (7:1–40). The second, dealing with food sacrificed to idols (8:1–11:1), is sometimes alleged to include one or two excursuses, but the general line of argument is fairly clear. In 8:1–13, Paul insists that divisions of opinion as to whether it is proper to eat food that has been sacrificed to idols must be resolved on the basis of self-sacrificial love, not claims to superior knowledge. Chapter 9, cast in part as Paul's defense of his apostolicity, shows that Paul perceives the connection between this problem and the divisiveness he treated in chapters 1–4: in both cases a raw triumphalism prevails. Paul combats this evil and addresses both problems by pointing to his own commitment to self-denial as the very hallmark of his apostolicity: despite his many rights as an apostle, he voluntarily lays them aside so as to win as many as possible to Christ. This model of self-control and self-denial must characterize all Christians (9:24–27). The negative example of Israel thus becomes directly relevant: it is all too easy to begin well but not persevere, and thus to fall under God's judgment (10:1–13). If idolatry is to be avoided, Christians should not participate in the worship of pagan temples (10:14–22).

The next three problems that Paul treats have to do with the public meetings of the Corinthian Christians. The first deals with the relationship between men and women, especially as it was surfacing in a dispute over the issue of head covering for women (11:2–16). The second addresses abuses at the Lord's Supper (11:17–34). And the third deals with the distribution and exercise of the Spirit's gifts (12:1–14:40), especially the relative value of prophecy and tongues (14:1–25). Here the apostle insists on the need for diversity in unity (chap. 12), the utter necessity and permanence of love, the "more excellent way" (chap. 13), the importance of intelligibility in the church (14:1–25), and the proper ordering of the church's corporate meetings so far as the exercise of the gifts is concerned (14:26–40). In the most distinctly theological chapter, Paul deals with the resurrection of believers (chap. 15), insisting that the proper prototype is the resurrection of Jesus Christ, denying that any wedge can be driven between these two resurrections so far as kind is concerned, thereby forcing his readers to direct their gaze and their aspirations to the triumph at the end. Paul brings his handling of the Corinthians' written agenda to a close by clearing up some questions on the collection (16:1–11) and on the coming of Apollos (16:12).

The epistle concludes with some final exhortations (16:13–18) and greetings (16:19–24).

2 Corinthians

Following the salutation (1:1–2), there is a lengthy thanksgiving (1:3–11). Such thanksgiving sections are characteristically placed after the salutation in many Hellenistic letters, including twelve of the thirteen letters in the Pauline corpus (the exception is Galatians); but this one is particularly long and emotional and focuses rather more on Paul's experiences (of "a deadly peril") than is usually the case.

Paul plunges into a defense of his travel plans (1:12–2:13). He denies that he has acted in a worldly or fickle manner (1:12–14). After reviewing his plans (1:15–22), he explains the reason why he changed them: he was reluctant to cause the Corinthians as much grief as he had on an earlier visit (1:23–2:4). This leads to instruction how to forgive and comfort someone the congregation had properly punished, apparently for opposing Paul and thereby damaging the Corinthian believers (2:5–11). Paul then begins the recital of the events that have led to the writing of the present letter (2:12–13), but the recital is broken up by an outburst of praise and a lengthy articulation of the nature and purpose of his ministry (2:14–7:4).

Paul begins this long section by insisting that God himself has made him competent for this ministry, which divides people around him as he serves as "the aroma of Christ among those who are being saved and those who are perishing" (2:14–3:6). This leads to a comparison and contrast between ministry under the old covenant and under the new (3:7–18). Since Paul has received this new-covenant ministry by the mercy of God, he is committed to integrity in the proclamation of the "gospel of the glory of Christ," regardless of how he himself is received (4:1–6). The treasure is Christ; the earthenware vessel in which the treasure is contained is Paul and his ministry (4:7–18). That does not mean this earthenware vessel will always be poor and perishing: the ultimate prospect is the transformation that comes when the "heavenly dwelling" swallows up Paul's mortality in life (5:1–10). With such a prospect before him, Paul's motives in life and ministry are to please Christ, not those to whom he ministers; yet far from suggesting indifference toward his hearers, this gospel and this view of ministry ensure that it is nothing less than the love of Christ that compels him to serve as Christ's ambassador, proclaiming reconciliation and a new beginning on the basis of Christ's sacrifice for sins (5:16–21). Therefore Paul pleads with the Corinthians to have an open heart to God and to God's ambassador, so as not to receive God's grace in vain (6:1–13); for they must understand that proper response to God is exclusive (6:14–7:1). So Paul brings his appeal to a close (7:2–4).

At this point, Paul resumes his account of the return of Titus and the encouraging report he brought with him (7:5–16). Paul is almost euphoric with transparent relief that the Corinthians have responded with repentance and godly sorrow to the earlier rebukes by visit and letter. This means it is possible for Paul to bring up a matter of constant concern to him at this stage of his ministry, namely, the collection for the Christians in Jerusalem and the Corinthians' part in it (8:1–9:15). The Macedonians had set a high standard by their sacrificial giving (8:1–6); the Corinthians, who had been the first to respond, are now exhorted to bring the project to completion as well as they began it (8:7–15). Titus's mission is designed to further the cause (8:16–24) and to prepare the Corinthians for a visit by Paul himself, possibly accompanied by some Macedonians (9:1–5). Paul concludes by setting the collection within a theological framework that ties this ministry to the gospel and to the glory of God (9:6–15).

The nature of the relationship between chapters 1–9 and 10–13 is disputed (see the section "Occasion" below), but the latter seem to depict Paul's response to a fresh outbreak of opposition at Corinth. Paul appeals for a faith that is obedient (10:1–6) and condemns the opposition for its ugly boasting and one-upmanship (10:7–18). In 11:1–15 he exposes the false apostles who have usurped authority in the church and denounces their false criteria. Then, answering fools according to their folly, Paul engages in a little boasting of his own—by inverting all the criteria of his opponents and boasting in things they would despise (11:16–33). In fact, Paul boasts in weakness, so that the power of God may powerfully operate through him (12:1–10). The Corinthians themselves are to blame for not taking decisive action against these opponents. Paul contrasts his own motives (12:11–21), begging the Corinthian believers to reconsider their course and warning them that if necessary, he will take strong action when he arrives on his third visit (13:1–10). The epistle ends with a final appeal, greetings, and the words of "the grace" (13:11–13 [vv. 11–14 in NIV]).

AUTHOR

Paul is identified as the author in the opening verses of both epistles, and few have contested the claim. In the case of 2 Corinthians, various partition theories have been proposed (discussed below). In most such theories, the various sections are nevertheless ascribed to Paul. The most persistent exception is 2 Corinthians

6:14–7:1; a number of scholars judge this unit to be a later interpolation written, perhaps, by someone in the Pauline school. The theory can be tested only by jointly weighing the corresponding reconstructions of Paul's relationships with the Corinthian church and the literary evidence advanced to justify this partition. These matters will be treated shortly.

DESTINATION

Corinth was located on the isthmus that connects the Peloponnese with the rest of Greece. Not only was it ideally situated to control north-south trade, but because the port of Lechaeum lay a mile and a half to the north (on the Gulf of Corinth) and Cenchrea (Rom. 16:1) was just over seven miles to the east on the Saronic Gulf, it also provided an indispensable land link between east and west.

The wealthy and ancient city of Corinth was utterly destroyed by the Romans in 146 B.C., and its citizens were killed or sold into slavery. Roman might ensured that the prohibition against rebuilding it was respected. Nevertheless, a century later Julius Caesar founded the city afresh, this time as a Roman colony, and from 29 B.C. on, it served as the seat of a proconsul and the capital of the senatorial province of Achaia. The new city was populated by people from various parts of the empire, doubtless not a few of them retired soldiers. According to Strabo *Geog.* (8.6.23c), many were freedmen from Rome, whose status was only a cut above slaves. Jews were certainly included in the new citizenry (a broken inscription of uncertain date, with the words "Synagogue of the Hebrews," has been discovered, confirming Acts 18:4). Some Greeks were also residents of the new Corinth, perhaps large numbers of them; but the Romans dominated the scene with their laws, culture, and religion. Much of the empire had been thoroughly Hellenized, however, so not only was the lingua franca Greek but doubtless many ties—religious, philosophical, and cultural—were quickly reestablished with the rest of the Greek peninsula. From Asia and Egypt came various mystery cults. Because there was no landed aristocracy in the new Corinth, there arose an aristocracy of wealth. Inevitably, the poor were correspondingly despised or ignored (see 1 Cor. 11:17–22).

It is important not to read the old city's character into the new city (as Pausanius 2.3.7 already makes clear). Old Corinth had such a notorious reputation that "to Corinthianize" could mean "to fornicate," and "Corinthian girl" was a way of referring to a whore. Clay votives of human genitals have come down to us from the old city. They were offered to Asclepius, the god of healing, in the hope that that part of the body, suffering from venereal disease, would be healed. Probably Strabo's description of the one thousand temple prostitutes of the old city's temple of Aphrodite was exaggerated,[1] but the reality must have been bad enough to win such an egregious reputation. Even so, it is far from clear that such associations were carried across to the new city; but traditions like that die hard, and as a great port city it is unlikely that new Corinth established a reputation for moral probity (see 1 Cor. 6:12ff.).

---

[1] H. Conzelmann, "Korinth und die Mädchen der Aphrodite: Zur Religionsgeschichte der Stadt Korinth," *NAG* 8 (1967–68): 247–61; Jerome Murphy-O'Connor, *St. Paul's Corinth: Texts and Archaeology* (Wilmington, Del.: Glazier, 1983), pp. 55–57.

OCCASION

Historical Reconstruction

Paul first preached the gospel in Corinth during his second missionary journey (Acts 18). Supporting himself with his trade as a tentmaker or leatherworker, he lived with Aquila and Priscilla, who had recently moved to Corinth from Rome (Acts 18:1–3). As usual, Paul began his ministry by trying to convince all who attended the synagogue, Jews and Gentiles alike, that Jesus was the promised Messiah (v. 4). Once Timothy and Silas rejoined him, Paul's ministry increased, possibly in part because they brought gifts from the Macedonian churches that freed him to devote more time to preaching (v. 5). As his ministry increased, so did the opposition. Paul was forced to move his ministry next door to the house of Titius Justus. So fruitful was his evangelism that not only many pagans but Crispus himself, the synagogue ruler, and his entire family believed in the Lord Jesus (vv. 7–8).

Only recently delivered from bruising punishment in Philippi (Acts 16), and having just barely escaped similar battering in Thessalonica and Berea (Acts 17), Paul approached Corinth "in weakness and fear, and with much trembling" (1 Cor. 2:3), but was encouraged by a dream in which the exalted Christ assured him of safety and much fruit (Acts 18:9–10). Paul stayed a year and a half, laying the only possible foundation, Jesus Christ himself (1 Cor. 3:10–11). After seeing the church well established, Paul left Corinth by ship (probably in the spring of A.D. 51: see discussion below in the section "Date"), crossing the Aegean Sea with Priscilla and Aquila, whom he left in Ephesus while he headed for Jerusalem— hoping, perhaps (if we follow the Western text of Acts 18:21), to arrive there before the Feast (Passover or Pentecost). He did not remain long in Jerusalem but soon returned to his home church in Antioch and shortly after returned to Ephesus. There he began an enormously fruitful ministry of two and a half years (probably the autumn of 52 to the spring of 55); during that period he wrote 1 Corinthians.

Meanwhile, others had come to build on the foundation that Paul had laid in Corinth. Apollos worked there (1 Cor. 3:6), and probably Peter as well.[2] There is no evidence that these or other leaders had fostered a party spirit, consciously attempting to form a coterie of personal devotees. Nevertheless, doubtless owing to factors still to be examined, the spiritually immature Corinthians formed partisan groupings that claimed to follow this or that leader (1 Cor. 1:11). The church as a whole was less than satisfied with Paul's leadership (1 Cor. 4:3, 15; 9:1–2), and the integrity of its life was marred by abuses at the Lord's Table (11:17–34), at least one notorious case of immorality (5:1–5; cf. 6:12–20), public litigation among members (6:1–8), uncertainties about the place of marriage (chap. 7) and the propriety of eating food that had been offered to idols (chap. 8), infatuation with the more spectacular of the charismatic gifts without any profound commitment to mutual love (chaps. 12–14), and a decidedly aberrant view of the resurrection (chap. 15).

---

[2] See C. K. Barrett, "Cephas and Corinth," in *Abraham unser Vater: Juden und Christen im Gespräch über die Bibel*, Fs. Otto Michel, ed. O. Betz, M. Hengel, and P. Schmidt, AGSU 5 (Leiden: Brill, 1963), pp. 1–12.

How Paul first came to hear of some of these problems we cannot be sure, but apparently in response to a communication from them, he wrote them a letter (referred to in 1 Cor. 5:9), most of whose contents are lost, but which forbade association with immoral people. This letter, sometimes referred to as the previous letter, we may designate Corinthians A. Most scholars agree that it has not survived (though see discussion below). Perhaps the Corinthians had posed a question about church discipline, and Paul assumed this question as the context of his response, while in fact some of his readers took his response in the widest sense and thus misinterpreted him (1 Cor. 5:9–13).

At some point during his Ephesian ministry, Paul received reports from "some from Chloe's household" (1:11) about the ugly factionalism in Corinth. The three official delegates of the church—Stephanas, Fortunatus, and Achaicus (16:17)— brought not only the gift from the Corinthians but also the church's letter and their own verbal reports, which together established Paul's agenda as he wrote 1 Corinthians (which might be designated Corinthians B).

When Paul sent off 1 Corinthians, he fully intended to remain in Ephesus until Pentecost (probably A.D. 55), then cross the Aegean to Macedonia, visit the churches there, and travel south to Corinth, where he expected to remain "awhile, or even spend the winter" (16:5–8). Meanwhile, he sent Timothy, exhorting the Corinthians to receive him warmly and "send him on his way in peace" (1 Cor. 16:10–11; cf. Acts 19:22) so that he could return to Paul, presumably with a report. After sending the letter, Paul changed his plans a little: he now proposed to visit Corinth twice, once on the way to Macedonia and once on the way back, intending to sail from Corinth to Judea (2 Cor. 1:15–16). On this return leg he hoped to collect considerable money from Macedonia and Achaia (including Corinth) for the relief of the believers in Jerusalem, who were suffering from famine and persecution.

When he formulated these plans, Paul apparently felt no urgency to get to Corinth. After all, he was in no hurry to leave Ephesus, since the "great door for effective work" (1 Cor. 16:9) was still open for him there. But when Timothy arrived in Corinth, he found the situation beyond his ability to manage. Even 1 Corinthians, the apostle's letter, had not had the good effect Paul had envisaged. Whether Timothy himself returned with a grim report, or Paul found out about the grim situation some other way, he abandoned any thought of further delay and immediately set out for Corinth. This turned into a distressing confrontation that Paul himself had warned the Corinthians they should avoid (1 Cor. 4:21)—a "painful visit," to use Paul's language (2 Cor. 2:1). We cannot determine whether or not Corinthians B (= 1 Corinthians) had helped the Corinthian believers resolve a number of matters, but it is quite clear that animus against Paul was still very strong and focused in one or two leaders whom the Corinthians either tacitly supported or refused to condemn. About the same time, and probably before the "painful visit," the church had been invaded by some self-designated Christian leaders. Probably they called themselves apostles (2 Cor. 11:13–15) and carried letters of recommendation with them (cf. 2 Cor. 3:1–3). They were not apostles in the way Paul was, a witness of the resurrection with a personal commission from Christ to evangelize where Christ was not known; they were probably apostles in the general sense that they were agents of others who had commissioned them. Probably they were in some sense Judaizers,[3] that is, those who were trying to bring the church more into line with Jewish piety and practice (see 2 Cor. 11:16ff.)—though doubtless they, like Paul, had also enjoyed considerable exposure to Hellenistic education and, unlike Paul, had absorbed more of the values of the Sophists than they realized (see further discussion below in the section "The Character of Paul's Opponents").

From Paul's perspective at the time, the "painful visit" was a complete fiasco. At least one of the opponents had attacked him in deeply insulting ways (2 Cor. 2:5–8, 10; 7:12); worse, the work of the gospel was in serious jeopardy. Why Paul left at this point is uncertain. Perhaps he hoped time would heal some of the wounds and bring the Corinthians to their senses; perhaps he had other pressing engagements. In any case, he resolved not to return immediately. This opened him up to the charge of being fickle, willing to change his commitments at a whim, even though the fundamental reason why he did not return was to spare them the pain of another confrontation (2 Cor. 1:16ff.). But this did not mean Paul was prepared to let the situation slide. He sent them another letter, which we may designate Corinthians C. Written "out of great distress and anguish of heart and with many tears" (2 Cor. 2:4), this letter assured the Corinthians of Paul's love for them but also laid down the standards he expected in the churches in his charge and sought to determine if they would meet those standards (2:9). For this reason, Corinthians C is sometimes called the "tearful letter" or the "severe letter." Delivered by Titus (who may have been a more forceful person than Timothy), this letter demanded the punishment of the ringleader who had maligned and opposed Paul so maliciously (2:3–9; 7:8–12). In all probability this letter has also been lost.[4]

Titus also had the responsibility to organize the collection for Jerusalem (2 Cor. 8:6). The fact that Paul could still expect the Corinthians to participate is evidence that he did not, despite the painful visit, regard the church as fundamentally apostate. He knew of their wealth and had boasted of their initial willingness not only to Titus (7:14) but also to the Macedonians (9:2). Probably he was afraid that some of the animus against him would degenerate into an unwillingness to cooperate in this financial assistance plan; probably he feared that the interlopers were by their strenuous demands for financial support (11:7, 12–20; 12:14) siphoning off funds that Paul felt should go to assist the poor believers in Jerusalem.

Meanwhile, Paul's ministry in Ephesus was providing another set of dangers

---

[3]The term "Judaizer" is problematic. In modern usage, the overwhelming majority of scholars apply it to Jews who in some sense accept Jesus as the Messiah but who insist that Gentiles convert to Judaism before (or at least as part of) coming to faith in Jesus (see also chap. 10, on Galatians). But in the first century, "to Judaize" meant "to live like a Jew (even though one wasn't a Jew)," and in this sense a "Judaizer" would be a Gentile trying to live like a Jew. In deference to modern usage, however, we have retained the term in the contemporary sense.

[4]This is much more likely that that the "severe letter" is in fact 1 Corinthians and that the person in question was the man guilty of incest (1 Cor. 5:1ff.), pace Philip E. Hughes, *Paul's Second Epistle to the Corinthians*, NICNT (Grand Rapids: Eerdmans, 1962), pp. xxviii–xxx. The passages in 2 Corinthians referring to Paul's demand for the discipline of the ringleader betray no hint of sexual immorality in the individual concerned. The offense was against Paul, and the critical question revolved around whether or not the church would rally to the apostle (7:12). Moreover, 1 Corinthians does not sound intense enough to be the letter described in 2 Cor. 2:4. For the view that Corinthians C is in reality 2 Cor. 10–13, see discussion below in the section "The Integrity of 1 and 2 Corinthians."

and challenges, a "deadly peril" such that he "despaired even of life," feeling upon himself "the sentence of death" (2 Cor. 1:8–10). We know nothing of the details. Shortly after the Demetrius riot (Acts 19:23–20:1), however, Paul left Ephesus for Troas (2 Cor. 2:12, 13—"Troas" might refer either to the port city or to the Troad region in which it lay), where he hoped not only to preach the gospel but to meet Titus returning with news of Corinth. Only the first of these hopes was happily realized. On the one hand, he "found that the Lord had opened a door" for him (2 Cor. 2:12); on the other, as he wrote, "I still had no peace of mind, because I did not find my brother Titus there" (2 Cor. 2:13). So Paul left Troas and headed for Macedonia (2:13); apparently he had established a contingency plan to meet Titus there, should the meeting at Troas not take place. In Macedonia Paul pursued both his pastoral ministry (Acts 20:1–2) and his organizing of the collection for the Jerusalem believers (2 Cor. 8:1–4; 9:2). These churches were themselves facing "the most severe trial" and "extreme poverty" (8:2), owing not least to active persecution; but worse still, from Paul's perspective, was that Titus had not yet shown up, so he still had no idea how his severe letter had been received in Corinth. "When we came into Macedonia, this body of ours had no rest, but we were harassed at every turn—conflicts on the outside, fears within" (7:5).

Titus soon arrived, and Paul's distress rapidly changed to near euphoria (2 Cor. 7:6–7). Immediately after sending the severe letter, he had suffered second thoughts, fearing that he might hurt the Corinthians unduly; but with Titus's encouraging report, Paul's fear was displaced by joy. If his letter had wounded them, it was "only for a little while" (7:8). "Godly sorrow brings repentance that leads to salvation and leaves no regret," Paul observes, "but worldy sorrow brings death" (7:10). Indeed, Paul's entire response, at least in 2 Corinthians 1–9, breathes an atmosphere of bruised relations that have recently eased. There is a noticeable sigh of relief that the worst is over.

That is what makes 2 Corinthians 10–13 so difficult to interpret: the tone in these chapters assumes that the situation in Corinth had become desperately dangerous yet again. Any further historical reconstruction is inextricably tied to questions about the integrity of the Corinthian epistles.

The Integrity of 1 and 2 Corinthians

The historical reconstruction developed so far, though in its main outline enjoying widespread support, depends on the integrity of 1 Corinthians and of 2 Corinthians 1–9. If parts of these letters were written at different times, perhaps by different authors, and somehow came together to constitute our present letters, then the reconstruction is without foundation. We would be left with too many unconnected fragments to make any widely believed reconstruction possible. Some of the points of dispute will shortly be surveyed, but first the contribution of 2 Corinthians 10–13 must be assessed.

The Place of 2 Corinthians 10–13 Despite widespread agreement on the main lines of the historical reconstruction just sketched in, there is equally widespread disagreement over the place of 2 Corinthians 10–13. Four principal theories address this issue.

1. Many argue that Paul, delighted by the news he received from Titus, immediately penned 2 Corinthians 1–9 (which thus becomes Corinthians D) and sent it off. They suggest that 2 Corinthians 10–13 is to be identified with Corinthians C, the severe and painful letter.[5]

The advantage of this theory is that it fully explains the remarkable difference in tone between 2 Corinthians 1–9 and 10–13. The former chapters transparently reflect the good news that Titus has brought with him. If Paul must still give some explanation of his movements (1:15–2:13) and outline again the nature of apostolic ministry (3:1–18), if he must still exhort the Corinthians to press on with the collection (chaps. 8–9), he does so with scarcely restrained joy and with restored confidence in the church's obedience and growing maturity. By contrast, the language and emphases in chapters 10–13 are alternately angry, broken, and scathingly ironic. Paul's joy has disappeared; his confidence in the maturity of the Corinthians has dissipated. No longer do we find Paul saying, "I am glad I can have complete confidence in you" (7:16); now he must say, "Examine yourselves to see whether you are in the faith; test yourselves. Do you not realize that Christ Jesus is in you—unless, of course, you fail the test?" (13:5). Moreover, proponents of this view argue that several passages in chapters 1–9 refer to statements *previously* made in chapters 10–13 (e.g., 1:23/13:2; 2:3/13:10; 2:9/10:6; 4:2/12:16; 7:2/12:17). And how, they ask, could Paul look forward to preaching the gospel "in the regions beyond you" (10:16) if he is already in Greece (more specifically, Macedonia) when he writes? Should he not have said "regions beyond *us*"? Surely it is easier to think he writes such words from Ephesus—which presupposes that they were written *before* chapters 1–9.

Nevertheless, the theory stumbles over several obstacles. First, no Greek manuscript of 2 Corinthians suggests that the epistle originally terminated at the end of chapter 9, or suggests that chapters 10–13 originally had a proem typical of the epistles Paul wrote to churches where he was known. This is not decisive, of course: one could argue that our 2 Corinthians was not published until the two parts had been fused together. But in that case one ought to be able to give convincing reasons why someone should have performed such fusion. Second, the expression "the regions beyond you" (τὰ ὑπερέκεινα ὑμῶν [*ta hyperekeina hymōn]*) does not demand that Paul not be writing from Greece. He may have thought of Achaia (where Corinth lay) as quite distinct from Macedonia; or he may have said "beyond you [Greeks]" in such a way as to refer to *their* land while excluding himself (as a Pole heading west might tell a German, on German soil, that he is going beyond "your country" on his way to France). Third, chapters 10–13 do not contain the one thing we are certain must have been in the severe letter, namely, the demand that a certain offender be punished (2:5–6; 7:12).

[5]So, e.g., A. Plummer, *A Critical and Exegetical Commentary on the Second Epistle of St Paul to the Corinthians*, ICC (Edinburgh: T. & T. Clark, 1915), pp. xxvii–xxxvi; R. H. Strachan, *The Second Epistle of Paul to the Corinthians*, MNTC (London: Hodder & Stoughton, 1935), p. xix; R. Bultmann, *The Second Letter to the Corinthians* (ET Minneapolis: Augsburg, 1985), p. 18; H. D. Wendland, *Die Briefe an die Korinther*, NTD 7 (Göttingen: Vandenhoeck & Ruprecht, 1965), p. 8; W. Schmithals, *Gnosticism in Corinth: An Investigation of the Letters to the Corinthians* (ET Nashville: Abingdon, 1971), p. 96.

Fourth, chapters 10–13 promise an imminent visit (12:14; 13:1), but Corinthians C, the severe letter, was sent *instead* of another painful visit (1:23; 2:1). Fifth, 12:18 clearly assumes that Titus had paid at least one visit to Corinth to assist in the collection; in other words, it presupposes either 8:6a or 8:16–19. Either way, it becomes hard to believe that chapters 1–9, where these two passages are embedded, were written *after* chapters 10–13, where 12:18 is located.

Still on the collection, if Paul was charged with using the funds himself (12:16), how could he later boast so freely to Titus (7:14) and to the Macedonians (9:2) about the Corinthians' generosity, without making some allusion to a patching up of misunderstanding on the point? It seems best to conclude that this first theory introduces more problems than it solves.

2. Some argue for the essential unity of 2 Corinthians: the entire book was written at one time.[6] Certainly this coheres with the textual evidence. If some reason must be given for the remarkable change in tone between chapters 1–9 and 10–13, there is no shortage of theories. Perhaps Paul had a sleepless night before composing the second part; perhaps the two parts of the book betray the ups and downs of a mercurial temperament; perhaps Paul finally exposes his deepest and hitherto repressed emotions on these matters. Better yet, Hughes argues that the difference in tone between the two parts of the book is greatly exaggerated: there is really no problem to solve. He draws comparisons between 1:13 and 10:11; 1:17 and 10:2; 2:1 and 12:14, 21 (see also 13:1–2); 2:17 and 12:19; 3:2 and 12:11; 6:13 and 11:2 (see also 12:14); 8:6, 8, 22 and 12:17–18.[7]

Similar lists of comparisons, however, could be drawn between 2 Corinthians 10–13 and 1 Corinthians, but no one would be brash enough to suggest they show that 2 Corinthians 10–13 once belonged to 1 Corinthians. Doubtless there is a difficult question of judgment involved: Are the two principal parts of our 2 Corinthians sufficiently different in tone to throw doubt on the assumption that they were written at the same time, under the same circumstances, in one letter? In our judgment, the differences in tone and emphasis are sufficiently strong that some account must be given of them, and the psychological solutions are not very satisfying. Was Paul's temperament so mercurial that it seriously affected his pastoral stance toward his converts, with no other cause than the day Paul happened to be writing? Is there any evidence that Paul was so emotionally immature and so full of repressed resentments that he was prone to losing control of himself? A more sympathetic reading is that Paul is constantly aware of what image he is projecting and takes it into account (see 1 Cor. 4:21). In 2 Corinthians 1–9, Paul is primarily engaged in building bridges toward the Corinthians, encouraging them, removing any obstacle in the way of their understanding; even the rebukes he administers are part of that design. By contrast, in chapters 10–13 Paul deploys sharp irony and dire threat, and whatever encouragement he offers is part of this pattern.

---

[6]E.g., E. B. Allo, *Saint Paul: Seconde épître aux Corinthiens* (Paris: Gabalda, 1956), pp. lii–liii; H. Lietzmann, supplemented by W. G. Kümmel, *An die Korinther I, II*, HNT 9 (Tübingen: J. C. B. Mohr, 1969), pp. 139–40; R. V. G. Tasker, *The Second Epistle of Paul to the Corinthians*, TNTC (Grand Rapids: Eerdmans, 1958), pp. 30–35; Hughes, *Second Corinthians*, pp. xxiii–xxxv; Kümmel, pp. 287–93; W. H. Bates, "The Integrity of II Corinthians," *NTS* 12 (1965–66): 56–59.

[7]Hughes, *Second Corinthians*, xxxi–xxxv.

Harris offers a variation on this theory.[8] He suggests that when Paul received Titus's good report, he did not immediately write any part of 2 Corinthians. Instead, he continued his pastoral work in Macedonia and quite possibly engaged in pioneer evangelism along the Egnatian Way and right around to Illyricum (see Rom. 15:19–21). When he returned to Macedonia, he heard of fresh problems in Corinth and wrote the entire epistle. This has the effect of explaining the tone of 2 Corinthians 10–13, but the cost is high: it fails to explain why 2 Corinthians 1–9 is so positive, why there is such euphoria in Paul's words at the reception of Titus's good report (7:6–16). Like the other theories that argue for the essential unity of 2 Corinthians, this one does not adequately grapple with the differences in stance between chapters 1–9 and 10–13.

3. The most popular theory among recent commentators is that chapters 10–13 were written after 1–9. In this view, chapters 10–13 constitute the whole or part of another letter, Corinthians E. After Paul heard from Titus, he immediately wrote Corinthians D (= 1 Cor. 1–9) and sent it off. Shortly after, however, he learned that the basically positive report brought by Titus was either premature or obsolete. The Corinthians had succumbed again to their carping criticism of Paul and had been wooed by the interlopers into a stance that was threatening the very integrity of the gospel. Once more they were taking decisive action against these leaders, and they were succumbing to the blandishments of the intellectual and cultural arrogance typical of Sophists. Paul therefore responds with his fifth letter to the Corinthians, namely, 2 Corinthians 10–13.[9]

The primary advantage of this explanation—and it is very weighty—is that it fully accounts for the profound difference in stance between chapters 1–9 and 10–13. Correlatively, it explains why in 12:19–13:10 Paul envisages a third trip to Corinth, a visit that will be characterized by stern justice or (Paul hopes) happy reconciliation, but which is a visit unforeseen in and inappropriate to chapters 1–9. Some also argue that this theory best accounts for Paul's references to Titus's behavior in 12:17–18. There Paul, expecting a negative answer, asks the Corinthians if Titus or any other of his emissaries had ever exploited them, presumably in connection with the collection. This, it is argued, presupposes that chapters 10–13 were written *after* 8:6, 16–24 and 9:3–5, where Paul tells his readers he is about to send Titus.

This last point is surely not very strong, since the first part of 8:6 demonstrates that Titus had been sent on an *earlier* visit to Corinth in connection with the collection, and 12:17–18 may refer to that earlier trip, thereby removing any need to postulate a time gap between 8:6, 16–24; 9:3–5, and 12:17–18. That no manuscript tradition supports the division of 2 Corinthians into two letters is important, though not decisive, since it might be argued that the two parts were published together: perhaps (it is suggested) they were copied onto the same scroll. If so, why should the conclusion of 1 Corinthians 1–9 be lost, along with

---

[8]Murray J. Harris, "2 Corinthians," in *EBC* 10:305–6. However, in a private communication, Dr. Harris indicates that in his forthcoming NIGTC commentary on 2 Corinthians he has changed his mind and followed much the same line adopted in this *Introduction*.

[9]So F. F. Bruce, *1 and 2 Corinthians* (London: Oliphants, 1971), pp. 166–70; Victor Paul Furnish, *II Corinthians*, AB 32A (Garden City, N.Y.: Doubleday, 1984), pp. 30–41; Ralph P. Martin, *2 Corinthians*, WBC 40 (Waco, Tex.: Word, 1986), p. xl; Colin G. Kruse, *The Second Epistle of Paul to the Corinthians*, TNTC (Grand Rapids: Eerdmans, 1987), pp. 29–35.

the greetings, salutation, and thanksgiving of 2 Corinthians 10–13? In short, this theory is possible, and better than the other two, but it has to rely rather heavily on a stupid scribe early in the manuscript tradition.

4. Perhaps a minor modification to the third theory would improve it. If Paul was as eager to hear from Titus as 2 Corinthians 2:13 suggests, it is altogether natural to assume that, once he heard Titus's good report, he immediately set about communicating his relief to the Corinthians. He was grateful that his severe letter (= Corinthians C) had not done the damage he feared, delighted that the Corinthians had responded with repentance and obedience, and encouraged to learn that his most obstreperous and dangerous opponent had been disciplined. But even if he set to writing (or dictating) immediately, there is no reason to think he finished it promptly. This epistle is fairly long, and Paul was at this time extraordinarily pressed by his ministry in Macedonia. It is not unreasonable to suppose that the completion of the letter was delayed for weeks, or even longer: the phenomenon of unfinished letters is not entirely unknown today, and our letters are usually much shorter than 2 Corinthians! If during that time Paul received additional information about the situation in Corinth and learned that it had once again plummeted into the disastrous state presupposed by 2 Corinthians 10–13, the abrupt change of tone that begins at 10:1 would be accounted for. In other words, one might reasonably postulate that after finishing chapters 1–9, but before completing the letter and sending it off, Paul received bad news from Corinth and changed his tack in the final chapters of his epistle.

Several objections have been raised against this reconstruction.

1. It has been argued that if Paul had received bad news from Corinth before chapters 1–9 had been sent, he would have torn them up and begun a new letter. But this overlooks how much of chapters 1–9 is valuable in its own right. Indeed, if Paul left some markers in chapters 10–13 that he *had* received fresh information about the disastrous turn the Corinthians were taking (see discussion below), then the Corinthian readers would become aware of the startling contrast between Paul's joy at Titus's report and his broken indignation at their recent defection. This would have the effect of turning even the earlier chapters into an *implicit* rebuke, since the causes of Paul's joy—Corinthian repentance, obedience, and zeal—would no longer be operative.

2. The only serious difficulty with this theory is that nowhere in 2 Corinthians 10–13 does Paul explicitly state that he has received fresh information. It must be remembered (a point frequently forgotten) that this difficulty also attaches itself to the third theory, which meets it by positing that part of Corinthians E was lost when it was joined with Corinthians D to form 2 Corinthians. But it is possible to construct an alternative explanation as to why Paul makes no direct mention of the arrival of additional information. For instance, if some new report came to him in which many Corinthian believers, influenced by the false apostles (2 Cor. 11:13–15), were accusing Paul of showing too much meekness and gentleness to be a true apostle, then his opening words in 2 Corinthians 10:1 would be sufficient to draw attention to his knowledge of the latest in their list of theological fads: "By the meekness and gentleness of Christ, I appeal to you. . . ." If charges were now widely circulating in Corinth that Paul's formal credentials left a great deal to be desired, in comparison with those of the interlopers (10:12–18), that he could not be much of a teacher because he refused to charge for his services (11:7–12;

12:13), that his apostolic status could not amount to much because he did not talk much about the supernatural visions of which others were eager to speak (12:1–10), then his responses in all these areas would be enough to alert his readers that these latest developments had reached his ears.

3. We have already seen that some think the movements of Titus can be explained only if we postulate a break between chapters 9 and 10 (cf. 8:6, 16–24; 9:3–5, and 12:17–18). But the pressure is eased if 12:17–18 refers to Titus's *earlier* trip to Corinth (8:6a).

4. Some find it unlikely that the Corinthian church could have tumbled so quickly into such disarray. A slightly cynical response might be that such critics have not witnessed very closely much contemporary church life. More important, neither 1 Corinthians nor 2 Corinthians 1–9 encourages us to think that this was a very stable church. The Corinthian believers seem to have been characterized by various forms of arrogance, prone to attach themselves to various leaders, rather overconfident of their own spiritual discernment, and badly compromised with the surrounding culture. Nor is this the end of the evidence. Forty years later, Clement of Rome finds it necessary to write to the Corinthian church and speak against their dissensions and anarchy.

In short, the evidence is not sufficient for giving a decisive account of 2 Corinthians 10–13. On the whole, however, the fourth theory seems marginally stronger than the third, which is considerably more believable than either of the other two.

We may well ask if Paul's Corinthian correspondence succeeded in turning the situation around, at least temporarily. Again, no decisive answer can be given. But there is some hope for an optimistic answer in the fact that, when the threatened third visit actually took place (2 Corinthians 13:2–3), Paul found the time and tranquility to write his epistle to the Romans. That letter betrays some anxiety about the future (Rom. 15:30–31), but none about his present circumstances. It is unlikely that Paul would still be planning his trip to Spain (Rom. 15:24–28) if he thought his presence was still chronically necessary in Corinth (see 2 Cor. 10:15–16a). And the Corinthians did contribute to the collection for the poor believers in Jerusalem (Rom. 15:26–27), though how much this may reflect a healed relationship with Paul it is impossible to say.

Other Alleged Interpolations in 2 Corinthians It cannot be too strongly emphasized that "the literary and historical hypotheses stand or fall together."[10] In other words, those who find interpolations (a literary phenomenon) in 2 Corinthians usually provide a reconstructed history to account for the alleged interpolations—the more so if these interpolations include references to Paul's movements. The principal theories of interpolation focus on three passages.

2 Corinthians 2:14–7:4. Some scholars argue that these chapters (usually without 6:14–7:1; see below) constitute the whole or a part of a separate letter. They note that excellent flow is achieved by reading 7:5 immediately after 2:13: the subject of Titus's itinerary and Paul's trip to Macedonia is continued. Some think that 2:14–7:4 once belonged with chapters 10–13 to constitute the severe

---

[10]C. K. Barrett, *A Commentary on the Second Epistle to the Corinthians*, BNTC/HNTC (London: Black, 1973), p. 17.

letter (= Corinthians C);[11] others suggest that this is part of yet another letter, written before the severe letter, before the Corinthians had been taken over by Paul's opponents.[12]

But although 7:5 follows 2:13 rather nicely from a thematic point of view, other literary indications suggest there is a break. For instance, the words that begin 7:5 ("For when we came into Macedonia . . ."), although they pick up the theme of 2:13 ("So I said good-by to them and went on to Macedonia"), would be unduly repetitive if they followed on immediately. They sound much more as if Paul is *resuming* a theme, knowing he has digressed. Morever, several linking words tie 7:4 with 7:5–7 (παράκλησις (*paraklēsis*, "comfort"); χαρά/χαρῆναι (*chara/charēnai*, "joy"/"to be joyful"), θλῖψις/θλιβόμενοι (*thlipsis/thlibomenoi*, "troubles"/"being harassed"). There are also thematic ties: for example, "I have great confidence in you" (7:4) and "I am glad I can have complete confidence in you" (7:16). Moreover, any view that ties 2:14–7:4 to chapters 10–13 confronts all the problems discussed earlier that are associated with the entirely different pastoral stances reflected in the two sections.

To argue that 2:14–7:4 is an integral part of chapters 1–9 still leaves one with the responsibility of explaining why the line of thought from 2:13 to 7:5 is in some measure broken up. Many suggestions have been put forward. Some of them are convincing; most are not mutually exclusive but rather mutually supportive. Many have suggested that the mere mention of Titus's name (2:13) prompts Paul to make a conscious digression to express gratitude to God for the relief he felt when Titus did show up,[13] or to leap forward to a happy, theological articulation of the basis on which his restored relationship with the Corinthians must now rest. It has been argued that, just as 1:8–11 draws a contrast between human weakness and the power of God, so the same theme is repeated when Paul moves from the admission of his own weakness in 2:12–13 to the triumphant note of 2:14–17.[14] Others propose that Paul is concerned not to make the Corinthians feel guilty for the anxiety they caused him. Therefore, after so frankly admitting his anxiety (2:12–13), he quickly turns to emphasizing the victorious progress of the gospel everywhere (including Troas) and thus signals that he himself suffered no disastrous personal defeat for which they should feel responsible.[15] One writer thinks that the length of the interposing passage, 2:14–7:4, is occasioned by the fact that 2:14–16 is a second "traditional thanksgiving period" (all but one of the canonical Pauline Epistles contain at least one, normally right after the salutation; see 1:3–7). Typically, these thanksgiving periods anticipate the direction of Paul's argument, and in this way, 2:14–16 foreshadows the content of the following chapters.[16] Above all, one of the major themes of 2 Corinthians 1–9 is the assurance of God's comfort in our affliction, an idea

---

[11]So J. Weiss, *Earliest Christianity: A History of the Period* A.D. *30–150*, 2 vols. (New York: Harper & Row, 1959), 1:349; Bultmann, *Second Corinthians*, p. 18.

[12]Wendland, *Briefe an die Korinther*, p. 9; Schmithals, *Gnosticism in Corinth*, pp. 98–100; G. Bornkamm, "The History of the So-called Second Letter to the Corinthians," *NTS* 8 (1961–62): 259–60.

[13]E.g., Plummer, *Second Corinthians*, p. 67; Kümmel, p. 291; Harris, "2 Corinthians," pp. 303, 331; Allo, *Saint Paul*, p. 45.

[14]P. Bachmann, *Der zweite Brief des Paulus an die Korinther* (Leipzig: Deichert, 1922), pp. 126–27.

[15]With various emphases, Zahn 3:343 n. 1; Hughes, *Second Corinthians*, pp. 76–77.

[16]Margaret E. Thrall, "A Second Thanksgiving Period in II Corinthians," *JSNT* 16 (1982): 111–19.

found not only before and after this alleged interpolation (1:3–11; 7:5–7, 12–13) but throughout it (e.g., 4:7–5:8; 6:1–10; 7:4).[17] In short, there do not appear to be adequate reasons for taking 2:14–7:4 as an interpolation, while there are sufficient reasons to explain the superficial hiatus.

2 *Corinthians 6:14-7:1.* Within the larger section 2:14–7:4, these six verses are often taken to be a further interpolation,[18] and possibly non-Pauline.[19] The reasons most commonly advanced are as follows: (1) the passage constitutes a self-contained unit without any unambiguous references to the situation in Corinth; (2) it contains six hapax legomena (i.e. words or expressions that occur only here in the New Testament);[20] (3) the combination of body (σάρξ [*sarx*], "flesh," and spirit (7:1) in this context is said to be un-Pauline, since he normally opposes the two; (4) the passage seems to interrupt the flow from 6:13 to 7:2, which make excellent sense if they are simply joined; (5) some hold that it betrays an exclusivism more characteristic of Pharisaism than of the apostle of liberty; and (6) some also hold that the apocalyptic dualism—righteousness/iniquity, Christ/Belial, light/darkness—is more typical of Qumran than of Paul.

The arguments that take the passage to be non-Pauline are not so strong as they first seem. It has often been noted that "Pauline outbursts containing a high percentage of *hapax legomena* are not uncommon (1 Cor 4:7–13 has six *hapaxes* and 2 Cor 6:3–10 [the verses preceding the passage under consideration] has four."[21] Hughes observes that there are about fifty hapax legomena in 2 Corinthians alone.[22] Moreover, if (as Fee suggests) we query the significance of those unique words where elsewhere Paul uses a cognate term, only one remains, namely, "Beliar," which is so common in Jewish writings that it is impossible to think Paul did not know the term.[23] Although Betz finds the exclusivism of this passage so remarkable[24] he judges it to be an *anti*-Pauline fragment (surely a strange judgment when one recalls such passages as Rom. 8:9; 1 Cor. 6:12–20; 10:14–22; Gal. 1:8–9). Qumran offers somewhat parallel formal dualism to the fourth gospel, but almost no one today suggests that John is made up of Qumran fragments: there is simply insufficient evidence to support Fitzmyer's view[25] that this passage is an Essene composition reworked by some unknown Christian.[26] Moreover, although it is true that Paul regularly places "flesh" (σάρξ [*sarx*]) over against "spirit" where the spirit refers to the Holy Spirit (e.g., Gal. 6:16–25), here

---

[17]Kruse, *Second Corinthians*, p. 37.

[18]By the majority of contemporary scholars, including Wendland, *Briefe an die Korinther*, p. 212; and Schmithals, *Gnosticism in Corinth*, pp. 94–95.

[19]By a minority of contemporary scholars, including Bultmann, *Second Corinthians*, p. 180 and n. 202; and J. Gnilka, "2 Cor 6:14–7:1 in Light of the Qumran Texts and the Testaments of the Twelve Patriarchs," in *Paul and Qumran*, ed. J. Murphy-O'Connor (London: Chapman, 1968), pp. 48–68.

[20]Namely, ἑτεροζυγοῦντες (*heterozygountes*), μετοχή (*metochē*), συμφώνησις (*symphōnēsis*), Βελιάρ (*Beliar*), συγκατάθεσις (*sugkatathesis*), and μολυσμός (*molysmos*).

[21]Martin, p. 192.

[22]Hughes, *Second Corinthians*, p. 242.

[23]Gordon D. Fee, "II Corinthians vi.14–vii.1 and Food Offered to Idols," *NTS* 23 (1977): 144–45.

[24]H. D. Betz, "2 Cor.6:14–7:1: An Anti-Pauline Fragment?" *JBL* 92 (1973): 88–108.

[25]J. A. Fitzmyer, "Qumran and the Interpolated Paragraph in 2 Cor 6:14–7:1," in *Essays on the Semitic Background of the New Testament* (London: Chapman, 1971), pp. 205–17.

[26]See Bruce, *1 and 2 Corinthians*, p. 214, who notes that such dualisms are not exclusive to Qumran.

the entire expression "body and spirit" refers to the whole person. In short, the arguments in favor of the view that this is a non-Pauline fragment do not seem very convincing.

Still, the distinctiveness of the passage demands some explanation, and it is not entirely surprising that some have suggested that this is a Pauline excerpt from another letter, perhaps from the "previous" letter (= Corinthians A, referred to in 1 Cor. 5:9).[27] Quite apart from the difficulty of imagining why anyone (Paul or a later redactor) would interpolate such a passage here, there is another obvious hurdle: the "previous" letter forbade the believers from enjoying fellowship with *believers* who were behaving immorally; by contrast, this passage forbids believers from enjoying close fellowship with *unbelievers,* especially in the matter of idolatrous worship (see 1 Cor. 10:14–22).

A strong contingent of scholars insist on the authenticity and integrity of the passage,[28] though their explanations of the abruptness of its beginning and ending vary (most of which are not mutually exclusive). It has often been observed that 7:2 sounds more like a resumption of 6:13 than a mere continuation of it, which suggests that 6:14–7:1 is not an accidental digression. Some envisage a pause in dictation at 6:13;[29] Barrett suggests that Paul, aware of false apostles lurking in the background, opens his heart to urge restored relationships between the Corinthians and himself but warns them that this will entail a break with the world.[30] Dahl's view is similar (though he thinks the passage originated in a Qumran community and was reworked by Paul).[31] Hughes suggests that, having rearticulated the nature of his spiritual authority in the previous chapters, Paul now uses it to warn against the ever-pressing threat of paganism, but in a spirit entirely free of censoriousness, as the surrounding verses attest.[32] Fee notes the many parallels with 1 Corinthians 10:14–22 and reconstructs a development to argue that this passage is still dealing with the question of food offered to idols.[33] In short, to accept the basic integrity of 2 Corinthians at this point seems considerably less problematic than the alternatives.[34]

2 Corinthians 8–9. Several scholars have argued that chapter 8 is an interpolation,[35] or that chapter 9 is,[36] or that each is a separate letter and that both have

---

[27]E.g., Wendland, *Briefe an die Korinther,* p. 212; Strachan, *Second Corinthians,* pp. xv, 3–5; Schmithals, *Gnosticism in Corinth,* pp. 94–95.

[28]E.g., Plummer, *Second Corinthians,* pp. xxiii–xxvi, 208; Lietzmann, *An die Korinther,* p. 129; Allo, *Saint Paul,* pp. liii, 193–94; Hughes, *Second Corinthians,* pp. 241–44; Bruce, *1 and 2 Corinthians,* p. 214; Barrett, *Second Corinthians,* p. 194, Harris, "2 Corinthians," p. 303.

[29]Lietzmann, *An die Korinther,* p. 129; cautiously, Harris, "2 Corinthians," p. 303.

[30]Barrett, *Second Corinthians,* p. 194.

[31]N. A. Dahl, "A Fragment and Its Context: 2 Corinthians 6:14–7:1," in *Studies in Paul* (Minneapolis: Augsburg, 1972), pp. 62–69.

[32]Hughes, *Second Corinthians,* p. 244.

[33]Fee, "II Corinthians vi.14–vii.1."

[34]The suggestion of J.-F. Collange, *Enigmes de la deuxième épître de Paul aux Corinthiens,* SNTSMS 18 (Cambridge: Cambridge University Press, 1972), pp. 282–84, 302–17, that Paul wrote two editions of a letter that began at 2:14, one ending with 6:13 (to the Corinthians) and the other running to 6:2 and then adding 6:14–7:4 (to other Christians in Achaia) is completely unverifiable and has not been adopted by anyone else.

[35]Esp. Weiss 1:353.

[36]So Bornkamm, p. 260; Schmithals, *Gnosticism in Corinth,* pp. 97–98.

been interpolated into 2 Corinthians.[37] The issues are extraordinarily complex, and we review here the principal turning points.

1. It is argued that chapter 9 introduces the subject of the collection as if no mention has been made of it already. Chapter 9 must therefore follow chapter 7, and chapter 8 is an independent document with its conclusion lost (Weiss). This demands that Weiss reconstruct just when chapter 8 was written. He thinks chapter 8 commended Titus and two unnamed believers much earlier, before the arrival of Timothy with the bad news, indeed before those from Chloe's house had arrived (1:11). It was the spontaneous enthusiasm of believers in Macedonia that "prompted [Paul] to press the matter with renewed zeal in Corinth. . . . [The Corinthians] had already a year ago, earlier than the Macedonians, made a beginning not only to 'will', but also to 'do' (viii.10). They should now carry out their program to completion (viii.11)."[38] But this is unlikely. Barrett has observed that 2 Corinthians 8:10 does not say that the Corinthians made a beginning not only to will but also to do, but the reverse: they made a beginning not only to do but also to will, reflecting the spontaneity of their initial response and the subsequent resolution that grew out of it.[39] Moreover, it is unlikely that there was any trip by Titus encouraging a collection before 1 Corinthians 16:1–4, not only because Titus is not mentioned there, but also because these verses presuppose that Paul's plans for the collection are still in the beginning stages.

2. The opening words of chapter 9, περὶ μὲν γάρ (peri men gar, "so now concerning," or the like), are often taken to be an introductory formula used to introduce new subjects, and therefore constitute evidence that chapter 8 (and perhaps chapter 9) is an interpolation. Certainly Paul elsewhere uses a similar, though not identical, formula to introduce new subjects (1 Cor. 7:1; 8:1; 12:1; 16:1, namely, περὶ δέ [peri de], "now concerning").

This argument, however, fails to take into account several important considerations. First, the two constructions are quite different, as Betz himself recognizes,[40] and the latter is in any case specifically introductory only because we are told that the apostle is taking up one topic after another seriatim, in response to the agenda established by a letter from the Corinthians (1 Cor. 7:1). Second, to label περὶ μὲν γάρ (peri men gar) an "introductory formula" already begs the issue, for it prompts the reader to take the expression as a whole (because it is a "formula"), rather than to consider the semantic contribution of each word. There is no evidence that this string of words constitutes a formula, introductory or otherwise, that would have been recognized as such in the first century. Third, this observation becomes important when Betz,[41] for instance, argues that γάρ (gar, "for"), which almost always connects its clause with something preceding, insists that that need not be the case here, since it is linked with the particle μέν (men), which points forward to the δέ (de) in verse 3 (overtranslating, this becomes "on the one hand . . . on the other hand"—i.e., "On the one hand, I know you need no reminder . . . but just the same I am sending . . ."). That simply does not

---

[37]Hans Dieter Betz, 2 Corinthians 8 and 9, Hermeneia (Philadelphia: Fortress, 1985).
[38]Weiss 1:353.
[39]Barrett, Second Corinthians, p. 20.
[40]Betz, 2 Corinthians 8 and 9, p. 90.
[41]Ibid.; see also Hans Windisch, Der zweite Korintherbrief, KEK 6 (1924; reprint, Göttingen: Vandenhoeck & Ruprecht, 1970), pp. 286ff.

follow. The μὲν...δέ construction makes its own semantic contribution; the preposition περί (*peri*, "concerning") brings up the subject (i.e., "this service to the saints"); and γάρ (*gar*, "for") connects this clause with what precedes, either so as to say "I can make confident boasts about you, *for* . . ."[42] or, perhaps, so as to say "I have been speaking about the collectors, *for* it is unnecessary to speak about the collection itself."[43] In other words, there is no compelling evidence that περὶ μὲν γάρ should be taken as an introductory formula. The expression reads much better as a resumptive, following the travel arrangements that take up 8:16–24, a resumptive that also, because of the μὲν . . . δέ construction, prepares for the next step in the argument.

3. It is sometimes argued that Paul's appeal in 8:1–5 to the Macedonians to stir up the Corinthians and his appeal in 9:1–2 to the Corinthians to stir up the Macedonians are in conflict unless the respective chapters were once separate documents. This is ingenuous because it fails to recognize the various markers of sequence. In chapter 8, Paul tells of a *completed* work by the Macedonians, hoping to stir up the Corinthians to *complete* what they had already set out to do; in chapter 9, Paul tells how he had appealed to this *earlier readiness* of the Corinthians to stimulate the Macedonians to *undertake* the action they had now *completed*.

4. Some find that the different purposes for sending the envoys, articulated in the two chapters, constitute evidence that they were written at different times. In chapter 8, Paul says he is sending well-accredited envoys so as to avoid any suspicion of impropriety in the matter of the collection; in chapter 9 he says he is sending them to ensure that everything will be ready by the time he himself arrives. It is simpler to assume that Paul had complementary reasons for sending the envoys.

5. In support of the unity of chapters 8-9, it can be argued that the way "the brothers" are referred to in 9:3 rather presupposes that their credentials have already been introduced—which introduction is provided in chapter 8. Moreover, many commentators have sought to demonstrate that there is a logical progression of thought through these chapters as they now stand in 2 Corinthians.

In short, despite the various leaps in Paul's thought from time to time, a phenomenon for which he is noted, the evidence supports the basic integrity of 2 Corinthians 1–9.

The Integrity of 1 Corinthians Relatively few voices question the Pauline origins of 1 Corinthians. Some have argued that 14:33b–35 is a non-Pauline interpolation (see comments below in the section "Text"). Others have suggested the same for 1:2b, on the grounds that, since the letter was specifically written for the Corinthians, the words "together with all those everywhere who call on the name of our Lord Jesus Christ—their Lord and ours," are utterly out of place.[44] This misreads Paul rather badly, on two grounds.

First, the Corinthian church was constantly tempted to think itself a cut above other churches, quite free to act without consideration of what other churches

---

[42]Barrett, *Second Corinthians*, p. 232.
[43]H. L. Goudge, *The Second Epistle to the Corinthians*, WC (London: Methuen, 1927), p. 86.
[44]So, e.g., Schmithals, *Gnosticism in Corinth*, p. 258.

thought. Correspondingly, Paul repeatedly stresses that what he is teaching them "agrees with what I teach everywhere in every church" (4:17); this "is the rule I lay down in all the churches" (7:17)—so much so that if anyone "wants to be contentious" about what Paul is saying, he or she must face the brute fact that "we have no other practice—nor do the churches of God" (11:16; see also 14:33b). In this framework, Paul's firm linking in 1:2 of the Corinthian church to all believers everywhere has a great significance.

Second, there is evidence that Paul self-consciously writes with authority that transcends that of a pastor for a church he has planted, that at least on some occasions the content of his writing is nothing less than "the Lord's command" (1 Cor. 14:37).[45] There lies at least the potential for an authoritative reach that extends beyond the local congregation.

But some scholars who do not doubt the authenticity of the entire epistle nevertheless suggest that it is a pastiche of Pauline fragments. The impetus for this analysis largely derives from three bits of evidence: the reference to a previous letter in 5:9, the influence of various partition theories in 2 Corinthians, and the topical, not to say fragmented, nature of 1 Corinthians. Numerous competing theories have been advanced.[46]

Without detailing them at length, the following factors tell heavily against such theories.

1. The fragmented nature of 1 Corinthians is, as we have seen, best accounted for by the fact that Paul is responding to reports brought by those from Chloe's house, by Stephanas, Fortunatus, and Achaicus, and also to a letter sent from the Corinthian church that raised a number of questions. Paul's agenda was already set for him.

2. The partition theories on 1 Corinthians agree on so few points, and gain so few adherents, that it seems best to conclude that none of them has the cogency their individual proponents see in them.

3. The alleged contradictions between parts of 1 Corinthians, contradictions that give warrant to the partition theories, are in every case patient of convincing exegetical resolutions. This is true, for instance, of the relation between 8:1–13 and 10:23–33, and between 11:2–16 and 14:33b–36.

4. Collins[47] and Fee[48] have shown that some of the unease about the smoothness of the flow of argumentation in this letter stems from the failure to recognize the frequency with which Paul makes use of an A-B-A pattern. That is, in the first A section Paul deals with the topic at hand within a broad theological framework; in the B section he partially digresses into some crucial explanation of

---

[45]See further D. A. Carson, *Showing the Spirit: A Theological Exposition of 1 Corinthians 12–14* (Grand Rapids: Baker, 1987), pp. 131–34.

[46]See discussion in C. K. Barrett, *A Commentary on the First Epistle to the Corinthians*, BNTC/HNTC, 2d ed. (London: Black, 1971); and Kümmel, pp. 275–78. Perhaps the most widely discussed of the recent theories is that of J. C. Hurd, *The Origin of I Corinthians*, 2d ed. (Macon, Ga.: Mercer University Press, 1983).

[47]John J. Collins, "Chiasmus, the 'ABA' Pattern, and the Text of Paul," in *Studiorum Paulinorum Congressus Internationalis Catholicus 1961*, 2 vols., AnBib 17–18 (Rome: BIP, 1963), 2.575–84.

[48]Gordon D. Fee, *The First Epistle to the Corinthians*, NICNT (Grand Rapids: Eerdmans, 1987), pp. 16–17.

an integral component of his argument; and in the second A section he returns to the topic but addresses it very specifically.[49]

The Character of Paul's Opponents in 1 and 2 Corinthians

The diversity of theories as to the nature of Paul's opponents in these two epistles makes it necessary to begin by enumerating pitfalls to be avoided.

1. One must not read the situation of 2 Corinthians back into 1 Corinthians—at least, not without observing several distinctions. In particular, there is no evidence whatsoever that at the time of writing 1 Corinthians the apostle Paul was facing a church that had been taken over by leaders *from the outside*. By the time of 2 Corinthians 10–13, that has certainly happened.

2. Protestations to the contrary, there is no evidence that the root cause of the opposition behind 1 Corinthians was the influence of Judaizers (as defined above). Paul's insistence on his own Jewish credentials, in order to minimize their importance, does not take place until 2 Corinthians 11:16ff., and they are presented so as to confront the false apostles (2 Cor. 11:13–15), who, so far as we know, have not arrived on the scene at the time 1 Corinthians was written. More important, the argumentation in 1 Corinthians is not slanted to refute Jews—certainly not Jews from any conservative background. For instance, those who are wary of eating meat offered to idols (chaps. 8,10) do not hesitate because of Jewish scruples, but because they were once idolators themselves, and now they want to avoid what has been offered to idols (8:7; that is why they have a "weak conscience"). This means that before their conversion they were pagans, not religiously observant Jews. Those in 1 Corinthians 8 who feel perfectly free to eat such meat are also unlikely to be Jews. Both groups, in other words, spring from non-Jewish backgrounds. Again, as we shall see, the reasons why many Corinthians did not affirm the reality of the resurrection (1 Cor. 15) did not lie in, say, the theological commitments of (Jewish) Sadducees, but in a thought world indebted to certain forms of Greek philosophy.

3. Despite the strenuous arguments of Schmithals[50] and a few others,[51] there is no satisfactory evidence that the dominant problem confronting Paul was Gnosticism, in the sense usually understood of the full-blown movement that can be traced in the second and third centuries (see discussion in chap. 21, on the Johannine Epistles). Too much evidence has accumulated to allow us to read later sources back into the New Testament.[52] None of the essential features of mature Gnosticism are present in the Corinthian epistles, except some elements of the

---

[49]E.g., (1) *A*: 8:1–13, *B*: 9:1–27, *C*: 10:1–22; (2) *A*: 1:10–2:5, *B*: 2:6–16, *C*: 3:1–23; (3) *A*: chap. 12, *B*: chap. 13, *C*: chap. 14.

[50]Schmithals, *Gnosticism in Corinth*; idem, *Paul and the Gnostics* (New York: Abingdon, 1972).

[51]E.g., U. Wilckens, *Weisheit und Torheit* (Tübingen: J. C. B. Mohr, 1959); R. Jewett, *Paul's Anthropological Terms: A Study of Their Use in Conflict Settings*, (AGJU 10 (Leiden: Brill, 1971).

[52]E.g., R. M. Wilson, "How Gnostic Were the Corinthians?" *NTS* 19 (1972–73): 65–74; B. A. Pearson, *The* Pneumatikos-Psychikos *Terminology in 1 Corinthians: A Study in the Theology of the Corinthian Opponents of Paul and Its Relation to Gnosticism*, SBLDS 12 (Missoula, Mont.: SP, 1973), especially pp. 51–81; Edwin M. Yamauchi, *Pre-Christian Gnosticism: A Survey of the Proposed Evidences*, 2d ed. (Grand Rapids: Baker, 1983); L. D. McCrary, "Paul's Opponents in Corinth: An Examination of Walter Schmithals' Thesis on Gnosticism in Corinth" (Ph.D. diss., Southwestern Baptist Theological Seminary, 1985).

dualism between spirit and body, which can be accounted for on other grounds—in particular, the pervasive influence of neoplatonism. Doubtless this was the sort of soil in which Gnosticism would later mushroom, but for the period in question, Hengel is surely right: "It is time to stop talking about Gnosticism in Corinth."[53]

More positively, we can state several things about Paul's opponents.

1. The opponents are simultaneously divided against each other and, in some measure, opposed to Paul. The former point is customarily stressed in the commentaries. The division within the community is apparent on the very surface of 1:10–4:21. If believers were taking each other to court (chap. 6), it is not hard to imagine that support for each side could be found within the church. If some were sexually promiscuous (6:12–20), others thought it best to be entirely celibate (chap. 7). Some thought they should not eat meat offered to idols; others thought it to be a matter of indifference—perhaps, even, a means of demonstrating their liberty. By the balanced way the arguments are put in 11:2–16, it appears that there were competing opinions in the church over the appropriateness of the head covering for women. Some differences were socioeconomic (11:18–19). Certainly there were differences of opinion over the relative status of various spiritual gifts (chaps. 12–14). These internal divisions go some way toward explaining what some have called the "yes, but" form of some of Paul's arguments (e.g., 7:1–2; 8–9; 8:1–6, 7; 14:5, 18–19).

In contrast, Fee minimizes the amount of internal division and stresses the opposition of virtually the entire church to Paul.[54] Certainly such opposition accounts, in part, for the defense of Paul's apostleship (chaps. 4, 9), for his insistence that they submit to his authority (14:37–38), and for his addressing himself, on issue after issue, to the *entire* church and its letter to him (7:1ff.). Fee's approach is a salutary correction and explains the continuing, festering relationship between Paul and the Corinthians alluded to in the "painful visit," the "severe letter" and especially in 2 Corinthians 10–13. The fact remains, however, that they have written to Paul and sought his opinion on a number of matters, and he feels free to instigate the collection among them (16:1–4): the breakdown between Paul and the Corinthians was far from total. More important, internal divisions and a fundamental misapprehension about Paul are not mutually exclusive faults, and it appears that Fee has minimized the latter.

2. The heart of the Corinthian opposition turns on several tightly held and intertwined positions. The Corinthians are convinced they are spiritual (see esp. chaps. 12–14), but this has less to do with conduct and ethics than Paul insists on, and more to do with status. They appear to treat baptism and the Lord's Supper as almost magical rites guaranteeing life, regardless of conduct (10:1–5; 11:17–34). They are puffed up and arrogant (4:6, 18; 5:2). But their view of what is spiritual is influenced by a neoplatonic depreciation of the material. That is probably what makes it possible for some of them to view sexual intercourse with a prostitute as morally indifferent (6:12–20); that is also why they take the stance they do regarding the resurrection. They do not deny that there is a future resurrection, as did the Sadducees; nor do they deny that Jesus rose from the dead.

---

[53]Martin Hengel, *Crucifixion* (ET London: SCM, 1977), p. 18 n. 10.

[54]Fee, *First Corinthians*, esp. pp. 5ff. In this he is largely returning to the stance of A. Robertson and A. Plummer, *A Critical and Exegetical Commentary on the First Epistle of St Paul to the Corinthians*, ICC (Edinburgh: T. & T. Clark, 1914).

Rather, they think they have already been raised, that such "resurrection" pertains to their present spiritual existence, and what they will be at the end is nothing other than what they are now, minus their physical body. This unswerving confidence in their own spirituality is tied, as well, to a brand of "overrealized" eschatology that assumes that all or most of the blessings of the age to come are already being experienced in their fullness.[55] That accounts not only for Paul's scathing outburst in 1 Corinthians 4:8–13 but also for the kind of moral indifferentism and supercilious arrogance (4:6, 18; 5:2) that will not easily listen to the apostle (9:3; 14:37–38) precisely because he speaks so much of perseverance and self-denial in the context of a world order that is still fallen and opposed to God and his gospel. Paul would not for a moment want to depreciate the presence and power of the Spirit in the believer's life and in the church in the present age. But for him this means the body is the Spirit's temple (6:19–20) and therefore must serve God wholly; and the resurrection is still to come.

3. From what source did the Corinthians derive their spurious notions of spirituality? Perhaps the dominant theory today is that the Corinthian distortion derives from wisdom speculation in Hellenistic Judaism.[56] Certainly many remarkable parallels can be found in the literature of Hellenistic Judaism to what is assumed to be the language of the Corinthians that calls forth these Pauline Epistles. What one must ask, however, at least of 1 Corinthians, is whether what is most convincing in these parallels is determined by Hellenistic Judaism or by Greek pagan thought more generally. It remains wholly unlikely that Paul's intended readership was substantially Jewish (see 6:9–11; 8:7; 12:2, and discussion above). Moreover, as Fee points out,[57] Paul explicitly assigns "wisdom" to the Greek quest, while Jews demand "miraculous signs" (1:22). It is inadequate, with Davis, to dismiss the dichotomy on the grounds that it is merely an instance of Paul's rhetoric.[58] "Even as rhetoric, the statement is quite explicit, while the idea that the section reflects a Jewish midrashic homily against wisdom is speculative at best."[59] It appears that the most likely source of the spurious Corinthian approach to wisdom and spirituality is their own pagan past.

4. We can be more specific. Winter has convincingly argued that one of the underlying problems of the Corinthian church was its reliance on the Sophist movement.[60] By the first century A.D., the "second sophistic" had begun.[61] It was characterized by rhetors whose skill and training in oratory attracted public admiration, not to mention students to their schools. By this period, the particular

---

[55]See esp. A. C. Thiselton, "Realized Eschatology at Corinth," *NTS* 24 (1977–78): 510–26.

[56]E.g., Pearson, *Terminology*. R. A. Horsley, in a number of articles, has argued in favor of the personified wisdom found in Philo; see esp. his "Wisdom of Word and Words of Wisdom in Corinth," *CBQ* 39 (1977): 224–39; "Pneumatikos vs. Psychikos: Distinctions of Spiritual Status Among the Corinthians," *HTR* 69 (1976): 269–88. By contrast, J. A. Davis finds the closest parallels in the "Torah Wisdom" at Qumran and in Sirach. See his *Wisdom and Spirit: An Investigation of 1 Corinthians 1.18–3.20 Against the Background of Jewish Sapiential Traditions in the Greco-Roman Period* (Lanham, Md.: UPA, 1984).

[57]Fee, *First Corinthians*, pp. 13–14.

[58]Davis, *Wisdom and Spirit*, p. 189 n. 26.

[59]Fee, *First Corinthians*, p. 14.

[60]B. W. Winter, "Are Philo and Paul Among the Sophists? A Hellenistic Jewish and a Christian Response to a First Century Movement" (Ph.D. diss., Macquarie University, 1988).

[61]See esp. G. W. Bowersock, *Greek Sophists in the Roman Empire* (Oxford: Oxford University Press, 1969).

philosophy held by rhetors was relatively incidental; it was their power to expatiate on it, to declaim in public assembly, to speak convincingly and according to strict conventions in legal, business, religious, and political contexts that won them their acclaim. Their influence in the Mediterranean world was enormous, not least in Corinth. They thought themselves wise, the purveyors of wisdom.

Winter argues that, especially in 1 Corinthians 1–4, Paul self-consciously frames his argument to counter Sophist claims (not least in 2:1–5). Many other themes in the Corinthian epistles—Paul's denunciation of "jealousy and quarreling" (3:3), the stratification of society prompted in part by sharp divisions between benefactors and those dependent on them, arrogant boasting about knowledge, the place of boasting—can be tied to Paul's confrontation with the Sophist movement. Against this background, one can also understand the high place many in Corinth assigned to Apollos.

5. As we have seen, by the time 2 Corinthians was complete, the Corinthian church had been invaded by outsiders. Although they were Jews, steeped in Hebrew language and culture (2 Cor. 11:21ff.), they were well familiar with the Hellenistic world (as Paul was), and they espoused many Sophist values and rhetorical devices.[62] These Paul eschewed, judging them inimical to the gospel itself (11:4). Thus 2 Corinthians presents us with a new kind of Judaizing: a Hellenistic Jewish movement that opposed Paul but was less concerned (so far as we know) with circumcision and with detailed observance of the Mosaic law than with prestige and power in accord with the contemporary values of the Sophists. Paul's ultimate response (2 Cor. 10–13) is the most intense, revealing, and emotional of all his writings.

DATE

Quite apart from constraints imposed on the dating of these epistles by the need to fit Paul's movements and writings together, there is one fixed point. There is an inscription recording a rescript of the Emperor Claudius to the people of Delphi that mentions Gallio as holding the office of proconsul in Achaia during the period of Claudius's twenty-sixth acclamation as *imperator*[63]—a period known from other inscriptions[64] to cover the first seven months of A.D. 52.[65] Proconsuls normally began their tour of duty on July 1, which means that Gallio probably ascended to the proconsulship on July 1, 51. However, it is possible that the rescript belongs to the very end of the seven-month period, in which case Gallio may have taken up his duties on July 1, 52. The latter date leaves only one month for the rescript, so the former date is perhaps marginally more likely.[66]

If the Jews made their united attack on Paul (Acts 18:12) fairly early during Gallio's proconsulship, then probably it was in the autumn of A.D. 51. After the

---

[62]See E. A. Judge, "The Conflict of Aims in NT Thought," *JCE* 9 (1966): 32–45; idem, "Paul's Boasting in Relation to Contemporary Professional Practice," *AusBibRev* 16 (1968): 37–50; S. H. Travis, "Paul's Boasting in 2 Corinthians 10–12," *SE* 6:527–32; D. A. Carson, *From Triumphalism to Maturity: An Exposition of 2 Corinthians 10–13* (Grand Rapids: Baker, 1984), pp. 16–27.

[63]See E. M. Smallwood, *Documents Illustrating the Principates of Gaius, Claudius, and Nero* (Cambridge: Cambridge University Press, 1967), p. 105 no. 376.

[64]*CIL* 3.476; 6.1256.

[65]For the bearing of this evidence on Pauline chronology generally, see chap. 7 above.

[66]It is also possible that Gallio served a second year as proconsul, but this is unlikely.

case was dismissed, Paul stayed in Corinth for some time (Acts 18:18) and then sailed for Syria, probably in the spring of 52. Paul's two-and-a-half-year stint in Ephesus would have taken him to the autumn of 55. Paul wrote 1 Corinthians while he was in Ephesus, some time before Pentecost (16:8), probably during his last year—that is, early in 55, with 2 Corinthians being complete within the next year or so. By that time he was in Macedonia (2 Cor. 2:12–13; 7:5; 8:1–5; 9:2). Primarily because of the uncertainty over the beginning date of Gallio's proconsulship, all of these dates could be advanced by one year.

TEXT

The position with respect to the transmission of the text of both Corinthian epistles is inherently the same as in the rest of the Pauline Epistles. The Alexandrian text type is represented by the Chester Beatty papyrus p^{46} (with some Western readings), by the uncials ℵ, B, and C, and by some minuscules. The Western text is represented by D, F, G, Old Latin, and Western church fathers; the Byzantine text by the overwhelming majority of (later) witnesses.

Although, as usual, there are many textual decisions to be made, the text of both epistles is in relatively good form. Some of the difficulties in 2 Corinthians stem from the fact that Paul, especially in chapters 10–13, is writing under enormous stress, which is reflected in his sometimes tortured Greek, certainly the most difficult Greek in the Pauline corpus.

In 1 Corinthians, the view that 14:34–35 is a gloss was very much a minority position, until Fee defended it in his recent commentary.[67] Fee's stature as a textual critic has served to make this view more acceptable. The fact remains that although some witnesses place verses 34–35 after verse 40, not one omits it; and despite Fee, convincing reasons can be given not only as to why a minority of witnesses transposed this passage to the end of verse 40, but also as to how it should be understood within its context.[68]

ADOPTION INTO THE CANON

First Corinthians is already being cited in the last decade of the first century (by Clement of Rome: *1 Clement.* 37:5; 47:1–3; 49:5) and in the first decade of the second (by Ignatius: *Eph.* 16:1; 18:1; *Rom.* 5:1; *Phil.* 3:3). There was never any dispute about its admission to the canon.

The situation with 2 Corinthians is very different.[69] Although it is just possible that 1 Timothy 2:13–15 alludes to 2 Corinthians 11:1–3, and barely possible that 2 Corinthians finds an echo in Ignatius (*Eph.* 15:3 [2 Cor. 6:16]; *Trall.* 9:2 [2 Cor. 4:14]; *Phil.* 6:3 [2 Cor. 1:12; 11:9–10]), there is only disputed evidence of 2 Corinthians in *1 Clement*,[70] and no certain attestation of 2 Corinthians until

---

[67]Fee, *First Corinthians*, pp. 699–708.

[68]See D. A. Carson, "'Silent in the Churches': On the Role of Women in I Cor. 14:33b–36," in *Recovering Biblical Manhood and Womanhood*, ed. Wayne Grudem and John Piper (Westchester: Crossway, 1990), pp. 140–153, 487–90.

[69]See esp. Furnish, *II Corinthians*, pp. 29–30.

[70]See *1 Clement.* 5:5–6 (2 Cor. 11:25); 38:2 (2 Cor. 9:12; but cf. 1 Cor. 16:17). See Donald A. Hagner, *The Use of the Old and New Testaments in Clement of Rome*, SuppNovT 34 (Leiden: Brill, 1973), esp. pp. 212–13.

Marcion's canon (c. A.D. 140). From about the middle of the second century there is undisputed evidence that 2 Corinthians was viewed as part of the Pauline corpus. The majority of scholars are surely right to insist that this by itself does not cast doubt on the authenticity of 2 Corinthians and that it should not be used to justify partition theories. (Kümmel, p. 292, points out that even Galatians is unattested in Ignatius.) The puzzling question is why 2 Corinthians did not apparently circulate as widely and as rapidly as 1 Corinthians.

1 AND 2 CORINTHIANS IN RECENT STUDY

The greatest part of the scholarly energy expended on these epistles is tied up with the kinds of issues already explored (see section "Occasion" above), or with the exegesis of particular passages and attempts to delineate specific situations or backgrounds to such passages. Four other areas are prominent in recent literature on the Corinthian epistles.

1. There is a wide-ranging debate over Paul's view of the law (see esp. the chapters in this book on Romans and Galatians), and inevitably Paul's epistles to the Corinthians play a part in that debate. This owes something to a few passages that specifically address the issue (notably 1 Cor. 9:19–23), but more to a perception that in these epistles Paul imposes some restraints, where in other passages he seems to see himself as free from law.

2. There is a rising concern to locate Paul, and these epistles in particular, against the backdrop of the social and anthropological conventions of the first-century Greco-Roman world.[71] Such studies are useful; occasionally they too greatly ignore what the epistles themselves say; and in some instances they slip from responsible social history into fairly uncontrolled and speculative projections of sociology.[72]

3. Doubtless owing to the worldwide growth of the so-called charismatic movement, numerous essays and books on 1 Corinthians 12–14 and related matters have attempted to break new ground on the nature of prophecy, the place of the χαρίσματα (charismata, "grace-gifts"), and the theology of the Spirit.[73]

4. Owing to the influence of the various feminist movements in the Western world, and assorted responses to them, a large body of literature has also grown up around 1 Corinthians 11:2–16 and 14:33b–36.[74]

THE CONTRIBUTION OF 1 AND 2 CORINTHIANS

Because so many of the topics treated in these epistles are occasional and closely related to particular cultural circumstances, 1 and 2 Corinthians offer potent opportunities to observe how the unchanging gospel, taught in the languages and

---

[71]E.g., Abraham Malherbe, *Social Aspects of Early Christianity* (Philadelphia: Fortress, 1983); Bruce J. Malina, *Christian Origins and Cultural Anthropology: Practical Models for Biblical Interpretation* (Atlanta: John Knox, 1986). Cf. Murphy-O'Connor, *St. Paul's Corinth.*

[72]E.g., Gerd Theissen, *The Social Setting of Pauline Christianity: Essays on Corinth* (ET Philadelphia: Fortress, 1982).

[73]See the bibliographies in David E. Aune, *Prophecy in Early Christianity and the Ancient Mediterranean World* (Grand Rapids: Eerdmans, 1983); Wayne Grudem, *The Gift of Prophecy in 1 Corinthians* (Lanham, Md.: UPA, 1982); Carson, *Showing the Spirit.*

[74]See bibliography in Grudem and Piper, *Recovering Biblical Manhood and Womanhood.*

cultures of the first century, was first applied to changing circumstances. For instance (to use the example of Childs, pp. 275, 279–81), the particular form of the Corinthian denial of the resurrection may not be popular in the twentieth century (although, arguably, an adaptation of it is returning in some sectors of the New Age movement), but Paul's strenuous insistence on the historical reality of the resurrection of Jesus as part of the nonnegotiable "given" of the gospel may be applied in many circumstances.

No part of the Pauline corpus more clearly illuminates the character of Paul the man, Paul the Christian, Paul the pastor, and Paul the apostle than do these epistles. He thereby leaves us some substance in his invitation to imitate him, and thereby imitate Christ (1 Cor. 11:1).

Because 1 and 2 Corinthians directly confront overrealized eschatology and all forms of professed spirituality that presuppose independence from the realms of ethics and conduct, these epistles speak volumes to contemporary Western Christianity. First Corinthians makes an enormous contribution to the doctrine of the church—its nature, unity, diversity, characteristics, conduct, interdependence, and discipline—even though there is very little in this epistle on church government (apart from inferences drawn from such passages as 5:1ff.). Also, 1 Corinthians 15 constitutes not only the earliest written list of the witnesses of Jesus' resurrection but the most important New Testament treatment of the nature of the resurrection.

These two epistles constitute the most telling condemnation of arrogance, self-promotion, boasting, and self-confidence in the Pauline corpus; conversely, they describe in practical terms the nature of Christian life and witness, emphasizing service, self-denial, purity, and weakness as the matrix in which God displays his strength. Perhaps the high-water mark is the emphasis on love as "the most excellent way" (1 Cor. 12:31–13:13) all Christians must pursue.

BIBLIOGRAPHY

E. B. **Allo**, *Saint Paul: Première Épître aux Corinthiens*, EBib (Paris: Gabalda, 1934); idem, *Saint Paul: Seconde Épître aux Corinthiens*, EBib (Paris: Gabalda, 1956); David E. **Aune**, *Prophecy in Early Christianity and the Ancient Mediterranean World* (Grand Rapids: Eerdmans, 1983); P. **Bachmann**, *Der zweite Brief des Paulus an die Korinther* (Leipzig: Deichert, 1922); C. K. **Barrett**, "Cephas and Corinth," in *Abraham unser Vater: Juden und Christen im Gespräch über die Bibel*, Fs. Otto Michel, ed. O. Betz, M. Hengel, and P. Schmidt, AGSU 5 (Leiden: Brill, 1963), pp. 1–12; idem, *A Commentary on the First Epistle to the Corinthians*, BNTC/HNTC, 2d ed. (London: Black, 1971); idem, *A Commentary on the Second Epistle to the Corinthians*, BNTC/HNTC (London: Black, 1973); H. D. **Betz**, "2 Cor. 6:14–7:1: An Anti-Pauline Fragment?" *JBL* 92 (1973): 88–108; idem, *2 Corinthians 8 and 9*, Hermeneia (Philadelphia: Fortress, 1985); G. **Bornkamm**, "The History of the Origin of the So-called Second Letter to the Corinthians," *NTS* 8 (1961–62): 258–64; G. W. **Bowersock**, *Greek Sophists in the Roman Empire* (Oxford: Oxford University Press, 1969); F. F. **Bruce**, *1 and 2 Corinthians* (London: Oliphants, 1971); idem, *Paul: Apostle of the Free Spirit* (Exeter: Paternoster, 1977); R. **Bultmann**, *The Second Letter to the Corinthians* (ET Minneapolis: Augsburg, 1985); D. A. **Carson**, *From Triumphalism to Maturity: An Exposition of 2 Corinthians 10–13* (Grand Rapids: Baker, 1984); idem,

Showing the Spirit: A Theological Exposition of 1 Corinthians 12–14 (Grand Rapids: Baker, 1987); idem, " 'Silent in the Churches': On the Role of Women in I Cor. 14:33b–36," in *Recovering Biblical Manhood and Womanhood*, ed. Wayne Grudem and John Piper (Westchester, Ill.: Crossway, 1990), pp. 140–153, 487–90; Brevard S. **Childs**, *The New Testament as Canon: An Introduction* (London: SCM, 1984); J.-F. **Collange**, *Enigmes de la deuxième épître de Paul aux Corinthiens*, SNTSMS 18 (Cambridge: Cambridge University Press, 1972); John J. **Collins**, "Chiasmus, the 'ABA' Pattern and the Text of Paul," in *Studiorum Paulinorum Congressus Internationalis Catholicus 1961*, 2 vols., AnBib 17–18 (Rome: BIP, 1963); H. **Conzelmann**, *1 Corinthians*, Hermeneia (Philadelphia: Fortress, 1975); idem, "Korinth und die Mädchen der Aphrodite: Zur Religionsgeschichte der Stadt Korinth," *NAG* 8 (1967–68): 247–61; N. A. **Dahl**, "A Fragment and Its Context: 2 Corinthians 6:14–7:1," in *Studies in Paul* (Minneapolis: Augsburg, 1972), pp. 62–69; J. A. **Davis**, *Wisdom and Spirit: An Investigation of 1 Corinthians 1.18–3.20 Against the Background of Jewish Sapiential Traditions in the Greco-Roman Period* (Lanham, Md.: UPA, 1984); Gordon D. **Fee**, *The First Epistle to the Corinthians*, NICNT (Grand Rapids: Eerdmans, 1987); idem, "II Corinthians vi.14–vii.1 and Food Offered to Idols," *NTS* 23 (1977): 140–61; J. A. **Fitzmyer**, "Qumran and the Interpolated Paragraph in 2 Cor 6:14–7:1," in *Essays on the Semitic Background of the New Testament* (London: Chapman, 1971), pp. 205–17; Victor Paul **Furnish**, *II Corinthians*, AB 32A (Garden City, N.Y.: Doubleday, 1984); J. **Gnilka**, "2 Cor 6:14–7:1 in Light of the Qumran Texts and the Testaments of the Twelve Patriarchs," in *Paul and Qumran*, ed. J. Murphy-O'Connor (London: Chapman, 1968), pp. 48–68; H. L. **Goudge**, *The Second Epistle to the Corinthians*, WC (London: Methuen, 1927); Wayne **Grudem**, *The Gift of Prophecy in 1 Corinthians* (Lanham, Md.: UPA, 1982); Wayne **Grudem** and John **Piper**, eds., *Recovering Biblical Manhood and Womanhood* (Westchester, Ill.: Crossway, 1990); Donald A. **Hagner**, *The Use of the Old and New Testaments in Clement of Rome*, SuppNovT 34 (Leiden: Brill, 1973); Murray J. **Harris**, "2 Corinthians," in *EBC* 10 (Grand Rapids: Zondervan, 1976); Martin **Hengel**, *Crucifixion* (ET London: SCM, 1977); R. A. **Horsley**, "Pneumatikos vs. Psychikos: Distinctions of Spiritual Status Among the Corinthians," *HTR* 69 (1976): 269–88; idem, "Wisdom of Word and Words of Wisdom in Corinth," *CBQ* 39 (1977): 224–39; Philip E. **Hughes**, *Paul's Second Epistle to the Corinthians*, NICNT (Grand Rapids: Eerdmans, 1962); R. **Jewett**, *Paul's Anthropological Terms: A Study of Their Use in Conflict Settings*, AGJU 10 (Leiden: Brill, 1971); E. A. **Judge**, "The Conflict of Aims in NT Thought," *JCE* 9 (1966): 32–45; idem, "Paul's Boasting in Relation to Contemporary Professional Practice," *AusBibRev* 16 (1968): 37–50; Colin **Kruse**, *2 Corinthians*, TNTC (Grand Rapids: Eerdmans, 1987); H. **Lietzmann**, supplemented by W. G. Kümmel, *An die Korinther I, II*, HNT 9 (Tübingen: J. C. B. Mohr, 1969); L. D. **McCrary**, "Paul's Opponents in Corinth: An Examination of Walter Schmithals' Thesis on Gnosticism in Corinth" (Ph.D. diss., Southwestern Baptist Theological Seminary, 1985); Abraham **Malherbe**, *Social Aspects of Early Christianity* (Philadelphia: Fortress, 1983); Bruce J. **Malina**, *Christian Origins and Cultural Anthropology: Practical Models for Biblical Interpretation* (Atlanta: John Knox, 1986); Ralph P. **Martin**, *2 Corinthians*, WBC 40 (Waco, Tex.: Word, 1986); Leon **Morris**, *The First Epistle of Paul to the Corinthians*, 2d ed., TNTC (Leicester: IVP, 1985); Jerome **Murphy-O'Connor**, *St. Paul's Corinth: Texts and Archaeology* (Wilmington, Del.: Glazier, 1983); B. A. **Pearson**, *The Pneumatikos-Psychikos Terminology in 1 Corinthians: A Study in the Theology of the Corinthian Opponents of Paul and Its Relation to Gnosticism*, SBLDS 12 (Missoula, Mont.: SP, 1973); A.

1 AND 2 CORINTHIANS   287

Plummer, *A Critical and Exegetical Commentary on the Second Epistle of St Paul to the Corinthians,* ICC (Edinburgh: T. & T. Clark, 1915); A. **Robertson** and A. **Plummer,** *A Critical and Exegetical Commentary on the First Epistle of St Paul to the Corinthians,* ICC (Edinburgh: T. & T. Clark, 1914); W. **Schmithals,** *Gnosticism in Corinth: An Investigation of the Letters to the Corinthians* (ET New York: Abingdon, 1971); idem, *Paul and the Gnostics* (New York: Abingdon, 1972); E. M. **Smallwood,** *Documents Illustrating the Principates of Gaius, Claudius, and Nero* (Cambridge: Cambridge University Press, 1967); R. H. **Strachan,** *The Second Epistle of Paul to the Corinthians,* MNTC (London: Hodder & Stoughton, 1935); R. V. G. **Tasker,** *The Second Epistle of Paul to the Corinthians,* TNTC (Grand Rapids: Eerdmans, 1958); Gerd **Theissen,** *The Social Setting of Pauline Christianity: Essays on Corinth* (ET Philadelphia: Fortress, 1982); A. C. **Thiselton,** "Realized Eschatology at Corinth," *NTS* 24 (1977–78): 510–26; Margaret E. **Thrall,** "A Second Thanksgiving Period in II Corinthians," *JSNT* 16 (1982): 101–24; S. H. **Travis,** "Paul's Boasting in 2 Corinthians 10–12," *SE* 6: 527–32; J. **Weiss,** *Earliest Christianity: A History of the Period* A.D. *30–150,* 2 vols. (New York: Harper & Row, 1959); H. D. **Wendland,** *Die Briefe an die Korinther,* NTD 7 (Göttingen: Vandenhoeck & Ruprecht, 1965); U. **Wilckens,** *Weisheit und Torheit* (Tübingen: J. C. B. Mohr, 1959); R. M. **Wilson,** "How Gnostic Were the Corinthians?" *NTS* 19 (1972–73): 65–74; Hans **Windisch,** *Der zweite Korintherbrief,* KEK 6 (Göttingen: Vandenhoeck & Ruprecht, 1924; reprint, 1970; B. W. **Winter,** "Are Philo and Paul Among the Sophists? A Hellenistic Jewish and a Christian Response to a First Century Movement" (Ph.D. diss., Macquarie University, 1988); Edwin M. **Yamauchi,** *Pre-Christian Gnosticism: A Survey of the Proposed Evidences,* 2d ed. (Grand Rapids: Baker, 1983); Günther **Zuntz,** *The Text of the Epistles: A Disquisition upon the Corpus Paulinum* (London: Oxford, 1953).

10

Galatians

CONTENTS

In a concise greeting, Paul insists on his status as an apostle sent by God and reminds his correspondents that Christ gave himself to deliver us from "the present evil age" (1:1–5). He expresses astonishment that the Galatians are deserting the gospel, a step he vehemently opposes (1:6–10). He insists that his gospel was given him by revelation from Christ and relates his persecuting activities and his few contacts with the earlier apostles to show that his gospel could not have derived from mere reliance on what they said (1:11–2:5). He points to a division of labor, with Peter at work as apostle to the Jews, while he was the apostle to the Gentiles, apparently with the implication that Gentiles would not be required to keep the Mosaic law (2:6–10). When later Peter withdrew from table fellowship with Gentile Christians, Paul took issue with him and pointed out that even Jews were not saved by works of the law but by faith in Christ (2:11–16). Sinners who are justified in Christ have died to the law and live "by faith in the Son of God" (2:17–21).

In an emotional appeal, Paul reminds the Galatians that the Spirit was given to them not on account of their observance of the law but on account of their faith in Christ (3:1–5). Abraham was an example of faith (3:6–9), whereas the law brings a curse on sinners that Christ has borne for them (3:10–14). The law cannot replace the covenant God made with Abraham 430 years earlier; the law was given until the coming of Christ (3:15–25). The primacy of faith means that in our approach to God all human distinctions are removed; there is one great family of God (3:26–29). Christ's redeeming work has brought believers into the place of sons, not slaves, in that family (4:1–7).

In their observance of the law the Galatians were going back into the kind of slavery from which they had been rescued, and Paul pleads again that they not persist in rejecting his teaching (4:8–20). He reminds them from the ancient Scripture that Abraham had a son by Hagar (a slave woman) and one by Sarah (who was free). These, he insists, represent two covenants. By submitting to the law's requirements, the Galatians are going back to the old covenant, though they are really children of the free woman (4:21–31). They should live in the freedom that Christ has won for them and not undergo the circumcision that means bondage (5:1–12). Paul contrasts life in the Spirit with that in the flesh (5:13–

26), which leads to instruction about right living (6:1–10). Paul takes up the pen himself to close with an impassioned reminder that neither circumcision nor uncircumcision matters—but God's new creation does (6:11–18).

AUTHOR

The letter claims to have been written by Paul (1:1), and the claim rings true. It is the outpouring of a concerned evangelist and pastor over some tragic false teaching that had arisen among his converts. As Kümmel says, "That Galatians is a genuine, authentic Epistle is indisputable."[1] It is not easy to be sure of where Paul was when he wrote the letter, but that he wrote it is not in serious dispute.

DESTINATION

During the third century B.C. some Gauls migrated to the inner plateau of Asia Minor and established a kingdom. Under Amyntas (first century B.C.) this extended to Pisidia, Lycaonia, and other places in the South, and most of these remained when, on the death of Amyntas (25 B.C.) the Romans took over and made it into the province of Galatia. The problem for us is whether the "Galatians" to which this epistle is addressed refers to ethnic Galatians in the north of the province or to the southerners of various races who were included in the Roman province. Toward the end of the third century, the southern area was detached and the province reduced to the northern sector. Traditionally "Galatia" has thus been understood of the northern area. But was this the way Paul used the term? The apostle visited the southern area on his first missionary journey (Acts 13–14), but he is never explicitly said to have visited the northern area—though many think that this is meant in Acts 16:6 and 18:23.

In favor of South Galatia, note the following ten considerations:

1. We have information about people and places Paul knew and visited in the southern region, but none at all in the North (at best Acts 16:6 and 18:23 *may* indicate work in the North, but neither passage says that Paul founded churches). This is in striking contrast to his work in other areas.[2] If Paul was writing to people in the North, we would expect some firm indication that he had been there at some time. It would be curious, to say the least, to have no information about churches to which such an important letter was sent.

2. The unusual expression "the region of Phrygia and Galatia" through which Paul traveled (Acts 16:6) is best understood of the area through which the apostle would go when he left Lystra and Iconium (Acts 16:2), that is, "the Phrygio-

---

[1] Kümmel, p. 304. This does not mean that there have been no dissentients (Kümmel himself cites Bruno Bauer, "the radical Dutch critics," and R. Steck). See also J. C. O'Neill, who thinks that Paul wrote only about two-thirds of Galatians (*The Recovery of Paul's Letter to the Galatians* [London: SPCK, 1972]). But today most scholars would agree with Kümmel.

[2] J. B. Lightfoot, who, like the other older commentators, favored the North Galatian theory, nevertheless comments: "It is strange that while we have more or less acquaintance with all the other important Churches of St Paul's founding, with Corinth and Ephesus, with Philippi and Thessalonica, not a single name of a person or place, scarcely a single incident of any kind, connected with the Apostle's preaching in Galatia, should be preserved in either the history or the epistle" (*Saint Paul's Epistle to the Galatians* [London: Macmillan, 1902], p. 21).

Galatic territory."³ Those who hold the North Galatian theory take this to mean "Phrygia and the Galatian country": Ernst Haenchen argues that Φρυγία (*Phrygia*) is an adjective of two terminations and cannot qualify χώρα (*chōra*).⁴ But C. J. Hemer has shown conclusively that it has three terminations and thus may well qualify χώρα.⁵ F. F. Bruce's careful examination yields the conclusion that the expression can mean only "the territory through which Paul and his friends passed after leaving Lystra, the territory in which Iconium and Pisidian Antioch were situated."⁶ The similar expression in Acts 18:23 seems to mean much the same.

3. Paul normally (though not invariably) uses Roman imperial names for the provinces, and "Galatians" would be the way he would refer to people in Lycaonia and other districts. Against this are the facts that Paul's usage is not invariable; in any case, "Galatians" would include the ethnic Gauls in the North.

4. "Galatians" was the only word available that embraced the people in all the cities: Antioch, Lystra, Iconium, and Derbe. Of course, this does not exclude the possibility that the term might be used of those in the North.

5. Paul speaks of "the Galatian churches" as included among the contributors to his collection for the believers in Jerusalem (1 Cor. 16:1), and in Acts 20:4 he lists a Berean, two Thessalonians, two South Galatians, and two Asians, who look suspiciously like the party bearing the gift. But Luke does not actually say so, and in any case there are no Corinthians in the list, so it may be incomplete.

6. The northern part of the country was not opened up like the southern area, through which a continual stream of commerce flowed. It is unlikely that Paul preached in this difficult mountainous country "because of an illness" (Gal. 4:13). A convalescent would look for a place much easier of access.

7. It is urged that it is unlikely that Paul's Jewish opponents would have pursued him into this difficult northern country and much more likely that they would have followed him to the southern cities. But how fanatical were they?

8. The words "you welcomed me as if I were an angel of God, as if I were Christ Jesus himself" (Gal. 4:14) are said to be an allusion to Paul's being welcomed as Hermes at Lystra (Acts 14:12). This is somewhat spoiled, however, by the fact that afterward the Lystrans stoned him (though this, too, is sometimes taken up into the argument with a reference in Gal. 6:17 to "the marks of Jesus" on Paul's body). The fact that he was welcomed as an angel is also sometimes used as an argument the opposite way: Paul could not have looked much like an angel when he came to the Galatians as a sick man!

9. Ramsay, who did more than anybody to establish the southern theory, argued that the church developed along the great lines of communication, and these went through the southern parts of Galatia, not the North.⁷

10. Barnabas is mentioned three times (2:1, 9, 13), which seems to mean that

---

³τὴν Φρυγίαν καὶ Γαλατικὴν χώραν (*tēn Phrygian kai Galatikēn chōran*).
⁴Ernst Haenchen, *The Acts of the Apostles* (Oxford: Blackwell, 1971), p. 483.
⁵C. J. Hemer, "The Adjective 'Phrygia,'" *JTS* 27 (1976): 122–26; idem, "Phrygia: A Further Note," *JTS* 28 (1977): 99–101.
⁶F. F. Bruce, "Galatian Problems. 2. North or South Galatians?" *BJRL* 52 (1970): 258.
⁷W. M. Ramsay, *The Church in the Roman Empire* (London: Hodder & Stoughton, 1893), pp. 10–11. Moffatt, however, cites Ramsay's question regarding Lystra: "How did the cosmopolitan Paul drift like a piece of timber borne by the current into this quiet backwater?" (p. 99).

he was known to the readers. But he accompanied Paul only on the journey when the South Galatian churches were established. It is objected that Barnabas is mentioned in 1 Corinthians 9:6, though we have no evidence that he was ever in Corinth. We should also bear in mind that Peter is mentioned (Gal. 2:7–8), though there is no evidence that he was ever in the North. The point carries little weight.

Those who favor a reference to North Galatia have advanced at least eight reasons.

1. In the speech of the day, "Galatia" meant the place inhabited by the Gauls in the North. Against this, as we have seen, it was also used of the whole province.

2. In Acts, Antioch is called "Pisidian" (Acts 13:14), while Lystra and Derbe are cities of Lycaonia (Acts 14:6). Luke, it is said, uses such terms to denote geographic locations. Thus when he refers to "the region of Phrygia and Galatia" (Acts 16:6), we must understand him to mean geographic Phrygia and geographic Galatia—that is, North Galatia.

3. Galatia would not be used of Phrygians and the like because it would remind them of their subjection to Rome. This, however, is scarcely valid. Paul referred to himself as a Roman citizen. In any case, "Galatia" was the only term that covered all the cities mentioned. Some have pointed out that in modern times an audience of Welsh, Scots, and English people would be addressed as British, with none of them objecting—that is the only term that covers them all. So with ancient Galatia.

4. A similar objection is that "Paul could not possibly have addressed Lycaonians or Pisidians 'O foolish Galatians' (3:1), particularly since this linguistic usage is generally not attested."[8] But what usage is attested? As noticed in the previous section, "Galatians" was the only term available to cover all the inhabitants of the province of Galatia.

5. The fickle and superstitious character of the Galatians suits a Gallic origin. But such a description scarcely applied to Galatians only. What of the Corinthians, for example?[9]

6. "The region of Phrygia and Galatia" (Acts 16:6; so also 18:23) is understood to mean "Phrygia and the Galatian region,"[10] which is taken to mean that Galatia was quite distinct from Phrygia (and presumably other districts such as Lycaonia). But as we saw have seen, the probable meaning is "the Phrygio-Galatic territory." It does not prove a distinction.

7. Paul writes, "Later I went to Syria and Cilicia" (Gal. 1:21), on which Marxsen comments, "According to the South Galatian hypothesis he must have founded the Galatian churches at that time, but there is no mention of this."[11] But because Syria and Cilicia were not in the province of Galatia, this is irrelevant; it

---

[8]Kümmel, p. 298.

[9]F. F. Bruce points out that the argument reduces itself to this syllogism: "The Gauls were fickle and superstitious. Paul's Galatians were fickle and superstitious. Therefore: Paul's Galatians were Gauls."

He adds that "the argument would be valid only if fickleness and superstition were not characteristic of other nations than the Gauls (and Galatians)" (*The Epistle to the Galatians* [Exeter: Paternoster; Grand Rapids: Eerdmans, 1982], p. 8).

[10]Moffatt holds that "διέρχεσθαι [*dierchesthai*] in 16⁶, taken along with 18²³, implies preaching-activity, not simply travelling" (p. 95). This would indicate that Paul evangelized North Galatia.

[11]Marxsen, p. 46.

appears to refer to a trip different from that on which Paul founded the churches of southern Galatia (one made in the period subsequent to Acts 9:30).[12]

8. There is not the slightest hint in Galatians that Paul had experienced strong opposition when he preached in the Galatian cities. But Acts makes it clear that there was persecution in most of the cities the apostle visited.

From all this it appears that there is no final proof for either the North Galatian or the South Galatian theory. But it surely seems that, while the South Galatian theory comes short of complete demonstration, the arguments in its favor are more compelling than those for the North.[13]

DATE

If the South Galatian theory is adopted, an early date is possible. It is supported by such considerations as the following:

1. In protesting that he had a divine commission and not one derived "from any man" (1:12), Paul lists his contacts with the Jerusalem apostles. These include a visit to Peter (1:18) and "fourteen years later" a visit again "in response to a revelation" (2:1–2; "again" indicates a second visit). These correspond to the visits in Acts 9:26; 11:28–30. Paul's list must be complete, else his argument would be vitiated (see 1:20).

2. Paul does not mention the decrees of the Council of Jerusalem (Acts 15), which would have been very suitable for his purpose. This points to a visit before the council.

3. Peter's withdrawal from table fellowship with the Gentiles (2:12) is more likely before than after the council.

4. This date is not invalidated by Paul's words "I first [τὸ πρότερον (to proteron)] preached the gospel to you" (4:13), which some suggest means "on the first of my two visits" (NEB mg.) and points to a date later than Paul's second missionary journey. In classical Greek the expression means on the former of two occasions, but in Hellenistic Greek it signifies "formerly, in the past" (as in John 6:62; 9:8; Heb. 4:6, etc.).[14] In any case, Paul visited his South Galatian churches twice during his first expedition (see Acts 14:21).

In contrast, a date during Paul's third missionary tour is favored by many. The early date is excluded by those who hold the North Galatian theory, for on this view Paul had not been to Galatia until this time. A later date is supported by such arguments as these:

1. The style and the thoughts expressed show an affinity with the Corinthian correspondence and with Romans, so the epistle to the Galatians accordingly

---

[12]F. F. Bruce locates it in this period ("Galatian Problems. 1. Autobiographical Data," *BJRL* 51 [1969]: 301–2).

[13]F. F. Bruce points out that neither view can be said to be proven to the extent that the other is ruled out. But he concludes an important discussion of the problem by saying, "the weight of the evidence, it seems to me, favours the South Galatian view" ("Galatian Problems. 2. North or South Galatians?" *BJRL* 52 [1970]: 266). J. A. T. Robinson is another who sees "the weight of scholarly opinion" as favoring the South Galatian view (*Redating the New Testament* [Philadelphia: Westminster, 1976], p. 55).

[14]On this passage BAGD remarks that "fr. a lexical point of view it is not poss[ible] to establish the thesis that Paul wished to differentiate betw[een] a later visit and an earlier one" (p. 722).

should be dated close to them, say at Ephesus during Paul's third journey (Acts 19) or even on the subsequent journey through Greece.

2. The visit to Jerusalem in Galatians 2 is so closely connected with the subject matter of the Council of Jerusalem of Acts 15 that the two must be regarded as independent accounts of the same visit (though some who favor the South Galatian theory see these as two different visits and simply hold that Paul wrote later than the council). It is reasoned that Paul did not mention the famine visit of Acts 11:30 because on that occasion his business was with the elders, not the apostles. But one short verse can scarcely be taken as a full account of all Paul did in Jerusalem.[15]

3. Paul has already visited Galatia twice (4:13), perhaps the visits of Acts 16:6 and 18:23. But we have already seen that the language does not necessarily mean two visits (see comments on Gal. 4:13, above).

4. In 1 Corinthians there is little about persecution, but there is much in 2 Corinthians. Romans is calm; evidently the trouble is largely in the past. Galatians fits into this sequence between 2 Corinthians and Romans.[16]

The main point at issue is whether Paul is writing before or after the Council of Jerusalem (Acts 15). Those who advocate a late date say that he writes later, and they emphasize what they see as discrepancies between Acts and Paul's letters. They hold that Paul would never have accepted such an arrangement as the Council of Jerusalem reached according to the description in Acts; indeed, they find his recollection of what happened in Galatians 2. They point out that, though they are treated from different points of view, in both accounts the points at issue are circumcision and the relation of the Christian to the law. This view entails the further point that Paul has omitted one of his visits to Jerusalem (or, alternatively, that Luke has wrongly inserted one).

But it is much simpler to accept both accounts.[17] Paul's two visits to Jerusalem are those of Acts 9 and 11 (Gal. 2 will refer to private contacts on the famine visit on this view; it is hard to date Peter's vacillation after Acts 15), and Paul wrote Galatians just prior to the council. If this is rightly dated A.D. 48,[18] then this is the date of Galatians. That the letter precedes the Jerusalem Council seems indicated by the fact that Paul makes no mention of its verdict. Even if he did not make it his main argument, it is hard to see why he should omit all mention of such a significant support to his argument against accepting the whole Jewish Torah.

---

[15]Klijn finds "a striking parallel between Gal. 2,1–10 and Acts 11, 25–30" (p. 94).

[16]Lightfoot argues this and finds support in "Finally, let no one cause me trouble, for I bear on my body the marks of Jesus" (6:17), which seems like "the language of one, who has lately passed through a fiery trial . . . Does it not seem to follow naturally *after* the tumult of affliction, which bursts out in the Second Epistle to the Corinthians?" (*Galatians*, p. 51). Bruce very carefully examines the relationship between Galatians and other Pauline epistles and finds nothing inconsistent with the view that this is the earliest of Paul's letters (*Galatians*, pp. 45–55).

[17]If we do, the early date follows. According to J. Knox, "If we could trust entirely the accuracy of the Acts account of Paul's visits to Jerusalem, the case for the early dating would be unassailable" ("Galatians, " in *IDB*, 2:342).

[18]This is the date given by George Ogg, *The Chronology of the Life of Paul* (London: Epworth, 1968), p. 200. It is also favored by Ronald Y. K. Fung; see his *Epistle to the Galatians* (Grand Rapids: Eerdmans, 1988), p. 28; John W. Drane, *Paul: Libertine or Legalist?* (London: SPCK, 1975), pp. 140–43; see also chap. 7 above.

OCCASION

From Acts 13–14 we learn that Paul and Barnabas evangelized the southern part of the province of Galatia by going first to the synagogues, where they preached to Jews and God-fearing Gentiles. But in each city Jews stirred up opposition, and the preachers turned to the Gentiles and made converts from among them. We need not doubt that, if the North Galatian theory is correct, the evangelization of the northern areas was brought about in much the same way. Throughout the region the church was no doubt predominantly Gentile.

But after Paul and Barnabas left the scene, apparently some Jewish Christians came into the area and taught that those who embrace the Christian salvation must submit to Jewish law, the Torah. So far as we know, local Jews did not teach this; they simply opposed the Christians. Paul distinguishes the false teachers from the congregation (1:7; 4:17, etc.; perhaps they had a strong leader, 1:9; 5:10); indeed, he can imply that they were not Christians at all (1:6–7). Their emphasis on keeping the Mosaic law makes it almost certain they were Jews. Doubtless they thought of themselves as Jewish Christians; Paul is prepared to question the "Christian" component if they set up as necessary to salvation any rival to Jesus.

From Galatians we gather that *Paul's authority* was undermined by the argument that he was inferior to the earlier apostles. Paul seems to have this in mind from first to last: "sent not from men nor by man, but by Jesus Christ and God the Father" (1:1); "let no one cause me trouble, for I bear on my body the marks of Jesus" (6:17).

Circumcision was insisted on: they "are trying to compel you to be circumcised" (6:12; see also 5:2–6). Paul points out that the acceptance of circumcision means the acceptance of the obligation to carry out the whole law of which it is a part (5:3), whatever the false teachers may have said. The keeping of the law was apparently insisted on, for he also writes, "You are observing special days and months and seasons and years!" (4:10).[19] He also speaks of his converts as wanting "to be under the law" (4:21) and as "trying to be justified by law" (5:4). Putting all this together, it seems that the false teachers saw Christianity as a modified Judaism; they were teaching that to be in covenant relationship to God means to submit to the requirements of the law of God. Therefore they were persuading the Galatians to submit to the way of the law instead of enjoying freedom in Christ.

Whether or not they were Christians in Paul's eyes, *the false teachers* evidently sprang from the Jewish-Christian camp. Christians had opposed Peter (Acts 11:2–3), and at a later time James could speak of "many thousands of Jews" who believed, "and all of them are zealous for the law" (Acts 21:20). Clearly there was a strong group of these people, and at least on occasion they could be active propagandists, as when they went from Judea to Antioch and taught the new converts, "Unless you are circumcised, according to the custom taught by Moses, you cannot be saved" (Acts 15:1). If they followed Paul to Antioch, it is not unlikely that they followed him to Galatia. They may not have been many in number, for Paul writes, "A little yeast works through the whole batch of dough"

---

[19]This may refer to "planetary powers or astrological signs of the zodiac" (Martin, 2:153). The στοιχεῖα (*stoicheia*, "basic principles") to which both Jews (4:3) and Gentiles (4:9) had been subjected are best understood in terms of "legalism as a principle of life" (Bruce, *Galatians*, p. 203).

(Gal. 5:9). Sometimes it is contended that Paul's opponents were Gentiles who had accepted circumcision and wanted others to do the same. But this supposition scarcely outweighs the evidence that there were zealous Jewish Christians, anxious to insist on the law. G. Howard thinks that they may not have been opponents in the strict sense but that they claimed that Paul was really teaching what they taught.[20] The vehemence with which Paul opposes them makes this unlikely.

Libertinism is sometimes detected in 5:13ff. with such exhortations as "do not use your freedom to indulge the sinful nature" and "live by the Spirit, and you will not gratify the desires of the sinful nature." But it is better to see this as a perversion of Paul's teaching that in Christ believers are free. In every age it has been easy to deduce that if we are saved by grace, it does not matter how we live. Paul would have none of this, and he denounces such teaching vigorously.

Criticisms of Paul seem to have been made. "If I am still preaching circumcision" (5:11) appears to mean that Paul had been accused of preaching circumcision when it suited him (see his circumcision of Timothy [Acts 16:3]). "Am I *now* trying to win the approval of men, or of God? Or am I trying to please men?" (1:10) indicates that it had been said that the apostle was simply interested in human approval. In the life of a man who became "all things to all men," including becoming like a Jew in order to win Jews (1 Cor. 9:20–22), there could not lack incidents that gave opponents the opening to charge him with inconsistency.

Galatian religion may have been such as to welcome the Judaizers. Lightfoot thinks there was an original "passionate and striking ritualism expressing itself in bodily mortifications of the most terrible kind" that was "supplanted by the simple spiritual teaching of the Gospel." But after a time the Galatians "began to yearn after a creed which suited their material cravings better, and was more allied to the system they had abandoned."[21] There may be something in this, but it is certainly largely speculative.

The gospel was seriously compromised by this new teaching. Paul complains that his correspondents were "turning to a different gospel," immediately adding, "which is really no gospel at all" (1:6–7). What the Galatians were doing was not adding some interesting new insights into the meaning of Christianity but denying the essential Christian message. They were substituting Jewish teaching for the truth of the gospel.

The epistle to the Galatians is the result of news of these happenings reaching Paul. He immediately recognized that what his converts were doing meant that they were renouncing the heart of the Christian way, and he wrote straightaway to correct the situation. He did not observe all the niceties of correct letter writing but sent off an impassioned appeal to the Galatians to return to the faith in which they had been saved. This lively letter has become a classic expression of the meaning of justification by faith in Christ alone.[22]

---

[20]Thus Howard says, "The agitators at Galatia were Jewish Christians, Judaizers from Jerusalem who were forcing the Galatians to be circumcised and to keep the law. They did not themselves oppose Paul but insisted that he like them taught circumcision" (*Paul: Crisis in Galatia* [Cambridge: Cambridge University Press, 1979], p. 19). On the use of the term "Judaizer," see n. 3 in chap. 9, above.

[21]Lightfoot, *Galatians*, p. 30.

[22]Howard has a useful if brief summmary of a good deal of work on this letter, esp. with regard to Paul's opponents (*Paul: Crisis*, pp. 1–7).

TEXT

Galatians contains an average number of minor variants, but on the whole there are no serious doubts about the text of this letter, as is shown by the fact that in UBS3 there are only five passages graded D. There is some confusion between the Aramaic name Cephas and the Greek name Peter in 1:18: 2:9, 11, 14, but in each case there seems to be nothing more than the substitution of the better-known Greek name for the unfamiliar Aramaic form. It is not certain whether we should add "of Christ" after "grace" in 1:6 or whether the subject "God" should be read before the verb "was pleased" in 1:15, but the sense is not greatly affected by these and similar variants. We have this letter substantially as Paul wrote it.

ADOPTION INTO THE CANON

Galatians was accepted from very early days. There seem to be reminiscences of expressions from this letter in Barnabas, *1 Clement*, Polycarp, Justin Martyr, and other early writers. No dispute about its genuineness seems to have arisen in early times. Burton's verdict is to be endorsed: "There is no other letter which has any better claim to be regarded as [Paul's] work than Galatians."[23] It appears first in some lists of the Pauline Epistles (as Marcion's), which points to a recognition of its importance as well as its authenticity.

GALATIANS IN RECENT STUDY

There is general agreement that Galatians is an authentic Pauline epistle and that it is very important for an understanding of Pauline thought. But there is considerable dispute about the location of the Galatian churches, and many recent scholars hold to the North Galatian theory (though South Galatia has many able supporters). If this is coupled with a suspicion of Lukan accuracy in Acts, the date of the letter is put late, in the general period in which the Roman and Corinthian letters were written. Knox even suggests that it may have been written from prison and therefore be one of Paul's latest letters.[24] But there is also strong support for the view that the letter is early, possibly the earliest of Paul's letters.[25]

Discussion continues as to the identity of the teachers Paul is opposing, and some recent writers are suspicious of the term "Judaizers." We have already noted[26] that some scholars have argued that Paul's opponents should be understood as libertines (see 5:13, 16) or even that they were Gnostics of some sort; sometimes they are thought to have been syncretists embracing features of both Judaism and Hellenism. A few have suggested that they were not Jewish but may even have been some of Paul's own converts,[27] their further studies in the Old Testament Scriptures to which Paul had introduced them having led them to think that keeping of the law was indispensable.

All this raises the question whether there is more than one group that Paul is

---

[23]E. de Witt Burton, *A Critical and Exegetical Commentary on the Epistle to the Galatians*, ICC (Edinburgh: T. & T. Clark, 1921), p. lxv.
[24]Knox, "Galatians," pp. 342–43.
[25]So, e.g., Bruce, *Galatians*, pp. 43–56.
[26]See n. 20 above.
[27]J. Munck, *Paul and the Salvation of Mankind* (Richmond: John Knox, 1959), pp. 87ff.

opposing or whether he is engaging in a unified argument. Despite the contentions of some, who seem to be indulging in speculations that are not justified by the evidence, there is no real evidence in Galatians that Paul is fighting on two fronts; his enemies appear to have been one determined group. Most likely, the false teachers were Jews or Jewish Christians who came in from outside and advocated some form of Judaism.[28]

Rising interest in rhetorical criticism has raised questions about the literary genre of this epistle. Thus H. D. Betz sees Galatians as "an example of the 'apologetic letter' genre."[29] He says that in antiquity rhetoric "has little in common with the truth, but it is the exercise of those skills which make people believe something to be true."[30] It is not easy to see this as a fair description of what Paul is doing. His deep concern for truth is evident on every page. Even less acceptable is Betz's contention that Galatians is a "magical letter." Paul speaks of a curse on false preachers (1:9) and a blessing on "all who follow this rule" (6:16). Betz sees this as meaning that the letter itself bears the blessing and the curse.[31] But there is some doubt as to whether antiquity did in fact recognize the category of "magical letter," and there is even more doubt that, if it did, Paul would have used it. It is hard to think of anyone more opposed to magic than Paul was.[32]

A good deal of recent discussion centers on the arguments put forward by E. P. Sanders,[33] who rejects the idea that the Jews of the day saw the keeping of the law as the means whereby they merited salvation. Sanders argues for what he calls "covenantal nomism": the Jews were saved because of their membership in the people with whom God had made a covenant, and the law was simply to regulate their life in the covenant community. Obedience to the law is conceived as important for *remaining in* the covenant community. This has served as a salutary corrective of some harsh and anachronistic views about Jewish beliefs in the first century, but it stands in serious need of qualification. Specifically, it has been objected that Sanders does not take seriously enough Jewish teaching about the rewards of righteousness and the punishment of sin;[34] nor is his exegesis of Paul above criticism.[35] Sanders has given a useful corrective to some earlier views, but he cannot be said to have come up with a universally acceptable solution to the problem.[36]

---

[28]E. P. Sanders sees it as "likely that they were 'right wing' Jewish Christians" who would emphasize such passages as Gen. 17:9–14 (*Paul, the Law, and the Jewish People*[Philadelphia: Fortress, 1985] p. 18).

[29]H. D. Betz, *Galatians*, Hermeneia (Philadelphia: Fortress, 1979), p. 14.

[30]Ibid., p. 24.

[31]Ibid., p. 25.

[32]According to Childs, "Betz's argument is here very weak. Not only is the category of 'magical letter' in itself highly suspect, but its application to Galatians is tenuous in the extreme" (p. 302).

[33]See esp. E. P. Sanders, *Paul and Palestinian Judaism* (Philadelphia: Fortress, 1977); idem, *Paul, the Law, and the Jewish People*.

[34]E.g., the strand of Jewish teaching that refers to judgment day with the imagery of weighing people's merits and demits in scales. Beth Hillel stressed the mercy of God in saying, "He that abounds in grace inclines (the scales) to grace" (*b. R. H.* 17a). Sanders puts his emphasis on those saved either because their good deeds outweigh their bad deeds or because, the scales being evenly balanced, God either pushes up the demerit side or pushes down the merit side. But there is a third class, those whose bad deeds outweigh their good deeds, and the rabbis saw them as lost. Sanders simply denies that this is representative. But it is part of the evidence and should not be overlooked.

[35]E.g., see R. H. Gundry, "Grace, Works, and Staying Saved in Paul," *Bib* 66 (1985): 1–38.

[36]Stephen Westerholm has a very useful survey of the contributions of a wide range of scholars to

Sanders thinks that the fundamental distinction between Paul and Judaism does not turn on justification, but on Christology. Christians accepted Jesus as Messiah; most Jews did not. Sanders rejects the commonly held view that Paul means that people cannot keep the law. "The whole thrust of the argument is that righteousness was never, in God's plan, intended to be by law . . . the problem with the law is not that it cannot be fulfilled. Paul has a view of God's intention which excludes righteousness by the law." Jews generally insisted that those who would become members of the people of God must become full proselytes, with the consequent acceptance of the law of Moses. But for Paul those who are "of works of law" are under a curse (Gal. 3:10).[37]

Sanders's views have been popularized and expounded at many levels. For instance, one recent essay questions "the Protestant understanding of Galatians," which it sees as "the clear, deliberate expression of the Pauline gospel of justification by faith, as opposed to works."[38] Gordon prefers to put the emphasis on the opposition of the Torah to faith in Christ and asks, "Shall the people of God be identified by Torah or by Christ?"[39] In this he is undoubtedly drawing attention to an important truth, but it must not be forgotten that Galatians does speak significantly often of being justified by faith (2:16 bis; 3:8, 11, 24) or "justified in Christ" (2:17), not by works of law (2:16 [three times]; 3:11). In correcting a view that overlooks the contrast between Christ and Torah and simply opposes faith to works, we must not overlook the truth that justification by faith in Christ is by its very nature opposed to any view of justification by works, those of the Torah or any other.

Whether or not his work is accepted without criticism, Sanders has so set the agenda of recent Pauline studies that a substantial part of current work largely presupposes his findings and proceeds to build on them. For instance, in his recent monograph, Barclay thoughtfully examines Paul's ethics as expressed in Galatians.[40] At the level of his exegesis of large parts of Galatians 5 and 6, Barclay's work is careful and stimulating; how he relates it to the rest of the epistle, however, turns in large part on adopting, rather uncritically, large parts of Sanders's structure. It is rather rare to find a book like that of Thielman,[41] who argues against Sanders at a pressing point. Because Sanders thinks the fundamental difference between (unconverted) Jew and Christian in Paul is Christology, therefore on matters such as sin and grace and forgiveness, Paul is really arguing "from solution to plight": that is, Paul knows the solution, namely Jesus, and then argues back to the plight. Thielman argues that when Paul in Galatians and Romans professedly sets out the plight (i.e. sin, or rebellion against God and his

---

our understanding of the subjects dealt with in this epistle (*Israel's Law and the Church's Faith: Paul and His Recent Interpreters* [Grand Rapids: Eerdmans, 1988]). See further the section "Romans in Recent Study," in chap. 8 above.

[37]According to Sanders, "God sent Christ; he did so in order to offer righteousness; this would have been pointless if righteousness were already available by the law (2:21); the law was not given to bring righteousness" (*Paul, the Law, and the Jewish People*, p. 27).

[38]T. David Gordon, "The Problem at Galatia," *Int* 41 (1987): 32.

[39]Ibid., p. 40.

[40]John M. G. Barclay, *Obeying the Truth: A Study of Paul's Ethics in Galatians* (Edinburgh: T. & T. Clark, 1988).

[41]Frank Thielman, *From Plight to Solution: A Jewish Framework for Understanding Paul's View of the Law in Galatians and Romans*, SuppNovT 61 (Leiden: Brill, 1989).

law) and then turns to the solution, he is not resorting to a pedagogical device but is borrowing from a standard pattern in both the Old Testament and in the Judaism of his day. Although Thielman's work barely begins to satisfy the need for more probing of the extraordinarily complex questions surrounding Paul's understanding of the law, it is a useful reminder that the synthesis proposed by Sanders can be challenged at many points.

The influence of Sanders should not allow us to overlook other topics of debate over the epistle to the Galatians. Paul begins the letter by asserting his apostleship and its importance. W. Schmithals has given a good deal of attention to the nature of the apostolate and has strongly argued that there were Gnostic apostles ranged in opposition to Paul.[42] The difficulty with his position is that there is no evidence for developed Gnosticism during Paul's lifetime. That Paul valued his apostleship highly is clear, and that he faced opposition is not in doubt. But that Gnosticism is involved is highly improbable on the basis of the facts available to us.[43]

Again, Cosgrove has argued that the question Paul is addressing in this epistle is explicitly articulated in Galatians 3:5 (our translation): "Does the one who supplies you with the Spirit and works wonders among you do so because of works of the law or because you heard [the gospel] and believed?" In others words, Paul and his readers share a charismatic background, and the question that now exercises the Galatians is the *ground* of Christian life in the Spirit.[44] Although Cosgrove attempts to justify his choice of Galatians 3:5 as the pivotal art᠎iculation of the epistle's theme, his methodological rationale is far from convincing. Moreover, it is hard to believe that the Galatians are concerned about the law (including such initiatory matters as circumcision), not with respect to conversion, but exclusively with respect to progress in the life of the Spirit.

THE CONTRIBUTION OF GALATIANS

This short letter has an importance out of all proportion to its size. There is always a tendency for people to think that their salvation (however it is understood) is something that is to be brought about by their own achievement. How they understand salvation may vary, and the kind of achievement they see as necessary may correspondingly vary. But that their eternal destiny rests in their own hands seems a truism, so obvious that it scarcely needs stating. Christianity has often been understood as nothing more than a system of morality, as the careful observance of a sacramental system, as conformity to standards, as a linking up with others in the church, and so on. There is always a need for Paul's forthright setting out of the truth that justification comes only through faith in Christ. This must be said over against those who stress the importance of works done in accordance with the Torah or any other achievement of the sinner.

The Christian way stresses what God has done rather than what sinners do to

---

[42]W. Schmithals, *The Office of Apostle in the Early Church* (Nashville: Abingdon, 1969).

[43]John W. Drane remarks that "the whole of Schmithals's argument here (and, indeed, throughout the whole of his work) is based on the assumption that Gnosticism as a system was of pre-Christian origin." He goes on to say that this belief "simply cannot be substantiated on the basis of any known evidence" (*Paul: Libertine or Legalist?* p. 17).

[44]Charles H. Cosgrove, *The Cross and the Spirit: A Study in the Argument and Theology of Galatians* (Macon, Ga.: Mercer University Press, 1989).

bring about salvation. There can be no improvement on the divine action by any human achievement, by way of either ritual observance or moral improvement. The cross is the one way of salvation, and no part of Scripture makes this clearer than does Galatians.[45]

We should not miss the importance of Paul's appeal to Abraham (3:6–29). This takes the reader back to a time when the law had not been given; the covenant established with Abraham takes precedence over the law (3:17). The law cannot annul the promise of God. Those who were forsaking simple reliance on the promise of God were turning from the divinely appointed way and mistaking the real purpose of the law (3:19). If Paul's Galatian friends would give proper consideration to the example of Abraham, they would see the serious error into which they were falling when they began to rely on the Torah.[46] If we read the account of Abraham and his faith in its proper sequence in the unfolding history of redemption, instead of anachronistically assuming, with many Jews, that Abraham must have kept the law, it becomes clear that God's way has always been the way of promise and faith. This brings Paul to the magnificent thought that all human distinctions have now become irrelevant (3:28–29). Christ came at the appointed time to redeem enslaved sinners (4:4–5), and Paul makes an important point when he says that he did this work of redemption "by becoming a curse for us" (3:13). This is a significant contribution to our understanding of the atonement.

Along with the emphasis on justification by faith in Christ is an emphasis on Christian freedom: "It is for freedom that Christ has set us free" (5:1); believers are literally to "walk in [NIV live by'] the Spirit" (5:16). Even those who are justified by faith in Christ sometimes find it easy to subject themselves to the slavery of a system. Paul's words remain the classic expression of the liberty that is the heritage of everyone who is in Christ.

Galatians is a constant reminder of how important it is to understand what the Christian faith implies for Christian living. Even Peter and Barnabas could go astray. Paul does not complain of their theology, but of their practice when "those who belonged to the circumcision group" induced them to withdraw from table fellowship with Gentiles (2:11–14). No letter makes as clear as this one does the importance of living out all the implications of salvation through the cross.

BIBLIOGRAPHY

John M. G. **Barclay**, *Obeying the Truth: A Study of Paul's Ethics in Galatians* (Edinburgh: T. & T. Clark, 1988); M. **Barth**, "The Kerygma of Galatians," *Int* 21 (1967): 131–46; H. D. **Betz**, *Galatians*, Hermeneia (Philadelphia: Fortress, 1979); idem, "The Literary Composition and Function of Paul's Letter to the Galatians," *NTS* 21

---

[45]Cf. Johnson's questions: "Is God ultimately a passive bookkeeper who, after shaping the world, lets it alone, concerned only to tally the relative merits of his creatures? Or is God one who is at every moment creating anew, redeeming, sanctifying, the source of all that is, and the goal toward which all things tend? Does God act in strange and unexpected ways, or is God locked into his own past?" (p. 305).

[46]"By grounding his argument in the faith of Abraham, Paul removes the debate from the sphere of merely contingent history. The Galatians have just not made a human misjudgment, but committed themselves to an alternative which severed their continuity with the father of the faith" (Childs, p. 308).

(1974–75): pp. 353–79; A. C. M. **Blommerde**, "Is There an Ellipsis Between Gal. 2,3 and 2,4?" *Bib* 56 (1975): 100–102; P. **Borgen**, "Paul Preaches Circumcision and Pleases Men," in *Paul and Paulinism, Fs.* C. K. Barrett, ed. M. D. Hooker and S. G. Wilson (London: SPCK, 1982), pp. 37–46; Udo **Borse**, *Der Brief an die Galater*, RNT (Regensburg: Friedrich Pustet, 1984); F. F. **Bruce**, "'Abraham Had Two Sons': A Study in Pauline Hermeneutics," in New *Testament Studies, Fs.* Ray Summers, ed. H. L. Drumwright and C. Vaughan (Waco, Tex.: Word, 1975), pp. 71–84; idem, *Commentary on Galatians*, NIGCT (Grand Rapids: Eerdmans, 1982); idem, "The Conference in Jerusalem—Galatians 2:1–10," in *God Who Is Rich in Mercy, Fs.* D. B. Knox, ed. P. T. O'Brien and D. G. Peterson (Homebush West, NSW: Anzea, 1986), pp. 195–212; idem, "The Curse of the Law," in *Paul and Paulinism, Fs.* C. K. Barrett, ed. M. D. Hooker and S. G. Wilson (London: SPCK, 1982), pp. 27–36; idem, "Galatian Problems," *BJRL* 51 (1968–69): 292–309; 52 (1969–70): 243–66; 53 (1970–71): 253–71; 54 (1971–72): 250–67; 55 (1972–73): 264–82; idem, "Paul and the Law of Moses," *BJRL* 57 (1974–75): 259–79; E. de Witt **Burton**, *A Critical and Exegetical Commentary on the Epistle to the Galatians*, ICC (Edinburgh: T. & T. Clark, 1921); D. A. **Carson**, "Pauline Inconsistency: Reflections on I Corinthians 9.19–23 and Galatians 2.11–14," *Churchman* 100 (1986): 6–45; Charles H. **Cosgrove**, *The Cross and the Spirit: A Study in the Argument and Theology of Galatians* (Macon, Ga.: Mercer University Press, 1989); idem, "The Law Has Given Sarah No Children (Gal. 4:21–30)," *NovT* 29 (1987): 219–35; Charles B. **Cousar**, *Galatians*, Interpretation (Atlanta: John Knox, 1982); John W. **Drane**, *Paul: Libertine or Legalist?* (London: SPCK, 1975); J. D. G. **Dunn**, "Once More—Gal 1 18: ἱστορῆσαι Κηφᾶν: In Reply to Otfried Hofius," *ZNW* 76 (1985): 138–39; idem, "The Relationship Between Paul and Jerusalem According to Galatians 1 and 2," *NTS* 28 (1981–82): 461–78; idem, "Works of the Law and Curse of the Law, *NTS* 31 (1984–85): 523–42; Gerhard **Ebeling**, *The Truth of the Gospel: An Exposition of Galatians*, trans. David Green (Philadelphia: Fortress, 1985); W. **Foester**, "Die Δοκοῦντες in Gal. 2," *ZNW* 36 (1937): 286–92; Ronald Y. K. **Fung**, *The Epistle to the Galatians* (Grand Rapids: Eerdmans, 1988); idem, "Justification, Sonship, and the Gift of the Spirit: Their Mutual Relationships as Seen in Galatians 3–4," *CGSTJ* 3 (1987): 73–104; T. David **Gordon**, "The Problem at Galatia," *Int* 41 (1987): 32–43; R. H. **Gundry**, "Grace, Works, and Staying Saved in Paul," *Bib* 66 (1985): 1–38; Ernst **Haenchen**, *The Acts of the Apostles* (Oxford: Blackwell, 1971); Richard B. **Hays**, "Christology and Ethics in Galatians: The Law of Christ," *CBQ* 49 (1987): 268–90; idem, *The Faith of Jesus Christ*, SBLDS 56 (Chico, Calif.: SP, 1983); C. J. **Hemer**, "The Adjective 'Phrygia,'" *JTS* 27 (1976): 122–26; idem, "Phrygia: A Further Note," *JTS* 28 (1978): 99–101; J. D. **Hester**, "The Rhetorical Structure of Galatians 1:11–2:14," *JBL* 103 (1984): 223–33; D. **Hill**, "Salvation Proclaimed: IV. Galatians 3:10–14," *ExpTim* 93 (1981–82): 196–200; O. **Hofius**, "Gal 1:18: ἱστορῆσαι Κηφᾶν," ZNW 75 (1984): 73–85; M. D. **Hooker**, "Paul and Covenantal Nomism,'" in *Paul and Paulinism*, pp. 47–56; G. **Howard**, *Paul: Crisis in Galatia* (Cambridge: Cambridge University Press, 1979); J. J. **Hughes**, "Hebrews ix 15ff. and Galatians iii 15ff.: A Study in Covenant Practice and Procedure," *NovT* 21 (1979): 27–96; R. **Jewett**, "The Agitators and the Galatian Congregation," *NTS* 17 (1970–71): 198–212; G. D. **Kilpatrick**, "Peter, Jerusalem, and Galatians 1:13–2:14," *NovT* 25 (1983): 318–26; J. B. **Lightfoot**, *Saint Paul's Epistle to the Galatians* (London: Macmillan, 1902); Andrew T. **Lincoln**, *Paradise Now and Not Yet*, SNTSMS 43 (Cambridge: Cambridge University Press, 1981); D. J. **Lull**,

" 'The Law Was Our Pedagogue': A Study in Galatians 3:19–25," *JBL* 105 (1986): 481–98; D. J. **Moo**, " 'Law,' 'Works of the Law,' and Legalism in Paul," *WTJ* 45 (1983): 73–100; J. **Munck**, *Paul and the Salvation of Mankind* (Richmond: John Knox, 1959); George **Ogg**, *The Chronology of the Life of Paul* (London: Epworth, 1968); J. C. **O'Neill**, *The Recovery of Paul's Letter to the Galatians* (London: SPCK, 1972); W. M. **Ramsay**, *The Church in the Roman Empire* (London: Hodder & Stoughton, 1893); P. **Richardson**, "Pauline Inconsistency: I Corinthians 9:19–23 and Galatians 2:11–14," *NTS* 26 (1979–80): 347–62; J. A. T. **Robinson**, *Redating the New Testament* (Philadelphia: Westminster, 1976); E. P. **Sanders**, "On the Question of Fulfilling the Law in Paul and Rabbinic Judaism," in *Donum Gentilicium, Fs.* D. Daube, ed. E. Bammel, C. K. Barrett, and W. D. Davies (Oxford: Oxford University Press, 1980), pp. 103–26; idem, *Paul and Palestinian Judaism* (Philadelphia: Fortress, 1977); idem, *Paul, the Law, and the Jewish People* (Philadelphia: Fortress, 1985); T. R. **Schreiner**, "Is Perfect Obedience to the Law Possible? A Re-examination of Galatians 3:10," *JETS* 27 (1984): 151–60; idem, "Paul and Perfect Obedience to the Law: An Evaluation of the View of E. P. Sanders," *WTJ* 47 (1985): 245–78; G. M. **Taylor**, "The Function of πίστις Χριστοῦ in Galatians," *JBL* 85 (1966): 58–76; Frank **Thielman**, *From Plight to Solution: A Jewish Framework for Understanding Paul's View of the Law in Galatians and Romans*, SuppNovT 61 (Leiden: Brill, 1989); P. **Vielhauer**, "Gottesdienst und Stoicheiadienst im Galaterbrief," in *Rechtfertigung, Fs.* E. Käsemann, ed. J. Friedrich, W. Pöhlmann, and P. Stuhlmacher (Tübingen: Mohr, 1976), pp. 543–55; M. **Wilcox**, "The Promise of the 'Seed' in the New Testament and the Targums," *JSNT* 5 (1979): 2–20; S. K. **Williams**, "Justification and the Spirit in Galatians," *JSNT* 29 (1987): 91–100; R. M. **Wilson**, "Gnostics—in Galatia?" *SE* 4: 358–67; N. H. **Young**, "Paidagōgos: The Social Setting of a Pauline Metaphor," *NovT* 29 (1987): 150–76.

ephesians

CONTENTS

After the opening greeting (1:1–2) there come praise to God for his predestining and redeeming activity in Christ (1:3–14) and thanksgiving and prayer for the letter's recipients (1:15–23). Chapter 2 reminds them of their sinfulness and of their salvation by grace (2:1–10), then addresses the peace and the unity Christ brings (2:11–22). Paul speaks of "the mystery of Christ" with the Gentiles being brought into membership of the one body with God's ancient people Israel (3:1–6) and of the way God's eternal purpose was worked out in Christ (3:7–13). This leads into prayer for the readers, ending in a doxology (3:14–21).

The importance of keeping "the unity of the Spirit" is stressed (4:1–6), as are the gifts of God to the church, enabling growth in love (4:7–16). The readers are exhorted to live as children of light (4:17–5:21). Directions for family life follow, with exhortations to wives and husbands (5:22–33), to children and parents (6:1–4), and to slaves and masters (6:5–9). Paul urges his readers to put on the armor God provides (6:10–18), concluding with a request that they use the weapon of prayer on his behalf (6:19–20). The letter closes with final greetings (6:21–24).

AUTHOR

That Ephesians is an authentic Pauline letter is the traditional view, but in modern times this is widely denied. The view that Paul wrote it is supported by such arguments as the following:[1]

1. The letter claims to have been written by Paul, not only in its opening (1:1) but also in the body of the letter (3:1). Any letter coming down from antiquity, it is said, should be held to be by the author it mentions unless there is strong evidence to the contrary. There are many personal notes: for example, the writer has heard of the readers' faith and love (1:15), and he gives thanks and prays for them (1:16); he calls himself "the prisoner of Christ Jesus" (3:1; 4:1); he asks the

---

[1]In addition to the standard commentaries and introductions, see A. van Roon, *The Authenticity of Ephesians*, SuppNovT 39 (Leiden: Brill, 1974); and the thoughtful review by A. T. Lincoln, *WTJ* 40 (1977–78): 172–75.

readers' prayers (6:19–20). This sort of thing is not proof, but it indicates that the man who claims to be Paul was known to the readers and was confident that his claim would not be overthrown.

2. From early days the letter was in wide circulation, and its authenticity does not seem to have been doubted. It was accepted by Marcion (as the letter to the Laodiceans); it is in the Muratorian Canon and was used by heretics as well as the orthodox. No one seems to have queried Pauline authorship.

3. Pauline features abound. The structure is like that of the undisputed epistles, and there is a good deal of Pauline language, including words that occur in this letter and the undisputed writings of Paul but nowhere else in the New Testament.[2] H. J. Cadbury has asked an interesting question: "Which is more likely—that an imitator of Paul in the first century composed a writing ninety or ninety-five per cent in accordance with Paul's style or that Paul himself wrote a letter diverging five or ten per cent from his usual style?"[3] Robert M. Grant noticed this question and posed one of his own: "Which is more likely,' we might well ask —that we can determine the authenticity of a letter written ninety or ninety-five per cent in accordance with Paul's style, and his outlook, or that we cannot?' *This* question, it would appear, can be answered. We are not in a position to judge, and since the authenticity of the letter cannot be disproved it should be regarded as genuine."[4]

4. The relationship to Colossians may be argued in more ways than one. Those who reject Pauline authorship hold that it would not be possible for one person to write two letters with such resemblances (e.g., the words about Tychicus; see Eph. 6:21–22 and Col. 4:7–8), but also with such significant differences (e.g., the "mystery" is the unity of Jews and Gentiles in Christ in Eph. 3:3–6, whereas it is Christ in Col. 2:2). But those who see Paul as the author "are equally emphatic that two minds could not have produced two such works with so much subtle interdependence blended with independence."[5] Ephesians is not so much a copy of parts of Colossians as a development of it. There may be similar vocabulary, but there are also curious differences. It is not unreasonable to think of Paul as producing Colossians with a specific situation in mind, and not long after as writing Ephesians with broader purposes. It is also possible that he made use of an amanuensis and allowed him some freedom in one or other of the letters. But against this is the fact that the other Pauline letters give no evidence of secretarial latitude, or at least of such secretarial latitude as this theory requires. Why should Paul treat this letter differently from the others?[6]

5. Paul is not mentioned in Revelation, which was addressed to the church at Ephesus among others (see Rev. 2:1; cf. 2 Peter 3:15). The question may be asked: Why should an author, writing pseudonymously, select the name of Paul in

---

[2]"It is difficult to believe that an imitator could have produced a work so like the writings of Paul and yet so splendid and original: difficult to believe some other spiritual genius was to be found in the Church at this time whose mind was so like Paul's and whose thought was so sublime" (Clogg, p. 96).

[3]H. J. Cadbury, "The Dilemma of Ephesians," *NTS* 5 (1958–59): 101.

[4]Grant, p. 202.

[5]Guthrie, p. 511.

[6]Johnson finds two major weaknesses in the argument that an imitator of Colossians produced this letter: "If Colossians was followed so assiduously, why does the usage even of the shared vocabulary differ in such interesting ways? And if the forger had available to him other genuine letters, why weren't they used in a more effective and convincing way?"(p. 369).

writing to an area where, granted the failure of Revelation to mention Paul, there is no evidence that the apostle was still highly revered?[7] In any case, the practice of writing letters in the name of someone else does not seem to have been as widely practiced in the early church as some claim. (See the section "Pseudonymity" in chap. 15.)

6. Many of the themes of Ephesians have the closest parallels in the undisputed Pauline epistles—for example, justification by faith, the place of grace, the dominance of flesh in the unredeemed, the work of Christ as reconciliation, the place of the Jews and of the law. Those who oppose Pauline authorship argue that this results from imitation, but that is to be proved. There is undoubtedly Pauline teaching in this letter.

7. Paul was a prisoner when he wrote the letter (3:1; 4:1) which accords well with this claim. There is development from the earlier letters, but this is natural enough as the apostle gets closer to the end of his life. The letter is very naturally understood as Paul's words to a church he sees as needing instruction on some of the important aspects of the faith, some of which he has not enunciated previously, at least in the form he now uses. Such an understanding seems to many scholars a better way of seeing the letter than the alternatives that are suggested. No suggested pseudepigraphical situation has anything like the aptness of the view that Paul is writing from his final imprisonment.

But many modern scholars are not persuaded by such considerations. They hold that the evidence points to someone other than Paul as the writer.

1. The theology of Ephesians is said to be such that we cannot ascribe the writing to Paul. There are Pauline features, such as the clear statement of justification by faith (2:5–8), but there are some doctrines we do not find in Paul, for example, the cosmic function of the church (3:10). Again, in Ephesians believers are "built on the foundation of the apostles and prophets" (2:20), whereas Paul sees Christ as the one foundation (1 Cor. 3:11). But these are not really in contradiction; in 2:20 Christ is "the chief cornerstone," which surely accords with the passage in 1 Corinthians. Others note that in Ephesians ἐκκλησία (*ekklēsia*) always refers to the universal church, while Paul normally uses the word for the local congregation. Paul refers to the parousia in all his undisputed letters, but it is absent from Ephesians (but is this fair to 1:14; 4:30; 5:6; 6:8?). This letter pictures Paul as commissioned to bring about the unity of Jews and Gentiles in the church (3:2–6), whereas Paul saw himself as the apostle of the Gentiles (but in Rom. 11:17–24 he has both Jews and Gentiles in the one olive tree). Ephesians uses marriage as a picture of the union between Christ and the church (5:23–33), which is said to be quite impossible for the author of 1 Corinthians 7. Clearly all of this is subjective. What appears to some as impossible for one mind is for others quite a possibility for such a wide-ranging and inventive mind as Paul's.[8]

2. The language of Ephesians includes words not found elsewhere in Paul, for

---

[7]Most of those who argue for the pseudonymity of Ephesians date the epistle as late as c. A.D. 90, almost thirty years after Paul's death and not long removed from the most likely date for the composition of the Apocalypse.

[8]F. W. Danker, under the heading "Theology," begins, "Beyond question this Epistle fits within boundaries largely familiar in other Pauline letters"; he demonstrates this with references to Paul's letters ("Ephesians," in *ISBE* 2:113–14).

example, ἀσωτία (asōtia, "wantonness"; but cf. Titus 1:6), πολιτεία (politeia, "citizenship," "commonwealth").[9] This argument is somewhat spoiled by Harrison's examination of the hapax legomena (words that occur in no other writing in the New Testament). He finds that in Ephesians there are on the average 4.6 such words to the page, which is in line with the figures for other letters, such as 5.6 in 2 Corinthians, and 6.2 in Philippians.[10] It is also pointed out that in this letter different expressions are used for the same thing. For example, whereas in other writings Paul uses οἱ οὐρανοί (hoi ouranoi) for "heaven," in Ephesians we have ἐν τοῖς ἐπουρανίοις (en tois epouraniois) as well. So also in this letter we find Christ called ὁ ἠγαπημένος (ho ēgapēmenos, "the One [God] loves," Eph. 1:6) and the verb χαριτόω (charitoō, lit. "to endue with grace"; cf. Eph. 1:6) where Paul normally has χάριν δίδωμι (charin didōmi, lit. "I give grace"). Paul usually refers to Satan, but in this letter we find "the devil." Such differences are interesting, but they come far short of proof, especially with a writer as versatile as Paul.[11]

3. The style of this letter is very different. The length of the sentences is specially noteworthy. In any modern translation these long sentences tend to be broken up, with the result that the reader does not realize the length. But 1:15–23 is one sentence, as is 3:1–7 (see KJV). Ephesians often has a quick use of synonyms; thus in 1:19 there are four words denoting power.

4. Ephesians is taken as an "early catholic" writing. It is suggested that the author looks back on the apostles as a closed group (2:20; 3:5) and that there is an un-Pauline interest in various orders of ministry (4:11; but should we not bear in mind 1 Cor. 12:28–30?). The use of the name of Paul, it is said, means that the writer is seeking to pass on the genuine apostolic tradition.

5. The relationship to Colossians is considered such that the same writer could not have produced the two. Colossians is usually held to be a genuine Pauline letter, and Ephesians is thought to be the work of an imitator who used Colossians for some of his thoughts and language. Indeed, on occasion the same word is used with different meanings (e.g., μυστήριον [mystērion]; cf. Eph. 3:2–13 and Col. 1:25–2:3). But as we saw earlier, this line of argument is unconvincing. We must allow any writer some flexibility, and the best explanation to many seems to be that the same man wrote Colossians and Ephesians a little later, with many of the same thoughts running through his head and with a more general application of the ideas he had so recently expressed.

It is possible to regard both Colossians and Ephesians as inauthentic. But in this case Colossians appears to use only Philemon to lead people to think of it as a genuine Pauline product, and Ephesians looks like another work by the same pseudepigrapher. This time, however, he does not bother to use personal references, and he also introduces some curious stylistic differences. All in all, such a procedure seems improbable.

---

[9] By contrast, some think that Ephesians is *too* Pauline: it contains reminiscences of too many Pauline letters (see G. Johnston, "Ephesians," in *IDB* 2:110–11).

[10] P. N. Harrison, *The Problem of the Pastoral Epistles* (London: Oxford University Press, 1921), p. 20.

[11] L. Cerfaux asks how an imitator can "avoid betraying himself by awkward phrases, wordiness, or allusions which correspond to his own interests. The forgers or plagiarists of antiquity have not accustomed us to such skill. As an example of their lack of it, let anyone read the so-called *Letter to the Laodiceans!*" (Robert/Feuillet, p. 503).

Markus Barth recognizes four schools of thought today: those who accept Paul as the author, those who see Paul as responsible for an original script that has been augmented by an editor,[12] those who reject Pauline authorship, and those who think that there is not enough evidence to decide.[13] While he recognizes the strength of the other views, he produces an argument "which more than others favors the authenticity of Ephesians and encourages the reader to understand the letter on the basis of its Pauline origin."[14]

PROVENANCE

This letter seems to have been written from the same place as Colossians, and its provenance is discussed under that for Colossians.

DATE

The letter speaks of Paul as in prison (3:1; 4:1). This is usually taken to refer to his imprisonment in Rome toward the end of his life, which would mean a date in the early 60s. Those who reject Pauline authorship usually date Ephesians in the period 70–90, the period during which the Pauline letters are thought to have been collected. If it was not written by Paul, it must belong to the immediate postapostolic period, but there are no criteria for locating it with precision. It cannot be much later than about 90, for it seems to be referred to by Clement of Rome, who is usually thought to have written his letter c. A.D. 96.

DESTINATION

There is a problem posed by the fact that "in Ephesus" is absent from 1:1 in some of the best MSS (p^{46}, ℵ, B, 424ᶜ, 1739), in Basil and Origen, apparently also in Marcion (who called the letter "the epistle to the Laodiceans"), and in Tertullian. The tone of the letter is impersonal, and some parts of it seem to indicate that the writer did not know the readers—for example, "ever since I heard about your faith in the Lord Jesus" (1:15) and "surely you have heard . . ." (3:2; 4:21). But Paul had evangelized the Ephesians and had spent quite a long time among them (Acts 19:8, 10; 20:31). The warmth of his affection for them and theirs for him is plainly evident in their last farewell (Acts 20:17–38, esp. vv. 36–37). It is very difficult to imagine that Paul would have written such a calm and impersonal letter to such dear friends. The words, however, are included by almost all MSS and by all the ancient versions; even the MSS that lack the words have "To the Ephesians" in the title.[15]

---

[12]Cf. Martin's view that "it was Luke who published this letter under the apostle's aegis" (2:224).
[13]Markus Barth, *Ephesians*, AB (New York: Doubleday, 1974), p. 38.
[14]Ibid., p. 41.
[15]Kümmel confidently says, "The superscription comes first from the time of the collecting of the Pauline letters, and therefore merely passes on an early Christian interpretation of those to whom it was addressed" (p. 353). This may conceivably be true, but how can we possibly know? We have no copies of MSS as early as the time of the collection of the Epistles, so we have no information about superscriptions then or before. In any case, should not some respect be accorded a Christian opinion as early as this? This is not to argue that we should accept the assignation to the Ephesians, but simply for care in the use of the evidence.

The suggestion is accordingly put forward that this was originally meant as a circular letter, probably conveyed by Tychicus, who would supplement it with his own comments (Eph. 6:21). It happens that the copy meant for the Ephesians is the ancestor of almost all the MSS that survive. A variant of this view is that a letter without an address was kept by the church at Ephesus, and in time it was assumed that it had been sent to that church. It would accord with the circular-letter hypothesis that there are no references to specific problems or disputes.

There is nothing decisive against the view that one letter was sent to a number of churches, but some objections are urged. An important one is that a circular letter with no name attached is very feasible in an age familiar with photocopiers (and even in one that had to depend on carbon paper), but it makes little sense in an age in which every copy had to be laboriously made by hand. If the whole had to be handwritten, there seems no reason for omitting the two words for the name of the individual church.[16] The saving in time would be miniscule. It is also to be borne in mind that the copies with the omission lack "in" as well as the place name: surely "in" would remain in each copy of the circular. It is further urged that it would be very curious if no copy of a circular survived other than that to one particular church: even those MSS that lack "in Ephesus" do not have another name inserted. Furthermore, some critics hold that a circular for churches in the general area of Ephesus might be expected to receive some greetings of a general character. At the same time, attention is also drawn to personal touches in Ephesians. Would Paul write to *every* church, "I ask you, therefore, not to be discouraged because of my sufferings for you, which are your glory" (3:13)?[17]

Perhaps the best form of the circular-letter theory is that which sees Paul as having sent such a letter with Tychicus when he sent Colossians and that the letter was copied and circulated from Ephesus. Since it was a circular, there would be a blank instead of the name of the recipients, but the letter would be known to be associated with Ephesus, and in time that name was attached to it.[18]

Another suggestion is that this letter was really meant for the Laodiceans, as Marcion thought. If it is held that it is the Laodicean copy of a circular letter, it is open to all the objections noted; furthermore, whereas there are many copies existent with the address to Ephesus, not one survives addressing Laodicea. And if it is held that it is the letter referred to in Colossians 4:16, there is the further problem that Ephesians and Colossians are so like one another that one wonders why the churches should go through the process of exchanging them. In any case, most scholars hold that Ephesians is later than Colossians; and if this judgment is correct, then Colossians 4:16 refers to another writing.

E. J. Goodspeed has suggested that the letter was written as an introduction to the whole Pauline corpus. The thought is that when some loyal Paulinist first made a collection of the Pauline Epistles, he wrote this letter in the style of his

---

[16]"[The] supposition of a letter with a gap in the prescript or a subsequent insertion of the address is without any parallel in antiquity" (Kümmel, p. 355).

[17]Francis Lyall adduces an argument from the legal allusions he finds in Ephesians. He points out that Ephesus was a main seat of government, a place where Roman law was known, and notes that "the Epistle to the Colossians, addressed to a smaller church outside Ephesus, does not contain the same measure of legal allusions as Ephesians" (*Slaves, Citizens, Sons* [Grand Rapids: Zondervan, 1984], p. 232).

[18]Wikenhauser makes this suggestion (p. 426).

beloved master as a way of introducing readers to some of Paul's thinking. Possibly the collection was first made at Ephesus, which would explain why so many MSS bear this address.[19]

There are difficulties in the way of this hypothesis. One is that we have no record of Ephesians ever standing first in a collection of the Pauline letters. There is variation in the order of Paul's epistles, but no order has Ephesians standing in the position of an introduction to the whole. There is also the resemblance to Colossians. These two letters resemble each other more than any other two in the Pauline corpus. If someone was writing an introduction, why should this one epistle receive so much attention? And why should the words about Tychicus (6:21–22) be included? They fit quite well in a letter to an individual church or in a circular letter to be carried by Tychicus, but it is not easy to see why they should be included in an introduction. In most forms of this hypothesis it is held that the Pauline letters fell into neglect and that the appearance of Acts stirred up interest in the great apostle. But there is no real evidence of the supposed neglect, or that the publication of Acts would have had such an immediate influence throughout the church that a collection of Pauline writings would be made. It cannot be said that the theory has compelling force.

In the end we must probably conclude that we do not know for sure for whom the letter was originally intended. The evidence of the great mass of the MSS and the improbabilities of all the other views may drive us back to the view that it was meant for the church at Ephesus. If we feel that the absence of characteristic Pauline expressions of warmth (which would be probable in a letter to a church where he had spent as much time as he did at Ephesus) and of references to concrete situations are significant, then we will probably think of some form of circular. But we are left with difficulties whatever view we adopt.

PURPOSE

There is no unanimity in understanding the letter's aim. Clearly it is meant to give instruction to the readers, but the instruction is not given in the way with which we are familiar from the Pauline writings generally. Most of Paul's letters are occasional, written for a specific purpose on a specific occasion, but it is not easy to see any particular occasion that called forth this letter.[20] Indeed, some question whether it should be called a letter at all.[21] N. A. Dahl rejects such views: "It belongs to a type of Greek letters—genuine and spurious—which substitute for a public speech rather than for private conversation."[22]

But what is the occasion of this public speech? Some point to a possible tension between Jewish and Gentile Christians and think Paul is trying to secure unity. Another suggestion is that the letter is meant to instruct Gentile converts in

[19]Harrison discusses this view, noting some cogent objections (pp. 337–39).

[20]Some scholars classify an epistle such as Romans as a "tractate letter": see Richard N. Longenecker, "On the Form, Function, and Authority of the New Testament Letters," in *Scripture and Truth*, ed. D. A. Carson and John D. Woodbridge (Grand Rapids: Zondervan, 1983), pp. 101–14.

[21]"Presumably the author has no particular church in mind. He is meditating, and developing certain thoughts—and clothes them in the form of a letter"; "it is not really a letter, but a treatise or a 'wisdom address'" (Marxsen, p. 192).

[22]N. A. Dahl, "Ephesians," in *IDBSup*, p. 268. He also says, "Ephesians has been seen as the mature fruit of Paul's thought, as the beginning of its distortion, or an inspired re-interpretation" (ibid.).

important aspects of their new faith. Some who date the writing later than Paul propose that it was written to further the ecclesiastical interests of early catholicism. Others have suggested that it is an attempt to set out some of the greatest truths for which the early Christians stood. Faced with such diversity, some scholars give up altogether the attempt to find "one" aim and think there are several purposes behind the letter.

All this means that there is a solemnity about the letter and an absence of specifics that show it is devoted to a general articulation of what is profitable for believers. We must not specify a concrete situation or a concrete problem and say that the letter is addressed exclusively to this. By contrast, we may discern a heresy that is being countered by the epistle to the Colossians, but there is no specific false teaching against which Ephesians is aimed. We can say that it is an important statement of Christian truth that may well have been greatly needed in more than one first-century situation.

TEXT

As we have already noted, there is the practically insoluble question of whether to include "in Ephesus" in 1:1. But apart from that one passage the text is reasonably straightforward. There are a few problems, such as whether to read πάντας (pantas, "everyone") in 3:9, and ἰδίαις (idiais, "own") in 4:28, but such variations are minor. Apart from the destination in the opening sentence, we can say that we are not in real doubt about anything substantial in the letter.[23]

ADOPTION INTO THE CANON

We have no record of anyone in the early church raising a question about the canonicity of Ephesians. There were disputes about its destination, Marcion claiming that it was written to the Laodiceans and Basil later saying that in ancient copies it was addressed not to the Ephesians but to the saints who are also faithful in Christ Jesus. Clement of Rome probably refers to it, though without mentioning the author. Ignatius quotes from it, as do Polycarp and others. It appears in Marcion's canon (where, as we have seen, it is said to be addressed to the Laodiceans) and in the Muratorian Canon. No serious doubt about its authenticity has come down to us from the Fathers.

EPHESIANS IN RECENT STUDIES

A good deal of attention has been paid to the question of authorship in recent studies. The relation to Colossians has been scrutinized closely, and new considerations have been produced, such as the parallels between Ephesians and some of the Qumran writings. This points to traditions shared by some parts of Judaism and by some early Christians,[24] and many recent scholars detect common

---

[23]T. K. Abbott offers a series of notes "on some readings peculiar to one or two MSS" in which he looks at the most important readings in a selected group of important MSS (A Critical and Exegetical Commentary on the Epistles to the Ephesians and to the Colossians, ICC [Edinburgh: T. & T. Clark, 1897], pp. xl–xlv).

[24]Markus Barth points to passages in Ephesians reflecting traditions in the Old Testament, in

tradition underlying both Colossians and Ephesians. This means that similarities are not necessarily to be explained by direct borrowing: there may well be independent use of the common stock of tradition. This will not account for all the similarities, and in the end there must be some more direct relationship, but it puts the problem in another perspective.

There is a tendency on the part of some students to find elements of Gnosticism behind most of the New Testament writings, so it is not surprising that some have found it here. Thus Bultmann finds "the Gnostic Redeemer-myth" and specifically "the descent and re-ascent of the Redeemer" in 4:8–10. In the quotation from Psalm 68:19 he finds "the idea that he conquered the inimical spirit-powers by his journey to heaven" (with the idea of victory over the cosmic powers also in Col. 2:15).[25] It is "Gnostic language" when the writer refers to "the prince of the power of the air" (2:2; so also 1:21; 3:10) and to the "spiritual hosts of wickedness in the heavenly places" (6:12).[26] Terms such as πλήρωμα (plērōma, "fullness," 1:23 etc.) are frequently found in Gnostic literature. That the author has on occasion used language that also occurs in the later Gnostics can scarcely be denied, but that he is either indebted to Gnosticism or that he is writing in opposition to it has not been demonstrated. It is not along such lines that a fruitful understanding of this letter is to be sought.[27]

The letter's emphasis on the church is unmistakable; Ephesians clearly tells us more about the church universal than do other writings in the Pauline corpus. This has generated a great deal of discussion.[28] For many, this focus on the church is a natural and acceptable development, but for Käsemann (among others) it is a distortion of the real Christian message. In Ephesians, he writes, "the gospel is domesticated." The world "may be its sphere. But it is so only as the frame into which the picture of the church fits." He goes on to complain that here "Christology is integrated with the doctrine of the church. . . . Christ is the mark towards which Christianity is growing, and no longer in the strict sense its judge."[29]

More theologically telling are those studies that recognize distinctive emphases in Ephesians but relate such emphases to central themes in the Pauline corpus. For example, Lincoln examines what it means to be seated with Christ in the heavenly realms (Eph. 2:6) and concludes that it is a kind of spatial equivalent of inaugurated eschatology.[30] Caragounis[31] and Bockmuehl[32] have examined the

intertestamental Judaism, in Jewish worship, in Qumran, in the worship of the early Christians, in early Christian hymns and paraenetic traditions, in traditions of a Gentile origin and character, etc. ("Traditions in Ephesians," NTS 30 [1984]: 3–25). Clearly many traditions are reflected in the letter. Peter T. O'Brien finds that much of the language of the prayers in Ephesians can be paralleled in the Qumran literature ("Ephesians 1: An Unusual Introduction to a New Testament Letter," NTS 25 [1978–79]: 515).

[25] Rudolf Bultmann, Theology of the New Testament, 2 vols. (London: SCM, 1952–55), 1:175.

[26] Ibid., p. 173.

[27] "There has emerged a growing consensus shared even by its defenders that the interpretation of the traditions underlying Ephesians cannot be restricted to Gnostic influence" (Childs, p. 318).

[28] See the bibliography in D. A. Carson, ed., The Church in the Bible and the World (Grand Rapids: Baker, 1987).

[29] Ernst Käsemann, Jesus Means Freedom (Philadelphia: Fortress, 1972), p. 89.

[30] Andrew T. Lincoln, Paradise Now and Not Yet: Studies in the Role of the Heavenly Dimension in Paul's Thought, with Special Reference to His Eschatology, SNTSMS 43 (Cambridge: Cambridge University Press, 1981).

"mystery" language in the Pauline corpus, especially rich in Ephesians; the latter's work, cast against the backdrop of first-century understanding of the nature of revelation, is especially suggestive.

THE CONTRIBUTION OF EPHESIANS

The letter begins with a section putting strong emphasis on the divine action in bringing salvation. Paul refers to the spiritual blessings in Christ that believers enjoy and goes on to speak of God as having chosen them before the creation of the world (1:4; see also v. 11). Their salvation did not take place because they earned it but because God planned it, a truth that is otherwise expressed in terms of predestination that is linked with God's will and pleasure (1:5) and again with his plan (1:11). This opening also includes references to sonship through Christ, redemption through his blood, and sealing with the Holy Spirit (1:5, 7, 13). This massive emphasis on the place of the divine is expanded with continuing references to grace.[33]

Christ's saving work is stressed in the opening, a work that has significant implications for Christology. This emphasis persists throughout the letter: it is plain everywhere that who Christ is and what he does is at the heart of the Christian way. It is he who brings about the reconciliation of Jew and Gentile in the church, in the notable section on the breaking down of hostility and the making of peace between them (2:11–22). Christ "himself is our peace" (2:14). This is more than the overcoming of human hostility. Part of Christ's work is "to bring all things in heaven and on earth together under one head, even Christ" (1:10). The powers in the heavenlies are to know "the manifold wisdom of God" through the church (3:10). There is an importance in Christ's saving work that we cannot fathom, and there is an importance in the very existence of the church that we are not able to comprehend.[34]

Ephesians emphasizes the importance of the Christian's growth in knowledge, and this is expressed in a variety of ways. Sometimes it comes out in simple statements about knowledge, as when Paul says that God "made known to us the mystery" (1:9; cf. "the mystery of the gospel," 6:19). "Mystery" ($\mu\nu\sigma\tau\acute{\eta}\rho\iota\nu$ [*mystērion*]) does not mean something difficult to work out (as in our use of the term) but something impossible to work out. In Paul's use, however, there is mostly the further thought that what we could never work out for ourselves God has now made known (cf. 3:3 and the making known of God's "manifold wisdom" [3:10]). It is significant, accordingly, that the word occurs more often in Ephesians than in any other book of the New Testament; this book emphasizes the divine disclosure. The same basic idea may be conveyed with the concept of enlightenment: "I pray also that the eyes of your heart may be enlightened in

---

[31]Chrys C. Caragounis, *The Ephesian* Μνστήριον: *Meaning and Content* (Lund: Gleerup, 1977).

[32]Markus N. A. Bockmuehl, *Revelation and Mystery in Ancient Judaism and Pauline Christianity*, WUNT 2.36 (Tübingen: J. C. B. Mohr [Paul Siebeck], 1990).

[33]Χάρις (*charis*, "grace") occurs twelve times in Ephesians, a total exceeded in the New Testament only in Acts, Romans, and 2 Corinthians, all of which are considerably longer.

[34]Clogg sees this as very relevant to our modern situation. We feel ourselves "in the grip of a vast mechanism and of inexorable laws of physics and the like, and human freedom seems to have no meaning in the face of cosmic forces. We learn from this epistle to believe that all these but subserve a spiritual purpose, and that spiritual purpose is summed up in Christ" (p. 101).

order that you may know . . ." (1:18), which is to be seen against the background of the darkness of the Gentiles (4:18). The readers are "light in the Lord" and they are to live as "children of light" and "find out what pleases the Lord" (5:8–10); they are to "understand what the Lord's will is" (5:17). No one who has grappled with the thought of this letter can doubt the importance of growing in knowledge.

One of the important things the readers must know is expressed in the prayer that they may be "rooted and established in love" and be able "to grasp how wide and long and high and deep is the love of Christ, and to know this love that surpasses knowledge" (3:17–19). The word ἀγάπη (agapē, "love") occurs more often in this book than in any other in the New Testament except 1 Corinthians and 1 John. The reader sees the wonderful thing that Christian love is and the importance of living in love in a world that knows so little of it.

The church is "a holy temple in the Lord," a building in which Christ is "the chief cornerstone" and in which "God lives by his Spirit" (2:20–22). From another point of view, church members are both "fellow citizens with God's people and members of God's household" (2:19; cf. 1:5), a household that derives its name from the Father and that has members in heaven as well as on earth (3:14–15). The bringing of Gentiles as well as Jews into membership of the one body is explained as a mystery (3:4–6), a deep and hidden truth that none of us could have worked out but that has now been revealed by God. There is a unity that believers should strive to preserve (4:3); indeed, Paul draws attention to a whole series of unities, including one Spirit, one Lord, one God and Father, one body and one hope, one faith, one baptism (4:4–6), even though there are diverse gifts of apostles, prophets, and others in the church (4:11–13). Clearly the writer wants his readers to catch the splendid vision of one church, thoroughly united in the Lord, though it contains members of various races and is equipped by God to render significant service in this world.

A considerable section of the letter is given over to an emphasis on the importance of lives lived in conformity with the salvation that God has given believers. The kind of life the Gentiles live is contrasted with the new life believers live (4:17–5:21); the darkness of the old way is set over against the light there is in the Lord (5:8). This has important entailments for specific groups—wives and husbands, children and parents, slaves and masters (5:22–6:9). Wives are to be subject to their husbands, though we should bear in mind that the verb "submit" is not found in 5:22; it must be understood from the preceding verse, so that the submission of wives is one example of the wider duty of believers to submit to one another. Paul has much more to say about the obligations marriage lays on husbands. They are to have a Christlike love for their wives. This is not merely an erotic passion but a sacrificial love like the love with which Christ gave himself up for the church. Such a love prevails over other ties, such as those that bound a man to his parents. This kind of love leads Paul to speak of "a profound mystery—but I am talking about Christ and the church" (5:32). The section on the Christian's armor is a further incentive to wholehearted Christian service as well as a reminder that there is full provision made for those who engage in Christian service (6:10–18).

In this letter we cannot miss the supreme place of God, who brings salvation despite the unworthiness of sinners. Nor can we overlook the greatness of Christ or the fact that the church, his body, occupies an important place in God's working out of his great purpose.

BIBLIOGRAPHY

T. K. **Abbott**, *A Critical and Exegetical Commentary on the Epistles to the Ephesians and to Colossians*, ICC (Edinburgh: T. & T. Clark, 1897); M. **Barth**, *Ephesians*, AB (Garden City, N.Y.: Doubleday, 1974); idem, "Traditions in Ephesians," *NTS* 30 (1984): 3–25; P. **Benoit**, *Les épîtres de saint Paul aux Philippiens, à Philémon, aux Colossiens, aux Ephésiens*, 2d ed. *(Paris: du Cerf, 1953)*; E. **Best**, "Ephesians 1:1 Again," *in Paul and Paulinism*, ed. M. D. Hooker and S. G. Wilson (London: SPCK, 1982), pp. 273–79; Rudolf **Bultmann**, *Theology of the New Testament*, 2 vols. (London: SCM, 1952–55); H. J. **Cadbury**, "The Dilemma of Ephesians," *NTS* 5 (1958–59): 91–102; D. A. **Carson**, ed., *The Church in the Bible and the World* (Grand Rapids: Baker, 1987); H. **Conzelmann**, *Der Brief an die Epheser*, NTD (Göttingen: Vandenhoeck & Ruprecht, 1965); F. L. **Cross**, ed., *Studies in Ephesians* (London: Mowbray, 1956); E. J. **Goodspeed**, *The Key to Ephesians* (Chicago: University of Chicago Press, 1956); idem, *The Meaning of Ephesians* (Chicago: University of Chicago Press, 1933); P. N. **Harrison**, *The Problem of the Pastoral Epistles* (London: Oxford University Press, 1921); E. **Käsemann**, *Jesus Means Freedom* (Philadelphia: Fortress, 1972); A. T. **Lincoln**, review of *The Authenticity of Ephesians*, by A. van Roon, *WTJ* 40 (1977–78): 172–75; A. **Lindemann**, "Bemerkungen zu den Adressaten und zum Anlass des Epheser- briefes," *ZNW* 67 (1976): 235–51; Richard N. **Longenecker**, "On the Form, Function, and Authority of the New Testament Letters," in *Scripture and Truth*, ed. D. A. Carson and John D. Woodbridge (Grand Rapids: Zondervan, 1983), pp. 101–14; Francis **Lyall**, *Slaves, Citizens, Sons* (Grand Rapids: Zondervan, 1984); C. Leslie **Mitton**, *The Epistle to the Ephesians* (Oxford: Clarendon Press, 1951); P. T. **O'Brien**, "Ephesians 1: An Unusual Introduction to a New Testament Letter," *NTS* 25 (1978–79): 504–16; J. Armitage **Robinson**, *St. Paul's Epistle to the Ephesians*, 2d ed. (London: Clark, 1922); M. **Santer**, "The Text of Ephesians 1:1," *NTS* 15 (1968–69): 247–48; R. **Schnackenburg**, *Der Brief an die Epheser*, EKKNT (Zürich: Benziger Verlag; Neukirchen-Vluyn: Neukirchener Verlag, 1982); E. F. **Scott**, *The Epistles of Paul to the Colossians, to Philemon, and to the Ephesians*, MNTC (New York: Harper, 1930); A. **van Roon**, *The Authenticity of Ephesians*, SuppNovT 39 (Leiden: Brill, 1974); B. F. **Westcott**, *St. Paul's Epistle to the Ephesians* (London: Macmillan, 1906).

12

philippians

CONTENTS

After the normal opening greetings (1:1–2) Paul thanks God for the Philippians and prays for them (1:3–11). He goes on to point out that his imprisonment has advanced the gospel (1:12–18), and he looks forward to being set free in response to their prayers (1:19–26). He urges them to live as Christians should, even though this means suffering (1:27–30). In a magnificent hymn Paul urges his readers to be humble and to follow the example of Christ, who, although he was "in very nature God," became man and underwent death on a cross. God therefore exalted him to the highest place (2:1–11). This leads to a further confident exhortation to his readers to serve God faithfully (2:12–18).

Paul expresses his hope to send Timothy (whom he praises warmly) to them soon and indeed to come himself (2:19–24). He also speaks of sending Epaphroditus, who had been very near to death but had apparently recovered from his illness (2:25–30). The apostle warns against people who were evidently advocating circumcision; he himself had had every reason for confidence in his life as a Jew, but he now sees all that as "loss for the sake of Christ"; to know Christ is much more important (3:1–11). Paul makes it clear that he has not reached perfection: he is still pressing on toward the goal. He invites the Philippians to join with him and not to follow the example of people he castigates as "enemies of the cross of Christ" (3:12–4:1).

With the main part of the letter over, there come greetings to people who have worked with the apostle (4:2–3), a call to rejoicing in the Lord, to prayer without anxiety but with the assurance that God's peace will guard them (4:4–7). They should practice Christian virtues wholeheartedly (4:8–9). Paul goes on to thank the Philippians for sending him help in his troubles, the only church to have done so (4:10–20). This leads into final greetings and the grace (4:21–23).

AUTHOR

The letter claims to have been written by Paul, and no serious doubt is raised against this claim. The style is Pauline, and while it is difficult to assign the letter to a specific point in the life of Paul, the situation presupposed rings true. Paul was the kind of man who would have found himself in this situation and written such a letter.

One problem is the authorship of the hymn in Philippians 2:5–11. Some of the vocabulary is unusual—μορφή, (morphē, "form," vv. 6, 7), ἁρπαγμός (harpagmos, "something to be grasped," NIV v. 6), ὑπερυψόω (hyperypsoō, "to exalt [him] to the highest place," v. 9), and other words are not found elsewhere in Paul—and the rhythmic style is not common in Paul, though it is the kind of thing we find in religious Hebrew poetry. Both the language and the rhythm would perhaps fit if the passage was a Greek translation of a Hebrew or Aramaic composition.[1] The passage speaks of Christ as "a servant" (v. 7), and Vincent Taylor sees this as "the strongest argument" that the passage is pre-Pauline.[2] Both before and after the hymn Paul exhorts the Philippians to right conduct, and it is urged that the apostle would not stop in his exhortations to compose such an exquisite song and then go right back to them. Nor would he have omitted such characteristic themes as redemption through the cross, the resurrection, and the place of the church.

This kind of reasoning leads some scholars to the view that the hymn is a pre-Pauline composition, perhaps coming from the early Palestinian church. It is fairly countered that there are passages that are undoubtedly Pauline that have as many unusual words in a comparable space and that there are Pauline passages with a rhythmic style (e.g., 1 Cor. 1:26–31; 2 Cor. 11:21–29). As for the early Palestinian flavor, Paul's mother tongue was Aramaic (Acts 22:2; 2 Cor. 11:22), so this does not preclude his authorship. The contention that the passage uses a Servant theology whereas Paul does not is countered by the fact that the passage has a very Pauline reference to "death on a cross" (v. 8—this is a characteristic Pauline expression; indeed, those who deny Pauline authorship of the whole often see it as a Pauline insertion). It is not easy to take seriously the view that the interruption of the hortatory sequence rules out Paul as author. Paul's letters sometimes take unexpected turns, and it is not legitimate to expect that a letter will always follow a given line without deviation. Moreover, this view does not reckon with the possibility that Paul had composed the hymn at an earlier time and simply inserted it at this point in the argument. The absence of characteristic Pauline themes is surely not very significant. There is no place where Paul mentions them all; his selection is always due to the needs of the moment, and perhaps at this point he chose not to use themes he found significant elsewhere.

The arguments are thus fairly evenly balanced. Although the passage is doubtless too short for us to be able to give a final proof or disproof of Pauline

---

[1] R. P. Martin has made a detailed study of the passage, and he cites E. Lohmeyer for the view that "the poet's mother-tongue was Semitic"; "Lohmeyer contrived to show that the Greek text must be based on an underlying Semitic original" (Carmen Christi, SNTSMS 4 [Cambridge: Cambridge University Press, 1967], p. 46). In his first remarks on authorship Martin finds the arguments "finely balanced" (p. 45) but after a detailed exegesis decides that Paul has made use of an earlier hymn. He thinks of the passage as "a missionary manifesto of some Christian or Christian group whose outlook reaches forth to the world beyond the confines of Jewish Christianity and sees that the cosmic Christ, the universal Lord, is the one true answer to the religious quests of the Graeco-Roman world" (pp. 298–99).

[2] Vincent Taylor, The Person of Christ in New Testament Teaching (London: Macmillan, 1959), p. 63. Elsewhere Taylor speaks of Paul's "comparative neglect of the Servant-conception of Isaiah lii.13–liii" (The Atonement in New Testament Teaching [London: Epworth, 1945], p. 65).

authorship, we should probably see it as coming from Paul, for (1) it is found in a writing undoubtedly penned by the apostle, and (2) there is no convincing reason for either rejecting Paul as the author or assigning the hymn to anyone else.

PROVENANCE

When Paul wrote this letter, he was a prisoner (1:7, 13, 17), but he does not say where his prison was located. He recognizes that death might be the outcome of his predicament (1:20; 2:17), but on the whole he anticipates a speedy release and looks forward to rejoining his Philippian friends (1:25–26; 2:23–24). These facts are interesting, but they tell us nothing of the location of the prison.

We read of Paul's being held at Caesarea for two years (Acts 23:33; 24:27), as well as at Rome (Acts 28:16). The apostle himself says that he had been in prison "more frequently" than others (2 Cor. 11:23), which makes it clear that he had undergone more imprisonments than those mentioned in Acts (Clement of Rome says that Paul was in jail seven times [*1 Clem.* 5:6]). There are thus three possibilities: the imprisonment at Caesarea, that at Rome, and an incarceration on one of the other occasions, of which no record has survived.

Traditionally it has been held that this imprisonment was at Rome. There is a reference to "the Praetorium" (1:13, JB), which is naturally understood to refer to the praetorian guard, which was centered at Rome. There Paul lived in his rented house with a soldier to guard him (Acts 28:16, 30–31). This would fit the situation in Philippians, as would the reference to "those who belong to Caesar's household" who send greetings through Paul (4:22). From the letter we gather that Paul was in a position to organize his coworkers; he could send Timothy and Epaphroditus to Philippi (2:19, 25), and this accords with the situation at Rome. So does the fact that a good number of "the brothers in the Lord" had been encouraged by Paul's chains to preach the gospel (1:14), which seems to mean that there was a well-established church there. The Marcionite prologue is usually cited as early evidence that Rome was the place of origin of the letter. Another line of argument is that in Philippians the apostle is faced with death or release (1:20), but elsewhere than in the capital city he could appeal to Caesar against an adverse verdict.

All this makes for a strong case, and it is not surprising that Rome has very often been judged to be the place from which the letter was written. But a difficulty is the problem posed by the journeys mentioned or implied in the letter. One journey is necessary for whoever brought the Philippians the news of Paul's imprisonment, a second for Epaphroditus as he brought their gift to Paul (2:25), a third for the news of Epaphroditus's illness to get to Philippi, and a fourth for the concern of the Philippians to have been reported to the sufferer (2:26). Paul envisages three more journeys, apparently all to be accomplished in the near future: those of Timothy to Philippi and back with news (2:19) and that of Epaphroditus (2:25). Philippi is a long way from Rome (about 1,200 miles), and it is urged that such journeys would take months, so that it is likely that the place of imprisonment was much closer to Philippi than was Rome. The list may possibly be shortened a little by contending that we need not assume that the Philippians had heard that Paul was in prison: they may have heard of Paul's appeal to Caesar and dispatched Epaphroditus to Rome to await him. There was plenty of time, for Paul was delayed by being shipwrecked and spending the winter in Malta. This possibility may be conceded, but it is conjecture, and the argument from the journeys is still a weighty one.[3]

A further objection arises from Paul's stated intention of going to Philippi if he is released (2:24). When he wrote to the Roman church, he said that he intended going on to Spain after he had been with them (Rom. 15:24, 28). He may have changed his mind, but if so, we would expect some reference to a change of plan. We should also notice the comment that the Philippians had had no opportunity of sending a gift to him until the one for which he gives them thanks (4:10). If Paul is writing from Rome toward the end of his life, this is very curious.[4]

The objections to Rome as the place of origin are weighty enough to cause a number of recent scholars to look at the evidence for some other place, and two candidates have been put forward: Caesarea and Ephesus. Caesarea is favored by the fact that we know that Paul was imprisoned there for two years (Acts 24:27).[5] The praetorium may well have been Herod's praetorium (see Acts 23:35), where Paul was placed when he was taken to that city. It is further urged that the polemic against false teachers is similar to that against Judaizers[6] in earlier letters and that Philippians must accordingly be seen as early. (There is no such polemic in Romans, and it is likely that the Judaizers were not active by the time Paul got to Rome.) Against Caesarea is its distance from Philippi; we are up against much the same problem in fitting in the journeys as in the Roman hypothesis. The argument that the church in the center from which Paul wrote must have been of some size is a difficulty, for we have no reason for thinking of a strong church at Caesarea. Moreover, the contention about the Judaizers loses force when we reflect that the imprisonment at Caesarea immediately preceded that in Rome; there was no considerable interval for a change in the false teachers being opposed. There seems no convincing reason for holding that Caesarea was the place of origin.[7]

There have been strong advocates of Ephesus. We have no explicit statement that Paul was ever imprisoned in that city, but there are the apostle's words about his many imprisonments (2 Cor. 11:23) and the fact that he was at one time in very serious trouble there (1 Cor. 15:32; see also 2 Cor. 1:8–11), which may well have meant time in prison, among other hardships. Ephesus was not far from Philippi (about one hundred miles), and the journeys mentioned in the letter

---

[3]It must be admitted, however, that some weigh the evidence from geography rather differently. Thus Moisés Silva, observing that not more than three communications have taken place at the time of writing (one of which may have occurred even before Paul reached Rome) allows two months per trip—a generous estimate—and concludes that not more than four to six months are required. Silva contends that the argument from geography should be dropped (*Philippians*, WEC [Chicago: Moody, 1988], pp. 5–8).

[4]"If he is writing from Rome, it is ten years or so since they sent to him: and it seems strange they had had no opportunity to send to him in so long a time. And during that time he had passed through Philippi twice (Acts xx.1, 3, 6)" (Clogg, p. 77).

[5]L. Johnson argues that the captivity letters were written during this period ("The Pauline Letters from Caesarea," *ExpTim* 68 [1956–57]: 24–26).

[6]On the ambiguity surrounding this term, see n. 3 in chap. 9 above.

[7]Gerald F. Hawthorne does not find that the evidence points conclusively to any city but argues that "it seems best for the sake of the understanding and explanation of Philippians to make a decision about where it was written and to exegete the text in the light of that decision. Hence, the assumption made in this commentary is that Philippians was written by Paul from prison in Caesarea." (*Philippians*, WBC [Waco, Tex.: Word, 1983], p. xliii). By contrast, Childs remarks, "Caesarea has been virtually eliminated as a possibility" (p. 331).

would not have been difficult; indeed, one of them may be mentioned in Acts, for Paul sent Timothy to Macedonia from Ephesus (Acts 19:22; as far as we know, Timothy was not with Paul in Rome). He himself went to Macedonia from Ephesus (Acts 20:1—which might well be the fulfillment of his confident hope, mentioned in Phil. 2:24). The literary affinities of Philippians are usually held to be with Galatians, Corinthians, and Romans rather than with the later letters, Ephesians and Colossians, though this may not mean much. A similar comment could be made about the suggestion that the Judaizing controversy is behind this letter and that this suits the earlier period better than the time Paul was in Rome, for we actually know little about what the Judaizers were doing at that later time. Attention is drawn to inscriptions showing that a section of the praetorian guard was stationed at Ephesus, which means that the reference to the praetorium would suit that city. Representatives of the emperor at Ephesus might well be who Paul has in mind when he refers to the saints of Caesar's household (4:22). Some scholars hold that certain parts of Philippians show that Paul had not been back to that city since he founded the church there (1:30; 4:15–16; see also 1:26; 2:12, 22), which would not be true at the time of the Roman imprisonment (cf. Acts 20:1–6). Others, probably correctly, do not think that Philippians proves so much. Another factor that is variously evaluated is the failure of Philippians to mention Luke, who certainly spent time with Paul in Rome (2 Tim. 4:11). The silence may be linked with the fact that Paul's Ephesian ministry is not in one of the "we" sections in Acts.[8]

This represents a strong but not conclusive case for Ephesus as the place of Paul's imprisonment. It is objected that at the time Paul was in Ephesus he was giving a good deal of emphasis to the collection for the poor saints in Jerusalem. He mentions it in every letter known to have been written during that period, but there is no reference to it in Philippians. Furthermore, Paul speaks of the church in the city from which he wrote as divided, some supporting him and some being very opposed to him (Phil. 1:15–17), but the church at Ephesus, a church of Paul's own founding, seems to have strongly supported him (see Acts 20:36–38). Most of the evidence can be interpreted in more than one way, and there seems no decisive reason for holding that this or any other city is proven. The traditional view has many supporters, but this is also the case for Ephesus. Perhaps there is a little more to be said for Ephesus than for Rome, but we can say no more than this (and many would hold that we are not entitled to say even this).[9]

DATE

Dating this epistle depends, of course, on identifying the imprisonment during which Paul wrote it. If it was written during his time under guard in Rome, we must date it toward the end of his life; if it came from Caesarea, then its date will

---

[8]G. S. Duncan argued the case strongly in his *St. Paul's Ephesian Ministry* (New York: Scribners, 1929); he reiterated his view with minor modifications in "Were Paul's Imprisonment Epistles Written from Ephesus?" *ExpTim* 67 (1955–56): 163–66.

[9]Guthrie, who favors Rome as the site, says of Ephesus, "The cumulative effect of this evidence is undoubtedly strong but it falls short of proof. If the Roman hypothesis were proved untenable the Ephesian would probably be unchallenged as an alternative theory" (Guthrie, p. 555). Kümmel, however, says that "the probability of the Ephesian hypothesis is the slightest" (p. 235).

be a little earlier. If we could be sure that Paul wrote it at Ephesus or at Corinth, it would be a few years earlier still. In view of our uncertainties, we can scarcely do better than say that it was written during the late 50s or early 60s.

OCCASION

We can discern a number of factors that may have called forth this letter. First, there is the matter of Epaphroditus. This man had been sent to Paul by the Philippian church "to take care of [Paul's] needs" (Phil. 2:25). He apparently had discharged his task but had fallen ill, so ill indeed that he nearly died. The Philippians had heard of the illness, and Epaphroditus was upset about this (2:26–27). Paul repeats his reference to the serious nature of the illness (2:30). The Philippians perhaps had not realized just how serious Epaphroditus's illness had been, or perhaps some were critical of the time he had stayed with Paul. So Paul tells them to honor people like this man (2:29). It is also possible that there had been some criticism of Paul for keeping Epaphroditus with him instead of sending him back earlier. Whatever the exact circumstances, Paul writes to make clear to the Philippians that their messenger had done his task well and that he had undergone great danger in discharging it. Paul is sending him back with a warm commendation.

Then there is the fact that the Philippian church had sent a gift to Paul (4:14–18; cf. 2:25). Since he leaves mention of this until quite late in the letter, it is probable that this is not the first time Paul has expressed his thanks. But it is plain that he greatly appreciated the help that this church had given him; he writes warmly about their generosity. A genuine appreciation of all that the Philippians had done for him is certainly part of the reason for this letter.

Third, Paul gives the Philippians news about his own circumstances (1:12ff.). The Philippians had been praying for him (1:19), and Paul recognizes them as partners with him in the gospel (1:5). Accordingly, he acquaints them with enough of his circumstances for them to see the way the gospel had been advanced by what was happening to him.

Fourth, although the Philippian church was in general a thriving Christian community, there were some problems. Paul recognizes their need for unity and specifically pleads with two women to be at peace with each other (4:2). His exhortation to wholehearted service (1:27–2:18) may be connected with a recognition that all is not well. Paul offers warnings against false teachers (3:2–4), people who are "enemies of the cross of Christ" (3:18).

A further reason for writing may have been to commend Timothy to them and possibly to prepare the way for a visit he himself would pay (2:19–24). His commendation of Timothy suggests that the Philippians did not know him well. Paul wants to ensure that his young colleague will receive a warm welcome when he comes to Philippi.

TEXT

"The epistle presents no textual questions of importance," wrote Marvin R. Vincent almost a century ago.[10] At one level, nothing that has happened since then disturbs this verdict. Thus in the entire epistle the UBS3 text has only one reading with a D rating (whether to read "the word," "the word of God," or "the word of the Lord" in 1:14). There is no reason for doubting that we have the letter substantially as Paul wrote it. Text-critical study, however, has become far more sophisticated since Vincent's day, so that even variants judged relatively minor when taken in isolation begin to assume importance as part of an exegetical and textual tradition as soon as they are placed within the *pattern* of variations of a MS or a text type. Recent study has carefully classified the 112 variants (not itself an exhaustive list) reported in NA[26].[11]

ADOPTION INTO THE CANON

This is one of the letters about whose canonicity there appears to have been few doubts. Echoes of the epistle have been discerned in *1 Clement* and Ignatius, while Polycarp speaks of Paul as having written letters to the Philippian church (*Phil.* 3:2). It is included in Marcion's canon, and there is no evidence that anyone entertained doubts about its being part of the Pauline corpus.

PHILIPPIANS IN RECENT STUDY

Four main areas have featured in recent study of this epistle: questions surrounding the hymn in 2:6–11, the location of Paul's imprisonment at the time he wrote the letter, the unity of the letter, and the identification of Paul's opponents. There is nothing approaching unanimity on any of these.

The Hymn in 2:6–11

In an earlier day this was often taken as a solemn doctrinal pronouncement of the apostle and made the basis for kenotic theories of the incarnation. In more recent times close attention has been given to its form, and it is now widely agreed that we should see it both as poetry and as liturgy—in short, as a hymn. But there is wide disagreement as to whether there are three strophes or four or five or six, or whether we should think of six couplets. Each view tends to be supported by treating words and phrases as secondary additions, probably made by Paul when he adapted the original to his argument.[12] It is difficult to resist the conclusion that

---

[10]Marvin R. Vincent, *A Critical and Exegetical Commentary on the Epistles to the Philippians and to Philemon*, ICC (Edinburgh: T. & T. Clark, 1897), p. xxxvii.

[11]So Silva, *Philippians*, pp. 22–27.

[12]Not much more than that it is a hymn is agreed. "It quickly becomes apparent . . . that although much has been written on these verses there is little that can be agreed upon, whether the topic discussed is the precise form of this section, its authorship, its place and purpose in the letter, the sources used in its composition, and so on" (Hawthorne, *Philippians*, p. 76). Hawthorne is so impressed by the lack of agreement on insertions and the like that he treats it all as part of the original hymn.

many modern scholars have insisted far too strongly that a first-century Christian hymn must conform to modern standards of versification.

Paul has inserted this hymn into his argument urging the Philippians to be Christlike, and specifically to live in humility. It is pointed out that the hymn as commonly understood is the earliest example known to us of a division of Christ's life into preexistence, his life on earth, and his exaltation to heaven. This analysis, however, is disputed by some. G. S. Duncan, for example, points to the Peshitta (The Bible in Syriac, from the early fifth century) to justify understanding verse 6 as "He was in the image of God" (i.e., truly man; Gen. 1:26).[13] So understood, the passage contrasts Jesus, who deliberately took the lowly way, with Adam (or perhaps with fallen angels), who pursued the path of self-aggrandizement, which led to disaster. But other study has convincingly shown that Philippians 2:6 must be understood to mean that Christ's "equality with God" was not something he *exploited*: That is, such equality was intrinsically his, but so great was his humility and subservience to the will of his Father that he chose not to exploit it but took the path of humiliation, incarnation, and death on a cross.[14]

That Paul made use of an existing hymn is usually accepted, and while some students hold that Paul wrote it, the more common opinion is that Paul has taken someone else's composition and adapted it to his purpose. Thus H. Koester holds that the background for the Christology of the hymn "was provided by a version of the Suffering Servant theme which developed in the speculative wisdom of Judaism."[15] Paul has taken up what was originally written about wisdom and used it of Christ. This has meant some reshaping of the hymn with the insertion of a number of prose phrases, which means that "it is no longer possible to reconstruct the original poetic form."[16]

Largely building on the work of E. Käsemann,[17] Ralph Martin rejects the commonly accepted view that the hymn is used as a lesson in humility. The introduction should be understood, he thinks, not as in the KJV ("Let this mind be in you which was also in Christ Jesus"), but rather to say, "Act as befits those who are in Christ Jesus." The controlling motive in Paul's ethics "is not imitation, but death and resurrection." Besides, the end of the hymn with Christ in glory and honor is a curious way of inculcating humility. Martin sees the hymn as meaning, rather, "Become in your conduct and church relationships the type of persons who, by that *kenosis*, death and exaltation of the Lord of glory, have a place in His body, the Church."[18] But against this C. F. D. Moule can say, "I see the whole

---

[13]G. S. Duncan, "Philippians," in *IDB*, 3:791. Similarly, James D. G. Dunn relies on such Adam-Christology to justify his conclusion that the preexistence of Christ is not taught in this passage (*Christology in the Making* [London: SCM, 1980], pp. 114–21).

[14]See Roy W. Hoover, "The Harpagmos Enigma: A Philological Solution," *HTR* 64 (1971): 95–119; and esp. N. T. Wright, "ἁρπαγμός and the Meaning of Philippians 2:5–11," *JTS* 37 (1986): 321–52. Christ "did not regard being equal with God as . . . something to use for his own advantage" (Hoover, "Harpagmos Enigma," p. 118).

[15]H. Koester, "Philippians," in *IDBSup*, p. 666.

[16]Ibid.

[17]E. Käsemann, "A Critical Analysis of Philippians 2:5–11," in *God and Christ: Existence and Province*, ed. Robert W. Funk, *JTC* 5 (New York: Harper & Row, 1968), pp. 45–88. (Käsemann originally wrote this article in 1950, in German.)

[18]Martin, *Carmen Christi*, pp. 288, 291. Martin thinks that the hymn may have been used in a baptismal context. He also holds that it portrays "a soteriological drama." These verses "are not a piece of Christological speculation which answers our question who Christ was, but the record of a series of

passage as an exhortation to follow the example of Christ";[19] similarly J. L. Houlden heads his discussion of the passage: "Christ the Model of Humility."[20] It cannot be said that there is unanimity on the point, but recent study has rather convincingly exposed the weaknesses of the strand of interpretation set in motion by Käsemann.[21] In any case, what cannot easily be gainsaid is that Paul is urging the importance of humility.

The Location of Paul's Imprisonment

As discussed above under the heading "Provenance," the evidence is not conclusive for any locale. The result is that scholars weigh differently the location of Paul's imprisonment, with supporters of each of the three centers contending vigorously for the place of their choice. But there is no consensus, nor apparently any likelihood of one. Other suggestions have been made, notably Corinth,[22] but none has won wide support. In the end we must probably say that the place of origin is an insoluble problem, given our present knowledge.

The Unity of the Letter.

Until comparatively recent times there has not been much discussion of the unity of Philippians. Some awkward sequences have been noticed, but these have been accepted as what we can expect in a dictated letter from a man like Paul. But in recent days there has been a tendency to see two or even three letters in what had been taken as a unity (Childs dates this tendency from 1950). A number of considerations are urged in support of the hypothesis.

1. In some places the break in sense is quite marked, notably at 3:1 and 4:9. There is little doubt that the author was Paul, but there has been much discussion of whether we are confronted with one letter composed as such, or a number of Paul's writings that have been joined together. Thus 3:1 appears to be leading into the end of a letter, but 3:2 goes off on a warning against false teachers; is it perhaps part of another letter? The transition from 4:9 to 4:10 also seems to many to require an explanation.

2. Epaphroditus is reported as very ill in 2:25–30, but there is no indication of this when the same man is referred to in 4:18. It is argued that there has been a change in his health, and that change presupposes a lapse of time.

3. Paul's opponents are not the same throughout the letter. There is a sharp, even merciless, attack on false teachers in 3:2–4, but nothing in the preceding part of the letter prepares us for anything like this. The conclusion is drawn that fragments from more than one letter have been combined.[23]

---

events of saving significance which declare what He did" (p. 295). See also discussion of this hymn in Martin's *Philippians*, NCB (Greenwood, S.C.: Attic, 1976). This, of course, does not mean that we may not draw some conclusions about the nature of the person who could accomplish all this.

[19]C. F. D. Moule, "Further Reflexions on Philippians 2, 5–11" in *Apostolic History and the Gospel*, ed. W. Ward Gasque and Ralph P. Martin (Exeter: Paternoster, 1970), p. 269.

[20]J. L. Houlden, *Paul's Letters from Prison* (London: SCM, 1977), p. 67.

[21]See esp. Wright, "ἁρπαγμός."

[22]E.g., see the discussion in Hawthorne, *Philippians*, pp. xl–xli.

[23]T. E. Pollard, however, compares chap. 3 with the rest of the letter and concludes that there are

4. Some scholars discern fragments in 4:1–9, 20–23. Both of these could be construed as appropriate ends of original letters.

5. Polycarp speaks of Paul as having written "epistles" to the Philippians (*Phil.* 3.2). This is evidence that more than one such letter was written, and it therefore opens the way for the hypothesis that some have been combined in our present Philippians.

Evidence of this sort leads a number of scholars to the conclusion that parts of two or perhaps three letters were put together by an unknown hand.[24] It is not uncommon to see the first letter as 4:10–20 (thanks for the Philippians' gift), a second as 1:1–3:1; 4:4–7, 21–23 (warning against division), and a third as 3:2–4:3, 8–9 (attack on false teachers).

But the evidence is far from compelling. Sudden breaks in sense are not altogether unknown in Paul (note the several breaks in Rom. 16:16–27), and those in Philippians are no greater than we might expect in a letter put together by this writer. The argument demands much more consistency in following a theme than Paul (or for that matter anyone else) always shows. It is better to see this as one letter with the abrupt changes of subject that we all tend to introduce from time to time. The references to Epaphroditus are quite in order; there is no reason why the man's illness should be brought up every time he is mentioned. That a number of things in chapter 4 might be suitably used toward the end of a letter does not mean that any of them was deliberately intended to be so used. And the letters of which Polycarp speaks were not necessarily combined. We need suppose no more than that only one of them survives. (Most of Paul's correspondence has surely been lost; we cannot think that a man who could write so powerfully wrote no more than thirteen letters throughout the whole of his ministry.)[25]

Paul's Opponents

Paul writes of opponents who "preach Christ out of envy and rivalry" (Phil. 1:15) and who try to stir up trouble for him (1:17). This makes it seem as though they are church members, but a little later he refers to them as opposing the church and goes on to speak of his readers as suffering for Christ (1:28–29). In 3:2 they are "dogs," and the subsequent references to circumcision and to Paul's fleshly qualifications in Judaism indicate that they are Judaizers of some sort. Paul goes on to say that he has not attained perfection (3:12), which makes it seem as though the false teachers claimed that they did. Later he writes of "enemies of the cross of Christ" and insists that "their god is their stomach, and their glory is in their shame" (3:18–19).

It is possible that all this refers to one group of people. Klijn refuses to see a variety of opponents: "The most acceptable solution for the problem is to assume

---

"marked verbal agreements between chapter iii as a whole and the rest of the letter" ("The Integrity of Philippians," *NTS* 13 [1966–67]: 66).

[24]"The composition breaks abruptly at 2,19; 3,2; 4, 2 10. It is possible—but cannot be proved—that Phil. is a conflation of various writings which Paul composed and sent to Philippi at various times" (Wikenhauser, p. 437). He adds, "At any rate, the entire Epistle bears the stamp of Paul's language and style."

[25]B. S. Mackay has a strong refutation of the idea that Philippians is made up of three letters ("Further Thoughts on Philippians," *NTS* 7 [1960–61]: 161–70).

that the persons referred to are Jews."[26] This view has not won wide acceptance, and it certainly seems more likely that Paul is confronted by people who are in some sense Christians.[27] How else would they be preaching the gospel, however maliciously (1:15; Klijn does not bring this verse into his argument)? The references to libertarianism ("their god is their stomach") and to perfectionism point some critics to a form of Gnosticism or to some kind of pre-Gnostic teaching. The latter is a possibility, but evidence that full-blown Gnosticism was in existence in Paul's day is lacking. Another view is that the opponents were Judaizers and that "their god is their stomach" refers to Jewish food laws. We can say only that in the present confused discussion, several possibilities are regularly canvassed in the literature.

It is likely that Paul envisages opponents of more than one kind. He seems to be fighting on two fronts, being opposed within the church by some who did not agree with his preaching and outside it by some who made the whole church suffer. The references to Jewish practices make it clear that either Jewish opponents or Judaizers were involved, who may well have held to some opinions that were later taken up into the great Gnostic systems.[28]

THE CONTRIBUTION OF PHILIPPIANS

Many of Paul's letters were called forth by the need to set things right in a given church, to oppose false teaching, or to correct lax practice. But Philippians is that comparative rarity: a letter to a church of Paul's own foundation with which he is well pleased. It reveals something of the apostle's satisfaction when his converts made progress in the faith. He does oppose false teaching here as elsewhere, but the main thrust of the letter lies elsewhere. As he is writing, he makes some comments on the opponents he and the Philippian church faced, but for the most part he is taken up with more enjoyable things.

Outstanding, of course, is the hymn in 2:6–11. There has been endless controversy about the meaning of most parts of it, but even so, the passage brings readers a clear message about the greatness of Christ and his condescension in taking a lowly place to bring salvation. It we can accept the NIV's rendering of the opening, Paul was referring to one who was "in very nature God," who took the lowest place and died on the cross to bring salvation. Now he is exalted to the highest possible place, and Paul looks forward to the time when every knee will bow to him and every tongue confess him as Lord. Moreover, on any reading this hymn is early—at least as early as Philippians, and maybe earlier—so it constitutes powerful evidence for the confession of a high Christology at a very early date in the church's life.

The letter is also an encouragement to Christians who find others preaching the gospel in ways they do not like. It is of permanent value to us all to have it laid down so firmly that what matters is that the gospel be preached (1:12–18). Paul

---

[26]Klijn, p. 110. He concludes his discussion of the point by noting, "The opponents, therefore, are Jews who will not tolerate Paul in their own missionary territory."

[27]H. Koester argues that the people opposed in chap. 3 are "Christian missionaries of Jewish origin and background" ("The Purpose of the Polemic of a Pauline Fragment," *NTS* 8 [1961–62]: 331).

[28]Johnson thinks that they may not have been Paul's opponents at all and that he refers to them as a counterexample to show his correspondents what they must not do (p. 346).

rejoices in this, and indeed the note of joy is sounded throughout this letter (the noun χαρά [*chara*, "joy"] occurs five times and the verb χαίρειν [*chairein*, "to rejoice"] nine times in this short letter; only Luke with twelve has more occurrences of the verb). That Christians are a rejoicing people is important.

Also significant is what Paul calls "partnership in the gospel" (1:5). Throughout the letter there is a harmony between writer and readers and a series of glimpses of what it is to work together in the cause of Christ. Paul encourages his friends, assures them of his affection for them, teaches them lessons from his own circumstances, and adds to their knowledge of the Christian way. He prays for them, warns them about false teaching, exhorts them to steadfastness in the Christian life, and sends Timothy to them. In the nature of the case, we do not learn as much of what the Philippians contributed to the relationship, but it is clear that they had a concern and affection for Paul, that they sent one of their number to look after him when he was in trouble, that they sent him gifts at a time when no other church helped him, and that they obeyed his directions. It is a beautiful picture of Christian harmony.

The epistle has a notable section in which Paul emphasizes the importance of concentrating on the essentials over against "confidence in the flesh" (3:4). He stresses the place of the cross and the resurrection in Christian salvation. The suffering of the Christian fits in with this. Paul draws attention to the way the gospel is advanced through his own sufferings (1:14–18; cf. 2:16–17), and he sees the sufferings of the Philippians, as they experience the same struggle as he, as God's gift to them (1:29–30). The important thing is the service of Christ. Then at the end of the letter he records his magnificent assurance that "my God will meet all your needs according to his glorious riches in Christ Jesus" (4:19).

BIBLIOGRAPHY

F. W. **Beare**, *The Epistle to the Philippians*, HNTC (New York: Harper & Bros., 1959); P. **Bonnard**, *L'épître de saint Paul aux Philippiens et l'épître aux Colossiens*, CNT (Neuchâtel: Delachaux & Niestlé, 1950); F. F. **Bruce**, *Philippians*, GNC (San Francisco: Harper & Row, 1983); idem, "St. Paul in Macedonia: 3. The Philippian Correspondence," *BJRL* 63 (1981): 260–84; C. O. **Buchanan**, "Epaphroditus' Sickness and the Letter to the Philippians," *EQ* 36 (1964): 157–66; G. B. **Caird**, *Paul's Letters from Prison* (Oxford: Oxford University Press, 1976); W. J. **Dalton**, "The Integrity of Philippians," *Bib* 60 (1979): 97–102; S. **Dockx**, "Lieu et date de l'épître aux Philippiens," *RevBib* 80 (1973): 230–46; G. S. **Duncan**, *St. Paul's Ephesian Ministry* (New York: Scribners, 1929); idem, "Were Paul's Imprisonment Epistles Written from Ephesus?" *ExpTim* 67 (1955–56): 163–66; James D. G. **Dunn**, *Christology in the Making* (London: SCM, 1980); G. **Friedrich**, *Der Brief an die Philipper*, NTD (Göttingen: Vandenhoeck & Ruprecht, 1962); Joachim **Gnilka**, *Der Philipperbrief*, HTKNT (Freiburg: Herder, 1976); Gerald F. **Hawthorne**, *Philippians*, WBC (Waco, Tex.: Word, 1983); Roy W. **Hoover**, "The Harpagmos Enigma: A Philological Solution," *HTR* 64 (1971): 95–119; J. L. **Houlden**, *Paul's Letters from Prison* (London: SCM, 1977); R. **Jewett**, "Conflicting Movements in the Early Church as Reflected in Philippians," *NovT* 12 (1970): 362–90; L. **Johnson**, "The Pauline Letters from Caesarea," *ExpTim* 68 (1956–57): 24–26; E. **Käsemann**, "A Critical Analysis of Philippians 2:5–11," in *God and Christ: Existence and Province*, ed. Robert W. Funk, *JTC* 5 (New York: Harper & Row, 1968), pp. 45–88; H.

Koester, "The Purpose of the Polemic of a Pauline Fragment" *NTS* 8 (1961–62): 317–32; J. B. **Lightfoot,** *St. Paul's Epistle to the Philippians* (1868; reprint, Grand Rapids: Zondervan, 1965); B. S. **Mackay,** "Further Thoughts on Philippians," *NTS* 7 (1960–61): 161–70; A. J. **Malherbe,** "The Beasts at Ephesus,," *JBL* 87 (1968): 71–80; Ralph P. **Martin,** *Carmen Christi,* SNTSMS 4 (Cambridge: Cambridge University Press, 1967); idem, *Philippians,* NCB (Greenwood, S.C.: Attic, 1976); C. F. D. **Moule,** "Further Reflections on Philippians 2, 5–11," in *Apostolic History and the Gospel,* ed. W. Ward Gasque and Ralph P. Martin (Grand Rapids: Eerdmans, 1970), pp. 264–76; T. E. **Pollard,** "The Integrity of Philippians," *NTS* 13 (1966–67): 57–66; B. D. **Rahtjen,** "The Three Letters of Paul to the Philippians," *NTS* 6 (1959–60): 167–73; Wolfgang **Schenk,** *Die Philipperbrief des Paulus: Kommentar* (Stuttgart: Kohlhammer, 1984); Moisés **Silva,** *Philippians,* WEC (Chicago: Moody, 1988); Vincent **Taylor,** *The Atonement in New Testament Teaching* (London: Epworth, 1945); idem, *The Person of Christ in New Testament Teaching* (London: Macmillan, 1959); Marvin R. **Vincent,** *Critical and Exegetical Commentary on the Epistles to the Philippians and to Philemon,* ICC (Edinburgh: T. & T. Clark, 1897); N. T. **Wright,** "ἁρπαγμός and the Meaning of Philippians 2:5–11," *JTS* 37 (1986): 321–52.

13

COLOSSIANS

CONTENTS

The opening greeting (1:1–2) is followed by thanksgiving for the faith and the love of the Colossian Christians (1:3–13). Paul then launches into a magnificent section on the greatness of Christ (1:15–20) in which he brings out the truth that he is "the image of the invisible God," that he was active in the creation of all things—indeed, we are also told (uniquely in the New Testament) that all things were made *for* him—and that he is the head of the church. The apostle goes on to Christ's reconciling work (1:21–23) and relates something of his own sufferings as he works for Christ, of his struggling for believers such as those in Colossae and Laodicea whom he has not met (1:24–2:5).

Paul exhorts his readers to live in Christ and warns them against being taken captive by a "hollow and deceptive philosophy" (2:6–8). He comes back to the greatness of Christ, in whom "all the fullness of the Deity lives," and reminds them of the salvation Christ has brought about (2:9–15). In the light of this they should not submit to people's ideas about food laws and religious festivals (2:16–23). This leads to the truth that believers have been "raised with Christ"; they should live in accordance with this great fact. Paul goes into some detail about the things they should avoid and the things they should do (3:1–17); he gives directions about the way people should live in Christian households, speaking of wives, husbands, children, fathers, slaves, and masters (3:18–4:1). He rounds this section off with injunctions to pray and to be wise in their behavior toward outsiders (4:2–6).

Tychicus, he says, will bring the Colossians news of him, as will Onesimus. This leads to greetings from a number of Paul's companions to the Colossian Christians (4:7–15). There is an injunction about the reading of the letter and exchanging it with one to the Laodiceans, a command for Archippus (4:16–17), and a short form of the usual Pauline ending to a letter (4:18).

AUTHOR

The authorship of this letter has been the subject of considerable discussion. Until the last century no serious question about Pauline authorship seems to have been raised. Even then questions were raised only by a minority of scholars. In the period between the two wars in this century, Bultmann and others began to speak of Colossians as "deutero-Pauline," and that tendency has grown since 1945. It is plain enough that there is a connection with Paul, but many recent scholars think that a follower of Paul rather than the apostle himself actually penned the book. No new evidence has been adduced; the considerations urged against the traditional view have simply come to be seen as more weighty. Some still argue for Paul as the author, including Kümmel, Moule, Bruce, and O'Brien,[1] but others think "deutero-Pauline" a better description.[2]

The letter claims to have been written by Paul in the opening (1:1), in the "I, Paul" of 1:23, and in "I, Paul, write this greeting in my own hand" (4:18; this is "the distinguishing mark in all my letters" [2 Thess. 3:17]). This claim has usually been accepted through the centuries, but in modern times it has been disputed on three main grounds: language, theology, and the relation to Ephesians.[3]

Language and Style

Colossians has quite a number of hapax legomena, but this is not a strong argument against the authenticity of this epistle, for the same is true of all of Paul's letters. Harrison has shown that Colossians in this respect falls well within the normal Pauline range.[4] Synonyms are joined together, such as "wisdom and understanding" (1:9) and "teach and admonish" (3:16), a phenomenon alleged to be un-Pauline, as is the verbose style. The latter judgment is somewhat subjective; indeed, it is precarious to lay down how far Paul can differ from the style we find in the generally accepted letters. All the more is this the case in that Colossians contains a number of stylistic features found elsewhere in the New Testament only in Paul.[5] Differences in vocabulary may be accounted for in part at least by his use

[1]Kümmel, pp. 340–46; C. F. D. Moule, *The Epistles of Paul the Apostle to the Colossians and to Philemon* (Cambridge: Cambridge University Press, 1962); F. F. Bruce, *The Epistles to the Colossians, to Philemon, and to the Ephesians*, NICNT (Grand Rapids: Eerdmans, 1984); Peter T. O'Brien, *Colossians, Philemon*, WBC (Waco, Tex.: Word, 1982).

[2]E.g., Charles Masson, *L'épître aux Colossiens*, CNT (Paris: Delachaux & Niestlé, 1950); E. Lohse, *Colossians and Philemon*, Hermeneia (Philadelphia: Fortress, 1971); E. Schweizer, *The Letter to the Colossians: A Commentary* (Minneapolis: Augsburg, 1982; German original, EKKNT, 1976); Joachim Gnilka, *Der Kolosserbrief*, HTKNT (Freiburg: Herder, 1980); Marxsen, pp. 176–86; Perrin/Duling, pp. 207–18.

[3]Also advanced are one or two fairly idiosyncratic reasons for denying the authenticity of this epistle. For instance, Marxsen finds "the most serious doubts as regards the Pauline authorship" arising from the link between 1:21–23 and the statements about Epaphras: "the authority of Paul is claimed for the authorization of other men." Marxsen speaks of the letter's "emphasis upon the apostolate— tantamount in effect to the doctrine of 'apostolic succession' " (p. 180). This is more than curious. The only use of "apostle" is in 1:1, and the only references to Epaphras are in 1:7 (where we learn that he is a "dear fellow servant" and "a faithful minister of Christ on our behalf," and that he brought news) and in 4:12 (he is "one of you" and "a servant of Christ Jesus," and he sends greetings). This is a remarkably slender basis on which to erect such a far-reaching doctrine as apostolic succession. It surely presents no serious obstacle to seeing Paul as the author. Although E. Lohse does not argue for Pauline authorship, he points out that in Colossians "teaching is described as a charge of the entire church" and thus not of successors of the apostles; "the church is not bound to a definite order of office and of offices" ("Pauline Theology in the Letter to the Colossians," *NTS* 15 [1968–69]: 216).

[4]P. N. Harrison, *The Problem of the Pastoral Epistles* (London: Oxford University Press, 1921), pp. 20–22.

[5]Kümmel lists such features as pleonastic καί (*kai*, "and") after διὰ τοῦτο (*dia touto*, lit. "on account of which," 1:9), οἱ ἅγιοι αὐτοῦ (*hoi hagioi autou*, "his saints," 1:26), ἐν μέρει (*en merei*, here with the rare meaning "concerning" or "with regard to," 2:16) and others. He concludes by saying, "The

of words needed to oppose a new heresy, and in style because he makes use of poetic forms. Furthermore, most scholars hold that there is a good deal of traditional matter in this letter, and this will account for some unusual vocabulary and style.

Theology

This objection comes in two forms: the absence of important Pauline concepts, and the presence of concepts of which Paul makes no use elsewhere. Under the first head is the absence of such characteristic Pauline terms as justification, law, salvation, and righteousness. But this proves little, because a similar observation may be made about some of Paul's other epistles. There was no need (and no place) for the use of every Pauline concept in every letter. Actually this argument may be used in favor of Pauline authorship. Although Paul himself did in fact omit some of his characteristic doctrines in each of his letters, it is very difficult to think of someone professing to write in Paul's name who would omit all the Pauline topics that are absent from this letter. Surely it would be an elementary precaution to use the apostle's most characteric doctrines.

Under the second head, this letter refers to cosmic aspects of Christ's person (1:16–19; also 2:9–10) and to his headship over the church, viewed as his body (1:18; 2:19). It is also suggested that 1:15–20 is the adaptation of a pre-Christian hymn. This latter is no real objection, for if a pre-Christian writing has been adapted, this could just as easily have been done by Paul as by an imitator.

As for the cosmic Christ, while what is said in Colossians is an advance on what we see in the undisputed Pauline letters, we surely have the beginnings of the concept in such expressions as "one Lord, Jesus Christ, through whom all things came and through whom we live" (1 Cor. 8:6), and "at the name of Jesus every knee should bow, in heaven and on earth and under the earth" (Phil. 2:10; cf. also the στοιχεῖα [stoicheia, perhaps "basic principles"] from whom Christ set believers free [Gal. 4:3, 9]). The development in Colossians is real, but it is not divorced from its roots in earlier Pauline writings. Furthermore, Paul has the idea of the church as a body in a number of writings (Rom. 12:4–5; cf. Gal.3:28; the concept is developed in 1 Cor. 12). It is but a step from this to the idea that Christ is the head of the body.[6] We cannot judge such objections as these decisive.

Relation to Ephesians

Doubtless Ephesians and Colossians stand in close relationship. Some scholars argue that one person would never produce two such similar writings: the resemblances mean that the author of one of these letters has written in imitation of the other. This is a very subjective argument. It may be countered by saying

language and style of Colossians, therefore, give no cause to doubt the Pauline origin of the Epistle" (p. 241).

[6]It is, nevertheless, a distinct step to move from picturing the church as a body whose members are the members of the church and that is animated by the Spirit, to picturing the church as a body of which Christ is the head. See the useful essay by Edmund P. Clowney, "Interpreting the Biblical Models of the Church: A Hermeneutical Deepening of Ecclesiology," in *Biblical Interpretation and the Church*, ed. D. A. Carson (Exeter: Paternoster, 1984), pp. 64–109.

that the two epistles are best understood as the expressions of the one writer, more or less repeating some of the same thoughts on two occasions not very far removed from one another. In any case it is a curious argument that we should reject a writing as Pauline because of its resemblances to another writing in the Pauline corpus.

It seems, then, that the arguments against Pauline authorship are not decisive. They do not reckon sufficiently with the fact that a mind like Paul's was capable of adaptation to new situations and to the adoption of new vocabulary and new concepts where older ones do not meet the need.[7] They also fail to give a reason for addressing the letter to the unimportant town of Colossae. Surely an imitator would have selected a city of some importance, such as Laodicea or Hierapolis. In view of the letter's claim and of the many undoubtedly Pauline features it manifests, we should accept it as an authentic Pauline writing. This is supported by a number of links with Philemon, which is surely a genuine letter of the apostle. In both epistles, greetings are sent from Aristarchus, Mark, Epaphras, Luke, and Demas who plainly were with Paul when he wrote (Col. 4:10–14; Philem. 23–24). Onesimus, the slave at the center of the letter to Philemon, is sent with Tychicus and referred to as "one of you" (Col. 4:9). Archippus, "our fellow soldier" (Philem. 2), is given a message to "complete the work" he has received in the Lord (Col. 4:17). In the light of such references it is difficult to argue that Colossians was not written by Paul.

PROVENANCE

When he wrote this letter, Paul was in prison (Col. 4:3, 10, 18). For the general possibilities of Rome, Caesarea and Ephesus, see the discussion above on Philippians (chap. 12, the section "Provenance"). It is probable that Ephesians, Colossians, and Philemon were written from the same place. The personal links mentioned in the previous paragraph are clear evidence that Colossians and Philemon were written at much the same time, while the case for Ephesians rests on the general similarities to Colossians. But there are no such personal links or general resemblances in Philippians, and that letter may well have been written from a different place.[8]

Paul's request for a guest room to be prepared (Philem. 22) favors Ephesus as the place of origin of Colossians and Philemon, for Colossae was not far from that city, while preparations for a guest room might be premature if Paul was in Rome. Against this is the fact that Luke and Mark are mentioned as being with Paul when he wrote, but Acts does not include the Ephesian ministry among the "we" sections, and Mark was not with Paul on the second missionary journey (Acts 15:36 -41). The runaway slave Onesimus had come to know Paul in his prison, and he would find it easier to get to Ephesus from Colossae than to Rome. He

---

[7]L. Cerfaux has commented: "It is not wise to attempt a priori to set limits on the potentialities of a thought as original and powerful as that of St. Paul, which changes very rapidly and rises to new syntheses. It is plausible that the reaction against the syncretism of Colossae was a powerful stimulant to Paul's thought" (Robert/Feuillet, p. 490).

[8]Bo Reicke argues that Philippians was written from Rome and the other three from Caesarea ("Caesarea, Rome, and the Captivity Epistles," in *Apostolic History and the Gospel*, Fs. F. F. Bruce, ed. W. Ward Gasque and Ralph P. Martin [Exeter: Paternoster, 1970], pp. 277–86).

may have preferred, however, to go further away and lose himself in the anonymity of populous Rome. If Ephesians was written in the same general period as Colossians, it is unlikely that Paul would write to the Ephesian church while he was in jail in that very city. But this can be countered by arguing that Ephesians was originally a circular and could have been written anywhere. The arguments for and against Ephesus seem to cancel each other out.[9]

Caesarea is a possibility, but it is hard to envisage a reason Onesimus would choose that city to flee to. Furthermore, we do not know that Paul had there the same kind of liberty to engage in evangelism that he enjoyed in Rome (Acts 28:30–31; but cf. Acts 24:23). Again, Paul's request for accommodation is not likely from Caesarea, for when he wrote Colossians, he was hoping for speedy release; while he was in Caesarea, however, his only hope of release lay in an appeal to Caesar. Moreover, if Paul were writing from Caesarea, we might have expected him to include Philip among those Jews who "have proved a comfort to me" (Col. 4:11 cf. Acts 21:8).

Objections to these other centers leave us with Rome, though we must bear in mind Paul's plan to go to Spain, not Colossae, after Rome. He may have abandoned that plan, but there is no evidence that he did (unless the Pastorals be held to indicate this). Luke was with Paul in Rome (Acts 28:14; 2 Tim. 4:11) and apparently Aristarchus also (Acts 27:2; cf. Col. 4:10). We cannot say that any center is strongly favored by the evidence, but perhaps a little more can be said for Rome than for anywhere else.

DATE

There is not much evidence for the date, and clearly a good deal depends on our conclusion about the place of imprisonment. If we can think that Rome was the place, we will have a date in the early 60s; if elsewhere, probably in the late 50s.

OCCASION

The church at Colossae was not of Paul's foundation (2:1). Epaphras had apparently been the preacher who brought the Christian gospel to that city (1:7). Paul describes him as "a faithful minister of Christ on our behalf" (1:7), which seems to mean that Paul had sent him to Colossae. Paul could not preach in every place, and it made sense to send trusted fellow workers to proclaim the gospel in places where he could not go himself. If so, he would retain an interest in the progress of such a church, and this letter may well have arisen out of such an interest. The apostle had heard that some false teachers had come to Colossae, so he wrote to refute their errors, lest the new little church be harmed.

The precise nature of the false teaching is not clear (as is always the case when we have none of the teaching itself, but only what is written to refute it), but some things are fairly plain. Paul puts emphasis on the supremacy of Christ (1:15–19), so it seems that the false teachers detracted in some way from a high Christology. Evidently they thought that Christ was no more than a beginning; to go on to spiritual maturity, it was necessary to follow their rules and practices. They may

---

[9]Martin, however, favors an imprisonment near Ephesus (2:216–22).

well have spoken of Christ in warm terms, but in the last resort they saw him as a created being and therefore as less than God. In the face of such teachings Paul insists that Christ is "the image of the invisible God" and the Father's agent in bringing creation about (1:15–16). Every created thing owes its existence to him, even the angelic powers that these teachers invited people to worship. All God's "fullness" dwells in Christ (1:19; 2:9). He is supreme over all, and there is no way of going on to some higher spirituality by deserting him.

Paul also speaks of "hollow and deceptive philosophy" (2:8). Unfortunately for us he does not explain what this means (the Colossians knew quite well, so why should he?). It seems that the false teaching had a Hellenistic aspect: "wisdom and knowledge" (2:3) may point to Greek roots, as perhaps do asceticism ("harsh treatment of the body" [2:23]) and "fullness" ($\pi\lambda\dot{\eta}\rho\omega\mu\alpha$ [plērōma], 1:19). There are puzzling references in 2:8, 20 to what NIV calls "the basic principles of this world" ($\tau\grave{\alpha}\ \sigma\tauo\iota\chi\epsilon\hat{\iota}\alpha\ \tauo\hat{\upsilon}\ \kappao\sigma\mu\omega$ [ta stoicheia tou kosmou]), an expression that some take to mean "elemental spirits" (RSV) and some, "elementary teaching" (KJV "rudiments"; cf. Heb. 5:12).[10] "Elemental spirits" would mean that the false teaching found a place for the worship of spirits, "elementary teaching" that the Colossians had failed to progress in the faith and were still taken up with elementary things.

But we must not see the error as simply a Greek aberration, for the references to circumcision (Col. 2:11; 3:11) show that there were Jewish elements in it as well.[11] "Human tradition" (2:8) may also point to Jewish teaching, perhaps the tradition of the elders. The Jews did not worship angels, but they had quite an interest in them; "the worship of angels" (2:18) may refer to some development of Jewish speculation about these celestial beings. Sabbath observance (2:16) was plainly Jewish, and the religious festivals and new-moon celebrations with which it is linked may also be Jewish in origin. The food regulations (2:16, 21) may be Jewish, but many religions had such regulations, so we cannot insist on it.

Our best understanding of the false teaching, then, is that it was a blend of Jewish and Hellenistic teachings.[12] Such syncretism was a feature of the ancient world, and it need not surprise us that when it appeared, it constituted an

---

[10]$\tau\grave{o}\ \sigma\tauo\iota\chi\epsilon\hat{\iota}o\nu$ (to stoicheion) originally meant "one of a row" and was used of such things as the alphabet (letters placed in a row), which leads to elementary teaching in general (the ABCs of the subject). Again, letters are the elements of which words are made up, and the word came to be used of the elements of which the universe is composed ("the elements" of 2 Peter 3:10, 12). The word occurs again in Gal. 4:3, 9. Bruce holds that in both Galatians and here we should think that "in the divine providence there was a time when the *stoicheia* fulfilled a supervisory role in the lives of the people of God, as a slave-attendant looked after a freeborn child till he came of age. The coming of age of the people of God coincided with the advent of faith in Christ: to remain under the control of the *stoicheia* after that was a sign of spiritual immaturity" (*Epistles*, p. 100). There is an excellent treatment of the term in O'Brien, *Colossians, Philemon*, pp. 129–32.

[11]G. Bornkamm finds several strands: "It originates in a gnosticized Judaism, in which Jewish and Iranian-Persian elements, and surely also influence of Chaldean astrology, have peculiarly alloyed themselves and have united with Christianity" ("The Heresy of Colossians," in *Conflict at Colossae*, ed. Fred O. Francis and Wayne A. Meeks [Missoula, Mont.,: SP, 1975], p. 135) This leads Andrew J. Bandstra to ask, "Is not the syncretistic nature of the religion Bornkamm and others have pictured so unusual that one may legitimately ask whether such a religion ever actually existed?" ("Did the Colossian Errorists Need a Mediator?" in *New Dimensions in New Testament Study*, ed. Richard N. Longenecker and Merrill C. Tenney [Grand Rapids: Zondervan, 1974], p. 330).

[12]There is a useful summary of opinions on the so-called Colossian heresy in O'Brien, *Colossians, Philemon*, pp. xxx–xli.

attraction for new and imperfectly instructed Christians: it was the sort of teaching that attracted first-century people.[13] Indeed, it is precisely because of the prevalence of such syncretism that Morna D. Hooker can question whether there was any Colossian heresy. She points out that if we find a modern Christian pastor telling people that Christ is greater than any astrological forces and that if Christians read their horoscopes in the newspaper they are succumbing to the pressures of contemporary society, we do not think of an invasion of the church by false teachers.[14] She thinks the situation in Colossae may have been something like that. Paul is concerned enough about it to spend time pointing the Colossians to right practices and right thinking, but he evidently does not think that the church is in a parlous state. His general satisfaction with the Colossian believers shines through the letter (see 1:3–5; 2:5; 3:7). But whether or not Hooker is right, we may be reasonably sure that Paul judges the believers in Colossae to be in danger of popular syncretism and writes in part to protect them from the threat.

TEXT

There is no reason to doubt that we have the text of the letter substantially as Paul wrote it. There are a few places where it is impossible to be sure of the right reading, but they do not affect the sense as a whole. As an example, in 3:6 after "the wrath of God is coming," quite a few MSS add "upon those who are disobedient." It is not easy to decide whether the additional words were added by scribes who remembered Ephesians 5:6, or whether they were accidentally dropped by a copying mistake. But whatever reading we adopt, the sense is much the same. There are problems with 2:18, 23, but these appear to center on the meanings of unusual vocabulary rather than uncertainty about the text. So with other disputed readings.[15]

ADOPTION INTO THE CANON

There may be a reference to Colossians in the *Epistle of Barnabas*, but otherwise we must come down to Justin Martyr in the middle of the second century for references to this letter. But it is accepted by Marcion, included in the Muratorian

---

[13]Thus Martin Dibelius holds that "the church was threatened with danger from a syncretistic movement, one of the numerous eclectic cults of Asia Minor which flourished at that critical moment in the history of religion" (*A Fresh Approach to the New Testament and Early Christian Literature* [London: Ivor Nicholson & Watson, 1936], p. 167).

[14]Morna D. Hooker, "Were There False Teachers in Colossae?" in *Christ and Spirit in the New Testament*, Fs. C. F. D. Moule, ed. B. Lindars and S. S. Smalley (Cambridge: Cambridge University Press, 1973), pp. 315–31. Kirsopp and Silva Lake said some time ago, "There is room for doubt as to whether Paul is arguing against Gentile Christians—in other words, against heresy—or against Gentiles who are endeavouring to convert Christians to their way of thinking. This point has, perhaps, not met with sufficient attention, and writers have spoken too lightly of the Colossian 'heresy' " (Lake, p. 151).

[15]It is difficult to understand why Enslin says that "the text of the letter is in a very bad state of preservation" (p. 292). He cites only 2:18–19 (which he says is "completely unintelligible") to support his view, whereas UBS3 gives the only disputed words in these verses a B rating. O'Brien recognizes differences of opinion about details here but says "the general drift of Paul's thought is reasonably clear" (*Colossians, Philemon*, p. 141). Ralph P. Martin agrees: "These verses abound with difficulties both linguistic and conceptual. Mercifully the drift of Paul's thought is clear" (*Colossians and Philemon*, NCB [London: Oliphants, 1974], p. 92).

Canon, found in the Syriac and Old Latin versions, and cited by authors such as Irenaeus, Clement of Alexandria, and Tertullian. No real doubt as to its canonicity appears to have been raised in antiquity, and the church seems to have had no difficulties in recognizing it as Scripture.

COLOSSIANS IN RECENT STUDY

It is strongly urged by some that the actual authorship of the letter does not matter. It is agreed that there is a Pauline connection; at the very least the author must have come from the devoted followers of Paul, and he has given a Pauline viewpoint in this letter. Such scholars tend to give most attention to the way the letter adapts the Pauline position to the situation in which the author finds himself.

As Childs emphasizes, "The letter to the Colossians is firmly anchored to the apostle Paul, both to his person and to the gospel which he proclaimed."[16] He is not arguing that Paul necessarily wrote the letter, but that whether he did so or not, there is a strong connection between the apostle and the writing. Neither Timothy nor Epaphras can be thought of as the author, he maintains, and the letter identifies with Paul in the opening and closing and in the body as well (1:23–2:5). He points to the way the Colossians are told to remain in the tradition that Paul represents and that was delivered to them. Childs holds that conservatives have been too ready to insist on Pauline authorship. Much more important, he thinks, is the fact that "in Colossians a false teaching called forth a specific apostolic response which used the heresy as a transparency through which to unfold a new and positive witness to the truth of the gospel."[17]

There has been a good deal of interest in the false teaching at Colossae. The problem is how to work up all that Paul says about the errors into a coherent system. It is most common these days to see the Colossians as opposed by some form of Gnosticism—all the more so, since Gnosticism was syncretistic, gathering in from many sources. Indeed, Kümmel says, "Today there are hardly any differences in basic opinion. Paul, with obvious correctness, sees in the heretical teaching Gnosticism, secret wisdom of a syncretistic sort (2:8, 18), which combines ascetic, ritualistic worship of the elements with Jewish ritualism and Jewish speculation about angels."[18] But this is too sweeping. Childs is more correct in saying, "Although there is a wide agreement that some form of Jewish syncretism is represented, there remains a continuing disagreement on the precise nature of the opposition."[19] As if to establish yet another pole, N. T. Wright argues that "all the elements of Paul's polemic in Colossians make sense as a warning against Judaism."[20]

Kümmel may speak for those scholars with whom he is aligned, but for no more. Mature Gnosticism is a series of systems propagated in the second century by great teachers such as Valentinus and Basilides. It featured a great number of

---

[16]Childs, p. 344.
[17]Ibid., p. 346.
[18]Kümmel, p. 239.
[19]Childs, p. 343.
[20]N. T. Wright, *The Epistles of Paul to the Colossians and to Philemon* (Grand Rapids: Eerdmans, 1986), p. 27.

heavenly intermediaries, or aeons, emanations from deity bridging the gap from the high good God to this material creation. Typically there was a contrast between spirit (which was good) and matter (which was evil). Gnosticism was eclectic, gathering teachings from a variety of sources, and we need not doubt that some of those teachings were to be found in the first century. But its characteristic teachings, such as those just mentioned, were not.[21] Behind Colossians there certainly lie some teachings that were later found in some of the forms of Gnosticism, but that does not mean that Gnosticism as such was the problem in this city.

Childs is nearer the mark when he finds "continuing disagreement." The problem is that we do not know of any teachers who combined all the features Paul is opposing. A given scholar may select certain features and say that they give us the essentials, but others will not agree with the selection. Morna Hooker's reminder that much of what we read in this letter we can recognize as features of first-century pagan or Jewish life is important. The Colossians were new Christians. They had not long left paganism or Judaism, and it was all too easy for them to revert to practices and ways of thinking to which they had been accustomed in their pre-Christian days, which they still encountered, and whose attractiveness they found impossible to deny. In the opinion of most recent writers, this will not account for the whole situation, yet it certainly is part of it and makes it more difficult to outline the essentials of the teaching Paul is opposing. But without some further information coming to light, we cannot identify the false teachers with any certainty, nor can we say with assurance whether they had a unified system, or whether Paul is referring to more than one set of teachings.

A further feature of recent discussion has been an interest in what is seen as traditional and liturgical material that the author has taken up and used to advance his argument. There has been a concentration on 1:15–20, which is widely seen as a hymn, adapted by the author to set forward important teaching about Christ and his functions. O'Neill, however, denies that it is a hymn; he does not find hymnic structure, but finds evidence that Paul is citing traditional matter.[22] There is room for further discussion of this point.

THE CONTRIBUTION OF COLOSSIANS

The false teachers interposed a barrier between God and God's people. They thought of the elemental spirits who stood in the way and permitted access to God only by the path of asceticism. In the face of all such claims, Paul stresses the supremacy of Christ, who is "the image of the invisible God," the one who brought creation about and holds it together, supreme over creation, preeminent in everything. And together with all this he is "the head of the body, the church," the one who made peace by the blood he shed on the cross (1:15–20). This combination of the greatness of Christ and of his saving work for believers runs through the epistle. It makes nonsense of any claim that other powers are involved

---

[21]See discussion in chap. 21 below.
[22]J. C. O'Neill, "The Source of the Christology in Colossians," *NTS* 26 (1979–80): 87–100.

in bringing people to God, or that meritorious practices like asceticism pave the way.

Christ has reconciled believers (1:22), he is in them "the hope of glory" (1:27). There is an unusual way of looking at the atonement when Paul says that God forgave us our sins, "having canceled the written code, with its regulations, that was against us and that stood opposed to us; he took it away, nailing it to the cross" (2:14). The adequacy of Christ's atonement is thus brought out in a fresh way. Again, in Christ are "all the treasures of wisdom and knowledge" (2:3); "all the fullness of the Deity lives" in him "in bodily form" (2:9) and believers "have been given fullness in Christ" (2:10). When they were dead in sins, God made them alive with Christ (2:13). They died with Christ "to the basic principles of this world" (2:20), and they have been raised with him (3:1). Christ "is all, and is in all" (3:11), and they are "God's chosen people" (3:12). They give thanks to God the Father through Christ (3:17). The great themes of Christ's outstanding excellence and the completeness of the salvation that he brought about in dying for his people on the cross run through this letter. They are not put in quite this way elsewhere, and Colossians accordingly has something to say that is distinctive. It is not enough to argue about authorship and the exact nature of the false teaching that is opposed.[23] What matters is the wonder of the love of God in Christ and the magnificence of the salvation that he has brought about for his people.

None of this means that Colossians tells of a different God or a different Christ or a different salvation. This letter is essentially Pauline, and it is the same God, the same Savior, and the same salvation as we see throughout the Pauline corpus. What is different is the way it is all expressed, with some new insights like being rescued "from the dominion of darkness" and brought into "the kingdom of the Son he loves" (1:13). Colossians is full of the teaching of Paul, even though there are new aspects to meet new needs of believers confronted with a new challenge from the Evil One.

Paul insists on the supremacy of Christ over all the supernatural forces the Colossians were treating with such respect. Some of us may miss part of the relevance of what he is saying because we do not believe in those forces in the way the Colossians did. But with rising occultism in the West, our skepticism is being mocked; and in any case it has often been pointed out that in modern times there is a widespread belief that we are the creatures of our heredity and our environment and that in the grip of such powers we can never be really free. It is part of the message of Colossians that in Christ we can overcome anything. The cross means a disarming of all the powers opposed to God's purpose (2:15), and this remains an important part of the Christian way.

Paul had never been to Colossae and had not met members of the church there (2:1). The love and the tender concern for them that comes through in every line

---

[23]Childs is scarcely fair at this point. He refers to those who "argue that it was Paul himself who 'translated' his message into a different idiom to meet the new situation" and then adds, "In my judgment, the philological and stylistic evidence speaks against the position." Child goes on to refer to "the intensity of the conservatives' defence of a direct Pauline authorship" as stemming "from a traditional hermeneutic which ties the book's authority to the author's intentionality" (p. 349). But Childs's "in my judgment" by itself settles nothing. Furthermore, at least some conservatives are more concerned with the evidence than with intensity, traditional hermeneutics, and the like.

of the letter are all the more significant. This letter brings out, as perhaps no other New Testament writing does, the truth that all believers form one church. Paul is emphatic that in the church there is "no Greek or Jew, circumcised or uncircumcised, barbarian, Scythian, slave or free, but Christ is all, and is in all" (3:11). We belong together, we who are members of the body of Christ, and we cannot be indifferent to the concerns and the interests of other members. The letter makes clear for all of us the importance of concern for the whole church and not only that little segment in which we live.

But along with that emphasis on the oneness of the church, we should heed the teaching of the letter that there are differences that distinguish believers. Paul gives directions to wives and husbands, children and fathers, slaves and masters (3:18–4:1). All are servants of Christ and must live as such, but that does not obliterate relationships in society. Our positions differ, and while a common obligation to live out the faith rests on all of us, the precise form that takes differs according to our circumstances.

In every generation Christians are tempted to go along with the philosophy of the times. It is never a comfortable thing to be out of step with what our community holds to be the best thinking of the day. But that thinking may be out of step with God, who made us all. Paul's warning about "hollow and deceptive philosophy, which depends on human tradition and the basic principles of this world" (2:8) is never out of season. At the same time, we should listen to the warnings about distracting religious practices, the observance of religious festivals that detract from what is central (2:16), and the habit of making rules the essence of religion (2:20–21). Such practices generate a false humility and really promote unspirituality (2:18). Nothing can make up for losing connection with the head (2:19).

BIBLIOGRAPHY

T. K. **Abbott**, *The Epistles to the Ephesians and to the Colossians*, ICC (Edinburgh: T. & T. Clark, 1897); E. **Bammel**, "Versuch zu Col 1:15–20," *ZNW* 52 (1961): 88–95; Andrew J. **Bandstra**, "Did the Colossian Errorists Need a Mediator?" in *New Dimensions in New Testament Study*, ed. Richard N. Longenecker and Merrill C. Tenney (Grand Rapids: Zondervan 1974), pp. 329–43; G. **Bornkamm**, "The Heresy of Colossians," in *Conflict at Colossae*, ed. Fred O. Francis and Wayne A. Meeks (Missoula, Mont.: SP, 1975), pp. 123–45; F. F. **Bruce**, *The Epistles to the Colossians, to Philemon, and to the Ephesians*, NICNT (Grand Rapids: Eerdmans, 1984); G. B. **Caird**, *Paul's Letters from Prison* (Oxford: Oxford University Press, 1976); C. C. **Caragounis**, *The Ephesian Mysterion: Meaning and Content* (Lund: Gleerup, 1977); W. **Carr**, "Two Notes on Colossians," *JTS* 24 (1973): 492–500; Edmund P. **Clowney**, "Interpreting the Biblical Models of the Church: A Hermeneutical Deepening of Ecclesiology," in *Biblical Interpretation and the Church: Text and Context*, ed. D. A. Carson (Exeter: Paternoster, 1984), pp. 64–109; Martin **Dibelius**, *A Fresh Approach to the New Testament and Early Christian Literature* (London: Ivor Nicholson & Watson, 1936); J. **Ernst**, *Pleroma und Pleroma Christi: Geschichte und Deutung eines Begriffs der paulinischen Antilegomena*, BU 5 (Regensburg: Pustet, 1970); Fred O. **Francis** and Wayne A. **Meeks**, eds., *Conflict at Colossae* (Missoula, Mont.: SP, 1975); Joachim **Gnilka**, *Der Kolosserbrief*, HTKNT (Freiburg: Herder, 1980); P. N. **Harrison**, *The Problem of* *the Pastoral Epistles* (London: Oxford, 1921); Morna D. **Hooker**, "Were There False Teachers in Colossae?," in *Christ and Spirit in the New Testament, Fs.* C. F. D. Moule, ed. Barnabas Lindars and Stephen S. Smalley (Cambridge: Cambridge University Press, 1973), pp. 315–31; S. E. **Johnson**, "Unsolved Questions About Early Christianity in Anatolia," in *Studies in New Testament and Early Christian Literautre, Fs.* Allen P. Wikgren, ed. D. E. Aune, SuppNovT 33 (Leiden: Brill, 1972), pp. 181–93; E. **Käsemann**, *Essays on New Testament Themes* (London: SCM, 1964), pp. 149–68; J. B. **Lightfoot**, *Saint Paul's Epistles to the Colossians and to Philemon*, 9th ed. (London: Macmillan, 1890); Eduard **Lohse**, *Colossians and Philemon*, Hermeneia (Philadelphia: Fortress, 1971); idem, "Pauline Theology in the Letter to the Colossians," *NTS* 15 (1968–69): 211–20; G. H. C. **Macgregor**, "Principalities and Powers: The Cosmic Background of St Paul's Thought," *NTS* 1 (1954–55): 17–28; Ralph P. **Martin**, *Colossians and Philemon*, NCB (London: Oliphants, 1974); Charles **Masson**, *L'épître aux Colossiens*, CNT (Paris: Delachaux & Niestlé, 1950); C. F. D. **Moule**, *The Epistles of Paul the Apostle to the Colossians and to Philemon* (Cambridge: Cambridge University Press, 1962); Peter T. **O'Brien**, *Colossians, Philemon*, WBC (Waco, Tex.: Word, 1982); J. C. **O'Neill**, "The Source of the Christology in Colossians," *NTS* 26 (1979–80): 87–100; T. E. **Pollard**, "Colossians 1:12–20: A Reconsideration," *NTS* 27 (1980–81): 572–75; Bo **Reicke**, "Caesarea, Rome, and the Captivity Epistles," in *Apostolic History and the Gospel, Fs.* F. F. Bruce, ed. W. Ward Gasque and Ralph P. Martin (Exeter: Paternoster, 1970), pp. 277–86; Eduard **Schweizer**, *The Letter to the Colossians: A Commentary* (Minneapolis: Augsburg, 1982; German original, EKKNT, 1976); H. **Weiss**, "The Law in the Epistle to the Colossians," *CBQ* 34 (1972): 294–314; N. T. **Wright**, *The Epistles of Paul to the Colossians and to Philemon* (Grand Rapids: Eerdmans, 1986).

14

1 and 2 thessalonians

CONTENTS

Thessalonians

Paul links Silas and Timothy with him in the salutation (1:1) and gives thanks for the faith, love, and hope of the Thessalonian Christians (1:2–3), pointing out that the way they had lived out the Christian faith had made them a model to others (1:4–10). He reminds them of the example he and his companions had set them when they evangelized the city (2:1–12) and gives thanks for their response, even when they suffered from Jewish opposition (2:13–16).

Paul speaks of his longing to see them (2:17–20) and reminds them that he had sent Timothy to them and that Timothy had reported that they were standing firm in the Lord (3:1–10). Paul breaks out into a short prayer (3:11–13), exhorting his readers to continue to make progress in the Christian way (4:1–2). He mentions sexual purity (4:3–8), brotherly love (4:9–10), and earning one's living (4:11–12).

Evidently some of these new believers had problems with the parousia. Paul tells them that they need not be without hope for believers who had died. When the Lord comes back, the deceased believers will be raised first, and the remaining believers will then be caught up to meet the Lord (4:13–18). The time of all this is not known (5:1–3), but they should live so that the day will not catch them unprepared (5:4–11). The letter closes with some general exhortations (5:12–27) and the grace (5:28).

2 Thessalonians

As in the first letter, Silas and Timothy are joined with Paul in the salutation (1:1–2), after which Paul gives thanks for the Thessalonians (1:3–5), speaks of God's judgment on those who trouble them (1:6–10), and prays for them (1:11–12). He urges them not to be unsettled by people who speak of "the day of the Lord" as already present (2:1–2) and, in a noteworthy and difficult passage, deals with "the man of lawlessness" and those who follow him (2:3–12). He urges the Thessalonians to stand firm (2:13–15) and utters a brief prayer for them (2:16–17). He asks them to pray for him and his associates (3:1–2), reminds them of the faithfulness of God (3:3–5), warns them against idleness (3:6–13) and disobedience (3:14–15) and closes the letter with another prayer (3:16), his autograph (3:17), and the grace (3:18).

AUTHOR

Both letters claim Paul as author. No serious objection has been raised to his authorship of 1 Thessalonians (other than by the Tübingen School, and their objections have not won acceptance).[1] The vocabulary and style are Pauline,[2] as are the ideas put forward. While there have occasionally been scholars who deny the Pauline authorship of 1 Thessalonians, this has always been rare, and today it is widely recognized that the reasons put forward are unconvincing. If it is not genuine, it is not easy to see why it was composed. As a letter to a young church in need of guidance, it rings true. But why should anyone write a letter like this and claim that it came from Paul? It is hard to think of a reason. The letter shows that the church to which it was written had no complex organization, which points to an early date. So does the discussion of the fate of those who died before the parousia, for this question must have arisen in the church in very early times. It is hard to think that a later writer would have ascribed to Paul words like those in chapter 4, which might be understood to mean that the parousia would take place during his lifetime. It has also been pointed out that the very existence of 2 Thessalonians, whether written by Paul or by someone else, is evidence for the existence of 1 Thessalonians.

Objections are sometimes raised on the grounds that what is said in the letter does not always agree with what we read in Acts. Thus Luke says that Paul spoke in the synagogue for three Sabbaths (Acts 17:2), whereas Paul says that he worked at his trade in the city, which implies (it is argued) a longer period (1 Thess. 2:7–9). This is often supported by saying that Paul received help from the Philippians more than once while he was in Thessalonica (Phil. 4:16), but it has been shown that the Greek means "both (when I was in Thessalonica) and more than once (when I was elsewhere) you sent. . . ."[3] In any case, we should be clear that neither Paul nor Acts says how long he was in the city. Acts may well give the time he spent among the Jews, after which he preached among the Gentiles. In any case his evangelistic campaign seems to have been short. We get no further with objections such as that in Acts 17:4 the converts are both Jews and Gentiles, while in the letter we read of people turning from idols and thus being Gentiles (1 Thess. 1:9). There were doubtless converts from both groups, and these

---

[1]On the Tübingen School, see the section "Date" in chap. 6 above.

[2]J. E. Frame has made a detailed examination of the words and phrases used in these two letters and shows conclusively that the language points to Pauline authorship of both. He reinforces this by an examination of what he calls the "Personal Equation," indications of the personality back of the words. (*A Critical and Exegetical Commentary on the Epistles of St. Paul to the Thessalonians*, ICC [Edinburgh: T. & T. Clark, 1912], pp. 28–37).

[3]See Leon Morris, "ἄπαξ καὶ δίς," *NovT* 1 (1956): 205–8. The phrase ἄπαξ καὶ δίς (*hapax kai dis*) seems to mean "more than once"; with καὶ (*kai*) prefixed, it signifies "both in Thessalonica and more than once (elsewhere)." There is no contradiction even if Acts gives the total time Paul spent in Thessalonica.

statements are not contradictory. The accounts are independent, but this gives no reason for ruling out Pauline authorship of the letter.[4]

There are more who regard 2 Thessalonians as inauthentic.[5] It is urged that the eschatology of this letter is incompatible with that of the first, and indeed with what Paul writes elsewhere. In the first letter the parousia will take place suddenly, whereas in the second there will be signs and the appearance of the lawless one. This objection demands a consistency that we do not find in the apocalypses, which often combine the thoughts of the imminence of the End and of preparatory signs. That there is no parallel to the man of lawlessness in the other Pauline letters is no objection, for there is no exact parallel elsewhere either, and Paul is just as likely as anyone to come up with a novel idea or expression. Paul does not elsewhere face the contention that "the day of the Lord has already come" (2:2), so it is not surprising that the solution he here proposes does not occur elsewhere.

Some students find a marked difference in tone between the two writings and conclude that one author would not have written in two such different ways. They point to the first letter as warm and colorful and find the second colder and more formal. The difference can be exaggerated. In fact it rests on a few expressions such as "we ought always to thank God for you" (2 Thess. 1:3) and "we command you" (2 Thess. 3:6). We should also bear in mind that the most colorful part of the first letter comes in the section where Paul is defending himself against his critics (2:1–3:13); take that away, and the difference is not very marked. But in any case we should ask why Paul should always write in the same tone. Does anybody?

The principal reason urged for seeing 2 Thessalonians as inauthentic is the combination of likeness and unlikeness to the first letter. In places, not only the ideas being expressed are similar but even the words in which the ideas are expressed are similar.[6] A writer as able as Paul, it is urged, would not repeat himself in this way, and these passages are seen as evidence of deliberate imitation. If this sort of thing is taken along with such differences as those we have just noticed in eschatology, it is maintained that we should see someone other than Paul as the writer of 2 Thessalonians. Against this conclusion, some have urged that when we have all Pauline ideas, style, and vocabulary in this second letter, it is better to think of the same author than to posit another. We should notice moreover that passages with similar wording are used differently. Thus in both letters the writer speaks of working with his own hands, but whereas in the first this comes early and shows his love for the converts and his determination not to be a burden to them (2:9), in the second it comes late and is "in order to make ourselves a model for you to follow" (3:7–9). We should also bear in mind that a good deal of the resemblance in language comes in the literary framework—the

---

[4]Moffatt reminds us to take a commonsense attitude to problems like this: "It is capricious to pronounce the epistle a colourless imitation, if it agrees with Acts, and unauthentic if it disagrees" (p. 71).

[5]Typical is J. A. Bailey, who strongly argues that 2 Thessalonians was not written by Paul but in the last decade of the first century by a writer who opposed Gnostic teaching and insisted on the place of apocalyptic in the Christian message ("Who Wrote II Thessalonians?" *NTS* 25 [1978–79]: 131–45).

[6]B. Rigaux offers lists of such passages (*Les Epîtres aux Thessaloniciens* [Paris: Gabalda, 1956], pp. 133–34).

opening and the closing. A further consideration is the detailed knowledge of the situation at Thessalonica presupposed by what is said in 3:6–15.

Thus there seem to be no decisive objections to the Pauline authorship, and in view of the positive reasons, we should hold that 2 Thessalonians is an authentic writing of the apostle.[7] If we think of this letter as being written a short time after the first letter in response to some difficulties that had arisen, we have as good a solution to the problem as has been offered. We should also allow for the possibility that Paul has made use of a secretary who may well have been responsible for some of the wording.[8] We should also bear in mind that the second letter ends with "I, Paul, write this greeting in my own hand, which is the distinguishing mark in all my letters. This is how I write" (3:17).[9] If this letter is not genuine, it is a forgery.[10] There is no possibility that the author is an honest man, writing in the name of Paul to express ideas he thinks the apostle would have been pleased to accept. The letter carries a signature it explicitly claims to be that of Paul. Would a forger produce a letter as Christian as this?[11]

PROVENANCE

These letters appear to be quite early and to have been written from Athens or Corinth. After founding the church in Thessalonica and fleeing from the city when the Jews started a riot (Acts 17:1–9), Paul had a somewhat similar experience in Berea that resulted in his being sent on to Athens (Acts 17:10–15). In that city he preached but apparently with little result, after which he went on to Corinth (Acts 18:1). He must have been a very discouraged man. After good beginnings in Philippi, Thessalonica, and Berea, his work had been disrupted by fanatic opponents and then had been followed by little success in Athens. Small wonder that he could say to the Corinthians, "I came to you in weakness and fear, and with much trembling" (1 Cor. 2:3). But then Silas and Timothy came to him (Acts 18:5) with news that the believers in Thessalonica were standing firm. That meant that despite the setbacks he had experienced, God was truly blessing his work.

Paul refers to Timothy as having "just now come to us from you" (1 Thess. 3:6). It is possible to understand this to mean that Timothy had just joined him in

---

[7]Johnson remarks, "Second Thessalonians is sometimes considered inauthentic, although it is difficult to make that case convincing" (p. 266). E. Best observes, "It is curious how the vast majority of the commentators accept the letter as genuine while its rejectors are found among those who approach the letter from the aspect of 'introduction'" (*A Commentary on the First and Second Epistles to the Thessalonians* [London: Adam & Charles Black, 1977], p. 52) Robert Jewett has a useful survey of arguments about authenticity. He sees the first epistle as Pauline and the second as probably authentic also (*The Thessalonian Correspondence* [Philadelphia: Fortress, 1986], pp. 3–18). On the latter he says, "While the likelihood of definitely proving Pauline authorship of 2 Thessalonians remains at a modest level, the improbability of forgery is extremely high" (pp. 17–18).

[8]"Is not the role of a secretary (cf. 2 Thes. 3:17) an important factor in solving the difficulties?" (Harrington, p. 230).

[9]McNeile remarks that "the boldness, or worse, of adding iii.17 is greater than we can admit to be possible, even in an age when pseudonymity was a recognized literary artifice" (p. 117).

[10]"This is an extremely blatant forgery, if it is not Pauline" (D. E. Whiteley, *Thessalonians* [London: Oxford University Press, 1969], p. 11).

[11]Holland Hendrix, in a review of Jewett's book, points out that if inauthenticity is to be established, "the explicit avowal of Paul's signature as a practice in *all* of his letters (2 Thess 3:17) must be rendered comprehensible as an authenticating tactic on the forger's part" (*JBL* 107 [1988]: 765).

Athens, for when he arrived in that city, he sent a request for Silas and Timothy to come to him (Acts 17:15), and they may have reached him there. If so, he sent them back, for when he was in Corinth, they came to him from Macedonia (Acts 18:5). But the most likely understanding of all this is that Paul wrote 1 Thessalonians shortly after Timothy reached him in Corinth. The longer period seems needed for the situation to develop to the position we discern in 1 Thessalonians and for the faith of the believers to become known "everywhere" (1 Thess. 1:8).[12] As 2 Thessalonians seems to have been written not long after the first letter, it will also have originated in Corinth.

DATE

What we have said about provenance yields the essential matter about dating these letters. They both seem to have been written at Corinth during Paul's evangelistic campaign in that city. That the organization of the church presupposed by these letters is of the simplest agrees with this reconstruction. There are no references to officials such as presbyters or deacons, only to "those . . . who are over you in the Lord" (1 Thess. 5:12). This also agrees with the passage about the parousia (1 Thess. 4:13–18) that has been understood by some (mistakenly in our view) to mean that the second coming would take place in Paul's lifetime. It is difficult to think that the statement would have been worded in this way if it was composed after Paul's death.

It can be argued from an inscription that the proconsul Gallio (before whom Paul was brought in Corinth [Acts 18:12]) reached Corinth in the early summer of A.D. 51.[13] As Paul had exercised a ministry in Corinth before Gallio's arrival, the apostle most likely came to Corinth early in 50. The first letter to the Thessalonians would have been written soon after that, and the second some months later. These letters are thus among the earliest letters of Paul to survive. Some date Galatians earlier, but none of the others.

As we noticed earlier, it is sometimes urged that Paul's stay in Thessalonica must have been longer than it would appear from the account given in Acts. Support is found for this in Paul's statement that he worked night and day (1 Thess. 2:7–9) so that he would not be a burden to the Thessalonians and his further statement about the aid the Philippians sent him while he was in Thessalonica (Phil. 4:16), which are said to demand a longer time. But even making full allowance for what these considerations tell us about the length of his stay, it still remains that Paul cannot have been in Thessalonica for more than a matter of months. His letters to the church there would still be quite early.[14]

Those who deny the Pauline authorship of 2 Thessalonians tend to date it rather later. Thus Enslin thinks it was written "after Paul's death, perhaps in the

---

[12]Moffatt finds the references to Achaia (1 Thess. 1:7–8) "enough to prove" that the letter was written from Corinth (p. 73).

[13]See chap. 7 above. See also Leon Morris, *The First and Second Epistles to the Thessalonians*, NICNT (Grand Rapids: Eerdmans, 1959), pp. 24–26.

[14]E.g., R. H. Fuller draws attention to the considerations noted above (and comments on the Philippian gifts to Paul, "two in a fortnight is rather a lot!"), but he still dates 1 Thessalonians in A.D. 50 (p. 20). In any case Fuller and those who agree with him on two gifts to Philippi while Paul was at Thessalonica are interpreting the Greek too confidently. It probably refers to no more than one gift at Thessalonica. See the section "Contents" above, along with n. 3.

early years of the second century." He argues this on the ground that the epistle was written after Paul's death by someone who wanted to get Paul's authority for his letter, in which he was setting forward "later views of the Parousia."[15] This is scarcely convincing evidence for a late date, Moreover, Enslin does not even examine the question of how on his view the letter could have been recognized as canonical by the time of Marcion.[16] Marxsen dates it "soon after A.D. 70,"[17] but cites no evidence.

RELATION BETWEEN 1 AND 2 THESSALONIANS

The letters are both addressed to the church at Thessalonica, and the contents fit the address. There is no reason for doubting this. But why should two such letters be sent to the same church within a short space of time? What are we to make of the way such resemblances and differences came to be combined in the two? A number of suggestions have been made.

A Division Between Jewish and Gentile Christians

A. Harnack tried to solve the problem in terms of destination. He thought that there was tension between the Jewish and Gentile members of the church and that Paul, in recognition of this, wrote two letters, 1 Thessalonians being addressed to the Gentile section and 2 Thessalonians to the Jewish Christians.[18] The reference to turning from idols (1 Thess. 1:9) marks the first letter as being directed toward former pagans, and Harnack thought there is a Jewish coloring in the second that makes it suitable for people who know their Old Testament. This Jewish tone, however, has not been apparent to all. Some point out, for example, that in 2 Thessalonians there is not one quotation from the Old Testament.

A related argument depends on accepting the reading "God chose you as his firstfruits" instead of "from the beginning God chose you" (2 Thess. 2:13; the NIV has the "firstfruits" reading in the margin). In what sense could the Thessalonians be labeled firstfruits? They were not the first Christians, not even the first in Macedonia (that honor went to the Philippians). But the Jews could be said to be the first in Thessalonica (Acts 17:4), and this observation has fueled the argument that 2 Thessalonians was written exclusively to the Jewish component of the church. Even if the variant "firstfruits" was accepted, however, it would not necessarily follow that the epistle is so narrowly directed. In James 1:18, all believers are the firstfruits of God's creation; in Revelation 14:4 faithful witnesses and martyrs are the firstfruits of humankind. In the context before us, it is quite likely that the church as a whole is the firstfruits (if that is the correct reading) of

---

[15]Enslin, p. 244.

[16]Perrin/Duling see this letter as "a deliberate imitation of 1 Thessalonians by a member of a Pauline school" and locate it at "the stage we know from the book of Revelation, itself a text from the end of the first Christian century" (pp. 208–9) But they do not mention the difficulty of its inclusion in Marcion's canon if written as late as this.

[17]Marxsen, p. 44.

[18]A Harnack, "Das Problem des zweiten Thessalonicherbriefs," *SAB* 31 (1910): 560–78. Kirsopp and Silva Lake argue that 1 Thessalonians was written mainly to Greeks and 2 Thessalonians "exclusively to the Jews." They see the second letter as written to the Jewish Christians when Paul found that the first letter would not satisfy them (Lake, pp. 134–35).

humankind to God.[19] But more important, there is every reason to hold that the NIV is right: "from the beginning" should be read and not "as his firstfruits."[20] Conversely, there is no greater substance in the argument that, since Paul insists in 1 Thessalonians that "all" be greeted with a holy kiss and that the first letter be read to "all" (1 Thess. 5:26–27), it must have been written to both Jews and Gentiles. Such directions are quite natural in a letter to all the church, without concrete reference to groups within the church.

Quite apart from such arguments it is quite unthinkable that Paul would accept a situation in which a church was so divided that it could not even meet as a whole. When he faced division in the Corinthian church, he delayed dealing with everything else until he had made it clear that he was totally opposed to any such division as cliques within the group. Such a division is contradicted by all that we know of the apostolic church. There were differences of opinion, indeed, but not such that believers separated off from one another. Paul's approval of the Thessalonians is manifestly impossible to reconcile with bitter division. Furthermore, the addresses of the two letters are practically identical; certainly there is no suggestion that they were addressed to different groups of believers within the church. There are other difficulties. On Harnack's view Paul holds up to Gentile believers the example of Jewish churches in Judea and commends them for being imitators of those churches (1 Thess. 2:14). Difficulties multiply; the hypothesis should be rejected.

There is perhaps more to be said for the idea of Martin Dibelius that the letter "was sent only to a special circle of the church,"[21] or that of E. Earle Ellis that we should take "the brothers" as a designation of Paul's Thessalonian coworkers and see the first epistle as sent to the whole church and the second as sent to "the brothers."[22] Ellis draws attention particularly to the designation "firstfruits," which is applied specifically to "the brothers" (2 Thess. 2:13), pointing to them as set apart for the work of God. He also sees the "idlers" (2 Thess. 3:6–15) as people "receiving financial support or, at least, communal meals," and Ellis thinks Paul is urging them to follow his example.[23] But it may be doubted whether Ellis has made out his case. The textual evidence for "firstfruits" is scarcely sufficient, and it is hard to see the strong denunciation of the idlers as referring to a class of church workers.

A problem in the way of all hypotheses that 2 Thessalonians is written for a different group of people than 1 Thessalonians is the address. As it stands, the letter is sent "to the church of the Thessalonians," an expression that is identical with that at the head of 1 Thessalonians. There is no evidence that this replaces

---

[19]So F. F. Bruce, *1 and 2 Thessalonians*, WBC (Waco, Tex.: Word, 1982), p. 190.

[20]The difference is between ἀπαρχήν (*aparchēn*, "as [his] firstfruits") and ἀπ᾽ ἀρχῆς (*ap' archēs*, "from [the] beginning"). The MSS evidence is divided, and good support may be urged for either view. Transcriptional probability favors "from the beginning," for this is not a typical Pauline expression, whereas "firstfruits" is (and therefore scribes would tend to alter "from the beginning" to "firstfruits" rather than the reverse). Paul never elsewhere links firstfruits with election, but he does tend to join election with some expression placing it in the beginning. R. V. G. Tasker favors "from the beginning," as this seems "in keeping with Paul's thought" (*The Greek New Testament* [Oxford: Oxford University Press and Cambridge University Press, 1964], p. 440)

[21]Martin Dibelius, *A Fresh Approach to the New Testament and Early Christian Literature* (London: Ivor Nicholson and Watson, 1936), p. 152.

[22]E. Earle Ellis, "Paul and His Co-Workers," *NTS* 17 (1970–71): 449–51.

[23]Ibid., p. 450.

any other form of address. Two questions arise. First, if the two letters were originally sent to two different groups of Christians, why are they addressed to the same group? Second, if originally there was a different address for one letter, why was it changed? When we add that the contents of both letters are very suitable in epistles to the whole Thessalonian church, it seems that the case has not been made out.

Co-Authorship

Silas and Timothy are linked with Paul in the openings of both letters, and this opens the way for the suggestion that one or other of them was responsible for one or both of the letters. If either wrote both, we have the same problem as with Paul. If Paul wrote 1 Thessalonians and one of them wrote 2 Thessalonians, we have the problem of the resemblances between the two letters, and also the fact that Paul signed 2 Thessalonians. While we know little about the exact role of an amanuensis in the first century,[24] it seems that suggestions along these lines are in danger of explaining the obscure by the more obscure.

Reversal of Order

Some have suggested that 2 Thessalonians preceded 1 Thessalonians.[25] There can be no a priori objection to the reversal of order; it is a matter of evidence. Neither letter claims to be before or after the other, and the traditional order could have arisen for no more profound reason than the greater length of 1 Thessalonians. There was a tendency in the early church to arrange letters in order of length, with the longer ones first. So we must look at the arguments adduced.

Some scholars think our problems arise mainly because we read the letters in the traditional order, assuming that 2 Thessalonians is overshadowed by 1 Thessalonians. But 2 Thessalonians is much more appealing as a first letter, and as it leaves quite a few things unsettled, it calls for a fuller letter to follow. The contention is supported by a number of considerations. Thus the tribulations that are at their height in 2 Thessalonians are over in the first letter (see 1 Thess. 2:14). The church's internal difficulties are a new happening in the second letter, but familiar in the first. The directions about the autograph (2 Thess. 3:17) are useful in a first letter, but not in a later one.[26] That the believers need not be instructed about dates (1 Thess. 5:1) would follow the teaching given in the second letter. Paul would have sent a letter with Timothy when he sent him to Thessalonica (1 Thess. 3:2). This letter, it is urged, must be 2 Thessalonians.

These and other considerations are not sufficiently persuasive. It is not at all certain that the trials were over when 1 Thessalonians was written (see 1 Thess. 3:3). Guthrie makes the point that "since 1 Thessalonians was designed partly to

---

[24]See Richard N. Longenecker, "On the Form, Function, and Authority of the New Testament Letters," in *Scripture and Truth*, ed. D. A. Carson and John D. Woodbridge (Grand Rapids: Zondervan, 1983), pp. 101–14.

[25]The hypothesis is argued, e.g., by T. W. Manson, *Studies in the Gospels and Epistles* (Manchester: Manchester University Press, 1962), pp. 268–78.

[26]By contrast, W. Hendriksen emphasizes "*every* letter" (NIV "in all my letters") and comments that this "is easier to understand if this were a *second* than if it were a first letter" (*New Testament Commentary: Exposition of I and II Thessalonians* [Grand Rapids: Baker 1955], p. 17).

encourage, some trials were still expected in the future."²⁷ Again, there is no real evidence of new internal difficulties in 2 Thessalonians. And that an autograph need not be explained in a first letter is shown by the fact that no such explanation is found in any of Paul's other letters (most of which are first letters).²⁸ Its use here argues for unusual circumstances at Thessalonica (see 2 Thess. 2:2). The argument from eschatology amounts to little; it could be worded to support the priority of either letter. Timothy would scarcely have been the bearer of a letter of which he was one of the authors.

Against the view that the Thessalonian epistles must be inverted, it is urged that the problems arising from persecution, the parousia, and idleness all seem to be more urgent in 2 Thessalonians.²⁹ It is also pointed out that there are references in that letter to a letter of Paul's (2 Thess. 2:15; 3:17), which seem to point us to 1 Thessalonians. The warmer tone of the first letter would be a natural result of the news Timothy had just brought, and the somewhat cooler tone of 2 Thessalonians would be natural later. Wikenhauser is impressed by the strength of Paul's expressions when he speaks of his being separated from the Thessalonians (1 Thess. 2:17–3:6); he says forthrightly that according to this passage 1 Thessalonians "is his first Epistle to the community."³⁰ It certainly reads like this.

It appears, then, that no sufficient reason has been given for reversing the order of the two letters. It is better to retain the traditional order.

OCCASION

Timothy had just come from Thessalonica, and some hold that he brought a letter to which 1 Thessalonians was Paul's reply. They point to the words "now about" (4:9, 13; 5:1), which Paul uses when answering points raised in a letter to him from the Corinthians (1 Cor. 7:1, 25; 8:1). They suggest that Paul deals with some topics as though he would prefer not to (1 Thess. 4:9; 5:1), which means he is answering points they had raised in a letter.

There may have been such a letter, but we do not have sufficient evidence to be sure. "Now about" is used in other ways than in answering letters, and we must all sometimes deal with topics we do not choose, even when not answering a letter. What is clear is that Paul is writing to meet the needs of the Thessalonians as they had come before him in Timothy's report.

It seems that Jewish opponents of the church were slandering Paul. If they could persuade the converts that Paul was simply trying to make money out of them and that his message was his own with no divine authorization, they would make it hard for the new Christians to hold on to their faith. So Paul spends a

---

²⁷Guthrie, p. 600.

²⁸Attention is drawn to the autograph in 1 Cor. 16:21, which is not Paul's first letter to the Corinthians (see 1 Cor. 5:9).

²⁹According to William Neil, "In each of the topics dealt with—persecution, Second Advent, idleness—there is an obvious intensification of the difficulties, and development of the situation, as described in the first letter, which make any alteration of the sequence impossible." Neil adds, "The personal reminiscences so characteristic of the first epistle are lacking here—they are no longer necessary in what is virtually an appendix" (*The Epistle of Paul to the Thessalonians* [London: Hodder & Stoughton, 1950], p. xx).

³⁰Wikenhauser, p. 370.

good deal of time in the first three chapters rebutting the kind of charge that might be brought against him. He aims to strengthen his friends in a time of persecution (1 Thess. 2:14) and to encourage them to live really Christian lives, not adopting pagan sexual standards (4:3–8). Some believers seem to have thought that Christ would come back soon, and when some of them died, the survivors thought the deceased would miss all the wonders of the parousia, so Paul wrote to put them right in this matter (4:13–18). Similarly there was need of teaching about the end times (5:1–11). Some of the believers apparently were idle, relying on others to support them (4:11–12). The authority of leaders was perhaps called in question (5:12–13), and the place of spiritual gifts was not clear to all (5:19–20).

In short, Paul wrote to meet the needs of his flock. They were a new church, not long enough in the faith to understand many things that more mature Christians would take for granted. Paul, their father in God, was concerned about them and wrote to help them go forward in the service of their Lord.

Second Thessalonians is basically more of the same. In some respects the first letter had been successful, and there was no need of repetition. Thus Paul spends a good deal of time in 1 Thessalonians defending himself against slanderous attacks, but none in the second letter.[31] Evidently he had quieted the opposition. But in other respects he faces the same problems. There is some new teaching (as in the matter of "the lawless one" [2:8]), but for the most part it seems that Paul is reinforcing what he wrote in the earlier letter. The problem of idleness had persisted, and it therefore receives greater emphasis in this second letter (2 Thess. 3:6–13). Misunderstandings about the parousia had to be set right, the timid had to be encouraged, sinners were to amend their ways. Second Thessalonians is another piece of pastoral counseling, a means of putting the young church on the right track.

TEXT

It is an indication of the generally good state of the text that in the eight chapters of these two epistles, UBS3 notes only twenty passages where variants warrant listing, and not one of these is sufficiently doubtful to warrant a D rating. This does not mean that there are no problems. There can be endless arguments about whether to read "gentle" or "babies" in 1 Thessalonians 2:7, where the MSS differ only as to whether to include or omit a Greek ν (the letter n). But the thrust of Paul's argument is not greatly affected, whichever we choose. So with other passages.

ADOPTION INTO THE CANON

The first epistle may be reflected in some passages in *1 Clement* and Ignatius, but this is not certain. What is clear is that it is included both in Marcion's canon[32]

---

[31]"His words went home; there is not the faintest echo of the *apologia* in the second epistle" (Frame, *Commentary*, p. 10).

[32]When Marcion is cited, we should bear in mind Kümmel's point that it is "very improbable that Marcion was the first to collect these epistles." According to Kümmel, "At least by the beginning of the

and in the Muratorian Fragment, and it is quoted by name in Ireneus. No doubts seem to have been raised by it. Second Thessalonians is attested by Polycarp, and possibly Ignatius and Justin. It is included in Marcion's canon and in the Muratorian Fragment. Ireneus quotes it by name.

Thus both letters were accepted in very early days; there seem to have been no doubts in the early church about their place in the canon.

THESSALONIANS IN RECENT STUDY

A feature of recent work on the Thessalonian correspondence is the attempt both to elucidate the *social history* of the context in which it was written and to erect *sociological models* to shed light on the church there. Writers such as R. Jewett,[33] A. J. Malherbe,[34] and W. A. Meeks[35] have stressed the importance of looking to the cultural background presupposed by these letters. Malherbe, for example, points to the importance of the "insula," common in the cities of the time: a row of shops faced the street, while owners, workmen, and their families lived above or behind the shops and formed a natural community in which the preachers could work and preach. He points to the pastoral care so clear in what Paul wrote and so absent from most of the letters that have come down to us from that day. Jewett looks at the political, social, economic, and religious conditions in the city. Such approaches shed new light on the correspondence and help us better to understand some of the things Paul wrote. In contrast, the swing toward imposing modern sociological models (Jewett devotes his ninth chapter to "The Millenarian Model") on first-century churches is frequently somewhat misleading. We have so little information from the first century, compared with the enormous statistical compilations where these modern models were first deployed. Sometimes these models become coersive, and subtle but important bits of information are ignored or deformed in the effort to make the model fit.

A few scholars have held that 1 Thessalonians is composite, sometimes seeing Paul as the author of fragments that have been pieced together and sometimes attributing parts of the letter to others than Paul. E. Best discusses,[36] for example, the views of K. Eckart[37] and W. Schmithals[38] but finds it difficult to accept such theories. "Paul was both too profound a thinker and too excitable a personality to be held within the categories of a fixed pattern of letter writing."[39] Once we accept the position that Paul cannot be bound to the conventionalities of the day for

---

second century, then, a collection of Pauline epistles was known in Asia Minor, and it is thoroughly probable that this canon already contained all of the ten epistles in Marcion's canon" (p. 338).

[33]R. Jewett, *The Thessalonian Correspondence* (Philadelphia: Fortress, 1986).

[34]A. J. Malherbe, *Paul and the Thessalonians* (Philadelphia: Fortress, 1987).

[35]W. A. Meeks, *The First Urban Christians* (New Haven, Conn.: Yale University Press, 1983).

[36]Best, *Commentary*, pp. 30–35. J. C. Hurd holds that "partition theories for 1 Thessalonians have seemed arbitrary and are certainly contradictory." He finds "somewhat more weight" behind the view that 2:13–16 is non-Pauline, but structural study "makes even this suggestion unlikely" ("Thessalonians, First Letter to," in *IDBSup*, p. 900).

[37]K. G. Eckart, "Der zweite echte Brief des Apostels Paulus an die Thessalonicher," *ZTK* 58 (1961): 30–44.

[38]W. Schmithals, "Die Thessalonicherbriefe als Briefkompositionen," in *Zeit und Geschichte*, Fs. Rudolf Bultmann, ed. E. Dinkler (Tübingen: Mohr, 1964), pp. 295–315.

[39]Best, *Commentary*, p. 35. W. Marxsen finds "the clear structure and inner consistency of the letter" an objection to the hypothesis of a combination of originally separate parts (p. 36).

letter writing, the problems alleged for 1 Thessalonians no longer appear so difficult. They certainly do not demand the hypothesis that the apostle wrote a number of letters that have been combined.

A good deal of attention has been given, especially in the United States, to the form of the letter and the function of the various parts that form criticism reveals. This aspect of Pauline studies is usually held to go back to the appearance in 1939 of P. Schubert's *Form and Function of the Pauline Thanksgiving*.[40] This leads to differences of opinion as to the centrality of the autobiographical part of 1 Thessalonians (chaps. 1–3) and the paraenetic section (chaps. 4–5). A number of writers have drawn attention to what is called the apostolic *parousia* (i.e. his presence, or his impending appearance)—a section that comes between the body of the letter and the exhortation, and that brings out something of the writer's desire to come to the recipients, the hindrance to this, perhaps the sending of an emissary, a seeking of divine approval, and some indication of the benefit that would result to the apostle, the recipients, or both. Thus H. Boers insists, "In 1 Thessalonians the purpose of the letter is disclosed by the inner connection of thanksgiving, apostolic apology and apostolic *parousia*."[41] A good deal of hard work has been put into such study of this letter, but with all respect to the participants, it is not easy to see that it has brought any significant increase in our understanding of the meaning of what Paul wrote.

A number of scholars have given attention in recent times to the problems connected with the authorship of 2 Thessalonians. As we saw earlier, there have been suggestions that one of Paul's assistants wrote the letter, that 2 Thessalonians really preceded 1 Thessalonians, or that the two were written for different audiences. Others have suggested that 2 Thessalonians was written to Philippi, or that it is made up of a number of fragments put together by a redactor. None of these positions has won wide acceptance. A number of scholars explore the view that 2 Thessalonians is pseudepigraphical. Sometimes they suggest that the aim was to replace 1 Thessalonians (some suggest this is in mind in 2 Thess. 2:2), which for various reasons displeased the pseudepigrapher.[42] Others think that the writer wrote out of esteem for Paul and tried in the spirit of the great apostle to add a message for his own day to what the apostle had written to meet the needs of an earlier day. But such hypotheses have not been notably more successful than the others we have noticed.

One problem is that no one seems to have come up with a convincing historical situation for a pseudepigraph. When was it written? To whom? For what purpose? The answers given to such questions satisfy few but the proponents of the hypotheses. Childs complains that "the two most recent attempts, by Trilling and Marxsen, to work out the pseudepigraphical hypothesis in the form of a commentary have demonstrated a new set of exegetical difficulties." He finds a problem in the situation envisaged in the letter; furthermore, "The effort to

---

[40]P. Schubert, *Form and Function of the Pauline Thanksgiving* (Berlin: Töpelmann, 1939).

[41]H. Boers, "The Form-Critical Study of Paul's Letters: 1 Thessalonians as a Case Study," *NTS* 22 (1975–76): 153.

[42]F. F. Bruce (*1 and 2 Thessalonians*, p. xl) examines the view of A. Lindemann ("Zum Abfassungszweck des Zweiten Thessalonicherbriefes," *ZNW* 68 [1977]: 35–47), who argues that an unknown writer who did not like the eschatology of 1 Thessalonians wrote 2 Thessalonians to replace it. The church did not go along with the rejection, but it accepted the pseudepigraph.

discover post-Pauline features, particularly to develop the idea of a portrait of Paul, seems often unconvincing and contrived." In Marxsen "a new form of psychologizing emerges."[43]

Childs goes on to raise the possibility of "II Thessalonians being written by someone under Paul's general direction, and signed by the apostle to legitimate the letter which was mediated in its actual composition by an associate."[44] He does not see the linking of Silvanus and Timothy with Paul in the opening as militating against this, and he proceeds to locate the letter "at a period considerably later than suggested by the traditional position." But when he comes to the situation that called forth this letter, he can say only that it was "a peculiar historical situation of one church, the exact details of which have been largely lost"[45]—which comes very close to the objection he has made to others who put forward the hypothesis of pseudepigraphy.[46]

Some have argued that these letters are rightly understood only when they are seen as dealing with the problem of Gnosticism. Marxsen argues this for 2 Thessalonians. He cites 2:2, "The day of the Lord has come, is present" and says, "The difficulty disappears if we recognize that here a Gnostic idea is being expressed apocalyptically." He goes on to say, "This provides us with a clue for understanding the whole situation."[47] But this is a very slender basis on which to erect a Gnostic superstructure: for centuries other explanations of the passage have been found quite satisfactory. Perhaps F. F. Bruce has it right when he says of this approach, "There is, in fact, nothing in the Thessalonian letters which requires explanation in terms of gnosticism; gnosticism can be read out of them only if it be first read into them."[48]

THE CONTRIBUTION OF THE THESSALONIAN EPISTLES

These letters make important contributions to our knowledge of eschatology. We learn from the first letter that there are no problems about believers who die before the parousia. When Jesus comes back, these people will be the first to rise from the dead, and they will come with him. Afterward believers who are alive at that time will be caught up to meet the Lord. "And so we will be with the Lord forever" (1 Thess. 4:17). No other part of Scripture is as explicit as this; however we understand the so-called rapture, it is this letter that tells us about it. And toward the end of every chapter in this letter there is a reference to some aspect of the second coming. But Paul does not encourage speculation about the date of the parousia. It will come unexpectedly (1 Thess. 5:1–2), and the important thing is

---

[43]Childs, p. 365.

[44]Ibid., p. 370.

[45]Ibid., p. 371.

[46]He has said of others, "It is far from obvious that the pseudepigraphical hypothesis has been successful in describing a suitable historical setting for the letter. The suggestions remain vague and hypothetical with little solid evidence on which to build" (Childs, p. 364). Surely this is a valid criticism to urge against his own view.

[47]Marxsen, p. 39. Marxsen's view involves the further assumption that the author of 2 Thessalonians was not Paul, on which Martin comments, "Marxsen's thesis falls down on the close linguistic connections between the two epistles" (2:168).

[48]Bruce, *1 and 2 Thessalonians*, p. xlvi. For an examination of the view of W. Schmithals that Paul is faced by a Gnosticism like that at Corinth, see Best, *Commentary*, pp. 16–19.

that "whether we are awake or asleep, we may live together with him" (1 Thess. 5:10).

In the same spirit, Paul in the second letter discourages becoming unsettled or alarmed by eschatological speculation (2 Thess. 2:2), and he goes on to point to events that will precede the parousia, notably the appearance of "the man of lawlessness" (2 Thess. 2:3). It may not be easy to combine these thoughts that the parousia will be totally unexpected when it occurs (like a thief in the night) and that it will be preceded by signs, but these two points occur elsewhere in the New Testament. What Paul laid down so clearly in these early writings is standard early Christian teaching. We should not overlook the further point that, while in other parts of the New Testament we have information about the Antichrist and about the evil that would coincide with his appearance, this is the only place where he is called "the man of lawlessness." Paul's account of what he will do and how he will be overthrown are also peculiar to the apostle. He is telling us something new, not repeating standard eschatological teaching.

Both letters give expression to the deep pastoral concern the apostle had for his converts and in so doing reveal to us something of the personality of the great apostle.[49] The Thessalonians were new Christians and found themselves the objects of some form of persecution for their faith. They thus needed guidance and encouragement, and Paul provided both. We should not fail to observe that this attitude is found so early in the history of Christianity. But with all his advice and his direct commands from time to time, Paul avoids paternalism. He had left Thessalonica shortly after the foundation of the church, and while he was ready to write letters that would help his converts, he trusted them to rely on the Lord, not on the apostle.

Paul had evidently been accused of a number of shortcomings: he had tricked the converts with his flatteries and the like, he was interested in their money rather than their spiritual progress, he had no love for them. In rebutting such accusations, Paul brings out for evangelists and pastors for all time important lessons about the kind of lives they should live (1 Thess. 2:1–10).

And he has important truths about the kind of lives people in Christian congregations should live. In a day like our own his teaching on sexual purity is important (1 Thess. 4:3–8). People today often think of loose sexual morality as something quite new and perhaps as a sign of modern enlightenment. They reason that Christianity was all right in earlier times when people lived more uprightly but that it is not adequate for a day like our own. We should bear in mind that the Roman world of the first century was very lax;[50] it has been well said that the only completely new virtue that Christians brought into the world was chastity. This very early letter points the way to deliverance from the subjection to lust that characterizes many people who think they are emancipated but who are in fact slaves to their own desires.

---

[49]"We are therefore given an insight into the nature of Paul the missionary. . . . Nowhere do we get a more human and lovable Paul" (Neil, *Thessalonians*, p. xxvii).

[50]W. E. H. Lecky summed up the Greek attitude: "A combination of circumstances had raised [the whole class of courtesans], in actual worth and in popular estimation, to an unexampled elevation, and an aversion to marriage became very general, and extra-matrimonial connections were formed with the most perfect frankness and publicity" (*History of European Morals from Augustus to Charlemagne*, 3d ed. 2 vols. [London: Longmans, Green, 1877], 2:297).

Paul is concerned that his converts live on all levels of life as "sons of the light and sons of the day" (1 Thess. 5:5). This means accepting high standards in all areas of life. In first-century Thessalonica this meant working for one's living (1 Thess. 4:11–12; 5:14). Apparently some of the converts were slow to learn this lesson, and in the second letter Paul has more to say about it (2 Thess. 3:6–12).

It is important to notice also that 2 Thessalonians makes it clear that we are all subject to the judgment of God. There is a graphic picture of what this means (2 Thess. 1:5–10); we must be clear that we are all responsible people. One day, Paul is saying, we must give account of ourselves to God, and that is no mere formality. Evil will be punished, and sinners should never think that they can get away with it. The blazing fire and the powerful angels of which Paul writes remind us of strength that will prevail in the end and the certainty of the final overthrow of evil.

Much of this is to be found elsewhere in the New Testament. But it is included here, since these letters are among the earliest Christian writings we have, possibly the earliest. We should not miss the revolutionary nature of their teaching, even if much has passed into the common stock of Christian knowledge.

BIBLIOGRAPHY

J. A. **Bailey**, "Who Wrote II Thessalonians?" *NTS* 25 (1978–79): 131–45; E. **Best**, *A Commentary on the First and Second Epistles to the Thessalonians* (London: Adam & Charles Black, 1977); H. **Boers**, "The Form-Critical Study of Paul's Letters: 1 Thessalonians as a Case Study," *NTS* 22 (1975–76): 140–58; F. F. **Bruce**, *1 & 2 Thessalonians*, WBC (Waco, Tex.: Word, 1982); idem, "St. Paul in Macedonia: 2. The Thessalonian Correspondence," *BJRL* 62 (1980): 328–45; Raymond F. **Collins**, "Apropos the Integrity of I Thes.," *EphThLov* 55 (1979): 67–106; L.-M. **Dewailly**, *La jeune église de Thessalonique: Les deux premières épîtres de Saint Paul* (Paris: du Cerf, 1963); Martin **Dibelius**, *A Fresh Approach to the New Testament and Early Christian Literature* (London: Ivor Nicholson & Watson, 1936); Karl Paul **Donfried**, "The Cults of Thessalonica and the Thessalonian Correspondence," *NTS* 31 (1985): 336–56; K. G. **Eckart**, "Der zweite echte Brief des Apostels Paulus an die Thessalonicher," *ZTK* 58 (1961): 30–44; E. Earle **Ellis**, "Paul and His Co-Workers," *NTS* 17 (1970–71): 437–52; J. E. **Frame**, *A Critical and Exegetical Commentary on the Epistles of St. Paul to the Thessalonians*, ICC (Edinburgh: T. & T. Clark, 1912); Charles H. **Giblin**, *The Threat to Faith: An Exegetical and Theological Re-examination of 2 Thessalonians 2*, AnBib 31 (Rome: Pontifical Biblical Institute, 1967); A. **Harnack**, "Das Problem des zweiten Thessalonicherbriefs," *SAB* 31 (1910): 560–78; W. **Hendriksen**, *Exposition of I and II Thessalonians* (Grand Rapids: Baker, 1955); R. F. **Hock**, "The Workshop as a Social Setting for Paul's Missionary Preaching," *CBQ* 41 (1979): 438–50; Robert **Jewett**, *The Thessalonian Correspondence* (Philadelphia: Fortress, 1986); Edwin A. **Judge**, "The Decrees of Caesar at Thessalonica," *RefThRev* 30 (1975): 1–7; Bruce N. **Kaye**, "Eschatology and Ethics in 1 and 2 Thessalonians," *NovT* 17 (1975): 47–57; W. E. H. **Lecky**, *History of European Morals from Augustus to Charlemagne*, 3d ed. 2 vols. (London: Longmans, Green, 1877); A. **Lindemann**, "Zum Abfassunszweck des Zweiten Thessalonicher-briefes," *ZNW* 68 (1977): 35–47; R. N. **Longenecker**, "The Nature of Paul's Early Eschatology," *NTS* 31 (1985): 85–95; idem, "On the Form, Function, and

Authority of the New Testament Letters," in *Scripture and Truth*, ed. D. A. Carson and John D. Woodbridge (Grand Rapids: Zondervan, 1983), pp. 101– 14; A. **Malherbe**, *Paul and the Thessalonians* (Philadelphia: Fortress, 1987); T. W. **Manson**, *Studies in the Gospels and Epistles* (Manchester: Manchester University Press, 1962); I. Howard **Marshall**, *1 and 2 Thessalonians* (Grand Rapids: Eerdmans, 1983); C. L. **Mearns**, "Early Eschatological Development in Paul: The Evidence of I and II Thessalonians," *NTS* 27 (1980–81): 137–57; Wayne **Meeks**, *The First Urban Christians* (New Haven, Conn.: Yale University Press, 1983); Leon **Morris**, "ἄπαξ καὶ δίς," *NovT* 1 (1956): 205–8; idem, *The First and Second Epistles to the Thessalonians*, NICNT (Grand Rapids: Eerdmans, 1959); B. Rigaux, *Les épîtres aux Thessaloniciens* (Paris: Gabalda, 1956); W. **Schmithals**, "Die Thessalonicherbriefe als Briefkompositionen," in *Zeit und Geschichte*, *Fs*. R. Bultmann, ed. E. Dinkler (Tübingen: Mohr, 1964), pp. 295–315; P. **Schubert**, *Form and Function of the Pauline Thanksgiving* (Berlin: Töpelmann, 1939); R. V. G. **Tasker**, *The Greek New Testament* (Oxford: Oxford University Press and Cambridge University Press, 1964).

15

the pastoral epistles

THEIR RELATIONSHIP TO OTHER PAULINE EPISTLES

The two epistles to Timothy and that to Titus are usually classed together under the title "Pastoral Epistles," a title that was apparently given to them by D. N. Berdot in 1703 and followed by Paul Anton in 1726.[1] The term is almost universally used in modern discussions. It is objected that the title is not completely appropriate because the letters are not taken up with pastoral duties. However, as they are directed to people with pastoral responsibility and with the task of appointing pastors, we should not cavil at the term. The three letters form a unit in that they are the only New Testament letters addressed to individuals with such responsibilities (Philemon is addressed to an individual, but not one in a position like that of Timothy or Titus).

There is, however, nothing to indicate that they were written at the same time or from the same place, or that the author intended them to be studied together. They are almost routinely treated as a group in modern studies, and it is necessary to consider the three together if we are to follow modern writing. But there are differences among them that may be important. For example, while 1 Timothy has quite a lot about the ministry of the church, 2 Timothy has practically nothing and Titus very little. False teaching is being opposed in all three letters, and it is usual to treat it as though it were the same in all cases,[2] but we need to ask if it really is. From another angle, Johnson points out that the Thessalonian correspondence might well look different if we decided to isolate these letters from all the other Pauline writings and treat them as a group on their own. He puts the other side of the coin in this way: "If Titus is read with other travel letters, or 2 Timothy with other captivity letters, their strangeness is greatly diminished."[3] In discussing problems that arise from these three writings, we should bear in

---

[1]So Donald Guthrie, *The Pastoral Epistles* (London: Tyndale, 1957), p. 11.

[2]This view is part of a sustained effort in recent scholarship to construct a definite and believable background to all three Pastoral epistles, taken together. It is forcefully presented (though from very different perspectives) by, among others, David C. Verner, *The Household of God: The Social World of the Pastoral Epistles*, SBLDS 71 (Chico, Calif.: SP, 1983); Gordon D. Fee, *1 and 2 Timothy, Titus*, GNC (San Francisco: Harper & Row, 1984); and Philip Towner, *The Goal of Our Instruction: The Structure of Theology and Ethics in the Pastoral Epistles*, JSNTSupp 34 (Sheffield: Sheffield Academic Press, 1989).

[3]Johnson, p. 382.

mind that things would look a lot different if we studied each of them by itself or in a different grouping.

Contemporary critical orthodoxy insists that the Pastorals were all written by someone other than Paul and at a time considerably later than that of the apostle. Considerations of style, vocabulary, attention to church order, and attitude to orthodoxy and to heretical teachings are some of the things that lead most scholars to hold that the letters are pseudonymous and that they do not fit into Paul's world. Despite all their differences, there are many links with Paul's teaching, so it is generally held that they come from a convinced Paulinist. The thought is that the writer is addressing the problems of his own day as one who has drunk deeply from the Pauline well. He is trying to say to the people of his own day what he thought Paul would have said, had he been confronted by the situation of that day. The following considerations are important.

Vocabulary

A strong argument is produced from the vocabulary differences between the three Pastoral epistles and the ten Pauline epistles. P. N. Harrison built on the work of scholars who preceded him and compiled some impressive statistics.[4] He pointed out that the three Pastorals make use of 902 words, of which 54 are proper names. Of the remaining 848 words, 306 do not occur in the other ten Pauline letters (more than a third of the total). Of the 306, no fewer than 175 occur nowhere else in the New Testament. The argument is then developed in two ways.

First, it is pointed out that this leaves 542 words shared by the Pauline letters and the Pastorals, of which no more than 50 are characteristic Pauline words in the sense that they are not used by other writers in the New Testament. Of the 492 words that are found in all three bodies—the Pastorals, the rest of Paul, and the rest of the New Testament—there are, of course, the basic words without which it would be impossible to write at all, and words that every Christian writer would necessarily use (e.g., "brother," "love," "faith"). Again, some words have different meanings from book to book. Paul, for example, uses ἀντέχομαι (antechomai) with the sense "to support," "to aid" (1 Thess. 5:14), the Pastorals with the meaning "to hold fast" (Titus 1:9); κοινός (koinos) means "Levitically unclean" in Paul (Rom. 14:14) and "common" (as in "the common faith") in the Pastorals (Titus 1:4).

Second, it is argued that many of the words in question are found in the apostolic fathers and the Apologists in the early second century. Of the 306 words in the Pastorals that are not in the Pauline Epistles, 211 are found in these second-century writings.[5] This kind of reasoning leads many to the conclusion that the author of the Pastorals was not Paul but probably a writer living in the early

---

[4]P. N. Harrison, *The Problem of the Pastoral Epistles* (London: Oxford University Press, 1921), pp. 20ff. Harrison's argument is refined and strengthened by K. Grayston and G. Herdan, who use an improved statistical method ("The Authorship of the Pastorals in the Light of Statistical Studies," *NTS* 6 [1959–60]: 1–15). More recently, A. Q. Morton and some of his colleagues have deployed statistical analyses of such features as the closing word in Pauline sentences, the length of sentences, the spread of different types of conjunction, and the like. This work is admirably assessed by Anthony Kenny, *A Stylometric Study of the New Testament* (Oxford: Clarendon, 1986).

[5]Harrison, *Problem*, p. 70.

second century. It is held to be unreasonable to think that in his old age Paul would suddenly produce a wealth of new words, words moreover that are found in a later period.

The argument sounds impressive, but it is not as convincing as it seems at first sight. Those who put it forward do not usually notice, for example, that most of the words shared by the Pastorals and the second-century writers are also found in other writings prior to A.D. 50.[6] It cannot be argued that Paul would not have known them, nor can it be argued that Paul's total vocabulary is the number of words in the ten letters (2,177 words). It is not necessary to argue that Paul produced hundreds of new words in his old age, for if he could use 2,177 words, there is no reason for supposing that he could not use another 306 words, most of which are known to have been current in his day. That some of the words are used with different meanings signifies no more than that the contexts are different. Paul uses words with different meanings in different contexts in the ten letters.

It is misleading simply to say that the Pastorals have 306 words that do not occur in the ten Paulines. On Harrison's own figures, of the 306 there are 127 that occur in 1 Timothy alone, 81 in 2 Timothy alone, and 45 in Titus alone.[7] This means that the vast majority are found in only one of the Pastorals and that the three differ from one another as much as (or more than) they differ from Paul. Are we to say that there were three pseudonymous writers? The statistics constitute no impressive argument for a single author. Or, to put the argument in a different way, if the figures show that the three Pastorals were written by one author, they also show that that author may well have been Paul.

This is to be borne in mind when related arguments are put forward. For example, it is pointed out that there are no more than half a dozen references to the Holy Spirit in the Pastorals, whereas Paul refers to him ninety times. This raises the question whether there are places in these letters where Paul must speak of the Spirit. He refers to him on those six occasions when it was appropriate, and we are not in a position to say that the Paul of the ten letters would have referred to him more often. We must be on our guard against taking up a position of omniscience about what went on in Paul's mind.

Style

P. N. Harrison makes a good deal of the fact that 112 particles, prepositions, and pronouns appear in the ten but not in the three.[8] He sees it as unlikely that "within a very few years we should find the same writer producing three epistles without once happening to use a single word in all that list—*one or other of which has hitherto appeared on the average nine times to every page that Paul ever wrote.*"[9] Once again he has produced what seems to be a very cogent argument. But Guthrie points out that he has not taken into consideration all the evidence. There

---

[6]So Donald Guthrie (*The Pastoral Epistles and the Mind of Paul* [London: Tyndale, 1956], p. 9), citing among others F. R. M. Hitchcock, "Tests for the Pastorals," *JTS* 30 (1928–29): 272–79; idem, "Philo and the Pastorals," *Hermatheua* 56 (1940): 113–35.

[7]Harrison, *Problem*, pp. 137–39. There are 75 words in 1 Timothy and not elsewhere in the New Testament, plus 52 in 1 Timothy and the non-Pauline New Testament books. For 2 Timothy the figures are 48 + 33 and for Titus 30 + 15.

[8]Harrison, *Problem*, pp. 36–37.

[9]Ibid., p. 35 (Harrison's italics).

are another 93 particles, prepositions, and pronouns, all but 1 appearing in the Pastorals, and all but 7 in Paul. He adds these to Harrison's list and points out that of the 205 there are 92 occurrences in the Pastorals, which compares favorably with the 131 occurrences in Romans, 113 in 2 Corinthians, 86 in Philippians, and so forth. He concludes that "Dr. Harrison's deductions from the connective tissue would seem to be invalid."[10]

On another level, the argument from style may be put this way: "One notes also that the dramatic vivacity of Pauline argumentation, with its emotional outbursts, its dialogue form of thought, its introduction of real or imaginary opponents and objections, and the use of metaphor and image, is replaced by a certain heaviness and repetitiousness of style."[11] Not everyone would put it in quite this way, but Beker draws attention to a very real difference. He has not, however, disposed of the fact that people use somewhat different styles in different circumstances. No one writes a business letter, for example, in the same style as a love letter. The question is whether the difference in style between the Pastorals and the ten Pauline letters is greater than the difference that might legitimately be expected between private letters to trusted fellow workers and public letters to churches usually addressing specific difficulties. So far this has not been shown. The arguments adduced have simply asserted either that Paul would not find it necessary to change style in moving from one type of letter to another or that Paul could not have written in the humdrum style of the Pastorals. But who has proven what the real Paul was capable of?[12]

Historical Problems

Many scholars draw attention to the difficulty of fitting the situations envisaged in the Pastorals into what we learn of the life of Paul from Acts and the Pauline letters. It is argued that this is quite impossible, and it is therefore suggested that the author of these letters has manufactured allusions that would give the impression of a historical setting. To this there are two rejoinders. One is that Acts finishes with Paul in prison in Rome, but with reasonable prospects of being released. Festus thought that Paul "had done nothing deserving of death" (Acts 25:25), while Agrippa held there was no case against him and that, had he not appealed to Caesar, he could have been freed (Acts 26:32). Even when he was in Rome, "Paul was allowed to live by himself, with a soldier to guard him" (Acts 28:16); he "stayed there in his own rented house and welcomed all who came to see him" (Acts 28:30); he was free enough to be able to summon Jewish leaders and hold a meeting with them. This does not look like the preliminary to an

---

[10]Guthrie, *The Pastoral Epistles and the Mind of Paul*, p. 13.

[11]J. C. Beker, "Pastoral Letters" in *IDB*, 3:670.

[12]It is, of course, possible that some of the style may be due to a secretary. C. F. D. Moule suggests "that Luke wrote all three Pastoral epistles. But he wrote them during Paul's lifetime, at Paul's behest, and, in part (but only in part), at Paul's dictation" ("The Problem of the Pastoral Epistles: A Reappraisal," *BJRL* 47 [1965]: 434). Harrison is another to favor the use of Luke as secretary, and he lists linguistic features common to Luke and the Pastorals (p. 363). The strength of this position is the very large number of words in the Pastorals that are found elsewhere in the New Testament only in Luke. See the list in S. G. Wilson, *Luke and the Pastoral Epistles* (London: SPCK, 1979), pp. 5–11. Wilson thinks that these epistles may have been planned as the third volume of a trilogy of which Luke-Acts were the first two volumes (pp. 139–40).

execution. There is nothing improbable about Paul being set at liberty and engaging in further activities of the sort envisaged in the Pastorals. The other possibility arises from the fact that we know so little of what Paul did during the years of his ministry. When did he undergo his frequent imprisonments, his five beatings at the hands of the Jews, his three shipwrecks, and the other sufferings that he mentions once only (2 Cor. 11:23–27)? One may say, "I cannot see how to fit the incidents mentioned in the Pastorals into Paul's earlier life," but one may not say, "Those incidents *cannot* be fitted into Paul's earlier life." We simply do not have enough information. Especially if we do not take the Pastorals as a unit but consider the letters individually, there is no insuperable difficulty.[13]

We should not overlook the difficulty of fitting the personal reminiscences in the Pastorals into the framework envisaged by those who see the letters as pseudonymous. Why then should we read of Paul's cloak and his scrolls (2 Tim. 4:13)? Or of his leaving Timothy in Ephesus when he went to Macedonia (1 Tim. 1:3)? Of his hope to come to Timothy soon but with no certainty that he would not be delayed (1 Tim. 3:14–15)? What is the point of saying that Onesiphorus searched for Paul in Rome and found him (2 Tim. 1:16–17)? Or of his instruction to Titus to help Zenas the lawyer and Apollos (Titus 3:13)? It is not easy to see what to make of these and other such references on the theory that the letters come from the second century and from an author who did not know Paul's situation. Surely any such writer would fit his reminiscences into what is known of Paul's life. No convincing reason has been suggested for the manufacture of hypothetical situations of this nature. Moreover, all such references in all three of these letters bear the stamp of historical particularity. There is nothing like the legendary touches that are such a feature of, say, the second-century *Acts of Paul*. The Pastorals are much more akin to the accepted letters of Paul than they are to the known pseudonymous documents that circulated in the early church.

The False Teachers

It is usually assumed that the same false teaching is opposed in all three letters. This may or may not be the case, but some of it at any rate certainly included a strong Jewish element. There are references to "teachers of the law" (1 Tim. 1:7), "the circumcision group" (Titus 1:10), "Jewish myths" (Titus 1:14), and "arguments and quarrels about the law" (Titus 3:9). There is a warning against "what is falsely called knowledge" (1 Tim. 6:20), which along with references to "myths and endless genealogies" (1 Tim. 1:4; cf. 4:7; Titus 3:9) is often taken to refer to Gnostic systems. This is supported by passages mentioning ascetic practices (e.g., 1 Tim. 4:3). But full-blown Gnosticism belongs to a time well into the second century, and these letters do not belong there. There is nothing in the way of false teaching as described in these letters that does not fit into what is

---

[13]A number of writers have suggested ways in which in the information in the Pastorals can be fitted into what we know of Paul's movements from other sources. See e.g., J. A. T. Robinson, *Redating the New Testament* (Philadelphia: Westminster, 1976), pp. 67–85, and the literature there cited. See esp. C. Spicq, *Les épîtres Pastorales*, 4th ed., 2 vols. (Paris: Gabalda, 1969), and S. de Lestapis, *L'énigme des Pastorales de Saint Paul* (Paris: Gabalda, 1976).

known during the time of Paul's ministry.[14] Though some will continue to see the heresy as belonging to the second century, there are no real grounds for saying that it could not have arisen while Paul was actively engaged in his life's work.

The Ecclesiastical Organization

Many scholars believe that the understanding of church life that is presupposed in these letters could not have appeared during Paul's lifetime. Specifically they see a strongly organized church with an ordained ministry.

We should first notice that Paul seems to have had some interest in the ministry, for he and Barnabas appointed elders in the churches they had founded (Acts 14:23), and again he writes to the bishops and deacons at Philippi as well as to the saints there (Phil. 1:1).

Second, to find an interest in the ministry in the Pastorals we must exclude 2 Timothy, for in that letter there is nothing about an ordained ministry or any form of church organization. Paul does speak of God's χάρισμα (*charisma*) which is in Timothy through the laying on of his hands (2 Tim. 1:6), but this may well be the equivalent of the later confirmation rather than of ordination (it leads on to thoughts of "power, of love and of self-discipline," which are just as relevant to the Christian life as to the Christian ministry). In Titus there is a direction to "appoint elders in every town" (Titus 1:5) and an indication of the kind of people who should be made elder or bishop (the two terms appear to denote the sam office). It is in 1 Timothy that we get any considerable teaching about the ministry. Here we find mention of the qualities that are to be sought in bishops and deacons (chap. 3) and an indication that elders are honored persons, to be treated with respect and to be paid for their work (5:17–20). The elder seems clearly to be equated with the bishop in Titus 1:5–7, and there is nothing in the other two letters to indicate any other system. Despite the inferences drawn by some, there is really nothing in any of the Pastorals that demands any more organization than the "bishops [NIV, overseers] and deacons" of Philippians 1:1. Against a second-century date is the writer's concentration on the qualities looked for in elders and deacons. By the second century these would surely have been well known, whereas it would have been useful to have them spelled out in the days of Paul. There is also a "list of widows" (1 Tim. 5:9), but it is not clear what this means (in any case, widows seem to have had a special place from the beginning [Acts 6:1]). Clearly none of this amounts to much in the way of organization, certainly to nothing more than can have appeared in the church in comparatively early days.[15]

Theology

Many contend that these three letters contain quite a number of Hellenistic terms for the salvation event, terms that Paul would not have used. Thus we read

---

[14]Kümmel says that the heresy opposed in these letters is "quite conceivable in the lifetime of Paul" (p. 267)

[15]Bo Reicke draws attention to the *mebaqqer* of the Qumran scrolls, who exercised superintendency functions not unlike those of the Christian bishop. This is "not a question of taking over a specific office or particular functions, but rather an example of similar types of internal development" (in *The Scrolls and the New Testament*, ed. Krister Stendahl [London: SCM, 1958], p. 155). The *mebaqqer* shows that in Jewish circles a functionary like the bishop could appear quite early. It is nonsense to say it *demands* a late date.

of "the appearing of our Savior, Jesus Christ, who has destroyed death and has brought life and immortality to light through the gospel" (2 Tim. 1:10); there is "one mediator between God and men" (1 Tim. 2:5); "the grace of God that brings salvation has appeared to all men" (Titus 2:11). These and other such expressions, however, often incorporate Pauline terms—perhaps used in a different way, but still Pauline. And there are many terms used as Paul uses them, such as Christ's coming to save sinners (1 Tim. 1:15); salvation because of divine mercy, not our works (Titus 3:5); the importance of faith in Christ (1 Tim. 3:13), of election (Titus 1:1), and of grace (2 Tim. 1:9). The discussion along these lines is inconclusive. Those who think of an author other than Paul are impressed by the number of new terms and the new uses of old ones; those who think Paul wrote the letters stress the number of common terms and see the new ones and new uses as no more than the legitimate variation in use that characterizes anyone writing in a variety of situations.

The problem may be illustrated by considering these words: "We know that the law is good if one uses it properly. We also know that the law is made not for the righteous but for lawbreakers and rebels" (1 Tim. 1:8–9). On this passage Moule comments, "It is astonishing that anyone could seriously attribute to Paul at any stage of his life the definition there offered of wherein the goodness of the law lies,"[16] while Zahn cites the same passage in support of Pauline authorship and goes on to speak of "the bold statement (1 Tim. i.9) that for the just man, and consequently for the sinner who has been made righteous by the mercy of the Saviour (1 Tim. i.13–16), there is no law."[17] When such diverse pronouncements can be made on the same passage, clearly it does not tell conclusively against Pauline authorship. The same may be said at many points. While some statements are confidently urged by objectors as proving that Paul could not have been the author, they are all accepted by others as things that Paul would have said.

But it is not only a matter of terminology. Many suggest that the entire piety of the Pastorals is different. There is a demand for "godliness" ($\varepsilon\dot{v}\sigma\acute{\varepsilon}\beta\varepsilon\iota\alpha$ [eusebeia], 1 Tim. 2:2 etc.), correct teaching (1 Tim. 6:3), and, above all, "sound doctrine" (2 Tim. 4:3). Kümmel speaks of "this rational, ethicized description of the Christian life and the Christian demand" and cites M. Dibelius, who "called this Christianity which is settling down in the world and which speaks a strongly Hellenistic language a 'bourgeois' Christianity," and Bultmann for the view that it is "a somewhat faded Paulinism."[18] There is no denying that there is a difference of emphasis in these letters, but the question is whether such writers as these are exaggerating. Granted that there is something of a change of pace, can it be seriously denied that Paul looked for such things as godliness (2 Cor. 1:12), correct teaching (Rom. 6:17), and sound doctrine (see his emphasis on knowledge, his repeated "I would not have you ignorant," and his fierce denunciations of false teaching)? Again we reach an impasse. To some the general

---

[16]Moule, "Problem," p. 432.

[17]Zahn 2:121. Zahn also comments, "Nowhere in these Epistles do we find sentences that sound so 'un-Pauline' as 1 Cor. vii.19, and which can be so readily mistaken as a fusion of genuine Pauline teaching with its opposite, as Gal. v.6" (ibid.).

[18]Kümmel, p. 270. This unimaginative view of the contents has been drawn into an argument for the authenticity of these letters. Would someone imaginative enough to produce pseudonymous letters produce this kind of writing?

tone of the Pastorals seems quite incompatible with that of the ten Paulines; to others it is no more than a development, appropriate enough in different circumstances.[19]

Some parts of these letters are very Pauline, and some scholars suggest that the author has made use of authentic fragments originally written by Paul. P. N. Harrison, for example, finds five such fragments,[20] but he has not won universal support for the hypothesis. No one seems to have been able to give a convincing reason for the fragments being preserved. (What happened to the letters of which they were parts? How did only parts survive?) Nor is it clear why the author should have inserted the fragments in the scattered places suggested. There is the further difficulty that the main reason for the identification of the fragments is that they fit in with what we know about some part of the life of Paul—but is that a sufficient criterion? Is there any reason why the particular epistle in which they occur should not have been written as a whole at that time? Or that the fragments should not fit into another part of Paul's life? It cannot be said that the hypothesis has a great deal to commend it. We should think of the entire corpus as coming from Paul or hold it all to be pseudonymous.

There is a problem about the view that these letters are pseudonymous that is rarely faced. According to Childs, "The purpose served by the Pastorals is strongly biased by its initial literary classification as pseudepigraphical. Its meaning cannot be obtained from the verbal sense of the text, but must be derived from a reconstruction of the author's 'real' intentions which have been purposely concealed. . . . The kerygmatic witness of the text is, thereby, rendered mute, and its interpretation is made dependent on other external forces which are set in a causal relationship."[21] There is no agreement on the exact situation of the pseudonymous author, no certainty about the problems he faced or the time he faced them or the ecclesiastical situation out of which he faced them. How then can we discover the real meaning of what he says?

Some of what is said seems unlikely from the pen of an admirer of Paul. Would such a person refer to Paul as the chief of sinners (1 Tim. 1:15)? Would he dredge up, many years after Paul's death, the fact that he had been "a persecutor and a violent man" (1 Tim. 1:13)? And we may wonder whether such a person would remind people that at a critical hour there was nobody who stood by the great apostle (2 Tim. 4:16). All the historical references in these letters ring true as statements coming from the life of Paul, but the same cannot be said of a date quite a long time after he had died.[22]

---

[19]This raises the whole question of "early catholicism," for which see chap. 4, above, the section "Luke in Recent Study." See also Moisés Silva, "The Place of Historical Reconstruction in New Testament Criticism," in *Hermeneutics, Authority, and Canon*, ed. D. A. Carson and John D. Woodbridge (Grand Rapids: Zondervan, 1986), pp. 105–33, 383–88.

[20]Harrison, *Problem*, pp. 115–27. Harrison later modified his theory to include only three fragments. Others have looked for genuine pieces of Pauline writing embedded in the letters. But none of them seems to agree with any of the others, which makes the whole endeavor seems suspect and subjective.

[21]Childs, pp. 382–83. It should be added that Childs is very sympathetic toward a pseudonymous understanding of these letters.

[22]From another point of view, Johnson comments, "Even those who like myself are not absolutely convinced that they come directly from Paul, think some of the reasons given for assigning their composition to a pseudepigrapher unconvincing" (p. 381) Johnson also points to the differences between the letters as a problem. "Why would three such letters be produced, each of which was

It is assumed by those who deny the Pauline authorship of the Pastoral Epistles that pseudonymous epistles were accepted as quite natural among the early Christian community. This view has been aided by the fact that pseudonymous writings of other sorts (apocalypses, gospels, acts) were certainly widely accepted in the first century. But the subject is not simple, so it is worth taking a little time to look at the whole issue of pseudonymous writings.

PSEUDONYMITY

In antiquity it was not uncommon for writings to appear bearing a claim to have been written by a given author but commonly understood not to be from that author. Apocalyptic writings, for example, are often said to have been written by Enoch or Moses or some other great person from antiquity. It is not known whether the first readers would have accepted the stated authorship as accurate or not, but later readers have not accepted them as coming from the great names they bear.[23] Writings other than apocalyptic were published under assumed names, among the Greeks and Romans as well as among the Jews and the Christians.

One noteworthy fact among the Jews and the Christians is the rarity of pseudepigraphic *letters*. Writers might claim great names as having been responsible for other kinds of literature, but only two pseudonymous letters have come down to us from Jewish sources, namely, the *Epistle of Jeremy* and the *Letter of Aristeas*, neither of which is really a letter. The former is a little sermon, and the latter an account of the translation of the Old Testament into Greek. There is no epistle among the canonical writings of the Old Testament, so there was no authoritative precedent to follow. A false claim to writing a letter would probably be easier to detect than, say, a false claim to writing an apocalypse. Whatever the reason, pseudepigraphic letters among the Jews are extremely rare.

Nor are they common among the Christians. If we may start with the New Testament itself, we find Paul instructing the Thessalonians to give no credence to any "prophecy, report or letter supposed to have come from us (2 Thess. 2:2) and telling them of "the distinguishing mark" in all his letters (2 Thess. 3:17). This suggests that pseudonymous letters were not entirely unknown; on the other hand, it certainly shows that the apostle did not agree with the practice of pseudonymity—at least in the case where someone was writing a letter in *his* name! He does not regard this as acceptable; in principle, he repudiates the practice, regarding pseudonymity as something to be guarded against, for he gives his readers a token whereby they might know which writings come from him and which make a false claim.

Some scholars give the impression that letters claiming to have been written by one person but actually written by another were in common circulation among adherents of the new faith. But this is not so. The Christians produced

---

directed to a situation that was internally consistent yet very difficult to make consistent with the situations the other two were directed to? Here we would have a forger able subtly to create the verisimilitude of an established church (in Ephesus) and a new church (in Crete), together with the appropriate sort of directions to each, and yet not able to imitate more convincingly the Pauline samples available to him" (pp. 388–89).

[23]As far as apocalyptic writings are concerned, the problem of pseudonymity is discussed in Leon Morris, *Apocalyptic*, 2d ed. (Grand Rapids: Eerdmans, 1973), pp. 51–54.

pseudonymous forms of other types of literature, such as gospels and acts, but very few epistles. M. R. James cites six only, mostly ranging from the fourth to the thirteenth century, and none that he dates anywhere near New Testament times. We can only conjecture the reasons for the rarity of epistles when there are so many examples of gospels, acts, and apocalypses. Perhaps the letter was a more personal and intimate writing. One might produce, for example, an apocalypse, sincerely written in the style one imagines some great person from the past would use and publish it in his name in order to give him honor. But to write a letter as coming from him might seem to claim too close an intimacy, too sure a knowledge of him. James suggests as a reason that "the Epistle was on the whole too serious an effort for the forger, more liable to detection, perhaps, as a fraud, and not so likely to gain the desired popularity as a narrative or an Apocalypse."[24] Whether any of these is the correct reason or not, we should not approach the New Testament epistles as though it were common for the early Christians to write letters in a name not their own. As far as our knowledge goes, there is not one such letter emanating from the Christians from anywhere near the New Testament period, and precious few even from later times. It may be correct that New Testament Christians commonly wrote letters in names not their own (an opinion that scholars routinely perpetuate), but we should be clear that it flies in the face of all the evidence we have about the way letters were written in first-century Jewish and Christian communities.[25] It is often said that the recipients of pseudepigraphic letters recognized the genre and were well aware that the letters they were reading did not come from Paul or Peter or some other putative author. But for this, too, there is no evidence.

The early Christians appear to have had no great urge to attach apostolic names to the writings they valued. More than half of the New Testament consists of books that do not bear the names of their authors (the four gospels, Acts, Hebrews, 1 John; even "the elder" of 2 and 3 John is not very explicit). Apparently the truth in the documents and the evidence that the Holy Spirit was at work in the people who wrote them carried conviction, and the attachment of apostolic names was not judged necessary. The onus is on upholders of theories of pseudonymous authorship to explain why this strong tradition of anonymity was discarded in favor, not of authors attaching their own names to what they wrote (as Paul did), but of other people's names.

The way the church dealt with those few spurious letters of which we have knowledge does not favor the view that pseudonymity was regarded as acceptable. We learn of one comparatively early spurious letter from the fact that it is quoted in the apocryphal *Acts of Paul*. As this book is referred to by Tertullian, it must have been written about the middle of the second century (James proposes c. A.D. 160). Among other things this *Acts* contains a letter Paul was supposed to have written to the church at Corinth ("3 Corinthians"), a letter that was so highly esteemed in parts of the church that for a time it was included in the canon of the Syrian and Armenian churches, evidently under the impression that Paul had

---

[24]M. R. James, *The Apocryphal New Testament* (Oxford: Clarendon, 1926), p. 476. He mentions also two other letters apparently not worth printing.

[25]Philip Carrington observes, "There seems to be no evidence at all that such missives were freely composed in the names of contemporary persons who had recently died" (*The Early Christian Church*, 2 vols. [Cambridge: Cambridge University Press, 1957], 1:259; cited also in Harrison, p. 332).

written it. Elsewhere, however, it was recognized that the writing was pseudonymous, and it was for that reason rejected; its edifying content was not enough to secure its recognition. Tertullian speaks of writings "which wrongly go under Paul's name" and tells us that "in Asia, the presbyter who composed that writing, as if he were augmenting Paul's fame from his own store, after being convicted, and confessing that he had done it from love of Paul, was removed from his office."[26] It did not matter that the work was seen as orthodox and edifying. It did not matter that it was done "from love of Paul." It claimed to have been written by Paul and was not. Its author was therefore a guilty man, and he was deposed from his honorable office.

Another spurious epistle ascribed to Paul is the *Epistle to the Laodiceans* (clearly an attempt to fill the vacuum created by the loss of the letter mentioned in Col. 4:16).[27] It is little more than a "worthless patching together of Pauline passages and phrases, mainly from the Epistle to the Philippians."[28] Its only value is that it is one of such a small number of letters circulating among Christians under a false name. There is no doubt that its author had a high regard for Paul. But there is also no doubt either that, although the letter was orthodox, it was not accepted by the Christian church. That church simply did not accept spurious letters.

The Muratorian Canon speaks of the letter to the Laodiceans with which it links one to the Alexandrians, "both forged in Paul's name." The document goes on to say that such "cannot be received into the Catholic Church; for it is not fitting that gall be mixed with honey."[29] This accords with what we have seen from other sources: pseudonymous letters were not received.

Mention should be made of Serapion, bishop of Antioch toward the end of the second century. He discovered that the *Gospel of Peter* was in use in the church at Rhossus, and although he seems not to have known the book, he at first allowed the church to continue to read it. When he later read the book and found that it was promoting heresy, he forbade its use. Clearly his permission to use it was predicated on the view that it was harmless, not that it was authoritative. He wrote, "For our part, brethren, we receive both Peter and the other apostles as Christ, but the writings which falsely bear their names we reject, as men of experience, knowing that such were not handed down to us."[30] There is, of course, a further difference in that we are now dealing with a spurious gospel, not a spurious epistle. But it is important to notice that Serapion made a sharp distinction between the apostolic writings he received wholeheartedly ("as Christ") and those that "falsely bear their names." The latter, if harmless, might be used, but they were not canonical. They had no place among the authoritative Scriptures.

Those who maintain that one or several of the New Testament epistles are pseudonymous should take a closer look at the evidence than they usually do. We do not say that it was impossible for New Testament Christians to use the

---

[26]Tertullian, *On Baptism*, 17.

[27]The text is given in Hennecke 2:131–32.

[28]Knopf-Krüger, cited in Hennecke 2:129.

[29]Cited from J. Stevenson, *A New Eusebius* (London: SPCK, 1963), p. 146. These letters are both heretical, which may be in mind in the comparison between gall and honey, but "forged" applies strictly to pseudepigraphy, and the canon roundly condemns it.

[30]Cited from Eusebius, *H.E.* 6.12.3.

pseudepigraphic method. We can easily imagine an early Christian feeling so sure he knew what Paul or Peter would have said in a given situation that he would write some piece, claiming the apostle's name for what he had himself composed. We should surely sympathize with the second-century presbyter who composed a "Pauline" writing "from love of Paul" and find little difficulty in imagining an earlier example of the same kind of thinking. The difficulty is not the idea of pseudonymity but the lack of *evidence* that the New Testament Christians gave any countenance to the idea. Nowhere is evidence cited that any member of the New Testament church accepted the idea that a pious believer could write something in the name of an apostle and expect the writing to be welcomed. The contrary, as we have seen, is often maintained. For example, in his standard textbook P. N. Harrison says that the pseudo-Paul who wrote the Pastorals "was not conscious of misrepresenting the Apostle in any way; he was not consciously deceiving anybody; it is not, indeed, necessary to suppose that he did deceive anybody. It seems far more probable that those to whom, in the first instance, he showed the result of his efforts, must have been perfectly well aware of what he had done."[31] But Harrison produces no evidence for this alleged practice; he simply says that it was so. This is scarcely good enough. The onus is on those who uphold the idea that the writing of pseudonymous letters was an accepted practice among the early Christians to produce some evidence for their view. On the contrary, the evidence we have is that every time such a writing could be identified with any certainty, it was rejected.

Sufficient attention is not given to this point in the recent study by David G. Meade.[32] Meade sees pseudonymity as rooted in Jewish religion, and he finds a series of pseudonymous writings associated with Isaiah, Solomon, and others. For him the Pastorals are simply the normal development of the tradition. Paul was a great teacher, and those who followed him carried on and developed the tradition that emanated from him.[33] Meade sees the process as "not mere reproduction, but an attempt to reinterpret a core tradition for a new, and often different *Sitz im Leben*."[34] He makes out a strong case for the development of an ongoing tradition in Judaism and early Christianity. But he takes little notice of the fact that this is not associated with letters. Indeed he holds that this process is independent of the kind of literature in which it is embedded.[35] But it is one thing to say that Jews

---

[31]Harrison, *Problem*, p. 12.

[32]David G. Meade, *Pseudonymity and Canon* (Grand Rapids: Eerdmans, 1987).

[33]But Meade assumes pseudonymity rather than proves it. In a review of Meade's book, Dan G. McCarney comments: "It simply remains unproven that biblical writers actually found pseudonymity acceptable and therefore employed it. Meade has only argued for its acceptability by biblical writers on the grounds of the a priori assumption that pseudonymity not only existed (which of course it does, outside the canon) but was knowingly accepted into the canon. This is arguing in a circle. On the other hand there is *direct* evidence that suggests the biblical writers took a dim view of someone else writing in their name (2 Thess 2:2)" (*WTJ* 51 [1989]: 171).

[34]Meade, *Pseudonymity and Canon*, p. 133.

[35]Meade has many statements such as this: "Attribution in the pseudonymous Pauline and Petrine epistles must be regarded primarily as an assertion of authoritative tradition, not of literary origin" (ibid., p. 193). But that is to be proved; strong assertion without evidence is not enough. Perhaps we should notice that Meade speaks of *1 Enoch* 91–103 as "The Epistle of Enoch" (p. 96), but there is nothing in that document like the epistolary forms with which we are familiar in the New Testament. It begins with, "Now, my son Methuselah, (please) summon all your brothers" and when they come, continues with, "Then he (Enoch) spoke to all of them" (*1 Enoch* 91:1, 3). Pseudonymous epistles are not as widespread as Meade would have us think.

and early Christians wrote pseudonymous apocalypses and acts and quite another to say that they wrote letters purporting to come from one person but actually written by someone else. For that we need evidence, and Meade supplies none.

There is an added problem with the Pastorals in that they all contain a warning about deceivers (1 Tim. 4:1; 2 Tim. 3:13; Titus 1:10), and in one passage the writer says that while in the past he had been a deceiver, that has all been changed now that he has been saved (Titus 3:3). Would a person who speaks of deceit like this put the name of Paul to a letter he himself had composed?[36] Would he say so firmly, "I am telling the truth, I am not lying" (1 Tim. 2:7)?[37]

Pseudonymity must be seen in the light of the church's discussions about canonicity. There were serious doubts in the early church about whether some books should or should not be received into the list of the accepted books, and those discussions tended to center on the question of authorship. In the case of 2 Peter, for example, the question discussed was whether the author was in fact the apostle Peter. If it was, then the book was accepted; if it was not, then the book was rejected. There appears to be no example of anyone in the early church accepting a book as truly canonical while denying that it was written by the author whose name it bears. A well-known example of the typical approach is Eusebius, who was prepared to accept Revelation if it could be shown that the author was the apostle John but who wholeheartedly rejected it if it was not apostolic. It apparently did not occur to him as a possibility that a pseudonymous writing could be accepted into the canon. And if this was so with regard to an apocalypse, much more was it the case with an epistle.

In the light of all this, we should exercise great care before we accept the view than any writing in the New Testament is pseudonymous. That there was pseudonymity in the ancient world is clear. That the Jews and the early Christians sometimes wrote pseudonymous apocalypses is also clear, as is the fact that the early Christians sometimes produced pseudonymous gospels and acts. But to this date there is no evidence that the church accepted any pseudonymous epistle. The very few examples of such literature that were produced were firmly rejected, and in the only case of which we have knowledge in which the author was identified, he was defrocked. We need much more evidence than we are usually offered before we can agree that any New Testament epistle is pseudonymous.[38]

---

[36]As Johnson points out, "The first generations of Christians . . . were very much concerned with the sources of spiritual teaching and with distinguishing between true and false teachers; they did not live in a charismatic fog (see only 1 Cor. 7:10–12; 14:29; 2 Cor. 11:13–15; 2 Thess. 2:2)" (p. 357). He agrees that pseudonymity was practiced in antiquity, but these words should give us pause when we are considering the practices of the early Christians.

[37]Even Meade agrees that this last passage "illustrates the difficulty of affirming the truth of Paul's authority and teaching by using a technique that involves deception" (*Pseudonymity and Canon*, p. 121). If the technique involves deception, what becomes of the assertion that pseudonymity was a transparent device in which readers recognized what was being done?

[38]Important articles on pseudepigraphy have been written by K. Aland ("The Problem of Anonymity and Pseudonymity in Christian Literature of the First Two Centuries," *JTS* 12 [1961]: 39–49 and Bruce M. Metzger ("Literary Forgeries and Canonical Pseudepigrapha," *JBL* 91 [1972]): 3–24). But neither of them produces evidence that the early church accepted letters that it knew to be pseudonymous.

1 TIMOTHY

Contents

The salutation (1:1–2) is followed by a warning against false teachers of the law who promote controversies rather than set forward God's work (1:3–11). There are thanks for the way God's mercy and grace have been at work in Paul (1:12–17). This epistle is designed to aid Timothy as he fights the good fight (1:18–20). Paul urges that prayer be offered for all, especially those in authority, so that they may promote conditions in which people will come to salvation (2:1–7). From the further thought of prayer in the right spirit, Paul moves to the way women should dress and live (2:8–15). Then he discusses the qualifications to be sought in bishops (3:1–7) and deacons (3:8–10, 12–13), with a short section on either deacons' wives or female deacons (3:11). He explains his concern for God's household and cites a little poem about the incarnation (3:14–16). There is a further warning about false teachers (4:1–5), followed by some exhortations to Timothy to be a good servant of Christ and not to neglect the gift he was given when hands were laid on him (4:6–16). Paul offers advice about how to treat older and younger men, older and younger women, and widows (5:1–16) and gives special instructions regarding elders (5:17–20), Timothy's own behavior (5:21–25), and slaves (6:1–2). Once again Paul warns against false teachers and the danger of the love of money (6:3–10); he urges Timothy to flee from all such conduct, charging him to live uprightly (6:11–16). Timothy should order rich people to do good and thus lay up treasure where it matters (6:17–19). The letter ends with another exhortation to Paul's young friend to be firm in the faith (6:20–21a). Finally, Paul appends the grace (6:21b).

Provenance

Not enough is known to identify the place of origin with certainty. The best suggestion is that the letter was written from Macedonia. Paul does not explicitly say that he was in that province when he wrote, but he does say, "As I urged you when I went into Macedonia, stay there in Ephesus" (1:3). This appears to mean that he had been with Timothy in Ephesus, from which point he went on to Macedonia, leaving his young assistant behind. Now in Macedonia, Paul writes reiterating the instruction he had given Timothy at the point of departure.

Date

If Paul was released from his imprisonment in Rome and wrote this letter during the course of his subsequent missionary activities, we should date it during the 60s, probably the early 60s. It has traditionally been held that the apostle was martyred under Nero (who died in 68). The chronology of his life is not absolutely certain, but it is usually thought that he arrived in Rome, as narrated in Acts, in about 59–61. Allowing for the couple of years of his imprisonment there (Acts 28:30), he would have been released in about 62. His letter to the Romans shows that he wanted to go to Spain, and he may have done this immediately on release and gone to Macedonia later. Or he may have gone immediately to the

East and left a trip to Spain until a later time. Many modern scholars think that we should place his death at the height of the Neronian persecution, say in 64, in which case 1 Timothy will be a year or two earlier. Eusebius says Paul died in 67; if this is correct, we could put the writing of the letter at 65 or even 66.

Another suggestion is that we should take the reference to Paul's departure for Macedonia (1:3) to be that mentioned in Acts 20:1, after the riot in Ephesus. Timothy was with Paul again in Acts 20:4, but evidently Acts 20:2 covers quite an interval of time, and there could have been a letter between Acts 20:1 and 20:4. J. A. T. Robinson thinks 1 Timothy may contain the gist of the charge Paul gave when he gathered the disciples and exhorted them (Acts 20:1). He dates the letter in the autumn of A.D. 55, when Timothy was quite a young man (cf. 1 Cor. 16:10–11, which Robinson thinks was written in the same year) and in need of the kind of directions Paul gives in this letter.[39] Not many have been convinced by this argument (the date seems to most students to be far too early), but it must remain a possibility.

Those who see the letter as pseudonymous generally locate it some time during the second century. Kümmel thinks of a time "just after the turn of the second century," for a later date is opposed by the strong Pauline teaching and what he sees as "the rudimentary character of the Gnosticism which is resisted."[40] Marxsen, however, makes it somewhat later. He dates all three Pastorals at "a time well into the second century."[41] If we remove this letter from the lifetime of Paul, there is clearly nothing very definite on which to fix our date. Everything then depends on our subjective estimate of the situation presupposed in the letter, and various second-century dates are suggested.

On the whole, it seems that there is most to be said for the first suggestion, that the letter was written somewhere in the middle 60s. We should at least bear in mind the possibility of Robinson's suggestion; if we see a situation in Paul's earlier ministry, this is as good a suggestion as any.

Destination

As it stands, the letter is a private communication to Timothy, written by his mentor to give him the guidance he needed for his work as a superintendent of churches. Those who see the letter as pseudonymous think of it rather as a general instruction to anyone in a place of authority and perhaps also as a letter to give guidance about the Christian way that would be suitable for the general Christian public. "Grace be with you" (6:21) is plural, and some have therefore argued that the letter was meant for others than Timothy. It is countered that Timothy would be expected to pass on to his congregations the counsel that this letter contains and that Paul is simply sending this little prayer for them all. It is not easy to think that the letter as a whole is meant for a wide public. In such a case, what are we to make of words such as "Timothy, my son" (1:18); "I hope to come to you soon" (3:14); "don't let anyone look down on you because you are young" (4:12); "stop drinking only water" (5:23)? This letter is surely a personal letter to an individual,

[39]Robinson, *Redating*, pp. 82–83.
[40]Kümmel, p. 272.
[41]Marxsen, p. 215.

whatever public use he might have been expected to make of the teaching given throughout it.

Text

There are variant readings, but for the most part the text is in reasonable shape. The best-known problem is whether to read ὅς (*hos*, "who") or θεός (*theos*, "God") in 3:16, but it is generally agreed that the former is correct. Another interesting variant is found twice, namely at 1:15 and 3:1, where most editors read πιστός (*pistos*, "faithful"), but where some witnesses have ἀνθρώπινος (*anthrōpinos*, "human"). The witnesses supporting the variant are mostly in Latin, though in 3:1 D lends its support. In favor of "human" is the consideration that in a number of places elsewhere in the Pastorals there are references to "faithful" sayings, and scribes may have been tempted to make this one conform. But this is not held to outweigh the solid textual support for πιστός (*pistos*). All told, Metzger discusses seventeen passages, which is not unduly large for a book of this length.[42]

Adoption into the Canon

This letter is quoted by Polycarp, Athenagoras, and later writers. Clearly it was widely regarded as written by Paul and accepted as canonical. It seems to have been rejected by Tatian (second half of the second century), but he had a very individualistic viewpoint and cannot be regarded as representative of any widely held opinion. Marcion also rejected it along with the other Pastorals (perhaps because of the respect it affords the Old Testament).[43] But he rejected so much that others accepted that we cannot take his omission as significant of wide hesitation in the church of his day. Apart from these idiosyncratic individuals, 1 Timothy seems to have been accepted universally as part of the correspondence of the apostle Paul. In modern times there have been serious doubts raised as to the authenticity of this and the other Pastoral Epistles, but this does not correspond to any widely held opinion in antiquity.

The Contribution of 1 Timothy

This is a very personal letter. From elsewhere in the New Testament we know that Paul was very fond of Timothy; he speaks of his love for the younger man and of his conviction that he was faithful (1 Cor. 4:17). Paul says further that Timothy could remind the Corinthians of Paul's way of life, which indicates a certain intimacy and shows that Paul trusted him. It accords with this that he likens Timothy's relationship to him to that of a son to his father (Phil. 2:22), and with a cheerful disregard for consistency speaks of him as a brother (and fellow worker, 1 Thess. 3:2). He links Timothy with himself in the opening greetings in some of his epistles (2 Cor. 1:1; Phil. 1:1; Col. 1:1; 1 Thess.1:1; 2 Thess. 1:1), which argues that he was a trusted colleague. Paul asks the Corinthians to ensure that Timothy "has nothing to fear" if he should visit them (1 Cor. 16:10), which

---

[42]Metzger, pp. 639–44.
[43]Tertullian, *Adv. Marc.* 5.21.

seems to indicate a certain diffidence about the young man. He sent him to the Thessalonians, he assures them, "to strengthen and encourage you in your faith" (1 Thess. 3:2), and he plans to send him to the Philippians, explaining, "I have no one else like him, who takes a genuine interest in your welfare" (Phil. 2:20).

All this gives point to Paul's greeting, "To Timothy my true son in the faith" (1 Tim. 1:2). The letter is written to a younger man for whom the apostle had a deep affection and whom he had for years entrusted with important missions. What Paul now says brings out the truth that Christians are linked in the service of the Lord and that there is significant help they can and should give to one another.

The letter is important also for the light it sheds on the ministry of the Christian church.[44] Throughout all the years of its history, the ministry has been of great importance. It has taken a variety of shapes, some very authoritarian, some egalitarian. It has been strongly hierarchical in some of its forms, and the very idea of a hierarchy has been rejected in others. However it has been understood, it has been seen as at the heart of ecclesiastical organization. It comes as something of a surprise to realize that, apart from the Pastoral Epistles, the New Testament has very little to say about it (and when it does, it speaks of forms like the apostle or the prophet, which have ceased to exist, at least as regular ministers). It is accordingly important that 1 Timothy has so much to say about ministers—more, indeed, than has any other New Testament writing.

It is significant that Paul says nothing about ordination in this letter, unless he has it in mind when he refers to "the prophecies once made about you" (1:18) or to the gift given when the elders "laid their hands on you" (4:14). In either case this is possible, but the point is that in neither case does Paul mention ordination, and both passages may be otherwise explained. However we understand these passages, clearly what matters to Paul is that those in the ministry should be upright people, leaders whose character is beyond reproach. So he gives instructions about the bishop (ἐπίσκοπος [episkopos], 3:1–7). NIV appropriately renders the Greek "overseer," for there is no reason for holding that in New Testament times the office discharged anything like the functions it came to have in the church and that arise in our minds when the word "bishop" is used today. But NIV obscures the fact that it was this office and no other that very shortly evolved into the monarchical bishop. It is one of our problems about the early history of the ministry that we do not know precisely what functions the New Testament "bishop" discharged. Paul is much more interested in his character than in his ecclesiastical activities. The church has all too often reversed this priority; 1 Timothy is of permanent value in pointing to the truth that it is the quality of Christian life that people show that fits them for office in the church.

It is usually agreed that the elder and the bishop were identical in the church of this period. Paul does not equate them in this letter as he does in Titus 1:5–7, but he does not differentiate them either, and there is no reason for taking 5:17–19 as referring to anyone other than the bishops of chapter 3. The elders, we learn, are active in directing the affairs of the church, though what form their direction took is not stated. Evidently some had administrative duties, and others were concerned

---

[44]J. B. Lightfoot's classic dissertation on "The Christian Ministry" still merits careful attention and has much to say about the teaching in the Pastorals (in *Saint Paul's Epistle to the Philippians* [London: Macmillan, 1885], pp. 181–259). See also Leon Morris, *Ministers of God* (London: IVP, 1964).

with preaching and teaching, these latter being singled out as worthy of special honor. Paul combines an Old Testament passage with a saying of Jesus to bring out the truth that the elders are to be paid for their work (5:18; cf. Deut. 25:4; Luke 10:7). And he makes it clear that the elder is a reverend personage, not to be accused lightly (5:19).

Paul also has something to say about deacons, and once again the emphasis is on character (3:8–10), with some emphasis on the importance of family life (3:12). Between these two references there is another that may refer to the wives of deacons or may tell us something about female deacons (3:11). Again the emphasis is on character and conduct.

The church has all too often neglected this emphasis. There have been battles as some have tried to exercise wide-ranging authority, and others have resisted this strenuously. There have been discussions as to whether the ministers in one church can recognize those in another; the validity of orders has been a matter of prime concern. Indeed, in the modern ecumenical movement the recognition of ministries has been a matter of profound interest. The strong emphasis on character in this letter is of the greatest importance, coupled as it is with a total bypassing of all that is implied in the term "the validity of orders." This does not mean that we can neglect proper arrangements in recognizing ministries. But Paul is teaching the whole church that there are more important considerations than the proper arrangements for a service of ordination.

While he thus has a good deal to say about the way those who are called into the ministry should live, he is not silent either about the conduct of others in the church. Paul insists on the importance of prayer (2:8) and on the way believers should behave, including women (2:9–15), believers generally (3:14–15), older and younger people (5:1–2), widows (5:3–16), slaves (6:1–2), and the rich (6:17–19). There are different duties for people in different stations, but all who profess to be Christians must be careful that their lives reflect their doctrines. The letter keeps reminding readers of the importance of upright Christian living.

First Timothy is also a protest against needless controversies. There are warnings against those who "devote themselves to myths and endless genealogies" (1:4; "godless myths," 4:7). Those who forbid marriage and introduce food laws are also condemned (4:3), and Timothy is warned against "an unhealthy interest in controversies and quarrels . . . that result in envy" (6:4). Perhaps some in the modern church should give heed to the warning against people who "think that godliness is a means to financial gain" (6:5), while the modern community is almost a classic illustration of the saying, "The love of money is a root of all kinds of evil" (6:10).

An interesting and permanently valuable part of this letter is the way Paul refers to the past in such a way as to afford guidance for the future. Thus he looks back to the time when he was with Timothy and to the teaching he then gave him; he exhorts him to continue in the course then urged (1:3–11). It is the same elsewhere: the instructions Paul has given in the past will enable Timothy to act in the future (3:14–15). Objectors to Pauline authorship often cavil at the insistence on sound doctrine, but they do not usually notice that this is derived from the essentials of the gospel: Paul writes of "the sound doctrine that conforms to the glorious gospel of the blessed God" (1:11). He refers to Jesus as the "one mediator between God and men" and goes on to say that he "gave himself as a ransom for all men." It was to spread this message that Paul "was appointed a herald and an apostle . . . and a teacher of the true faith to the Gentiles" (2:5–7). The writer is clear that the events that constitute the gospel form the basis of the whole Christian message. Whatever the circumstances in which Timothy finds himself, the gospel is to form the message he proclaims, the gospel that Paul preached and that is central to the life of the whole Christian church.

Even many who see the letter as pseudonymous make the point that the writer is still appealing to Paul. The letter stands as a reminder that there are some truths that persist from age to age. The meaning of the gospel of Christ is not to be modified in the interests of Christians living in circumstances very different from those of Paul. In other words, this letter points us to a "given" in the Christian message. There are great truths that are to be embraced in every age. The fact remains that the writer does not refute the heresies to which he makes reference. Rather he draws Timothy's attention to the *way* those heresies should be refuted—another important and continuing value of this writing.

2 TIMOTHY

Contents

This is a letter written at a time when Paul was contemplating his own death (4:6–8), so it has the character of a testamentary charge. There is a special solemnity about a letter written in such circumstances. It begins with a normal form of greeting (1:1–2) and moves to thanksgiving and encouragement (1:3–7). This leads to an exhortation to Timothy not to be ashamed of Paul, because Paul is not ashamed of the gospel (1:8–14). After some historical reminiscences (1:15–18), Timothy is urged to be strong in Christ's grace (2:1–7) and reminded of the essentials of the gospel (2:8–13). He is to be a workman who does not need to be ashamed, but one who teaches faithfully. With this is linked a warning about the false teachers and exhortations to upright living (2:14–26). Paul prophesies of troubles "in the last days," when all manner of evil flourishes (3:1–9). He gratefully confesses that the Lord has protected him in his troubles (3:10–13) and exhorts Timothy to continue in the teaching he has had from infancy, specifically the teaching from the Scriptures, which are God-breathed and valuable (3:14–17). This leads to a charge to Timothy to preach the word steadfastly (4:1–5). Paul speaks of his impending death and preparedness for it (4:6–8). There follow a series of remarks about individuals (4:9–15) and the information that Paul had been forsaken at his first defense (4:16–18). The letter closes with greetings and the grace (4:19–22).

Provenance

Paul writes in the consciousness that his life is nearly over (4:6). His word for "defense" ($\dot{\alpha}\pi o\lambda o\gamma\iota\alpha$ [*apologia*], 4:16) is often used of a defense in a law court. It seems, then, that we are to think of Paul as in prison faced with the prospect of speedy execution. He says that Onesiphorus searched for him and found him in Rome (1:16–17), which makes it likely that that was the place of his current imprisonment. Paul asks Timothy to come to him and pick up Mark on the way

(4:11), so we know that this imprisonment in Rome is not that related in Acts (Timothy was with him when he wrote Colossians, as was Mark [Col. 1:1; 4:10; Philem. 24; these two letters are generally held to have been written from Rome). Paul appears to have been in Asia Minor not long before he wrote, for he speaks of having left a cloak at Troas (4:13), of Erastus having stayed in Corinth, and of his having left Trophimus sick in Miletus (4:20). We learn from Acts that Paul had been in prison in Caesarea for two years (Acts 24:27) prior to being sent to Rome and that his journey there was via Crete and Malta. He had thus not been in Asia Minor for quite some time. It is unlikely that he is writing from his imprisonment in Caesarea (which would fit the references to Asia Minor), for Trophimus was with him in Jerusalem when he was arrested (Acts 21:29) and probably Timothy also (Acts 20:4).[45] It seems much more likely that Paul was released from the imprisonment mentioned in Acts and engaged in missionary activities for a period before being imprisoned again.[46] The probabilities are that 2 Timothy was written during this second imprisonment in Rome.

Date

The evidence bearing on the dating of the letter has largely been canvassed in the section on "Provenance." There we saw that the probabilities are that the letter was written from Rome during an imprisonment later than the one described in Acts. In that case, the letter was written in the middle 60s. If Eusebius is correct in dating the martyrdom of Paul in 67, then that or the preceding year will be the date of 2 Timothy.

Those who deny the Pauline authorship of the letter class it with the other Pastorals and usually date it some time in the second century. The three are normally discussed together, so the arguments are the same as those for 1 Timothy (see above).

Destination

The letter purports to have been written to Timothy (1:1–2), and the contents bear this out. Personal touches such as the references to Lois and Eunice (1:5) are very natural in such a letter and hard to explain otherwise. So with Timothy's tears (1:4) and Paul's laying hands on him (1:6) and with the references to Paul's being deserted (1:15; 4:10). The prayers for Onesiphorus together with the information that he made a hard but successful search for Paul and the reference to his previous activities in Ephesus (1:16–18) are the kind of thing we might expect in a private

---

[45]Robinson maintains that the letter was written from Caesarea (*Redating*, pp. 67–82). But he has to argue that Luke has confused Tychicus with Trophimus p. 76), for which there is no evidence.

[46]Clement of Rome says that Paul came "to the limit of the West" (*1 Clement* 5:7), which to a Roman would probably mean Spain, a trip that cannot be fitted into the Acts narrative. If Clement is referring to Spain his comment is evidence for Pauline missionary activity after the imprisonment described in Acts 28. As Clement wrote no more than about thirty years after Paul's death, this is important evidence. The Muratorian Canon speaks of "the departure of Paul from the City on his journey to Spain" (Stevenson, *New Eusebius*, p. 145; "the City" means Rome). Eusebius says that according to tradition, Paul defended himself after his two years in Rome and engaged in "the ministry of preaching" before being arrested again and suffering martyrdom under Nero; he specifically says that Paul wrote 2 Timothy during this imprisonment (*H.E.* 2.22.2).

letter. The same is true of personal admonitions to Timothy (2:1–2, 22–26; 3:14; 4:2, 5) and the little chatty section at the end when Paul gives news of friends and some information about himself (4:9–22). The letter is throughout so personal that it is probably the hardest of the three Pastorals to claim as pseudonymous.

Those who deny that it was a letter written to Timothy point to the plural in the grace at the end (4:22). But this surely means no more than that Paul extends his greetings to the Christians who were with Timothy at the time he wrote. There does not seem anything else on which to base a theory of other recipients than Timothy, unless we go along with the whole theory of pseudonymity, in which case we must say that we do not know to whom the letter was written.

Text

The text of this letter seems fairly well preserved. There are no great problems, and it is perhaps significant that the longest discussion in Metzger is that over the form of the grace in 4:22. All told, he discusses fifteen passages, but none of the variants gives us a significant difference of meaning. Westcott and Hort think that ὧν (hōn, "which") in 1:13 is a primitive corruption,[47] but the sense is not greatly changed if we accept their alteration to give the meaning "hold as a pattern the word (= teaching) which you heard from me."

Adoption into the Canon

There may be echoes of this letter in *1 Clement* and in the letters of Ignatius, though this is disputed. It seems clear, however, that Polycarp quoted some passages. There is not the slightest doubt that Ireneus refers to the letter, citing it as written by Paul to Timothy. Clement of Alexandria does the same, and from these early days, on the letter was universally accepted. Tatian seems to have rejected it along with 1 Timothy, while Marcion did not have any of the Pastorals in his canon—but then he rejected so much of the New Testament that this is not surprising. He probably did not like the high regard for the Old Testament that the letter reveals. None of the Pastorals is found in the Chester Beatty Papyrus p^{46}, which is dated c. A.D. 200, but the codex is incomplete and may originally have contained the letters. If it did not, it is worth noticing that it also omits Philemon, so that the reason may be that the codex contained only letters to churches. All three are included in the Muratorian Canon. The church in general seems to have had little hesitation over accepting 2 Timothy.

The Contribution of 2 Timothy

The deep conviction of the writer that he was about to be put to death for holding the Christian faith (4:6–8) is to be kept in mind in all discussions of this letter. Paul does not envisage writing anything further to Timothy, nor perhaps to anyone else. He hopes that Timothy will be able to reach him before the end (4:9), and his request for his cloak and his scrolls (4:13) shows that he anticipated

---

[47]WH, p. 135.

an interval before his execution. Nevertheless the letter is written in the shadow of the scaffold and is to be seen as what Paul considered to be important in his last communication to a trusted subordinate. Not the least of the letter's values is that it shows us the way a Christian martyr should face death. Those who live comfortably in secure communities should not belittle this contribution, for in many lands with anti-Christian governments, people still die for their faith. Indeed, a recent press report informs us that in our time an average of 330,000 Christians are martyred for their faith each year,[48] which means that there may well be more martyrs today than at any other period in history. Certainly martyrdom for the faith is much more common than most Western Christians realize, and accordingly it is well that we appreciate Paul's attitude to dying for Christ. It is important that modern Christians take heed to his calm contemplation of what lay ahead—and the quiet faith that undergirded all he was doing and his going about his necessary business. There is no fanaticism here, nor any attempt at grandstanding. The apostle writes from a lowly posture and sets the example of the way Christians should die for their faith. He writes also of how they should live for it, even if this means suffering along the way (e.g., 1:8).

Paul also brings out something of the importance of their heritage. He speaks of "the good deposit that was entrusted to you" (1:14; the same word "deposit" is used in v. 12, with possibly much the same meaning, so the RSV). In line with this, Paul has much to say about what God has done, such as his reference to the gospel, followed by the power of God, salvation, the call to a holy life, grace given in Christ "before the beginning of time" and now revealed in our Savior, the destruction of death, and the gift of life and immortality (1:8–10)—an enormous freight to be carried within three verses. It is of abiding importance that believers are not given a list of instructions as to what constitutes the path of the service of God and then left to themselves as they try to work it all out. The foundation of all Christian life is what God has already done, and Paul makes it clear that all that Christians are asked to do is to live out the consequences of God's saving act. This they can do without timidity, for God has given them "a spirit of power, of love and of self-discipline" (1:7). In line with this, the apostle exhorts Timothy to pass the teaching on "to reliable men who will also be qualifed to teach others" (2:2). There is a "given" about the Christian faith; it is something inherited from the very beginning of God's action for our salvation, and it is to be passed on as long as this world lasts. Paul is not arguing that believers should be insensitive to currents of thought and action in the world about them, nor is he saying that the Christian is a kind of antiquarian, interested in antiquity for its own sake. He is saying that there is that about the essence of the Christian faith that is not open to negotiation. God has said and done certain things, and Christians must stand by those things whatever the cost. We should bear in mind his notable statement about Scripture (3:16–17); God has spoken, and we neglect what he has said to our peril.

Paul is clear that the cost of discipleship may be great. He speaks of suffering, both his own and that of other believers (1:8, 12; 2:9, 12; 3:11–12). He likens Christian service to that of a soldier, an athlete, and a hardworking farmer (2:3–6). He leaves Timothy in no doubt that, while our salvation is a free gift from

---

[48]*The Australian Church Record* for June 8, 1987, citing David Barrett.

God, it is also demanding. In living out its implications, the believer is going to run into difficulties and will find that the God who sent his Son to die on the cross is always served at cost. Paul uses the illustration of the variety of articles in a large house—some costly, some cheap, some for noble purposes, and some for ignoble; the believer is to aim at being fit for noble purposes (2:20–21). Cleansing is costly.

The Christian will meet with opposition, sometimes from people who profess to be Christians themselves. Part of the value of this letter to us is its warning against those who wander from the truth (2:14–18). Especially is this true of "the last days," when there will be people who have a form of godliness but deny its power (3:1–5). In accord with this, Paul insists on the importance of "sound teaching" (1:13), which some people will reject, gathering teachers "to say what their itching ears want to hear" (4:3). Paul is not contending for adherence to some dead orthodoxy; rather, he insists that God has laid a "solid foundation" that stands firm (2:19).

TITUS

Contents

The opening greeting (1:1–4) is longer than Paul's usual greeting and contains a reminder that God has promised eternal life and brought it to pass in due course. Paul has left Titus in Crete to set things in order in the church, and he now urges him to appoint elders in every town, giving directions about the kind of person required for this office (1:5–9). There is a contrast with the "many rebellious people" to be found in Crete; Paul warns Titus against them (1:10–16). He goes on to detail what must be taught to older men (2:2), older women, who will teach younger women (2:3–5), young men (2:6–8), and slaves (2:9–10). All believers are to live uprightly, awaiting "the glorious appearing of our great God and Savior, Jesus Christ" (2:11–15). People in authority are to be obeyed (3:1–2). There is a contrast between the way people lived before they became Christians and the good lives that follow Christ's saving work in them (3:3–8). They should avoid foolish divisions (3:9–11). The letter is rounded off with some instructions about various individuals and then closing greetings (3:12–15).

Provenance

The only other references to Crete in the New Testament are in the account of Paul's voyage to Rome in Acts 27, a time when the apostle was briefly in the harbor of Fair Havens (Acts 27:8), but it is impossible to think of him as doing significant evangelism on the island at that time. But from 1:5 we learn that he had left Titus to complete what had to be done, which seems to imply that he had done work there himself and had left Titus to complete it. Unfortunately we have no information as to when this took place. At the time of writing Paul was in or on the way to Nicopolis, where he planned to spend the winter (3:12), but we do not know when he was there either. There are considerable gaps in the story Acts tells of Paul's missionary journeys, but it is plausibly argued that had he done such a work in Crete as this letter presupposes, it could scarcely have been omitted in its entirety. While certainty is unattainable, it seems probable that, as in the case of 2 Timothy, we should think that Paul was released after the Roman imprisonment narrated in Acts and that he engaged in a further period of missionary activity. Whereas 2 Timothy presupposes a further arrest of Paul, Titus comes from the period of active missionary service.

Date

Robinson reminds us that Titus was in Corinth, busy about the collection (2 Cor. 8; 12:17–18), and that he was probably not with Paul when Romans was written, since he is not mentioned in the greetings of Romans 16:21–23, as Timothy is. Paul was finishing off the collection himself (Rom. 15:28), and he may at this point have sent Titus to Crete and left him there while he himself set off for Jerusalem. The letter to Titus, Robinson thinks, may have been written while Paul was on the way to Jerusalem, which gives a date of A.D. 57.[49] If we date this letter during Paul's ministry as described in Acts, this is as good a suggestion as any. It is perhaps supported by the fact that the church in Crete was a very young church, lacking even elders (Titus 1:5).

But to most scholars such a date seems very improbable. Acts puts Paul neither in Crete nor in Nicopolis, so it seems better to think of this letter, like the other Pastorals, as coming from a time after Paul's release from a first Roman imprisonment. In that case, it was written before 2 Timothy, and somewhere around the same period as 1 Timothy—that is, in the middle 60s.

Those who see the letter as pseudonymous, usually date it some time in the second century (see on 1 Timothy).

Destination

Little needs to be added to what was said under the other two Pastorals. The letter is addressed to Titus, and there is nothing in it inconsistent with this man being the recipient. There are not as many personal references as in the letters to Timothy, but the remarks at the end (3:12–15) ring true. Titus was evidently a trusted helper, and Paul looks to him to act responsibly.

Adoption into the Canon

There may well be an echo of Titus 3:1 in Clement of Rome, and certainly some second-century writers quote Titus, including Tertullian and Ireneus. It is interesting that although Tatian rejects both letters to Timothy, he accepts that to Titus. Like the other Pastorals, Titus is absent from Marcion's canon (probably for the same reasons) and present in the Muratorian Canon. From the end of the second century it was universally recognized. For its absence from p^{46}, see the comment on 2 Timothy.

---

[49]Robinson, *Redating*, pp.81–82.

The Contribution of Titus

This letter brings out something of what we might call the civilizing function of Christianity. Titus was clearly in charge of a very young church in a very unpromising situation. Elders had not yet been appointed, and Titus was to appoint them. (By contrast, the church was well established where Timothy was, and there a bishop was not to be "a recent convert" [1 Tim. 3:6].) In Crete, where Titus found himself, there was the possibility that a candidate for the eldership might have unconverted children or children who were "wild and disobedient" (1:6). The elder himself must be "not overbearing, not quick-tempered, not given to drunkenness, not violent, not pursuing dishonest gain" (1:7). He is to function in a community of which one of their own people said, "Cretans are always liars, evil brutes, lazy gluttons" (1:12), a testimony with which Paul agrees. In that situation it would seem that neither Paul nor Titus had a moment's hesitation about establishing the church. The letter is clear evidence that the Christian church is not intended to function only in cozy, respectable, middle-class environments. The gospel is for the most unpromising of people.

This is seen also in the instructions to those who have been converted. The older women are not to be addicted to wine (2:3), the younger are to love their husbands and children (2:4), slaves are not to steal from their masters (2:10), people are to respect authority and do what is good and not to engage in slander (3:1–2). All this is surprising in directions to a group of Christians. It shows both that these Cretans were unpromising material and that Paul expected them nevertheless to produce qualities of Christian character.

Moreover, the gospel is to be taken to such people, despite the strong opposition of rival teachers. Some of these are successful, for they are "ruining whole households," even though they aim only at their own dishonest gain (1:11). Apparently there was quite a Jewish flavor to the false teaching: its adherents are "of the circumcision group" (1:10), they teach "Jewish myths" (1:14), they "claim to know God," even though their actions show this to be a lie (1:16), they argue about the law and engage in foolish controversies (3:9). But this letter makes it clear that the strength and the nature of the opposition make no difference: Christian teachers are to press on with their task of evangelism and of leading the converts into a lifestyle that brings glory to God.

Paul takes up no position of superiority but makes it plain that he owes everything to "the kindness and love of God our Savior" and specifically to what God has done in Christ (3:3–7). He puts the highest standard before the Cretans, "for the grace of God that brings salvation has appeared to all men" (2:11). The letter makes it plain that the Christian way is an urging of people not to pull themselves up by their bootstraps, but rather to rely on the grace of God. This grace "teaches" (2:12); it educates people like the Cretans—and any other group.

We should not miss Paul's reference to the parousia, as he waits for "the blessed hope—the glorious appearing of our great God and Savior, Jesus Christ" (2:13; note here the way he speaks of Christ). The letter emphasizes what God has done to bring salvation and the certainty of its culmination when Christ comes back.

BIBLIOGRAPHY:

K. **Aland**, "The Problem of Anonymity and Pseudonymity in Christian Literature of the First Two Centuries," *JTS* 12 (1961): 39–49; C. K. **Barrett**, *The Pastoral Epistles*, NClarB (Oxford: Clarendon, 1963); J. H. **Bernard**, *The Pastoral Epistles* (Cambridge: Cambridge University Press, 1899); M. M. **Bourke**, "Reflections on Church Order in the New Testament," *CBQ* 30 (1968): 493–511; N. **Brox**, *Die Pastoralbriefe*, RNT, 4th ed. (Regensburg: Pustet, 1969); R. **Bultmann**, *Theology of the New Testament*, 2 vols. (London: SCM, 1952–55), 2:95–118; P. **Carrington**, *The Early Christian Church*, 2 vols. (Cambridge: Cambridge University Press, 1957); idem, "The Problem of the Pastoral Epistles: Dr. Harrison's Theory Reviewed," *ATR* 21 (1939): 32–39; M. **Dibelius** and H. **Conzelmann**, *The Pastoral Epistles*, Hermeneia (Philadelphia: Fortress, 1972); E. Earle **Ellis**, "The Authorship of the Pastorals: A Résumé and Assessment," *EQ* 32 (1960): 151–61; Gordon D. **Fee**, *1 and 2 Timothy, Titus*, GNC (San Francisco: Harper & Row, 1984); K. **Grayston** and G. **Herndon**, "The Authorship of the Pastorals in the Light of Statistical Studies," *NTS* 6 (1959–60): 1–15; Donald **Guthrie**, "Pastoral Epistles," in *ISBE* 3:679–87; idem, *The Pastoral Epistles* (Grand Rapids: Eerdmans, 1957); idem, *The Pastoral Epistles and the Mind of Paul* (London: Tyndale, 1956); A. T. **Hanson**, "The Domestication of Paul: A Study in the Development of Early Christian Theology," *BJRL* 63 (1981): 402–18; idem, *The Pastoral Epistles*, NCP (Grand Rapids: Eerdmans, 1982); idem, *Studies in the Pastoral Epistles* (London: SPCK, 1968); P. N. **Harrison**, "The Authorship of the Pastoral Epistles," *ExpTim* 67 (1955–56): 77–81; idem, *Paulines and Pastorals* (London: Villiers, 1964); idem, *The Problem of the Pastoral Epistles* (London: Oxford University Press, 1921); F. R. M. **Hitchcock**, "The Pastorals and a Second Trial of Paul," *ExpTim* 41 (1929–30): 20–23; "Tests for the Pastorals," *JTS* 30 (1928–29): 272–79; idem, "Philo and the Pastorals," *Hermatheua* 56 (1940): 113–35; idem, "Tests for the Pastorals," *JTS* 30 (1928–29): 272–79; J. L. **Houlden**, *The Pastoral Epistles: I and II Timothy, Titus*, PNTC (London: Penguin, 1976); M. R. **James**, *The Apocryphal New Testament* (Oxford: Clarendon, 1926); R. J. **Karris**, "The Background and Significance of the Polemic of the Pastoral Epistles," *JBL* 92 (1973): 549–64; J. N. D. **Kelly**, *A Commentary on the Pastoral Epistles*, HNTC (New York: Harper, 1963); Anthony **Kenny**, *A Stylometric Study of the New Testament* (Oxford: Clarendon, 1986); S. **de Lestapis**, *L'énigme des Pastorales de Saint Paul* (Paris: Gabalda, 1976); J. B. **Lightfoot**, "The Date of the Pastoral Epistles," in *Biblical Essays* (London: Macmillan, 1904), pp. 397–410; idem, *Saint Paul's Epistle to the Philippians* (London: Macmillan, 1885); W. **Lock**, *A Critical and Exegetical Commentary on The Pastoral Epistles*, ICC (Edinburgh: T. & T. Clark, 1924); David G. **Meade**, *Pseudonymity and Canon* (Grand Rapids: Eerdmans, 1987); B. **Metzger**, "Literary Forgeries and Canonical Pseudepigrapha," *JBL* 91 (1972): 3–24; idem, "A Reconsideration of Certain Arguments Against the Pauline Authorship of the Pastoral Epistles," *ExpTim* 70 (1958–59): 91–94; Leon **Morris**, *Apocalyptic*, 2d ed. (Grand Rapids: Eerdmans, 1973); idem, *Ministers of God* (London: IVP, 1954); C. F. D. **Moule**, "The Problem of the Pastoral Epistles: A Reappraisal," *BJRL* 47 (1965): 430–52; J. D. **Quinn**, "The Last Volume of Luke: The Relation of Luke-Acts to the Pastoral Epistles," in *Perspectives on Luke-Acts*, ed. C. Talbert (Danville, Va.: Association of Baptist Professors of Religion, 1978), pp. 62–75; W. M. **Ramsey**, "Historical Commentary on the First Epistle to Timothy," *Exp* 7 (1909): 481–94; 8 (1910): 1–21, 167–85, 264–82, 339–57, 399–416, 557–68; 9 (1910): 172–87, 319–33, 433–40; J. A. T. **Robinson**,

Redating the New Testament (Philadelphia: Westminster, 1976); E. F. **Scott**, *The Pastoral Epistles*, MNTC (London: Hodder & Stoughton, 1936); Moisés **Silva**, "The Place of Historical Reconstruction in New Testament Criticism," in *Hermeneutics, Authority, and Canon*, ed. D. A. Carson and John D. Woodbridge (Grand Rapids: Zondervan, 1986), pp. 105–33, 383–88; C. Spicq, *Epîtres Pastorales*, 4th ed., 2 vols. (Paris: Gabalda, 1969); Krister **Stendahl**, ed., *The Scrolls and the New Testament* (London: SCM, 1958); J. **Stevenson**, *A New Eusebius* (London: SPCK, 1963); Philip H. **Towner**, *The Goal of Our Instruction: The Structure of Theology and Ethics in the Pastoral Epistles*, JSNTSupp 34 (Sheffield: Sheffield Academic Press, 1989); David C. **Verner**, *The Household of God: The Social World of the Pastoral Epistles*, SBLDS 71 (Chico, Calif.: SP, 1983); S. G. **Wilson**, *Luke and the Pastoral Epistles* (London: SPCK, 1979).

16

philemon

CONTENTS

This intensely personal letter begins with a greeting from Paul and Timothy to Philemon, Apphia, Archippus, and the church "in your home" (1–3). A prayer of thanksgiving follows, stressing the faith and the love of the addressee (4–7).

On the basis of love Paul appeals for Onesimus, whom he calls "my son," adding "who became my son while I was in chains" (8–10). Playing on the meaning of the name Onesimus (= "profitable") Paul says that this man had been unprofitable but will now be profitable (11). Paul is sending him back, even though he would like to keep him with him. Now he is better than a slave: he is "a dear brother" (12–16). Paul asks that Onesimus be welcomed and adds that if Onesimus has wronged Philemon, he, Paul, will repay it. He is confident that Philemon will do more than he has asked. He further asks that a guest room be prepared for him, as he hopes to come soon (17–22), and ends with greetings and the grace (23–25).

AUTHOR

There has never been serious doubt that this letter is a genuine writing of the apostle Paul (as it claims to be). It is the nearest approach to a purely private letter in the Pauline correspondence. It reads like a natural product of the situation it presupposes, and its freshness and naturalness are impressive. We should take this as a genuine Pauline letter.

PROVENANCE AND DATE

There are connections with Colossians: in both Paul is a prisoner (1, 9; Col. 4:3, 10, 18), the people sending greetings are mostly those who do so in Colossians (23–24; Col. 4:10–14), and Onesimus who features in this letter is mentioned as one of the Colossians and as going to that city with Tychicus (Col. 4:7–9). Clearly this letter is written from the same place as Colossians. Two features of this letter bear on this relationship. One is the fact that Paul asks Philemon to prepare a guest room for him (22), which argues that his place of imprisonment is not far from Colossae. The other is the fact that Onesimus seems fairly clearly to be a runaway slave, and the question arises, To which city would such a slave be likely to flee from Colossae? Both considerations are said to favor Ephesus, but the second could be evidence for Rome. It is just as likely that a slave would flee to Rome because it was a long way away, as that he would go to Ephesus because it was close. In the end our decision must be that this letter was written from the same place as Colossians and that, while Ephesus cannot be entirely ruled out, Rome is a little more likely. As in the case of Colossians, the date will be in the early 60s if written from Rome, in the late 50s if from Ephesus.

ADDRESSEE(S)

A problem arises from the address. The epistle is addressed "to Philemon our dear friend and fellow worker, to Apphia our sister, to Archippus our fellow soldier and to the church that meets in your home" (1–2). Philemon, mentioned first, is clearly the principal addressee, and Apphia may well be his wife, as is often assumed. We have no means of knowing whether Archippus was related to them or not (he is sometimes said to be their son). "Your" is singular in the Greek and doubtless refers back to Philemon.[1] While the letter has many of the characteristics of a private communication, this opening shows that a house church is involved in its message, as well as its host. There is no convincing reason for denying that the letter was written to Philemon (though with two other people and a house church also included as recipients of the apostle's message).

OCCASION

The letter seems to show that Onesimus, a slave of Philemon, had run away from his master, probably robbing him in the process (18). The alternative is to think that his master had sent him on a mission and that he had failed to return when he should have. Sometimes in antiquity (at least among the Greeks) a slave would flee from his master and claim sanctuary at an altar, which might be a household altar. In that case the householder was under obligation to get the slave to go back, and if the slave refused, then the householder was to sell him and send the money to the owner. If the situation is understood in this way, Onesimus robbed Philemon only in the sense that by refusing to go back, he deprived Philemon of the services he should have rendered him.

We have no way of knowing how Onesimus came into contact with Paul, but clearly he had done so and had been converted as a result (10). Now Paul is sending him back to his owner as the law required, but the letter is an appeal to Philemon not to employ the full rigor of the law. He is entitled to punish Onesimus, but Paul urges him instead to receive him "as a dear brother" (15–16). Clearly Paul had valued Onesimus's presence and his help in evangelism (see 13). It is quite possible that he wants Philemon to send the slave back to him. But he does not specifically ask that, and we can say for certain no more than that he urges Philemon to receive his slave with kindness.

Did Philemon respond as Paul wished? We may safely assume that he did.

---

[1] John Knox argues that we should take "your" to refer to Archippus, who is named immediately before it. He thus sees Archippus as the person who owned Onesimus and to whom the request in the letter was made (*Philemon Among the Letters of Paul* [London: Collins, 1950], pp. 49–61).

Otherwise he would surely have suppressed the letter, and we would know nothing about it.

TEXT

There are a few textual variants (UBS3 notes only four), but none causes much argument, and none seriously affects the sense. We may take it that we have the text substantially as Paul wrote it.

ADOPTION INTO THE CANON

A short letter dealing with what is mostly a private matter is not likely to be quoted very much, and we do not have many references to it in early literature. But it appears in early lists of the canon, such as that of Marcion and the Muratorian Fragment. Tertullian in his refutation of Marcion shows that he accepts it, and Origen quotes it as authoritative. There seems to have been no serious questioning of its canonicity in early days. J. B. Lightfoot notes "a strong bias against it" in the fourth century by people who "had no sympathy with either the subject or the handling."[2] But even then there were strong defenders, including Jerome and Chrysostom. The letter's canonicity is beyond question.

PHILEMON IN RECENT STUDY

A good deal of recent discussion turns on Knox's argument that this letter is the one described as "the letter from Laodicea" (Col. 4:16). He thinks that Philemon was a Laodicean, the leader of the churches in the Lycus valley and a man to whom the Colossians would look for guidance. Because of the light it would shed on the position and future of Onesimus, it was important that this little letter be read at Colossae, but it was sent to Philemon at Laodicea first. With this Knox takes the view that it was Archippus who was the owner of Onesimus and to whom the pleas in the epistle to Philemon would be addressed. But it would help in having him respond if Philemon of Laodicea added his weight to what Paul had written.[3] A few scholars see this as a fruitful line of approach, but Knox and those who think with him have not been able to convince the world of scholarship that all this is really credible. It is not the natural way to interpret Philemon 1–2 and Colossians 4:16, nor does it reckon with the fact that Marcion knew a letter to Laodicea as well as a letter to Philemon.

Others start with the premise that Colossians is inauthentic and suggest that Philemon was published to induce people to think of Colossians as genuine. This, too, has attracted little support. It seems an unlikely explanation of a letter as full of human interest as Philemon.

---

[2] J. B. Lightfoot, *St Paul's Epistles to the Colossians and to Philemon* (London: Macmillan, 1876), p. 316.

[3] Knox, *Philemon, passim.*

THE CONTRIBUTION OF PHILEMON

This little letter does not expound major doctrinal themes, but it has something important to say in the realm of personal relationships. In the first century slavery was an accepted part of the order of life. No one thought of abolishing it. And a slave could be considered a living tool, not a person. But when Paul urges Philemon to receive Onesimus "no longer as a slave, but better than a slave, as a dear brother" and goes on to speak of him "both as a man and as a brother in the Lord" (16), he makes slavery meaningless. Paul does not appeal to Philemon to take action on such grounds as compassion or private concern (important as these undoubtedly are), but on the basis of love (9), the outworking of the gospel. Paul could say that each person should "retain the place in life that the Lord assigned to him," that the slave is "the Lord's freedman" (1 Cor. 7:17, 22), and that in Christ there is "neither . . . slave nor free" (Gal. 3:28; Col. 3:11). In Philemon we see what that meant in practice.[4] Paul is saying something of permanent significance about the way Christians live in the society of which they are members.[5]

This little letter also sheds light on the character of Paul. The apostle has received criticism in some quarters: he is seen as a hard-liner, intolerant of those who differed from him and rigorous in enforcing conformity to his arbitrary standards. It is good to have this glimpse of a compassionate man, pleading for a runaway slave and ready to pay the cost. It tells us something of his attitude to Philemon, too, and the manner in which he could open up the way for his friend to be magnanimous.

BIBLIOGRAPHY

F. F. **Bruce**, "St. Paul in Rome. 2. The Epistle to Philemon," *BJRL* 48 (1965–66): 81–97; E. R. **Goodenough**, "Paul and Onesimus," *HTR* 22 (1929): 181–83; H. **Greeven**, "Prüfung der Thesen von J. Knox zum Philemonbrief," *TLZ* 79 (1954): 373–78; John **Knox**, *Philemon Among the Letters of Paul* (London: Collins, 1960); J. B. **Lightfoot**, *St Paul's Epistles to the Colossians and to Philemon* (London: Macmillan, 1876); Eduard **Lohse**, *Colossians and Philemon*, Hermeneia (Philadelphia: Fortress, 1971); F. **Lyall**, "Roman Law in the Writings of Paul: The Slave and the Freedman," *NTS* 17 (1970–71): 73–79; Ralph P. **Martin**, *Colossians and Philemon*, NCB (London: Oliphants, 1974); C. F. D. **Moule**, *The Epistles to the Colossians and to Philemon* (Cambridge: Cambridge University Press, 1968); Peter T. **O'Brien**, *Colossians, Philemon*, WBC (Waco, Tex.: Word: 1982); William J. **Richardson**, "Principle and Context in the Ethics of the Epistle to Philemon," *Int* 22 (1968): 301–16; Peter **Stuhlmacher**, *Der Brief an Philemon*, EKKNT (Zürich: Benziger; Neukirchen-Vluyn: Neukirchner, 1975); W. L. **Westermann**, *The Slave Systems of Greek and Roman Antiquity* (Philadelphia: American Philosophical Society, 1955).

---

[4]"The letter effectively shaped early Christian attitudes toward slavery for four centuries" (W. G. Rollins, "Philemon," in *IDBSup*, p. 663).

[5]According to Ralph Martin, the teaching in this letter "is more of how the Christian life is to be lived in a social context" than about the treatment to be given a law-breaking slave (*Colossians and Philemon*, NCB [London: Oliphants, 1974], p. 150).

17

ҺEBREWS

CONTENTS

The book begins without the salutation and the naming of writer and addressees that characterize all New Testament epistles except 1 John and that are common in epistles of the Greco-Roman period. Yet the book concludes in a typically epistolary way, with a benediction, some personal remarks, and a final farewell (13:20–25). Moreover, judging by the specificity of the warnings and moral exhortations that punctuate the document, the writer has specific readers in mind (see 5:12; 6:10; 10:32); the natural way to take 13:22 is that the writer is referring to the entire book (though he does not actually call it an "epistle" or "letter," despite the NIV). It seems justifiable to designate this book an epistle,[1] not least because that is how it has been classified throughout most of its history in the church.

"Epistle" or "letter" in the New Testament period, however, was an extremely broad category (see chap. 7 above). The wealth of rhetorical devices in Hebrews has suggested to many (probably rightly) that this work was originally a homily or series of homilies that have been turned into the published form of a somewhat anomalous letter.[2] This seems considerably more likely than the suggestion that the opening lines were somehow lost or that the present conclusion was added later—suggestions for which there is no textual evidence. In any case, it has been shown that Hebrews 13 is integral to the work as a whole.[3]

The general theme of Hebrews is not in dispute: the unqualified supremacy of God's Son, Jesus Christ, a supremacy that brooks no challenge, whether from angelic or human beings. Correlatively, the covenant he has inaugurated is superior to any covenant that has preceded it, his priesthood is better than Levi's, the sacrifice he has offered is superior to those offered under the Mosaic code, and in fact the very purpose of antecedent revelation was to anticipate him and point to him and to all the blessings he has brought with him. This theme of the supremacy of Christ is not the stuff of an abstract essay; its purpose is repeatedly

---

[1]See esp. C. Spicq, *L'épître aux Hébreux*, 2 vols., EBib (Paris: Gabalda, 1952–53), 1:19–20.

[2]F. F. Bruce calls Hebrews "a homily in written form, with some personal remarks added at the end" (*The Epistle to the Hebrews*, NICNT, rev. ed. [Grand Rapids: Eerdmans, 1990], p. 389.

[3]Harold W. Attridge, *The Epistle to the Hebrews*, Hermeneia (Philadelphia: Fortress, 1989), pp. 13–21.

disclosed by the paraenetic passages (2:1–4; 3:7–4:11; 4:14–16; 5:11–6:12; 10:19–39; 12:1–13:17) designed to warn the readers not to turn back from the Christian faith to the forms of piety they once knew.

It is also widely agreed that this book has been carefully constructed. What is not agreed is the shape of that structure. Some have focused on large thematic movements, concluding that the argument for the superiority of Jesus and of the Christian faith extends from 1:1 to 10:18, after which exhortations take over (10:19–13:25).[4] Most find this suggestion too undiscriminating: exhortations abound in the earlier section, and the argument continues in the later. By drawing attention to catchwords, literary inclusions, and the like, some have argued that the body of the book is nestled between an introduction (1:1–4) and a conclusion (13:20–21), to which have been added the glosses of an accompanying letter (13:19, 22–25), and that this body is made up of five chiastically arranged divisions (i.e. 1:5–2:18, the name higher than the angels; 3:1–5:10, Jesus the merciful high priest; 5:11–10:39, Jesus the high priest in the order of Melchizedek; 11:1–12:13, faith and endurance; 12:14–13:19, the peaceful fruit of righteousness).[5] This has been shown to be a bit contrived;[6] nor does it explain the book's intensity, its passion. Others believe there is a lengthy prologue (1:1–4:13) and a lengthy epilogue (10:19–13:25), between which are two expositions of Jesus as high priest (4:14–6:20; 7:1–10:18).[7] Still others appeal to rhetorical devices to justify various outlines, which vary enormously.[8] Some of them, at least, are not very convincing, such as the view that the book's structure is controlled by the paraenetic passages, which stand in parallel forms at the beginning and end of each large division (in Kümmel's scheme, 1:1–4:13; 4:14–10:31; 10:32–13:17, followed by an epistolary conclusion). But it is far from clear that the paraenetic passages should be divided up (e.g., Do 10:26–31 and 10:32–39 belong in separate divisions?), and some paraenetic passages are thereby largely ignored (e.g., 2:1–4).

Attridge rightly observes that most of the smaller units are well marked and that there is little dispute over them.[9] The question is how to tie these units into the larger structure of the book. His own attempt seeks a balance between the "static organizational principles of the discourse" and its "dynamic, developmental features," that is, the movement of thought; but the result diminishes the concrete contrasts the epistle repeatedly draws.[10] For example, Attridge says that 1:5–2:18 presents Christ the eternal Son as the high priest whose perfected or exalted status was achieved through suffering; the comparison between Christ and the angels is merely a "superficial rubric" used to develop this theme.

In the light of continuing debates on the structure, the following summary

[4]E.g., Guthrie, pp. 717–21; idem, *The Letter to the Hebrews*, TNTC (Grand Rapids: Eerdmans, 1983), pp. 58–59.

[5]So A. Vanhoye, *La structure littéraire de l'épître aux Hébreux*, SN 1 (Paris: Desclée de Brouwer, 1963); Hugh Montefiore, *A Commentary on the Epistle to the Hebrews*, HNTC (San Francisco: Harper, 1964).

[6]See Attridge, *Hebrews*, pp. 15–16.

[7]E.g., Hans Windisch, *Der Hebräerbrief*, HNT 14, 2d ed. (Tübingen: Mohr, 1931).

[8]E.g., Barnabas Lindars, "The Rhetorical Structure of Hebrews," *NTS* 35 (1989): 382–406.

[9]Attridge, *Hebrews*, p. 14.

[10]Ibid., p. 17–21.

surveys the flow of thought with as few judgments as possible on the best way to form a hierarchy of the individual units.

The exordium (1:1–4) stresses the superiority and finality of the divine revelation that appeared in God's Son, Jesus Christ. Verse 4 is transitional, preparing the way for the first sustained argument of the superiority of the Son: he is superior to angelic beings (1:5–14). The first warning or admonition section immediately follows: if this revelation is superior, it is desperately important not to drift away from the gospel it brings, especially when we bear in mind the terrible judgments that befell those who ignored even the earlier, lesser revelation (2:1–4). Chapter 2 briefly continues the contrast between Jesus and the angels (2:5, 9), but only to remind the readers that human destiny transcends that of the angels and that in order to bring humanity to that destiny, Jesus has identified himself with mortal, fallen human beings (2:5–18). In short, he has become their "merciful and faithful high priest in service to God" (2:17).

Before turning to the theme of high priest, however, the author shows in what way Jesus is faithful, and thereby introduces another contrast. Both Moses and Jesus were faithful in their service, but Jesus as the son of the household (3:1–6). Mention of Moses' service in God's household leads to a stern warning not to fall away into unbelief, as many of Moses' generation did (3:7–19). But this is cast in terms of an exposition of Psalm 95:7–11 (Heb. 3:7–11) and of the relation between the rest to which the psalm's readers are invited, the rest intrinsic to entering the land of Canaan, and even the rest God enjoys from the time of the completion of his initial creative work (3:7–4:11). Joshua led his generation into the promised land, but the fact that later Scripture writers promise more rest proves that possession of the land cannot be the ultimate "rest." The rest Jesus provides is superior to that of Joshua's day and is of a piece with the "rest" of God himself. Any thought of escaping the perceptive authority of this revelation is therefore utter folly (4:12–13).

The author returns to the theme of Jesus as high priest, stressing the encouragement Christians enjoy in coming to One who is so able to sympathize with their weaknesses (4:14–16). The same qualifications that applied to the high priests of the old covenant (5:1–4) are superlatively found in Christ (5:5–10) for our encouragement. The section ends by referring to Jesus as the "high priest in the order of Melchizedek," but before the significance of this title is explored, the author again intrudes into the discussion a stern warning (5:11–6:20): he condemns spiritual immaturity (5:11–6:3), warns that apostates cannot be recovered (6:5–8), and encourages his readers to persevere (6:9–12) in light of the certainty of God's promise (6:13–20). The writer then picks up the theme of the Melchizedekian priesthood (7:1–28), linking Genesis 14:18–20 and Psalm 110 so as to demonstrate the superiority of the priesthood of Melchizedek above that of Levi, and to show that Jesus belongs to the former. The crucial point to which the argument leads is the permanent efficacy of Jesus' sacrifice. Unlike the sacrifices of the old covenant, which made nothing perfect (7:19), the sacrifice of Jesus is able "to save completely those who come to God through him" (7:25). Indeed, perfection in this epistle is essentially a matter of completion—in particular, the completion of God's plan of salvation.[11] In that light, the Levitical

---

[11]See esp. David Peterson, *Hebrews and Perfection: An Examination of the Concept of Perfection in the "Epistle to the Hebrews,"* SNTSMS 47 (Cambridge: Cambridge University Press, 1982).

high priest and the old sanctuary are but shadows of the new covenant and the new high priest that the Old Testament prophets themselves foresaw (Heb. 8:1–13; Jer. 31:31–34). Indeed, the announcement of the new covenant had already in principle made the Mosaic covenant old and obsolete (8:13). That truth leads to an exposition of the ritual of the tabernacle, especially the Day of Atonement (9:1–10), in order to show that Christ's sacrifice achieves a permanent effect that the old sacrifices never aspired to (9:11–28). In fact, the old order was designed to be a shadow of the reality that has been introduced by the new (10:1–10). Even the enthronement of the new high priest attests the finality and permanent efficacy of his sacrificial work.

Once again there is a lengthy paraenetic section (10:19–11:39) designed to encourage the readers to press on with their Christian profession. To turn aside is profoundly dangerous in light of the exclusive sufficiency of the new covenant. What is required is persevering faith; and this, too, has been modeled by the Scriptures (11:1–40). The readers must look to Jesus, the pioneer (not "author") and perfecter of our faith (12:1–3)—the one who has both opened up the way to God and completed (or perfected) all that was necessary. In that light, any trials they face are to be borne as discipline from the loving hand of God (12:4–11); to fall away from want of persistence is to align oneself with Esau (12:12–17). Eager to draw further contrasts between the old covenant and the new in order to foster perseverance, the author sets off the heavenly Zion, to which Christians come, with the earthly Sinai of the old covenant (12:18–29), thus tightly merging biblical exposition and paraenesis.

The concluding exhortations (13:1–17) are doubtless shaped to counter particular ways in which the readers' incipient backsliding is in danger of manifesting itself. There are ethical injunctions to obey (13:1–6). The readers will do well both to follow the example of those who first brought them the gospel (13:7–8) and to submit to their current leaders (13:17). Intertwined with this practical encouragement is the exhortation to offer the "sacrifice of praise," a sacrifice contrasted with the sacrifices of the old covenant, since they are fulfilled in the sacrifice of Jesus "outside the camp" (13:9–16). If this entails sharing his disgrace, so be it: the implication is that it is infinitely better to share his disgrace than to defect from his grace.

The author concludes with a request for prayer (13:18–19), his own prayer and doxology (13:20–21), some personal notes (13:22–23), and final greetings and a benediction (13:24–25).

AUTHOR

In the earliest text of Hebrews that has come down to us—p^{46} (early third century)—this epistle is placed in the Pauline corpus, right after Romans.[12] This undoubtedly reflects the conviction of the Eastern church, itself dependent on the more cautious assessment of several notable Alexandrian scholars, whose opinions are largely preserved by Eusebius. In particular, both Clement of Alexandria (c. A.D. 150–215) and Origen (185–253) preserve the tradition that Paul is the author of Hebrews, even though they recognize the difficulties attached to the

---

[12]For the diversity of placement in the manuscripts, see Metzger, pp. 661–62.

view. The Greek of Hebrews is more polished than that of Paul, and the consistent quality of the rhetoric quite remarkable. Doubtless because of similarities between the Greek of Hebrews and the Greek of Luke-Acts, Clement supposes that Paul wrote to the Hebrews in Hebrew and suggests that our Greek text is Luke's translation (*H.E.* 6.14.2). Clement explains the lack of a Pauline superscription by saying that Paul was writing for Hebrews who had formed strong biases against him, and therefore he prudently left his name off. Although Origen insists that the content of Hebrews is not inferior to what is found in Paul's acknowledged letters (*H.E.* 6.25.12), he suggests that one of Paul's disciples took notes of what the apostle said and wrote the material up for him (*H.E.* 6.14.13). He is aware that some think this unnamed party is Luke, and others Clement of Rome, but Origen himself refuses to speculate: "But who wrote the epistle, in truth God knows" (*H.E.* 6.25.14).

In the Western church, Pauline authorship was resisted until the latter half of the fourth century. The Muratorian Canon, Ireneus, and Hippolytus of Rome all agree that Paul was not the author. But the only alternative suggestion is that of Tertullian (in the second century). He insists that Hebrews has more authority than the *Shepherd* of Hermas, owing to the eminence of its author, whom he identifies as Barnabas, as if he is making an ascription that is commonly agreed in his circles (*On Modesty* 20). When Eusebius wrote (c. 325), many in Rome still did not consider Hebrews to be Pauline.

It was the combined opinion of Jerome and Augustine that shifted opinion in the West. Here it was not so much the weight of literary criticism that persuaded them as the fact that admission of a book to the canon was greatly helped by recognition of apostolic authorship. Both Jerome (*Epistle* 129.3) and Augustine (*Forgiveness of Sins* 1.50) refer to the prestigious opinion of the Eastern churches; the former acknowledges that many in the West still had doubts and says that it does not matter who the author really was, since the work is "honored daily by being read in the churches." Despite such weighty support for Pauline authorship, Western synods initially preserved some distinction between Hebrews and the generally recognized Paulines. Both the Synod of Hippo (A.D. 393) and the Third Synod of Carthage (397) enumerate, "Of Paul the apostle, thirteen epistles; of the same to the Hebrews, one." By the Sixth Synod of Carthage (419), fourteen epistles are ascribed to Paul. By and large, Pauline authorship is thereafter affirmed in the West, although even so, the most learned commentators raise caveats. Thus Thomas Aquinas affirms that Luke translated the epistle into excellent Greek.[13]

Not until the Reformation questioned countless ancient traditions was this one submitted to forceful reexamination. Calvin (on 13:23) argued for Clement of Rome or Luke as the author; Luther proposed (for the first time, so far as we know) Apollos. The (Roman Catholic) Council of Trent responded by insisting there are fourteen Pauline epistles—though few Catholic scholars would espouse that view today.

The last major defense of the Pauline authorship of Hebrews was written more than half a century ago.[14] Today virtually no one would repeat the effort. Quite

---

[13]Thomas Aquinas, *Preface to the Epistle to the Hebrews*, quoted by Spicq, *Hébreux* 1:198 n. 1.
[14]William Leonard, *The Authorship of the Epistle to the Hebrews: Critical Problem and Use of the Old Testament* (Rome: Vatican Polyglot Press, 1939).

apart from the differences in vocabulary, Greek style, and rhetoric, which cannot of themselves disprove Pauline authorship but certainly make it a less plausible alternative, the absence of a self-identifying salutation at the beginning of the document—Paul's normal practice—makes it hard to believe that Paul wrote it. Moreover, numerous common Pauline themes are missing, and conversely, the high priesthood of Christ, so central to Hebrews, does not figure largely in the acknowledged Pauline epistles. Above all, it is almost impossible to believe that Paul would identify himself as one of those who heard the gospel not from the Lord but from "those who heard him" (2:3; cf. Gal. 1:11–12).

Neither Luke nor Clement of Rome draws many votes today. The points of connection between Luke and Hebrews are too slight to support a theory of common authorship. Clement of Rome must be dismissed as a likely candidate, not only because he appears to quote Hebrews in several places (though doubtless one could argue that he is quoting his own work!), but especially because his treatment of several themes is so widely removed from the approach of Hebrews. For example, he chooses to buttress his arguments about the nature of the church's ministry by appealing to the ceremonial laws of the Old Testament—a stance utterly at variance with the arguments of Hebrews.

At least in the case of Paul, Luke, and Clement of Rome, there are some extant writings that can be compared with the epistle to the Hebrews. Evidence in support of other writers is entirely circumstantial, since no undisputed document from their pens has come down to us. There are four principal options.

1. Those who suggest Barnabas is the author point out that he was a Levite from Cyprus (Acts 4:36) and therefore a member of the Hellenist party in the Jerusalem church.[15] On this ground, it is suggested he may have shared the antitemple perspectives of Stephen (Acts 7:48–50). For a time he was a close collaborator of Paul (Acts 9:27; 11:30; 13:1–14:28), and since he was called υἱὸς παρακλήσεως (huios parakleseōs, "Son of Encouragement," Acts 4:36), it is entirely appropriate that he should write [τὸν λόγον] ([ton logon] τῆς παρακλήσεως tēs paraklēsōs, a "word of exhortation," Heb. 13:22).

But παράκλησις (paraklēsis, "encouragement" or "exhortation") is sufficiently common in the New Testament that it cannot be restricted to an association with only one person. The epistle to the Hebrews is not so much antitemple as interested in demonstrating the obsolescence in principle of the *biblical* cultus. That Barnabas was a Hellenistic Jew makes him at least potentially qualified to write a Christian book so deeply interacting with the LXX but hardly identifies him as the author.

2. Luther's suggestion of Apollos has gathered a fair bit of support.[16] He is described as ἀνὴρ λόγιος (anēr logios, "a learned man"—more probably, "an eloquent man") with "a thorough knowledge of the Scriptures" (Acts 18:24). He was a native of Alexandria, and many writers have found numerous connections between the epistle to the Hebrews and the writings of Philo of Alexandria. Judging by the Corinthian correspondence (esp. 1 Cor. 1–4), he had some sort of connection with the Pauline mission.

---

[15]See the extended bibliography in Spicq, *Hébreux* 1:199 n. 8, to which may be added J. A. T. Robinson, *Redating the New Testament* (Philadelphia: Westminster, 1976), pp. 200–220.

[16]See bibliography in Attridge, *Hebrews*, p. 4.

But although Luther's suggestion is a brilliant guess, there is insufficient evidence to make it testable. Moreover, many have pointed out that although Hebrews shares some important vocabulary with Philo, the basic elements of his thought are far removed from the neoplatonism and Stoicism that undergird so much of Philo.[17] Of course, Apollos may have transformed the categories in which he was trained as he improved his knowledge of the Christian way. But this is to pile speculation on speculation.

3. From the time of Harnack, a number of scholars have suggested that Priscilla is the author, perhaps in conjunction with her husband Aquila in the minor role.[18] That might account for the interchange between "we" and "I" in the book (the former is more common). They were sufficiently informed that they undertook the teaching of Apollos (Acts 18:26), and they must have known Timothy (see Heb.13:23), since, like them, he worked with Paul in Corinth and Ephesus (Acts 18:5; 19:22; 1 Cor. 16:10, 19). The disappearance of the author's name might then be accounted for by appealing to antifeminist tendencies in the church. Once again, however, there is too little evidence to support the thesis. Above all, this theory seems to be ruled out by the self-reference in the masculine singular in 11:32.

4. Similar objections can be raised against theories that advance as the author of this book Silas, Timothy, Epaphras, the deacon Philip, or Mary the mother of Jesus.

It is far better to admit our ignorance. We do not know who wrote it; almost certainly the first readers did. In all likelihood the author was a Hellenistic Jew who had become a Christian, a second-generation believer (Heb. 2:3). He was steeped in the LXX (none of his numerous quotations from the Old Testament depends on the Hebrew) and, judging by his excellent vocabulary and Greek style, had enjoyed a good education.

PROVENANCE

If we are uncertain who the author of the epistle to the Hebrews was, we are still less certain about the book's geographic provenance. The only explicit clue is found in 13:24: "Those from Italy send you their greetings." Unfortunately, the expression is unclear. It may refer to a group of Italian believers who left their native land and were sending their greetings home (in which case the epistle was sent "to" Italy, but we cannot specify the place from which it was sent),[19] or it may refer to believers *in* Italy (in which case we cannot identify the destination, but the author is writing *from* Italy).[20] Because we cannot be certain which is meant, the ambiguity in the NEB rendering is attractive: "Greetings to you from our Italian friends."

Even if we could be reasonably certain who wrote the book, that would not

---

[17]See esp. Ronald Williamson, *Philo and the Epistle to the Hebrews*, ALGHJ 4 (Leiden: Brill, 1970).

[18]Adolph von Harnack, "Probabilia über die Addresse und den Verfasser des Hebräerbriefes," *ZNW* 1 (1900): 16–41; Ruth Hoppin, *Priscilla: Author of the Epistle to the Hebrews* (New York: Exposition, 1969).

[19]See RSV: "those who come from Italy."

[20]Alexander Nairne translates, "Those who are in Italy and send their greetings with mine from Italy" (*The Epistle of Priesthood* [Edinburgh: T. & T. Clark, 1913], p. 433).

necessarily establish its geographic provenance, since the writer may have moved around quite a bit (as Paul did). As for the book's conceptual provenance, in a work as clearly polemical and paraenetic as this one it is important to recognize that much of the argument may be shaped less by the author's personal interests than by the author's perception of his readers' critical needs. In that case, analysis of the book's conceptual categories may reveal more about the work's intended readers than about the author.

DATE

It is difficult to be certain about the date of Hebrews. The principal points in the debate are these:

1. That the addressees and apparently the author himself belong to the second generation of Christians (2:3) does not yield much concrete information, since "second generation" must be understood not chronologically but genealogically. Probably one should infer that the epistle was not written before A.D. 50; most would insist not before 60.

2. Although some of the quotations of Hebrews in 1 Clement are disputed, it is exceedingly difficult to dismiss the repeated references to Hebrews 1 in 1 Clement 36:1–6.[21] The overwhelming majority of scholars date 1 Clement to A.D. 96. If accepted, this would put a terminus ad quem on the date of Hebrews. It must be admitted, however, that the primary reason for dating 1 Clement so precisely is that some words from the first chapter—"the sudden and repeated misfortunes and calamities which have befallen us"—refer to persecution of Christians under the Emperor Domitian. Evidence for such persecution is slight (see discussion in the section "Date" in chap. 23 below). If it is discounted, the range of possible dates for 1 Clement is opened up from about 70[22] to about 140,[23] with several mediating positions. The very late dates are unlikely, since 1 Clement is cited as an authoritative source by Clement of Alexandria, and the 96 date still seems most plausible; but it is important to recognize the limits of our knowledge.

3. If, as seems likely, the Timothy mentioned in Hebrews 13:23 is the younger companion of Paul, then the epistle to the Hebrews must have been written within his lifetime. Paul co-opted him into missionary service c. A.D. 49, but we do not know how old he was at the time. Still, this probably establishes the upper limit for Hebrews to be about 100, very close to the upper limit imposed by the traditional dating of 1 Clement.

4. Many have attempted to tie the words of Hebrews 12:4 ("in your struggle against sin, you have not yet resisted to the point of shedding your blood") to the particular period of persecution leading up to the persecution under Nero. If the language is figurative, signaling nothing more than strenuous opposition to sin, the passage has no bearing on the date of the book. But even if the passage is

---

[21]See esp. Donald A. Hagner, *The Use of the Old and New Testaments in Clement of Rome*, SuppNovT 34 (Leiden: Brill, 1973), pp. 179–95; Paul Ellingworth, "Hebrews and 1 Clement: Literary Dependence or Common Tradition," *BZ* 23 (1979): 437–40; Herbert Braun, *An die Hebräer*, HNT (Tübingen: Mohr, 1984), pp. 3, 32.

[22]So Robinson, *Redating*, pp. 327–34, largely dependent on G. Edmundson, *The Church in Rome in the First Century*, BL (Oxford: Oxford University Press, 1913), pp. 188–202.

[23]So Elmer T. Merrill, *Essays on Early Christian History* (London: Macmillan, 1924), pp. 217–41; Laurance L. Welborn, "On the Date of 1 Clement," *BR* 29 (1984): 35–54.

understood, somewhat more naturally, to refer to the death of martyrs, it is exceedingly difficult to draw certain inferences. For example, one might conclude that this rules out the church in Rome during or immediately after Nero's persecution, because Christians at that time did lose their lives. That might suggest a date *earlier* than Nero's persecution (A.D. 64). Alternatively, one might suppose this was written to believers elsewhere in the empire who had heard what their fellow believers had *already* suffered under Nero but who had not themselves faced opposition that had gone so far. In that case, the book was written *after* Nero. Similar arguments have been mooted with respect to the reign of Domitian. Above all, opposition from the synagogue sporadically broke out here and there in every decade of the first century, after A.D. 30, making it rather hazardous to use Hebrews 12:4 to isolate a particular date.

5. Perhaps the most important discussion turns on the occurrence of present-tense verbs in connection with the ritual (7:8; 9:6–7, 9, 13; 13:10). In English translation, they read as if the ceremonies are continuing at the time the author is writing. There are two flaws in this argument. First, the present tense in Greek, even in the indicative, does not necessarily refer to present time. Even traditional approaches to Greek grammar observe the frequency of the so-called historic present in Greek; a more linguistically informed approach, appealing to aspect theory, doubts that the (morphological) "present tense" has any immediate bearing on time.[24] Second, Clement of Rome, writing after the destruction of the temple, uses present tenses to describe similar ritual (*1 Clem.* 41); similarly, Josephus alternates between present and past tenses in his discussion of the tabernacle and its furnishings (*Ant.* 4.102–50) and of the vestments of the priests (*Ant.* 4.151–87). Some also point out that the epistle to the Hebrews never specifically mentions the temple: its focus is the biblical tabernacle, and this suggests (they argue) that the destruction of the second temple would not have been of great interest to the author. Therefore silence as to its destruction is no evidence of an early date.

But although the linguistic argument is not decisive, another form of this argument is far stronger. When Josephus, for instance, describes the tabernacle, furnishings, and priestly vestments, he is not engaged in a theological argument about their principal obsolescence, about their utter replacement by the corresponding realities of the new covenant; but that lies at the very heart of the argument in Hebrews. When the author cites Jeremiah's prophecy of a new covenant (Jer. 31:31–34; Heb. 8:7-12), he concludes that by calling this covenant new, God through Jeremiah "made the first one obsolete; and what is obsolete and aging will soon disappear" (8:13). The law-covenant "can never, by the same sacrifices repeated endlessly year after year, make perfect those who draw near to worship. If it could, would they not have stopped being offered?" (10:1–2). It is difficult not to conclude that the sacrifices were still being offered when the author wrote such lines as these. Although he does not directly refer to the temple, he could not have spoken in such terms if he did not see the sacrifices at the temple in fundamental continuity with those established for the tabernacle. By

---

[24]See Stanley E. Porter, *Verbal Aspect in the Greek of the New Testament*, SBG 1 (Bern: Peter Lang, 1989).

the same token, if the sacrifices of the temple had ended (as they did in A.D. 70),[25] it is hard to imagine how he could have resisted pointing this out. As Lindars indicates, the thrust of his rhetoric is to establish the exclusive finality of Christ's sacrifice,[26] and to prevent his readers from returning to the sacrificial system from which they had been weaned when they first became Christians. Had the temple sacrifices already ceased, his argument would have had to be cast in a different guise. True, this is an argument from silence; but it is a powerful argument from silence because, given the nature of his polemic, we expect noise: it is hard to imagine how the author could maintain such silence if he were writing after the destruction of the temple. Although not conclusive, this constitutes strong support for a date before 70 for Hebrews.[27]

6. The strongest argument for a late date turns on the attempt to plot where this book should lie on the trajectory of the development of early Christianity. For instance, it is often argued that the Christology of Hebrews (esp. 1:1–3) reflects the same sort of high Christology found in, say, Luke-Acts, 1 Peter, or the Pastorals, all of them frequently dated to 75–90. But not only is the dating of these documents also disputed, with many scholars insisting on a date before 70 for one or more of these books, but more important, the Christology of Hebrews 1:1–3 is certainly no "higher" than that found in such passages as 1 Corinthians 8:6, Philippians 2:6–11, or Colossians 1:15–20. The overwhelming majority of scholars recognize these passages to be pre-70, and many of them think they represent *pre*-Pauline thought.

Thus, although one cannot decisively rule out any date between about A.D. 60 and 100, the preponderance of evidence favors a date before 70.

DESTINATION

Because the author refers to experiences in the lives of his readers (e.g., 10:32–34), we are right to assume that he has a specific group in mind as he writes. Many ancient commentators, and some moderns,[28] think the addressees lived in Palestine, perhaps even in Jerusalem. The strength of this view turns on the repeated references to the cultus. The complete silence on the temple (as opposed to the tabernacle), however, slightly weakens this theory. The epistle is written in polished Greek, and none of the Old Testament quotations and allusions unambiguously depends on Hebrew or Aramaic: from this we must conclude either that the author knew no Semitic tongue or that his readers, if in Jerusalem,

---

[25]The attempt of Kenneth W. Clark in "Worship in the Jerusalem Temple After A.D. 70," *NTS* 6 (1959–60): 269–80, to prove what his title announces is entirely unconvincing; similarly Otto Michel, *Der Brief an die Hebräer*, KEK, 12th ed. (Göttingen: Vandenhoeck & Ruprecht, 1966), pp. 56–58. Cf. Robinson, *Redating*, pp. 202–3.

[26]Lindars, "Rhetorical Structure."

[27]Modern supporters of a date before A.D. 70 include Bruce, *Hebrews*, pp. 20–22; George Wesley Buchanan, *To the Hebrews*, AB (Garden City, N.Y.: Doubleday, 1972), p. 261; August Strobel, *Der Brief an die Hebräer*, NTD (Göttingen: Vandenhoeck & Ruprecht, 1975), p. 83; Philip Edgcumbe Hughes, *A Commentary on the Epistle to the Hebrews* (Grand Rapids: Eerdmans, 1977), pp. 30–32; and Donald A. Hagner, *Hebrews*, GNC (San Francisco: Harper, 1983), pp. xviii–xix.

[28]E.g., Buchanan, *Hebrews*, pp. 255–56; Hughes, *Commentary*, p. 19. Sir William Ramsay suggested that Hebrews was written to the Jerusalem church from Caesarea while Paul was imprisoned there (c. A.D. 57–59), penned by one of Paul's companions, possibly Philip the evangelist (*Luke the Physician* [London: Hodder & Stoughton: 1908], pp. 301ff.).

were all expatriots, Greek speakers choosing to live in Jerusalem or the surrounding area. In any case, judging by the large numbers of Jews from around the empire that visited Jerusalem at the high feasts, especially Passover, there were countless Jews who did not live in Palestine who nevertheless looked to the cultus in Jerusalem for cleansing and a secure relationship with God. If that is so, it is hard to see what evidence in the book supports Jerusalem or Palestine as the destination, above many other places in the empire.

Although many other candidates for destination have been advanced, including Alexandria, Antioch, Bithynia and Pontus, Caesarea, Colossae, Corinth, Cyprus, Ephesus, and Samaria, the only other suggestion that has garnered a fair measure of support is Rome.[29] In the literature that has come down to us, this is the first place the epistle was known (in the writings of Clement of Rome; see the section "Provenance" above). The fact that the Roman church, and the West in general, took so long to ascribe it to Paul, may argue that they enjoyed positive information that it was *not* written by the apostle. As we have seen, this view entails taking "those from Italy" (Heb. 13:24) to refer to some Italians who left Italy and at the time of writing were living elsewhere (like Priscilla and Aquila), and the Greek certainly allows that interpretation. Both Harnack[30] and William Manson[31] have attempted to tie this theory into the early history of Christianity at Rome, Harnack envisaging that the addressees were in a house church in Rome and Manson envisaging a conservative Jewish-Christian faction there.

Doubtless Rome is as good a guess as any, but it is not much more than a guess. Fortunately, few exegetical issues depend on determining the geographic location of the addressees. The situation that calls forth this epistle is far more important.

PURPOSE

Any assessment of the purpose of Hebrews is inextricably tied to one's understanding of who the addressees were: one cannot discuss the purpose without presupposing some things about the addressees, and vice versa. In the earliest form of the text that has come down to us, p^{46}, this book had the title Πρὸς Ἑβραίους (*Pros Hebraious*, "To [the] Hebrews"). Apparently Clement of Alexandria, writing c. A.D. 180, knew the book under this title, since he speaks of it as having been written Ἑβραίοις (*Hebraiois*, "for Hebrews"; *H.E.* 6.14.3–4). Most scholars assume that this is a later editorial label attached to the work for convenient reference and therefore should not influence our efforts to establish the identity of the addressees. This may be too skeptical (cf. comments in chap. 2 above on the author of Matthew). In any case, it is the content of the book that must finally determine the direction of the discussion, not least because, even if the title was original, it has some ambiguity (e.g., it could refer to Jewish Christians

---

[29]Commentators support Rome with varying degrees of confidence; see Bruce, *Hebrews*, pp. 10–14; Robinson, *Redating*, pp. 205–13; Simon J. Kistemaker, *Exposition of the Epistle to the Hebrews*, NTC (Grand Rapids: Baker, 1984), pp. 17–18; Raymond E. Brown and John P. Meier, *Antioch and Rome* (New York: Paulist, 1983), pp. 139–58; see also the next two notes.

[30]Harnack, "Probabilia."

[31]William Manson, *The Epistle to the Hebrews: An Historical and Theological Reconsideration* (London: Hodder & Stoughton, 1951).

whose mother tongue is Hebrew/Aramaic [Acts 6:1] or to Christians who are Jewish by birth, irrespective of their mother tongue [Phil.3:5]).[32]

All agree that the book is written for Christians, who are urged to maintain their confession (e.g., 3:6, 14; 4:14; 10:23). Their ethnic background is more disputed. Although the book is steeped in Old Testament allusions and Levitical ritual, it does not necessarily follow that either the author or the readers are Jewish Christians; doubtless some Gentile believers immersed themselves in the Greek Old Testament. It is often pointed out that the author's knowledge of Jewish ritual, like the knowledge that he presupposes of his readers, is a literary knowledge: it is drawn from the Old Testament and perhaps other Jewish texts, not (so far as the epistle shows) from any close observation of or participation in the temple ritual in Jerusalem. A number of scholars take this line.[33] Some argue that the warnings against turning "away from the living God" (3:12) better suit former pagans in danger of apostasy than Jews who, if they relapsed into Judaism, would still be serving the living God of their fathers. Others suggest that these are Gentile Christians in danger of abandoning the exclusive claims of Christ and seeking a deeper way in Judaism, a variation on the "Judaizing" controversy. Some think Hebrews attempts to adapt Jewish apocalyptic to a Jewish environment, or tries to dissipate misplaced sacramental piety.

These lines of reasoning have not proved convincing to the majority of scholars. When the author warns against turning "away from the living God" (3:12), he adduces the example of the Israelites under Moses' leadership who turned away from God. If such language applies to ancient Israelites, it is hard to imagine a reason why it could not be applied to first-century Jews. The "elementary teachings" of 6:1 presuppose a background in Judaism, and the author's driving insistence that the old covenant has been eclipsed by the new makes sense only if the readers are still trying to live under it, or if they imagine that, having passed beyond it, they may legitimately revert to it. Moreover, as Bruce points out,[34] nothing in this epistle suggests that the problem the author confronts is Judaizing propaganda.[35] In particular, the nonmention of circumcision makes sense if the epistle is directed to a Jewish-Christian community but would be quite surprising if the readers are Gentile believers in danger of being seduced by the so-called Judaizers.

Furthermore, the author cites the Greek Old Testament as if he assumes that his readers will recognize its authority. That would be true of Hellenistic Jews who had converted to Christianity. Even if they were tempted to modify some elements of their Christian belief and return in some measure to their erstwhile commitment to Judaism, their confidence in what we call the Old Testament would not be shaken. Pagans who had converted to Christianity, should they be

---

[32]See Zahn 2:296.

[33]E.g., Marcus Dods, "The Epistle to the Hebrews," in *EGT*; J. Moffatt, *A Critical and Exegetical Commentary on the Epistle to the Hebrews*, ICC (Edinburgh: T. & T. Clark, 1924); Windisch, *Hebräerbrief*; E. F. Scott, *The Epistle to the Hebrews* (Edinburgh: T. & T. Clark, 1922); G. Vos, *The Teaching of the Epistle to the Hebrews* (Grand Rapids: Eerdmans, 1956); Ernst Käsemann, *The Wandering People of God: An Investigation of the Letter to the Hebrews* (ET Minneapolis: Augsburg, 1984 [from 2d ed., 1957]); Gerd Theissen, *Untersuchungen zum Hebräerbrief*, SNT 2 (Gütersloh: Mohn, 1969).

[34]Bruce, *Hebrews*, p. 6 n. 13.

[35]On the difficulties surrounding the terms "Judaizing" and "Judaizers," see chap. 9, n. 3.

tempted to return to their paganism, would surely also be tempted to abandon their submission to the Scriptures that had contributed to their becoming Christians. Moreover, not a few of the author's arguments for the superiority of Jesus turn on challenging the assumption that the cultic regulations of the Sinai code were final (e.g., 7:11). Christians in danger of reverting to paganism would scarcely need that kind of argument; Christians in danger of reverting to Judaism certainly would.

Among those who believe the intended readers are Jewish Christians, many have attempted to identify a particular subset of Jews. Bornhaüser infers from 5:12 (the author's insistence that by this point his readers should be teachers) that they were not ordinary Jewish-Christians but some of the "large number of priests" who "became obedient to the faith" (Acts 6:7).[36] Spicq at first defended this theory[37] and then modified it by suggesting that they were "Esseno-Christians," including former members of the Qumran community.[38] Several scholars have urged variations on this theme.[39] But the most that can reasonably be said is that the Jewish background of the readers was probably not so much in the conservative rabbinic traditions of Palestine as in Hellenistic Judaism influenced by various nonconformist Jewish sects, of which the Essenes are but one example.[40]

Others think that the readers have been attracted, not to a form of Jewish faith and practice independent of Christianity, but to a form of Jewish Christianity more conservative than what the author himself approves.[41] There is a sense in which this appears to be correct, and another in which it seems quite false. It is probably correct in that there is no conclusive evidence that the readers thought of themselves as apostates. They probably did not set out to abandon the Christian gospel and return to Judaism. In that sense the readers are turning to a form of "Jewish Christianity" more conservative than what the author himself approves. But the author's point is that what the readers are in danger of adopting is *in fact* no Christianity at all. It is nothing less than apostasy: hence the strong paraenetic passages. The lengthy expositions intertwined with the paraenesis provide the grounds for this judgment. To return to reliance upon the cultic structures of the old covenant is not only to fail to appreciate the way in which they pointed to Christ across the years of redemptive history, it is implicitly to assign to them a redemptive effectiveness that they never possessed and simultaneously to depreciate the exclusive significance of Christ and his sacrifice.

The reasons the readers have for reverting to some form of Judaism (overlaid, perhaps, with continuing protestations of faithfulness to Christianity) are not

---

[36]Karl B. Bornhäuser, *Empfänger und Verfasser des Briefes an die Hebräer*, BFCT 35,3 (Gütersloh: Bertelsmann, 1932).

[37]Spicq, *Hébreux* 1:226ff.

[38]C. Spicq, "L'épître aux Hébreux: Apollos, Jean-Baptiste, les héllenistes, et Qumrân," *RevQ* 1 (1958–59): 365–90, esp. p. 390.

[39]E.g., Hans Kosmala, *Hebräer-Essener-Christen*, SPB 1 (Leiden: Brill, 1959); Hughes, *Commentary*, pp. 10–15.

[40]See F. F. Bruce, " 'To the Hebrews' or 'To the Essenes'?" *NTS* 9 (1962–63): 217–32. See the excellent discussion of conceptual backgrounds in R. M. Wilson, *Hebrews*, NCB (Grand Rapids: Eerdmans, 1987), pp. 18–27.

[41]So J. V. Dahms, "The First Readers of Hebrews," *JETS* 20 (1977): 365–75; Brown and Meier, *Antioch and Rome*, pp. 151–58.

spelled out in detail; they are simply hinted at. For instance, it appears they were tired of bearing the shame of living outside the mainstream of their cultural heritage (13:13). They were in danger of focusing on novel teachings (13:9) at the expense of the apostolic gospel (13:7–8). It is also possible that fear was a contributing motivation. The religion of the Jews was recognized by the Romans; Christianity was not. To be seen to return to the fold of Judaism might alleviate the threat of persecution by the state authorities. In any case, the discipline of the Christians was apparently fading as they withdrew from regular meetings (10:25; this *may* signal that the readers belonged to a house church that was no longer meeting with the rest of the church). But whatever their reasons, it is not so much the *reasons* that interest the author as the *outcome*: Christ, his sacrifice, and his priestly work are so relativized that they are effectively denied, and apostasy is only a whisker away. It is to prevent just such a calamity that the author writes this epistle.

TEXT

The major witnesses are nicely set out by Attridge.[42] The manuscript tradition is not unlike that of the Pauline corpus, though somewhat idiosyncratic by comparison. The most important witnesses are overwhelmingly Alexandrian.[43] The Byzantine tradition is represented by the uncials K and L (both ninth century) and many later minuscules; the Western text type is represented by D (Codex Claromontanus, sixth century) and the Old Latin. On the whole, the text of Hebrews is well preserved, though difficult decisions are called for in several passages (e.g., 1:8; 11:17, 37; 12:3, 7).

ADOPTION INTO THE CANON

In the Western church, as we have seen above in the section "Authors," although the epistle to the Hebrews was widely known and quoted, it was not at first received as canonical. In addition to the evidence from Clement of Rome, a number of other early Western fathers allude to it or cite it (e.g., Ignatius, *Phil.* 9:1; *Shepherd* of Hermas 2.3.2; Justin Martyr, *Dial.* 116.1), but none treats it as apostolic or canonical. The Muratorian Canon (c. A.D. 170–80) excludes Hebrews.

Doubtless when it was incorporated into the Pauline corpus—probably in Alexandria, in the second century—it was being acknowledged to have canonical status. Indeed, its canonicity was never (so far as we know) doubted in Alexandria or in the Eastern church, whatever doubts may have been entertained about its authorship (by Origen and others, as we have seen). Eusebius (*H.E.* 3.3.5) includes Hebrews among the "acknowledged" books, though he is aware of doubts in the West. The Syrian fathers never dispute its canonical status. And eventually, as we have seen, the convictions of the Eastern church won out in the West, owing to the influence of Jerome and Augustine.[44]

[42]Attridge, *Hebrews*, pp. 31–32.
[43]See Frank W. Beare, "The Text of the Epistle to the Hebrews in p^{46}," *JBL* 63 (1944): 379–96; and esp. Spicq, *Hébreux* 1:412–32.
[44]For a brief overview of Reformation responses, see Hughes, pp. 23–24; Bruce, *Hebrews*, pp. 24–25.

HEBREWS IN RECENT STUDY

In addition to studies that continue to probe the setting and circumstances that called forth this epistle, we may mention the considerable scholarly interest in the following areas:

1. The peculiar Christological emphases of Hebrews capture the attention of many scholars.[45] There are clear links with John and Paul (e.g., in the "Son" language and in the high Christology of Heb. 1:1–3), but the exposition of the priestly work of Christ, both on earth and in heaven, is much fuller here than anywhere else in the New Testament. Hebrews also displays firm interest in the historical Jesus.[46]

2. In particular, considerable attention has been devoted to what this epistle says about Melchizedek and to comparison of this treatment with other Jewish traditions about him, not least in the Dead Sea Scrolls.[47]

3. The epistle's interest in Melchizedek is part and parcel of its detailed appeal to many Old Testament texts. Only Matthew in the New Testament rivals this book for the range and hermeneutical complexity of the Old Testament texts it cites. Inevitably, this phenomenon has drawn much scholarly attention.[48]

4. Several themes in Hebrews attract continual attention, either because they are more prominent in Hebrews than elsewhere in the New Testament, or because the treatment of them is distinctively nuanced. They include perfection,[49] (Sabbath)-rest (Heb. 4),[50] and faith (Heb. 11).[51]

THE CONTRIBUTION OF HEBREWS

Much of the canonical contribution peculiar to Hebrews lies in the distinctive emphases of the book that also draw scholarly attention, just outlined. The epistle to the Hebrews greatly enriches New Testament Christology, especially with respect to Jesus' priestly work, the finality of his sacrifice, the nature of his sonship, the importance of the incarnation (see esp. chap. 2), and his role as "pioneer" (ἀρχηγός [archēgos]).

Similarly, because of its extensive use of Old Testament texts, this epistle enables us to explore the hermeneutical assumptions of first-century Christians, so as

---

[45]See the bibliography in Attridge, Hebrews, p. 25 n. 197; and esp. William R. G. Loader, Sohn und Hoherpriester: Eine traditionsgeschichtliche Untersuchung zur Christologie des Hebräerbriefes, WMANT 53 (Neukirchen-Vluyn: Neukirchener, 1981).

[46]See Bertram L. Melbourne, "An Examination of the Historical-Jesus Motif in the Epistle to the Hebrews," AUSS 26 (1988): 281–97.

[47]E.g., Fred L. Horton, The Melchizedek Tradition: A Critical Examination of the Sources to the Fifth Century A.D. and in the Epistle to the Hebrews, SNTSMS 30 (Cambridge: Cambridge University Press, 1976); Paul J. Kobelski, Melchizedek and Melchireša', CBQMS 10 (Washington, D.C.: Catholic Biblical Association, 1981).

[48]E.g., Simon J. Kistemaker, The Psalm Citations in the Epistle to the Hebrews (Amsterdam: Soest, 1961); Friedrich Schröger, Der Verfasser des Hebräerbriefes als Schriftausleger, BU 4 (Regensburg: Pustet, 1968).

[49]E.g., Peterson, Hebrews and Perfection.

[50]E.g., Otfried Hofius, Katapausis: Die Vorstellung vom endzeitlichen Ruheort im Hebräerbrief, WUNT 11 (Tübingen: Mohr, 1970); A. T. Lincoln, "Sabbath, Rest, and Eschatology in the New Testament," in From Sabbath to Lord's Day: A Biblical, Historical, and Theological Investigation, ed. D. A. Carson (Grand Rapids: Zondervan, 1982), pp. 197–220.

[51]E.g., Erich Grässer, Der Glaube im Hebräerbrief (Marburg: Elwert, 1965).

better to learn how to read the Old Testament. The nature of typology, the understanding of prophecy that goes far beyond merely verbal prediction, the interplay between exegesis of specific texts, and the constraints of redemptive history are all exemplified in Hebrews. It thus also provides many of the working elements for developing biblical theology.

The epistle joins other New Testament books (e.g., Acts and Galatians) in providing an independent slant on the difficult movement from an understanding of Israel as the locus of the people of God, constrained by the law-covenant of Sinai, to the church as the people of God, constrained by the covenant sealed by Jesus and his death and resurrection. Finally, Hebrews links with some other New Testament books (e.g., 1 John) that are vitally interested in the problem of the perseverance of Christians and the nature and danger of apostasy.

BIBLIOGRAPHY

Harold W. **Attridge**, *The Epistle to the Hebrews*, Hermeneia (Philadelphia: Fortress, 1989); Frank W. **Beare**, "The Text of the Epistle to the Hebrews in p^{46}," *JBL* 63 (1944): 379–96; Karl B. **Bornhäuser**, *Empfänger und Verfasser des Briefes an die Hebräer*, BFCT 35,3 (Gütersloh: Bertelsmann, 1932); Herbert **Braun**, *An die Hebräer*, HNT 14 (Tübingen: Mohr, 1984); Raymond E. **Brown** and John P. **Meier**, *Antioch and Rome* (New York: Paulist, 1983); F. F. **Bruce**, *The Epistle to the Hebrews*, NICNT, 2d ed. (Grand Rapids: Eerdmans, 1990); idem, " 'To the Hebrews' or 'To the Essenes'?" *NTS* 9 (1962–63): 217–32; George Wesley **Buchanan**, *To the Hebrews*, AB (Garden City, N.Y.: Doubleday, 1972); Kenneth W. **Clark**, "Worship in the Jerusalem Temple After A.D. 70," *NTS* 6 (1959–60): 269–80; J. V. **Dahms**, "The First Readers of Hebrews," *JETS* 20 (1977): 365–75; Franz **Delitsch**, *Commentary on the Epistle to the Hebrews*, 2 vols. (Edinburgh: T. & T. Clark, 1871 [reprint], Minneapolis: Klock & Klock, 1978); Marcus **Dods**, "The Epistle to the Hebrews," in *EGT*/4; G. **Edmundson**, *The Church in Rome in the First Century*, BL (Oxford: Oxford University Press, 1913); Paul **Ellingworth**, "Hebrews and 1 Clement: Literary Dependence or Common Tradition," *BZ* 23 (1979): 437–40; Erich **Grässer**, *Der Glaube im Hebräerbrief* (Marburg: Elwert, 1965); idem, "Der Hebräerbrief, 1938–1963," *ThR* 30 (1964): 138–226; Rowan A. **Grier**, *The Captain of Our Salvation* (Tübingen: Mohr, 1973); Donald **Guthrie**, *The Letter to the Hebrews*, TNTC (Grand Rapids: Eerdmans, 1983); Donald A. **Hagner**, *Hebrews*, GNC (San Francisco: Harper, 1983); idem, *The Use of the Old and New Testaments in Clement of Rome*, SuppNovT 34 (Leiden: Brill, 1973); Adolph von **Harnack**, "Probabilia über die Addresse und den Verfasser des Hebräerbriefes," *ZNW* 1 (1900): 16–41; Jean **Héring**, *The Epistle to the Hebrews* (London: Epworth, 1970); Otfried **Hofius**, *Katapausis: Die Vorstellung vom endzeitlichen Ruheort im Hebräerbrief*, WUNT 11 (Tübingen: Mohr, 1970); Ruth **Hoppin**, *Priscilla: Author of the Epistle to the Hebrews* (New York: Exposition, 1969); Fred L. **Horton**, *The Melchizedek Tradition: A Critical Examination of the Sources to the Fifth Century A.D. and in the Epistle to the Hebrews*, SNTSMS 30 (Cambridge: Cambridge University Press, 1976); Graham **Hughes**, *Hebrews and Hermeneutics: The Epistle to the Hebrews as a New Testament Example of Biblical Interpretation*, SNTSMS 36 (Cambridge: Cambridge University Press, 1979); Philip Edgcumbe **Hughes**, *A Commentary on the Epistle to the Hebrews* (Grand Rapids: Eerdmans, 1977); Ernst **Käsemann**, *The Wandering People of God: An Investigation of the Letter to the Hebrews* (ET Minneapolis: Augsburg, 1984 [from 2d ed., 1957]); Simon J. **Kistemaker**,

Exposition of the Epistle to the Hebrews, NTC (Grand Rapids: Baker, 1984); idem, *The Psalm Citations in the Epistle to the Hebrews* (Amsterdam: Soest, 1961); Paul J. **Kobelski**, *Melchizedek and Melchireša'*, CBQMS 10 (Washington, D.C.: Catholic Biblical Association, 1981); Hans **Kosmala**, *Hebräer-Essener-Christen*, SPB 1 (Leiden: Brill, 1959); William **Leonard**, *The Authorship of the Epistle to the Hebrews: Critical Problem and Use of the Old Testament* (Rome: Vatican Polyglot Press, 1939); A. T. **Lincoln**, "Sabbath, Rest, and Eschatology in the New Testament," in *From Sabbath to Lord's Day: A Biblical, Historical, and Theological Investigation*, ed. D. A. Carson (Grand Rapids: Zondervan, 1982), pp. 197–220; Barnabas **Lindars**, "The Rhetorical Structure of Hebrews," *NTS* 35 (1989): 382–406; William R. G. **Loader**, *Sohn und Hoherpriester: Eine traditionsgeschichtliche Untersuchung zur Christologie des Hebräerbriefes*, WMANT 53 (Neukirchen-Vluyn: Neukirchener, 1981); William **Manson**, *The Epistle to the Hebrews: An Historical and Theological Reconsideration* (London: Hodder & Stoughton, 1951); Elmer T. **Merrill**, *Essays on Early Christian History* (London: Macmillan, 1924); Otto **Michel**, *Der Brief an die Hebräer*, KEK, 12th ed. (Göttingen: Vandenhoeck & Ruprecht, 1966); J. **Moffatt**, *A Critical and Exegetical Commentary on the Epistle to the Hebrews*, ICC (Edinburgh: T. & T. Clark, 1924); Hugh **Montefiore**, *A Commentary on the Epistle to the Hebrews*, HNTC (San Francisco: Harper, 1964); Alexander **Nairne**, *The Epistle of Priesthood* (Edinburgh: T. & T. Clark, 1913); David **Peterson**, *Hebrews and Perfection: An Examination of the Concept of Perfection in the "Epistle to the Hebrews,"* SNTSMS 47 (Cambridge: Cambridge University Press, 1982); V. C. **Pfitzber**, *Hebrews* (Adelaide: Lutheran Publishing House, 1979); Sir William **Ramsay**, *Luke the Physician* (London: Hodder & Stoughton: 1908); J. A. T. **Robinson**, *Redating the New Testament* (Philadelphia: Westminster, 1976); Friedrich **Schröger**, *Der Verfasser des Hebräerbriefes als Schriftausleger*, BU 4 (Regensburg: Pustet, 1968); E. F. **Scott**, *The Epistle to the Hebrews* (Edinburgh: T. & T. Clark, 1922); C. **Spicq**, *L'épître aux Hébreux*, 2 vols., EBib (Paris: Gabalda, 1952–53); idem, "L'épître aux Hébreux: Apollos, Jean-Baptiste, les héllenistes, et Qumrân," *RevQ* 1 (1958–59): 365–90; August **Strobel**, *Der Brief an die Hebräer*, NTD (Göttingen: Vandenhoeck & Ruprecht, 1975); James **Swetnam**, *Jesus and Isaac: A Study of the Epistle to the Hebrews in the Light of the Aqedah*, AnBib 94 (Rome: Pontifical Biblical Institute, 1981); R. V. G. **Tasker**, *The Gospel in the Epistle to the Hebrews* (London: Tyndale, 1950); Gerd **Theissen**, *Untersuchungen zum Hebräerbrief*, SNT 2 (Gütersloh: Mohn, 1969); A. **Vanhoye**, *La structure littéraire de l'épître aux Hébreux*, SN 1 (Paris: Desclée de Brouwer, 1963); G. **Vos**, *The Teaching of the Epistle to the Hebrews* (Grand Rapids: Eerdmans, 1956); Laurance L. **Welborn**, "On the Date of 1 Clement," *BR* 29 (1984): 35–54; Brooke Foss **Westcott**, *The Epistle to the Hebrews*, 3d ed. (London: Macmillan, 1909); Ronald **Williamson**, *Philo and the Epistle to the Hebrews*, ALGHJ 4 (Leiden: Brill, 1970); R. M. **Wilson**, *Hebrews*, NCB (Grand Rapids: Eerdmans, 1987); Hans **Windisch**, *Der Hebräerbrief*, HNT 14, 2d ed. (Tübingen: Mohr, 1931).

18

James

CONTENTS

The letter of James, a series of loosely related homilies, resists clear structural demarcation. But five general sections can be discerned.

Trials and Christian maturity (1:1–18). After the address and salutation (1:1), James opens with a section in which he attacks several issues, among which Christian suffering ("trials") is the most prominent (1:2–18). He encourages his readers to find meaning and purpose in their suffering (1:2–4), to pray in faith for wisdom (1:5–8), and to apply a Christian worldview to poverty and wealth (1:9–11). After coming back to the subject of trials (1:12), he moves into the issue of temptation (1:13–15), a transition eased by the fact that the words $\pi\epsilon\iota\rho\acute{\alpha}\zeta\omega$ (*peirazō*) and $\pi\epsilon\iota\rho\alpha\sigma\mu\acute{o}\varsigma$ (*peirasmos*) can connote either "trials" or "temptations." The section concludes with a reminder of God's goodness in giving (1:16–18).

True Christianity seen in its works (1:19–2:26). The second section of the letter is marked out by a focus on three key words: "word [of God]" (esp. 1:19–27), "law" (esp. 2:1–13), and "works" (esp. 2:14–26). After a warning about loose speech and anger (1:19–20), James encourages his readers to "accept the word planted in you" (1:21) and then expands this exhortation by showing that true receiving of God's word involves *doing* it (1:22–27). As an important instance of "doing the word," James cites the need for Christians to be impartial in their treatment of others. Only so will they fulfill the "royal law" and escape judgment (2:1–13). The significance of Christians' actions in avoiding judgment sparks James's famous discussion of faith and works (2:14–26). James insists that true faith is always marked by obedience and that only such faith evidenced in works will bring salvation.

Dissensions within the community (3:1–4:12). No obvious breaks distinguish the third section of the letter. But we may view James's warnings about improper speech (3:1–12; 4:11–12) as indicative of an *inclusio* in which James focuses generally on the problem of dissensions among Christians and its roots in envy. Harking back to a topic touched on earlier (1:19–20, 26), James uses a series of vivid and memorable images to warn Christians about the power and danger of the tongue (3:1–12). He then tackles the problem of dissensions headon, tracing such external unrest to the wrong kind of wisdom (3:13–18) and to frustrated desires (4:1–3). The passage 4:4–10 issues a stern warning about a compromising kind of Christianity and summons the readers to repentance. The section ends with a final exhortation about speech (4:11–12).

Implications of a Christian worldview (4:13–5:11). This section is the least obvious, but we may suggest that its major general theme has to do with a Christian worldview. One such implication is the need to take God into account in all the plans we make (4:13–17). Another is the recognition that God will judge the wicked rich (5:1–6) and reward the righteous (5:7–11) at the time of the Lord's return.

Concluding exhortations (5:12–20). James finishes with exhortations about oaths (in keeping with Jesus' teaching, James urges that they be avoided [5:12]); prayer, especially for physical healing (5:13–18); and the responsibility of believers to look after one another's spiritual health (5:19–20).

AUTHOR

The letter claims to have been written by "James, a servant of God and of the Lord Jesus Christ" (1:1). The lack of elaboration points to a well-known James, and it is natural to think first of those men by this name who are mentioned in the New Testament. There are at least four: (1) James the son of Zebedee, brother of John, one of the Twelve (see, e.g., Mark 1:19; 5:37; 9:2; 10:35; 14:33); (2) James the son of Alphaeus, also one of the Twelve (see Mark 3:18; he may be the same as "James the younger" [Mark 15:40]); (3) James the father of Judas (Luke 6:16; Acts 1:13);[1] (4) James, "the Lord's brother" (Gal. 1:19), who plays a leading role in the early Jerusalem church (see Acts 12:17; 15:13; 21:18).

Of these four, the last is by far the most obvious candidate for the authorship of this letter. James the father of Judas is too obscure to be seriously considered; the same is true, to a lesser degree, of James the son of Alphaeus. James the son of Zebedee, on the other hand, is given a prominent role among the Twelve, but the date of his martyrdom—c. A.D. 44 (see Acts 12:2)—is probably too early to allow us to associate him with the letter. We are left, then, with James the brother of the Lord, who is certainly the most prominent James in the early church.

A circumstance that corroborates this decision is the striking similarities between the Greek of the epistle of James and that of the speech attributed to James in Acts 15:13–21.[2] Also in keeping with this identification are the frequent allusions to the teaching of Jesus within the letter, the Jewish atmosphere of the book, and the authority assumed by the author in addressing "the twelves tribes in the dispersion." Early Christian testimony is not unanimous on the point but tends to favor the same identification. Origen identifies "James the apostle" as the author,[3] but only the sometimes unreliable Latin translation of Origen by Rufinius explicitly mentions the brother of the Lord. Eusebius claims that the letter was

---

[1]In the expression Ἰούδαν Ἰακώβου (*Ioudan Iakōbou*, lit. "[he called] . . . Judas of James," Luke 6:16), the genitive Ἰακώβου (*Iakōbou*) probably indicates "son of" ("Judas son of James") but could mean "brother of."

[2]For these parallels and discussion, see particularly J. B. Mayor, *The Epistle of St. James* (London: Macmillan, 1913), pp. iii–iv.

[3]Origen, *Comm. on John*, frag. 126.

generally attributed to James the Lord's brother but that there were some dissenters (*H.E.* 3.25.3; 2.23.25).[4]

The case for identifying the letter with James the brother of the Lord is, then, quite strong. Despite this, alternative theories of authorship have been propounded, and these must now be considered.

1. A few scholars have attributed the letter to an unknown James.[5] But while this is possible and would conflict with nothing in the letter itself, the simplicity of the author's identification points to a well-known individual—and so well known a person is likely mentioned in the New Testament.

2. The most important alternative is that the letter is pseudonymous—that it was written by an unknown early Christian in the name of James.[6] Advocates of this view agree that the "James" in the salutation points to James the brother of the Lord but are convinced that this James could not have written this letter. They base this conclusion on four main arguments:

It is thought to be inconceivable that a brother of the Lord would have written such a letter without alluding to his special relationship to Christ or to his confrontation with the resurrected Christ (cf. 1 Cor. 15:7). This objection presupposes, however, that blood relationship to Christ was highly valued in the early church. But this is doubtful, particularly in the case of James, who derived no spiritual benefit from his earthly relationship to Christ (see John 7:1–5). It is noteworthy in this respect that the author of Acts never calls James "the brother of the Lord." In fact, the importance of physical ties to Christ emerged only later in the history of the church; the reticence of the letter in this respect favors an early date.[7]

Another reason for denying the letter to James the brother of the Lord is the language and cultural background of the letter. It is written in fairly good Hellenistic Greek and evidences certain literary touches in its choice of vocabulary and style (e.g., the incomplete hexameter in 1:17). Moreover, the author alludes to concepts derived from Greek philosophy and religion (e.g., the phrase ὁ τροχὸς τῆς γενέσεως [*ho trochos tēs geneseōs*, "the whole course of his life"] in 3:6). Could a Galilean Jew with the reputation of being a conservative Jewish Christian and who, as far as we know, never left Palestine, write such Greek with such sophisticated allusions? Many answer no.

But this answer is not so obviously the right one, for three reasons. First, while the Greek of the letter is undoubtedly well polished, its quality should not be exaggerated. Ropes concludes that "there is nothing to suggest acquaintance with the higher styles of Greek literature."[8] James's style is not that of a literary Atticist, but that found in other Hellenistic-Jewish works of his day, such as *Testaments of*

---

[4]Guthrie, pp. 723–26.

[5]E.g., Erasmus; Luther; Hunter, pp. 168–69 (though cautiously); J. Moffat, *The General Epistles: James, Peter, and Judas* (London: Hodder & Stoughton, 1928), p. 2.

[6]Some of the more important presentations of this view are Kümmel, pp. 411–14; James Hardy Ropes, *A Critical and Exegetical Commentary on the Epistle of St. James*, ICC (Edinburgh: T. & T. Clark, 1916), pp. 43–52; Martin Dibelius, *Commentary on the Epistle of James*, Hermeneia, rev. by H. Greeven (Philadelphia: Fortress, 1976), pp. 11–21; Sophie Laws, *A Commentary on the Epistle of James*, HNTC (San Francisco: Harper & Row, 1980), pp. 38–42.

[7]See the important article of Gerhard Kittel, "Der geschichtliche Ort des Jakobusbriefes," *ZNW* 41 (1942): 73–75.

[8]Ropes, *James*, p. 25. Zahn minimizes the quality of the Greek even more (1:112).

the Twelve Patriarchs and Sirach. Second, we must not underestimate the extent to which Palestinian Jews in the first century were conversant with Greek. Recent discoveries suggest that Greek was a language widely used in Palestine and that someone like James would have had ample opportunity to become fluent in the language.[9] Indeed, J. N. Sevenster uses James as a test case for his investigation into Greek influence in Palestine and concludes that the brother of the Lord could very well have written the letter.[10] Third, the religious and philosophical concepts alluded to in James are of the sort that would have been fairly widespread among the general population.[11] We conclude, then, that the language of the letter is no obstacle to identifying the brother of the Lord as its author.

A theological reason for thinking that James the brother of the Lord could not have written this epistle has to do with the way the Old Testament law and Judaism generally are treated.[12] In both Galatians (2:12) and Acts (21:17–25), it is argued, James appears to be a spokesman for a conservative Jewish-Christian position on these matters. Later legend magnifies this characteristic, where James is seen as zealous for the law and respected by most of his Jewish contemporaries.[13] Yet the letter takes a somewhat liberal view of the law, ignoring its ritual demands and calling the law "the law of liberty" (1:25; 2:12).

A response to this argument would be to note that both sides of the polarity just sketched are exaggerated. On the one hand, the legends that picture James as a hidebound Jewish traditionalist are probably tendentious.[14] Nor is the New Testament evidence about James's theological position clear. Galatians 2:12 tells us only that the Judaizers in Antioch *claimed* to come from James, and Acts 21:17–25 betrays no extreme Jewish viewpoint. On the other hand, James's rather liberal pronouncement on the question of the law and circumcision in Acts 15 paints a very different picture. Moreover, the letter of James, while not encouraging obedience to the ritual law, does not prohibit it—and we can surmise that this may have been a nonissue for James and his readers. Nor does the view of the law in the letter conflict in any way with what we can assume to have been James's position.

The final main reason for thinking that James must be pseudonymous turns on the relationship between Paul and the letter of James on the doctrine of justification. As is well known, the letter of James (2:20–26) takes an approach to this issue that many find to be at variance with Paul's view. Yet it is also generally thought that what James says fails to meet Paul's position directly—that he is arguing with a garbled or misunderstood form of Paul's teaching on this matter. These circumstances, it is argued, can be accounted for only by presuming that the

---

[9]See esp. J. N. Sevenster, *Do You Know Greek? How Much Greek Could the First Jewish Christians Have Known?* (Leiden: Brill, 1968).

[10]Ibid., p. 191; see also J. H. Moulton, W. F. Howard, and Nigel Turner, *A Grammar of New Testament Greek*, 4 vols. (Edinburgh: T. & T. Clark, 1908–76), 4:114.

[11]Martin Hengel has demonstrated the degree to which first-century Palestine was permeated with Hellenistic concepts (*Judaism and Hellenism*, 2 vols. [Philadelphia: Fortress, 1974]). With respect to James, see also Hengel's article "Der Jakobusbrief als antipaulinische Polemik," in *Tradition and Interpretation in the New Testament*, Fs. E. Earle Ellis, ed. G. F. Hawthorne and Otto Betz (Grand Rapids: Eerdmans, 1987), p. 252.

[12]Dibelius labels this the decisive argument against the traditional position (*James*, pp. 17–18).

[13]We are dependent on Hegesippus's account of James's death as recorded in Eusebius (*H.E.* 2.23) for much of this information.

[14]See J. B. Lightfoot, *The Epistle of St. Paul to the Galatians* (London: Macmillan, 1890), p. 366.

letter of James was written considerably later than Paul. Kümmel succinctly summarizes the point: "The debate in 2:14ff. with a misunderstood secondary stage of Pauline theology not only presupposes a considerable chronological distance from Paul—whereas James died in the year 62—but also betrays a complete ignorance of the polemical intent of Pauline theology, which lapse can scarcely be attributed to James, who as late as 55/56 met with Paul in Jerusalem (Acts 21:18ff.)."[15]

The relationship between James 2:14–26 and Paul's teaching is the most vexing theological issue in the letter, and we consider this later (see the section "The Contribution of James"). But assuming that the relationship between James 2 and Paul is as described above (that James 2 responds to a misunderstood form of Paul's teaching), the point to be made here is that there is an alternative explanation for the situation. Could not the letter of James have been written at a time during which Paul's teaching was beginning to have an impact on the church, yet *before* James and Paul had met?[16] Such a circumstance would explain the fact that James seems to have Paul's distinctive emphasis on justification by faith in mind, yet does not fairly grapple with Paul's real point with the doctrine. In other words, James's contact with Paul's doctrine would be only indirect, coming from those who have misunderstood Paul's teaching and taken the idea of justification by faith alone as an excuse for moral laxity. It is to this garbled form of Paul's teaching that James responds because he is writing before he had the opportunity to learn from Paul himself just what Paul means by the doctrine. If this situation is possible (and it makes more sense of James 2 than to suppose that someone with Paul's letters in hand would so seriously misunderstand him), then the teaching of James 2 offers no difficulty to thinking that the Lord's brother could have written it.

3. A third general position on the authorship of James admits the force of both the evidence for identifying the writer of the letter with the brother of the Lord *and* of the objections brought against that identification. A mediating position is therefore adopted, according to which James's teaching lies at the base of the letter but has undergone a later editing that has put it in the form we now have it.[17] The main objection to this view is that it is unnecessary. We have seen that the arguments against the ascription of the letter to James the brother of the Lord do not hold water. It is far simpler, then, to view James as the author of the letter in the form that we now have it than to hypothesize levels of redaction for which there is no textual or solid historical evidence.

We conclude, then, that James the brother of the Lord is the author of the letter. This is the natural implication of the letter's own claims, it is corroborated by New Testament and early Christian evidence, and it has no decisive argument against it.

---

[15]Kümmel, p. 413.

[16]For this argument, see particularly Kittel, "Der geschichtliche Ort," pp. 96–97; see also Walter Wessel, "James, Letter of," in *ISBE* 2:965.

[17]See esp. Peter Davids, *The Epistle of James*, NIGTC (Grand Rapids: Eerdmans, 1982), pp. 12–13; Ralph P. Martin, *James*, WBC (Waco, Tex.: Word, 1988), pp. lxix–lxxviii; Wiard Popkes, *Adressaten, Situation, und Form des Jakobusbriefe*, SBS 125/126 (Stuttgart: Katholisches Bibelwerk, 1986), pp. 184–88.

PROVENANCE

If the author of the letter is unknown, then almost any provenance for the letter is possible. Laws, for instance, noting resemblances between James and several works of Roman origin—1 Peter, *1 Clement*, Hermas—thinks the letter may have been written in Rome.[18] If, as we think, James the brother of the Lord is the author of this letter, then it was probably written from Jerusalem during his tenure as leader of the Christian church in Jerusalem (tradition makes James the first bishop of Jerusalem). While it may say as much about the readers as the author, the social and economic backdrop assumed in the letter also fits a Palestinian provenance: merchants ranging far and wide in search of profits (4:13–17), absentee landlords taking advantage of an increasingly poor and landless labor force (2:5–7; 5:1–6), and heated religious controversy (4:1–3).

DATE

The explanation offered above for the relationship between the teaching of James 2:14–26 and Paul requires that James be dated sometime after Paul's teaching had begun to have an influence and before James and Paul met at the Jerusalem Council (Acts 15). Paul was engaged in a ministry of teaching and preaching from the time of his conversion (c. A.D. 33), and the Jerusalem Council is probably to be dated in 48 or 49. If, then, we allow some time for Paul's teaching of justification by faith to develop and become known, the most likely date for the letter of James is sometime in the early or middle 40s.[19] Such a date fits the circumstances and emphases of the letter very well. There is no hint of conflict between Jewish and Gentile Christians (such as we would have expected if the letter was written after the Jerusalem Council), and the theology of the letter is relatively undeveloped.

There are two main alternatives to this dating. Others who identify James the brother of the Lord as the author date the letter toward the close of his life (he was martyred in A.D. 62). Alleged in favor of this date are (1) the need to have Paul's letters sufficiently well known that James could be responding to Paul's teaching, and (2) the typical second-generation problem of worldliness that James confronts in the letter.[20] Yet worldliness hardly needs a period of time to develop, and as we have argued, James 2:14–26 makes better sense if James has never heard Paul or read any of his letters. A date sometime toward the end of the first century is generally adopted by those who think the letter is pseudonymous.[21]

DESTINATION/ADDRESSEES

James has been included among the so-called General Epistles because it does not address a specific church. Yet the letter was almost certainly intended for a specific audience. Several features of the letter make it clear that the addressees

---

[18]Laws, *James*, pp. 25–26.

[19]For this dating, see, inter alia, Zahn 1:125–28; Guthrie, pp. 749–53; Mayor, *James*, pp. cxliv-clxxvi; Wessel, "James," p. 965; and esp. Kittel, "Der geschichtliche Ort," pp. 71–102.

[20]F. J. A. Hort, *The Epistle of St. James* (London: Macmillan, 1909), p. xxv; R. V. G. Tasker, *The General Epistle of James*, TNTC (Grand Rapids: Eerdmans, 1956), pp. 31–33.

[21]E.g., Kümmel, p. 414.

were Jewish Christians:[22] the unself-conscious way in which the Old Testament law is mentioned (1:25; 2:8–13), the reference to their meeting place as a synagogue (2:2), and the widespread use of Old Testament and Jewish metaphors. Furthermore, passages such as 5:1–6 suggest that most of the readers were poor—although a good case can be made that 1:9–11, 2:1–4, and 4:13–17 presume the presence of some wealthier Christians among the readers.

The letter's address gives more detailed information: "to the twelve tribes scattered among the nations" (1:1). But this designation is so general as to be of little help in identifying the addressees. "Twelve tribes" need not even indicate a Jewish-Christian audience, since the phrase may have been one of many drawn from the Old Testament to designate the church as the new covenant people of God.[23] The word translated "scattered among the nations"—διασπορά (*diaspora*, "Diaspora")—was used to denote Jews living outside of Palestine (see John 7:35) and, by extension, the place in which they lived. The word had a metaphoric meaning, characterizing Christians generally as those who live away from their true heavenly home (1 Peter 1:1). Nevertheless, the early date and Jewishness of James favors the more literal meaning.[24]

The word perhaps has an even more specific force. Acts tells us of Christians from Jerusalem who were "scattered"(from the verb διασπείρω [*diaspeirō*], a word cognate to "Diaspora" in James 1:1) because of persecution and "traveled as far as Phoenicia, Cyprus and Antioch, telling the message only to Jews" (11:19).[25] Identifying James's readers with these early Jewish Christians would fit the date of the letter and would furnish an explanation of the circumstances that called it forth: James, the leader of the Jerusalem church, must minister to his scattered flock by mail. While tentative, this suggestion is better than most in explaining the circumstances of the letter.

NATURE/GENRE

While the letter of James has a typical epistolary introduction, it lacks the usual epistolary postscript. Moreover, it does not contain any personal touches such as greetings, travel plans, or prayer requests. All this suggests that James is best viewed as what we might call a literary letter. Probably it was intended for those several communities in which James's scattered parishioners had settled. More precise identification of the genre of James demands that we give attention to four further features of the letter.

The first is the flavor of pastoral admonition that pervades the letter. Imperative verbs occur with greater frequency in James than in any other New Testament

---

[22]The view that James was originally written to Jews and Christianized at a later date (argued by, among others, A. Meyer, *Das Rätsel des Jakobusbriefes* [Berlin: Töpelmann, 1930]) is no more than a scholarly curiosity.

[23]After the exile, the twelve tribes no longer existed physically, but the phrase became a way of denoting the regathered people of God of the last days (see Ezek. 47:13; Matt. 19:28; Rev. 7:4–8; 21:12).

[24]See, e.g., Mayor, *James*, pp. 30–31; Hort, *James*, pp. xxiii–xxiv; J. B. Adamson, *The Epistle of James*, NICNT (Grand Rapids: Eerdmans, 1976), pp. 49–50; Douglas J. Moo, *The Letter of James*, TNTC (Grand Rapids: Eerdmans, 1985), p. 58.

[25]Tasker draws attention to this parallel (*James*, p. 39).

book. James rebukes and exhorts his readers, and any theology that is taught comes only in conjunction with this overriding purpose.

A second feature that must be considered is its looseness of structure. We have suggested a division of the letter into five main parts. Yet these divisions are by no means well defined, as is clear from the diversity of suggested outlines for the letter. The difficulty arises from the fact that James moves rapidly from topic to topic; sometimes he will spend a paragraph or so on a given topic (e.g., 2:1–13, 14–26; 3:1–12), but more often he appears to change subjects after only a few verses.

James's extensive and very effective use of metaphors and figures of speech is a third noteworthy feature of his letter. The images James uses to make his points— the billowing sea, the withered flower, the brushfire—are universal in their appeal and go a long way toward accounting for the popularity of the letter.

A fourth feature of the letter is the degree to which James shares words and ideas with other teachings and works of literature of his day. The most important of these sources is the teaching of Jesus. The degree to which James is permeated by parallels to Jesus' teaching can be accounted for only if James so thoroughly knew that teaching—probably in oral form—that it had molded his own views and attitudes.[26] But James also shares vocabulary and concepts with early Jewish works, especially the *Testaments of the Twelve Patriarchs*, Sirach, and, to a lesser extent, Philo and Wisdom of Solomon. The nature of these parallels does not suggest direct borrowing; rather, they appear to result from James's sharing of a similar background with the authors of these works.

Do these features enable us to define the genre of James more definitely? Ropes suggests "diatribe," a popular format used for instruction and debate among some Greek authors.[27] More popular is the identification of James as parenesis. Dibelius, who is the best-known advocate of this identification, notes four features of this genre, all of which he finds in James: eclecticism (borrowing from traditional material), the unstructured stringing together of moral admonitions, repetition, and general applicability.[28] That these features are evident in James is clear, but it must be questioned whether they need be confined to a specific genre or style. Perhaps a better way of viewing James is to see it as a homily, or series of homilies, put into a letter in order to address Christians at a distance from their "pastor."[29]

The last paragraph raises the question of structure in James. Luther accused James of "throwing things together . . . chaotically,"[30] a judgment echoed in another form by Dibelius, who, in focusing on independent units to the exclusion of the whole, takes what we might call a form-critical approach to James. A reaction to this approach has arisen in more recent work, where the concern has been with the final form of the letter, sometimes viewed as the work of a redactor. Davids well exemplifies this trend, finding three key themes in the letter—testing,

---

[26]A list of the parallels between James and the teaching of Jesus can be found in Davids, *James*, pp. 47–48.

[27]Ropes, *James*, pp. 10–16.

[28]Dibelius, *James*, pp. 5–11. See also L. G. Perdue, "Paraenesis and the Epistle of James," *ZNW* 72 (1981): 241–56.

[29]See esp. G. H. Rendall, *The Epistle of St. James and Judaistic Christianity* (Cambridge: Cambridge University Press, 1927), p. 33; Davids, *James*, p. 23; and esp. Wessel, "James," p. 962 (who is summarizing the results of his doctoral dissertation).

[30]Luther, "Preface to the New Testament" (1522) (*LW* 35:397).

wisdom/pure speech, and poverty/wealth—that are treated in three main sections.[31] Probably the truth lies somewhere between these options. James certainly displays more continuity of thought than Dibelius allows, but it is questionable whether the diverse material of James can be fairly summarized under three (or more) topics. Rather, in his pastoral concern to deal with a number of problems, James moves fairly rapidly from one subject to another. Certain themes recur, wholeness or maturity being perhaps the most important (1:4, 6–8; 2:4; 3:2, 8, 11–12, 16–17; 4:4–5, 8), but they are just that—themes, or motifs, and not topics under which James's admonitions can be organized.

ADOPTION INTO THE CANON

The letter of James appears to have influenced several late-first-century works, among them the *Shepherd* of Hermas and *1 Clement*.[32] Clement of Alexandria is said to have written a commentary on James, but no such work has survived.[33] Origen is the first to cite James as Scripture, and other third-century works show acquaintance with the letter. Eusebius cites James frequently and accords it canonical status. But by classifying it among the "disputed books" (see *H.E.* 3.25.3), he also serves notice that some in his day questioned its status. He may be referring to some in the Syrian church who were slow to accept as canonical all the General Epistles. But James is included in the Syriac translation, the Peshitta, and is quoted approvingly by Chrysostom (d. 407) and Theodoret (d. 458). The Western part of the early church witnesses to a similar situation, although acceptance of James came a bit later. James is not found in either the Muratorian Canon or the Mommsen catalogue (reflecting the African canon c. 360).[34] The earliest clear references to James date from the fourth century (Hilary of Poitiers and Ambrosiaster). Decisive for the acceptance of James in the Western church was Jerome's full acceptance of the book.

James thus came to be recognized as canonical in all parts of the ancient church, and while there were hesitations on the part of some, no one rejected the book outright. Should these hesitations give us pause about the status of James? No. They were probably the product of a combination of uncertainty about the identity of the author (which James?) and the relative neglect of the book. Being practical and Jewish in its flavor, James was not the sort of book that would have been widely used in the doctrinal controversies of the early church.

James came in for its most severe criticism at the hands of Luther. His passionate embracing of Paul's teaching on justification by faith alone as the heart of Scripture made it difficult for him to accept James. He therefore relegated it to a secondary status in the New Testament, along with Jude, Hebrews, and

---

[31]David, *James*, pp. 22–29. He is using F. O. Francis's description of a literary letter ("The Form and Function of the Opening and Closing Paragraphs of James and 1 John," *ZNW* 61 [1970]: 110–26).

[32]See the discussion in Mayor, *James*, pp. lxix–lxxi, lxxxviii–cix. He discerns allusions to James in many more New Testament and early Christian writings, but most of these are probably indirect.

[33]See B. F. Westcott, *A General Survey of the History of the Canon of the New Testament* (London: Macmillan, 1889), pp. 357–58.

[34]Some think, however, that the omission of James from the Muratorian Canon is accidental, since the text of the canon is damaged (Westcott, *History of the Canon*, pp. 219–20). See, for the contrary opinion, Franz Mussner, *Der Jakobusbrief* (Freiburg: Herder, 1981), p. 41.

Revelation. Nevertheless, Luther did not exclude James from the canon, and despite his criticisms, he quoted James approvingly many times.[35] Compared with those "chief books" that clearly taught justification by faith, James appeared to Luther to be an "epistle of straw" (i.e. one made of straw; his allusion is to 1 Cor. 3:12). But he can also say, "I would not prevent anyone from including or extolling him as he pleases, for there are otherwise many good sayings in him."[36] We do not wish to minimize Luther's criticism of James: he clearly had difficulties with it. But his difficulties arose from a somewhat imbalanced perspective induced by his polemical context. Considered in a more balanced way, James can be seen to be making an important contribution to our understanding of Christian theology and practice, one that in no way conflicts with Paul or any other biblical author (see "Contribution" below). On both historical and theological grounds, James fully deserves the canonical status that the church has accorded it.

JAMES IN RECENT STUDY

As we have seen, there has been renewed interest in the compositional history of James, with several scholars proposing that the present form of the letter is due to a redactor who worked over earlier material (see above, "Nature/Genre"). James's very strong condemnation of the rich (esp. 5:1–6) has naturally made his letter a favorite of those who are propounding various forms of liberation theology.[37] Perhaps the most interesting development, however, has been the attention given to the social setting of the letter. In keeping with a renewed interest in this matter in New Testament studies generally, scholars have sought to identify the historical and social setting of the letter and then to use this reconstruction as a hermeneutical key in their interpretation. One such reconstruction views James as directed to oppressed and impoverished Jewish Christians who are attracted by the revolutionary philosophy that eventually led to the zealot movement. James champions their cause (e.g., 5:1–6) and the rights of oppressed poor people, at the same time as he cautions them about using violent means to ease their situation (4:1–3).[38] Such reconstructions can be illuminating, but we must be careful not to be more definite than the text allows us to be, lest we force the letter into a single mold that it was not meant to fill.[39]

THE CONTRIBUTION OF JAMES

Chief among James's contributions is his insistence that genuine Christian faith must become evident in works. He resolutely opposes the tendency all too common among Christians to rest content with a halfhearted, compromising faith that seeks to have the best of both this world and the next. Double-mindedness is

---

[35]D. Stoutenberg, "Martin Luther's Exegetical Use of the Epistle of St. James," (M.A. thesis, Trinity Evangelical Divinity School, 1982), p. 51.

[36]*LW* 35:397.

[37]E.g., P. V. Maynard-Reid, *Poverty and Wealth in James* (Maryknoll, N.Y.: Orbis, 1987).

[38]Martin, *James*, pp. lxii–lxix.

[39]The subjectivity involved in such reconstructions is evident from the fact that another recent attempt to identify James's setting comes to very different conclusions: James's readers were members of a Hellenistic, Pauline-influenced missions church (Popkes, *Adressaten, Situation, und Form des Jakobusbriefes*, p. 71).

the basic sin for James (see 1:8; 4:8), and he insists that Christians repent of it and get back on the road to the whole and perfect character that God desires.

The very strength of James's assertions on this point raise questions about the theological standpoint of the letter, particularly when James pursues his point to the extent that he ties justification to works (2:14–26). For at this point he appears to contradict Paul's insistence that justification comes by faith alone (see Rom. 3:28). Many are content to find here an indication of the deep diversity within the New Testament, thinking that Paul and James say different *and conflicting* things about how a person is justified before God.[40] But so damaging an admission in unnecessary; there are at least two legitimate ways of harmonizing James and Paul on this point. The first, and more popular of the two, argues that James is using the verb "justify" (δικαιόω, [*dikaioō*]) in the sense "vindicate before people" (the verb is used this way in, e.g., Luke 7:29). Paul and James, then, are talking about different things: Paul of the declaration of our righteousness and James of the demonstration of our righteousness. Another possibility is to take "justify" in James to mean "vindicate at the last judgment," a force the word often has in Judaism (see Matt. 12:37). On this view, both Paul and James are referring to the sinner's righteousness before God, but Paul is focusing on the initial reception of that status and James on the way that status is vindicated before God in the judgment.[41]

Such theological harmonization is, we think, absolutely necessary, but it should not lead us to ignore the important contribution made either by Paul or by James. When faced with legalism, with the attempt to base salvation on human works, Paul needs to be heard—as he was so powerfully at the time of the Reformation. But when faced with quietism, with the attitude that dismisses works as unnecessary for Christians, James needs to be heard—as he was equally powerfully in the time of the Wesleys.

BIBLIOGRAPHY

J. B. **Adamson**, *The Epistle of James*, NICNT (Grand Rapids: Eerdmans, 1976); John **Calvin**, *Commentaries on the Catholic Epistles*, reprint ed. (Grand Rapids: Eerdmans, 1948); J. **Cantinat**, *Les épîtres de Saint Jacques et de Saint Jude* (Paris: Gabalda, 1973); Peter **Davids**, *The Epistle of James*, NIGTC (Grand Rapids: Eerdmans, 1982); Martin **Dibelius**, *Commentary on the Epistle of James*, rev. by H. Greeven, Hermeneia (Philadelphia: Fortress, 1976); James G. D. **Dunn**, *Unity and Diversity in the New Testament* (Philadelphia: Westminster, 1977); F. O. **Francis**, "The Form and Function of the Opening and Closing Paragraphs of James and 1 John," *ZNW* 61 (1970): 110–26; Martin **Hengel**, "Der Jakobusbrief als antipaulinische Polemik," in *Tradition and Interpretation in the New Testament*, ed. G. F. Hawthorne and Otto Betz (Grand Rapids: Eerdmans, 1987), pp. 248–78; idem, *Judaism and Hellenism*, 2 vols. (Philadelphia: Fortress, 1974); F. J. A. **Hort**, *The Epistle of St. James* (London: Macmillan, 1909); Gerhard **Kittel**, "Der geschichtliche Ort des Jakobusbriefes," *ZNW* 41 (1942): 71–105; R. J. **Knowling**, *The Epistle of St. James*, 2d ed. (London: Methuen, 1910); Sophie **Laws**, *A Commentary on the Epistle of James*, HNTC (San Francisco:

---

[40]E.g., James G. D. Dunn, *Unity and Diversity in the New Testament* (Philadelphia: Westminster, 1977), pp. 251–52.

[41]See Moo, *James*, pp. 44–48, 108–16.

Harper & Row, 1980); Ralph P. **Martin**, *James*, WBC (Waco, Tex.: Word, 1988); P. V. **Maynard-Reid**, *Poverty and Wealth in James* (Maryknoll, N.Y.: Orbis, 1987); J. B. **Mayor**, *The Epistle of St. James* (London: Macmillan, 1913); A. **Meyer**, *Das Rätsel des Jakobusbriefes* (Berlin: Töpelmann, 1930); C. L. **Mitton**, *The Epistle of St. James* (Grand Rapids: Eerdmans, 1966); J. **Moffat**, *The General Epistles: James, Peter, and Judas* (London: Hodder & Stoughton, 1928); Douglas J. **Moo**, *The Letter of James*, TNTC (Grand Rapids: Eerdmans, 1985); J. H. **Moulton**, W. F. **Howard**, and Nigel **Turner**, *A Grammar of New Testament Greek*, 4 vols. (Edinburgh: T. & T. Clark, 1908–76); Franz **Mussner**, *Der Jakobusbrief* (Freiburg: Herder, 1981); L. G. **Perdue**, "Paraenesis and the Epistle of James," *ZNW* 72 (1981): 241–56; Wiard **Popkes**, *Adressaten, Situation, und Form des Jakobusbriefe*, SBS 125/126 (Stuttgart: Katholisches, 1986); G. H. **Rendall**, *The Epistle of St. James and Judaistic Christianity* (Cambridge: Cambridge University Press, 1927); James Hardy **Ropes**, *A Critical and Exegetical Commentary on the Epistle of St. James*, ICC (Edinburgh: T. & T. Clark, 1916); J. N. **Sevenster**, *Do You Know Greek? How Much Greek Could the First Jewish Christians Have Known?* (Leiden: Brill, 1968); R. V. G. **Tasker**, *The General Epistle of James*, TNTC (Grand Rapids: Eerdmans, 1956); Walter **Wessel**, "James, Letter of," in *ISBE* 2:959–65; B. F. **Westcott**, *A General Survey of the History of the Canon of the New Testament* (London: Macmillan, 1889).

19

1 PETER

CONTENTS

After the opening greeting (1:1–2) the letter praises God for the hope and salvation he has given in Christ (1:3–12). This forms the basis for an exhortation to obedient and holy living (1:13–16) and a reminder of Christ's redeeming work (1:17–21), with a further reminder of the importance of living in a holy and loving manner (1:22–2:2). Christ is then presented as the one in whom the "stone" prophecies of the Old Testament are fulfilled (2:4–8), and the church is described in terms used of the people of God in the Old Testament (2:9–12). Christians are to live in due submission to the authorities (2:13–17). There are separate exhortations to slaves, wives, and husbands (2:18–3:7). The Christian community generally is urged to live in harmony and love (3:8–12) and to take Christ's example as pointing the way for them to suffer, if need be, when they have done no wrong (3:13–22). Believers have left their sinful way of living (4:1–6); they are to live in a way that brings praise to God (4:7–11). The readers are undergoing a painful trial, but they are to bear suffering in the right way (4:12–19). Then come exhortations to the elders (5:1–4), to young men (5:5–6), and to all (5:8–9), leading into a doxology (5:10–11) and a normal epistolary ending (5:12–14).

AUTHOR

The letter claims to have been written by "Peter, an apostle of Jesus Christ" (1:1); the author is "a fellow elder, a witness of Christ's sufferings" (5:1). The claim to be a witness is supported by a number of expressions scattered through the letter, so that Selwyn can say, "This impression of eyewitness runs through the Epistle, and gives it a distinctive character."[1] He cites a number of expressions that would come very naturally from one who had been with Jesus during his earthly ministry. For example, he refers to 2:20–25, which contains references to buffeting (see Mark 14:65), following Jesus (Mark 8:34), following his footsteps

---

[1]E. G. Selwyn, *The First Epistle of St. Peter* (London: Macmillan, 1949), p. 28. See also Robert H. Gundry, "*Verba Christi*" in 1 Peter," *NTS* 13 (1966–67): 336–50; Ernest Best, "I Peter and the Gospel Tradition," *NTS* 16 (1969–70): 95–113; Robert H. Gundry, "Further *Verba* on *Verba Christi*," *Bib* 55 (1974): 211–32.

(Mark 10:32), and Jesus being the Shepherd (Mark 14:27) and bearing sins (see reference to redemption in 1:18; Mark 10:45). There are many such resemblances.

There are likewise some noteworthy resemblances between this letter and words attributed to Peter in Acts. Thus Christ is the "stone" of Psalm 118:22 (Acts 4:10–11; 1 Peter 2:7–8) and his cross is "the wood" (τὸ ξύλον [to xylon], Acts 10:3, 9; 1 Peter 2:24).[2] Such examples do not, of course, prove Petrine authorship. But they show that the letter is compatible with the claim made in its opening words.

The Petrine authorship is, however, denied by many recent scholars.

1. They point to the excellent Greek, which they think could not have been written by an "unschooled, ordinary" man (Acts 4:13). To this it is retorted that the description in Acts should be taken to mean that Peter and John were not skilled in rabbinic learning, not that they were uneducated. Greek was widely spoken in Palestine, and we have no real reason for saying that a Galilean could not have considerable competence in the language.[3] In any case, we are told that the letter was written[4] "with the help of Silas" (5:12; the name is really Silvanus), which may mean that Silvanus was the secretary who polished up the language (this seems better than viewing him as the bearer of the letter).[5]

A kindred objection is that the use of the Septuagint translation of the Old Testament is inconsistent with a Galilean author. This sounds as though it might have force, but what do we really know about the text a Greek-speaking Galilean would use? As the letter is written in Greek, it is not in the slightest surprising that the Greek version of the Old Testament is the one that is used.

2. The letter is said to be too dependent on Pauline theology to have been written by the apostle Peter. To this we should say that the differences between Petrine and Pauline teaching have probably been exaggerated.[6] There is no reason for affirming that they were in contradiction on the essentials of the faith, and at least some of the passages in 1 Peter that are said to have been derived from Paul are better understood as part of the common tradition of the early church.[7] We

---

[2]For other examples, see Selwyn, First Peter, pp. 33–36; Alan M. Stibbs and Andrew F. Walls, The First Epistle General of Peter (London: Tyndale, 1959), pp. 35–36.

[3]At the turn of the century J. H. Moulton likened the situation to that in modern Wales, where English is handled competently even by very many who speak Welsh. Of Jesus and the apostles he says, "They would write as men who had used the language from boyhood, not as foreigners painfully expressing themselves in an imperfectly known idiom" (A Grammar of New Testament Greek, vol. 1 [Edinburgh: T. & T. Clark, 1906], p. 8). Johnson holds that "Peter could have improved his Greek during the years of his ministry. To deny him this capacity is cultural condescension. Two of the great English stylists of the twentieth century (Conrad and Nabokov) learned and mastered English only as adults" (pp. 432–33).

[4]The author says "I wrote," not "I sent" (ἔγραψα [egrapsa], not ἔπεμψα [epempsa] or ἀπέστειλα [apesteila].

[5]See esp. Peter H. Davids, The First Epistle of Peter, NICNT (Grand Rapids: Eerdmans, 1990), pp. 3–5.

[6]More than fifty years ago, Enslin insisted, "It is not an overstatement to say that [1 Peter] is saturated with Pauline ideas. In fact, it actually stands closer to Paul's thought than do some letters which bear his name" (p. 322). This is clearly an exaggerated estimate and lacks support today.

[7]According to Klijn, "If Peter's authorship be accepted, the letter becomes an important document of the life of the primitive church in general and more specifically of the relationship between Peter and Paul. For it appears, then, that these two apostles drew on the same traditions, which indicates a oneness in their preaching that has often been denied" (p. 158).

should also bear in mind N. Brox's warning "against too sharp a contrast between Pauline and Petrine theology which would be anachronistic if projected back into the first century."[8] Moreover, Paul wrote a very significant letter to the Roman church. If Peter was linked with that church before his death, it would not be surprising if he had become acquainted with the teaching of Romans. We should also recall the parallels with the letter of James, for example the links between 1:6–7 and James 1:2–3, 1:24 and James 1:10–11, 4:8 and James 5:20, 5:5–6 and James 4:6–7. We should not minimize the amount shared in the common Christian tradition.

3. There is no evidence of a knowledge of the events in Jesus' life, which would have been natural in a letter coming from Peter. There are general references to Jesus' sufferings, but Peter would have been more explicit. But this is a very subjective objection. Selwyn has cited a number of expressions that come naturally from Peter.[9] In any case the author was not indulging in "reminiscences of life with Jesus" but "encouraging you and testifying that this is the true grace of God" (5:12). There is no real reason why Peter should have included more references to Jesus.

4. There are four passages referring to persecution (1:6; 3:13–17; 4:12–19; 5:9), and these are said to demand a persecution like that under Domitian or Trajan. We know of no such persecution during the lifetime of the apostle. Against this is the fact that traditionally most students have found these references compatible with the Neronic persecution, which Peter experienced. Actually the letter nowhere says that there was an empirewide persecution: "There are no tribunals, nor judges, not even confiscation."[10] In fact, the letter includes statements that view the civil authorities very favorably (e.g., 2:13–14, 17), statements that are unlikely to have been made while the whole church was being persecuted. Local officials may well have played havoc with particular congregations; indeed there are passages that seem to show that private individuals, not the state, were responsible for the trouble in which the Christians found themselves (e.g., 2:12; 4:4). All the indications are that there were scattered and local persecutions in many places, and no first-century Christian can have felt very safe (see 5:9).[11] But this does not mean that the emperor had instigated a worldwide suppression of Christianity at the time of this letter.

Despite the confidence with which some scholars deny that Peter wrote the letter, it seems that we should accept it as coming from that apostle. The definite claim made in the opening words and the Petrine language throughout the letter, together with the inconclusive nature of the objections, mean that the verdict

---

[8]The words are taken from the summary of Childs, p. 453; the reference is to N. Brox, *Der erste Petrusbrief,* EKKNT (Zürich: Benziger Verlag, 1979; 2d ed. 1986), p. 51. John H. Elliott, sees a fresh approach to 1 Peter in which "a more judicious distinction between tradition and redaction is beginning to clarify the peculiar features of the document." This peculiarity "argues positively for the liberation of 1 Peter from its 'Pauline bondage'" ("The Rehabilitation of an Exegetical Step-Child: 1 Peter in Recent Research," *JBL* 95 [1976]: 248).

[9]Selwyn, *First Epistle,* pp. 28–31.

[10]Robert/Feuillet, p. 576.

[11]Ernest Best holds that "the evidence is satisfied by the situation in which Christians lived at all times and in which violence might break out against them at any moment—in this they might suffer death, or the loss of goods, or be regarded as murderers or just mischief-makers" (*1 Peter,* NCB [Grand Rapids: Eerdmans, 1982], p. 39).

should go in favor of Peter as the author. We should not overlook the fact that no convincing reason seems ever to have been brought forward as to why the name Peter was attached to the writing if Peter was not the author. As Childs says, "No obvious reason—historical, sociological, doctrinal—has been established for assigning the letter to the apostle. Nor is there any clear legitimating function provided by the appeal to Peter's authority." [12]

PROVENANCE

"She who is in Babylon" sends greetings (5:13), which seems to indicate that Rome was the place of origin. "Babylon" was a symbolic way of referring to Rome, a name that expressed something of Rome's pride, luxury, immorality, and godlessness.[13] It is highly unlikely that the Babylon of the Old Testament is meant, for the Jews were chased out of that city well before this time (see Josephus, *Ant.* 18.371–79), and anyway Babylon was in decline. We have no reason for thinking that Peter's missionary journeys ever took him to this area, and in any case it is hard to think of a reason that would bring Peter, Mark, and Silvanus there at the same time. There was a military strong point in Egypt called Babylon, but there seems no reason for thinking this location is in view (though Klijn does so). Rome is usually accepted, and rightly so.[14]

DATE

If we accept the apostle Peter as the author, the letter was probably written in the 60s. Persecution was in the air, and this points to Nero's reign, the traditional time and occasion of Peter's death. There is little in the way of ecclesiastical organization, an indication that the letter is early. Everything fits together if the letter was written from Rome not long before the apostle was put to death.[15] Those who reject Petrine authorship mostly look ahead to the persecution under Domitian (toward the end of the first century) or to that in the time of Trajan (early second century).

DESTINATION

The letter is addressed to "God's elect, strangers in the world, scattered throughout Pontus, Galatia, Cappadocia, Asia and Bithynia" (1:1), where the names may be those of the ancient districts or of the provinces into which the Romans organized their empire. There is no evidence to decide the point. The

---

[12]Childs, p. 455. It should be added that Childs does not argue that Peter was the author.

[13]Fuller says, "The use of Babylon as a cryptogram points likewise to a period of official state persecution" (p. 158). But this is surely reading far too much into the use of a name.

[14]"We may conclude that, given the apostolic authorship whether direct or indirect, the Roman origin of this Epistle stands without serious challenge" (Martin 2:335).

[15]W. C. van Unnik holds that "the comparison in i.18–19 can only have its full force if the letter was written before the fall of the Temple in A.D. 70"; he goes on to reason, "There are no cogent arguments which prevent us from seeing in Peter the mind which directed the hand of Silvanus (v.12)" ("The Teaching of Good Works in 1 Peter," *NTS* 1 [1954–55]: 92–110). Without being specific, J. H. L. Dijkman has argued that the letter must be early ("1 Peter: A Later Pastoral Stratum?" *NTS* 33 [1987]: 265–71).

places named are in the northern part of modern Turkey (unless Galatia includes the southern areas with that name). It is unlikely that the readers had been evangelized by Peter, for he speaks of "those who have preached the gospel to you" (1:12) rather than identifying himself with the evangelists.

In earlier days it was often thought that the recipients were Jewish Christians (in agreement with Peter's commitment to work among Jews [Gal. 2:9]). But there is little indication of this in the letter itself, and it cannot be held that Peter never ministered to Gentiles. That Gentiles are addressed seems clear from 1:18, which speaks of the readers as having been redeemed "from the empty way of life handed down to you from your forefathers." It is difficult to see this as a description of a way of life based on the teachings of the Old Testament. Literally translated, the addressees are described as "elect sojourners of the dispersion" (1:1): probably words characteristically used of the Jews as the people of God are transferred to Christians. The writer envisages heaven as the home of God's people, so that while on earth they are no more than sojourners. It seems that the writer is concerned neither with Jews nor Gentiles as such, but with those who in Christ have become the people of God. We need not doubt that most who came from the provinces named were Gentiles, although there would have been some Jewish converts.[16] But the emphasis is on what they have become, not on what they were originally.

We should notice further that the destinations named mean that the letter was a circular letter from the beginning. This does not mean that it is not a genuine letter, sent to a specific audience. The references to the experiences of the recipients (e.g., 1:6–9) show that Peter has definite people in mind, as do his use of "dear friends" (2:11; 4:12), his words to the elders (5:1–4), and the closing section with its greetings (5:13).[17] But he does not confine himself to the parochial concerns of a small community or communities. From the first, the letter was surely intended to be applicable to the needs of believers in many places. Peter surely knew that what he had to say was relevant to Christians generally. While his letter was originally addressed to Christians in specific places, it is so worded that it is useful for believers everywhere.

ADOPTION INTO THE CANON

The first reference to this letter is that in 2 Peter 3:1, but from this we learn no more than that Peter had written a letter. There are many coincidences of language with *1 Clement*, which may indicate that Clement used the letter (or that they shared common material), and there are further examples in Barnabas, Polycarp (there seems no doubt about quotations in Polycarp), Hermas, and others. The first to quote it explicitly as a writing of Peter is Ireneus, and thereafter it is routinely accepted in the church—apart from its exclusion, along with all the

---

[16]This is a far more likely assessment than that of J. H. Elliott, who argues that Jews were one of the persecuting groups (*A Home for the Homeless: A Sociological Exegesis of 1 Peter, Its Situation and Strategy* [Philadelphia: Fortress, 1981], esp. pp. 80–81), On this reading, the lack of any anti-Jewish polemic is decidedly strange. The wholesale application in this epistle of Old Testament (Jewish) categories to the church appears to be to the church as a whole and is part of a distinctively Christian reading of the Old Testament attested in many New Testament documents.

[17]Moreover, the provinces in 1:1 are listed in the order in which a messenger might visit them; see C. J. Hemer, "The Address of 1 Peter," *ExpTim* 89 (1977–78): 239–43.

other Catholic Epistles, from the Syriac Canon. It is not listed in the Muratorian Canon, but Selwyn and others think that the text of that writing is not complete.[18] If the omission is deliberate, we have no indication of the reason, nor is there record of any objection to this letter in antiquity. Eusebius includes it among the authentic writings (H.E. 3.3.25). There never seems to have been serious doubts in the church about 1 Peter.

1 PETER IN RECENT STUDY

A certain amount of discussion has focused on the question of authorship, with a tendency to see the letter as pseudepigraphic.[19] But if we ask why the author should have written in the name of Peter rather than in his own name, nobody seems to have come up with a convincing reason. The writing contains orthodox teaching of the kind that any member of the early church might have been happy to claim. There is nothing that might have demanded authorization from some strong source before it stood a chance of being accepted in the church at large. Nor is it apparent why Peter should be held to be writing to the churches in the provinces named.

The one consideration with some force behind it is the allegation that the persecutions the readers are undergoing could not have taken place during Peter's lifetime and that therefore we must place the letter during one of the persecutions that we may fairly say afflicted the provinces in question. Furthermore, the letter places special emphasis on suffering simply "because of the name of Christ" or "as a Christian" (4:14, 16) rather than for specific crimes. This, it is urged, means the time of Domitian or Trajan (there is documentary evidence of persecution in part of the area Peter names during Trajan's reign).

But the argument is not cogent. There is no real evidence of an empirewide persecution under these emperors, and the references in 1 Peter do not correspond to what is known of the persecutions under the emperors named. Thus Pliny writes to Trajan about the official inquiries he has made into the Christians, and he speaks of tortures he has inflicted, neither of which features in 1 Peter.[20] This aspect of modern discussions overlooks the widespread suspicion of Christians from much earlier times, and the fact that, if an enemy wronged them or accused them falsely, they could rarely look to government officials with confidence for protection. On the contrary, they could almost always be safely assailed, and this must have led to a good deal of oppression by petty local officials. It should perhaps be added that Peter calls on his readers to share in Christ's sufferings (4:13), but not his death. There is no martyr piety in this letter.

Some recent writers link the epistle with baptism, seeing it as a baptismal homily or liturgy. In 1911 R. Perdelwitz pointed to a break in the letter's argument at 4:11. He thought that the sufferings of the Christians were spoken of

---

[18]B. F. Westcott similarly argues, "The present form of the Fragment makes the idea of a chasm in it very probable" (A General Survey of the History of the Canon of the New Testament, 6th ed. [Cambridge: Macmillan, 1889], p. 289).

[19]On pseudonymity in general, see the section "Pseudonymity" in chap. 15 above.

[20]G. Edmundson writes, "The Rescript of Trajan merely confirmed in writing the practice, which had subsisted since the time of Nero, of treating the very name of Christian as a crime against the State" (The Church in Rome in the First Century [London: Longmans, 1913], p. 139 n. 1; cited also in Martin 2:333).

earlier as potential, but as actual from 4:12; joy is present in 1:6, 8 and future in 4:12ff. "Briefly" (5:12) would not be a good description of the whole letter, which is of respectable length by the standards of the day, but would apply to the part from 4:12 on.[21] Having separated the two, he drew attention to the baptismal motifs in the first part and suggested that it was a baptismal homily. H. Preisker has taken this view further with the suggestion that this part of 1 Peter is in fact the baptismal liturgy of the Roman church, the actual words that would be used when a candidate was baptized. On such views the baptism would take place after 1:21, the act not being mentioned because of the church's policy of keeping such things secret.[22] F. L. Cross sees it as the liturgy for an Easter baptism.[23]

Some of the arguments put forward in support of such hypotheses overlook important parts of the evidence. First, baptism is mentioned once only in the entire letter (3:21), which is very strange if it is at the heart of the writing. Again, a key part of the argument is the assertion that the tenses of the verbs in 1:3–21 show that sanctification is future, whereas in 1:22 we have the past: the baptism has now been accomplished, and the baptized person is "sanctified." But this overlooks the fact that as early as 1:3 the past tense in "he has given us new birth" shows that the writer is addressing people who have already been brought into the church.[24] And there is no reason for understanding the present participle in 1:5 (translated "are shielded") as though it were future. The language does not sustain the argument.

Baptismal views also overlook the variety in the earlier part of the letter. While those who advocate them have done us a service in emphasizing the possibility of linking some of the letter's teaching with baptism, they have not demonstrated that all that is said points to a baptismal homily or a baptismal liturgy. The early church seems to have been quite interested in baptism and all that it means, for it was indeed the decisive step in turning away from paganism and identifying oneself with God's people. So we find references to it in a number of epistles where there is no question of liturgy (e.g., Rom. 6:3; 1 Cor. 1:13–17; Col. 2:12). Nor do proponents face the difficulty that there is no evidence that a fixed liturgy was in use as early as this letter. And if there was, they give no reason the Roman liturgy should be sent to Asia Minor. For all the learning and the devotion with which the thesis is argued, we must surely say that its adherents have overemphasized some of the evidence and soft-pedaled what does not fit their theory.[25] This is not the way 1 Peter should be understood.

---

[21]R. Perdelwitz, *Die Mysterienreligionen und das Problem des I. Petrusbriefes*, RVV 11.3 (Giessen: Töpelmann, 1911). Without referring to its originator by name, Wikenhauser says that this partition theory "is brilliant rather than well-founded" (p. 504).

[22]In H. Windisch and H. Preisker, *Die katholischen Briefe*, HNT, 3d ed. (Tübingen: Mohr, 1951), esp. pp. 156ff.; Contra, e.g., Guthrie, pp. 789–90; J. Ramsey Michaels, *1 Peter*, WBC (Waco, Tex.: Word, 1988), p. 73.

[23]F. L. Cross, *1 Peter: A Paschal Liturgy* (London: Mowbray, 1954).

[24]Even under a strictly aspectual reading of the Greek verb, in which the tense in itself is not understood to provide any *necessary* reference to time, the context clearly argues that this new birth is something in the readers' past.

[25]J. N. D. Kelly comments, "Both Preisker's and Cross's theories are impressive in their breath-taking ingenuity"; he adds, "It is impossible, however, to feel much confidence either in the detail of their analyses or in their schemes as wholes" (*A Commentary on the Epistles of Peter and of Jude*, HNTC [New York: Harper, 1969], p. 18) See also T. C. G. Thornton, "1 Peter, a Paschal Liturgy?" *JTS* 12 (1961): 14–26.

A good deal of modern discussion is taken up with the liturgical interest that many see in the letter. It is widely agreed that phrases from the liturgy are to be found in many of the New Testament writings, and 1 Peter is seen to have its share. There may also be fragments from Christian creeds. The identification of such phrases is a rather subjective matter, and there cannot be said to be wide agreement as to precisely which are the liturgical expressions. But passages such as 1:3–12; 2:4–8, 21–25; 3:18–22 frequently come into the discussions, and there is widespread agreement that the liturgy must be understood to stand behind the letter. So also with the early church's paraenesis. First Peter clearly includes some of the teaching that was as a matter of course imparted to converts to the Christian way. This does not mean that we are to think of a number of documents having been put together to make up this writing. Partition theories are not widely accepted, and scholars usually affirm the unity of the letter, whatever expressions from liturgical sources the author may have chosen to include.

This has its effect on some of the earlier controversies, for example, those that deny Petrine authorship on the grounds that there is too much Paulinism in the letter. It is widely accepted that both Paul and Peter include a good deal of the common stock of Christian teaching, and it becomes perilous to argue that either writer depends on the other. Rather, both are members of the early church, and they write out of the common concerns of its membership.

THE CONTRIBUTION OF 1 PETER

As Martin points out, "Probably no other document in the New Testament is so theological as 1 Peter, if we understand 'theological' in the strict sense as teaching about God."[26] Statistically the writing has the word "God" thirty-nine times, which means an average of once in every forty-three words. The only other New Testament writings to compare with this are 1 John (once in thirty-four) and Romans (once in forty-six). Statistics are not everything, but these make it clear that there is an unusual number of references to God in this letter. God is "the living God" (1:23),[27] whose will is done (2:15; 3:17), who foreknows who are his (1:2) and whose Word stands forever (1:25). God is the Father (1:2); he is holy (1:15), the judge of all (4:5), and the faithful Creator (4:19). He is "the God of all grace" (5:10), and indeed "grace" is a frequent idea in this letter (ten times). It is due to God's great mercy that Christians have new birth and a living hope (1:3). The church is related to God in several ways: it is "the people of God" (2:10), "the family of God" (4:17), "God's flock" (5:2), and its members are "servants of God" (2:16). There is more, but this is sufficient to make it clear that Peter is giving us a full and satisfying understanding of who God is and what he is doing.[28]

---

[26]Martin 2:344.

[27]The participle "living" may be attached to "word" (as in the NIV and many commentators). But perhaps F. J. A. Hort was correct in attaching "living" to God. He drew from this the inference, "It is in effect God Himself speaking, speaking not once only, but with renewed utterance, kindling life not by a recollection but by a present power" (*The First Epistle of St Peter I.1–II.17* [London: Macmillan, 1898], p. 92). But even if we accept the NIV, God is still seen as vitally concerned with his Word.

[28]F. W. Beare finds in this letter "the thought of God as Creator, Father, and Judge, as the One whose will determines all that comes to pass, who shapes the destiny and determines the actions of those whom He has chosen for His own, who sustains them through the sufferings which He sends to

Peter puts a good deal of emphasis on the sufferings of Christ. He uses the verb πάσχω (*paschō*) twelve times, whereas it is found only eleven times in all the rest of the New Testament epistles (the next most frequent is the much longer Luke, with six). He leaves no doubt that it was through what he suffered that Christ brought salvation to sinners. He wastes no time in getting to this thought, in his second verse referring to the sprinkling of the blood of Jesus. Blood, of itself, might be held to refer to no more than death by violence, but sprinkling of blood took place in the Levitical sacrifices: Peter is saying that Christ was a sacrifice for his people. That death may be spoken of as redemption (1:18–19), and there is specific mention of price, with a denial that it is "silver or gold." The reference to Christ as "a lamb without blemish or defect" (1:19) links redemption with the sacrifices: the process of salvation is complex. And when Peter goes on to speak of Christ as "chosen before the creation of the world" (1:20), he is saying that Christ's death was in the eternal divine purpose.

So, too, Christ left his people an example of how to bear suffering (2:21), which must have been important for people situated like Peter's readers evidently were. It is important in every age that the passion be our example, for there is no Christian who does not have to suffer at some time. Peter stresses the thought that Jesus did not respond to insults with insults or threats but committed himself to the Father. Indeed, Christ "himself bore our sins in his body on the tree" (2:24), a way of looking at the cross that is found elsewhere in the New Testament only once (Heb. 9:28). The concept is found frequently in the Old Testament, however, where bearing sins clearly means bearing the penalty of sins. The Israelites, for example, are told that they would bear their sins by wandering in the wilderness for forty years (Num. 14:34; the NIV translation "you will *suffer for* your sins" is a rather idiomatic rendering of what literally reads "you will *bear* your sins," as in the KJV).[29] There are also coincidences of language with Isaiah 53, so that probably Peter was thinking here of Jesus fulfilling all that the suffering servant means.

The atonement is also in mind when Peter says, "Christ died for sins once for all, the righteous for the unrighteous, to bring you to God" (3:18). It is the death of Jesus that removes sins and enables sinners to approach God. This is also behind the statement that "Christ suffered in his body" (4:1) and other such references. Peter is clear that the death of Jesus on the cross was no tragic accident but the fulfillment of the purpose of God in dealing with the sins of the race. This is the thought also in the "stone" passage (2:4–8). Christ fulfills the Old Testament Scriptures that refer to the stone the builders rejected, which was put in the supreme place (Isa. 8:14; 28:16; Ps. 118:22; cf. 1 Peter 2:4–8). The prophets predicted his sufferings but also the glories that would follow (1:11). Clearly Peter is giving expression to a deep conviction that Christ was the very revelation of God and that it is in him alone that people are brought to salvation.

Peter does not have so much to say about the Holy Spirit, but he begins the letter with a reference to his sanctifying work (1:2) and presently tells us that he is "the Spirit of Christ" (1:11) and that the early preachers preached the gospel "by

---

test them, and who at the last will vindicate them and reward them eternally" (*The First Epistle of Peter* [Oxford: Blackwell, 1947], p. 33).

[29]See further Leon Morris, *The Cross in the New Testament* (Grand Rapids: Eerdmans, 1965), pp. 322–25.

the Holy Spirit sent from heaven" (1:12). "The Spirit of glory and of God" rests on believers (4:14).

Throughout this writing we are met by the tension between the "now" and the "not yet." The passages surveyed about Christ's saving work show very clearly that salvation is a present possession. Believers have already purified themselves (1:22); they have been born again (1:23). But salvation is also "ready to be revealed in the last time" (1:5); "the end of all things is near" (4:7). Readers are told of the day of God's visitation (2:12) and reminded of "the crown of glory" they will receive "when the Chief Shepherd appears" (5:4). In the light of this prospect, Peter has a good deal to say about the ethical virtues that should characterize believers. They should have love for one another (1:22; 2:17, etc.), and they should turn away from the evil desires that they indulged in their pre-Christian days (1:14). That means being rid of "all malice and all deceit, hypocrisy, envy, and slander of every kind" (2:1). There are solid blocks of teaching about the high moral standards that should be evident in the lives of those who follow Christ (2:13–3:12). We must not think of all this as individualistic (though there is much of which the individual must take note), for there is a strong emphasis on the church, for example, when the writer takes a series of epithets originally used of the people of God in the Old Testament and applies them to believers generally (2:9–10). In this letter there is nothing like the problem of the place of the Jews with which Paul wrestled in Romans 9–11; for Peter there is no doubt that the church is the people of God, the true Israel. Gentiles have been called out of the darkness and brought into God's marvelous light.

This is a short letter, but it covers a surprisingly wide range. It has teaching of great and permanent importance about God and the salvation he has brought about through Christ. It emphasizes the changed lives that follow when people come to a place of faith and to the wonder of their corporate existence.

BIBLIOGRAPHY

D. L. **Balch**, *Let Wives Be Submissive: The Domestic Code in 1 Peter*, SBLMS 26 (Chico, Calif.: SP, 1981); F. W. **Beare**, *The First Epistle of Peter* (Oxford: Blackwell, 1947); Ernest **Best**, *1 Peter*, NCB (Grand Rapids: Eerdmans, 1982); idem, "I Peter and the Gospel Tradition," *NTS* 16 (1969–70): 95–113; C. A. **Bigg**, *A Critical and Exegetical Commentary on the Epistles of St. Peter and St. Jude*, 2d ed. (Edinburgh: T. & T. Clark, 1902); G. W. **Blenkin**, *The First Epistle General of Peter*, CGTC (Cambridge: Cambridge University Press, 1914); N. **Brox**, *Der erste Petrusbrief*, EKKNT, 2d ed. (Zürich: Benziger Verlag, 1986); H. J. B. **Combrink**, "The Structure of 1 Peter," *Neot* 9 (1975): 34–63; F. L. **Cross**, *1 Peter: A Paschal Liturgy* (London: Mowbrays, 1954); W. J. **Dalton**, *Christ's Proclamation to the Spirit: A Study of 1 Peter 3:18–4:6*, AnBib 23 (Rome: Pontifical Biblical Institute, 1965); Peter H. **Davids**, *The First Epistle of Peter*, NICNT (Grand Rapids: Eerdmans, 1990); J. H. L. **Dijkman**, "1 Peter: A Later Pastoral Stratum?" *NTS* 33 (1987): 265–71; G. **Edmundson**, *The Church in Rome in the First Century* (London: Longmans, 1913); John H. **Elliott**, *The Elect and the Holy: An Exegetical Examination of 1 Peter 2:4–10 and the Phrase* βασιλείαν ἱεράτευμα, SuppNovT 12 (Leiden: Brill, 1966); idem, *A Home for the Homeless: A Sociological Exegesis of 1 Peter, Its Situation and Strategy* (Philadelphia: Fortress, 1981); idem, "The Rehabilitation of an Exegetical Step-Child: 1 Peter in Recent Research," *JBL* 95 (1976): 243–54; L. **Goppelt**, *Der erste Petrusbrief*, KEK (Göttingen: Vandenhoeck & Ruprecht, 1978); Wayne A. **Grudem**, *The First Epistle of Peter*, TNTC (Grand Rapids: Eerdmans, 1988); R. H. **Gundry**, "Further *Verba* on *Verba Christi*," *Bib* 55 (1974): 211–32; idem, "Verba Christi in 1 Peter," *NTS* 13 (1966–67): 336–50; C. J. **Hemer**, "The Address of 1 Peter," *ExpTim* 89 (1977–78): 239–43; F. J. A. **Hort**, *The First Epistle of St Peter I.1–II.17* (London: Macmillan, 1898); J. N. D. **Kelly**, *A Commentary on the Epistles of Peter and of Jude*, HNTC (New York: Harper & Row, 1969); A. R. C. **Leaney**, "1 Peter and the Passover: An Interpretation," *NTS* 10 (1963–64): 238–51; J. Ramsey **Michaels**, *1 Peter*, WBC (Waco, Tex.: Word, 1988); Leon **Morris**, *The Cross in the New Testament* (Grand Rapids: Eerdmans, 1965); C. F. D. **Moule**, "The Nature and Purpose of 1 Peter," *NTS* 3 (1956–57): 1–11; idem, "Some Reflections on the 'Stone Testimonia' in Relation to the Name Peter," *NTS* 2 (1955–56): 56–59; J. H. **Moulton**, *A Grammar of New Testament Greek*, vol. 1 (Edinburgh: T. & T. Clark, 1906); W. **Munro**, *Authority in Peter and Paul*, SNTSMS 45 (Cambridge: Cambridge University Press, 1983); F. **Neugebauer**, "Zur Deutung und Bedeutung des 1. Petrusbriefes," *NTS* 26 (1979–80): 61–86; R. **Perdelwitz**, *Die Mysterienreligionen und das Problem des I. Petrusbriefes*, RVV 11.3 (Giessen: Töpelmann, 1911); K. H. **Schelkle**, *Die Petrusbriefe, Der Judasbrief*, HTKNT, 5th ed. (Freiburg: Herder, 1980); E. G. **Selwyn**, *The First Epistle of St. Peter* (London: Macmillan, 1949); idem, "The Persecutions in 1 Peter," *BSNTS* (1950): 39–50; Alan M. **Stibbs** and Andrew F. **Walls**, *The First Epistle General of Peter* (London: Tyndale, 1959); C. H. **Talbert**, ed., *Perspectives on First Peter* (Macon, Ga.: Mercer University Press, 1986); T. C. G. **Thornton**, "1 Peter, a Paschal Liturgy?" *JTS* 12 (1961): 14–26; W. C. **van Unnik**, "The Teaching of Good Works in 1 Peter," *NTS* 1 (1954–55): 92–110; B. F. **Westcott**, *A General Survey of the History of the Canon of the New Testament*, 6th ed. (Cambridge: Macmillan, 1889); H. **Windisch** and H. **Preisker**, *Die katholischen Briefe*, HNT, 3d ed. (Tübingen: Mohr, 1951).

20

2 PETER

CONTENTS

The address (1:1–2) leads into a reminder of the good gifts Christ has given (1:3–4), which forms the basis of an exhortation to develop Christian qualities (1:5–11). Peter has not long to live (1:14), and he wants the readers to be able to recall the truth after his death (1:15). He insists that the message about Jesus Christ was not "cleverly invented stories"; he personally attests hearing the words spoken at the transfiguration (1:16–18). He goes on to locate Scripture in the work of the Holy Spirit in prophets (1:19–21). He brings together false prophets of old and false teachers of the future (2:1–3) and reminds his readers that God has judged angels and ungodly people but rescued godly Lot (2:4–10). The false teachers especially in mind are arrogant (2:10–12), but they will be punished for their evil way of life (2:13–22). Peter reminds his readers of what he has written to them in an earlier letter (3:1) and expresses his desire to recall them to the teachings of the prophets and of Jesus, given through the apostles (3:2). Scoffers will arise in the last days (3:3–7), but the Lord's coming is sure, even though it is on his own time scale, not ours (3:8–10). This forms the basis of an exhortation to godly living (3:11): Christians must live in the prospect of the time when the heavens will be destroyed by fire and the elements will melt in the heat, leading into the appearing of a new heaven and earth (3:12–13). Peter reminds his readers of what Paul has written and continues to urge them to live uprightly (3:14–18).

AUTHOR

The style of this letter is not like that of 1 Peter, and the language is quite different. R. J. Bauckham points out that 2 Peter has the highest proportion of hapax legomena of any New Testament book. Of the fifty-seven words not found elsewhere in the New Testament, thirty-two do not occur in the LXX, that is, they are not biblical in any sense—even though many of them occur in Hellenistic Jewish writers of the period. He suggests that "2 Peter belongs to the sphere of Hellenistic Jewish Greek."[1] Those who see Peter as the author hold that this may

---

[1] Richard J. Bauckham, *Jude, 2 Peter*, WBC (Waco, Tex.: Word, 1983), pp. 135–36.

result from the use of different secretaries. They point out that little is known about what a secretary might contribute[2] and that if Peter used different secretaries or if he wrote one letter himself and used a secretary for the other, the stylistic differences are adequately accounted for. They hold also that any writing that comes down to us from antiquity bearing the name of its author should be accepted as coming from that author unless there is strong evidence that the attribution is erroneous.

In modern times most scholars hold that there is such strong evidence. Kümmel, for example, bluntly says, "Peter cannot have written this Epistle."[3] A variety of considerations is put forward for this conclusion, including (1) the idea that the relation of this letter to Jude forbids Petrine authorship, (2) the differences in literary style and vocabulary between this epistle and 1 Peter, (3) the reference to Paul's letters as Scripture (3:15–16), (4) the references to the apostles as "in the past" (3:2) and to "our fathers" as having died (3:4)— references that are said to point to a time later than the apostle. The message of Peter that we get in the letter is said to be the product of an emerging tradition from a later period, rather than personal recollections of the apostle. Some point out that there were several books attributed to Peter, such as the *Gospel of Peter*, the *Acts of Peter*, and the *Apocalypse of Peter*. There is no reason for ascribing these writings to the apostle, and (it is suggested) 2 Peter is simply another product of the thinking that multiplied writings said to have been written by Peter.

Generally speaking, conservative scholars have held to the Petrine authorship, but scholars of other points of view have held that Peter was not the author. Interestingly Bauckham, whose general stance is quite conservative, accepts the view that the letter is pseudonymous, but he argues that the original readers would have recognized what the writer was doing; there was no intention to deceive. Bauckham says they "must have expected it to be fictional," and again, "the Petrine authorship was intended to be an entirely *transparent* fiction."[4] Perhaps this view does not give enough attention to the fact that in the early church the debates over whether it should be accepted or not raged over whether it was written by an apostle or not. If the fiction was really transparent, the question arises, "Why was it that so many in the early church did not realize it?"

We must consider several points in determining the authorship of 2 Peter.

External Attestation

E. M. B. Green takes from Westcott the point that while no book of the New Testament is as poorly attested in the early church as 2 Peter, this epistle "has incomparably better support for its inclusion than the best attested of the rejected books."[5] This is perhaps as far as we can go along this line. Those who reject Petrine authorship will point to the weakness of the attestation; those who accept it point out that no noncanonical book has as much acceptance. They also remind

---

[2]For discussion, see Richard N. Longenecker, "On the Form, Function, and Authority of the New Testament Letters," in *Scripture and Truth*, ed. D. A. Carson and John D. Woodbridge (Grand Rapids: Zondervan, 1983), pp. 101–14.

[3]Kümmel, p. 302.

[4]Bauckham, *Jude, 2 Peter*, p. 134.

[5]E. M. B. Green, *2 Peter Reconsidered* (London: Tyndale, 1961), p. 5.

us that in the nature of the case—owing to both its brevity and its content—2 Peter is unlikely to be quoted or even referred to as often as most of the other New Testament writings. Even today those who accept it fully do not often find themselves in a position where they must quote it.

Allusions to Peter

The letter plainly indicates that Peter was the author. The writer calls himself "Simeon [or Simon] Peter," adding "a servant and apostle of Jesus Christ" (1:1). The form "Simeon" is not generally used of Peter (in the New Testament only in Acts 15:14, and apparently not in the apostolic fathers or the Christian pseudepigraphic literature).[6] It would be more natural for Peter himself to use the original form of his name than for an imitator to employ a form used of the apostle practically nowhere else. By definition an imitator would surely use the form found in 1 Peter.

The writer says that the Lord had shown him that his death was close (1:14), or "swift" (the meaning the word has in 2:1), and he goes on to say that he was an eyewitness of the transfiguration and to quote the words of the heavenly voice (1:16–18). He says that he has previously written a letter to the same recipients (3:1), and he calls Paul "our dear brother Paul" (3:15), which seems to betoken a certain closeness to that apostle. It is suggested by some that a reference to the transfiguration rather than, say, the resurrection is unlikely from an apostle. But it is just as unlikely from a pseudepigraphic writer. In favor of Peter it might be said both that the transfiguration must have been a high point for him and that there are slight differences from the way the incident is reported in the Gospels (here there is no mention of Moses and Elijah, no "hear him," the emphatic $\grave{\varepsilon}\gamma\acute{\omega}$ [egō] is used, etc.).

Church Tradition

Such tradition uniformly ascribes the letter to Peter. There is no other name linked with it in the tradition.

Paul and the "Other Scriptures"

For some scholars the reference to Paul makes it impossible for them to conclude that Peter wrote this letter. They hold that the reference to Paul's writings (3:15–16) presupposes an authoritative collection of the Pauline Epistles and that this was unlikely during Peter's lifetime. But 2 Peter says nothing about a collection, authoritative or otherwise; "all his letters" need mean no more than all his letters known to Peter. The fact that this writing shows so little knowledge of characteristic Pauline doctrines indicates that there was, as yet, no authoritative collection. The reference to Paul's letters as Scriptures is the major problem in this statement. It is, of course, possible to take γραφάς (graphas) in the sense of "writings," in which case there is no insuperable difficulty. But it is more likely that the word means "Scriptures," which brings us face-to-face with the problem

---

[6]So Guthrie, p. 820.

of how early the Pauline writings were classed in this category. Paul himself clearly thought his writings inspired (1 Cor. 7:40; 14:37) and authoritative (1 Cor. 2:16; 7:17; 14:37–38; 2 Thess. 3:14). Many recent scholars hold that this estimate was not widely accepted in the primitive church. They often hold that there was a time when Paul's writings were widely neglected and that it took quite a long time for them to be generally accepted. This may be so, but it must be insisted that there is no evidence to support it. Paul's view may have been accepted in very early days. In any case, there seems no reason for saying that Peter would not have been in the forefront in recognizing the hand of God in what Paul wrote. One thing in favor of the expression as coming from Peter himself is the candid admission that he found Paul's writings "hard to understand." Would someone choosing Peter as the one in whose name he would write go out of his way to introduce a doubt as to that apostle's ability to understand Paul?

The Fathers

For many, the lifetime of Peter was too early for Christians to be referring to their early leaders as "the fathers" (3:4; NIV's "our fathers" is based on inferior MSS). Perhaps it was, but we should bear in mind that nowhere else in the New Testament is the expression "the fathers" used of the early Christians. It is much more likely that here, as elsewhere, it refers to the Jewish patriarchs. And a pseudepigraphist would not be likely to assume that in Peter's day the first Christians were called "the fathers." Even if we assume that the writer made a slip, we should bear in mind that he is not using the expression of himself but ascribing it to the false teachers, which would mean a generally accepted way of speaking. The objection is not decisive.

The Use of Jude

It is argued that an apostle would not have made use of a writing by a nonapostolic person, and this writer's use of Jude thus rules out the possibility of Peter's being the author. But there are two assumptions here. The first is that Jude is the source of the corresponding passages in 2 Peter. This is not impossible, but it is not certain, and some have felt that the dependence was the other way (see the discussion below in "Relation of 2 Peter to Jude"). The second assumption is that an apostle would not use a nonapostolic writing. But we are in no position to say what writings an apostle would or would not use. There is no reason for holding that Peter would not incorporate any useful words, no matter where he found them.

The False Teaching

A common objection is that the writer is opposing Gnostic teaching, which does not make its appearance until well after Peter's day. But there is no Gnostic system known to us that matches what 2 Peter says; to say that the writer is opposing Gnosticism is to go beyond the evidence.[7] It must always be borne in

---

[7]Jerome H. Neyrey can speak of a time when "it was fashionable to identify 2 Peter's opponents as

mind that when we meet Gnosticism in the second century, it is a group of eclectic systems that gathered their teachings from a variety of sources. There is no doubt that some of the teachings that were later to appeal to the Gnostics go back to apostolic times, but this does not mean that Gnosticism does.[8] The fact that this writer opposes such teaching is no reason for saying he was not Peter.

Motive

If the writing is pseudepigraphic, the question arises, Why was it written? There were Christian writings in which a great name of the past was used to give respectability to what was said, but these seem all to be books that promote unorthodox teaching. Second Peter does nothing of the sort. Its teaching is quite respectable and in line with what other Christian teachers have said. It could quite easily go out under its author's real name, or indeed under no name. We need a reason for choosing to send the little letter out under Peter's name if we are to accept the pseudepigraphic hypothesis, and so far no sufficient reason seems to have appeared. It is usually said that the author chose Peter's name to give authority to what he was writing. But he was writing orthodoxy, and for that no great name was needed.

It cannot be said that all the problems have been overcome by any who have written on this letter. So far as historical inquiry is concerned, we are reduced, in the end, to the probabilities. No conclusive reason has been given for denying that the letter is by the author it claims as its writer. None of the objections can be sustained, and it seems better to accept it at face value, as a genuine writing of the apostle Peter.

RELATION OF 2 PETER TO JUDE

Most of Jude is included in 2 Peter, no less than nineteen of his twenty-five verses being represented in the longer writing. It is difficult to hold accordingly that there is no relationship, although exactly what that relationship was is not easy to determine. While the subject matter of Jude is almost all to be found in 2 Peter, the wording is rarely identical. Guthrie has done some word counts and observes that the passages containing matter common to the two letters run into 297 words in 2 Peter and into 256 words in Jude but that only 78 words are common to the two accounts. Thus if 2 Peter was the borrower, he has changed 70 percent of Jude's words and added some of his own, while if Jude took over a section of 2 Peter, he has changed a somewhat higher percentage and has reduced the length of the excerpt. Guthrie says that of twelve parallel sections, Jude is longer than 2 Peter on five occasions, which means that neither writer is consistently more concise than the other.[9] Whichever writer borrowed from the other, there was thus no slavish copying; the borrower shaped what he borrowed to make it fit his purpose.

Most writers hold that 2 Peter used Jude, largely on the grounds that it is

---

Gnostics," while he himself says flatly, "the opponents are not Gnostics" ("The Apologetic Use of the Transfiguration in 2 Peter 1:16-21," *CBQ* 42 [1980], p. 506).

[8] For fuller discussion of Gnosticism, see chap. 21.

[9] Guthrie, p. 925, n. 1.

difficult to imagine that a writer who on this hypothesis had so little to say as Jude would take an extract from the longer writing and do no more than simply add a few words. But such a procedure cannot be ruled out as impossible. Jude tells us that he wrote in a hurry (v. 3), and it may have suited him to make use of whatever material he happened to have by him.

Most of the arguments for the priority of either writing are subjective. Thus Jude arranged his work in triplets, which means to some that his work is the earlier one, with 2 Peter adapting the form to his own needs, and to others that Jude has taken over 2 Peter and arranged it more artistically. Jude uses the Apocrypha, which some see as a mark of earliness, with 2 Peter omitting allusions to such writings as not suitable in an apostolic letter, while others argue that 2 Peter has in fact alluded to Apocryphal writings without quoting them and Jude decides to indicate the source. Other considerations are urged, but in practically every case it is possible to take up either position. Because we lack any firm indication of the relative dates of the two writings, we cannot say for certain which of the two borrowed from the other.

Actually it is not certain that either did this, for it is possible that they both made use of some earlier document. There is a good deal of common matter in Matthew and Luke, but most scholars think the explanation is not that one of them copied from the other but that they both made use of a source or sources, Mark and Q. Something of the same may have happened here. If so, the common source has been lost. Michael Green argues for a common source,[10] but the hypothesis has not widely commended itself.

It seems, then, that there is not sufficient evidence to enable us to draw a firm conclusion. The large amount of common matter shows that there is a connection between the two writings, but the reasons for preferring either as the original source or both as using a common source are largely subjective.

PROVENANCE

There is not much to go by if we are looking for the place of origin of 2 Peter. If it was written by the apostle, it is likely that it came from Rome, for that is where tradition places Peter toward the end of his days. Such a place is favored by the strong stand against false teaching, for Rome early became a bastion of orthodoxy. Defenders of this view also point to the picture given of the writer's relations with Paul (for both men were in Rome under Nero's rule), and they find a hint at the gospel of Mark in 1:15. We can certainly say that there is nothing in the letter that decisively contradicts such an origin, but Rome is far from having been proven. As with so much about this letter, in the end we have to say, "We do not know. There is no evidence."

DATE

If Peter was the writer, the letter's date has an upper limit imposed by the apostle's death, which can scarcely have been later than about A.D. 68 (though a

---

[10]Michael Green, *The Second Epistle General of Peter and the General Epistle of Jude*, 2d ed. (Grand Rapids: Eerdmans, 1987), pp. 58–64.

few scholars set the upper limit at A.D.). But it was apparently written not long before that death, for Peter speaks of it as imminent. The references to Paul show that several (perhaps all) of that apostle's letters had been written, and that may suggest that he was dead. These considerations would support such a date.

If the letter is pseudepigraphic, it may have been written later, and most scholars who take this view date it in the second century. It must be earlier than c. 150, for it was used by the author of the *Apocalypse of Peter*, which must have been written at about that time. Kümmel thinks of it as coming from "the second quarter of the second century," though he admits, "Every clue to a precise dating of II Peter eludes us."[11]

DESTINATION

It is much the same with the letter's destination as with its origin and date: there is so little to go by. If 3:1 refers to 1 Peter, then this letter is addressed to the same people as that epistle: "God's elect . . . scattered throughout Pontus, Galatia, Cappadocia, Asia and Bithynia" (1 Peter 1:1). If the reference is to some other writing, we have little to go on, though many have thought that these Asian provinces are still the most likely destination, on such grounds as the letter's reception in that area and the fact that heresies of the kind opposed developed there in due course. Obviously we are not in a position to be very definite. Christians in the Asian provinces are a good guess, but we can scarcely say more.

We should also notice that 2 Peter is addressed to "those who through the righteousness of our God and Savior Jesus Christ have received a faith as precious as ours" (1:1). There is no proper epistolary ending; the writing simply closes with a doxology to Christ (a feature found also in 2 Tim. 4:18, but nowhere else in the New Testament). Clearly we lack the information that would enable us to tie down the intended recipients, and perhaps the author intended this from the first. The epistle has come down to us as one of the so-called general letters, and its opening shows that there was some intention of this kind from the very beginning. We may say that it was sent first to Christians in Pontus and the other places listed, but it is clear that its author did not intend it to be limited to them. He was writing with the whole church in mind: however widely or narrowly his letter would circulate, his message was intended for the church at large.

TEXT

The Greek text of this letter is not in good shape (Bigg refers to "the extremely bad state of the text").[12] In the nature of the case, this book would not have had as wide a circulation as many of the other New Testament writings; with fewer copies around, the errors that were bound to creep in would have been harder to correct. Some of the problems are very difficult. Some seem so intractable that even cautious scholars will propose emendations. Thus, Westcott and Hort cite 2 Peter 3:10 as an example of a primitive corruption. They hold that εὑρεθήσεται (*heurethēsetai*) "is the most original of recorded readings" but that it

[11]Kümmel, p. 305.
[12]Charles Bigg, *A Critical and Exegetical Commentary on the Epistles of St. Peter and St. Jude*, ICC (Edinburgh: T. & T. Clark, 1902), p. 211.

cannot be right.[13] However, there is nothing that leads us to think that the meaning of the epistle as a whole has been seriously affected by the state of the text. Reasonable solutions have been offered for most of the problems, and those that remain do not greatly affect the sense.

The language of 2 Peter is unusual. This letter has the highest proportion of hapax legomena of any New Testament book, and a few of them are not cited anywhere else in the whole of Greek literature. It seems that the writer was competent in the Greek that was the lingua franca of the world of his day—at least if his vocabulary is any indication.

ADOPTION INTO THE CANON

"No NT document had a longer or tougher struggle to win acceptance than 2 Peter," writes Kelly.[14] The subject matter of the book was not such as to make it wildly popular, and there were certainly doubts as to whether the book was really written by the apostle Peter. So the church hesitated. Kelly finds evidence of its acceptance first in the East, where it is present in the early Coptic version (c. A.D. 200) and in the early-third-century p^{72}. According to Rufinus's Latin translation of Origen, that Father says it was a disputed writing, but he cites it and apparently regards it as authoritative. Eusebius accepts 1 Peter, "but the so-called second Epistle we have not received as canonical, but nevertheless it has appeared useful to many, and has been studied with other Scriptures" (*H.E.* 3.3.1). Of all the writings bearing the name of Peter, he says "I recognize only one as genuine" (3.3.4). He includes 2 Peter in his list of "the Disputed Books which are nevertheless known to most" (*H.E.* 3.25.3). The book does not appear to have been used by Chrysostom or Theodore of Mopsuestia, but it does appear in Athanasius's festal letter of 367. In the West it seems to have been unknown or overlooked for quite a long time. Jerome says that Peter "wrote two epistles which are called Catholic, the second of which, on account of its difference from the first in style, is considered by many not to be by him" (*De vir. ill.* i). But evidently it won its way, and after Athanasius it seems to have been generally accepted.

2 PETER IN RECENT STUDY

Modern writers do not pay a great deal of attention to 2 Peter, often regarding it as a comparatively mediocre writing and thus unworthy of serious attention. Debates over authorship have mostly died down with the wide acceptance of the view that the writing is pseudonymous. It is held that it is an example of the ascription of a testament to a great figure of the past, in this case a testament that bears its witness to "early catholicism" and helps to shape the church in that model. Ernst Käsemann gives it serious attention in "An Apologia for Primitive Christian Eschatology,"[15] in which he argues that "the Second Epistle of Peter is

---

[13]WH, pp. 279–80.

[14]J. N. D. Kelly, *A Commentary on the Epistles of Peter and of Jude*, HNTC (New York: Harper, 1969), p. 224.

[15]This was a lecture given at the Beinrod Convention in 1952. It is published in an ET in Ernst Käsemann, *Essays on New Testament Themes* (London: SCM, 1964), pp. 169–95. Käsemann sets his

from beginning to end a document expressing an early Catholic viewpoint and is perhaps the most dubious writing in the canon."[16] He argues that faith for this writer means no more than "the saved state of the citizens of heaven,"[17] and with an element of caricature to bring out the meaning, "revelation is now a piece of property which is at the community's disposal."[18] The Christian community no longer distinguishes between Spirit and letter.[19] The meaning of "apostle" has changed so that instead of being the messenger of the gospel, he has become "the guarantor of the tradition."[20] Most students have seen in the letter an emphasis on eschatology, but Käsemann denies this. He sees the Pauline view of the parousia as pointing us to God's final triumph: "The *Kyrios* comes to take possession of his creatures and his world,"[21] but in 2 Peter there is the thought of the partaking of the divine nature (1:4), and its eschatology means no more than that "the Judge of the world has become the instrument of the apotheosis of the pious man."[22]

While many recent scholars endorse what Käsemann has said, there are other viewpoints. Childs cites A. Vögtle as one "who describes the letter as offering a significant key to the phenomenon by which the apostolic tradition was rendered into scripture."[23] Most of the New Testament writings were in fact occasional writings, but they have come down to us as sacred Scripture. None of the writers of the early church tells us how this change comes about, but Vögtle's point is that we learn more about the process in 2 Peter than we do in most other places. Childs himself goes along with the modern consensus that the epistle did not come from Peter; his main hesitation is apparently not with the view itself but with the way this is interpreted. His reluctance to use the term "pseudepigraphy" with respect to this letter arises from the fact that it leads people to concentrate on the motivation of the man who adopted the pseudonym instead of engaging in "a close reading of the text which has with great freedom assigned an astonishing variety of functions to the putative author of the apostolic tradition in performing its particular canonical role."[24] In other words, Childs is deeply concerned that those who write about pseudonymity here are more interested in drawing attention to what they see as the letter's limitations and its failure to conform with what they think Peter would have written than in its important achievement. Whoever wrote the letter (and whenever he wrote it), he performed a significant service to the church by the part he played in establishing the canon and the criteria by which canonicity is to be determined.

---

estimate of the value of the letter over against those of G. Wohlenberg, who found it "full of originality" and "displaying a gift for acute observation" (Käsemann, p. 191).

[16]Ibid., p. 169.

[17]Ibid., p. 174.

[18]Ibid.

[19]Ibid., p. 195.

[20]Ibid., p. 177.

[21]Ibid., p. 182.

[22]Ibid., p. 183.

[23]Childs, p. 465. He is referring to A. Vögtle, "Die Schriftwerdung der apostolischen Paradosis nach 2 Petr. 1,12–15," in *Neues Testament und Geschichte, Fs.* O. Cullmann, ed. H. Baltensweiler et al. (Zürich: TVZ; Tübingen: Mohr, 1972), pp. 297–306.

[24]Childs, p. 471.

THE CONTRIBUTION OF 2 PETER

This letter still has some important things to say to the church. Its opening greeting looks for an abundance of grace and peace for its readers "through the knowledge of God and of Jesus our Lord" (1:2), and its closing exhortation is to "grow in the grace and knowledge of our Lord and Savior Jesus Christ" (3:18). The writer is clear that there is no place in the church for those who decline to increase their knowledge of their Savior. Christians are to be continually learning. They are to add knowledge to goodness (1:5).

A particularly important part of Christian knowledge is that Scripture occupies a unique place. No prophecy of Scripture originated in human will ("came about by the prophet's own interpretation"), but "men spoke from God as they were carried along by the Holy Spirit" (1:20–21). This is understood by many modern scholars to mean that it is the church that tells its members how to interpret the Bible (cf. "no one can interpret any prophecy of Scripture by himself" [1:20, NEB]). But the passage says nothing about the church; it speaks of what God has done by his Holy Spirit. The writer is affirming the divine origin of Old Testament Scripture. Later he goes on to speak of what "our dear brother Paul also wrote" and says that "ignorant and unstable people distort" his writings "as they do the other Scriptures" (3:15–16). Clearly Peter is not bolstering up the place of the church as an authoritative interpreter, but affirming in strong language the divine origin of the prophetic writings and the place of Paul among the writers of Scripture. It is not so much the church as the divine revelation on which the writer is placing his emphasis.

It agrees with this that he repeatedly calls on his readers to remember. His whole letter is a reminder to them (3:1), and he says he will "always remind" them of the things he is writing about (1:12). He is refreshing their memory (1:13) and wants them always to be able to remember these things, even after his death (1:15). He has some new things to say to the readers, but his really important point is that God has spoken in Scripture and that it is important that they bear this in mind. In view of the way the place of the ministry came to be stressed in the church, not least its connection with Peter, it is all the more significant that Peter here makes no reference to the official ministry. And in view of the way the church has often stressed the place of tradition as distinct from written Scripture, it is important that our writer makes no such distinction. For him it is the apostolic traditions that God has caused to be written in Scripture that are important.[25] It is Scripture that is authoritative, and in making this point Peter has his eye on future generations of believers as well as on those to whom he writes immediately (1:15). The words that "men spoke from God as they were carried along by the Holy Spirit" (1:21) are clearly of more than local and temporary concern.

Peter shares with Jude a strong denunciation of false teachers (chap. 2). No heretical teaching is known from antiquity that has exactly the characteristics he singles out, and it is probably wasted effort to try to track it down. What matters in any case is not precisely who taught these things but the fact that even in the earliest days of the church there were people who departed from the teaching God gave through his prophets and apostles. Indeed, departure from the true way is as

---

[25]According to Childs, "II Peter's concern is to address the question of how the fixed apostolic traditions represented by the figure of Peter function as written scripture for later generations of Christians" (p. 492).

old as the flood generation (2:5), and it extends even to the angels (2:4). But whoever those people are who have sinned have undergone punishment, Peter leaves his readers in no doubt that later sinners will also undergo the punishment they deserve (2:12). An interesting feature of his treatment of the judgment theme is his inclusion of Noah and Lot (2:5, 7), for in the midst of destruction "the Lord knows how to rescue godly men from trials and to hold the unrighteous for the day of judgment" (2:9). Judgment is real, but it is not indiscriminate. There is deliverance for those who serve God.

Then there is an important section on the second coming (3:3–13). Even in those early days there were teachers who took the delay in Christ's parousia to mean that he would never come back (3:4). Their contention that things have always been much as they are now is refuted first by the reminders that "the earth was formed out of water and by water" (3:5) and that the flood destroyed the world of its day (3:6). Created beings should never forget that the present heaven and earth will in due course be destroyed (3:7) and that God does not measure time as we do (3:8). Since the created universe is temporary and will one day be destroyed, "what kind of people ought you to be?" (3:11). The writer is driving his readers to reflect on the implications of who God is and what he has revealed. They are not to be led astray by false teaching, no matter how plausible. The purposes of God will infallibly be accomplished in God's good time.

We should not overlook Peter's teaching about the importance of upright Christian living. He has a notable list of qualities that should characterize the Christian (1:5–7); his denunciation of the wicked together with his announcement of their punishment carries with it the thought that God's people should be living very different lives. The second coming is not to be taken as a curious piece of information but as an incentive to holiness of living (3:11).

BIBLIOGRAPHY

Richard J. **Bauckham**, *Jude, 2 Peter*, WBC (Waco, Tex.: Word, 1983); Charles **Bigg**, *A Critical and Exegetical Commentary on the Epistles of St. Peter and St. Jude*, ICC (Edinburgh: T. & T. Clark, 1902); E. M. B. **Green**, *The Second Epistle General of Peter and the General Epistle of Jude*, 2d ed. (Grand Rapids: Eerdmans, 1987); idem, *2 Peter Reconsidered* (London: Tyndale, 1961); E. **Käsemann**, "An Apologia for Primitive Christian Eschatology," in *Essays on New Testament Themes* (London: SCM, 1964), pp. 169–95); J. N. D. **Kelly**, *A Commentary on the Epistles of Peter and of Jude*, HNTC (New York: Harper, 1969); R. **Knopf**, *Die Briefe Petri und Judä*, KEK, 7th ed. (Göttingen: Vandenhoeck & Ruprecht, 1912); Richard N. **Longenecker**, "On the Form, Function, and Authority of the New Testament Letters," in *Scripture and Truth*, ed. D. A. Carson and John D. Woodbridge (Grand Rapids: Zondervan, 1983), pp. 101–14; J. H. **Neyrey**, "The Apologetic Use of the Transfiguration in 2 Peter 1:16–21," *CBQ* 42 (1980): 504–19; idem, "The Form and Background of the Polemic in 2 Peter," *JBL* 99 (1980): 407–31; Bo **Reicke**, *The Epistles of James, Peter, and Jude*, AB (New York: Doubleday, 1964); K. H. **Schelkle**, *Die Petrusbriefe, der Judasbrief*, HTKNT (Freiburg: Herder, 1961); E. M. **Sidebottom**, *James, Jude, and 2 Peter*, NCB (London: Thomas Nelson, 1967); A. **Vögtle**, "Die Schriftwerdung der apostolischen Paradosis nach 2 Petr. 1,12–15," in *Neues Testament und Geschichte*, *Fs.* O. Cullmann, ed. H. Baltensweiler et al. (Zürich: TVZ; Tübingen: Mohr, 1972), pp. 297–306.

21

1, 2, 3 John

CONTENT AND STRUCTURE

1 John

Like the epistle to the Hebrews, 1 John does not exhibit any of the formal characteristics that are normally associated with the openings of letters written in Greek in the first century. Nevertheless, the personal references, the common ties the author shares with his readers, and the explicit historical referents (e.g., 2:19) make it clear that this writing was not intended to be an abstract paper, a mere brochure,[1] or a tractate for all Christians everywhere:[2] it was meant to be read as a pastoral letter to a congregation, or to a number of congregations. There is something to be said for the view that its atypical form is a reflection of its author's intention to send it to several congregations along with an accompanying note personalizing each delivery: 2 John could be one such note (3 John does not qualify nearly so well) and may be the only one that has come down to us.

The structure of 1 John is disputed, largely because John takes up a number of themes and keeps returning to them in slightly different connections. The best survey of structure is by Marshall,[3] though his own proposal—that no structure is believable because John probably connects his various sections by virtue of mere associations of ideas—sounds more haphazard than the flow of the epistle will allow. Although most see between the prologue (1:1–4) and the conclusion (5:14–21) two large sections (1:5–2:29; 3:1–5:13) broken down in various ways, Schnackenburg's suggestion of three divisions has much to commend it: the first treats fellowship with God as walking in the light (1:5–2:17), the second deals directly with the present situation of the church or churches to which John addresses himself (2:18–3:24), and the third divides those who belong to God from the "world" by the tests laid out in the epistle (4:1–5:12).[4] Virtually all sides agree that John lays down three tests: (1) true believers must believe that Jesus

---

[1]Stephen S. Smalley, *1, 2, 3 John*, WBC (Waco, Tex.: Word, 1984), p. xxxiii. For a survey of the discussion on 1 John's literary genre, see R. E. Brown, *The Epistles of John*, AB (Garden City, N.Y.: Doubleday, 1982), pp. 86–92.

[2]Contra Kümmel, p. 437.

[3]I. Howard Marshall, *The Epistles of John*, NICNT (Grand Rapids: Eerdmans, 1978), pp. 22–27.

[4]R. Schnackenburg, *Die Johannesbriefe*, HTKNT (Freiburg: Herder, 1975), pp. vii–viii, 10–11. His subdivisions are less insightful.

truly is the Christ come in the flesh, and this belief must work itself out in (2) righteousness and (3) love.

2 and 3 John

It is widely agreed that these two short epistles bear the form of letters. Ostensibly written to "the chosen lady and her children," 2 John is directed to another congregation—whether to a house–church within the same city or to the church of another city is unclear—to warn against the dangers inherent in traveling preachers, some of whom are "deceivers, who do not acknowledge Jesus Christ as coming in the flesh" (7). But even here, John insists that true believers walk not only in the truth but in transparent love for one another, in line with the command "you have heard from the beginning" (6). This message occupies the central section (4–11) between the introduction (1–3) and the conclusion (12–13).

By contrast with 2 John, which mentions no one by name except Jesus Christ, 3 John is addressed to Gaius about the activities of Diotrephes, who not only "loves to be first" (9) but has become so powerful that he is even refusing the emissaries of the writer, ejecting from the church those who take a softer line. John encourages Gaius (who may have belonged to the church where Diotrephes held court) to follow instead the example of Demetrius and warns that he is coming to expose Diotrephes.

AUTHOR

The external evidence is consistent and can be briefly stated. Possible allusions are found in many of the documents from the end of the first century and the first half of the second century. The most likely are the following: (1) Clement of Rome describes God's elect people as being "perfected in love" (*1 Clem.* 49:5; 50:3, c. A.D. 96; cf. 1 John 2:5; 4:12, 17–18); (2) the *Didache* (estimated date ranges from 90 to 120) has something similar (10:5), a parallel made more impressive in this case by the mention in the next verse of the world passing away (10:6; cf. 1 John 2:17); (3) the *Epistle of Barnabas* (c. 130) speaks of Jesus as "the Son of God come in the flesh" (5:9–11; 12:10; cf. 1 John 4:2; 2 John 7); (4) Polycarp warns against deceiving false brothers in these terms: "For everyone who does not confess Jesus Christ to have come in the flesh is Antichrist" (*Phil.* 7:1, c. 135), surely dependent on 2 John 7 and 1 John 4:2–3; cf. 1 John 2:22. Numerous other allusions are proposed, most of them less plausible than these.[5]

However, the first author to refer specifically to a Johannine epistle as the work of John is Papias of Hierapolis in the middle of the second century, who, according to Eusebius (*H.E.* 3.39.17), "used testimonies drawn from the former Epistle of John." It is important to note that "former" is Eusebius's word, not Papias's; one cannot deduce from it that Papias knew of more than one Johannine epistle. By the time of Ireneus (c. A.D. 180), at least the first and second epistles are explicitly attributed to John, the disciple of the Lord and the author of the fourth

---

[5]The evidence is conveniently set out in A. E. Brooke, *A Critical and Exegetical Commentary on the Johannine Epistles*, ICC (Edinburgh: T. & T. Clark, 1912), pp. liiff. See Brown, *Epistles of John*, pp. 6ff., for a slightly more skeptical view of the evidence.

gospel (*Adv. Haer.* 3.16.18). Writing about the same time, Clement of Alexandria knows of more than one Johannine epistle, since he refers to "the greater epistle" and ascribes it to the apostle John (see *Strom.* 2.15.66; cf. 3.4.32; 3.5.42; 4.16.100). Thereafter the evidence becomes plentiful.

The external evidence for 2 and 3 John is not as strong as for 1 John, partly owing to the fact that they are so brief and somewhat less theologically focused, and thus they would be unlikely to be quoted so often. We have already noted that 2 John is linked with 1 John by Ireneus and that Clement knows of more than one Johannine epistle. So far as our records go, it is Origen (d. A.D. 253) who first mentions all three epistles, but according to Eusebius (*H.E.* 6.25.10), he does so in part to acknowledge that not everyone accepted the authenticity of 2 and 3 John. Origen's pupil Dionysius of Alexandria (d. 265) insisted that John the apostle wrote the fourth gospel and 1 John (but not Revelation) and knew about 2 and 3 John. See further the section "Adoption into the Canon," below. Never is any of the three Johannine epistles attributed to anyone other than John the son of Zebedee.

As for the internal evidence, nothing in any of the epistles points unambiguously to a specific author. All the arguments finally turn on the relation of these epistles to the fourth gospel. Methodologically, it is easiest first to deal with the relation of 1 John to the gospel, and then to consider the relation of 2 John and 3 John to 1 John.

A superficial reading of the fourth gospel and of 1 John reveals many striking similarities in theme, vocabulary, and syntax.[6] The same stark polarities prevail: light and darkness, life and death, truth and lie, love and hate—with no third alternative. The same relatively simple syntax is found in both, combined with a marked penchant for parallelism. Poythress has shown that the prevalence of asyndeton and the relative infrequency of intersentence conjunctions in both documents argue for the same author.[7] Stott has demonstrated that the same "scheme of salvation" pervades both 1 John and the fourth gospel.[8] To offer but a few examples drawn from several score: In our unredeemed state we are "of the devil," who has sinned and lied and murdered "from the beginning" (1 John 3:8/John 8:44); we are "from the world" (2:16; 4:5/8:23; 15:19). We therefore "sin" (3:4/8:34) and "have" sin (1:8/9:41), "walk in the darkness" (1:6; 2:11/8:12; 12:35) and are "dead" (3:14/5:25). God loved us and sent his Son to be "the Savior of the world" (4:14/4:42) so that "we might live" (4:9/3:16). Believing in him or in his "name" (5:13/1:12), we pass from death to life (3:14/5:24). We "have life" (5:11, 12/3:15, 36; 20:31), for life is in the Son of God (5:11–12/1:4; 14:6). This is what it means to be "born of God" (2:29; 3:9; 5:4, 18/1:13). There is much more of the same.

---

[6]The most comprehensive lists of linguistic similarities and dissimilarities are still found in Brooke, *Johannine Epistles*, pp. i–xix, 235–42, and in Robert Law, *The Tests of Life* (1914; reprint, Grand Rapids: Baker, 1979), pp. 341–63.

[7]Vern Poythress, "The Use of the Intersentence Conjunctions *De, Oun, Kai,* and Asyndeton in the Gospel of John," *NovT* 26 (1984): 312–34; idem, "Testing for Johannine Authorship by Examining the Use of Conjunctions," *WTJ* 46 (1984): 350–69. Cf. discussion in chap. 5 on the fourth gospel.

[8]John R. W. Stott, *The Letters of John,* TNTC (Grand Rapids: Eerdmans, 1988), pp. 21–23.

Those who argue for a different author for the two documents usually appeal to two kinds of phenomena.[9]

1. There are subtle but significant differences between John and 1 John in both doctrine and wording, even when they are formally parallel. For instance, it is commonly argued that only in John is the λόγος (*logos*, "Word") personal (see John 1:1, 14); in 1 John 1:1–4, the "word" is the "word of life," and it is the life that is personal. In the fourth gospel, the Holy Spirit is the παράκλητος (*paraklētos*, "Paraclete" or "Counselor," John 14–16); in 1 John 2:1, it is Jesus himself. John affirms that "God is Spirit"; 1 John says, rather, that he is light (1:5) and love (4:8, 16). In the fourth gospel, the death of Jesus is presented as his being "lifted up" and "glorified"; in the epistle, the purpose of Jesus' death is propitiatory (2:2; 4:10). It is often argued that in the fourth gospel the eschatology is profoundly "realized" (i.e. people enjoy eternal life already), while in 1 John much more place is given to Jesus' future, personal coming (2:28; 3:2; 4:17).

On close examination, these and similar objections carry little weight. It is true that the prologue to the gospel uses λόγος (*logos*) to refer to the preincarnate Son of God, but it uses the same word numerous times throughout the gospel with its more common meaning of "message" (e.g., 8:31), and some scholars think that even in 1 John the personal usage has not disappeared (i.e. they understand the text to say that it is the "word of life," not the "life," that has appeared). That Jesus should be called the παράκλητος (*paraklētos*) in 1 John is scarcely surprising, for Jesus in John insists he is sending *another* Paraclete (John 14:16): one could surely argue common authorship from this, rather than disparate authorship. The suggestion that the one who wrote that God is spirit is unlikely to have written that he is light and love is almost silly on the face of it. If the fourth gospel looks at Jesus' death as a "lifting up" and a "glorification," it is partly because it is focusing on the historical Jesus, and partly because it is intent on showing that the cross was not the defeat that some Jews thought it was. If 1 John casts Jesus' death in terms of its propitiatory significance, that owes much to his polemical purpose: he is concerned to show that sin has serious effects, and the only way to remove those effects is by the provision that God himself has made. In any case, the presentation of Jesus' death in the fourth gospel is not univocal: other themes intrude there and overlap with those of 1 John (see John 1:29; 3:14–16, 36; 6:51; 10:11, 15; 11:49–52; etc.). We should speak of complementarity of vision and thought, of differentiation in application, not of mutual contradiction. Finally, although the eschatological emphases of the two books are not identical, the complementary truth is also found in both books: the fourth gospel reserves space for futurist eschatology (5:28–29; 6:39–40, 44, 54; 11:24–26; 12:48; 14:3), while 1 John insists that those who believe may have confidence that they experience eternal life as a present possession.

2. There are words and expressions in John not found in 1 John, and vice versa (see Brooke's commentary). Today most scholars acknowledge that nothing decisive can be based on these lists. The divergent vocabularies enjoy greater similarity than those of, say, Luke and Acts, known to come from the same pen, or

---

[9]See esp. C. H. Dodd, *The Johannine Epistles*, MNTC (London: Hodder & Stoughton, 1946), esp. pp. xlviiff.

of Ephesians and Colossians, or of 1 Timothy and Titus. "The variations in phrase suggest common authorship rather than servile, or even intelligent, copying."[10]

Although a few scholars have argued that 2 John and 3 John came from some pen other than that which wrote 1 John, not many have been persuaded by them. The links of both vocabulary and theme are too many (granted the brevity of the second and third epistles) to justify such skepticism (e.g., "Jesus Christ has come in the flesh" [2 John 7/1 John 4:2]; "deceiver" and "antichrist" [2 John 7/2:23]; those who love and do good show that they are "from God" [3 John 11/3:10; 4:4, 7]).

More difficult to explain, on the traditional view, is why the author of 2 John and 3 John should refer to himself as ὁ πρεσβύτερος (*ho presbyteros*, "the elder"). This certainly does not give justification to the position of Eusebius, and of many modern scholars who have followed him, who argue that the fourth gospel and the Johannine Epistles were written not by John the apostle but by John the elder (see discussion in the section "Author" in chap. 5). Note, however, that there is nothing anomalous about an apostle designating himself as an elder (1 Peter 5:1; cf. Papias, in the discussion just reported). Furthermore, the term "elder" can refer to an old man (see Philem. 9, using the cognate term πρεσβύτης, [*presbytēs*]). If the author is John the son of Zebedee, the last of the apostles, it is not inappropriate for him to make a dual allusion. This interpretation may be strengthened by observing the article: John refers to himself as "*the* elder." He could scarcely refer to himself as "the apostle": that would surely sound a trifle pompous, even if he was the last of the Twelve to survive. He was simply *an* apostle (note the usage of Paul in Rom. 1:1, and of Peter in 1 Peter 1:1). But he could be *the* elder in the Ephesus region, precisely because he was not just an ordinary elder.

Two other factors argue for apostolic authorship.[11]

1. Although in most of the "we" passages in the Johannine Epistles the pronoun includes the Christian readers and is set over against the "they" of the "world" (i.e. non-Christians, including heretics—e.g., 2:3; 3:2, 11; 4:19), in a few passages the most reasonable exegesis suggests that the "we" refers to the author and his fellow eyewitnesses over against the "you" of the Christian readers. This is particularly true in 1:1, 3; 4:14; 5:6–7. Despite vigorous protests to the contrary, in these passages the author distinguishes himself not only as writer from his readers but as eyewitness from second-generation believers and as authoritative teacher from those who are being taught.

2. The latter distinction (between authoritative teacher and those being taught) deserves expansion. It is not simply the sweep and tone of the writer's authority that is at issue, though that is impressive (e.g., 2:1–2, 8, 15, 17, 23, 28; 3:6, 9; 4:1, 8, 16; 5:21), not least when he brands certain people as liars, deceivers, and antichrists (cf. Gal.1:8, 9). Rather, it is that he does so *across congregations* (2 and 3 John). Indeed, it is this fact that prompts Käsemann to argue that the author of the Johannine Epistles was not the apostle John but the first of what became

[10]Brooke, *Johannine Epistles*, p. xvi.

[11]These points are argued in detail by such commentators as B. F. Westcott (*The Epistles of St John* [1892; reprint, Appleford: Marcham Manor, 1966], Marshall (*Epistles of John*), and Stott (*Letters of John*).

monarchical bishops, leading directly to the stance of Ignatius that the church exists where the bishop is.[12] That means, of course, that it is Diotrephes who is trying to preserve the more primitive pattern of local church autonomy. Few have agreed with Käsemann; the more obvious motive for Diotrephes's power play is simply that he loved to be first (3 John 9)—a problem not unknown in either the ancient church (see 2 Cor. 10–13) or the modern. But that means that the most obvious explanation for this cross-congregational authority is that the author of these epistles was an apostle, since elders per se did not, so far as we know, enjoy such authority.

Almost inevitably, the most fundamental reasons advanced today for rejecting Johannine authorship of these epistles turn not on the hard evidence or on source theories[13] that have almost universally been abandoned but on reconstructions of the development of the Johannine "circle" or "community" or "school." This reconstruction exercises such controlling power in contemporary discussion that the possibility of apostolic authorship is prematurely ruled out of court, in favor of a document refracting the light from community beliefs. These matters are treated at some length in chapter 5 above on the fourth gospel, and they also have a bearing on our understanding of the purpose of these epistles (see the section "Purpose" below).

PROVENANCE

Whether one thinks in terms of apostolic authorship or of a Johannine school, the most likely provenance is Ephesus. The evidence that John the son of Zebedee (and for that matter Philip the evangelist and his daughters) moved to Ephesus at the time of the Jewish War (A.D.66–70) and ultimately died there is not overwhelming, but it is consistent. It depends in large part on the witness of Polycrates, bishop of Ephesus, writing to Victor, bishop of Rome, c. 190 (so Eusebius, *H.E.* 3.31.3; 5.24.2), and the witness of Ireneus (*Adv. Haer.* 3.1.1), who knew both Papias and Polycarp. Several witnesses could also point to the tombs of Philip and his daughters and of the beloved disciple. (See discussion in chaps. 5 and 23.)

Those who judge the external evidence to be late and unreliable deny any connection with Ephesus and postulate other centers, largely on the ground of conceptual links with literature thought to come from those centers. Thus, on the ground that the Johannine Epistles are tied in some way to the fourth gospel and that the fourth gospel shares some conceptual links with *Odes of Solomon*, thought to have originated in Syria, Kümmel cautiously postulates Syria.[14] Methodologically, this approach appears to be far too cavalier with specific historical witnesses and far too trusting of our ability to establish the closest conceptual links (not to mention our utter ignorance of how far a document such as the *Odes of Solomon* circulated toward the end of the first century).

---

[12]E. Käsemann, "Ketzer und Zeuge," *ZTK* 48 (1951): 292–311.

[13]In particular, J. C. O'Neill, *The Puzzle of 1 John* (London: SPCK, 1966); Rudolf Bultmann, *The Johannine Epistles*, ET Hermeneia (Philadelphia: Fortress, 1973); W. Nauck, *Die Tradition und der Charakter des ersten Johannesbriefes*, WUNT 3 (Tübingen: Mohr, 1957). Cf. Marshall, *Epistles of John*, pp. 27–30.

[14]Kümmel, p. 246–47, 445.

DATE

The date of the epistles of John is entirely bound up with the date of the fourth gospel and their relationship to it. As we have seen, although a few date the gospel of John before A.D. 70, and a majority assign it to the last decade of the first century, we have cautiously suggested 80–85. The question to be posed, then, is whether the epistles were written before or after the gospel.

Certainty is impossible; the decision depends, finally, on one's understanding of the respective purposes of the fourth gospel and of the Johannine Epistles. It will be argued here that the epistles, unlike the gospel, were written in part to establish and encourage the faith of Christians in the wake of rising controversy over proto-Gnosticism (see the section "Purpose" below). Since this movement was on the ascendency at the end of the first century (though it did not reach full flowering until well into the second century), it seems best to date the epistles *after* the fourth gospel. This judgment is confirmed by the evidence that suggests that at least some of the Gnostic heretics were using the fourth gospel for their own purposes: certainly John was a favorite of Gnostics in the second century (though John 1:14, "the Word became flesh," was ultimately destructive of their beliefs). Probably, therefore, some time elapsed between the publication of the fourth gospel and that of the epistles, enough at least to allow what John perceives to be the improper use of his earlier work to gain enough steam to cause schism in the church (see 1 John 2:19). Constrained at the other end by apparent allusions to 1 John in some of the subapostolic fathers, it appears best to date the epistles of John to the early nineties.

DESTINATION

First John mentions no addressee and preserves no specific greetings, formal thanksgiving, or any of the other formal touches that normally characterize a first-century letter. The second epistle is addressed to "the chosen lady and her children," almost certainly not a respected Christian matron and her family but a local congregation. It can scarcely be thought that this epistle is directed to the universal church, since it reports greetings from "your chosen sister," which must be understood to be salutations from another congregation: the universal church has no sister. Even so, it is just possible that the author chose this form of address not only for its symbolic connections but also because it was flexible enough to be used with respect to *several* congregations.[15] The third epistle is addressed to an individual, Gaius by name, not to be associated with Gaius of Corinth (1 Cor. 1:14; Rom. 16:23) or Gaius of Macedonia (Acts 19:29), and probably not Gaius of Derbe (Acts 20:4)—though a fourth-century document, the *Apostolic Constitutions* (7.46.9), makes this latter connection. The document is late, and "Gaius" was an exceedingly common name in the empire.

The geographic destination cannot be more than an inference from what is reconstructed of the documents' provenance. Probably, therefore, these epistles were sent to churches (and an individual) somewhere in the Ephesus area,

---

[15]See Judith M. Lieu, *The Second and Third Epistles of John* (Edinburgh: T. & T. Clark, 1986), pp. 64–68.

including, perhaps, the territory spanned by the seven churches of Revelation 2–3).

PURPOSE

A few scholars have argued that 1 John is pastoral and not polemical, that there is no need to reconstruct a group of heretics or secessionists. The first epistle was written to foster Christian assurance and to ward off possible developments in the community's theology that could have ultimately led to schism;[16] or, if there was trouble, it was caused by nothing more than the undisciplined exercise of prophetic gifts.[17]

Although John does intend to edify his readers, most scholars rightly reject this view as an inadequate explanation of the evidence. Some have already seceded (1 John 2:18–19), and John is writing to warn his readers about false teachers who are actively trying to deceive them (2:26). Paul's prophecy to the Ephesian elders (Acts 20:29–30), renewed to Timothy (2 Tim. 3:1–7; 4:3–4), was coming true: "savage wolves" were rending the flock, and John labels them "false prophets" (1 John 4:1), "deceivers" (2 John 7), and "antichrists" (1 John 2:18; 4:3; 2 John 7). Probably their secession owed much to their failure to convert more of the congregation(s) to which they once belonged (1 John 2:18–19): many Christians by their adherence to the truth had "overcome them" (1 John 4:4). Still, John finds he must reassure the faithful and explain in straightforward terms the differences between the two groups and thereby give them grounds for their own assurance and confidence before God (1 John 5:13) at a time when they were being made to feel inferior and spiritually threatened.

The differences between John's readers and John's opponents are substantial. The secessionists denied that Jesus was the Christ (2:22)—not apparently meaning that they disbelieved that Jesus was the Messiah of Old Testament expectation, but that the human Jesus really was the Christ, the Son (2:23; 4:15; 2 John 9). They denied that Christ had come in the flesh (4:2; 2 John 7). Judging by 1 John 1:6–10, they also denied that they were in any sense dominated by or even subject to sin: it did not inhere in their nature, display itself in their behavior, or hinder their fellowship with God. Meanwhile their own conduct was so haughty, loveless, and schismatic that they denied the very gospel they claimed that only they understood, prompting some of the more hesitant amongst those left behind to wonder at times if they had the Spirit at all (see 2:26–27).

What, then, could account for this matrix of errors? External evidence commonly leads commentators to postulate one of three movements.

Gnosticism. This theosophical potpourri was anchored in neoplatonic dualism, which fostered a dichotomy between matter (evil) and spirit (good). In the classic Gnostic myth that comes down to us from third-century sources (see *DBI*, pp. 264–66), there is an ultimate Father from whom a variety of spiritual beings emanate. One of these, Wisdom, tries to act independently from another, Thought, and unintentionally produces a misshapen being, Wisdom's son

---

[16]So Judith M. Lieu, " 'Authority to Become Children of God': A Study of 1 John," *NovT* 23 (1981): 210–28.

[17]So F. Büchsel, *Die Johannesbriefe*, THNT (Leipzig: Deichert, 1933), pp. 4–5; cf. G. M. Burge, *The Anointed Community: The Holy Spirit in the Johannine Tradition* (Grand Rapids: Eerdmans, 1987).

Ialdabaoth, who steals enough of her power to become the creator of the spiritual powers who rule this world, and with whose help the physical universe, including Adam and Eve, comes into being. The biblical stories are then retold to accommodate the changes. The fall narrative (Gen. 3), for instance, becomes an attempt to impart true knowledge (*gnōsis*) to those imprisoned in evil matter by the action of their evil creator. Adam ultimately begets Seth, who receives some pure spirit. This sets up a dichotomy in the human race: some have their origins in this spirit-life, and others are nothing but matter. Later versions of the myth tell of a Gnostic redeemer who explains their origins to the "elect" (i.e., not to those who are *chosen* by God, but to those who are *choice* by virtue of their possession of spirit-life, and who therefore have the capacity to receive this "knowledge," thereby liberating them). The structure of Gnostic myths varies considerably. Valentinus, in the second century, taught that the Godhead is comprised of thirty "aeons," regarded as male and female pairs. Among them, Intellect and Truth produced Word and Life, who in turn produced Man and Church. Whatever the precise structure, some scholars argue that the heretics presupposed by 1 and 2 John have been influenced by Gnosticism and are concerned with deliverance from the flesh by the acquisition of knowledge.

Docetism. More particularly, a branch of Gnosticism known as Docetism (from δοκέω, [*dokeō*], "it seems") applied the same reasoning so as to reject the incarnation. Docetism asked, How can a spirit-being, "Christ" or the "Son of God," good by definition, actually become flesh, which is evil by definition? Although such a spirit-being may temporarily *assume* it, it could never *become* it. Docetists so misconceived the true locus of evil that they fell into sin and puffed themselves up with Gnostic pride.

The heresy of Cerinthus. No less commonly, appeal is made to Cerinthus, about whom we learn chiefly from Ireneus and Eusebius. Eusebius, for instance, preserves Polycarp's report that John the apostle fled the bathhouse in Ephesus when he found that Cerinthus was in it, on the ground that God could at any time reach down and destroy this "enemy of the truth" (*H.E.* 3.3.4; cf. 3.28.6; 4.14.6). Ireneus gives an account of Cerinthus's heretical views (*Adv. Haer.* 1.16.1; 3.2.1, 7, 8), which severed the man Jesus from the divine Christ (or from the Spirit, according to Epiphanius's report of the heresy (*Ref. Haer.* 28.1). The Christ (or the Spirit) came upon Jesus at his baptism and left him to suffer alone on the cross (since the Christ/Spirit himself is impassible).

The explanatory power of these proposed backgrounds is considerable, but caution must be exercised. For example, Marshall points out that some of what we know about Cerinthus (e.g., his belief that Jesus was the son of an inferior creator-god) is not reflected in the Johannine Epistles, while some of what the epistles oppose (e.g., the claim to sinlessness) is not known to have been associated with Cerinthus.[18] Schnackenburg, who favors a background in Docetism of the kind opposed by Ignatius a mere decade or two later (e.g., *Smyr.*1–3; *Magn.* 11; *Trall.* 9–10), nevertheless acknowledges that there are critical differences: for example, the Docetists opposed by Ignatius are tied to Jewish rites and beliefs, of which there are no traces in the Johannine Epistles.[19]

---

[18]Marshall, *Epistles of John*, p. 18.
[19]Schnackenburg, *Die Johannesbriefe*, pp. 19ff.

Above all, the dates of Gnosticism itself are hotly disputed. Full-blown Gnosticism is almost certainly an amalgam of Jewish, Christian, and pagan deviations, an amorphous movement whose flowering is not only later than the New Testament but also so diverse in its manifestations that very few generalizations can be made. The most plausible conclusion is that the movement was gaining strength when John wrote his epistles, and some of the contours of the particular form it took in this case can be hesitantly delineated from these letters. Doubtless this form cannot be precisely identified with any of the manifestations that have come down to us independently. The point is that rather few have been preserved for us, and the most we can say is that, so far as the epistles of John go, the discernible errors and abysmal practices that are being opposed have much in common with the Docetism and Cerinthianism of which we know all too little.

Many contemporary scholars, however, pay little attention to this external evidence and seek to trace out divergent streams of "Johannine Christianity" largely by establishing trajectories from the fourth gospel (or from perceived distinguishable traditions in the fourth gospel) to a complex situation that can be retrieved from the epistles.[20] Virtually all of these scholars exhibit far more sympathy for John's opponents than John did, and sometimes more for the opponents than for John himself.

Smalley, who at least is sympathetic to the epistles, nevertheless insists that distinctions between heresy and orthoxy have not yet been made at this period in the church's life—an extraordinary judgment when Paul was making them almost half a century earlier (see Gal. 1:8–9; 2 Cor. 11:4; see further John 14:6; Acts 4:12). Houlden thinks the fourth gospel is adventurous and speculative and judges that the "dissidents" simply wanted to go a little further in the same direction, while the epistles are a conservative "rearguard action" to reassert traditional doctrine. Smalley postulates three groups—one that denies Jesus' humanity, another that denies Jesus' deity, and a group of seceders (who may have overlapped with the others)—all quite apart from the traditionalists.

Brown engages in considerable speculation and uncontrolled inferences to tease out the contours of two groups, divided not in their acceptance of the authority of the fourth gospel but in its interpretation, especially in the areas of Christology, ethics, eschatology, and pneumatology (with his commentary primarily focusing on the first two). Brown does not think it is possible for the historian to judge which group understood the fourth gospel correctly. Because of this stance, Brown argues, for instance, that the secessionists did not deny the humanity of Jesus (since they held John 1:14 to be authoritative) but denied that the humanity of Jesus was significant for revelation or salvation. Perhaps; but the texts do not say so, and a great deal is made to rest on the postulate that both sides adopted the fourth gospel. Brown thinks that in the aftermath of the struggle the "secessionists" (he cannot think of them as heretics) drifted off into the later "heretical" movements (Cerinthianism, Montanism, Docetism, etc.), while those remaining "were swallowed up by the 'Great Church.' "[21]

---

[20]E.g., Brown, Epistles of John; Smalley, 1, 2, 3 John; Kenneth Grayston, The Johannine Epistles, NCB (Grand Rapids: Eerdmans, 1984); J. L. Houlden, The Johannine Epistles, BNTC (London: Black, 1973); Pierre Bonnard, Les épîtres johanniques, CNT (Geneva: Labor & Fides, 1983); Georg Strecker, Die Johannesbriefe, KEK (Göttingen: Vandenhoeck & Ruprecht, 1989).

[21]Brown, Epistles of John, p. 103.

Detailed evaluation is not possible in short compass. Methodologically, the heart of the problem is the heaping up of merely possible inferences (see discussion in chap. 5 and below in the section "The Johannine Epistles in Recent Study") and the too-ready distancing from the external sources. It still seems best to conclude that John is combating proto-Gnosticism, an embryonic Docetism or Cerinthianism that has already divided Christians. Over against the emphases of his opponents, emphases that he frankly aligns with all that is non-Christian, John stresses the truth that Jesus is Christ come in the flesh and that genuine belief in this Jesus works itself out in obedience to the commands of God and in love for God's people.

If this is approximately correct, the purpose of 2 John is primarily to warn a congregation or house church against admitting traveling teachers who espouse such false teaching. Although many have attempted to find similar heresy behind 3 John (whether in Diotrephes or in the writer!), the epistle itself betrays no such aberrations and is perhaps nothing other than an apostolic warning against someone who is attempting to amass all local authority. Even so, we would have to conclude that this was taking place against the background established by the other two epistles. We might therefore speculate that Diotrephes was using the danger of heresy to build his own power base. But it is hard to imagine that he himself is a heretic, or John would surely have denounced him for it.

TEXT

The detailed work of Richards,[22] supplemented marginally by that of Amphoux,[23] has shown that in all probability the text of the Johannine Epistles is supported by three text types—Alexandrian (with three subgroups), Byzantine (seven subgroups) and Mixed (three subgroups)—not two or four, as some have argued.

Only a few passages contain variants of substantial exegetical significance, the most notorious being the addition of the "Trinitarian witnesses" at 1 John 5:7–8a: "For there are three that bear record in heaven, the Father, the Word, and the Holy Ghost: and these three are one. And there are three that bear witness in earth"(KJV). This is certainly a gloss. It is found in no Greek manuscript before the fourteenth century, except for one eleventh- and one twelfth-century manuscript, where the words have been added in the margin by a much later hand. None of the early Greek fathers quotes the words, and it is quite certain that had they known of them, they would have used them in the ancient Trinitarian debates. None of the ancient versions supports the gloss, including the early editions of the (Latin) Vulgate. The words first appear in a fourth-century Latin treatise (not a biblical manuscript), after which some Latin fathers start to use them.

---

[22]W. L. Richards, *The Classification of the Greek Manuscripts of the Johannine Epistles*, SBLDS 35 (Missoula, Mont.: SP, 1977).

[23]B. Amphoux, "Note sur le classement des manuscrits grecs de 1 Jean," *RHPR* 61 (1981): 125–35.

ADOPTION INTO THE CANON

The earliest witnesses to the Johannine Epistles have already been surveyed.[24] The first mention of all three epistles is in a context that reports at least some hesitation as to the suitability of 2 and 3 John for inclusion in the canon: Origen (c. A.D. 231) writes that John "left an epistle of a very few lines and, it may be, a second and a third, for not all say that these [i.e. the second and the third] are genuine" (quoted by Eusebius, *H.E.* 6.25.10). Eusebius (c. 325) includes 1 John among the *homologoumena*, the acknowledged books, but places 2 and 3 John among the *antilegomena*, the disputed books (*H.E.* 3.25.2–3)—though he says they are "well known and acknowledged by most," whether they were written by John the apostle or by "another of the same name" (certainly referring to the "John the elder" theory, which depends at least in part on his misreading of Papias; see the section "Author" in chap. 5 above). He himself is persuaded that all three Johannine epistles were written by John the apostle (*H.E.* 6.25.10). The Muratorian Canon refers to two epistles by John, but probably 1 and 2 John are in mind, not 2 and 3 John.

First John belongs to a group of New Testament epistles often called catholic or general, because they are not addressed to a specific community or individual. Origen applies the term "catholic" to 1 John (*Comm. on Matt.* 17.19) and his disciple Dionysius, bishop of Alexandria, speaks of 1 John as John's "catholic epistle," possibly in contrast to 2 and 3 John (*H.E.* 7.25.7, 10). A little later, 2 and 3 John were reckoned among the seven catholic epistles (James, 1–2 Peter, 1–3 John, Jude—so Eusebius, *H.E.* 2.23.25), where "catholic" has come to mean almost "canonical"—that is, canonical in addition to the canonical epistles of Paul. All three Johannine epistles are included in Athanasius's list of twenty-seven New Testament books (A.D. 367) and in the lists approved by the Councils of Hippo (393) and of Carthage (397). The Peshitta included 1 John, but not 2 and 3 John; not until the next century, with the publication of the Philoxenian version (508), were the two shorter epistles (along with 2 Peter, Jude, and Revelation, which had also been omitted) included in a Syriac New Testament. In Reformation times, debates over the authorship of 2 and 3 John were again raised, both on the Roman Catholic side (Cajetan) and the Reform side (Erasmus), but not over their canonicity.

THE JOHANNINE EPISTLES IN RECENT STUDY

With few exceptions (though they are notable),[25] the driving force behind the most recent studies on the Johannine Epistles has been the attempt to delineate the contours—more, the trajectories of the changing contours—of the Johannine community.[26] We have already argued that this is a mistake.[27] It is not that

---

[24]See Lieu, *Second and Third Epistles*, pp. 5–36.

[25]E.g., Richards, *Classification*; Lieu, *Second and Third Epistles*; Edward Malatesta, *Interiority and Covenant: A Study of εἶναι ἐν and μένειν ἐν and μένειν ἐν in the First Letter of Saint John*, AnBib 69 (Rome: BIP, 1978).

[26]E.g., the commentaries by Brown, Smalley, and Strecker, and such books as John Bogaert, *Orthodox and Heretical Perfectionism*, SBLDS 33 (Missoula, Mont.: SP, 1977; D. Bruce Woll, *Johannine Christianity in Conflict*, SBLDS 60 (Chico, Calif.: SP, 1981); Rodney A. Whitacre, *Johannine Polemic: The Role of Tradition and Theology*, SBLDS 67 (Chico, Calif: SP, 1982).

nothing profitable can be said about the communities to which the epistles were sent; rather, it is that merely possible inferences regarding those communities must not be allowed to control the exegesis. Many of the criticisms Brevard Childs levels against Brown could rightly be applied to a number of modern commentaries.[28] According to Childs, Brown's exegesis of the Johannine Epistles is made to rest so entirely on his detailed reconstructions of his opponents, including not only their theology but their motives, that the edifice becomes precariously speculative. Since Brown argues that the competing perspectives of the epistles and of the secessionists turns on different interpretations of the fourth gospel, at every point he attempts to reconstruct the origin of each doctrinal stance and the riposte; but "what purports to be an historical investigation is actually an exercise in creative imagination with very few historical controls."[29] Every clause in the text of 1 John is historicized—not simply passages that call for it (e.g., 2:19). The result is a flattening of exegesis in which virtually every passage serves exclusively as polemic, and entire ranges of exegetical options are foreclosed; the necessary circularity in all historical reconstructions is in danger of becoming vicious. For instance, the sin unto death (5:16–17) is simply identified with the sin of the secessionists. There is a continuing need for treatments of the Johannine Epistles that are less speculative in their handling of historical reconstructions and more profound in their reflection on theological, canonical connections.

THE CONTRIBUTION OF THE JOHANNINE EPISTLES

Taken together, the epistles of John stand as a poised demonstration of the critical importance of testing all attempts to rearticulate the gospel by the immutables of the gospel revelation. Doubtless John's opponents saw themselves as being on the leading edge of Christian reflection (2 John 9); by contrast, John reverts to what was "from the beginning," to the testimony of the first eyewitnesses, to incontrovertible Christological givens, to the perennial newness of the "old" command to love one another, to the irrefragable connection between genuine faith and obedience. This stance has a bearing on what teaching a church will listen to (2 John). At the practical level, whether heresy stands behind 3 John or not, this holistic vision insists that there is no place for petty gurus in the church who will not bow to apostolic admonition and authority.

The Johannine Epistles make an important contribution to the doctrine of assurance (see 1 John 5:13). If other New Testament writings make it clear that the objective grounds of our confidence before God are in Christ and his death and resurrection on our behalf, such that Christian assurance is not much more than a concomitant of genuine faith, these epistles insist that a distinction must be made between genuine and spurious faith. Spurious faith does not have the right to assurance before God; genuine faith can be authenticated not only by the correctness of its object (in this case, the belief that Jesus is Christ come in the flesh) but also by the transformation it effects in the individual: genuine Christians learn to love one another and obey the truth. Christian assurance is not, for John,

---

[27]See esp. chap. 5 above.
[28]Childs, p. 482–85.
[29]Ibid., p. 483.

an abstract good; it is intimately tied to a continuing and transforming relationship with the covenant God, who has revealed himself in Jesus Christ.

The Johannine Epistles open an unrivaled window onto at least one part of the New Testament church toward the end of the apostolic age. They afford us the opportunity to draw some lines, however hesitantly, between the church as reflected in the earliest documents of the New Testament and the church at the end of the first century.

BIBLIOGRAPHY

Chr. B. **Amphoux**, "Note sur le classement des manuscrits grecs de 1 Jean," *RHPR* 61 (1981): 125–35; John **Bogaert**, *Orthodox and Heretical Perfectionism*, SBLDS 33 (Missoula, Mont.: SP, 1977); Pierre **Bonnard**, *Les épîtres johanniques*, CNT (Geneva: Labor & Fides, 1983); A. E. **Brooke**, *A Critical and Exegetical Commentary on the Johannine Epistles*, ICC (Edinburgh: T. & T. Clark, 1912); Raymond E. **Brown**, *The Epistles of John*, AB 30 (Garden City, N.Y.: Doubleday, 1982); F. **Büchsel**, *Die Johannesbriefe*, THNT (Leipzig: Deichert, 1933); Rudolf **Bultmann**, *The Johannine Epistles*, ET Hermeneia (Philadelphia: Fortress, 1973); G. M. **Burge**, *The Anointed Community: The Holy Spirit in the Johannine Community* (Grand Rapids: Eerdmans, 1987); C. H. **Dodd**, *The Johannine Epistles*, MNTC (London: Hodder & Stoughton, 1946); Kenneth **Grayston**, *The Johannine Epistles*, NCB (Grand Rapids: Eerdmans, 1984); J. L. **Houlden**, *The Johannine Epistles*, HNTC (San Francisco: Harper, 1973); E. **Käsemann**, "Ketzer und Zeuge," *ZTK* 48 (1951): 292–311; Robert **Law**, *The Tests of Life* (1914; reprint, Grand Rapids: Baker, 1979); Judith M. **Lieu**, "Authority to Become Children of God': A Study of 1 John," *NovT* 23 (1981): 210–28; idem, *The Second and Third Epistles of John* (Edinburgh: T. & T. Clark, 1986); Edward **Malatesta**, *Interiority and Covenant: A Study of εἶναι ἐν and μένειν ἐν in the First Letter of Saint John*, AnBib 69 (Rome: BIP, 1978); I. Howard **Marshall**, *The Epistles of John*, NICNT (Grand Rapids: Eerdmans, 1978); W. **Nauck**, *Die Tradition und der Charakter des ersten Johannesbriefes*, WUNT 3 (Tübingen: Mohr, 1957); J. C. **O'Neill**, *The Puzzle of 1 John* (London: SPCK, 1966); Vern **Poythress**, "Testing for Johannine Authorship by Examining the Use of Conjunctions," *WTJ* 46 (1984): 350–69; idem, "The Use of the Intersentence Conjunctions *De, Oun, Kai*, and Asyndeton in the Gospel of John," *NovT* 26 (1984): 312–34; W. L. **Richards**, *The Classification of the Greek Manuscripts of the Johannine Epistles*, SBLDS 35 (Missoula, Mont.: SP, 1977); Rudolf **Schnackenburg**, *Die Johannesbriefe*, HTKNT (Freiburg: Herder, 1975); Stephen S. **Smalley**, *1, 2, 3 John*, WBC (Waco, Tex.: Word, 1984); John R. W. **Stott**, *The Letters of John*, TNTC (Grand Rapids: Eerdmans, 1988); Georg **Strecker**, *Die Johannesbriefe*, KEK (Göttingen: Vandenhoeck & Ruprecht, 1989); B. F. **Westcott**, *The Epistles of St John* (1892; reprint, Appleford: Marcham Manor, 1966); Rodney A. **Whitacre**, *Johannine Polemic: The Role of Tradition and Theology*, SBLDS 67 (Chico, Calif.: SP, 1982); D. Bruce **Woll**, *Johannine Christianity in Conflict*, SBLDS 60 (Chicoc Calif.: SP, 1981).

22

JUÐE

CONTENTS

The letter follows the address (1–2) with a reference to godless and immoral men who have appeared among the readers (3–4). In the past, God has punished a variety of sinners, unbelieving Israelites, angels, and Sodom and Gomorrah (5–7), but these men are worse; they do not respect their own limitations as did the archangel Michael, so they do things that destroy themselves (8–10; their pride comes out again in v. 16). They lead fruitless lives, being interested only in their own profit (13), and they engage in flattery to gain their ends (16). Jude cites a prophecy of their destruction (14–15) and calls his readers to persevere, reminding them that Christ's apostles had foretold all this (17–19). He exhorts them to build themselves up in the faith and concludes with a magnificent benediction (20–25).

AUTHOR

The writer was probably a Jewish Christian, for he shows that he knows such Jewish writings as the *Assumption of Moses* (9) and the *Apocalypse of Enoch* (14). He calls himself "Jude, a servant of Jesus Christ and a brother of James" (1) and, though he does not say which James he has in mind, it is generally held that this must be James the brother of Jesus, on the grounds that no other James in the early church was eminent enough to be referred to in this way without qualification. If so, Jude is himself a brother of Jesus (Mark 6:3). We may wonder why he does not say this, but James does not say it either (James 1:1); it seems that the brothers preferred to see themselves as servants of Christ rather than to claim kinship. In a spirit of true Christian humility, they preferred to class themselves with other believers rather than to take up a position that might be thought to assume a specially close connection with Jesus.

Many recent scholars hold that the writing is pseudonymous,[1] but it is difficult to produce an argument for this. Why should anyone want to claim that a writing he had produced was written by Jude? As far as we know, Jude the brother of Jesus had no great reputation in the early church; certainly we cannot say that he

---

[1]"Obviously, the Epistle of Jude pretends to be written by this brother of Jesus" (Kümmel, p. 301).

was such a great man that people would naturally father their writings onto him. It is better to go along with the claim of the letter itself, that its author really was called Jude. There was a Jude among the apostles (Mark 6:3) and another Jude to whose name "Barsabbas" was added (Acts 15:22), but there is no reason for seeing the author as either of these. The probability is that the writer was Jude the brother of Jesus; if not, we have no way of knowing which Jude he was.

DATE

Practically nothing in this writing enables us to date it with any precision; most attempts at dating it are largely guesswork. One estimate is that it was written about the turn of the century (Kümmel), which is about as late as is consistent with authorship by the Lord's brother and is accepted by many who deny such authorship. But the brother of Jesus would have been very old by the end of the century, so if we hold that he wrote it, we should probably put the date somewhat earlier than this (Guthrie thinks between 65 and 80).[2] It is not among the earliest Christian writings, for we must allow time for the false teaching to develop.[3] Those who deny that the author was the Lord's brother sometimes hold to a second-century date. But there is no evidence to support a late date, and a date like Guthrie's is more probable. Sometimes it is urged that the words of verse 17 show that the writer is looking back on a past apostolic age and that therefore the letter must be late. But we should not overlook the words "they said to you" (18), which surely means that the readers had themselves heard the preaching of the apostles. The words argue for a comparatively early date.

DESTINATION

The address is "to those who have been called, who are loved by God the Father and kept by Jesus Christ" (1). This is very general and might apply to any Christians. But the writing gives evidence that the author had a specific audience in mind. He calls his readers "dear friends" and addresses them as "you" (3). To speak of false teachers as those who "secretly slipped in among you" looks like a reference to a specific situation rather than a description of the church as a whole. But neither what the writer says about the recipients nor what he says about the false teachers enables us to pin him down with any precision. We may guess, but in the end we are forced to say that we do not know who the original recipients were.

TEXT

There are some difficult problems with the text. Thus in verse 5 the strongest attestation is for the reading "Jesus,"[4] but it is so difficult to think that the writer

---

[2]Guthrie, p. 908. J. A. T. Robinson argues for a date before 62 (*Redating the New Testament* [Philadelphia: Westminster, 1976], pp. 197–98).

[3]Richard J. Bauckham, however, says of this letter, "Its character is such that it might very plausibly be dated in the 50s, and nothing requires a later date" (*Jude, 2 Peter*, WBC [Waco, Tex.: Word, 1983], p. 13). He is impressed by the absence of features of "early catholicism" and the lack of dependence on Paulinism.

[4]Metzger says, "Critical principles seem to require" its acceptance, but the majority of his committee rejected it on the grounds that "the reading was difficult to the point of impossibility" (p. 726).

holds that Jesus delivered Israel from Egypt that most reject the
there are difficulties with verses 22–23, where some MSS give u:
people (as NIV) and some two (as NEB) ; most scholars accept th
other variants in the letter are of relatively minor importance.

ADOPTION INTO THE CANON

There are apparently traces of this letter in Clement of Rome, Hermas,
Polycarp, Barnabas and perhaps the *Didache*, although none is so definite that we
can say with certainty that the writer was citing Jude as sacred Scripture. Jude is
mentioned in the Muratorian Canon along with two epistles of John, and some
critics think that the way the sentence is worded implies doubts about whether
these books should be included. But the canon cites them after some books that
are excluded and speaks of them in such a way as to indicate a contrast; on a
straightforward reading of the canon, they are included.[5] The letter is cited by
writers such as Tertullian and Clement of Alexandria, so that with Rome, Africa,
and Egypt using the book, it apparently had wide acceptance around A.D. 200.
After that it seems to have waned in popularity, but Origen uses it (though he
implies that some people did not), and Eusebius classes it among the disputed
books. But it won its way and was accepted except by the Syriac Canon (which
also excluded the other Catholic Epistles and Revelation). Those who had doubts
apparently were influenced by the fact that the author made use of Apocryphal
books: some in the early church were sure that no canonical writer would do this.
But in time it was seen that this is no sufficient reason for doubts, and acceptance
became universal.

JUDE IN RECENT STUDY

Jude is not the kind of book to be at the center of major theological discussions.
It is very short, and its subject matter is not such as to grip the attention of those
who lead the way in such discussions. Indeed, so little has it featured in modern
debate that Rowston calls it the most neglected book in the New Testament,[6] and
Bauckham can say, "No NT books have been more neglected by scholars than
Jude and 2 Peter. Most of the conventional scholarly opinions about them derive
from a past era of NT scholarship. This commentary is therefore an attempt to
drag the study of these two books into the 1980s."[7] We are not confronted with a
plethora of profound writings when we look for the modern treatment of these
two books. Occasionally scholars treat the obvious relationship between Jude and
2 Peter (see the discussion in chap. 20).

Those who discuss Jude are not usually impressed. They tend to see him as
unduly concerned to maintain a conservative attitude to the deposit of Christian
truth, as one who vigorously opposes those he sees as heretics. The writer emerges
as a dogmatic supporter of the old way and a bigoted opponent of those who
differ from him. But this is scarcely fair. There is more than dogmatism to Jude.

[5]See the discussion in C. Bigg, *A Critical and Exegetical Commentary on the Epistles of St. Peter and St.
Jude*, ICC (Edinburgh: T. & T. Clark, 1901), p. 14; Guthrie, p. 901.
[6]Douglas J. Rowston, "The Most Neglected Book in the New Testament," *NTS* 21 (1975): 554.
[7]Bauckham, *Jude, 2 Peter*, Preface (no page number).

In modern discussions of New Testament topics, there is a widespread interest in what is called "early catholicism," and Jude is often taken as an example of this. There are often derogatory associations with the term, for what is "early catholic" is not seen as authentic, primitive Christianity. But "early catholicism" is an expression of uncertain meaning (each interpreter seems to have his or her own understanding of what it signifies). We may, however, not be too far wide of the general consensus if we speak of it as including at least these three features: the fading of the hope of the parousia, an interest in the church as an institution, and the use of credal forms to summarize the faith. But none of these is to be found in Jude. Indeed, the hope of the parousia burns brightly, as we see from verses 6, 14, 21, 24; it cannot be said that there is any diminution of the lively expectation of the first Christians. As for the institution of the church, neither the church nor its officials rate a mention in Jude. When dealing with the false teachers, Jude might well have drawn attention to the sound doctrine of the official teachers who carried on the apostolic teaching and were accredited among believers. He is of course concerned for "the faith that was once for all entrusted to the saints" (3), but this is surely not so much a reference to an official body of teaching such that those who differed from it were to be rejected, as a way of drawing attention to the "given" that is bound up with the gospel. The writer is referring to the importance of being faithful to the earliest Christian teaching, not to a body of doctrine under the control of ecclesiastical officials. Moreover, as Childs reminds us, "One cannot even talk of a common salvation without setting it in the context of a fundamental repudiation of this hope."[8] Jude does not write as though the church were the custodian of lawful teaching in distinction from the heretics with their invalid forms. Rather, he insists on the truth of the gospel that leads people into godly lives, so different from the evil he discerns in his opponents.

Scholars who hold that Jude is later than apostolic times usually hold also that the writer is opposing some form of Gnosticism. Thus Rowston cites R. M. Grant's view that "prophecy led to apocalyptic after the Maccabean war and apocalyptic led to gnosticism after the Jewish war" and sees in Jude "a revival of apocalyptic" that "could well be an attempt to reinstate a genuine Paulinism in place of a post-apocalyptic antinomian gnosticism."[9] We must always be suspicious of an assertion that Gnosticism lies behind any New Testament writing, for full-blown Gnosticism as we know from its own sources is a series of systems that appeared well on into the second century. Gnosticism encompassed teachings from many sources, and some of those individual teachings existed in the New Testament period. But it is too much to call any of these pre-Gnostic teachings simply "Gnosticism."[10] There is nothing about Jude that proves it was written at a time when Gnosticism flourished. That there is apocalyptic in Jude does not justify us in calling it "a revival of apocalyptic"; there is apocalyptic in Paul and in Revelation, and Jude's apocalyptic may well be simply the normal early Christian apocalyptic.

---

[8]Childs, p. 492.
[9]Rowston, "Most Neglected Book," p. 561.
[10]For more discussion, see the section "Purpose" in chap. 21 above.

THE CONTRIBUTION OF JUDE

Jude is concerned both for the salvation Christians share and for the faith that was given once for all and entrusted to the saints (3). But his letter is not a systematic setting forth of the faith or of some aspect of the faith. Rather, he is calling his readers to consider what follows when people who profess to be followers of Christ deny the faith in teaching and in life. He is taking action in a situation where people with membership in the Christian church live such evil lives that they could be called godless and it could be said of them that they "deny Jesus Christ" (4). He does not proceed by the method of systematic discussion of the heretical teaching with a steady refutation of it point by point. His concern is not to show where it is wrong; he takes it for granted that his readers will not need such argumentation once they consider the kind of lives the heretics lived. People do not live licentiously and deny Christ as a result of the proclamation of the truth. Jude simply emphasizes that the judgment of God is certain. Those who live like the heretics of whom he is writing inevitably face eternal punishment.

Jude makes it clear that there is nothing new about wrong attitudes to God and wrong ways of living. He points out that back in the days when the Lord delivered the people from Egypt, there were some among them who did not believe, and in the same strain he draws attention to sinning angels and to the sinners of Sodom and Gomorrah (5–7). He later speaks of Cain, of Balaam, and of Korah and his associates (11). Jude's readers know of people who should be loyal servants of God, people who are aware of the great things God has done but who pursue their own selfish and sinful way. The apostles had specifically warned the infant church that heretics would arise (17–19). There was then nothing surprising in the situation in which Jude and his readers found themselves. But if they should not be surprised, they should not be complacent either. This little letter is a strong challenge to its readers to oppose resolutely all teachings and habits of life that profess to be Christian but deny the essence of the faith.[11]

This letter speaks to the modern world as to every previous age. In our century it is the fashion to be tolerant of anything that calls itself Christian, no matter how wide of the gospel it may be. Clearly tolerance is important, and there is danger whenever Christians are so sure of their own rectitude and sound faith that they proceed to sit in judgment on all who differ with them, even in comparatively minor matters. There are many ways of looking at the Christian life, and genuine Christianity finds a variety of forms of expression in the modern church. It is important not to be judgmental; it is important that we treat as brothers and sisters people whose thinking and practice form somewhat different manifestations of the authentic gospel. But Jude reminds us that there are limits. The modern church must realize that it is possible to refashion the gospel so radically that the heart is taken out of it. It is possible to reinterpret the Christian life so that it ceases to be too demanding and degenerates into a way of living indistinguishable from that of the world. In the face of such attitudes Jude's warnings are of continuing significance.

---

[11]Cf. Childs's summary: "The letter offers a theological description of the phenomenon of heresy rather than attacking a specific historical form of error" (p. 493).

BIBLIOGRAPHY

Richard J. **Bauckham**, *Jude, 2 Peter*, WBC (Waco, Tex.: Word, 1983); idem, "The Letter of Jude: An Account of Research," *ANRW* II 25.5 (1988): 3791–3826; C. **Bigg**, *A Critical and Exegetical Commentary on the Epistles of St. Peter and St. Jude*, ICC (Edinburgh: T. & T. Clark, 1901); M. **Desjardins**, "Portrayal of the Dissidents in 2 Peter and Jude: Does It Tell Us More About the 'Godly' Than the 'Ungodly'?" *JSNT* 30 (1987): 89–102; E. Earle **Ellis**, "Prophecy and Hermeneutic in Jude," in *Prophecy and Hermeneutic in Early Christianity: New Testament Essays*, WUNT 18 (Tübingen: Mohr, 1978), pp. 221–36; I. H. **Eybers**, "Aspects of the Background of the Letter of Jude," *Neot* 9 (1975): 113–23; J. **Fossum**, "Kyrios Jesus as the Angel of the Lord in Jude 5–7," *NTS* 33 (1987): 226–43; M. **Green**, *The Second Epistle General of Peter and the General Epistle of Jude*, TNTC, 2d ed. (Grand Rapids: Eerdmans, 1987); J. J. **Gunther**, "The Alexandrian Epistle of Jude," *NTS* 30 (1984): 549–62; R. **Heiligenthal**, "Der Judasbrief: Aspekte der Forschung in den letzten Jahrzehnten," *ThR* 51 (1986): 117–29; J. N. D. **Kelly**, *A Commentary on the Epistles of Peter and Jude*, HNTC (New York: Harper & Row, 1969); R. **Knopf**, *Die Briefe Petri und Judä*, KEK, 7th ed. (Göttingen: Vandenhoeck & Ruprecht, 1912); J. B. **Mayor**, *The Epistle of St. Jude and the Second Epistle of Peter* (London: Macmillan, 1907); Bo **Reicke**, *The Epistles of James, Peter, and Jude*, AB (New York: Doubleday, 1964); J. A. T. **Robinson**, *Redating the New Testament* (Philadelphia: Westminster, 1976); Douglas J. **Rowston**, "The Most Neglected Book in the New Testament," *NTS* 21 (1974–75): 554–63; K. H. **Schelkle**, *Die Petrusbriefe, der Judasbrief*, HTKNT (Freiburg: Herder, 1961); E. M. **Sidebottom**, *James, Jude, and 2 Peter*, NCB (London: Thomas Nelson, 1967); F. **Wisse**, "The Epistle of Jude in the History of Heresiology," in *Essays on the Nag Hammadi Texts*, Fs. Alexander Böhlig, ed. M. Krause (Leiden: Brill, 1972), pp. 133–43. Thomas **Wolthuis**, "Jude and Jewish Traditions," *CTJ* 22 (1987): 21–41;

23

Revelation

CONTENTS

The structure of Revelation is hotly debated, mainly because conclusions on this matter radically affect one's understanding of the historical referents and eschatology of the book. There is general agreement that 1:1–20 (or 1:1–8) and 22:6–21 are, respectively, the prologue and epilogue, and that the letters to the seven churches in chapters 2–3 form a separate unit. There seems to be some basis for this division in 1:19, where it is plausible to think that "what you have seen" refers to the vision in chapter 1, "what is now" to the letters in chapters 2–3, and "what will take place later" to chapters 4 and following.[1]

The material from 4:1 to 22:5 has been structured in many different ways. The simplest is to note the places where an interruption in the visionary mode occurs and where the seer is invited to "come and see." This would result in a threefold division, 4:1–16:21; 17:1–21:8; 21:9–22:5. Others think that the section divides in half, chapters 12–22 repeating the material of chapters 1–11.[2] The book of Revelation has been likened to a seven-act play, with seven scenes in each act.[3] Others find a chiastic structure.[4] More often, the three series of sevens—seals (6:1–17; 8:1), trumpets (8:2–9:21; 11:15–19), and bowls (15:1–16:21)—are used as the basis of the structure. Chapters 4–5 (or chap. 4 alone) are then viewed as an inaugural vision that sets the tone for what follows, with 17:1–22:5 giving the details of the eschatological denouement. Interrupting the sequence of events—that is, between the sixth and seventh seals (chap. 7), the sixth and seventh trumpet (10:1–11:14), and the seventh trumpet and the bowls (12:1–14:20)—are further visions that give the reader perspective on the unfolding of

---

[1]It is possible, however, that "what you saw" refers to all the visions of Revelation, which contain both "what is" and "what will follow" (see Robert H. Mounce, *The Book of Revelation*, NICNT [Grand Rapids: Eerdmans, 1977], pp. 81–82), or that there is no relationship between the phrases and the parts of the book (Jan Lambrecht, "A Structuration of Revelation 4,1–22,5," in *L'Apocalypse johannique et l'apocalyptique dans le Nouveau Testament*, ed. J. Lambrecht, BETL 53 [Louvain: Louvain University Press, 1980], pp. 79–80).

[2]Henry Barclay Swete, *The Apocalypse of St. John*, 3d ed. (London: Macmillan, 1911), pp. xxxvii–xliv.

[3]John Wick Bowman, "Book of Revelation," in *IDB* 4:64–65.

[4]Elisabeth Schüssler Fiorenza, *The Book of Revelation: Justice and Judgment* (Philadelphia: Fortress, 1985), pp. 174–77.

the septets of judgment. This last seems to provide the best approach to the structure, and we follow it in the outline of contents below.[5]

Prologue (1:1–20). The book opens with a brief introduction (1:1–3), address and salutation (1:4–8), and vision of the glorified Christ (1:9–20). (Some take this vision, with chaps. 2–3, as an introduction to the letters to the seven churches.)

Messages to seven churches (2:1–3:22). John is commanded by the risen Christ to address messages to seven churches in seven cities within the Roman province of Asia: Ephesus (2:1–7), Smyrna (2:8–11), Pergamum (2:12–17), Thyatira (2:18–29), Sardis (3:1–6), Philadelphia (3:7–13), and Laodicea (3:14–22). Each letter contains (1) a greeting to the ἄγγελος, (*angelos*, "angel" or "messenger") of the church; (2) a description of the risen Christ, drawn from the vision in 1:9–20; (3) praise for the church (except in the letter to Laodicea); (4) criticism of the church (except in the letters to Smyrna and Philadelphia); (5) a warning; (6) an exhortation, beginning, "He who has an ear . . . "; and (7) a promise.

A vision of heaven (4:1–5:14). John is taken up to heaven "in the Spirit," where he sees the sovereign God seated on the throne and receiving worship. The transcendence of God depicted in this vision sets the stage for the drama that unfolds: John sees a sealed scroll in God's hand, and only a "Lamb, looking as if it had been slain," is accounted worthy to break the seven seals and open the scroll (5:1–14).

The seven seals (6:1–8:5). John describes what he sees as each seal is opened by the Lamb: conquest (6:1–2), slaughter (6:3–4), famine (6:5–6), death (6:7–8), martyrs crying out for justice (6:9–11), and natural disasters, signifying the "wrath of the Lamb" (6:12–17). Then, before the seventh seal is described, John sees two visions, each of them depicting a great mass of people: 144,000 from the tribes of Israel who had been sealed by God (7:1–8), and an innumerable multitude who had "come out of the great tribulation" (7:9–17). The opening of the seventh seal brings silence in heaven and the introduction of the seven trumpets (8:1–5).

The seven trumpets (8:6–11:19). In his vision, John now observes the disasters that come upon the earth as angels blow each of the trumpets: hail and fire from heaven (8:7), a mountain thrown into the sea (8:8–9), a great star falling from the sky (8:10–11), astronomical changes (8:12–13), destructive locusts (9:1–12), and a huge conquering army (9:13–21). As was the case with the seals, John interjects two visions before he narrates the events connected with the seventh trumpet. John sees an angel with a little scroll that he is instructed to eat (10:1–11) and two witnesses, who prophesy, are killed, and are raised again (11:1–14). The seventh trumpet contains no specific event but inaugurates hymns that praise God for his triumph and judgments (11:15–19).

Seven significant signs (12:1–14:20). John interrupts his numbered septets to give a series of visions. But the number seven, so obviously basic to Revelation, is not abandoned, since the events narrated in these visions are seven in number: a woman who gives birth to a son (12:1–6); a war in heaven between Michael and

---

[5]For this outline, with minor modifications, see Leon Morris, *The Revelation of St. John,* TNTC, rev. ed. (Grand Rapids: Eerdmans, 1987), pp. 43–44.

his angels and a dragon, identified with Satan, who is cast out of heaven (12:7–12); a war on earth between Satan and the woman and her child (12:13–13:1a); the worldwide worship of a beast who comes out of the sea (13:1b–10); the worldwide domination of a beast who comes out of the earth (13:11–18); the praise of the Lamb from the 144,000 (14:1–5); and the harvesting of the earth, done by "one 'like a son of man'" and angels (14:14–20). As with the first two septets (seals and trumpets), there is a vision inserted between the sixth and the seventh in this series (see 14:6–13).

The seven bowls (15:1–16:21). John now sees "in heaven another great and marvelous sign: seven angels with the seven last plagues" (15:1). Those who had triumphed over the beast sing praises to God (15:2–4) as the angels come out of the temple with the plagues (15:5–8). These plagues are then described with the imagery of bowls that the angels pour out on the earth (16:1). The pouring out of the bowls brings, successively, painful sores "on the people who had the mark of the beast and worshiped his image" (16:2), a turning of the sea into blood (16:3), a turning of the rivers and springs of water into blood (16:3–7), scorching heat from the sun (16:8–9), destruction of the beast's dominion (16:10–11), the drying up of the Euphrates River and the coming of evil spirits in preparation for "the battle on the great day of God Almighty" at "Armageddon" (16:12–16), and, climactically, the "it is done" of utter earthly destruction (16:17–21).

The triumph of Almighty God (17:1–20:15). These visions describe and celebrate the triumph of God in the world, as his sovereignty, seen by John in heaven in chapter 4, is now manifested in the world. John depicts both the judgment of the wicked and the reward of the righteous. His first vision reveals the evil and destiny of "the great prostitute," "the great city that rules over the kings of the earth" (17:1–18). This great city, named Babylon to suggest an ungodly suppressor of God's people, is now condemned and destroyed, as those who profited from her mourn her (18:1–19:5). In the midst of judgment, however, is salvation, as John hears the praise of a great multitude who had been invited to share in the wedding supper of the Lamb (19:6–10). John next portrays the victory over the beasts and the assembled nations won by the rider on a white horse (19:11–21). There follows John's famous description of the "thousand years" (hence the "millennium"), during which Satan is bound, and which separates the "first" resurrection from the second (20:1–6). John then depicts the final rebellion and destruction of Satan (20:7–10) and God's judgment of all the dead before the great white throne (20:11–15).

A new heaven and a new earth (21:1–22:5). The passing of the first earth leads to John's vision of "a new heaven and a new earth." Here God resides with his people (21:2–5), and the righteous are separated from the wicked (21:6–8). In his vision, John sees the "bride, the wife of the Lamb," in the image of a new Jerusalem, whose features and dimensions are described in considerable detail (21:9–21). There will be no need for temple or sun or moon in this city, for God and the Lamb are there, and there will be no wickedness (21:22–22:5).

Epilogue (22:6–21). John is promised that the message contained in the visions he has seen is "trustworthy and reliable" and that there will be reward for those who are faithful and true. This reward is brought by Jesus himself, who is "coming quickly."

AUTHOR

Early Christian Testimony

As early as the middle of the second century, Revelation was ascribed to John, "one of the apostles of Christ" (Justin, *Dial.* 81). Other second-century works and writers make the same claim: a lost commentary on Revelation by Melito, bishop of Sardis (c. A.D. 165; see Eusebius, *H.E.* 4.26.2); Ireneus (c. 180; *Adv. Haer.* 3.11.1, 4.20.11, 4.35.2); and the Muratorian Canon (late second century). Whether Papias, an even earlier witness than these (d. c. 130), can be added to this list is disputed, but a good case can be made out that he both knew Revelation and attributed it to John.[6] The evidence of these writers is particularly strong in that two of them (three, if Papias is included) could well be reporting firsthand evidence. Sardis, where Melito was bishop, was one of the churches addressed in Revelation (1:11; 3:1–6). Ireneus was from Smyrna, also a church addressed in Revelation (1:11; 2:8–11), and claims to have heard Polycarp, who had talked with John the apostle himself. Papias knew John the apostle personally. The early tradition is confirmed by the third-century fathers Tertullian, Hippolytus, and Origen. Not only do these authors ascribe Revelation to John the apostle, they do so without any hint of there being a contrary claim. No New Testament book, concludes Gerhard Maier, has a stronger or earlier tradition about its authorship than does Revelation.[7]

Nevertheless, the association of John the apostle with Revelation, while early and widespread, is not unanimous. Marcion rejected the book (but then he rejected most of the New Testament, including the gospel of John). The second-century group called the Alogoi also rejected the apostolic origin of Revelation, suggesting that it was written by Cerinthus. But particularly clear and strong in his dissent from the tradition of apostolic authorship was Dionysius, a third-century bishop of Alexandria. As recorded by Eusebius (*H.E.* 7.25.7–27), Dionysius claimed on three grounds that John the apostle could not have written Revelation: (1) the author of Revelation makes no claim to be an apostle or eyewitness and does not describe himself, as does the author of the gospel of John, as "the beloved disciple"; (2) the conceptions and arrangement of Revelation are completely different from those of the fourth gospel and 1 John; and (3) the Greek of Revelation differs drastically from the Greek of the fourth gospel and 1 John. If, then (as Dionysius thought), John the apostle wrote the gospel and 1 John, he could not have written Revelation. Revelation must have been written by some other person named John; in fact, Dionysius had heard it said that there were two tombs of significant Christians named John in Ephesus.

Dionysius's views are shared by most contemporary scholars, and we will examine his arguments below. For the moment, we want to estimate the value of his witness as an ancient authority. This value is not great. Dionysius makes no claim to be passing on tradition; his rejection of apostolic authorship is based entirely on arguments from the content of Revelation. Moreover, his arguments themselves are motivated by theological bias. Several early Fathers (e.g., Justin,

---

[6]See esp. Gerhard Maier, *Die Johannesoffenbarung und die Kirche*, WUNT 25 (Tübingen: Mohr, 1981), pp. 1–69.
[7]Ibid., p. 107.

Ireneus, Tertullian) interpreted Revelation 20:1–6 as teaching what was called chiliasm: the doctrine that Christ would establish a thousand-year reign on earth (the doctrine is today usually called premillennialism). Other Fathers, however, found this doctrine abhorrent because of its alleged Jewish roots and materialism. Dionysius was one of these, and his rejection of apostolic authorship of Revelation has as its purpose the discrediting of its alleged chiliastic teaching.[8] This does not mean that Dionysius was wrong or that his arguments are therefore without force. But it does mean that his opinion, being independent of any tradition and motivated by polemical concerns, will be only as valuable as the arguments he uses to support it.

Contemporary Discussion

Internal Evidence Revelation claims to be written by "John" (1:1, 4, 9; 22:8). Addressing himself to his readers, he calls himself "your brother and companion in the suffering and kingdom and patient endurance that are ours in Jesus" (1:9). The author, however, never makes any other claims about himself, and this suggests that he was someone well known to his readers. What John would have been better known to the churches of Asia Minor in the late first century than John the apostle, whom reliable early church tradition places in Ephesus at the end of his life (see below)? The author's claim to be mediating prophetic words that are authoritative for the readers (e.g., 22:9, 18–19) has also been seen to be indicative of apostolic authorship.[9] While there is something to this argument, it must be admitted that people other than apostles were gifted with prophecy in the early church, that authority, even scriptural authority, does not depend on apostolic status (e.g., Mark, Luke, the author to the Hebrews), and that the authority of Revelation comes more from the One who revealed the visions to the author than from the author himself. Nevertheless, the author's assumption that what he relates will be accepted by the readers simply on the basis of his name alone points more naturally to an apostle than to someone else.

Arguments Against Apostolic Authorship Despite this internal evidence, the majority of contemporary scholars deny that John the apostle wrote Revelation. Their reasons for doing so are essentially the same as those of Dionysius.

Lack of apostolic claims. First, it is claimed that the author cannot be an apostle. The author never claims to be such, never alludes to gospel events, and never claims a special relationship with Christ. Furthermore, passages such as 18:20 and 21:14, with their allusions to the significant role of the apostles, show that the author was not numbered among the Twelve.[10]

This argument carries little weight. The author's failure to mention his apostolic status may well be because he knows so well those to whom he writes that such an identification is not needed. Reference to the events of Jesus' life or to any

[8]See ibid., pp. 96–107, and esp. p. 107, where Maier notes that Dionysius's judgment was motivated by church politics and dogmatics. See also Ned B. Stonehouse, *The Apocalypse in the Ancient Church* (Goes: Oosterbaan & Le Cointre, 1929).

[9]Guthrie, p. 936.

[10]So, inter alios, R. H. Charles, *A Critical and Exegetical Commentary on the Revelation of St. John*, 2 vols., ICC (Edinburgh: T. & T. Clark, 1920), 1:xliii–xliv.

personal relationship between the author and Jesus would be out of place in a book like Revelation. And the significance accorded to the apostles is no greater than that found in passages such as Ephesians 2:20 (and see Matt. 16:17–19).

Theological differences. Both other key arguments against John the apostle being the author of Revelation depend for their validity on the assumption that the apostle wrote the fourth gospel and the epistles of John. These arguments will, therefore, not be convincing to the many contemporary critics who deny that John the apostle wrote the fourth gospel or the epistles. But we have argued in this book that John the apostle did write these books, and we must, then, reckon with the problems that confront any attempt to establish unity of authorship for all the Johannine books.

The first of the problems is that the theology of Revelation appears to be quite distinct from the theology of the fourth gospel and of 1 John. This emerges particularly in three doctrines: theology proper, Christology, and eschatology. The God of Revelation, it is argued, is a God of majesty and judgment, while the God of the gospel and epistles is a God of love. A similar contrast is found in Christology: while the gospel focuses on Christ as revealer and redeemer, Revelation pictures Christ as conquering warrior and ruler. The fourth gospel is frequently said to exhibit what is called a "realized eschatology," a view of history and eternity in which "the last things" are viewed as completely realized in the incarnation, death, and resurrection of Christ. Revelation, on the other hand, focuses almost exclusively on a coming of Christ at the end of history. The same author, it is then concluded, cannot be responsible for both books; the theological perspective is too different.[11]

But the contrasts are both overdrawn and incapable of proving much. Both the gospel and Revelation teach that God is *both* loving and judging, that Christ is *both* redeemer and sovereign Lord, and that "the last things" have *both* been realized in Jesus' death and resurrection (at least in principle) and await the end of history for their consummation. Differences between the gospel and Revelation on these points have been magnified by a narrow and one-sided interpretation of the fourth gospel. That the theological emphases of the fourth gospel and of Revelation are different, no one can deny. But the different settings and purposes for the two books adequately explain these differences in emphasis. There is no reason on such grounds to think the same person could not have written both. Indeed, there is much evidence suggesting commonality of authorship: the description in both books of Jesus as "Word" (John 1:1; Rev. 19:13), "lamb" (John 1:29; Rev. 5:6 and elsewhere—although different Greek words are used) and shepherd; a "replacement of the temple" theme (John 4:21; Rev. 21:22); and a love of antithesis (darkness-light, truth-falsehood); and many others.[12]

Stylistic differences. Dionysius's third argument against unity of authorship between the gospel and Revelation is the most telling: the differences in the Greek. The Greek of Revelation, as R. H. Charles has commented, is "unlike any Greek that was ever penned by mortal man."[13] Particularly striking are the many grammatical solecisms, or irregularities. One example is the neglect of the proper

---

[11]E.g., Kümmel, p. 472.

[12]See esp. F. Godet, *Commentary on the Gospel of St. John*, 3 vols. (Edinburgh: T. & T. Clark, 1899–1900), 1:182–90.

[13]Charles, *Revelation* 1:xliv.

case after a preposition, as in 1:4: ἀπὸ ὁ ὤν καὶ ὁ ἦν καὶ ὁ ἐρχόμενος (*apo ho ōn kai ho ēn kai ho erchomenos*, NIV "from him who is, and who was, and who is to come"). Charles concluded that it was the Greek of one who was thinking in Hebrew while writing in Greek.[14] Stephen Thompson has shown further that it was biblical Hebrew or Aramaic, rather than postbiblical Hebrew or Aramaic, that has influenced the author, and that Revelation is almost certainly not a translation of an original Hebrew or Aramaic work.[15] In contrast, the Greek of the fourth gospel, while simple and having its share of Semitisms,[16] is accurate and clear.[17] Most contemporary scholars agree with Dionysius: the same person could not have written both books.[18]

Nevertheless, many scholars have attempted to explain the difference in a way that would be compatible with common authorship. Hort and Westcott suggested that a great amount of time intervened between the two books, John having written Revelation in the late sixties and the gospel in the nineties.[19] But it is doubtful that the books can be dated so far apart; nor does the passage of time in itself explain the difference. Others argue that the difference is due to the fact that John, exiled in Patmos, is writing without the aid of an amanuensis that he was able to use for the gospel and the epistles.[20] There may be some truth to this, but it is doubtful that the Greek of Revelation can be set down to inadequate knowledge of the language, for the author is not at all consistent in his breaking of grammatical rules. In the example cited above, for instance, the author goes on in the very same verse to use the correct case after the same preposition (ἀπὸ τῶν ἑπτὰ πνευμάτων [*apo tōn hepta pneumatōn*], NIV "from the seven spirits"). As Charles made clear in his magisterial treatment of the grammar of Revelation, the author follows certain rules of his own, and his solecisms appear to be deliberate. Many scholars therefore think that the author has deliberately chosen to write Greek as he has perhaps because of the immediacy of the visionary experience,[21] or as a protest against the upper classes.[22] Whatever his reason, if the author of Revelation has written as he has deliberately, then it is not clear that the person who wrote the fourth gospel could not also have written Revelation. As G. B. Caird says, "Because a man writes in Hebraic Greek, it does not inevitably follow that this is the only Greek he is capable of writing."[23] And, before leaving this

---

[14]See Charles's extensive discussion in *Revelation* 1:cxvii–clix. Note also Swete, *Apocalypse*, pp. cxx–cxxx.

[15]Stephen Thompson, *The Apocalypse and Semitic Syntax*, SNTSMS 52 (Cambridge: Cambridge University Press, 1985). It must be emphasized, however, that Thompson has greatly overplayed the evidence; see Stanley E. Porter, *Verbal Aspect in the Greek of the New Testament, with Reference to Tense and Mood*, SBG 1 (Berne: Peter Lang, 1989), pp. 111–56 and the literature there cited.

[16]Or, more commonly, Semitic enhancements. See n. 14 in chap. 2 above.

[17]Charles outlines the differences clearly (*Revelation* 1:xxix–xxxii).

[18]E.g., ibid. 1:xxix and G. R. Beasley-Murray, *The Book of Revelation*, NCB (London: Marshall, Morgan & Scott, 1974), pp. 35–36.

[19]F. J. A. Hort, *The Apocalypse of St. John I–III* (London: Macmillan, 1908), p. xii; B. F. Westcott, *The Gospel According to St. John* (reprint, Grand Rapids: Eerdmans, 1971), p. lxxxvi.

[20]George Eldon Ladd, *A Commentary on the Revelation of John* (Grand Rapids: Eerdmans, 1972), pp. 7–8; Morris, *Revelation*, p. 39.

[21]Zahn 3:432–33; Ibson T. Beckwith, *The Apocalypse of John: Studies in Introduction* (New York: Macmillan, 1919), p. 355.

[22]Adela Yarbro Collins, *Crisis and Catharsis: The Power of the Apocalypse* (Philadelphia: Westminster, 1984), p. 47.

[23]G. B. Caird, *A Commentary on the Revelation of St. John the Divine* (New York: Harper & Row, 1966), p. 5.

matter of the language, we must point out that, as in the case of the theology of the two books, the Greek style of the two shows many similarities.[24]

Conclusion

While the difference in Greek style is a problem, we are not convinced that the arguments of Dionysius or his latter-day followers make it impossible for the same person to have written both the fourth gospel and Revelation. We are thus inclined to accept the testimony of those who were in a position to know about these matters, and we attribute both books to John the apostle, "the beloved disciple."[25]

If this identification is rejected, then there are four other possibilities. First, Revelation could have been written by another well-known John in the ancient church. Dionysius, after suggesting (and properly rejecting) John Mark,[26] mentions a second John (in addition to the apostle John) buried in Ephesus. This second John is often identified with an "elder John" whom Papias mentions (see Eusebius, *H.E.* 3.39.4–5), and this "elder John" is thought by some to have written Revelation.[27] But it is doubtful whether Papias refers to two different men named John at all (see the section "Author" in chap. 5); the whole thesis is most improbable. Another well-known John in the early church was John the Baptist, and J. Massyngberde Ford has suggested that he could be responsible for much of Revelation.[28] But her theory is too far-fetched to command assent (see the section "Composition and Genre," below).

A second possibility is that Revelation, like Jewish apocalypses, is pseudonymous—written by an unknown person in John's name. But Charles has shown this hypothesis to be unlikely,[29] and it is rarely argued.

Much more popular of late has been a third option: that Revelation, like the other Johannine books, was written by an anonymous member of a Johannine "school" or "circle." Such a hypothesis seems to offer an attractive solution to the problem of explaining both the similarities and differences among these books.[30] Yet, as A. Y. Collins says, the hypothesis "is clearly not the result of careful historical-critical research, but a prior assumption that shapes the result of the research."[31] We have elsewhere argued that the "school" or "circle" hypothesis is untenable (see esp. chap. 5, the section "Stylistic Unity and the Johannine 'Community'").

We are left, then, as the only real alternative to John the apostle's authorship, authorship by an unknown John, and this is the explanation held by most who

---

[24]See Charles, *Revelation* 1:xxix–xxxvii, for a list.

[25]Apostolic authorship is hesitantly accepted by, among others, Guthrie, pp. 932–48; Mounce, *Revelation*, pp. 25–31; John F. Walvoord, *The Revelation of Jesus Christ* (Chicago: Moody, 1966), pp. 11–14.

[26]J. N. Sanders, however, appears to defend the idea ("St. John on Patmos," *NTS* 9 [1962–63]: 75–85).

[27]The solution was quite popular at the turn of the century but has lately fallen out of favor. See, however, John J. Gunther, "The Elder John, Author of Revelation," *JSNT* 11 (1981): 3–20.

[28]J. Massyngberde Ford, *Revelation*, AB (Garden City, N.Y.: Doubleday, 1975), pp. 3–37.

[29]Charles, *Revelation* 1:xxxviii–xxxix.

[30]An early advocate of the idea was Johannes Weiss, *Offenbarung des Johannes*, FRLANT 3 (Göttingen: Vandenhoeck & Ruprecht, 1904), pp. 146–64.

[31]Collins, *Crisis and Catharsis*. p. 33; see also Fiorenza, *Book of Revelation*, pp. 85–113.

demur from the traditional identification.[32] Yet we might question whether a John who is never mentioned in the abundant sources for first-century Asian church life would have had sufficient stature to write a book of this sort, so different from anything else in the New Testament, simply under his own name. Particularly does this seem unlikely when we recall that there *was* a John who was well known in this area at just this period. Guthrie's question is to the point: "Was the Asiatic church overrun with brilliant Christians by the name of John, who would only need to announce their name for the Christians to know which was meant?"[33]

PROVENANCE

John writes from Patmos, a rocky and rugged island about six miles wide and ten miles long, some forty miles southwest of Ephesus in the Aegean Sea. The island was used by Roman authorities as a place of exile (see Pliny, *Nat. Hist.* 4.23), and John indicates that this was his reason for being there: "because of the word of God and the testimony of Jesus" (1:9). Early tradition (e.g., Origen) says that the emperor himself condemned John to exile in Patmos, but it is more likely, considering John's extensive ministry in Asia Minor, that it was a local Roman official from this region who sent John to Patmos is order to get him out of the way.[34]

DATE

Early Christian Testimony

Early Christian writers date Revelation in the reign of one of four different Roman emperors. (See table 7.)

Contemporary Discussion

As can be seen from table 7, a date for Revelation in the reign of Domitian, and probably toward the end of that reign (say, 95–96), receives the most support from the early Fathers. Ireneus, who is a key source for this tradition, was in the position, as we noted above, to have direct information about the matter. Most scholars have been inclined to follow Ireneus in his dating of Revelation at the close of the reign of Domitian. Dates in the reign of Claudius or Trajan are, respectively, too early and too late, and have attracted virtually no adherents. A date shortly after the reign of Nero (68–69), however, has considerable support and is the main alternative to the Domitianic date.[35]There are six key areas of evidence to consider in coming to a decision.

---

[32]E.g., Kümmel, pp. 469–72; Wikenhauser, pp. 648–53; Collins, *Crisis and Catharsis*, p. 33. Charles called him "John the Prophet" (*Revelation* 1:xxxviii–l).

[33]Guthrie, p. 946.

[34]See Sanders, "St. John on Patmos," p. 76.

[35]The most important advocates of the early date are Hort, *Apocalypse I–III*, pp. xii–xxxiii, and J. A. T. Robinson, *Redating the New Testament* (Philadelphia: Westminster, 1976), pp. 221–53. See also Albert A. Bell, Jr., "The Date of John's Apocalypse: The Evidence of Some Roman Historians Reconsidered," *NTS* 25 (1979): 93–102; Kenneth L. Gentry, Jr., *Before Jerusalem Fell: Dating the Book of Revelation* (Tyler, Tex.: ICE, 1989).

Table 7
Early Christian Writings and the Date of the Revelation

Emperor	Ruled	Sources dating Revelation by emperor
Claudius	41–54	Epiphanius, *Haer*. 51.12
Nero	54–68)	Syriac versions of Revelation
Domitian	81–96	Ireneus (*Adv Haer*. 5.30.3) ("toward the end of the reign of Domitian"); Victorinus, *Apoc*. 10.11; Eusebius, *H.E*. 3.18; Clement of Alexandria (*Quis div*. 42) and Origen (*Matt*. 16.6) both locate Revelation in the reign of "the tyrant," probably referring to Domitian
Trajan	98–117	a synopsis of the life and death of the prophets, attributed to Dorotheus; Theophylact on Matt. 20:22

The persecution of Christians. While there are some dissenting voices,[36]the majority of scholars agree that Revelation was written at a time when Christians were being persecuted in an unusually strong way (see, e.g., 1:9; 2:13; 3:10; 6:9; 17:6; 18:24; 19:2; 20:4). Advocates of the Domitianic date have generally appealed to the early Christian tradition that pictured the years 95–96 as a period of intense persecution. Advocates of the earlier date, for their part, point out that the evidence for this persecution is quite slim. The clearest evidence comes from later writers (Orosius, Eusebius, Sulpicius Severus), while those more contemporary to Domitian's time, both Christian and pagan, say nothing about a systematic persecution of Christians. In contrast, evidence for a persecution of Christians under Nero is clear and irrefutable. We have no evidence that Nero's persecution extended beyond Rome, but if we are looking for a period when Christians in Asia Minor were likely to be persecuted, a time during which Christians were being persecuted elsewhere is more likely than a time when we are not sure that they were being persecuted at all.

Advocates of an early date have a point: many scholars have exaggerated the evidence for a persecution of Christians under Domitian. The evidence suggests rather that Domitian in the last years of his reign instituted a purge of Roman aristocrats who might challenge his power. The wife of one of those purged, Domitilla, whose husband, Flavius Clemens, was executed, was probably a Christian, but it does not seem that either she or her husband were singled out because of her faith.[37] There is little evidence, however, that the Neronian persecution of Christians in Rome had lasting effects or spread to the provinces. Advocates of neither date, then, can appeal to solid evidence for persecution in Asia Minor. We are shut up to assumptions, and the assumption of persecution of Christians in Asia Minor under Nero has no more to be said for it than a similar persecution under Domitian (see the next point).

Worship of the emperor. The conclusion just reached must be modified in light of another consideration: the assumption within Revelation that worship of the emperor had become an issue for Christians (see 13:4, 15–16; 14:9–11; 15:2;

[36]E.g., Collins, *Crisis and Catharsis*, pp. 69–73.
[37]See Dio Cassius, *Hist. Rom*. 68.14. Note the survey of the situation in M. R. Charlesworth, "The Flavian Dynasty," *CAH* 11 (1936): 41–42.

16:2; 19:20; 20:4).[38] We have no solid evidence for the date at which the emperors made worship of their own person a requirement, but there is clear evidence that Domitian stressed his deity, ordering that he be addressed as *dominus et deus* ("lord and god").[39] Domitian apparently made this confession a test of loyalty. It is possible, indeed, that some Christians tried to avoid the predicament this placed them in by taking refuge in the synagogue, where some of the traditional legal exceptions granted Jews in this regard still applied. This may help explain the tensions between Jews and Christians evident in the letters to the seven churches.[40] In response to this reasoning, advocates of the earlier date appeal to the fact that emperors since Augustus (d. A.D. 14) had made claims to deity and that it is quite possible, granted Nero's character, that he could have stressed such claims. But the fact remains that our hard evidence points to the last years of Domitian as being the time when Christians would most likely have collided with the claims of the emperor cult.

The conditions of the churches. Several elements in the letters to the seven churches are said to be much more compatible with a date in the nineties than one in the sixties: the spiritual stagnation in several of the churches; the wealth of the Laodicean church (the city was destroyed by an earthquake in A.D. 60–61); the existence of the church at Smyrna (the church may not have existed until 60–64); the lack of any mention of Paul, who had labored in Ephesus for so long, and perhaps as late at 64. Not all these points are equally persuasive,[41] but Colin Hemer, after an exhaustive study of the local settings of the churches, claims that his findings generally confirm the Domitianic date.[42]

The existence of a Nero myth. Popular hatred and fear of Nero led to stories circulating after his death to the effect that he would return to Rome leading a Parthian army. Passages in Revelation that speak of the beast recovering from a mortal wound (e.g., 13:3–4), it is argued, allude to a Nero-redivivus myth, and it must have taken time for the myth to circulate and become known. However, the Nero myth is not really very close to what is actually said of the beast in the Revelation, so the argument carries little weight. Moreover, many of those who argue that the number 666 in 13:18 is a cryptic reference to Nero hold that this link is entirely independent of such a myth.

The existence of the Jerusalem temple. Revelation 11:1–2, it is argued, presumes that the temple in Jerusalem was still standing at the time Revelation was written.[43] This argument is not without force, but it is mitigated by two considerations: the possibility that John is using a source and, more important, the possibility that John refers to a rebuilt or metaphoric temple rather than to the temple of Jesus' day.

Revelation 17:9–11. This passage enumerates seven kings, who are apparently to

---

[38]We should mention that we are not here presuming a so-called preterist interpretation of Revelation, in which everything in the book applies only to John's day. Some of these texts could be genuinely prophetic, envisaging a situation that did not prevail in the first century. Nevertheless, some of the texts suggest that the problem was real for John's readers (cf. Mounce, *Revelation*, p. 33).

[39]Cf. Suetonius, *Domitian* 13; Charlesworth, "Flavian Dynasty," pp. 41–42.

[40]Colin J. Hemer, *The Letters to the Seven Churches of Asia in Their Local Setting*, JSNTSupp 11 (Sheffield: JSOT, 1986), pp. 7–12.

[41]See Robinson for a rebuttal (*Redating*, pp. 229–31).

[42]Hemer, *Letters to the Seven Churches*, pp. 2–11.

[43]E.g., Robinson, *Redating*, pp. 238–42.

be taken as emperors of Rome (the allusion to the seven hills in v. 9 is unmistakably a reference to Rome). "Five," says John, "have fallen, one is, the other has not yet come; but when he does come, he must remain for a little while. The beast who once was, and now is not, is an eighth king. He belongs to the seven and is going to his destruction." The assumption of the text is that the sixth king in the sequence is now in power. Taking these data, and beginning with the first of the Roman emperors, Augustus, brings us to Galba, who reigned only a short time after the death of Nero. Here, then, is what appears to be a relatively objective indication that Revelation was written in A.D. 68–69.[44]

This argument carries some weight, but it is not decisive, because the text is not entirely clear. Is it referring to emperors in John's day or to future kings? Should we start counting the emperors from Augustus or from Julius Caesar, who first claimed imperial rights, or perhaps from Caligula, the first persecuting emperor?[45] should we include the three minor emperors, who reigned for only very brief periods in 68–69? None of these questions can be answered certainly.[46]

Conclusion

Various other minor points are disputed,[47] but these cover the main arguments. The last two factors appear to favor a date shortly after Nero, but the conditions generally presumed in Revelation are more likely to have existed in the reign of Domitian than earlier (the second and third points). We are inclined, then, to follow the oldest tradition on this point and date Revelation in the last years of Domitian.

DESTINATION

John directs the record of his visions to seven churches in the Roman province of Asia, which incorporated approximately the western third of Asia Minor. These churches were probably personally known to John from years of ministry in the area. His reason for selecting these seven churches, as well as the order in which the churches are listed, probably has to do with geography and communications. As Ramsay pointed out long ago, the cities in which the churches are located are all centers of communication; a messenger bearing Revelation to the cities would arrive from Patmos in Ephesus, travel by secondary road north to Smyrna and Pergamum, and then go east on the Roman road to Thyatira, Sardis, Philadelphia, and Laodicea.[48]

---

[44]E.g., Hort, *Apocalypse I–III*, p. xxvi; Robinson, *Redating*, pp. 242–48.

[45]For the last alternative, see A. Strobel, "Abfassung und Geschichtstheologie des Apokalypse nach Kp. 17, 9–12," *NTS* 10 (1963–64): 433–45.

[46]See the discussion in Collins, *Crisis and Catharsis*, pp. 58–64.

[47]E.g., Charles (*Revelation* 1:xlvi–l) and others have argued that early traditions indicate that John was martyred between A.D. 64 and 70. But this tradition is very much inferior to the one that has John ministering in Ephesus to a ripe old age (Leon Morris, *Studies in the Fourth Gospel* [Grand Rapids: Eerdmans, 1969], pp. 280–83; Beckwith, *Apocalypse*, pp. 362–93).

[48]William Ramsay, *The Letters to the Seven Churches of Asia* (London: Hodder & Stoughton, 1904), pp. 171–96. See also Hemer, *Letters to the Seven Churches*, pp. 14–15; Barry J. Beitzel, *The Moody Atlas of Bible Lands* (Chicago: Moody, 1985), p. 185.

COMPOSITION AND GENRE

Sources and Theories of Composition

Revelation borrows extensively from the Old Testament, more so than any other New Testament book.[49] Most of the references come not in explicit quotations but in allusions and conceptual borrowings. John also makes use of Jewish apocalyspses, though to a lesser degree than is sometimes thought. Some have thought that John also betrays a knowledge of several New Testament books: Charles lists Matthew, Luke, 1 Thessalonians, 1 and 2 Corinthians, Colossians, and Ephesians.[50] But this is not so clear, since almost all the similarities could have arisen from John's knowledge of the oral tradition of Jesus' life and teaching and of general early Christian teachings. Still, since it is likely that John had read at least Mark and Luke by this date (on their dates, see the section "Date" in chaps. 3 and 4 above), we must allow the possibility of direct borrowing.

During the heyday of source analysis of the Scriptures in the late nineteenth and early twentieth centuries, a number of scholars found evidence of sources behind the canonical book of Revelation. Charles, for instance, thinks one-fifth of the book is dependent on written sources, Greek and Hebrew in language and Jewish and Christian in origin.[51] He also argued that the author of most of the book died before finishing it and that "a faithful but unintelligent disciple" pasted together the material in 20:4–22:21, but in an order radically different from what the author intended.[52] But Charles's rearrangement of the material causes more problems than it solves. Neither has his identification of sources much to be said for it. Revelation demonstrates a consistency in style that prevents any inferences about sources on the basis of linguistic considerations. Moreover, the book is so thoroughly permeated with traditional language and conceptions that it is impossible to identify sources through these means either. Evidence for sources is often found in the existence of doublets, or passages that appear to be roughly parallel. But repetition of material is part of the nature of Revelation.

Undeterred by these hindrances, a number of scholars have gone even further and argued that the book of Revelation is made up of two or more large blocks of material. Boismard thinks that two parallel apocalypses have been combined.[53] J. Massyngberde Ford argues that chapters 4–11 stem from John the Baptist, 12–22 from a disciple of John, with 1–3; 22:16a, 20b; 21 being added by a Jewish-Christian disciple.[54] Neither theory has much positive evidence in its favor, but rests (particularly in Ford's case) on imaginative and implausible connections and inferences.

---

[49]See the lists of parallels in Charles, *Revelation* 1: lxviii–lxxxiii; Swete, *Apocalypse*, pp. cxxxix–clii; and esp. G. K. Beale, *The Use of Daniel in Jewish Apocalyptic Literature and in the Revelation of St John* (Lanham, Md.: UPA, 1984).

[50]Charles, *Revelation* 1: lxxxiii–lxxxvi.

[51]Ibid., pp. lxii–lxv.

[52]Ibid., pp. l–lv.

[53]M. E. Boismard, "The Apocalypse," in Robert/Feuillet, pp. 701–7.

[54]Ford, *Revelation*, pp. 3–37. A useful survey of source and compilation hypotheses can be found in Fiorenza, *Book of Revelation*, pp. 159–80.

Genre

As Beasley-Murray notes, the opening verses of Revelation appear to suggest three different genre identifications: "apocalypse" (1:1), "prophecy" (1:3), and epistle (1:4).[55] Each has its defenders, and each plays a role in the complex literary phenemenon of Revelation.

Identification with the genre "apocalypse" or "apocalyptic" is complicated by continuing debate over just what apocalyptic is: is it a type of eschatology, or is it a literary genre, or both? Current researchers generally answer that it embraces both but that we should distinguish the two, "apocalyptic" being used to describe a certain kind of eschatology, and "apocalypse" to denote a literary genre.

The literary genre "apocalypse" began to appear in the second century B.C. as a response to persecution and oppression. The authors of apocalypses claim to be passing on heavenly mysteries revealed to them by an angel or some other spiritual being.[56] Apocalypses are typically pseudonymous, written in the name of a great figure in Israel's past (Adam, Moses, Enoch, etc.). By so projecting themselves into the past, the authors of apocalypses can put historical surveys of God's dealings with his people and with the world in the form of prophecy. These historical surveys, which are found in many, though not all, apocalypses, culminate with the breaking in of God's kingdom, expected in the very near future.

The writers of apocalypses usually use extensive symbolism in their historical reviews. The kind of eschatology found in these books (though not confined to them) is then called apocalyptic. It is characterized by a dualistic conception of history: the present world, with its sin, rebellion against God, and persecution of God's people, is sharply contrasted with the world to come, when God will intervene to establish his kingdom.[57] Just at this point "apocalyptic" is often contrasted with "prophecy," which, it is argued, looks for God's salvation to be manifested through the processes of this world rather than through a breaking in of a new world. The prophet is also sometimes contrasted with the apocalypticist in his claim to speak directly from the Lord.

It takes only a casual acquaintance with Revelation to see that it possesses many of the features just described. Its message comes through visions given by angels. It is communicated through extensive use of symbols, strongly contrasts this world with the world to come, and looks for deliverance in the near future. Considering these similarities to Jewish apocalyptic and the apparent claim in 1:1 (the first three words in Greek are Ἀποκάλυψις Ἰησοῦ Χριστοῦ [*Apokalypsis Iēsou Christou*], NIV "the revelation of Jesus Christ"), it is no wonder that many

---

[55]Beasley-Murray, *Revelation*, p. 12.

[56]Christopher Rowland judges this to be the key to apocalyptic (*The Open Heaven* [London: SPCK, 1982], pp. 14, 21, 356–57).

[57]A collection of apocalypses in English translation can be found in J. H. Charlesworth, ed., *The Old Testament Pseudepigrapha*, vol. 1 (Garden City, N.Y.: Doubleday, 1983). Some of the key treatments of apocalyptic include H. H. Rowley, *The Relevance of Apocalyptic*, 2d ed. (London: Lutterworth, 1947); D. S. Russell, *The Method and Message of Jewish Apocalyptic* (London: SCM, 1964); Klaus Koch, *The Rediscovery of Apocalyptic* (London: SCM, 1972); Paul D. Hanson, *The Dawn of Apocalyptic*, 2d ed. (Philadelphia: Fortress, 1979); and Leon Morris, *Apocalyptic* (London: Tyndale, 1973). Three collections of important essays are *Semeia* 14 (1979); Paul D. Hanson, ed., *Visionaries and Their Apocalypses* (Philadelphia: Fortress, 1983); and D. Helmbold, ed., *Apocalypticism in the Mediterranean World and the Near East* (Tübingen: Mohr, 1983).

scholars are convinced that Revelation belongs in the literary genre "apocalypse." Yet there are problems with this identification. The most notable one is the fact that Revelation, unlike Jewish apocalypses, is not pseudonymous. John speaks in his own name. If, then, pseudonymity is considered essential to the genre apocalypse, Revelation clearly cannot be an apocalypse.[58] Others respond, however, by insisting that pseudonymity is not necessary to the genre and that Revelation is an apocalpyse "with a difference." Yet there is another vital difference: Jewish apocalyptists ground their hope in a future event, while John in the Revelation grounds his hope in the past sacrifice of Jesus Christ, the "Lamb that has been slain."[59] We are therefore reluctant to consider Revelation an apocalypse.

It is difficult, however, to find another genre to which Revelation belongs. John certainly suggests that he stands in a prophetic role, and there is a tendency in current scholarship to view Revelation as a prophecy. But a better suggestion is to find elements of both prophecy and apocalyptic in Revelation.[60] Despite the impression given by some scholars, no rigid distinction between these two is possible. They are combined in many Old Testament books (e.g., Daniel, Isaiah, Zechariah) and in our Lord's Olivet discourse.[61] In his consciousness of inspiration and of the authority that he assumes, John is truly a prophet. But his prophecy makes use of the forms current in Jewish apocalypses.

In terms of literary genre, however, "epistle" may be the best single categorization. This may seem odd at first, but the epistle was a very broad genre (see the section "Paul's Letters," in chap. 7 above), and Revelation, with its opening address and salutation (1:4–5, 9–11), presents itself as a circular letter to seven churches in Asia Minor. We may best view Revelation, then, as a prophecy cast in an apocalyptic mold and written down in a letter form.[62]

TEXT

Kurt and Barbara Aland claim, "In the book of Revelation the textual scene and its history differs greatly from the rest of the New Testament."[63] This is due to two factors. First, Revelation has far fewer Greek manuscript witnesses than any other New Testament book. Revelation originally circulated independently of the rest of the New Testament, and the nature of the book, combined with suspicions about it in the East, where the bulk of Greek manuscripts were produced, cut down the number of copies made. Extant are only five papyrus manuscripts, the longest containing eight chapters (p^{47}, from the third century), and eleven uncials, only six of which contain any substantial portion of text, and only three of which contain

---

[58]See, e.g., Bruce W. Jones, "More About the Apocalypse as Apocalyptic," *JBL* 87 (1968): 325–27. Also doubting the appropriateness of the apocalyptic classification is James Kallas, "The Apocalypse: An Apocalyptic Book?" *JBL* 86 (1967): 69–80.

[59]Kümmel claims that Revelation represents "a total recasting of the apocalyptic view of history out of the Jewish into the Christian mold" (p. 461).

[60]See, e.g., John J. Collins, "Pseudonymity, Historical Reviews, and the Genre of the Revelation of John," *CBQ* 39 (1977): 329–43; Fiorenza, *Book of Revelation*, pp. 133–58.

[61]See esp. George Eldon Ladd, "Why Not Prophetic-Apocalyptic?" *JBL* 76 (1957): 192–200.

[62]See esp. the discussion and conclusions in Fiorenza, *Book of Revelation*, pp. 164–70.

[63]Kurt Aland and Barbara Aland, *The Text of the New Testament*, 2d ed. (Grand Rapids: Eerdmans, 1989), p. 246.

the whole book (Sinaiticus [א], from the fourth century; Alexandrinus [A], from the fifth century, and 046, from the tenth century). The textual critic, then, has much less evidence on which to base decisions. At least the contemporary critic has more to go by than did Erasmus, who, in his first edition, for lack of *any* Greek manuscript evidence for some verses in the Revelation, translated the Latin Vulgate back into Greek![64]

A second factor that makes the text of Revelation unique is the value of the witnesses that are available. While in most of the New Testament, Sinaiticus (א) is considered to have a text superior to that found in Alexandrinus (A), the situation is reversed in Revelation: Alexandrinus, in combination with Ephraemi (C) (where it is extant), is considered the best text available.[65] Dependence on these uncials is all the more important because one of the most-respected uncials for the New Testament text, Vaticanus (B), does not include Revelation. The combination of few witnesses and variant text types requires that textual decisions in Revelation be based on methods appropriate to its own peculiar text situation.[66]

ADOPTION INTO THE CANON

Revelation may be alluded to by Ignatius (A.D. 110–117) and Barnabas (before 135) and is probably used by the author of the *Shepherd* of Hermas (c. 150).[67] As we noted above in the section "Author," Revelation is quoted as authoritative by (perhaps) Papias (d. 130), Justin (middle of the second century), Ireneus (180), and is found in the Muratorian Canon (end of the second century). Marcion rejected Revelation from his canon (see Tertullian, *Adv. Marc.* 4.5), but this is not surprising, since he rejected any New Testament book that smacked of the Old Testament or Judaism—and Revelation is filled with Old Testament allusions. Eusebius also mentions that Revelation was rejected by a Gaius, a church official in Rome at the beginning of the second century (*H.E.* 3.27.1–2). His reason was probably the use to which the Montanists, a Christian sect that stressed prophecy and the nearness of the eschaton, were putting Revelation. By denying canonical status to one of their most important books, Gaius could hope to discredit the movement.[68] The same reason probably lies behind the rejection of Revelation on the part of the group known as the Alogoi. In any case, these scattered rejections of Revelation in the Western church did not affect its canonicity, and from this point forward there is no hint of doubt about Revelation's full canonical status in the West.

The situation in the East was quite different. The authority accorded to Revelation by Papias and Justin was seconded by third-century scholars such as Clement of Alexandria and Origen. But the Egyptian bishop Dionysius disagreed.

---

[64]See Bruce M. Metzger, *The Text of the New Testament: Its Transmission, Corruption, and Restoration*, 2d ed. (New York: Oxford, 1968), pp. 99–100.

[65]Charles, *Revelation* 1:clx–clxvi; Aland and Aland, *Text*, p. 247.

[66]J. Delobel, "Le text de l'Apocalypse: Problèmes de méthode," in *L'Apocalypse johannique*, pp. 151–66. The two major studies of the text of Revelation are H. C. Hoskier, *Concerning the Text of the Apocalypse*, 2 vols. (London: Bernard Quaritch, 1929), and J. Schmid, *Studien zur Geschichte des griechischen Apokalypsetextes*, 3 vols. (Munich: Kaiser, 1955–56).

[67]Guthrie, pp. 929–30.

[68]See the discussion in the section "Author" in chap. 5 above, and in Maier, *Johannesoffenbarung*, pp. 79–85.

As we have seen, he questioned the apostolic authorship of the book in an effort to minimize its authority. His questions led other churchmen in the East to question its canonicity, among them Eusebius, who says that many in his day questioned its status (*H.E.* 3.25.1–4). The Council of Laodicea (360) did not recognize it as canonical, and it is omitted from the earliest editions of the Syriac Peshitta.

At first sight, these doubts about Revelation seem somewhat disturbing. But on closer examination, they can be seen to be somewhat extraneous to the issue of canonicity. As Maier has shown in great detail, the doubts about Revelation stemmed from no considered argument or historical knowledge, but were the result of distaste for the eschatology of the book.[69] Revelation seemed to teach, and was interpreted by many in the early church to teach, a doctrine of the last things that was too earthly focused, too materialistic, for many of the Eastern fathers. We should not, then, be much influenced by them in our assessment of the canonicity of the book. A similar point must be made about latter-day critics of the Revelation. Luther, for instance, relegated it to a secondary status in his New Testament, saying, "My spirit cannot accommodate itself to this book. There is one sufficient reason for the small esteem in which I hold it—that Christ is neither taught nor recognized."[70] One might wonder at this point if Luther was reading the same book that we have in our Bibles, the book that makes "the Lamb that was slain" the linchpin in God's plan for history and the end of history. At any rate, such theological prejudice should not be allowed to affect our judgments about the book's rightful place in the canon.

REVELATION IN RECENT STUDY

Scholarship on Revelation, in keeping with New Testament scholarship generally, has moved away from a concern with sources and historical background, to a concern with the final literary product and its setting.[71] Attention has been given to the genre of Revelation (see above) and to the genre of the letters to the seven churches,[72] as well as to the structure and literary techniques of the book.[73] The social-theological setting out of which the book arose has also been investigated, one of the more interesting theories being that the Revelation is the product of a Christian "prophetic circle."[74] Collins has used sociological theories to argue that John was writing to help his readers find a new identity and to learn to cope with their sense of having failed to meet their own expectations.[75] Study of

---

[69]Maier, *Johannesoffenbarung*, passim.

[70]From the preface to Luther's 1522 Bible.

[71]See Fiorenza, *Book of Revelation*, pp. 20–21. Her essay "Research Perspectives on the Book of Revelation" (pp. 12–32) gives a helpful overview of the terrain. See also U. Vanni, "L'Apocalypse johannique: État de la question," in *L'Apocalypse johannique*, pp. 21–46, and Jon Paulien, "Recent Developments in the Study of the Book of Revelation," *AUSS* 26 (1988): 159–70.

[72]John T. Kirby, "The Rhetorical Situations of Revelation 1–3," *NTS* 34 (1988): 197–207; D. E. Aune, "The Form and Function of the Proclamations to the Seven Churches (Revelation 2–3)," *NTS* 36 (1990): 182–204.

[73]E.g., Fiorenza, *Book of Revelation*, pp. 159–80; Lambrecht, "Structuration," pp. 77–104.

[74]See David E. Aune, "The Social Matrix of the Apocalypse of John," *BR* 26 (1981): 16–32; idem, "The Prophetic Circle of John of Patmos and the Exegesis of Revelation 22:16," *JSNT* 37 (1989): 103–16; Fiorenza, *Book of Revelation*, pp. 133–56.

[75]Collins, *Crisis and Catharsis*.

the Revelation continues to be affected also by continuing research into apocalyptic, which is now focusing on the wider dimensions of the movement and on its social matrix.[76]

Other studies, more traditional in their orientation, have also appeared. John's Greek continues to be the subject of interest, with two recent monographs on the subject.[77] Alan James Beagley, in a monograph on the enemies of the church in Revelation, concludes that Jewish-Christian antipathy plays a key role in the book.[78] Two studies stand out in particular. The first is Colin J. Hemer's study of the setting of the seven churches of the Revelation, in which the student of Revelation is provided with a cornucopia of background data that sheds new light on the text.[79] The second in the magisterial study by Gerhard Maier of the interpretation of, and attitude toward, Revelation in the history of the church.[80] His work puts to rest many of the theories about Revelation that tend to undercut its apostolic origin or canonical status.

THE CONTRIBUTION OF REVELATION

Methods of Interpretation

Any estimate of the contribution of Revelation to our understanding of Christ and the gospel demands some decision about the basic intent and subject matter of the book. What do John's visions refer to? What are we to learn from them? The church has never come to anything close to unanimity on this point. As Gerhard Maier says after his survey of interpretations, Revelation has been "the exercise field of hermeneutics par excellence."[81] We may categorize the majority of interpretations under the usual four headings.[82]

The preterist approach. This approach, also called the "contemporary-historical" (*zeitgeschichtlich*), is the most common today. It insists that the visions of John grow out of and describe events in John's own day. The symbols in the visions all refer to people, countries, and events in the world of that day, and John's purpose is to show his readers how God is about to bring judgment on that world that is oppressing them, and so deliver them into his eternal kingdom.

The historical approach. Several movements in the Middle Ages grew up in the conviction that the millennium was about to dawn. To buttress their beliefs, they found in the Revelation a sketch of history from the time of Christ to their own day. This approach (the *kirchengeschichtlich*) was popular with the Reformers also, enabling them to identify the beast in the Revelation with the papacy.

The futurist approach. A consistently futurist (or *endgeschichtlich*) approach holds that everything in the Revelation from chapter 4 to the end finds its fulfillment in

[76]See, e.g., Helmbold, *Apocalypticism.*

[77]G. Mussies, *The Morphology of Koine Greek As Used in the Apocalypse of John,* SuppNovT 27 (Leiden: Brill, 1971); Thompson, *Semitic Syntax.*

[78]Alan James Beagley, *The "Sitz im Leben" of the Apocalypse, with Particular Reference to the Role of the Church's Enemies,* BZNW 50 (Berlin: de Gruyter, 1987).

[79]Hemer, *Letters to the Seven Churches.*

[80]Maier, *Johannesoffenbarung.*

[81]Ibid., p. 622.

[82]See, e.g., Merrill Tenney, *Interpreting Revelation* (Grand Rapids: Eerdmans, 1957), pp. 135–46. R. H. Charles has a fine history of interpretation up to the early twentieth century in *Studies in the Apocalypse,* 2d ed. (Edinburgh: T. & T. Clark, 1915), pp. 7–78.

the very last days of human history. The view is also held in a more moderate form, according to which some of the events in these chapters—particularly the earlier ones—take place in history before the end.

The idealist approach. Some scholars are convinced that we are on the wrong track altogether in trying to identify the events portrayed in John's visions. The symbolism is designed, they argue, to help us understand God's person and ways with the world in a general way, not to enable us to map out a course of events. Revelation, then, teaches us "the action of great principles and not special incidents."[83]

Along with several recent commentators,[84] we find some truth in all four of these views. Yet it is the futurist approach that comes closest to doing justice to the nature and purposes of Revelation. As we have seen, Revelation adapts and modifies the apocalyptic perspective. Jewish apocalyptic writers projected themselves back into time so that they could describe the imminent breaking into history of God's eternal kingdom as the culmination of history. By writing in his own name, John discards the historical survey and confronts his readers with an elaborate vision of the establishment of Christ's reign in history. Revelation is about eschatology, not history.[85]

Nevertheless, the peculiar eschatological stance of the early church demands that we not ignore the degree to which John pictures this eschatological climax against the backdrop of events in his own day. It is likely, for instance, that John's depiction of the "great prostitute," "Babylon," that is doomed to fall, has some reference to the Roman Empire of his own day, and that the terrible persecution described in Revelation would remind John's readers of their own oppression. To some extent, then, John, while describing the end, describes it against the background of his first-century situation. But this is typical of biblical prophecy in both Old and New Testaments. While revealing his plan for history, God has not often revealed its timing; and biblical prophets have always pictured "the day of the Lord," the eschaton, in terms of their own time. Moreover, it is clear that history itself contains many prefigurements of that end; John himself reminds us that, while "the antichrist is coming, even now many antichrists have come" (1 John 2:18).[86]

The Contribution of Revelation

Revelation makes significant contributions to a number of areas of New Testament theology. It conveys a sense of the sovereignty of God that no other New Testament book approaches. The vision of God on his throne and of the worship he receives helps us to see beyond our earthly circumstances to the Lord of earth and heaven and reminds us that only God is ultimately worthy of our devotion and praise.

Revelation offers a high Christology, as Jesus is constantly portrayed in terms appropriate only to God. It is significant in this regard, as Beasley-Murray points

[83]William Milligan, *The Revelation of St. John*, 2d ed. (London: Macmillan, 1887), p. 153.

[84]E.g., Morris, *Revelation*, pp. 15–22; Mounce, *Revelation*, pp. 41–45; Tenney, *Interpreting Revelation*, pp. 145–46.

[85]Fiorenza, *Book of Revelation*, p. 46.

[86]See particularly Ladd, *Revelation*, pp. 10–14, for this approach.

out, that the opening vision of the book is not of God the Father but of Jesus Christ (1:12–20) and that both God the Father and Jesus Christ are called "the Alpha and the Omega" (1:8; 22:13).[87] In these ways and in many others, John makes clear that the sovereign God is accomplishing his purposes on earth through the Son, very God himself.

But while the Revelation focuses on Christ's glory, power, and his role in judgment, the cross is never lost sight of. The powerful rider on the white horse, we are constantly reminded, is none other than the "lamb that was slain." Without dwelling on the crucifixion of Christ, John makes clear that all that Christ does to wrap up human history is rooted in his sacrificial death. John has restructured the typical Jewish apocalyptic perspective with his Christological focus.[88]

If, as we have argued, Revelation focuses on the end of history, then it is in the area of eschatology that it makes its most important contribution. Nowhere are we given a more detailed description of the events of the end; and while many interpreters have been guilty of finding far more specifics in John's visions than his symbolism allows and of unwisely insisting that only their own circumstances fit those specifics, we should not go to the other extreme and ignore those details that John does make relatively clear.

But it is shortsighted to think of eschatology simply in the sense of what will happen in the end times. For the End, in biblical thought, shapes and informs the past and the present. Knowing how history ends helps us understand how we are to fit into it now. Particularly is this so because the New Testament makes clear that even now we are in "the last days." Thus, Revelation reminds us of the reality and severity of evil and of the demonic forces that are active in history. Beasley-Murray's comment is insightful: "It is ironical that the century which has witnessed the death of the Devil and the Antichrist in theology has experienced the most appalling manifestations of demonic statecraft, the most terrible desolation of war, and the most widespread oppression of the Christian faith in all history."[89]

John's visions also place in clear relief the reality of God's judgment. A day will come when his wrath will be poured out, when sins will have to be accounted for, when the fate of every individual will depend on whether or not his or her name is "written in the Lamb's book of life." Equally clear, of course, is the reward that God has in store for those who "keep the word of endurance" and resolutely stand against the Devil and his earthly minions, even at the cost of life itself. John's visions are a source of comfort for suffering and persecuted believers in all ages.

BIBLIOGRAPHY

Kurt **Aland** and Barbara **Aland**, *The Text of the New Testament*, 2d ed. (Grand Rapids: Eerdmans, 1989); D. E. **Aune**, "The Form and Function of the Proclamations to the Seven Churches (Revelation 2–3)," *NTS* 36 (1990): 182–204; idem, "The Social Matrix of the Apocalypse of John," *BR* 26 (1981): 16–32; idem, "The Prophetic Circle of John of Patmos and the Exegesis of Revelation 22:16," *JSNT* 37 (1989): 103–16; Alan James **Beagley**, *The "Sitz im Leben" of the Apocalypse,*

---

[87]Beasley-Murray, *Revelation*, p. 24.
[88]See Childs, pp. 311–12.
[89]Beasley-Murray, *Revelation*, p. 43.

with Particular Reference to the Role of the Church's Enemies, BZNW 50 (Berlin: de Gruyter, 1987); G. K. **Beale**, *The Use of Daniel in Jewish Apocalyptic Literature and in the Revelation of St John* (Lanham, Md.: UPA, 1984); G. R. **Beasley-Murray**, *The Book of Revelation*, NCB (London: Marshall, Morgan & Scott, 1974); Ibson T. **Beckwith**, *The Apocalypse of John: Studies in Introduction* (New York: Macmillan, 1919); Barry J. **Beitzel**, *The Moody Atlas of Bible Lands* (Chicago: Moody, 1985); Albert A. **Bell, Jr.**, "The Date of John's Apocalypse: The Evidence of Some Roman Historians Reconsidered," *NTS* 25 (1979): 93–102; Wilhelm **Bousset**, *Die Offenbarung Johannis*, rev. ed. (Göttingen: Vandenhoeck & Ruprecht, 1906); John Wick **Bowman**, "Book of Revelation," in *IDB*, 4:58–71: G. B. **Caird**, *A Commentary on the Revelation of St. John the Divine*, HNTC (New York: Harper & Row, 1966); R. H. **Charles**, *A Critical and Exegetical Commentary on the Revelation of St. John*, 2 vols., ICC (Edinburgh: T. & T. Clark, 1920) idem, *Studies in the Apocalypse*, 2d ed.(Edinburgh: T. & T. Clark, 1915); J. H. **Charlesworth**, ed., *The Old Testament Pseudepigrapha*, vol. 1 (Garden City, N.Y.: Doubleday, 1983); M. R. **Charlesworth**, "The Flavian Dynasty," *CAH* 11 (1936): 41–42; Adela Yarbro **Collins**, *Crisis and Catharsis: The Power of the Apocalypse* (Philadelphia: Westminster, 1984); John J. **Collins**, "Pseudonymity, Historical Reviews, and the Genre of the Revelation of John," *CBQ* 39 (1977): 329–43; J. **Delobel**, "Le text de l'Apocalypse: Problèmes de méthode," in *L'Apocalypse johannique et l'apocalyptique dans le Nouveau Testament*, ed. J. Lambrecht, BETL 53 (Louvain: Louvain University Press, 1980), pp. 151–66; A. **Feuillet**, *The Apocalypse* (Staten Island, N.Y.: Alba House, 1965); Elisabeth Schüssler **Fiorenza**, *The Book of Revelation: Justice and Judgment* (Philadelphia: Fortress, 1985); J. Massyngberde **Ford**, *Revelation*, AB (Garden City, N.Y.: Doubleday, 1975); Kenneth L. **Gentry, Jr.**, *Before Jerusalem Fell: Dating the Book of Revelation* (Tyler, Tex.: ICE, 1989); John J. **Gunther**, "The Elder John, Author of Revelation," *JSNT* 11 (1981): 3–20; Paul D. **Hanson**, *The Dawn of Apocalyptic*, 2d ed. (Philadelphia: Fortress, 1979); idem, ed., *Visionaries and Their Apocalypses* (Philadelphia: Fortress, 1983); D. **Helmbold**, ed., *Apocalypticism in the Mediterranean World and the Near East* (Tübingen: Mohr, 1983); Colin J. **Hemer**, *The Letters to the Seven Churches of Asia in Their Local Setting*, JSNTSupp 11 (Sheffield: JSOT, 1986); William **Hendriksen**, *More than Conquerors: An Interpretation of the Book of Revelation*, 6th ed. (Grand Rapids: Baker, 1952); F. J. A. **Hort**, *The Apocalypse of St. John I–III* (London: Macmillan, 1908); H. C. **Hoskier**, *Concerning the Text of the Apocalypse*, 2 vols. (London: Bernard Quaritch, 1929); Bruce W. **Jones**, "More About the Apocalypse as Apocalyptic," *JBL* 87 (1968): 325–27; James **Kallas**, "The Apocalypse: An Apocalyptic Book," *JBL* 86 (1967): 69–80; John T. **Kirby**, "The Rhetorical Situations of Revelation 1–3," *NTS* 34 (1988): 197–207; Klaus **Koch**, *The Rediscovery of Apocalyptic* (London: SCM, 1972); George Eldon **Ladd**, *A Commentary on the Revelation of John* (Grand Rapids: Eerdmans, 1972); idem, "Why Not Prophetic-Apocalyptic?" *JBL* 76 (1957): 192–200; Jan **Lambrecht**, "A Structuration of Revelation 4,1–22,5," in *L'Apocalypse johannique*, pp. 77–104; Gerhard **Maier**, *Die Johannesoffenbarung und die Kirche*, WUNT 25 (Tübingen: Mohr, 1981); Bruce M. **Metzger**, *The Text of the New Testament: Its Transmission, Corruption, and Restoration*, 2d ed. (New York: Oxford, 1968); William **Milligan**, *The Revelation of St. John*, 2d ed. (London: Macmillan, 1887); Paul S. **Minear**, *I Saw a New Earth* (Washington, D.C.: Corpus, 1968); Leon **Morris**, *Apocalyptic* (London: Tyndale, 1973); idem, *The Revelation of St. John*, TNTC, rev. ed. (Grand Rapids: Eerdmans, 1987); Robert H. **Mounce**, *The Book of Revelation*, NICNT (Grand Rapids: Eerdmans, 1977); G. **Mussies**, *The Morphology of Koine Greek As Used in the Apocalypse of John*,

SuppNovT 27 (Leiden: Brill, 1971); Jon **Paulien**, "Recent Developments in the Study of the Book of Revelation," *AUSS* 26 (1988): 159–70; Stanley E. **Porter**, *Verbal Aspect in the Greek of the New Testament, with Reference to Tense and Mood*, SBG 1 (Berne: Peter Lang, 1989); William **Ramsay**, *The Letters to the Seven Churches of Asia* (London: Hodder & Stoughton, 1904); Matthias **Rissi**, *Time and History: A Study of the Revelation* (Richmond, Va.: John Knox, 1966); J. A. T. **Robinson**, *Redating the New Testament* (Philadelphia: Westminster, 1976); Christopher **Rowland**, *The Open Heaven* (London: SPCK, 1982); H. H. **Rowley**, *The Relevance of Apocalyptic*, 2d ed. (London: Lutterworth, 1947); D. S. **Russell**, *The Method and Message of Jewish Apocalyptic* (London: SCM, 1964); J. N. **Sanders**, "St. John on Patmos," *NTS* 9 (1962–63): 75–85; J. **Schmid**, *Studien zur Geschichte des griechischen Apokalypsetextes*, 3 vols. (Munich: Kaiser, 1955–56); *Semeia* 14 (1979); Ned B. **Stonehouse**, *The Apocalypse in the Ancient Church* (Goes: Oosterbaan & Le Cointre, 1929); A. **Strobel**, "Abfassung und Geschichtstheologie des Apokalypse nach Kp. 17, 9–12," *NTS* 10 (1963–64): 433–45; Henry Barclay **Swete**, *The Apocalypse of St. John*, 3d ed. (London: Macmillan, 1911); Merrill **Tenney**, *Interpreting Revelation* (Grand Rapids: Eerdmans, 1957); Stephen **Thompson**, *The Apocalypse and Semitic Syntax*, SNTSMS 52 (Cambridge: Cambridge University Press, 1985); U. **Vanni**, "L'Apocalypse johannique: Etat de la question," in *L'Apocalypse johannique*, pp. 21–46; John F. **Walvoord**, *The Revelation of Jesus Christ* (Chicago: Moody, 1966); Johannes **Weiss**, *Offenbarung des Johannes*, FRLANT 3 (Göttingen: Vandenhoeck & Ruprecht, 1904).

the new testamen

INTRODUCTION

Etymologically, κανών (*kanōn*, "canon") is a Semitic loanword that originally meant "reed" but came to mean "measuring reed" and hence "rule" or "standard" or "norm." In the course of time it came to have the purely formal sense of "list" or "table." In ecclesiastical usage during the first three centuries, it referred to the normative doctrinal and ethical content of Christian faith. By the fourth century it came to refer to the list of books that constitute the Old and New Testaments.[1] It is this latter sense that predominates today: the "canon" has come to refer to the closed collection of documents that constitute authoritative Scripture.

The first Christians, of course, possessed no New Testament canon; they relied on the gospel that was being preached by the apostles and others, and on the books in what we now call the Old Testament canon. The *historical* question of the New Testament canon, then, is how the twenty-seven books that make up our New Testament came to be recognized as authoritative and distinctive from other literature. The answer depends on careful reading of the Fathers. This was done in a cursory way in the previous chapters, as the account of how each New Testament book was adopted into the canon was briefly related, and major studies put this material together and treat it in some detail.[2]

But the *theological* questions relating to the canon are in many ways more important, and certainly more disputed. What is the relation between canon and authority? Which comes first, a book's canonical status or its functional authority? What is the relationship between the authority of the text and the authority of the ecclesiastical body that recognizes (some would say "confers") its canonical status? Are the reasons (as opposed to the conclusions) adopted by the early church regarding the contours of the canon binding on us today? If not, are the conclusions themselves in jeopardy? In what follows, there is no attempt at

[1]See H. W. Beyer, "κανών," in *TDNT* 3:596–602.
[2]See esp. Theodor Zahn, *Geschichte des neutestamentlichen Kanons*, 4 vols. (Erlangen: A. Deichert'sche Verlagsbuchhandlung, 1888–92); Brooke Foss Westcott, *A General Survey of the History of the Canon of the New Testament*, 7th ed. (London: Macmillan, 1896); Bruce M. Metzger, *The Canon of the New Testament: Its Origin, Development, and Significance* (Oxford Clarendon, 1987); and, more briefly, David G. Dunbar, "The Biblical Canon," in *Hermeneutic, Authority, and Canon*, ed. D. A. Carson and John D. Woodbridge (Grand Rapids: Zondervan: 1986), pp. 297–360, 424–46; R. P. Meye, "Canon of the NT," in *ISBE* 1:601–6.

treatment of any of the subjects introduced; we present only the briefest of some of the most important points in the contemporary debate, and indication of the directions in which the evidence takes us.

THE RELEVANCE OF THE OLD TESTAMENT CANON

A New Testament introduction is not the place to review the complex questions about the development of the Old Testament canon. But one point of dispute must be raised, since it bears on how we conceive of the formation of the New Testament canon. Was there already a "closed" Old Testament canon that could serve as a model for the formation of the New Testament canon?

Until quite recently, the critical consensus of the past two centuries argued that the Old Testament came to be canonically recognized in three separate steps, corresponding to the three divisions of the Hebrew canon. The Torah (here understood to mean the Pentateuch) achieved canonical status toward the end of the fifth century B.C.; the Prophets achieved similar status about 200 B.C., and the Writings only toward the end of the first century A.D. at the Council of Jamnia (or Jabne).

This critical consensus is now breaking up. Among the more important turning points in the discussion are these:

1. The role—even the existence—of the Council of Jamnia is increasingly being questioned. Probably Lightstone goes too far when he dismisses the Jamnian picture of a college of rabbis in the last decade of the first century as nothing more than the imaginative product of third- and fourth-century traditions,[3] but it is now widely accepted that, assuming there was an academy of rabbis at Jamnia, it did not constitute an authoritative council that decisively ruled on a number of issues but was both a college and, to a lesser extent, a legislative body. For instance, Leiman argues that although Jamnia discussed whether Ecclesiastes and perhaps Canticles made the hands unclean (i.e. whether or not they were inspired), it was more by way of theological probing than binding decision, for the same topics were being discussed a century later.[4] Indeed, one might argue that the fact these books were so discussed in the first century demonstrates that they were already widely assumed to have some sort of canonical status; otherwise there would have been little to question. One thinks of Luther's later questioning of the status of James: his historical and theological probing was predicated on the virtually unanimous assumption of James's canonical status. So far as our sources go, there is no evidence whatsoever that Jamnia assigned canonical status to any book not previously recognized, or rejected any book previously accepted.

2. Although there is evidence from Josephus (*Contra Ap.* .1.37–42), Philo (*De Vita Contemp.* 3.25), and other sources that the tripartite division of the Hebrew canon was a commonplace in the first century A.D., evidence for the hypothesis

---

[3]Jack N. Lightstone, "The Formation of the Biblical Canon in Judaism of Late Antiquity: Prolegomenon to a General Reassessment," *SR* 8 (1979): 141–42. See also Jack P. Lewis, "What Do We Mean by Jabneh?" *JBR* 32 (1964): 125–32; Robert C. Newman, "The Council of Jamnia and the Old Testament Canon," *WTJ* 38 (1976): 319–49.

[4]Sid Z. Leiman, *The Canonization of the Hebrew Scriptures: The Talmudic and Midrashic Evidence* (Hamden, Conn.: Archon, 1976), pp. 121–24. See also Roger Beckwith, *The Old Testament Canon of the New Testament Church and Its Background in Early Judaism* (Grand Rapids: Eerdmans, 1985), pp. 276–77.

that the canonical process followed these three divisions sequentially is much harder to come by. It is altogether reasonable that the Pentateuch was viewed as a closed canon first, not to be added to; as for the rest of the process, there is far too little evidence of consistent groupings of the biblical books to allow much more than speculation.

3. One of the most frequently cited arguments in support of the view that the Pentateuch was recognized by about 400 B.C. and the Prophets not until about 200 B.C. lies in the fact that the Samaritans accepted only the Pentateuch as canonical, and the Samaritan schism is customarily dated to the close of the fourth century B.C. But this assumes, without evidence, that before the schism Jewish and Samaritan views of the canon were identical. Morever, many would agree with Coggins that the decisive period for the theological development of Samaritanism was from the third century B.C. to the first century A.D.[5]

4. One of the most entrenched arguments for the late dating of the Writings is the assumed Maccabean dating of Daniel and the fact that Daniel is placed among the Writings, not among the Prophets. But quite apart from the fact that many conservative scholars still argue for a sixth-century date for Daniel, John Barton has recently argued, rather convincingly, that apart from the Pentateuch,[6] there were no recognized sequences of Old Testament books. The fact that these books were in separate scrolls meant that ordered sequences were impossible. The various classifications that have come down to us reflect the organization of material on thematic grounds, not on the grounds of a corpus of books judged as a group to be canonical; and the Jewish grouping that excluded Daniel from the Prophets has to do with the fact that Jews preferred to see the prophets as "*tradents*, those who stand in a line of historical succession and hand on tradition from one generation to the next"[7]—which is why the so-called historical books were also listed with the prophets.

5. Nevertheless, there is ample evidence that in some contexts, both Jewish and Christian, Daniel was viewed as a prophet (as David could be viewed as a prophet, even though the Psalms ascribed to him constitute part of the Writings).[8] The simplest explanation is that "prophecy" and "prophets" could be viewed from several different angles: in terms of predictive content, access to divine mysteries, calling people back to the given revelation, and so forth.

6. But doubtless it goes too far to conclude that although the Prophets and the Writings were viewed in the first century as Scripture and therefore authoritative, they were not viewed as canonical, since "canonical" assumes a closed list. Only

---

[5]R. J. Coggins, *Samaritans and Jews: The Origins of Samaritanism Reconsidered* (Oxford: Blackwell, 1975), p. 164.

[6]Even this exception may be conceding too much. The ancient Hebrew-Aramaic list of the books of the Old Testament preserved in MS 54 of the library of the Greek patriarchate in Jerusalem (see J.-P. Audet, "A Hebrew-Aramaic List of Books of the Old Testament in Greek Transcription," *JTS* 1 [1950]: 135–54) preserves the following order: Genesis, Exodus, Leviticus, Joshua, Deuteronomy, Numbers, Ruth, Job, Judges. . . . Paul E. Kahle thinks this "is possibly the oldest list available to us" (*The Cairo Geniza* [Oxford: Blackwell, 1959], p. 218). See also Leon Morris, *Ruth*, TOTC (London: Tyndale, 1968), p. 231.

[7]John Barton, *Oracles of God: Perception of Ancient Prophecy in Israel After the Exile* (London: DLT, 1986), p. 15.

[8]See exp. ibid., pp. 35–37.

the Torah (it is argued) was viewed as canon: no one could add to the books of the Law.

Certainly the notion of a fixed list of canonical books assumes that the production of authoritative books has ceased, or is in abeyance. Arguably, however, that was part of the common belief in the first century. Josephus, in the passage already cited, is a strong witness to a *closed* canon in first-century Judaism, over against surrounding religions with multiplied holy books. That biblical books circulated in individual scrolls implies no definite sequence; it does not rule out the perception that the production of such books had ceased, that is, that the canon was closed.

7. Indeed, there is considerable cumulative evidence that pre-Christian Judaism held that classical prophecy had ceased. *First Maccabees* 9:23–27 (c. 100 B.C.) bemoans this cessation; Josephus ties the closing of the canon to the fact that the line of prophets had failed. The fact that the Qumran covenanters wrote commentaries only on biblical books suggests that they viewed them as a category apart. Josephus and others do refer to some individuals *after* the closing of the canon as prophets, as Aune points out;[9] but Aune himself admits that "canonical and eschatological prophecy had a special status that distinguished them from prophetic activity in the intervening period."[10] In other words, "prophet" and "prophecy" were not technical terms that always had precisely the same force, and there is ample evidence that, as used to refer to the phenomenon that had produced the Hebrew canon, "prophecy" was viewed in the first century as an activity that had ceased and that would not return until the time of eschatological promise. Opinions vary considerably over the date of the closing of the Old Testament canon, from about 500 B.C. (for Law and Prophets) to about A.D. 200.[11] Increasingly, however, it is recognized that any date later than the first century B.C. must fly in the face of too much evidence.

8. Some have argued that the LXX, which as it has come down to us in manuscripts from the fourth and fifth centuries A.D. includes most of the Apocryphal books,[12] constitutes evidence that Diaspora Judaism, or at least Alexandrian Judaism, had a different canon; and since most early Christians used Greek versions of the Old Testament (the LXX or something very much like it), therefore it is futile to look to Semitic sources for the delineation of the canon. But this argument is sharply questioned by Sundberg and others.[13] They point out that our evidence for the LXX is late (fourth and fifth centuries A.D. and later), certainly influenced by Christian scribes, and not supported by any independent attestation of the beliefs of Alexandrian or Diaspora Jews. Furthermore, the most natural reading of two Alexandrian Christian fathers, Origen and Athanasius, suggests

[9]David E. Aune, *Prophecy in Early Christianity and in the Ancient Mediterranean World* (Grand Rapids: Eerdmans, 1983), pp. 103–52.

[10]Ibid. p. 368 n. 2.

[11]The extremes are represented by David Noel Freedman and A. C. Sundberg respectively. For discussion, see Barton, *Oracles*, pp. 27–29.

[12]B (Codex Vaticanus, fourth century) includes all of the Apocrypha except 1 and 2 Maccabees; ℵ (Codex Sinaiticus, fourth century) includes Tobit, Judith, 1 and 2 Maccabees, Wisdom, and Ecclesiasticus; A (Codex Alexandrinus, fifth century) includes all of the Apocrypha, plus 3 and 4 Maccabees and the *Psalms of Solomon*.

[13]Albert C. Sundberg, Jr., *The Old Testament of the Early Church* (Cambridge: Harvard University Press, 1964).

that they held to a Jewish canon that differed but littl
(and Semitic) reckoning.[14] Sundberg himself deni
canonical (i.e. a *closed* corpus of Scripture) in either
the first century; whether or not scholars have foll
most have been persuaded by his demolition of th
canon.

9. There is ample evidence that the New Testame
books that constitute the Old Testament as Scripture, but there is no unequivocal
evidence that the New Testament writers viewed the Old Testament Scriptures as
a closed canon. Of course, that does not mean they did *not* so view it: arguments
from silence can be tricky. And there are several lines of evidence in the New
Testament that at least suggest that they recognized a closed canon.

First, the quotation patterns of the New Testament largely line up with
predominant Jewish evidence for the shape of the canon. New Testament writers
quote every book in the Pentateuch (in its Jewish, not Samaritan, form), and from
many of the other canonical books, from both the Prophets (Kings, Isaiah,
Jeremiah, Ezekiel, and the Minor Prophets) and the Writings (Psalms, Job,
Proverbs, Daniel, Chronicles). Even some Old Testament books not certainly
quoted in the New may be alluded to (e.g., Josh. 1:5 in Heb. 13:5; Judges in
Heb. 11:32).

Second, when literature outside the corpus of what is now recognized to be the
Old Testament canon is cited (e.g., Cleanthes in Acts 17:28; Menander in 1 Cor.
15:33; Epimenides in Titus 1:12; *1 Enoch* in Jude 14–15), it is not referred to as
Scripture (γραφή [*graphē*]) or assigned to the Holy Spirit or to God as the
ultimate author.

Third, there is no hint that the New Testament writers want to jettison any of
the canonical Old Testament as being incompatible with their developing
Christian faith. Paul goes so far as to insist that the reason why "the Scriptures"
were written was for the instruction and encouragement of Christians (Rom.
15:3–6; see also 1 Cor. 10:11; 2 Tim. 3:14–17; 1 Peter 1:10–12; Heb.
11:39–40).

Fourth, many New Testament passages, although cast as refutation or
correction of traditional Jewish theology, nevertheless appeal to what both sides
have in common, namely, agreed Scriptures (e.g., Mark 7:6–7, 10–13; 11:17;
12:10–11, 24; Luke 4:16–21; John 6:45; 10:34–35; 15:25; Acts 17:2–3, 11;
29:23; 18:28; 24:14–15; 26:22; Rom. 3:1–2; Gal. 3).

Fifth, it is probable, though not certain, that Jesus' reference to all the blood
from that of Abel to that of Zechariah son of Berekiah (Matt. 23:35) runs from
the first man to be killed to the last one in the Hebrew canon to be killed
(Zechariah son of Jehoiada, in 2 Chron. 24:20, 22). Zechariah was certainly not
the last to be killed on any chronological scale: within the period of time
represented by the Old Testament, the last chronologically was probably Uriah
son of Shemaiah (Jer. 26:20–23). If the identification with the Zechariah of
2 Chronicles 24:20, 22 is correct, he was chosen because of his place *in the
recognized canon.*

It appears, then, that there is adequate evidence to support the view that there

---

[14]Respectively, *H.E.* 4.26 (Origen as cited by Eusebius), and *Ep. List.* 39 (= NPNF2 4:552).

ed) canon of Scripture to serve as a model in the formation of the New
nt canon. Even if this point be disputed, there is entirely convincing
nce that the Torah and the Prophets were viewed as closed collections by the
t century A.D.

THE FORMATION OF THE NEW TESTAMENT CANON

If we think of the New Testament canon as a "closed" list of recognized books,
the principal turning points are well known and not largely in dispute. The first
such closed list to come down to us is that of Marcion. Heavily influenced by
Syrian dualism, he rejected the entire Old Testament and accepted only one
gospel—a highly edited edition of Luke—plus his edition of ten letters of Paul,
excluding the Pastorals. But although Marcion's list is the first, it is going too far
to say that the very idea of a Christian Bible is the work of Marcion.[15] Paul's letters
were already circulating in collected form, and probably the four canonical gospels
as well. More important, the idea of New Testament Scripture, certainly well
established in the first part of the second century, presupposes some sort of
canonical limit sooner or later.

Undoubtedly the work of Marcion and of other heretics spurred the church to
publish more comprehensive and less idiosyncratic lists. In the same vein, the
Montanist movement, which sought to elevate the voice of prophecy to a level of
supreme authority in the church—a level it did not enjoy even in Paul's day
(1 Cor. 14:37–38)—also served to force the church to make public decisions as
to the standard of orthodoxy. By the end of the second century, the Muratorian
list, though virtually valueless as a guide to the *origin* of the New Testament books
to which it refers, reflects the view of the great church in recognizing a New
Testament canon not very different from our own. The list is fragmentary, so that
Matthew and Mark do not appear, but doubtless they are presupposed, since Luke
is referred to as the third gospel, and John as the fourth. Luke is also recognized to
be the author of "the acts of all the apostles." Thirteen letters are recognized as
authentically Pauline. The list excludes an *Epistle to the Laodiceans* and another to
the Alexandrians (which some take to be Hebrews). Two Johannine epistles and
Jude are accepted. The apocalypses ascribed to John and to Peter are both
accepted, but the list admits that there was some opposition to the public reading
of the latter work. The *Shepherd* of Hermas is accepted for private but not for
public reading, on the grounds of its being such a recent compostion. Gnostic,
Marcionite, and Montanist writings are all rejected; a rather odd passage
recognizes the Wisdom of Solomon to be canonical.

The pattern by which this or that Father cites the various New Testament books
as Scripture has been lightly surveyed throughout this *Introduction*; but such a
pattern does not itself establish when the New Testament canon as a closed list of
books was recognized. For this, the most important source is probably Eusebius
of Caesarea (c. 260–340), whose views were largely indebted to the Alexandrian
fathers Clement and Origen. In discussing the New Testament canon, Eusebius

---

[15]So, rightly, F. F. Bruce, "New Light on the Origins of the New Testament Canon," in *New
Dimensions in New Testament Study*, ed. Richard N. Longenecker and Merrill C. Tenney (Grand
Rapids: Zondervan, 1974), p. 12, against the magisterial work of H. von Campenhausen, *The
Formation of the Christian Bible* (Philadelphia: Fortress, 1972), p. 148.

deploys a tripartite classification: the recognized books (*homologoumena*), the disputed books (*antilegomena*), and the books put forward by heretics in the name of the apostles but rejected by those Eusebius regards as orthodox. In the first category, Eusebius includes the four gospels, Acts, fourteen Pauline epistles (Eusebius includes Hebrews, though he is aware that the church in Rome did not hold Hebrews to be Pauline), 1 Peter, 1 John, and, apparently (though with some reservation) the Apocalypse. The disputed books Eusebius subdivides into those generally accepted (James, Jude, 2 Peter, and 2 and 3 John) and those that are not genuine (*Acts of Paul*, *Shepherd* of Hermas, *Apocalypse of Peter*, *Epistle of Barnabas*, the *Didache*, and, perhaps, the Apocalypse).[16] The third category, embracing clearly heretical writings, includes gospels such as those of Peter and Thomas, acts of Andrew and John, and similar writings (*H.E.* 3.25).

In other words, the four gospels, Acts, the thirteen Paulines, 1 Peter, and 1 John are universally accepted very early; most of the remaining contours of the New Testament canon are already established by the time of Eusebius. The Cheltenham manuscript, thought to represent North African views c. A.D. 360, includes all the New Testament books except Hebrews, James, and Jude. The first list that includes all and only the twenty-seven books of our New Testament is that of the Easter Letter by Athanasius in 367—clearly prescriptive rather than descriptive for the Alexandrian church. The sixtieth canon of the Council of Laodicea (c. 363) includes all twenty-seven books except the Apocalypse, but the manuscript evidence suggests this canon may have been a later addition (though in all probability still fourth century).[17] The Third Council of Carthage (397), attended by Augustine, recognized the twenty-seven New Testament books, and thereafter in the West there was little deviation from that stance.

The Eastern church, at least as represented by the Syriac (Peshitta), omitted 2 Peter, 2 and 3 John, Jude, and the Apocalypse, a pattern followed by the native (as opposed to the Greek-speaking) Syrian church today. Still, it is important to recognize that not a few Fathers from the Eastern church recognized exactly those twenty-seven books that constitute our canon today.[18] At the other extreme, the Ethiopian church recognizes not only the standard twenty-seven books but adds eight others, mostly dealing with church order.[19] Nevertheless, Dunbar is right to conclude:

> Yet it is fair to say that wherever Christians in particular localities have been concerned to know the extent of the New Testament and have searched for this knowledge in a spirit of open communication with the larger church, unanimity of opinion has generally been the result. So it is significant that the reopening of the questions of canon by the leaders of the Protestant Reformation led to a narrowing

---

[16]Uncertainty about where Eusebius places the Apocalypse turns on his own confused way of expressing himself. Although the Apocalypse was almost universally recognized as Scripture in the second century, it fell under suspicion in the Eastern church. Eusebius's stance seems to vary from initial acceptance of the Apocalypse as the work of the apostle John, to rejecting it completely as a forgery by the heretic Cerinthus, to accepting the canonical status of the book while denying its apostolic authorship. See the discussion of Robert M. Grant, *Eusebius as Church Historian* (Oxford: Clarendon, 1980), pp. 126–37.

[17]See Metzger, *Canon*, p. 210.

[18]See Westcott, *History of the Canon*, pp. 445–48.

[19]See R. W. Cowley, "The Biblical Canon of the Ethiopian Orthodox Church Today," *ÖstK* 23 (1974): 318–23.

of the Old Testament canon over against Roman Catholic usage but effected no similar change in the extent of the New Testament canon.[20]

Indeed, it is important to observe that although there was no ecclesiastical machinery like the medieval papacy to enforce decisions, nevertheless the worldwide church almost universally came to accept the same twenty-seven books. It was not so much that the church selected the canon as that the canon selected itself. This point has frequently been made, and deserves repeating.

> The fact that substantially the whole church came to recognize the same twenty-seven books as canonical is remarkable when it is remembered that the result was not contrived. All that the several churches throughout the Empire could do was to witness to their own experience with the documents and share whatever knowledge they might have about their origin and character. When consideration is given to the diversity in cultural backgrounds and in orientation to the essentials of the Christian faith within the churches, their common agreement about which books belonged to the New Testament serves to suggest that this final decision did not originate solely at the human level.[21]

Whatever the pressures that encouraged the church to issue canonical lists—including persecution, distance from the historical Jesus, the pressure of Montanism, the rise of Gnosticism and other movements with scriptures to be rejected—the *criteria* used by the church in discussions as to what books were canonical were primarily three:[22]

1. One basic requirement for canonicity was conformity to the "rule of faith" (ὁ κανὼν τῆς πίστεως [*ho kanōn tēs pisteōs*]; in Latin, *regula fidei*), conformity between the document and orthodoxy, that is, Christian truth recognized as normative in the churches. Although many scholars have denied that any clear distinction was made between "orthodoxy" and "heresy" in subapostolic times, let alone in the New Testament, it is hard not to detect the roots of the distinction in passages such as Galatians 1:8–9, Colossians 2:8ff., 1 Timothy 6:3ff. and 1 and 2 John. And already in Ignatius there is considerable concern to distinguish the true from the false. This concern rapidly increased with time.

2. Perhaps the most commonly mentioned criterion in the Fathers is apostolicity, which as a criterion came to include those who were in immediate contact with the apostles. Thus, Mark's gospel was understood to be tied to Peter; Luke was tied to Paul. When the Muratorian Fragment rejects the *Shepherd* of Hermas for public reading, it does so on the ground that it was too recent and therefore cannot find a place "among the prophets, whose number is complete, or among the apostles" ("the prophets" here refers to the Old Testament books, and

---

[20]Dunbar, "Biblical Canon," p. 317–18. In a footnote Dunbar points out that this is true even with Martin Luther, who raised the strongest questions about the *antilegomena* (p. 432 n. 117). It is often pointed out that the table of contents of Luther's translation of the Bible separates Hebrews, James, Jude, and Revelation from the rest of the books and discontinues counting them (e.g., Meye, "Canon," p. 605); it is not always pointed out that this configuration was in the 1522 edition but was dropped in subsequent editions, along with the most strident of his negative judgments on these books (expressed in his prefaces). Only his negative judgment on James continued to the end of his life. See Paul Althaus, *Theology of Martin Luther* (ET Philadelphia: Fortress, 1966), pp. 83–85.

[21]Barker/Lane/Michaels, p. 29.

[22]See Metzger, *Canon*, pp. 251–54.

"the apostles" to the New). For the same reason, wherever the Fathers suspect pseudonymity, they reject the work.

Thus, as we have seen (chap. 15), the New Testament itself betrays principled rejection of pseudonymous letters (esp. 2 Thess. 2:2; 3:17); now we observe that the Fathers universally reject pseudonymity as an acceptable literary category for documents bearing the authority of Scripture. This leaves very little space for the common modern assertion that pseudonymity was a widely acceptable practice in the ancient world. That pseudonymous apocalypses were widespread is demonstrable; that pseudonymous letters were widespread is entirely unsupported by evidence; that *any* pseudonymity was knowingly accepted into the New Testament canon is denied by the evidence.[23]

3. Scarcely less important a criterion is a document's widespread and continuous acceptance and usage by churches everywhere. Thus Jerome insists it does not matter who wrote Hebrews, for in any case it is the work of a "church-writer" (*ecclesiastici viri*, by which Jerome probably means someone writing in conformity with the truth taught in the churches, a variation of the first criterion) and is in any case constantly read in the churches (*Epist.* 129). If the Latin churches were slow to accept Hebrews and the Greek churches were slow to accept the Apocalypse, Jerome accepts both, in part because many ancient writers had accepted both of them as canonical.[24]

THE SIGNIFICANCE OF THE NEW TESTAMENT CANON

It must be admitted that this more or less traditional approach to the canon is in danger of giving a false impression, namely, that the church took inordinately long to recognize the *authority* of the documents that constitute the New Testament. This is entirely false. Discussion of the canon is discussion of a *closed* list of authoritative books. The books themselves were necessarily circulating much earlier, most of them recognized as authoritative throughout the church, and all of them recognized in large swaths of the church.[25]

There was an authoritative message from the beginning. Already in his early preaching Jesus set himself up as an authority on a par with, and in some sense fulfilling, Old Testament Scriptures (Matt. 5:17–48, esp. vv. 21ff.). The revelation of the good news, the gospel of God's dear Son, was so bound up with the life, ministry, death, and resurrection of Jesus that accounts of this "good news" came to be called gospels. This good news was passed on by apostles: in Acts 2, Luke insists that the believers who constituted the first church devoted themselves to the apostles' teaching. Already in 2 Corinthians 3:14, Paul writes of Jews reading the Scriptures of the *old* covenant.[26] By implication, a *new* covenant has dawned, the new covenant foretold by Jeremiah (esp. 31:31–34; cf. Heb. 8)

---

[23]See further the section "Pseudonymity" in chap. 15 above.

[24]Perhaps it should be mentioned that the Fathers do not recognize a work as canonical on the grounds that it is inspired, since they freely apply "inspiration" and related expressions to noncanonical books as well (see Metzger, *Canon*, pp. 254–57). "Inspiration" in modern theological discussion is a theological construct drawing from a number of important historical and theological structures and is commonly more tightly defined than in the rather flexible usage of the first centuries.

[25]Theo Donner, "Some Thoughts on the History of the New Testament Canon," *Themelios* 7, no. 3 (April 1983): 23–27.

[26]The reference is probably to the Torah, not the entire Old Testament; see v. 15.

and announced by Jesus in the words of institution on the night he was betrayed ("This cup is the new[27] covenant in my blood"). Implicitly, new covenant *Scriptures* are not far away. The epistle to the Hebrews begins by contrasting the former period of revelation with what has taken place "in these last days" in which God has revealed himself in his Son (Heb. 1:1–3). The locus and source of all authoritative new-covenant revelation rests, finally, in the Son. The apostles, in the narrower sense of that term,[28] were viewed as those who mediated such revelation to the rest of the church; but precisely because that revelation was tied to the Jesus who appeared in real history, an implicit closure was built into the claim. There could not be an unending stream of "revelations" about Jesus if those revelations were detaching themselves from the Jesus who presented himself in real history and who was confessed by the first eyewitnesses and apostles.

Thus there was both extraordinary authority and implicit closure from the very beginning. Extracanonical recognition of this pair comes as early as Ignatius. When he is challenged by some men (presumably Jews) who refuse to believe anything in the gospel that is not to be found in "our ancient records" (the Old Testament?), Ignatius responds, "But for my part, my records are Jesus Christ, for me the sacred records are his cross and death and resurrection and the faith that comes through him" (*Phil.* 8:2). Arguably, the genesis of the New Testament canon lies in the appeal to "gospel" and "apostle,"[29] with Jesus Christ himself ultimately standing behind both.

If, then, we pursue the question as to when and how the various New Testament books were read as authoritative witnesses to the gospel, instead of the question as to when and how the canon was *closed*, we are forced back, not to the closed lists prepared by Fathers who tend to be later, but to the use of the New Testament books (as compared with other sources) in the early Fathers. Then we discover that even most of the *antilegomena* are widely cited. Hebrews, for instance, is quoted extensively in *1 Clement* (probably A.D. 90–110); James is attested in *1 Clement* and Hermas (mid-second century). Indeed, even within the New Testament, an Old Testament passage and a gospel quotation can lie adjacent to each other and be introduced by "the Scripture says" (1 Tim. 5:18). Even if this gospel quotation is not from a written gospel, the passage is at least evidence that a teaching of the Lord Jesus enjoys the same authority status as Old Testament Scripture. In 2 Peter 3:16 the epistles of Paul are recognized as Scriptures.

Three other strands of evidence are important:

1. In the earliest stages of transmission, before efforts were made to provide written records (see Luke 1:1–4), the "tradition" was passed on orally. As has often been recognized,[30] "tradition" ($\pi\alpha\rho\dot{\alpha}\delta o\sigma\iota\varsigma$ [*paradosis*]) has no necessary negative overtones in the New Testament. For instance, in Paul traditions have bad overtones when they are simply human or are utterly divorced from the gospel

---

[27]"New" is retained in Luke and Paul (1 Cor.11:23–26), omitted by Matthew and Mark.

[28]See D. A. Carson, *Showing the Spirit* (Grand Rapids: Baker, 1987), pp. 88–91.

[29]See Donald Robinson, *Faith's Framework: The Structure of New Testament Theology* (Sutherland, NSW: Albatross, 1985).

[30]See esp. F. F. Bruce, "Scripture in Relation to Tradition and Reason," in *Scripture, Tradition, and Reason: A Study in the Criteria of Christian Doctrine, Fs.* Richard P. C. Hanson, ed. Richard Bauckham and Benjamin Drewery (Edinburgh: T. & T. Clark, 1988), pp. 35–64.

(Gal. 1:14; Col. 2:8); they are to be cherished and tightly held when they *are* the gospel, as passed on by an accredited messenger (1 Cor. 11:2; 2 Thess. 2:15; 3:6).

2. But this does not mean that oral tradition was widely viewed as intrinsically superior to the written documents that soon began to circulate. The one passage that everyone cites to justify the perception that the oral tradition was more highly cherished is a statement of Papias reported by Eusebius (*H.E.* 3.39.4), which in Campenhausen's translation reads, "That which comes from books seems to me not to be of such service as that which begins as living speech and remains so."[31] It has been convincingly argued that Papias magnifies the importance of oral tradition for his *commentary* on the words of the Lord, not for the actual content of those words.[32] The slighting reference to books probably refers to the writings of heretics who at this point were doing what Papias was: commenting on the received words of the Lord, but from their own theological perspective. Papias's response, in effect, is that he prefers to retain the traditional (oral) interpretations of the Lord's words. After all, elsewhere Papias rushes to deny that there is any error in Mark's gospel, even though that gospel is not a chronological presentation: surely this would be a strange maneuver if Papias disparaged *all* written records.

3. If we ask when and how the first collections of at least some of the New Testament books were made, the brief answer is that we do not know. We do know that by the middle of the second century at the latest, the four canonical gospels were being circulated together as the fourfold gospel "according to Matthew," "according to Mark," and so forth. Probably earlier still, the Pauline Epistles were in wide circulation. The process of circulating such materials was doubtless aided by the wide use that Christians made of the codex form of books. Until that time, valuable writings were normally published in scrolls; the adoption of the codex (more or less like modern books, with individual leaves sewn or glued on one edge) not only made the books more "user-friendly" but made it easier to publish several different books together in one volume.[33]

That Paul wrote other letters that have not come down to us is certain (see 1 Cor. 5:9; Col. 4:16), but the principles of selection, and the party or parties that put together the collection, have not been identified in any of our sources. Nevertheless, on the basis of a number of carefully drawn inferences, it is entirely plausible to suppose that the collection was put together by Paul's associates, such as Timothy, shortly after Paul's martyrdom.[34]

Finally, four contemporary approaches to the significance of the canon should be briefly noted.

1. Some (e.g., Koester) have argued that the notion of a canon should be abolished. There is no qualitative difference between the New Testament books and other early Christian literature, they say; whatever sources shed light on the early Christian movement should be treated the same way, so that James, say,

---

[31] See Campenhausen's discussion in *Formation*, pp. 130ff. Similarly, see Bruce, "Scripture," pp. 37–38.

[32] This line of interpretation appears to have originated with J. B. Lightfoot, *Essays on the Work Entitled Supernatural Religion* (London: Macmillan, 1893), pp. 156ff.

[33] See Moule, pp. 239–41.

[34] See Guthrie, pp. 986–1000.

should not be treated with more respect or as having more authority than, say, Clement of Rome.

Clearly, this view becomes plausible only if one rejects not only the notion of canon as a closed list of authoritative books but also the notion of Scripture. The view is also helped along by an easy willingness to abandon rather quickly the established heritage of the church, and especially by critical views that read several of the canonical books as late, pseudonymous writings, completed *after* a number of other early Christian sources that have come down to us.

2. There is at present a complex debate about the possibility of a "canon within the canon." All of us tend to lean rather more heavily on some parts of the canon than on others—just as Luther and Calvin made much more of Romans and Galatians than, say, of 1 Peter or the Apocalypse. Why not therefore make a virtue of necessity and recognize that different groups have the freedom, perhaps even the obligation, to define certain parts of the canon as being definitive for them? A more attenuated form of this theory suggests we should think of the canon as a spiral, with the outermost elements (James, 2 Peter) gradually giving way to the inner core, the very heart of genuine Christianity (John, Romans).[35]

But surely the notions of Scripture and canon forbid such approaches. True, preachers may more greatly stress one part than another, judging them to be more immediately relevant to their contexts than other parts. Some parts of the New Testament may continually wield greater influence because they are longer and more comprehensive. But to raise pragmatic pastoral choices and the accidents of composition to the obligation to relativize the canon is to deny that there is a canon that must stand as the test of our pastoral choices.

3. Traditional Roman Catholic theology has sometimes spoken of the church's role in *forming* (or *establishing*) the canon, and this in turn gives rise to a view of the church's authority rather different from that in Protestantism. The latter locates the deposit of the gospel in Scripture; conservative Catholicism locates the deposit of the faith in the church, Scriptures being one component of that deposit.

Some of the resulting debates are dissipating today, because both Protestantism and Roman Catholicism are in a state of enormous flux. But some of the problems associated with the Protestant position are largely alleviated if the distinction advocated here between Scripture and canon is carefully maintained. The church's role is not to *establish* what books constitute Scripture. Rather, the scriptural books make their own way by widespread usage and authority, and the church's role is to *recognize* that only certain books command the church's allegiance and obedience, and not others—and this has the effect of constituting a canon, a closed list of authoritative Scripture.

4. There has been considerable interest in the rise of so-called canon criticism. Although this branch of study has many forms,[36] the heart of its assumption is that, whatever sources and pressures have gone into making Scripture as we know it, the text as it stands represents the church's handling of its own traditions, including the peculiar interpretations established by inner-biblical connections, and these must be accepted as normative for the church.

---

[35]So C. K. Barrett, "The Centre of the New Testament and the Canon," in *Die Mitte des Neuen Testaments: Einheit und Vielfalt neutestamentlicher Theologie, Fs.* Eduard Schweizer, ed. Ulrich Luz and Hans Weder (Göttingen: Vandenhoeck & Ruprecht, 1983), pp. 5–21.

[36]E.g., Childs; James A. Sanders, *From Sacred Story to Sacred Text* (Philadelphia: Fortress, 1987).

There is much that is healthy about this movement. It r
effort to read the Bible as a whole, and to read biblical boo
In practice, however, some exponents of canon criticism te
truths that can be inferred from the text as a whole, but r
claims that have historical referents. This inconsistency conj
certain kind of raw fideism: adhere to the canon where it
reserve judgment where it can. This form of fideism makes canon criticism as
frequently practiced (at least in some circles) intrinsically unstable.

In short, that God is a self-disclosing, speaking, covenant-keeping God who has
supremely revealed himself in a historical figure, Jesus the Messiah, establishes the
necessity of the canon and, implicitly, its closure. The notion of canon forbids all
self-conscious attempts to select only part of the canon as the governing standard
of the Christian church: that would be to decanonize canon, a contradiction in
terms. Because the canon is made up of books whose authority ultimately springs
from God's gracious self-revelation, it is better to speak of recognizing the canon
than of establishing it. And canonical theology cannot rightly be divorced from
hard questions that tie God's revelation to real history.

BIBLIOGRAPHY

Paul **Althaus**, *Theology of Martin Luther* (ET Philadelphia: Fortress, 1966); J.-P. **Audet**, "A
  Hebrew-Aramaic List of Books of the Old Testament in Greek Transcriptions,"
  JTS 1 (1950): 135–54; David E. **Aune**, *Prophecy in Early Christianity and in the
  Ancient Mediterranean World* (Grand Rapids: Eerdmans, 1983); C. K. **Barrett**,
  "The Centre of the New Testament and the Canon," in *Die Mitte des Neuen
  Testaments: Einheit und Vielfalt neutestamentlicher Theologie*, Fs. Eduard Schweizer,
  ed. Ulrich Luz and Hans Weder (Göttingen: Vandenhoeck & Ruprecht, 1983),
  pp. 5–21; John **Barton**, *Oracles of God: Perception of Ancient Prophecy in Israel
  After the Exile* (London: DLT, 1986); Richard **Bauckham**, "Tradition in
  Relation to Scripture and Reason," in *Scripture, Tradition, and Reason: A Study in
  the Criteria of Christian Doctrine*, Fs. Richard P. C. Hanson, ed. Richard
  Bauckham and Benjamin Drewery (Edinburgh: T. & T. Clark, 1988), pp. 117–
  45; Roger **Beckwith**, *The Old Testament Canon of the New Testament Church and
  Its Background in Early Judaism* (Grand Rapids: Eerdmans, 1985); F. F. **Bruce**,
  "New Light on the Origins of the New Testament Canon," in *New Dimensions in
  New Testament Study*, ed. Richard N. Longenecker and Merrill C. Tenney (Grand
  Rapids: Zondervan, 1974), pp. 3–18; idem, "Scripture in Relation to Tradition
  and Reason," in *Scripture, Tradition, and Reason*, pp. 35–64; H. von **Campen-
  hausen**, *The Formation of the Christian Bible* (Philadelphia: Fortress, 1972); R. J.
  Coggins, *Samaritans and Jews: The Origins of Samaritanism Reconsidered* (Oxford:
  Blackwell, 1975); Theo **Donner**, "Some Thoughts on the History of the New
  Testament Canon," *Themelios* 7, no. 3 (April 1983): 23–27; David G. **Dunbar**,
  "The Biblical Canon," in *Hermeneutics, Authority, and Canon*, ed. D. A. Carson
  and John D. Woodbridge (Grand Rapids: Zondervan: 1986), pp. 297–360,
  424–46; Robert M. **Grant**, *Eusebius as Church Historian* (Oxford: Clarendon,
  1980); F. W. **Grosheide**, *Some Early Lists of the Books of the New Testament*
  (Leiden: Brill, 1948); Paul E. **Kahle**, *The Cairo Geniza* (Oxford: Blackwell,
  1959); Sid Z. **Leiman**, *The Canonization of the Hebrew Scriptures: The Talmudic
  and Midrashic Evidence* (Hamden, Conn.: Archon, 1976); Jack P. **Lewis**, "What
  Do We Mean by Jabneh?" *JBR* 32 (1964): 125–32; J. B. **Lightfoot**, *Essays on the*

Work Entitled Supernatural Religion (London: Macmillan, 1893); Jack N. **Lightstone**, "The Formation of the Biblical Canon in Judaism of Late Antiquity: Prolegomenon to a General Reassessment," *SR* 8 (1979): 135–42; Bruce M. **Metzger**, *The Canon of the New Testament: Its Origin, Development, and Significance* (Oxford: Clarendon, 1987); Leon **Morris**, *Ruth*, TOTC (London: Tyndale, 1968); Robert C. **Newman**, "The Council of Jamnia and the Old Testament Canon," *WTJ* 38 (1976): 319–49; Donald **Robinson**, *Faith's Framework: The Structure of New Testament Theology* (Sutherland, NSW: Albatross, 1985); James A. **Sanders**, *From Sacred Story to Sacred Text* (Philadelphia: Fortress, 1987); Albert C. **Sundberg, Jr.**, *The Old Testament of the Early Church* (Cambridge: Harvard University Press, 1964); Brooke Foss **Westcott**, *A General Survey of the History of the Canon of the New Testament*, 7th ed. (London: Macmillan, 1896); Theodor **Zahn**, *Geschichte des neutestamentlichen Kanons*, 4 vols. (Erlangen: A. Deichert'sche Verlagsbuchhandlung, 1888–92).

name index

Aland, Barbara, 479
Aland, Kurt, 479
Allison, Dale C., Jr., 76, 81
Ambrosiaster, 242, 417
Amphoux, 455
Amyntas, 290
Anderson, Norman, 150
Anton, Paul, 359
Apollinaris, Claudius, 139
Aquinas, Thomas, 395
Athanasius, 440, 456, 490, 493
Athenagoras, 374
Athenagorus, 139
Attridge, Harold W., 392, 404
Augustine, 20, 29, 31, 33, 34, 254,
  395, 404, 493
Aune, David E., 233, 490

Barclay, John M.G., 299
Barrett, K., 127, 150, 159, 174, 275
Barth, G., 82
Barth, Markus, 309
Barton, John, 489
Basil, 309, 312
Basilides, 151, 338
Bauckham, R.J., 433, 434, 461
Baur, F.C., 191, 202, 250
Beagley, Alan James, 482
Beare, W., 71, 82
Beasley-Murray, G.R., 478, 483–84
Beatty, Chester, 283, 379
Beker, J.C., 362
Berdot, D.N., 359
Best, Paul E., 353
Betz, H.D., 274, 276, 298
Beza, 43
Bigg, Charles, 439
Bockmuehl, Marcus N.A., 313–14
Boers, H., 354
Boismard, M.F., 477
Borgen, P., 157
Bornhauser, Karl B., 403
Bornkamm, Gunther, 41, 42, 82, 83

Bousset, Wilhelm, 222
Brandon, S.G.F., 100-101, 104
Brooke, A.E., 448
Brown, Raymond E., 145–46, 150,
  153, 454, 456–57
Brox, N., 423
Bruce, F.F., 114, 208, 291, 332, 355,
  402
Bultmann, Rudolf, 21, 22–23, 24, 44,
  49, 51, 151, 153, 221, 222, 248,
  313, 332, 365
Butler, B.C., 31

Cadbury, Henry J., 114, 186, 306
Caird, G.B., 471
Cajetan, 456
Calvin, John, 43, 254, 395, 498
Campenhausen, H. von, 497
Caragounis, Chrys C., 313–14
Carrington, Philip, 105
Carson, D.A., 166
Charles, R.H., 470–71, 472
Childs, Brevard, 52, 126, 211, 285,
  325, 338, 339, 354–55, 366, 424,
  441, 456–57
Chrysostom, 96, 389, 417, 440
Cicero, 232
Cleanthes, 491
Clement of Alexandria, 78, 92, 95, 96,
  140, 167, 186, 338, 379, 394, 395,
  397, 401, 417, 447, 461, 480, 492
Clement of Rome, 122, 151, 272, 283,
  309, 312, 319, 382, 395, 396, 399,
  401, 404, 425, 446, 461, 498
Coggins, R.J., 489
Collins, A.Y., 472, 481
Collins, John J., 278
Conzelmann, Hans, 41, 42, 123, 124,
  128, 132, 203, 204, 205
Cosgrove, Charles C., 300
Cross, F.L., 427
Cullman, Oscar, 150, 205
Culpepper, R.A., 154, 174

SUBJECT INDEX

A-B-A pattern, 278–79
Abel, 491
Abraham, 239, 243, 244, 289, 301
Achaia, as provenance of Luke, 116
Achaicus, 260, 265, 278
Acts of Paul, 363, 368, 493
Acts of Peter, 434
Acts of the Apostles, 54, 78, 79, 93, 95, 123, 124, 126, 128, 131, 181–211, 215–19, 234, 296, 297, 311, 321, 334, 382, 395, 400, 406, 415, 448, 492, 493
  addressees of, 195–99
  authorship of, 113–15, 185–90
  chronology of, 223, 224, 225, 226, 227, 228, 229, 230, 231, 241
  contents of, 181–85
  contribution of, 206–211
  date of, 190–94
  genre of, 181, 194–95, 204
  historicity of, 203–204
  literary approaches to, 204
  Mark and, 97, 98, 106, 192
  Pastorals and, 362
  1 Peter and, 422
  pseudonymity and, 368
  purpose of, 195–99
  recent studies of, 202–6
  sources for, 199–201
  speeches of, 209–10, 220
  text of, 81, 121, 201
  theology of, 198, 204–6, 210–11
  Thessalonians and, 344, 347
Adam, 240, 324, 453, 478
Agabus, 116
Alexander, 95
Alexandria,
  as destination of Hebrews, 401
  as provenance of John, 157–58
  as provenance of Matthew, 76
Alexandrian text type, 121, 283, 404, 455

Alexandrinus, 480
Alogoi, 141, 173, 468, 480
Amanuenses, 149
  Pauline Epistles and, 233–34
  Revelation and, 471
  Romans and, 241
Ambassadorial letters, 248–49
Ananias, 182
Andrew, 139, 142, 145, 162
Andronicus, 243
Annas, 120
Anonymity
  Hebrews and, 67, 157
  John and, 138
  Mark and, 92
  Matthew and, 66–67
  Synoptics and, 138
Anti-Marcionite prologue, 113, 115, 140, 181, 186, 319
Antinomianism, 80
Antioch,
  as destination of Hebrews, 401
  as provenance of John, 158
  as provenance of Luke, 115
  as provenance of Mark, 96
  as provenance of Matthew, 75–76
Antiochene source, 199
Antiquities (Josephus), 117, 191
Anti-Semitism
  in John, 171
  in Matthew, 73–74
Apocalypse, 83, 141, 143, 158, 493, 495, 498
Apocalypse of Enoch, 459
Apocalypse of Peter, 434, 439, 493
Apocalypses, 345, 367, 371, 472, 477, 478–79, 482, 484, 492, 495. See *also* specific works.
Apocalyptic dualism, 274
Apocryphal writings, 66, 138, 438, 461, 462, 490. See *also* specific works.

scripture index

1 CORINTHIANS

An Introduction to the New Testament was typeset by the
Photocomposition Department of Zondervan Publishing House,
Grand Rapids, Michigan on a Mergenthaler Linotron 202/N.
Compositor is Sue Koppenol.
Editor for Academie Books is Leonard G. Goss.

The text was set in 10 point Galliard, a face designed by
Matthew Carter for Mergenthaler in 1978, based on models of
sixteenth-century designer Robert Granjon. Galliard is one of the
best oldstyle faces specifically designed for photocomposition.
It is "A type of . . . artistic and scholarly merit" (from a
fascinating history of this typeface in Bigelow).
This book was printed on Lyons Falls 50-pound paper by
R.R. Donnelley & Sons, Harrisonburg, Virginia.